ENCYCLOPEDIA
OF
WESTERN
GUNFIGHTERS

ENCYCLOPEDIA
of
WESTERN
GUN-
FIGHTERS

by
Bill O'Neal

University of Oklahoma Press
Norman

Library of Congress Cataloging in Publication Data

O'Neal, Bill, 1942–
  Encyclopedia of western gunfighters.

  Bibliography: p. 349.
  Includes index.
  1. Outlaws—The West—Biography. 2. Frontier and
pioneer life—The West. 3. The West—Biography.
I. Title.
F596.O65   364.1'5'0922[B]   78-21380

Copyright © 1979 by the
University of Oklahoma Press, Norman,
Publishing Division of the University.
Manufactured in the U.S.A.
First edition, 1979;
second printing, 1980.

To Jessie Standard O'Neal
Mother of the author and granddaughter of a gunfighter

For three hundred dollars I'd cut anybody in two with a sawed-off shotgun.
Mannen Clements

In spite of the violence and outlawry through which I have lived, I firmly believe that an understanding Providence has watched over me. No matter how close the call has been, when I have looked to a higher power for assistance, it has never failed me. I will go further and say that at times, when it seemed that I could not avoid killing a man, some unseen power has intervened at the crucial moment. . . . It is true that I wounded one or two, and received two wounds in return, but I have never taken a human life.

George Coe

I, at no time, contemplated taking any chances [with Billy the Kid] which I could avoid with caution or cunning. The only circumstances under which we could have met on equal terms, would have been accidental, and to which I would have been an unwilling party.

Pat Garrett

The most important lesson I learned . . . was that the winner of a gunplay usually was the one who took his time. The second was that, if I hoped to live on the frontier, I would shun flashy trick-shooting—grandstand play —as I would poison. . . . In all my life as a frontier peace officer, I did not know a really proficient gunfighter who had anything but contempt for the gun-fanner, or the man who literally shot from the hip.

Wyatt Earp

Never try to run a bluff with a six-gun. Many a man has been buried with his boots on because he foolishly tried to scare someone by reaching for his hardware. Always remember that a six-shooter is made to kill the other fellow with and for no other reason on earth. . . . If you have to stop a man with a gun, grab the stock of your six-shooter with a death-grip that won't let it wobble, and try to hit him just where the belt buckle would be. That's the broadest target from head to heel.

Bat Masterson

I have been asked many times how my wife could stand being married to anyone who was shot at so often. I don't know that myself. I don't know how she ever lived through it.

Dee Harkey

As to killing, I never think much about it. I don't believe in ghosts, and I don't keep the lights burning all night to keep them away. That's because I'm not a murderer. It is the other man or me in a fight, and I don't stop to think—is it a sin to do this thing? And after it is over, what's the use of disturbing the mind?

Wild Bill Hickok

I don't believe the bullet was ever molded that will kill me.

Dallas Stoudenmire
[He was wrong.]

My first step was disobedience; next whisky drinking; next carrying pistols; next gambling, and then murder, and I suppose next will be the gallows.

Bill Longley
[He was right.]

Acknowledgments

My first debt in compiling this volume is owed to the numerous authors who have produced biographical books or articles about western gunfighters. A great amount of material has been written concerning individuals included in this study, and much of this material has proved to be a rich source of reliable information.

Dr. Ralph Goodwin, professor of history at East Texas State University in Commerce, directed my master's thesis, thereby introducing me to the possibilities and techniques of historical research through the accumulation and evaluation of biographical information.

Joyce Chapman, librarian at Panola Junior College, was unfailingly cooperative and resourceful in procuring needed books and miscellaneous material. Nyle H. Miller and Joseph W. Snell were responsible for a highly informative session at the Kansas State Historical Society in Topeka. Also helpful were several members of the staffs of the Main Library at the University of Texas in Austin, of the Dallas Public Library, and of the Stephen F. Austin University in Nacogdoches, Texas.

In collecting the photographs used in this book I am indebted to Eugene D. Decker of the Kansas State Historical Society; to June Witt, David Bagley, and Emily Myers of the Western History Collections of the University of Oklahoma Library; and to Lori Davisson of the Arizona Historical Society.

I acknowledge deep gratitude to Ruth Rhodes, Kathryn Deppe, Robin Howell, and Pam Golden for typing help, assistance in compiling statistics, and invaluable aid in preparing the index.

A final heartfelt word of thanks must go to my wife, Faye, who furnished numerous tips concerning style and grammar and who provided warmth and domestic comforts while overlooking long absences of person or mind during the completion of this book.

BILL O'NEAL

Carthage, Texas

Contents

Illustrations

ENCYCLOPEDIA
OF
WESTERN
GUNFIGHTERS

Introduction

An initial and continuing problem of this project has been to arrive at a definition of the gunfighter. Through movies, television, and novels the gunfighter has become the most celebrated and colorful of western characters, but so many misconceptions have developed about him that it is difficult to define the precise terms *gunfighter* and *gunfight.* What criteria should be used to identify a man as a western gunfighter? What time period should be involved? What states or territories should be included? What occupations characterized a gunman? How many gunfights qualified such a man as a gunfighter? How many victims must he have slain?

As my research progressed, it became increasingly evident that such qualifications would be difficult to determine. It was even hard to define a gunfight. Was a harmless exchange of shots a gunfight? Was a murder from ambush? Or could only a fast-draw showdown be considered a gunfight? I concluded that if showdown duels were the only legitimate gunfights this would be a very short book. Of the 587 gunfights described in these pages, a mere handful satisfy the choreography of countless shootouts depicted in motion pictures, television series, and novels.

The primary misconception revealed by this project concerns the fast draw. No western image is so deeply ingrained as the picture of two men approaching each other with their hands poised over their gun butts, bound to determine who could draw and fire faster. Suddenly there is a blur of motion and two nearly simultaneous gunshots, and one man drops, hit by the first bullet. Common variations of this myth include one gunman shooting his adversary in the hand or, with even greater sportsmanship, letting his opponent draw first.

In real gunfights, however, the primary consideration was not speed but accuracy. Gunfighters frequently did not even carry their weapons in holsters. Pistols were shoved into hip pockets, waistbands, or coat pockets, and a rifle or shotgun was almost always preferred over a handgun. The primary concern in a shootout was not hitting the other man first or in the right spot but just *hitting* him. In gunfight after gunfight, as the reader will see, men emptied

3

their weapons at their adversaries without wounding them, or inflicting only minor wounds. The speed of the draw was insignificant. As anyone knows who has tried to hit a moving target with a pistol or has tried to "fan" a revolver, a snap shot rarely hits anything but the ground or the sky. If western gunfighters were reincarnated today, they would be astonished by the emphasis on the fast draw; in their day it was so unimportant that it was hardly worth mentioning.

Another inaccuracy concerns the number of kills recorded by gunfighters. From Billy the Kid's twenty-one ("not counting Mexicans") to John Wesley Hardin's forty-plus, western gunfighters have been credited with so many homicides that to merit inclusion in this book a gunman would be required to have achieved a minimum of six or eight kills. Most gunfighters killed but few men during their careers. Bat Masterson, for example, killed only one man and was involved in just three shooting scrapes. There is no certainty that Billy the Kid dispatched more than four men, and in all likelihood Hardin killed not quite a dozen. The typical gunfighter fired his gun at other men only infrequently, and rarely in his career was he responsible for a fatality.

It also became clear to me that the gunfighter was typically a man who used his gun to help him earn a living. By occupation he was a law officer, detective, buffalo hunter, or army scout, or a rustler, thief, or hired killer. Gunmen often sold their services to both sides of the law, on the run one year and wearing a badge the next. Occasionally, however, men became gunfighters by accident. Cowboys became involved in range wars and associated shooting scrapes, and professional gamblers and men with a taste for saloon and whorehouse recreation found themselves firing away for their lives.

With these and various other factors in mind I decided, somewhat arbitrarily, to label a man a gunfighter if he had been involved in at least two verifiable shootouts—usually but not necessarily fatal ones—during the period from the Civil War to the turn of the century. I also decided to apply the classification to those engaged in some vocation requiring them to carry a gun in a western area during its frontier period. The shootings themselves I did not classify. They were simply that and nothing more: encounters in which men fired at other men—spontaneously, from ambush or hiding, or face to face. There are a few exceptions even to these loose criteria, but most of the gunmen included here were westerners who displayed a marked tendency toward violence. They shot people and were shot themselves. They exposed themselves to peril by wearing badges, robbing people, or associating with dangerous men in dangerous places. They fought and died in dusty little streets and in smoky barrooms, in the mountains and on the deserts and plains. They were the western gunfighters.

"Rating" the Gunfighters

Which gunfighters were the "greatest"? Which ones were overrated, and which were underrated? The thirty-three gunfighters listed below include the most active and successful ones, as well as several whose reputations clearly were exaggerated.

This survey indicated two things: (1) gunfighters killed comparatively few men, and (2) they participated in relatively few shootouts. Nevertheless, the number of people a gunman killed, as well as those he may have dispatched in a general fray, certainly is a means of determining his skill with a gun. Also of importance in rating a gunslinger is the number of verifiable shootouts he participated in, which serves to indicate his willingness to use his gun, as well as how accurate he was. While idealists may feel that a gunfighter who killed few men during his career was an expert and generous shot, a more practical gauge of his skill is how many deaths he caused. The more shooting scrapes a man fought in, the more individuals he should have killed, because his natural instincts for self-preservation dictated that he must kill his opponent or opponents as promptly as possible.

By these measurements among the deadlier gunmen are, as expected, Wes Hardin, Billy the Kid, Wild Bill Hickok, and Ben Thompson. But ranking surprisingly high are such men as Jim Miller, Harvey Logan, John Selman, and Henry Brown. Gunfighters whose reputations greatly exceeded their accomplishments include Wyatt Earp, Bat Masterson, Doc Holliday, and John Ringo.

Gunfighter Statistics

Gunfighter	Number of Killings	Number of Gunfights	Number of Possible Killings or Assists
Jim Miller	12	14	1
Wes Hardin	11	19	1
Bill Longley	11	12	2
Harvey Logan	9	11	0
Wild Bill Hickok	7	8	1
John Selman	6	8	0
Dallas Stoudenmire	5	8	2
Cullen Baker	5	7	3
King Fisher	5	4	0
Billy the Kid	4	16	5
Ben Thompson	4	14	2
Henry Brown	4	10	5
John Slaughter	4	8	2
Clay Allison	4	4	0
Jim Courtright	4	3	0

Gunfighter	Number of Killings	Number of Gunfights	Number of Possible Killings or Assists
John Hughes	3	12	8
Cole Younger	3	7	2
John Younger	3	4	1
Doc Holliday	2	8	2
Pat Garrett	2	6	2
Burt Alvord	2	6	1
Oliver Lee	2	5	2
Dave Mather	2	5	1
Luke Short	2	5	0
Heck Thomas	1	10	3
Jesse James	1	9	3
Bill Tilghman	1	7	0
Bat Masterson	1	3	0
Jack Slade	1	3	0
John Ringo	1	2	0
Jeff Milton	0	8	6
Wyatt Earp	0	5	5
Sundance Kid	0	4	0

Vital Statistics

Statistics concerning the births, deaths, and lifespans of western gunfighters reveal several interesting facts. For example, consider the average age of half the gunmen listed in these pages—and they lived comparatively long, considering the risky nature of their lives. The average date of birth was 1853, the average date of death was 1895, and the mean lifespan was a surprising forty-seven years. Sixty-one of the gunmen for whom statistics are available did not die violently, and their lifespans average a full threescore and ten. Those who were shot to death or executed, however, lived only half as long, meeting their fate at an average age of thirty-five.

Gunfighters followed a dangerous profession: two out of three met death by gunfire or in such other premature ways as by lynching or suicide. About one-third of all gunmen died peacefully: 23.5 percent of those listed in these pages died from natural causes, while most of the 12 percent whose deaths were not recorded presumably had unremarkable ends.

One obvious assumption was verified by the statistics: most professional gunfighters died in the states or territories in which the most shootouts occurred: Texas, Kansas, New Mexico, Oklahoma, California, Missouri, and

Colorado. It was also not surprising to learn that few gunmen of the period covered here were born in the western states. Texas, which had an influx of Americans in the 1820's, and Missouri, admitted to the Union in 1821, were the exceptions. They were settled early, and they provided the atmosphere in which gunfighters could thrive.

Birth, Death, Lifespan Statistics

Number of available birth dates: 138
Number of available death dates: 212
Average date of birth: 1853
Average date of death: 1895
Number of available lifespans: 125
Average lifespan (years):   47
Number of lifespans of gunmen who died violently: 79
Average lifespan of gunmen who died violently (years):   35
Number of lifespans of gunmen who died peacefully: 46
Average lifespan of gunmen who died peacefully (years):   70

Causes of Death

Causes	Number of Gunmen	Percentage of Gunmen
Shooting	145	57.0
Miscellaneous violence	5	2.0
Execution	14	5.5
Natural	61	23.5
Not known	30	12.0

Occupations of the Gunfighters

How did western gunmen make their livings? A large number of them pursued predictable occupations as law officers; train, bank, and stagecoach robbers; rustlers; gamblers; cowboys; ranchers; or range detectives. There were also saloonkeepers, soldiers, army scouts, and buffalo hunters who became accustomed to handling and using guns in their daily vocations and therefore were inclined toward violent solutions to their quarrels. Occasionally prospectors, con men, stage drivers, and bounty hunters engaged in shootouts, and at times many westerners forthrightly hired their guns to people or factions who desired a show of power or the death of an adversary. A surprising number of farmers and one-time farmers participated in gunfights, as did store clerks, schoolteachers, butchers, actors, and others of more prosaic pursuits. Below is a list of the occupations followed at various times by the men included in this book. It sheds considerable light on the vocational pursuits of the western gunfighters.

Occupations of Gunfighters

Law officer	110	Carpenter	3
Cowboy	75	Hotel owner	3
Rancher	54	Lawyer	3
Farmer	46	Politician	3
Rustler	45	Private detective	3
Hired gunman	35	Racketeer	3
Soldier	34	Sportsman	3
Bandit	26	Whisky peddler	3
Gambler	24	Con man	2
Laborer	22	Counterfeiter	2
Saloon owner	19	Customs collector	2
Clerk	17	Dance-hall owner	2
Train robber	14	Dispatch rider	2
Miner	10	Horse breeder	2
Prospector	10	Hunter	2
Army scout	9	Printer	2
Stage robber	9	Schoolteacher	2
Teamster	9	Speculator	2
Bank robber	8	Surveyor	2
Buffalo hunter	8	Arsonist	1
Range detective	7	Author	1
Stage driver	7	Baker	1
Actor	6	Blacksmith	1
Ranch foreman	6	Building contractor	1
Railroad employee	6	Businessman	1
Bartender	5	Cattle broker	1
Bronco buster	5	Dentist	1
Butcher	4	Doctor	1
Freighter	4	Engineer	1
Livery-stable owner	4	Express-company superintendent	1
Criminal	4	Ferryman	1
Bounty hunter	3	Gunsmith	1
Café owner	3	Harness maker	1

Indian agent	1	Realtor	1
Indian fighter	1	Sailor	1
Inspector	1	Salesman	1
Insurance executive	1	School superintendent	1
Inventor	1	Sheepherder	1
Irrigation manager	1	Shotgun guard	1
Jailer	1	Showman	1
Jeweler	1	Slave trader	1
Lecturer	1	Spy	1
Livery-stable employee	1	Stagecoach contractor	1
Movie producer	1	Stage-station employee	1
Movie scenarist	1	Telegraph runner	1
Newsboy	1	Tinsmith	1
Oil wildcatter	1	Trail boss	1
Packmaster	1	Train brakeman	1
Page	1	Trapper	1
Painter	1	Wheelwright	1
Postmaster	1	Whiskey smuggler	1
Prison warden	1	Wild-West-show performer	1
Racetrack employee	1	Woodcutter	1
Railroad guard	1		

Gunfighters' Relatives

Families commonly are advised, "Do things together." This advice was certainly taken to heart by western gunmen, who freely passed on their lethal inclinations and skills to sons, brothers, cousins, nephews, and in-laws. Frank and George Coe were cousins. So were Wes Hardin and the Clements brothers, as well as Bill and Jim Taylor and Doboy and Hays Taylor. Clint Barkley and Merritt Horrell were brothers-in-law, and so were Dallas Stoudenmire and Doc Cummings. Mannen Clements was the father of fellow gunman Mannie Clements. Hugh Beckwith, the father of Lincoln County gunslingers Bob and John Beckwith, killed William Johnson, his son-in-law. By far the most common kindred gunfighters were sets of brothers who followed the outlaw trail together or allied as law-enforcement officers. Among those brothers who complemented or rivaled each other as gunmen were Bob and John Beckwith; Billy and Ike Clanton; Bill, Bob, Emmett, and Grat Dalton; Morgan, Virgil, Warren, and Wyatt Earp; Ben, Martin, Merritt, Sam, and Tom Horrell; Frank and Jesse James; Harvey and Lonie Logan; Arthur and Mike McCluskie; Frank and Tom McLaury; Ed, Jim, and Bat Masterson; Bob and Wallace Olinger; Ed and Jim Tewksbury; Ben and Billy Thompson; and Bob, Cole, Jim, and John Younger.

Some of the men listed in these pages had brothers who sometimes displayed attributes of gunfighters, though their records did not measure up to gunfighter status. Among them were Will Christian's brother Bob; Mannen Clements' brothers Gyp, Jim, and Joe; Tom Ketchum's brother Sam; Jim Manning's brothers Doc, Frank, John, and William; John Sontag's brother George; and Port Stockton's brother Ike.

Gunfights

The 587 gunfights described in this book were not, of course, the only shooting scrapes that occurred in the West. The shootouts that are omitted from these pages were chance affairs between men. The gunfights included here involved men who proved themselves professionals, and these incidents reveal interesting patterns.

It is clear, for example, that gunfights were most common during the 1870's and early 1880's, with a brief revival of activity during the mid-1890's. The gunfighters' era did not really begin until after the Civil War, during which important technical improvements had been made in firearms, and thousands of young men had served in combat. Though the period ended at the turn of the century, in 1924 lawman Bill Tilghman was gunned down, and officers killed outlaw Roy Daugherty, final examples of western-style gunfighting to Americans of the Roaring Twenties.

Texas was the most violent western area; nearly 160 shooting scrapes took place there during the gunfighters' era. Kansas, whose cattle towns provided enticing arenas for gunmen, and New Mexico, where the Lincoln County War provoked more than 20 shootouts in 1878 alone, were the scenes of over 70 gunfights each. Vast, sparsely settled Arizona was the arena of nearly 60 shootings involving gunslingers, while in Oklahoma there were more than 50 gunfights, most of them during the 1880's and 1890's. California, which was relatively well policed during the gunfighters' heyday, was nevertheless the battleground of more than 20 gun battles. Colorado also produced a score of shootings between known gunmen, and Missouri and Wyoming each were the sites of more than a dozen shootouts. Gunfighters also managed to put their weapons into action in decidedly unwestern locales, from Florida to Bolivia.

Gunfight Statistics

Year	Number of Gunfights	Place
1854	1	Texas
1856	5	California

Year	Number of Gunfights	Place
1857	1	California
1858	2	Colorado, Texas
1859	4	Texas (2), California, Colorado
1860	2	Idaho, Louisiana
1861	3	Missouri (2), Nebraska
1862	4	Missouri, Tennessee, Texas, Wyoming
1863	4	Arizona (2), Montana (2)
1864	2	Arkansas, Texas
1865	6	California (3), Missouri, Oklahoma, Texas
1866	4	Missouri (2), Mexico, Texas
1867	10	Texas (6), Oklahoma (2), Wyoming (2)
1868	16	Texas (10), Nevada (2), Wyoming (2), Kansas, Missouri
1869	12	Texas (5), Kansas (3), Arkansas, Colorado, Missouri, Oklahoma
1870	6	Kansas (4), Texas (2)
1871	22	Kansas (8), Texas (5), California (2), New Mexico (2), Oklahoma (2), Iowa, Mississippi, Wyoming
1872	13	Kansas (6), Texas (2), California, Kentucky, Oklahoma, Utah, Wyoming
1873	27	Kansas (12), Texas (10), New Mexico (3), Colorado, Oklahoma
1874	14	Texas (6), Missouri (2), New Mexico (2), Oklahoma (2), California, Kansas
1875	13	Texas (9), New Mexico (3), Missouri
1876	22	Texas (11), New Mexico (5), Dakota (2), Minnesota (2), Arizona, Colorado
1877	21	Texas (12), Kansas (4), New Mexico (2), Arizona, Florida, Kansas
1878	36	New Mexico (23), Texas (10), Kansas (3)
1879	14	New Mexico (6), Kansas (4), Colorado (2), Texas (2)
1880	25	New Mexico (11), Arizona (3), Kansas (3), Texas (3), California, Colorado, Mexico, Nebraska, Nevada
1881	27	New Mexico (8), Arizona (7), Texas (5), Kansas (4), California, Colorado, Kansas
1882	15	Arizona (5), Texas (5), Missouri (2), New Mexico (2), Colorado
1883	9	Kansas (6), Nebraska, New Mexico, Texas
1884	17	Kansas (5), Texas (5), New Mexico (3), California, Colorado, Montana, Mexico

Year	Number of Gunfights	Place
1885	7	Oklahoma (3), Texas (2), Colorado, Kansas
1886	7	Texas (3), Oklahoma (2), Arizona, New Mexico
1887	20	Arizona (9), Texas (9), Oklahoma (2)
1888	10	Arizona (2), Kansas (2), Texas (2), Alabama, Illinois, Oklahoma, Tennessee
1889	9	Arizona (3), Texas (2), Kansas, New Mexico, Oklahoma, Tennessee
1890	9	Oklahoma (4), Colorado, Kansas, Louisiana, Texas, Utah
1891	10	Kansas (2), Oklahoma (2), Texas (2), Arkansas, California, Colorado, Wyoming
1892	13	Oklahoma (7), California (2), Colorado, Kansas, Washington, Wyoming
1893	11	Oklahoma (3), California (2), Arkansas, Kansas, Louisiana, Mexico, Texas, Wyoming
1894	14	Oklahoma (5), Texas (5), Arizona, Missouri, Montana, Utah
1895	19	Oklahoma (10), Texas (4), Colorado, Missouri, Montana, New Mexico, Utah
1896	19	Oklahoma (5), Texas (4), Arizona (3), Arkansas, California, Kansas, Mexico, Montana, New Mexico, Utah
1897	7	Kansas (2), Montana (2), Arizona, Texas, Utah
1898	8	Arizona (5), New Mexico (2), Colorado
1899	8	Arizona (3), Wyoming (2), Colorado, Texas, Utah
1900	12	Arizona (5), Colorado (2), Utah (3), Missouri, Wyoming
1901	9	Arizona (5), Oklahoma, Tennessee, Texas, Wyoming
1902	8	Arizona (3), Washington (3), Oregon, Texas
1903	2	Texas (2)
1904	6	Texas (2), Arizona, Colorado, New Mexico, Oklahoma
1905	5	Oklahoma (2), Bolivia, New Mexico, Texas
1906	2	Oklahoma, Mexico
1907	3	Arizona (2), Colorado
1908	4	New Mexico (2), Texas, Bolivia
1909	1	Oklahoma
1911	3	Texas (2), Georgia
1912	1	Wyoming
1915	2	Oklahoma, Texas
1917	1	Arizona
1924	2	Missouri, Oklahoma

Chronology of the Gunfighters' West

What events caused flurries of gossip and professional interest in the saloons, jail offices, bunkhouses, and hideouts where gunfighters congregated? The following occurrences highlighted the western calendar during the era of the gunmen, marking the demise of noted gunfighters, designating the more prominent feuds and range wars, and taking note of the most spectacular shootouts.

1861   Shootout between the "McCanles Gang" and Wild Bill Hickok (July 12, Rock Creek Station, Nebraska).

1864   Hanging of Henry Plummer and many of his Montana outlaws.
        Hanging of Jack Slade (March 10, Virginia City, Montana).

1865   Duel between Dave Tutt and Wild Bill Hickok (July 21, Springfield, Missouri).

1870   Fight between Wild Bill Hickok and Fort Hays cavalrymen (July 17, Fort Hays, Kansas).
        Killing of Bear River Tom Smith (November 2, near Abilene, Kansas).

1871   Mass shootout in Newton saloon (August 20, Newton, Kansas).
        Shooting between Wild Bill Hickok and Phil Coe (October 5, Abilene, Kansas).

1873   Vicious brawl between Arthur McCluskie and Hugh Anderson (June, Medicine Lodge, Kansas).
        Killing of Sheriff C. B. Whitney by Billy Thompson (August 15, Ellsworth, Kansas).
        Horrell War (Lincoln County, New Mexico).

1874   Gunfight between John Younger and detectives (March 16, Monegaw Springs, Missouri).
        Climax of Texas' Sutton-Taylor feud.

1876   Fight between Bat Masterson and Sgt. Ed King (January 24, Mobeetie, Texas).
        Murder of Wild Bill Hickok (August 2, Deadwood, D.T.)
        James-Younger raid on Northfield, Minnesota (September 7).

1877   Horrell-Higgins feud climaxes around Lampasas, Texas.

1878   Gunfight between Ed Masterson and Texans (April 9, Dodge City, Kansas).
        Battle between Texas Rangers and Sam Bass gang (July 19, Round Rock, Texas).
        Hanging of Wild Bill Longley (October 11, Giddings, Texas).
        Lincoln County War.

1880   Pat Garrett's violent manhunt for Billy the Kid and gang.

1881   El Paso gunfight featuring Dallas Stoudenmire and four fatalities (April 14).
        Billy the Kid shoots his way out of jail (April 28, Lincoln, New Mexico).
        Death of Billy the Kid (July 14, Fort Sumner, New Mexico).

Gunfight at the OK Corral (October 26, Tombstone, Arizona).

1882   Murder of Jesse James (April 3, St. Joseph, Missouri).

Killing of Johnny Ringo (July 14, Turkey Creek Canyon, Arizona).

Killing of Dallas Stoudenmire by the Manning brothers (September 18, El Paso, Texas).

Fight between Buckskin Frank Leslie and Billy Claiborne (November 14, Tombstone, Arizona).

1884   Death of Ben Thompson and King Fisher (March 11, San Antonio, Texas).

Attack on Elfego Baca (October, Frisco, New Mexico).

Medicine Lodge, Kansas, bank robbery (December 15).

1887   Fight between Luke Short and Longhaired Jim Courtright (February 8, Fort Worth, Texas).

Peaceful death of Doc Holliday (November 8, Glenwood Springs, Colorado).

Arizona's Pleasant Valley War.

1892   Dalton Gang raid on Coffeyville, Kansas (October 5).

Powder River War (Wyoming).

1893   Shootout between lawmen and the Doolin gang (September 1, Ingalls, Oklahoma).

1895   Killing of John Wesley Hardin by John Selman (August 19, El Paso, Texas).

1896   Death of Bill Doolin by a posse (August 25, Lawson, Oklahoma).

1898   Heyday of Butch Cassidy's Wild Bunch.

1900   Fight between Jeff Milton and Burt Alvord's gang (February 15, Fairbank, Arizona).

1904   Death of Harvey Logan (May 8, near Glenwood Springs, Colorado).

1908   Murder of Pat Garrett (February 29, near Las Cruces, New Mexico).

Fight between Bolivian soldiers and Butch Cassidy and the Sundance Kid.

1909   Lynching of Jim ("Killer") Miller (April 19, Ada, Oklahoma).

1924   Killing of Bill Tilghman (November 1, Cromwell, Oklahoma).

Nicknames

Westerners demonstrated a passion for nicknames. From Buffalo Bill Cody to Snakehead Thompson the inhabitants of the last frontier acquired sobriquets and assigned them to their contemporaries eagerly and prolifically. Gunfighters, among the most colorful and well-known westerners, were so liberally labeled with appellations that many of them are hardly known by their real names: Billy the Kid, for example, was rarely referred to as Henry McCarty, and it is popularly thought that he was christened William Bonney.

Jesse James was often referred to as Dingus, John Calhoun Pinckney Higgins was called Pink, George Weightman was dubbed Red Buck, John Long was inevitably named Long John, and Henry Andrew Thomas was always known as Heck. George Newcomb once worked for John Slaughter and subsequently was called Slaughter's Kid, and his frequent warbling of "I'm a wild wolf from Bitter Creek/And it's my night to howl" earned him the sobriquet "Bitter Creek." William Bartholomew Masterson became known as Bat because he struck lawbreakers over the head with a cane, or because of the middle name he later changed to Barclay, or because he was a battler.

There were also many varieties of "Bill": Buffalo Bill Brooks, Cherokee Bill (Crawford Goldsby), Curly Bill Brocius (William Graham), Wild Bill Hickok and Wild Bill Longley, Old Bill Miner, Billy the Kid Claiborne, Texas Billy Thompson, and Little Bill Raidler.

Physical characteristics and appearance dictated a number of appellations. There was Broken Nose Jack McCall, Flat Nose or Big Nose Curry, Long-haired Jim Courtright, Black Faced Charlie Bryant, Buckskin Frank Leslie, Red Hall and Red Beard, Big Steve Long, the Big Indian (Bob Olinger), Three-Fingered Jack Dunlap, and Cockeyed Frank Loving. Will Christian was known as Black Jack because of his dark complexion, and because of his weight he was often called 202.

Personality traits resulted in such sobriquets as Rowdy Joe Lowe, Happy Jack Morco, Bully Brooks, Mysterious Dave Mather, the Human Wildcat (Juan Soto), the Bearcat (Henry Starr), and Wild Charlie (Zip Wyatt).

There were any number of "Kids": Billy the Kid McCarty and Billy the Kid Claiborne, Harry the Kid (Harry Head), Slaughter's Kid (George Newcomb), the Mormon Kid (Matt Warner), Kid Curry (Harvey Logan), and the Sundance Kid (Harry Longabaugh).

Locations provided sobriquets for many gunfighters. Thomas Smith tamed the Wyoming railroad town of Bear River and thereafter was known as Bear River Tom. Roy Daugherty ran away from his Missouri home at the age of fourteen, claimed he was from Arkansas and adopted an alias to cover his trail, and became familiar as Arkansas Tom Jones. John Slaughter and William Thompson, although born in Louisiana and England, respectively, were reared in Texas and later referred to as Texas John and Texas Billy. Geography also labeled Turkey Creek Johnson, Tulsa Jack Blake, and Little Arkansas (Wes Hardin).

Occupational tendencies frequently were responsible for a man's nickname. Professional gambler John O'Rourke was known as Johnny-Behind-the-Deuce, and bank and train robber Dan Clifton became familiar as Dynamite Dick. Dentist John Holliday was universally called Doc, and so were Samuel Cummings, J. G. Scurlock, and C. W. Shores, although the last three were never medical practitioners. Rank titles labeled Cap Mossman and Cap Whitney, who respectively had commanded the Arizona Rangers and a militia company, but Commodore Perry Owens never held a naval commission. Jim Miller, a notorious assassin, was widely referred to as Killer Miller and Killin' Jim—although presumably not to his face.

The Gunfighters

What sorts of men were the gunfighters? What kinds of lives did they lead when not blazing away at other men with guns? The following register attempts to answer such questions about commonplace gunmen like Scott Cooley and Chris Evans and Sylvester Powell as well as such famous individuals as Wes Hardin, Wild Bill Hickok, and Billy the Kid.

In this register of 255 gunfighters I do not presume to have included every man who might have laid legitimate claim to the vocation of gunfighter. Because of the scarcity of information about certain periods and places of the West, a comprehensive list of gunfighters would be impossible to compile. But every effort has been made to collect as complete and representative a list as possible, and it is hoped that the reader searching for information on a particular gunfighter will find it within the following pages.

A standard format was adopted to arrange the information about each gunman in an orderly manner. The last name and first and middle names begin each man's section, followed by any nickname or prominent alias which he used. Next, the birthdate, the birthplace, the date and place of death, and the occupations the man pursued are given if these facts are available. The first narrative section details general information about each gunman's life. The next segment is a list, arranged in chronological order, of the verifiable gunfights the man participated in; the date and place of each shootout are included, as well as a description of each battle. When it became necessary to describe a gunfight two or more times, I attempted to depict the scrape from the point of view of each participant, and if possible different details are mentioned in each version of the same shootout. The final segment of each account is a list of sources that proved most useful in furnishing information about each man; complete publication facts of these sources are provided in the Bibliography.

The men listed below are frequently referred to by their aliases instead of their less familiar real names. There are other such men in this book, but the ones who follow are the primary gunmen about whom confusion might occur.

Alias	Real Name
Bell, Tom	Thomas Hodges
Bonney, William	Henry McCarty
Bowen, Bill	Clint Barkley
Brocius, Curley Bill	William Graham
Canton, Frank	Joe Horner
Cassidy, Butch	Robert LeRoy Parker
Chelson, Tom	Tom Hill

Alias	*Real Name*
Delaney, Arthur	Mike McCluskie
Jones, Arkansas Tom	Roy Daugherty
Pitts, Charlie	Samuel Wells
Warner, Matt	Willard Erastus Christianson
Wheeler, Ben	Ben F. Robertson
Wilson, Billy	D. L. Anderson

The Gunfighters

Allison, Robert A. Clay

(b. 1840, Waynesboro, Tennessee; d. July 1, 1887, Pecos, Texas. Farmer, soldier, cowboy, rancher, cattle broker.) Until the age of twenty-one Clay Allison lived and worked on his family's farm in Tennessee. At the outbreak of the Civil War, Allison ignored his club foot and defended his native state, serving throughout the conflict in various Confederate units. A few months after the war three of the Allison brothers—Clay, John, and Monroe—and a sister and brother-in-law—Mary and Lewis Coleman—left Tennessee and moved to Texas. Along the way, at a Red River crossing near Denison, Texas, the fractious Clay severely beat up ferryman Zachary Colbert in a fist fight.

Allison soon signed on as a cowhand with Oliver Loving and Charles Goodnight and was probably one of the eighteen herders who followed the two cattlemen on the 1866 drive through Texas, New Mexico, and Colorado which blazed the famous Goodnight-Loving Trail. During the late 1860's Allison also rode for M. L. Dalton and was trail boss for a partnership between his brother-in-law and Isaac W. Lacy. In 1870 Coleman and Lacy relocated in New Mexico on a spread in Colfax County, and Allison led their herd to

the new ranch for a payment of three hundred head of livestock. With this small herd he established his own ranch near Cimarron, New Mexico, and he eventually built it into a lucrative operation.

On October 7, 1870, Allison led a mob which broke into the jail in Elizabethtown, near Cimarron, and lynched an accused murderer named Charles Kennedy. Kennedy was hanged in the local slaughterhouse, and a wild-eyed Allison decapitated him and then placed the head on a pole in Henri Lambert's saloon in Cimarron. In January, 1874, Allison shot gunman Chunk Colbert to death, and he was suspected of killing Charles Cooper shortly afterward.

At about that time Allison, always a heavy drinker, had a drunken run-in with a hardy citizen named Mason T. Bowman. In a saloon Allison and Bowman determined to find out who was quicker on the draw, and Bowman repeatedly beat Clay. At that point both men stripped down to their underwear and conducted an inebriated, seminude dance in front of a captivated crowd. Finally, to see who was the better dancer, they began shooting at each other's feet, but fortunately they stopped short of any further violence.

On October 30, 1875, Allison became

Clay Allison, shown here at the age of twenty-six. He killed four men in as many gunfights. *(Courtesy Western History Collections, University of Oklahoma Library)*

involved in another Colfax County lynching, heading a mob which seized suspected murderer Cruz Vega. The terrified Vega confessed that Manuel Cardenas was the actual culprit, but he was hanged from a telegraph pole anyway and then shot in the back for good measure. Once again a bloodthirsty Allison abused the victim, tying the lynch rope to his saddlehorn and dragging the corpse over rocks and brush. Two days later Allison killed gunman Pancho Griego, a friend of Cruz's.

Allison next began to have trouble with his Colfax County neighbors, including his brother-in-law, and following a scathing editorial, Clay wrecked the office of the *Cimarron News and Press.* While escaping from an abortive attempt to steal a herd of army mules, Allison accidentally shot himself in the right foot, which aggravated his club foot and ne-

cessitated his use of a cane throughout the remainder of his life. In December, 1876, he killed a deputy sheriff in a wild dance hall shootout but later was released from custody. Two years later he shipped a herd of cattle east and engaged in the celebrated "East St. Louis Scrimmage," a brawl in which he trounced a man named Alexander Kessinger. Shortly afterward he sold his ranch and established himself in Hays City as a cattle broker.

By 1880 Allison had moved to a ranch in Hemphill County, Texas, and the next year he took a wife. He sired two daughters—Patsy, who was born crippled, and Clay, who was born following his death. In 1886 he established still another ranch in Lincoln County, New Mexico, and later that year he drove a herd to Rock Creek in Wyoming Territory. Legend reports that while there, he developed a toothache and went to nearby Cheyenne to find a dentist. The dentist began working on the wrong tooth, whereupon Clay went to another dentist for proper repairs. The enraged Allison then returned to the first man and forcibly—and, it may be assumed, inexpertly—had extracted one of the unfortunate man's front teeth and was working on another when the dentist's shrieks attracted a restraining crowd to the scene.

A year later Allison fell beneath a wagon about forty miles from Pecos, Texas, where he had gone to buy supplies. He fractured his skull on a front wheel, and he died within less than an hour.

Gunfights: *March, 1862, Waynesboro, Tennessee.* Allison was at home on medical leave because of a medical condition "of a mixed character, partly epileptic and partly maniacal." A corporal of the Third Illinois Cavalry determined to loot the Allison farm. After he broke one of Mrs. Allison's favorite pitchers, Clay produced a gun and relieved his mother's distress by shooting the soldier to death.

January 7, 1874, Colfax County, New Mexico. Chunk Colbert was a nephew of Zack Colbert, who had been pummeled by Allison in a fist fight nine years earlier, and a gunman who had shot men in past scrapes. At Tom Stockton's Clifton House, an inn and store at a river crossing near Allison's ranch, Clay and Colbert staged a horse race which was judged a dead heat. Following the race, Allison and Colbert, their disgruntlement thinly disguised, ate in the Clifton House along with Charles Cooper, a friend of Colbert's.

After finishing his meal, Colbert reached for another cup of coffee with one hand and with the other slowly raised a six-gun above the table. When Allison saw Colbert's gun, he went for his own weapon, and Chunk hurried his shot, blasting a slug into the tabletop. Allison fired a bullet into Colbert's face, drilling him just above the right eye.

Colbert died immediately and was buried behind the Clifton House. When asked why he had shared a meal with a man he intended to shoot, Allison crowed, "Because I didn't want to send a man to hell on an empty stomach."

It should be added that Cooper disappeared mysteriously about twelve days later, and it was widely assumed that Allison had murdered him. The last time Cooper was seen was on January 19, riding toward Cimarron. Allison would have had ample opportunity to kill Cooper and dispose of the body, and two years later he was formally charged with Cooper's murder. He was later released for lack of evidence.

November 1, 1875, Cimarron, New Mexico. Two days earlier Allison had been instrumental in the death of Cruz Vega, a friend and employee of Colfax County *pistolero* Pancho Griego. On the night of November 1 in front of Cimarron's St. James Hotel, Allison met Griego, Vega's eighteen-year-old son Luís, and Florencio Donahue, Griego's business partner. After a few words the men went inside to talk over drinks. A few minutes later Griego and Allison stepped into a corner of the saloon to speak privately. Within moments Allison palmed a revolver and fired three slugs into Griego. Suddenly the lights were extinguished, and as Griego fell dead, Allison escaped into the darkness.

December 21, 1876, Las Animas, Colorado. Clay and his brother John were raucously enjoying a drunken revel in the Olympic Dance Hall. Charles Faber, a deputy sheriff and local constable, asked the Allisons to check their guns, but they predictably ignored him. Soon there were complaints that the brothers were being belligerently insulting and were intentionally trampling the feet of other couples. Faber borrowed a shotgun, lined up two special deputies, and approached the Olympic.

At that point Clay was at the bar, his back to the entrance, while John still was capering on the dance floor. Faber entered the hall, and someone cried, "Look out!" Whirling just as Faber fired a barrel of the shotgun, John was staggered by buckshot in the chest and shoulder.

Clay pulled his six-gun and fired four slugs at Faber. The first bullet tore into the constable's chest, and although the other three went wild, Faber dropped in his tracks and died almost immediately. When Faber fell, the other barrel of the shotgun discharged, striking John in the leg and slamming him to the floor.

The two special deputies fled and were pursued by Clay, who emptied his gun at them from the front steps of the Olympic. Clay then dragged the mortally wounded Faber over to his fallen brother, repeatedly assuring John that the lawman was dead and vengeance was achieved. John was carried away, and Clay surrendered to the county sheriff. Eventually John recovered from his wounds, and Clay was released from custody.

Sources: Stanley, *Clay Allison;* Clark, *Clay Allison of the Washita;* Schoenberger, *Gunfighters,* 1–19, 171–73; Stanley, *Desperadoes of New Mexico,* 185–202; Coolidge, *Fighting Men of the West,* 71-84.

Alvord, Burt

(b. 1866; d. ca. 1910, Latin America. Livery-stable employee, law officer, cattle rustler, train robber, convict.) Alvord came West with his father, a justice of the peace, at an early age. As a teenager he worked as a stable hand at Tombstone's OK Corral, where he witnessed the famous shootout and, three years later, the lynching of John Heath. When John Slaughter was elected sheriff of Cochise County in 1886, the twenty-year-old Alvord became his deputy and right-hand man.

For the next four years Alvord helped Slaughter track down numerous thieves and rustlers, and, as an amiable frequenter of bars, he was particularly adept at ferreting out information concerning the whereabouts of various fugitives. During the mid-1890's Alvord drifted into Mexico and rustled cattle for a time, but soon he returned to the right side of the law as constable first of Fairbank and then of Willcox, Arizona.

Although respected as a lawman, Alvord used his position to mastermind a band of train robbers. After arrests in 1900 and in 1903 Alvord and Billy

Stiles, his deputy and accomplice, managed to escape. Alvord spread a rumor that he and Stiles had been killed, and he sent two coffins to Tombstone. The ruse did not work: Arizona peace officers continued the search for the two bandit leaders.

Alvord was recaptured in 1904, but after two years in prison at Yuma he was released and went to Latin America. He reportedly turned up in Venezuela, in Honduras, and in Panama as a canal worker, and he died about 1910.

Gunfights: 1885, *Tombstone, Arizona.* Young Alvord had a run-in with a man known in Tombstone as "Six-Shooter Jim." Gunplay climaxed the clash, and Alvord shot Jim to death.

May, 1888, Cochise County, Arizona. Sheriff Slaughter and deputies Alvord and Cesario Lucero had tracked three Mexican train robbers to the Whetstone Mountains. At dawn, while the fugitives were still in their blankets, Slaughter ordered them to surrender. When the outlaws tried to resist, the officers opened fire, and after one of the robbers was hit, the other two surrendered.

June 7, 1888, Cochise County, Arizona. Slaughter and Alvord and two Mexicans soon returned to the Whetstones in search of another group of bandits. Once again the outlaws were caught asleep, and once again shooting broke out. One fugitive was killed, and two were wounded, although one of the wounded men managed to escape on foot.

February, 1889, Tombstone, Arizona. Alvord was drinking with two men named Fuller and Fortino in a private home near John Slaughter's Tombstone town house. Fuller and Fortino began scuffling, and Fuller seized Alvord's pistol, fatally wounded his opponent, and fled with the deputy's gun. Slaughter immediately appeared on the scene and was enraged at Alvord's role in the fray.

1898, Willcox, Arizona. Constable Alvord had had difficulties with a cowboy named Billy King. King tried to patch up the problem by buying drinks, and Alvord asked him outside to talk. When the two men closed the back door of the saloon behind them, Alvord drew his pistol and emptied it into King's face, killing him on the spot.

February 17, 1904, Nigger Head Gap, Mexico. Two members of the Arizona Rangers slipped across the border into Mexico and cornered Alvord at Nigger Head Gap. Alvord tried to shoot his way past the lawmen, but he was wounded in the leg and foot and taken into custody.

Sources: Erwin, *John H. Slaughter,* 215–17, 227–28, 231–36, 239, 242–48, 262; Haley, *Jeff Milton,* 270, 302–12, 316; Sherman, *Ghost Towns of Arizona,* 53–54; Hunt, *Cap Mossman,* 198–204, 226–28.

Anderson, D. L.

("Billy Wilson")

(b. 1862, Trumbull County, Ohio; d. June 14, 1918, Sanderson, Texas. Cowboy, livery-stable owner, counterfeiter, rustler, rancher, law officer, customs inspector.) In his early teens Anderson, usually known as "Billy Wilson," moved with his family from Ohio to South Texas; after a short period as a cowboy he went to White Oaks, New Mexico, where he bought a livery stable in 1880. Within less than a year he sold his operation, supposedly was paid in counterfeit money, and began to pass the bogus bills in Lincoln. When he was indicted, he joined Billy the Kid's band of fugitives and rustlers.

Along with several cohorts, Wilson was arrested by Pat Garrett at Stinking Springs. Convicted in 1881, he soon escaped from custody in Santa Fe. Reverting to his real name, D. L. Anderson, he returned to Texas, started a ranch in Uvalde County, married, and began raising two children. Pat Garrett and others helped him to obtain a presidential pardon in 1896. He worked as a U.S. customs inspector for a time, then became sheriff of Terrell County, where he was killed in the line of duty in 1918.

Gunfights: November   29–31, 1880, near White Oaks, New Mexico. Near White Oaks a posse of eight men caught Billy the Kid and Wilson in the open. As soon as the outlaws saw them they opened fire, and a chase commenced. The horses of both fugitives were killed, but the Kid and Wilson managed to escape on foot.

The next day this bold pair, accompanied by Dave Rudabaugh, audaciously rode into White Oaks. One of them took a shot at Deputy Sheriff James Redman, who dove for cover. But a crowd of thirty or forty armed citizens surged into the street, and the outlaws galloped out of town.

At daybreak the next morning a posse of twelve men located the fugitives in a ranch house forty miles away. After a parley an exchange of hostages was agreed upon pending further negotiation: ranch owner Jim Greathouse and posse leader James Carlyle, a deputy sheriff, traded places. About midnight shooting erupted and Carlyle leaped through a window and then died with three bullets in his body. The fugitives burst outside as the posse gaped at Carlyle, and they mounted and thundered

away into the darkness, leaving the lawmen to vent their rage by burning the
ranch house.

*December 19, 1880, Fort Sumner, New
Mexico.* Late on a cold Sunday night
the Kid, Wilson, Rudabaugh, Charlie
Bowdre, Tom O'Folliard, and Tom
Pickett rode into Fort Sumner, where a
posse led by Pat Garrett waited in ambush. As the riders approached the old
hospital, Garrett and his men emerged,
and Garrett shouted, "Halt!" Garrett
and Deputy Lon Chambers immediately
opened fire. O'Folliard and Pickett, riding in front, were hit and Rudabaugh's
horse was shot out from under him.
O'Folliard, mortally wounded, died in
Fort Sumner within the hour. But
Rudabaugh vaulted up behind Wilson,
and the remainder of the gang retained
their freedom for the moment.

June 14, 1918, Sanderson, Texas. Wilson was asked to come to the railroad
depot to halt a disturbance caused by a
drunken cowboy, Ed Valentine. Wilson
knew the rowdy cowhand and was con-
fident that he could handle him without
trouble. As he approached the station,
however, Valentine ducked into a nearby baggage shed. Wilson stepped up to
the door and demanded that the youth
give up; instead, a shot rang out, and
the sheriff dropped to the ground, mortally wounded. Within an hour of Wilson's death, Valentine was lynched by a
mob.

Sources: Hutchinson and Mullin,
Whiskey Jim and a Kid Named Billie;
Fulton, *Lincoln County War,* 380,
384–85, 387–88; Keleher, *Violence
in Lincoln County,* 281–99, 305, 308,
323–24; Metz, *Pat Garrett,* 58–62, 68,
72, 74, 76, 78, 84, 98, 159.

Anderson, Hugh

*(b. Texas; d. June, 1873, Medicine Lodge,
Kansas.* Cowboy, bartender.) Anderson
was a cowboy who helped drive a herd
from Salado, Texas, to Newton, a raw
Kansas railhead, in 1871. En route he
helped three other men track murderer
Juan Bideno to Bluff City, Kansas, but
only Wes Hardin was involved in the
shootout which resulted in the Mexican's death.

While Anderson was in Newton, a
friend, Texas gambler William Bailey,
was killed by a tough railroad foreman
named Mike McCluskie. McCluskie left
town, and Anderson led the Texans in
vowing revenge if McCluskie ever returned. McCluskie was back within
days, and Anderson, true to his word,
shot him, igniting one of the bloodiest
gun battles in the history of the West.
A warrant was sworn for Anderson's
arrest, but friends spirited the wounded
Texan away—first to Kansas City, then
home to Texas. Within a couple of
years, however, he drifted back to Kansas. He was located in Medicine Lodge
by Mike McCluskie's revenge-minded
brother, and the two men killed each
other in a gory duel.

*Gunfights: August 20, 1871, New-
ton, Kansas.* Mike McCloskie returned
to Newton on Saturday, August 19, and
spent the evening at the faro layout in
Perry Tuttle's dance hall. About 1:00
A.M. Anderson, determined to have revenge for William Bailey's death, walked
up to McCluskie and shouted, "You are
a cowardly son-of-a-bitch! I will blow
the top of your head off." Anderson
shoved his pistol at the seated McCluskie
and fired a slug which hit the big man
in the neck.

McCluskie half rose and tried to
return Anderson's fire, but his gun

snapped on a defective cartridge, and his adversary pumped another bullet into his leg. The impact threw McCluskie to the floor, and as he fell, his gun discharged. But Anderson fired once again into his back, and McCluskie was out of action.

By this time several other cowboys had opened fire, and an erstwhile peacemaker, Texan Jim Martin, clutched his neck and stumbled outside to die. Suddenly Jim Riley, an eighteen-year-old friend of McCluskie's, fell on his comrade's assailants. When the bullets finally stopped flying, McCluskie was carried away to die within a few hours, and three other men lay mortally wounded: Patrick Lee, a friend of McCluskie's who was hit in the belly, and cowboys Henry Kearnes and Billy Garrett, who both died of chest wounds. In addition, another cowboy was shot in the leg, cowhand Jim Wilkerson was grazed on the nose, and Anderson was struck twice in the leg.

June, 1873, Medicine Lodge, Kansas. Anderson had returned to Kansas and was tending bar at Harding's Trading Post in an obscure cluster of shacks and cabins called Medicine Lodge. One summer day Mike McCluskie's brother, Arthur, rode into town accompanied by a guide named Richards. Richards entered the trading post, found Anderson, and told him that McCluskie wanted revenge for his brother's death. Richards relayed McCluskie's challenge to a knife or gun duel, and Anderson closed the bar, grimly announcing that he had "a chore to do." Anderson enlisted his boss, Harding, as a second and decided to fight the larger McCluskie with pistols.

A large crowd gathered at dusk, betting heavily on the outcome of the fight. Anderson and McCluskie stood twenty

paces apart, backs turned to each other, then whirled and fired when a signal shot split the air. Their first shots were too hurried, but McCluskie's second slug broke Anderson's arm. Anderson crumpled to his knees, then rallied and sent a bullet crashing into McCluskie's mouth.

In a rage of pain and fury, McCluskie roared, spat blood and teeth, and charged Anderson. The fallen man continued to fire, putting bullets into McCluskie's leg and abdomen. At last McCluskie went down, and the excited onlookers thought the fight was over. But McCluskie looked up, aimed his revolver, and shot Anderson in the stomach. Anderson tumbled onto his back, but he continued to breathe, and McCluskie clutched his knife and began to crawl painfully toward his foe. A few members of the crowd tried to intercede, but Harding insisted that the fight be concluded. As McCluskie inched toward him, Anderson struggled to a sitting position and drew his own knife. Anderson slashed McCluskie's neck, McCluskie stabbed Anderson in the side, and the bloodstained men finally relaxed in death.

Sources: Miller and Snell, *Great Gunfighters of the Kansas Cowtowns,* 65–72, 74; Yost, *Medicine Lodge,* 75–77.

Anderson, William

Bill Anderson was a habitué of Delano, the unrestrainedly wicked district near Wichita, Kansas. He was involved in two shootouts there in 1873, and the final one blinded him and ended his gunfighting days.

Gunfights: Spring, 1873, Wichita, Kansas. In a Wichita livery stable a quarrel broke out among several men, one of whom was Anderson. Guns were drawn, and Anderson squeezed off a shot which killed an onlooker. Anderson was later acquitted on grounds that the shooting was accidental.

October 27, 1873, Wichita, Kansas. On a Monday evening Anderson was standing at Rowdy Joe Lowe's bar in Delano, drinking and talking with bartender Walter Beebe. Suddenly a drunken Red Beard burst into the saloon and shot dance hall girl Annie Franklin in the stomach. An equally drunken Joe Lowe fired at Beard with a shotgun. There was a quick flurry of shots before Lowe chased Beard outside, and one of the slugs slammed into Anderson's head. The bullet passed behind Anderson's eyes, splattering the bar with blood and blinding him permanently.

Sources: Miller and Snell, *Great Gunfighters of the Kansas Cowtowns,* 158, 160–61, 163–64, 167.

Texas Ranger Captain John Armstrong, who tracked down John Wesley Hardin. *(Courtesy Western History Collections, University of Oklahoma Library)*

Armstrong, John Barclay

("McNelly's Bulldog")

(b. January, 1850, McMinnville, Tennessee; d. May 1, 1913, Armstrong, Texas. Law officer, rancher.) The son of a Tennessee doctor, Armstrong left home as a youth and drifted to Missouri, Arkansas, and later, in 1871, Austin, Texas. He married and eventually raised seven children. In 1875 he enlisted in the Texas Rangers under the command of the famed L. H. McNelly and became known as "McNelly's Bulldog." He accompanied McNelly on excursions into Mexico which resulted in notorious and comparatively large-scale clashes with Mexican forces at Palo Alto and Las Cuevas.

In 1876 Armstrong, by now a sergeant, helped gun down four men during a night filled with three shooting scrapes. The next year his reputation as a gunman was somewhat dimmed when he wounded himself while carelessly handling his own weapon. But that same year he was promoted to lieutenant, and he promptly proved himself a highly efficient and dangerous law enforcement leader. Armstrong recovered stolen livestock, curtailed the activities of such lethal badmen as King Fisher, and, in his most famous exploit, captured elusive killer John Wesley Hardin.

Armstrong collected a reward of four thousand dollars for Hardin's arrest, and he used that stake to establish a fifty-thousand-acre ranch in Willacy County, Texas. He served for a time as a U.S. marshal, but business increasingly absorbed his time. He died on his ranch in 1913.

Gunfights: October 1, 1876, near Carrizo, Texas. Sergeant Armstrong, conducting a ranger patrol into King Fisher's territory, closed in on an outlaw camp at Espinoza Lake. The desperadoes had learned that lawmen were nearby, and six men had fled, but four men were still in camp when Armstrong arrived at midnight, and they tried to resist arrest. A vicious gunfight ensued, and Armstrong and his men cut down all four of their adversaries. Three of the outlaws died, and the fourth was hit four times. That same night small detachments of Armstrong's squad killed two other outlaws in separate shootouts.

December 7, 1876, Wilson County, Texas. A large reward had been posted for accused murderer John Mayfield, and Armstrong and Ranger Leroy Deggs rode to Mayfield's ranch in Wilson County. Mayfield was in his corral when the rangers arrived, and when they tried to arrest him he went for a gun. Armstrong and Deggs both opened fire, killing Mayfield on the spot. Within moments an angry crowd of the dead man's relatives and friends had gathered, and the situation became so threatening that the rangers quickly withdrew. Mayfield was then buried secretly, with the result that the reward was never paid.

August 23, 1877, Pensacola, Florida. Again attracted by a large reward, Armstrong began to comb the Gulf states in search of John Wesley Hardin, the West's most dangerous killer. Following a lengthy investigation, Armstrong located Hardin, and when the fugitive's train pulled into Pensacola the ranger (who held no legal authority in Florida) was waiting with a hastily gathered posse.

Limping and using a cane, because he had recently shot himself in the leg, Armstrong eased into Hardin's coach, drew his long-barreled .45, and ordered

Hardin and his companions to surrender. Hardin gasped, "Texas, by God!" and went for his own pistol, but the hammer caught in his suspenders. Sitting beside Hardin, however, was nineteen-year old Jim Mann, who produced a six-gun and shot a hole in Armstrong's hat. The ranger coolly drilled the young man through the chest. Mann leaped out the window, staggered several steps, then fell dead.

Hardin kicked Armstrong backward, but the lawman pistol-whipped the fugitive into unconsciousness. Armstrong then arrested Hardin's other three companions, and within a short time the party was on a train headed to Texas.

Sources: Raymond, *Captain Lee Hall,* 49, 53, 86–88, 90, 107, 115, 129–31, 160, 170, 172; Webb, *Texas Rangers,* 291–92, 294–301.

Aten, Ira

(b. September 3, 1863, Cairo, Illinois; d. August 5, 1953, Burlingame, California. Law officer, ranch foreman.) Son of a Methodist minister, Ira and his family moved to a farm near Round Rock, Texas, after the Civil War. As a teen-ager Aten was in Round Rock when the mortally wounded Sam Bass was brought back to town and tended by Reverend Aten. Known locally as a crack shot, Ira joined the Texas Rangers at twenty and was assigned to border duty. After a fight with rustlers he was promoted to corporal and was sent to West Central Texas, where he was instrumental in breaking up widespread cattle rustling activities. In his handling of the arrests of Jim Epps and Rube Boyce he acquired a reputation for leniency as well as a further promotion to sergeant.

In 1887 a long manhunt by Aten and three shootouts resulted in the death of rustler-murderer Judd Roberts. In 1889 Aten was appointed sheriff of Fort Bend County during the violent feud between the "Jaybirds" and "Woodpeckers." Soon thereafter he was appointed sheriff of Castro County, where he took vigorous action against Panhandle rustlers. He next was superintendent of six hundred thousand acres of XIT ranchland from 1895 to 1904. After leaving the XIT he went to California with his wife and five children and resided there until his death in 1953 at the age of nearly ninety.

Gunfights: *May, 1884, Rio Grande River, Texas.* Seven rangers, including Aten, were hunting a gang of rustlers eighty miles below Laredo. Two cattle thieves were spotted, and Aten and two other lawmen raced to head them off before they crossed in Mexico. Ranger Ben Reilly drew near the desperadoes but was shot from the saddle with a shattered thigh, and Frank Sieker was struck in the heart. Working his Winchester from horseback, Aten wounded both outlaws: one was hit in the shoulder, and one in the hand. Aten and the other rangers rounded up the wounded bandits later in the day, but were themselves arrested on trumped-up charges by the crooked county sheriff, Dario Gonzalez. Aten remained in the Webb County jail for twenty-seven days.

April, 1887, Williamson County, Texas. Aten was searching Williamson and Burnet counties for Judd Roberts, a murderer who had escaped from jail in San Antonio. At a ranch near the Burnet-Williamson county line Aten concealed himself and surprised Roberts as the outlaw rode up. Roberts drew his gun and fired wild, and Aten shot him in the hand. Roberts dropped his six-shooter, but made good his escape by spurring away.

June, 1887, Liberty Hill, Texas. Two months later Aten was back in Burnet County, still on the trail of Roberts. He spent the night at the Liberty Hill ranch of John Hughes, who also had clashed with Roberts. At dawn a vengeful Roberts tried to creep up on the ranch house, but Aten alertly armed himself and told Roberts he was under arrest. Startled, Roberts squeezed off a shot, then again was wounded in the shooting hand by Aten. Once more, however, he galloped off to safety.

July, 1887, Texas Panhandle. For a month Aten and Hughes trailed Roberts. They finally located the outlaw courting a rancher's daughter at an isolated Panhandle spread. The two manhunters ambushed him near the ranch house. Once again Roberts tried to shoot his way out, but Aten and Hughes punctured him with six slugs, and the outlaw died in the arms of his hysterical sweetheart.

After the fight Aten persuaded Hughes to join the Texas Rangers, and in August the recruit began a distinguished twenty-eight-year career.

December 25, 1889, near Vance Texas. Alvin and Will Odle, rustlers and accused murderers, tried to fight their way out of an ambush set by Rangers Aten, John Hughes, and Bass Outlaw and Deputy Sheriff Will Terry. Illuminated by moonlight, the outlaw brothers were blasted off their horses and died within moments.

November, 1891, Dimmitt, Texas. A few months earlier Aten had moved to the vicinity and established a homestead. During a local election controversy Aten came to oppose a faction led by two land-grabbing brothers from Tennessee, Hugh and Andrew McClelland, who called a public meeting to denounce the former ranger. Aten boldly attended and was called a liar by Andrew, a lawyer and candidate for the position of county judge. After a heated election the Mc-Clelland "ring" was defeated, and Aten went immediately to the county seat, Dimmitt, to settle his account with Andrew McClelland. When Aten found him, the lawyer was unarmed.

"Andrew, you called me a liar not long ago," said Aten. "Do you still say it?"

"I still say it, Aten!" replied McClelland. "But I have to say it unarmed."

"Arm yourself," challenged Aten. "I'll wait."

McClelland ducked into a store and burst out a few moments later, flourishing a brace of new .45's. He snapped off two wild shots at the former ranger, and Aten calmly shot him in the arm, knocking him off his feet. McClelland fired wildly again, but Aten generously allowed his friends to carry him off.

Then, as Aten turned away, another slug went whizzing by his face. He whirled to spot Hugh McClelland ducking behind a nearby shack, firing as he moved. Aten fired, and the slug crashed through the flimsy pine planking to wound McClelland. McClelland shot again, and Aten once more fired through the shack to nick Hugh a second time. McClelland fled, and Aten surrendered himself to local custody.

Sources: Preece, *Lone Star Man— Ira Aten;* Martin, *Border Boss,* 33–38, 40–42, 55–66, 68–75, 82–84, 207, 215–16.

Baca, Elfego

(b. 1865, Socorro, New Mexico; d. 1945, Albuquerque, New Mexico. Laborer, clerk, law officer, politician, school superintendent, attorney.) Born in Socorro, Baca moved with his family to Kansas, where he spent his boyhood. When he was in his teens the family returned to New Mexico. In 1882 Baca's father, Francisco, killed two cowboys in a gunfight and was sentenced to a stiff prison term. Elfego finally found steady employment working in a store in Socorro, but he hoped to carry on his father's tradition as a hard case. He bought a mail-order badge and began sporting a pair of six-guns, which he soon put to desperate use. In 1884 he stood off eighty cowboys for thirty-three hours in what became one of New Mexico's most famous gunfights.

Following this "miracle of the jacal," Baca capitalized upon his reputation to secure a variety of public offices, including county clerk, deputy sheriff, county sheriff, mayor of Socorro, school superintendent, and district attorney. He also ran unsuccessfully for the post of district judge and governor of New Mexico and forged a career as one of the state's most prominent lawyers. Elected sheriff of Socorro County in 1919, he mailed letters to various neighborhood fugitives ordering them to surrender or suffer his lethal displeasure— and several wanted men actually complied. Baca died at the age of eighty in Albuquerque, with his boots off.

Gunfights: *October, 1884, Frisco, New Mexico.* A cowboy named McCarty was shooting up the town, concentrating his drunken efforts upon making the Mexican populace "dance" by firing at their feet. The nineteen-year-old Baca cockily pinned on his mail-order badge, pulled out his guns, and "arrested" McCarty. He then marched McCarty to the Middle Plaza, intending to leave at daylight for the county seat at Socorro, but several punchers led by McCarty's foreman, a man named Perham, confronted him and demanded that he release their friend. Baca waved his revolvers and retorted that he would give them until the count of three to leave town. He quickly counted, "One, two, three," and began firing. One cowboy took a slug in the knee, and Perham's horse reared and fell, fatally injuring the foreman.

In the morning a group of citizens led by J. H. Cook approached Baca and persuaded him to turn over his "prisoner" to the local justice of the peace. The justice fined McCarty five dollars, and a satisfied Baca turned to leave. But outside he was met by eighty cowboys led by Tom Slaughter, owner of the ranch for which Perham and McCarty worked. A shot was fired, and Baca ducked into an alley. He sprinted into a nearby jacal, a tiny building inhabited by a woman and two children, and pushed them outside just as rancher Jim Herne rushed the dwelling on foot, brandishing a rifle. Baca pumped two bullets into Herne, and the rancher collapsed, mortally wounded.

Herne's body was dragged away, and the cowboys began to pour systematic volleys into the jacal. The flimsy building was constructed only of posts and mud, but the floor was dug out about eighteen inches below ground level, and Baca crouched low as bullets whipped over his head. From time to time he managed to shoot back, and his aim was so deadly that his adversaries tied ropes between nearby buildings and draped blankets over them so that they could walk about in comparative safety. Baca placed a plaster replica of a saint in a window and dropped his hat on top of it to provide an alternate target.

About dusk a volley succeeded in collapsing part of the roof, and Baca was buried under the rubble, managing to dig himself out only after two hours of effort. At midnight a stick of dynamite demolished half the building, but

Baca survived in a far corner. At dawn he coolly began to cook breakfast, to the delight of a large group of Mexicans who had arrived to cheer him. One cowboy managed to close in behind a cast-iron shield made from a cookstove, but Baca sent him scampering away by grazing him on the skull.

It was claimed that more than four thousand bullets were fired into the little jacal, that the door had 367 holes in it, and that a broom handle had been hit eight times. But Baca fought grimly on, finally killing four men and wounding several others. At last Cook, followed by a deputy sheriff named Ross and Francisquito Naranjo, approached the ruined jacal and persuaded Baca to come out. He emerged at 6:00 P.M. after thirty-three hours under siege, having agreed to let the cowboys take him under custody to Socorro, but insisting that he be allowed to keep his guns. When they set out, the cowboys rode in the lead, followed by a buckboard, driven by Ross, in the rear of which Baca was seated with his guns alertly trained on his captors. Baca was tried twice for murder, but won acquittal on both occasions.

1915, El Paso, Texas. On a Sunday afternoon Baca and a companion were approached outside El Paso's Paso del Norte Hotel by an antagonist, Celestino Otero. The situation became ominous, and Baca and his friend, Dr. Romero, tried to drive away in the latter's automobile. But Otero and several companions crowded around, and Baca hopped out of the car. Otero squeezed off a shot which missed, and Baca pumped two slugs into his adversary's chest. Otero died immediately, and a jury later acquitted Baca.

Sources: Crichton, *Law and Order,*

Ltd.; Looney, *Haunted Highways,* 28, 126–32.

Baker, Cullen Montgomery

(b. June 22, 1835, Weakly County, Tennessee; d. January 6, 1869, south-western Arkansas. Farmer, soldier, ferryman, bandit.) Cullen Baker moved with his family to Texas when he was four; they settled finally on a farm in Cass County. As a youth Baker became a crack shot, a braggart, and a heavy drinker. In February, 1854, he married, but a few months later he killed a man and fled to Perry County, Arkansas. In 1856 he stabbed a man named Wartham to death, returned to Texas for his wife, then went back to Arkansas.

In 1860 Baker's wife died, and he returned home to leave their daughter with her grandfather. Two years later he remarried, but soon thereafter he entered the Confederate Army and was stationed in Little Rock. He deserted the Confederacy, served in the Union Army for a time, then deserted again and joined a gang of bandit raiders. After the war he operated a ferry across the Sulphur River in southwestern Arkansas until his second wife died in 1866. He erected an effigy of her clad in her clothing, but two months later he proposed to her sixteen-year-old sister—and was stiffly refused by her parents.

Baker was involved in a number of gunfights and was wanted for several murders, and further rewards were offered for him after he organized a gang of thieves. After a number of depredations Baker was hunted down and killed in 1869.

Gunfights: August, 1854, Cass County, Texas. A local farmer named Baily accused Baker of bullying an orphan, and Baker went to Baily's house and found him on his porch. Baily fired a pistol shot at Baker, who then opened up with his revolver. Baily staggered back with the impact of the first slug, and a second bullet slammed into his head and killed him in front of his horrified family.

Spring, 1864, Spanish Bluffs, Arkansas. Baker had recently deserted the Confederate Army and still was in uniform when four Union soldiers entered a bar where he was drinking. Baker instantly went for his gun, shot three troopers, and escaped. He fled north to Little Rock and there joined the Federal occupation force.

June 1, 1867, Cass County, Texas. Baker owed money to a storekeeper named Rowden, whose enterprise was located on a road in Cass County, Texas. Rowden pressed Baker for his money, and one night Cullen appeared at the store, shouting for the owner to come outside. Arming himself with a shotgun, Rowden emerged, and Baker opened fire with his pistol. He pumped four slugs into Rowden, and the merchant collapsed, dead before he hit the ground.

June, 1867, Pett's Ferry, Texas. At Pett's Ferry across the Sulphur River, Baker was approached by two suspicious soldiers. The sergeant soon decided that Baker was a fugitive and went for his gun, but Cullen produced a pistol and shot him to death. The private fled, and Baker escaped the scene.

October 10, 1867, Cass County, Texas. On the road between Linden and Boston, Baker held up a government supply wagon with a four-man escort. The driver tried to reach for his revolver, but Baker killed him. The four guards halfheartedly traded a few shots with Baker, then abandoned the wagon.

October, 1868, Boston, Texas. Baker antagonistically swaggered up to an army captain named Kirkham and announced: "I'm Cullen Baker. You looking for me?" Kirkham went for his gun, but was killed by a bullet in the head, and Baker then boldly escaped.

January 6, 1869, southeastern Arkansas. In the past Baker had bullied and threatened Thomas Orr, a schoolteacher with a crippled right hand. Orr led three men, including Baker's second father-in-law, in tracking Baker to southeastern Arkansas. They came upon Baker and a companion eating lunch beside the road, and immediately the posse charged with guns blazing. Baker and his friend both were killed, and on Baker's corpse were found a shotgun, four revolvers, three derringers, and six pocketknives.

Sources: Webb, *Handbook of Texas,* I, 98; Breihan, *Great Gunfighters of the West,* 66–87.

Barkley, Clint

("Bill Bowen")

(Cowboy, gunman.) Accused of a murder in Texas in 1873, Barkley adopted the alias Bill Bowen and fled to Lampasas to seek the help of Merritt Horrell, his brother-in-law. The five lethal Horrell brothers, all local cattlemen, gave Barkley shelter and a job, and when state policemen attempted to arrest him, the Horrells helped in gunning down the lawmen. Barkley next assisted the Horrells in staging a jail break, then accompanied them to New Mexico and further violence. He returned with them to Texas and fought actively in the Horrell-Higgins feud before dropping out of sight.

Gunfights: *March 19, 1873, Lampasas, Texas.* Sought by Captain Tom Williams and three state policemen, Barkley was informed by the Horrells that they would defend him with their guns. Barkley, Tom, Mart, and Sam Horrell and several other cowboys went into town to Jerry Scott's Matador Saloon. When Williams and his men entered the building, they were met by a hail of lead. Mart and Tom were wounded, but Williams and two policemen were shot to death. Mart was carried to his mother's home nearby, and the rest of the party went into hiding.

March, 1873, Georgetown, Texas. Mart Horrell and Jerry Scott were soon arrested and jailed in Georgetown, and within days a breakout was attempted. The Horrell faction rode into town, and while the others stood guard with rifles, Barkley assaulted the door with a sledgehammer. Townspeople opened fire, and Barkley was slightly wounded, but he kept swinging until the door shattered. When A. S. Fisher, a local lawyer, was seriously wounded, the citizens retreated, and the Horrell party made good their escape.

June, 1877, Lampasas County, Texas. Several members of the Horrell group attempted to raid a line camp of neighboring rancher Pink Higgins. While they were in the stock corral at dawn, two cowhands emerged from the line shack, and the rustlers opened fire. Both Higgins men were gunned down, and the Horrell party mounted and fled.

June 14, 1877, Lampasas, Texas. Barkley and his brother Tom; Mart, Sam, and Tom Horrell; and two other Horrell men encountered Pink Higgins, his chief lieutenant, Bill Wren, and several other members of his faction in the streets of Lampasas. Shooting immediately broke out, and Wren was dropped with a severe wound. Frank Mitchell, Higgins' brother-in-law, was killed, but before there were any more casualties local citizens prevailed upon the gunmen to cease fire.

July, 1877, Lampasas County, Texas. The Horrells and their men were attacked at their ranch headquarters by Higgins and fourteen gunhands. Two Horrell men were wounded, but the Horrell party vigorously fired back from inside the ranch building, and after a two-day siege Higgins ordered a withdrawal.

Sources: Gillett, *Six Years with the Texas Rangers*, 74–80; Rasch, "The Horrell War," *NMHR;* Webb, *Texas Rangers*, 334–39.

Barnes, Seaborn

("Seab," "Nubbins Colt")

(b. Cass County, Texas; d. July 19, 1878, Round Rock, Texas. Train and bank robber.) Seaborn Barnes was a hard-bitten gunman who won notoriety as Sam Bass's chief lieutenant. Barnes's father was the sheriff of Cass County, Texas, but died when Seab was an infant. Seab was raised near the village of Handley (nine miles east of Fort Worth), where his widowed mother, with her five children, moved to be among relatives. The origin of his nickname is unknown. At the age of seventeen Barnes fell into trouble over a shooting and spent a year in a Fort Worth jail.

Early in 1878 Bass, having recently eluded posses in Nebraska, began organizing a gang of thieves in the Dallas area. Barnes joined the gang and became Bass's most trusted accomplice. That spring the band pulled four train robberies, which gained Barnes almost as much lead as gold. The train jobs yielded comparatively little loot, the

robbers were frequently fired upon, and at Mesquite, Barnes was shot four times in the legs. A few months later he was gunned down in the streets of Round Rock and was buried in the cemetery near the gang's recent campsite. Three days later Bass died of wounds suffered in the same fight, and he was interred alongside Barnes. On Barnes's tombstone was inscribed: "He was right bower [sea anchor] to Sam Bass."

Gunfights: April 10, 1878, Mesquite, Texas. Bass, Barnes, and other members of the gang rode into Mesquite intent upon pulling another area train holdup. When they intercepted the train, however, they almost immediately met stiff resistance. A furious volley erupted from train passengers, railroad employees, and convict guards. Several of the robbers were hit, and Barnes suffered the worst damage. One slug entered his left leg, and three punctured his right, and he eagerly followed the rest of his cohorts as they galloped away from the depot.

June 13, 1878, Salt Creek, Wise County, Texas. Barnes and the rest of the Bass gang had been hotly pursued by posses and Texas Rangers. On June 13 a posse led by Sheriff W. F. Eagan and Ranger Captain June Peak found the outlaws camped at Salt Creek in Wise County. A sharp fight ensued, and train robber Arkansas Johnson was shot to death. The posse also shot or captured the gang's horses, but Barnes and the other survivors managed to escape on foot. They quickly found horses to steal and eluded their pursuers.

September 19, 1878, Round Rock, Texas. A few days earlier Barnes had camped near the Round Rock cemetery along with Bass, Frank Jackson, and Jim Murphy. The four outlaws planned to rob

Sam Bass (standing, at the left). Joe and Joel Collins are seated, Joel brandishing the cocked six-gun. J. E. Gardner is also standing. *(Courtesy Western History Collections, University of Oklahoma Library)*

the Round Rock bank, but Murphy had secretly begun informing to Texas Rangers about the activities of the Bass gang.

The robbery was planned for Saturday, July 20, and on Friday the robbers rode into town for a final look. Knowing that the town was filling with lawmen, Murphy cautiously dropped behind. The other three entered Round Rock, tethered their mounts in an alley, and strolled into a store next door to the bank. Soon they were approached by Deputy Sheriffs Morris Moore and

Ellis Grimes, who grabbed the back of Barnes's shoulder and asked if he was armed. There was a city ordinance against carrying firearms, and the deputies were inquiring about suspicious bulges beneath the strangers' coats. In reply Barnes pulled his gun and whirled around, and all three outlaws opened fire. Grimes was killed, and Moore was wounded in the chest.

Bass, Barnes, and Jackson then sprinted for their horses, but Texas Rangers and local citizens, alerted by the gunfire, ran into the street and began firing. Ranger Private Dick Ware emerged from a barber shop, bib around his neck and lather on his face, and squeezed off a shot as Barnes neared his horse. The slug caught Barnes in the head, and he collapsed and died in the street. Jackson and mortally wounded Bass managed to gallop out of town, and the question of the slain outlaw's identity was raised. Murphy soon arrived on the scene and described the bullet scars on Barnes's legs, and local curiosity was satisfied.

Sources: Gard, *Sam Bass,* 108–218, 225, 233, 238–39; Webb, *Texas Rangers,* 374, 379–80, 382–83, 386–89.

Bass, Samuel

(b. July 21, 1851, Mitchell, Indiana; d. July 21, 1878, Round Rock, Texas. Farmer, teamster, gambler, cowboy, saloon owner, miner, bank and train robber, laborer.) Sam Bass was orphaned while a child and reared by an uncle. Bass left Indiana in 1869, went to St. Louis, and after a brief stay drifted downriver to Rosedale, Mississippi, where he worked in a sawmill for a year. In 1870 he moved to Denton, Texas, and in time he was hired as a farmhand and teamster by Sheriff W. F. Eagan, who later participated in the manhunt

for Bass. Bass was a frugal, dependable employee, but in 1874 he acquired a racehorse and soon was successful enough to leave Eagan. The next year he won a string of ponies from an Indian at Fort Sill, Oklahoma, and when the owner refused to surrender the herd, Bass seized them at night and headed for San Antonio.

In August, 1876, Bass and Joel Collins led a herd of cattle to Kansas, shipped the steers to Sidney, Nebraska, then drove them to booming Deadwood, Dakota Territory. For a time Bass and Collins operated a freight line out of Deadwood, but they soon sold out and opened a casino and saloon. Next they bought a mine, but they went broke and decided to turn to thievery. Enlisting several eager desperadoes, they systematically robbed seven stagecoaches before deciding to leave the Black Hills for a more ambitious operation.

Assisted by James Berry, Jack Davis, Bill Heffridge, and Tom Nixon, the outlaws held up a train at Big Spring, Nebraska, on September 18, 1877. They seized more than sixty thousand dollars, most of it newly minted twenty-dollar gold pieces. The robbers split the money, but a week later Collins and Heffridge were gunned down, and twenty-five thousand dollars was recovered. Berry was soon shot as well, and before dying he revealed the names of his cohorts. But Bass made good his return to Texas, where he began organizing another band of robbers.

In the spring of 1878 Bass staged four train holdups in the Dallas area, but the robbers snared little loot, and a widespread manhunt ensued. In September, Bass's plan to rob a bank in Round Rock was foiled by Jim Murphy, a member of his gang who betrayed the outlaw leader to the Texas Rangers in exchange for leniency. Bass was shot in the streets of Round Rock, and he died two days later on his twenty-seventh birthday.

Gunfights: *April 10, 1878, Mesquite, Texas.* Just six days after pulling another area holdup, Bass and his gang tried to rob a train in Mesquite. They encountered unexpected resistance, however. Train employees, passengers, and convict guards poured forth a withering volley, and after several of the outlaws suffered minor wounds, the gang galloped away from the station.

June 13, 1878, Salt Creek, Wise County, Texas. Ranger Captain June Peak and Sheriff W. F. Eagan were leading a posse in pursuit of Bass and his gang, and over the weeks several skirmishes had occurred. The lawmen encountered the outlaw camp in Wise County, and the "Salt Creek Fight" erupted. The posse killed Arkansas Johnson and shot or captured all of the bandits' horses. Bass and his surviving gang members shot their way out of the camp and escaped on foot. They managed to steal some horses and fled to Denton County.

July 19, 1878, Round Rock, Texas. Bass, Seaborn Barnes, Frank Jackson, and Jim Murphy had encamped near Round Rock with the intention of robbing the local bank. Murphy, however, had informed on Bass, and the town was swarming with lawmen.

The outlaws already had cased the bank twice and had decided to rob it on Saturday, July 20. On Friday they rode into town for a last look, and Murphy managed to drop behind his companions, muttering something about buying corn for the horses. Bass, Barnes, and Jackson tied their horses in an alley, then went into the Koppel store adjacent to the bank to buy tobacco for Bass. There they were ap-

proached by deputy sheriffs Ellis Grimes and Morris Moore. Grimes placed a hand on Barnes and asked if he were armed. The three bandits whirled and opened fire, killing Grimes on the spot and downing Morris with a chest wound.

Bass, wounded in the hand, led a sprint for the horses, but the bandits were fired upon by several Texas Rangers and local citizens. Ranger Dick Ware killed Barnes, and Ranger George Harrell began firing as Bass and Jackson galloped by. A slug ripped into Bass on the right side of his spine and tore through his body, exiting to the left of his navel. Bass clung to the horn, but after another couple of hundred yards he dropped out of the saddle. Frank Jackson braved a hail of lead to pick up Bass, and the pair escaped into the approaching night. But Bass was unable to ride, and Jackson dropped him off under a tree outside of town.

Bass bound his wounds with strips of his shirt, and a posse found him sitting under the tree the next morning. He was taken into Round Rock, and he lingered until Sunday, stubbornly refusing to reveal any information. He was buried beside Barnes.

Sources: Gard, *Sam Bass;* Webb, *Texas Rangers,* 371–91.

Beard, Edward T.

("Red")

(b. ca. 1828, Beardstown, Illinois; d. November 11, 1873, Wichita, Kansas. Dance hall proprietor.) The son of the man who founded Beardstown, Illinois, Beard was well educated and married to a cultured woman from Virginia. Although he was a member of a prominent family and the father of three children, Beard abruptly pulled up stakes in 1861 and went West. He became a

footloose and somewhat notorious character in California, Oregon, and Arizona before being attracted to Kansas by the cattle boom. In Wichita he established a disreputable dance hall, and in 1873 he engaged in a series of wild shootouts, the last of which caused his death at the hands of Rowdy Joe Lowe.

Gunfights: *June 3, 1873, Wichita, Kansas.* In Beard's dance hall in Delano, just outside Wichita, several cavalrymen had a quarrel with a prostitute named Emma Stanley. After arguing over a small sum of money, one of the soldiers drew his revolver and inflicted a flesh wound in Emma's thigh. At the sound of the shot Beard produced a six-gun and rushed toward the trouble, firing indiscriminately at the soldiers. The man who shot Emma escaped and deserted that night, but two innocent troopers went down: Doley, with a slug in his throat at the base of the tongue, and Boyle, his right ankle shattered. Doley and Boyle survived, but their comrades were incensed at Beard.

June 5, 1873, Wichita, Kansas. The following night the soldiers sought revenge against Beard. Laying their plans carefully, they stationed a guard outside the sheriff's house and one at the river bridge, and another man was left with their horses. Then, about 2:00 A.M. the remaining thirty troopers marched in columns of four to Beard's dance hall. There was a flurry of shooting in which a dance hall girl and a man named Charles Leshhart were wounded, and Emma Stanley was shot again. In the end Beard's building was burned to the ground, and the soldiers filed away in orderly fashion.

October 27, 1873, Wichita, Kansas. Beard quickly rebuilt his dance hall, but he soon found himself at odds with Rowdy Joe Lowe, owner of a similar establishment adjacent to Beard's place. On a Monday evening Beard drank himself stupid in his building, quarreled with and threatened a prostitute named Jo DeMerritt (who later was convicted of forging a deed to a piece of property belonging to Beard). Red next fired through a window at Joe Lowe, then drunkenly mistook Annie Franklin for Jo DeMerritt and shot the poor woman in the stomach.

As Annie doubled over, an equally drunken Lowe barged inside and fired a shotgun at Beard, who returned the shot, then ran outside. Bill Anderson, standing at the bar, was wounded in the head by a stray slug, and Lowe suffered a minor wound in the neck. Lowe pursued Beard, shot him at the river bridge, then surrendered himself to local authorities. His right arm and hip shattered fearfully by buckshot, Beard held on to life for two weeks before dying at 3:00 A.M. on November 11.

Sources: Miller and Snell, *Great Gunfighters of the Kansas Cowtowns,* 42, 156–63; Drago, *Wild, Woolly & Wicked,* 151, 161–62.

Beckwith, John H.

(b. New Mexico; d. 1879, Seven Rivers, New Mexico. Rancher, law officer.) Beckwith was a native of New Mexico who, along with his brother Bob, started a cattle ranch on the east side of the Pecos River in the Seven Rivers country of Lincoln County. When the Lincoln County War erupted, the Beckwith boys were deputized to fight Billy the Kid and the rest of the McSween "Regulators." Bob was killed during the climactic battle in Lincoln in 1878, and John was shot to death the following year by John Jones.

Gunfights: February 18, 1878, near Lincoln, New Mexico. Beckwith's first job as a Lincoln County "deputy" was to assist the posse which seized a number of John Tunstall's livestock. The posse then met Tunstall on the road near Lincoln and killed him, thus touching off the Lincoln County War.

August 16, 1878, near Seven Rivers, New Mexico. At the ranch of Henry Beckwith, John's crusty old father, a simmering family quarrel exploded in the presence of a number of bystanders. Henry killed his son-in-law, William Johnson, with a shotgun blast, then had to be restrained from shooting John when the latter angrily tried to intervene. At that point Wallace Olinger, who was Johnson's partner in a nearby ranch, began firing at Henry Beckwith, hitting him in the cheek and nose. Olinger was arrested, but when Beckwith recovered he was released from custody.

August 26, 1879, Lincoln County, New Mexico. Beckwith fell into a quarrel with rustler John Jones over the ownership of a herd of cattle, and the two men quickly resorted to gunplay. After a brief flurry of shots Beckwith was fatally wounded.

Sources: Keleher, *Violence in Lincoln County,* 140–41, 159, 223, 233; Klasner, *My Girlhood Among Outlaws,* 64, 67, 172, 174; Fulton, *Lincoln County War,* 213, 216, 251, 333, 370.

Beckwith, Robert W.

(b. 1858, New Mexico; d. July 19, 1878, Lincoln, New Mexico. Rancher, law officer.) Beckwith was the son of a Southerner who had settled in New Mexico and who eventually established a ranch in Lincoln County. By 1876

Bob and his brother John were running a spread of their own, but when the Lincoln County War started a couple of years later the Beckwith brothers became involved with the Dolan-Murphy faction. Bob received an appointment as deputy sheriff, but was killed before his twentieth birthday during the big shootout in Lincoln.

Gunfights: February 18, 1878, near Lincoln, New Mexico. Beckwith was a member of the posse which attached a number of livestock belonging to John Tunstall. When the posse encountered Tunstall near Lincoln, shooting broke out, and the rancher was murdered.

April 30, 1878, near Lincoln, New Mexico. Beckwith was a prominent member of the "Seven Rivers crowd" which intercepted Regulator leader Frank McNab about eight miles from Lincoln. When McNab and his two companions, Frank Coe and Ab Sanders, stopped to water their horses at a stream, Beckwith and his cohorts opened fire. McNab and Sanders, who had dismounted, were hit in the first volley, but Coe had stayed in the saddle, and he promptly spurred his mount. Coe's horse was killed, however, and he was arrested after emptying his six-gun at his attackers. The posse returned and finished off McNab, who had tried to crawl away, but Sanders later recovered from his wounds.

July 15–19, 1878, Lincoln, New Mexico. Beckwith was active during the four-day siege of Alexander McSween's house. After the building was set ablaze during the evening of the final day, Beckwith and several of his companions moved in. Beckwith stepped into the open and shouted that he was a deputy sheriff and that he would protect the

McSween men inside. But as he approached the door, they began to shoot at him from inside, and when he tried to fire back, his gun jammed. He was hit in the wrist, then slammed to the ground by a bullet which entered his left eye. (Maurice Fulton writes that, when John Jones tried to shoot McSween, Beckwith intervened, but Jones's rifle slug passed through his wrist and into his eye.) The McSween men came out shooting, and McSween was killed, falling almost on top of Beckwith. But Beckwith was already dead and oblivious to the fighting which swirled around him.

Sources: Keleher, *Violence in Lincoln County,* 140–41, 144, 155, 159, 233–34, 251–52, 258–59, 261, 265, 276; Hunt, *Tragic Days of Billy the Kid,* 75–76, 101–103; Klasner, *My Girlhood Among Outlaws,* 67, 174, 179; Fulton, *Lincoln County War,* 23, 37–40, 119, 213, 216–17, 251, 271–74; Coe, *Frontier Fighter,* 82–84.

Bideno, Juan

(d. July 7, 1871, Bluff Creek, Kansas. Cowboy.) Bideno's known career as a gunman was compressed into a few violent days in the summer of 1871. Bideno killed his trail boss while herding cattle toward Abilene. A posse pursued Bideno, and he was killed in a shootout with John Wesley Hardin.

Gunfights: July 5, 1871, Cottonwood River, Kansas. Bideno had hired on to trail a herd of cattle from Texas to the Kansas railhead at Abilene. At the crossing of the Cottonwood, Bideno clashed with his trail boss, twenty-two-year-old Billy Cohron. When shooting broke out, Bideno mortally wounded Cohron and immediately fled south toward Indian Territory.

July 7, 1871, Bluff Creek, Kansas. Wes Hardin, Jim Rodgers, Hugh Anderson, and Cohron's brother John tracked Bideno to tiny Bluff Creek, where they located him eating in a café. Hardin walked inside while the others surrounded the place. When Hardin approached Bideno, the fugitive dropped his knife and fork and went for his gun, but Hardin shot him in the head at close range and he died on the floor.

Sources: Streeter, *Prairie Trails & Cow Towns,* 86–87; Schoenberger, *Gunfighters,* 82.

Blake, William

("Tulsa Jack")

(d. spring, 1895, near Dover, Oklahoma. Cowboy, bank and train robber.) Blake was a cowboy in Kansas during the 1880's, but later he wandered south and became a member of the Doolin gang. He was wanted for the deaths of two men. Blake was killed in the wild shootout between lawmen and the Doolin gang after a train robbery near Dover, Oklahoma.

Gunfights: September 1, 1893, Ingalls, Oklahoma. Blake fought in the Battle of Ingalls, shooting his way from the hotel to the stable and then galloping out of town with the rest of Doolin's Oklahombres.

May 20, 1895, Southwest City, Missouri. While the Doolin gang was robbing a bank in Southwest City, a gunfight erupted. Doolin was wounded in the head, and Bill Dalton killed a citizen named J. C. Seaborn. But Doolin made it to his horse, and the outlaws fought their way out of town.

Spring, 1895, near Dover, Oklahoma. A posse led by Chris Madsen located

Those who lived by the gun often died by it, as did Tulsa Jack Blake (extreme right, second row from the top). *(Courtesy Western History Collections, University of Oklahoma Library)*

the Doolin gang encamped on the Cimarron River. Blake was guarding the sleeping band when he spotted Deputy William Banks. Blake fired a shot, then a general engagement began. A bullet from the lawmen struck Blake's cartridge belt and exploded a shell, mortally wounding the outlaw. The rest of the gang managed to escape after a running gun battle.

Sources: Croy, *Trigger Marshal,* 177, 181; Drago, *Road Agents and Train Robbers,* 201, 205–207; Shirley, *Sixgun and Silver Star,* 91–93, 104–105, 145, 151–52, 159, 172–74, 179.

Blevins, Andy

("Andy Cooper")

(d. September 4, 1887, Holbrook, Arizona. Cowboy, rustler.) Blevins was a member of a ranching family from Texas who moved to Pleasant Valley, Arizona, and became involved in the local range war. Reported to have been a rustler and killer in Texas, Andy "Cooper" (an often-used alias) hired out his gun to the cattlemen's side. Andy killed two men, including the leader of the sheepherder's faction, but was himself shot to death two days later by Perry Owens, who also gunned down two of Andy's brothers and his brother-in-law.

Gunfights: September 2, 1887, Pleasant Valley, Arizona. Blevins and several other cowboys quietly closed in on a secluded sheep camp. After breakfast John Tewksbury, leader of the opposing sheepmen, and Bill Jacobs left the campfire to find their horses. Blevins opened fire, fatally wounding both men. Tewksbury's wife ran toward the scene, but Blevins fired again and drove her away. The other sheepmen managed to hold out from the shelter of a hut and that night slipped away into the darkness. The angry cowboys then allowed several hogs to eat the bodies of Tewksbury and Jacobs.

September 4, 1887, Holbrook, Arizona. As a result of the Pleasant Valley War, Andy's father and one of his brothers had been killed. Mrs. Blevins therefore had left the family ranch in Pleasant Valley and had moved to Holbrook, where she lived with three of her four surviving sons. (The fourth son, Charlie, was killed a short time later.)

Sheriff Perry Owens located the Blevins family and on a Sunday afternoon rode up to their house brandishing a rifle. Andy fired at him from behind a front door, but Owens shot from the hip and mortally wounded Blevins. Andy reeled back and collapsed, and his mother dragged him away from the line of fire. Andy's older brother John opened up on the lawman from the other front door, but Owens put him out of action with another hip shot. A Texan named Mose Roberts, brother-in-law to the family, dashed outside with a pistol, and Owens killed him on the spot. The youngest Blevins boy, sixteen-year-old Sam Houston, then came out with a revolver and was shot down by the deadly Owens. Only John Blevins, wounded in the shoulder, survived the fight.

Sources: Raine, *Famous Sheriffs and Western Outlaws,* 226–35; Drago, *Great Range Wars,* 101–102, 106–27, 130–31, 139, 146, 292; Coolidge, *Fighting Men of the West,* 123–32.

Bowdre, Charlie

(b. ca. 1859, Mississippi or Tennessee; d. December 23, 1880, Stinking Springs, New Mexico. Rustler, gunman, rancher.) A close cohort of Billy the Kid, Bowdre aligned with the "Regulators" in the Lincoln County War, participat-

ing in the assassination of Frank Baker, Billy Morton, and William McCloskey. A few weeks later he fired the shot which killed Buckshot Roberts at Blazer's Mill, and in July, 1878, he played a relatively minor role in the climactic shootout in Lincoln. He then became briefly involved with the Kid's band of rustlers and was inaccurately accused of the murder of Indian agency clerk Morris Bernstein.

But by this time Bowdre had married a native New Mexican and had begun trying to mend his fences. He became foreman of a ranch in the vicinity of Fort Sumner and soon acquired part ownership. A few weeks before his death he met with Pat Garrett to discuss the possibility of exoneration. But a federal warrant still demanded his arrest, and he rejoined the Kid and a handful of other fugitives, leaving his wife in Fort Sumner.

After nightfall on December 19 the half-dozen outlaws rode into Fort Sumner for a brief vacation, but they were jumped by Pat Garrett and a posse. Tom O'Folliard was killed, and so was Dave Rudabaugh's horse, but Rudabaugh vaulted onto Billy Wilson's mount, and the five fugitives escaped safely. They secured a horse for Rudabaugh and secluded themselves in a rock house near Stinking Springs, where Bowdre was killed by the posse on December 23. Bowdre was buried beside O'Folliard at Fort Sumner, and a few months later the two were joined by the remains of the Kid.

Gunfights: *May 12, 1877, Lincoln, New Mexico.* On a quiet Sunday afternoon Bowdre and Alabaman Frank Freeman, both of whom had been drinking heavily, imagined a grievance against cattle magnate John Chisum and sought him out at Alexander McSween's store.

Shouting for Chisum to come out, the drunken pair fired dozens of shots at the windows and doors of the store. Soon they repaired to a nearby café, where Freeman became irked at an army sergeant and shot him in the head.

Sheriff William Brady and a posse quickly confronted Freeman, and Brady pistol-whipped him and sent him sprawling in the street. Freeman jumped up and knocked Brady down with his fist, and Brady's companions came to his rescue. Bowdre tried to help his friend, but John Riley drew his gun and made him watch as Freeman was subdued and carried away. While Freeman was being transported to nearby Fort Stanton, however, he managed to escape.

April 4, 1878, Blazer's Mill, New Mexico. A large group of Regulators led by Dick Brewer had just ridden into Blazer's Mill and were awaiting a meal. A member of the opposing faction, Buckshot Roberts, armed with a brace of pistols and a Winchester, rode into their midst on a mule. Regulator Frank Coe tried to talk him into surrendering, but Bowdre, Henry Brown, and George Coe soon approached with more violent intentions.

Leveling a gun, Bowdre ordered Roberts to submit to arrest. But Roberts reached for the Winchester on his lap and snarled, "Not much, Mary Ann!" The two men fired simultaneously and Bowdre's slug tore through Roberts' middle. Roberts' bullet ricocheted off Bowdre's cartridge belt and shattered George Coe's hand. Roberts staggered back, but managed to shoot John Middleton in the chest as the Regulators dove for cover.

Roberts barricaded himself inside Blazer's sleeping quarters and killed Brewer with a shot in the head, but it was evident that he was near death. The posse therefore left him to die and rode off to seek medical help for Middleton and Coe.

May 14, 1878, Lincoln County, New Mexico. Bowdre was one of a large group of Regulators who attacked an opposition cow camp. The Regulators wounded two men, killed one, and seized a herd of horses.

December 23, 1880, Stinking Springs, New Mexico. With Pat Garrett on their trail, the hunted men took refuge in a small, abandoned rock house standing on the snow-covered banks of a small arroyo. Billy the Kid brought his mount inside, leaving the horses of Bowdre, Dave Rudabaugh, Billy Wilson, and Tom Pickett tethered outside. The only door had collapsed, and the five fugitives shivered through the night, not realizing that Garrett's posse was silently surrounding them.

At daybreak Bowdre emerged from the cabin, and Garrett and Lee Hall, who had stationed themselves near the door, raised their rifles and fired. Struck twice in the chest, Bowdre reeled back inside. Wilson shouted that Bowdre was dying and wanted to come out, and Garrett ordered him to have his hands up. But the Kid jammed Bowdre's pistol into his fist and said: "They've murdered you, Charlie, but you can get revenge. Kill some of the sons-of-bitches before you die."

Bowdre came out, but raised his hands and staggered toward Garrett. Strangling on his own blood, he fell into Garrett's arms. "I wish . . . I wish . . . I wish," he gasped. "I'm dying," he said with his last breath a few seconds later.

Sources: Keleher, *Violence in Lincoln County,* 19–20, 69, 99, 114–19, 131, 159, 184, 233, 286–93, 296, 308, 312, 325; Fulton, *Lincoln County War,* 66, 77–79, 84, 137, 140, 175, 186, 201, 225, 234, 260–61, 282, 333, 380, 384; Garrett, *Billy, the Kid,* 105–106, 114–25; Siringo, *Texas Cowboy,* 137–39, 170; Hunt, *Tragic Days of Billy the Kid,* 57–60, 90, 107–20, 123–26, 132, 148, 191, 217, 227–28, 232–47.

William M. Breakenridge, Indian fighter and lawman. In 1881 he shot Curly Bill Brocius in the mouth, thereby persuading Curly Bill to hang up his guns. *(Courtesy Arizona Historical Society)*

Breakenridge, William Milton

(b. December 25, 1846, Watertown, Wisconsin; d. January 31, 1931, Tucson, Arizona. Newsboy, teamster, page boy, laborer, telegraph messenger, soldier, train brakeman, storekeeper, law officer, prospector, rancher, county sur-

veyor, author.) Reared in Wisconsin, Billy Breakenridge quit school at fourteen to sell newspapers in Milwaukee. Two years later he ran away from home and enlisted as a teamster with the U.S. Army during the Civil War. Soon he went West, working at a variety of jobs in Denver, including service as a page boy for the Colorado legislature. In 1864 he joined Chivington's Third Colorado Cavalry and participated in the savage Sand Creek Massacre. After the war he worked as a train brakeman, but by 1867 he was employed as a storekeeper in Sidney, Nebraska.

He was soon wandering again, and in 1878 he turned up in Phoenix as a deputy sheriff. The next year he was attracted to booming Tombstone, where he hauled lumber for a time before again securing an appointment as a deputy sheriff. In 1883 he went into a ranch partnership, but he soon sold out and pinned on a deputy U.S. marshal's badge.

In 1888 Breakenridge was elected surveyor of Maricopa County, and later he became special officer for the Southern Pacific Railroad. Headquartered in Tucson, he performed detective and guard work for the railroad until his retirement at the age of seventy-two. In 1928 he published his reminiscences in *Helldorado,* and he basked in the book's publicity until his death three years later in Tucson.

Gunfights: May 25, 1881, Galeyville, Arizona. Deputy Sheriff Breakenridge rode into Galeyville and entered a saloon where Curly Bill Brocius and several other rustlers were drinking. Jim Wallace, a gunman who had participated in the Lincoln County War, drew his revolver and insulted the lawman. Breakenridge laughed it off and bought drinks for all present, and Curly Bill

talked Wallace into apologizing. But when Breakenridge tried to leave the saloon, Curly Bill began to quarrel with him and followed him out to his horse.

Breakenridge swung into the saddle, and when Curly Bill continued to shout abuse, the lawman drew his six-gun and fired a shot. The slug went into the left side of Bill's neck and came out his right cheek, knocking out a tooth in the process. Curly Bill recovered, but hung up his guns and left Arizona.

1882, near Tombstone, Arizona. A posse consisting of Breakenridge, John C. Gillespie, and two officers named Allen and Young were tracking Zwing Hunt and Billy Grounds, a pair of badmen who had committed murder during a recent robbery attempt in Charleston, near Tombstone. The lawmen located the outlaws at a ranch about ten miles from Tombstone. When the posse arrived at the ranch, they hid their mounts, then closed in on the cabin.

Suddenly Gillespie ran toward the front door and ordered the fugitives to come outside. The outlaws promptly threw open the door and began firing. Gillespie was cut down, mortally wounded, and Young was hit in the leg. A man named Lewis burst out of the cabin shouting that he was just an innocent ranch hand, but a bullet from the doorway ripped into his shoulder. Allen and Young also were wounded, but Breakenridge crouched behind a tree and leveled his shotgun at the doorway. He fired one barrel at the entrance, and the buckshot tore into Grounds's face, hurling him to the floor.

Hunt dashed out the back door, but Allen and Breakenridge opened fire, and a slug caught the outlaw in the back and knocked him off his feet. He regained his balance and kept running, but Breakenridge and Allen pursued and soon found him stretched out on the ground.

Sources: Breakenridge, *Helldorado;* Waters, *Earp Brothers of Tombstone,* 106–107, 189–90; Faulk, *Tombstone,* 145, 148, 156, 200, 205; Kellner, "W. M. Breakenridge," *Arizoniana.*

Brewer, Richard M.

(b. 1852, St. Albans, Vermont; d. April 4, 1878, Blazer's Mill, New Mexico. Farmer, horse breaker, ranch foreman, law officer, gunman.) Dick Brewer moved with his family in 1860 to a farm in Wisconsin. At the age of eighteen he left home and went West, arriving in Lincoln County in 1870. He established a farm, and his interest in horse breeding brought him in close contact with a neighbor, Englishman John Tunstall. He became foreman of Tunstall's ranch, and when his employer was murdered he led the so-called Regulators in revenge until he was himself killed.

Gunfights: September, 1877, Lincoln County, New Mexico. While Tunstall was away on a trip to St. Louis, rustlers Jesse Evans, Frank Baker, Tom Hill, and a Texan named Davis stole two of Brewer's horses and "a pair of magnificent mules" from the Tunstall ranch. Brewer and two hands pursued and overtook the thieves, who offered to return Brewer's mounts but insisted upon keeping the mules.

Brewer went to Las Cruces to seek aid, but the authorities were indifferent, and he returned to Lincoln, where he obtained a deputy sheriff's commission. He raised a posse of fifteen men, and on the second night out they tracked the rustlers to an isolated dugout. At dawn a shootout ensued, and Evans had three clear shots at Brewer. He missed by inches each time, and when the outlaws were told that the posse intended to kill them, they filed out with their hands in the air.

On the road back to Lincoln they encountered Tunstall, who accompanied the prisoners to Lincoln, where they were incarcerated in a hole in the ground. A few weeks later thirty-two hard cases boldly rode into town, easily freed their cohorts, and galloped out of town.

March 9, 1878, Steel Springs, New Mexico. Following the murder of John Tunstall, Brewer went in search of the assassins at the head of a posse of "Regulators" which included Billy the Kid, Henry Brown, Doc Scurlock, Charlie Bowdre, Frank McNab, Fred Wait, Sam Smith, Jim French, John Middleton, and William McCloskey. On March 6 they spotted Frank Baker and Billy Morton, two of the primary suspects in Tunstall's death. At one hundred yards' distance Baker and Morton spurred away, and a five-mile chase ensued.

When their horses collapsed, Baker and Morton made a stand, but they surrendered when they were promised that no harm would come to them. Brewer, however, grumbled that he was sorry they had given up before being killed, and other Regulators muttered similar sentiments. McCloskey, who brought up the rear of the procession with Middleton, expressed sympathy for the prisoners, and he was killed when they were.

Some said that Morton grabbed McCloskey's pistol and shot him, while others hold that McNab angrily cut him down. At any rate, McCloskey and the two prisoners were shot to death before the group reached Lincoln.

April 4, 1878, Blazer's Mill, New Mex-

ico. The Regulators, including the Kid, Brown, French, Wait, Middleton, Scurlock, Frank and George Coe, Bill Scroggins, Tom O'Folliard, and Stephen Stevens, and still led by Brewer, continued to prowl about and rode into Blazer's Mill to get a meal. Buckshot Roberts, a notorious character who had been a rustler with Jesse Evans, rode into the mill armed with a Winchester and two pistols. Frank Coe, who knew Roberts, tried to talk him into surrendering.

Suddenly Charlie Bowdre, brandishing a gun and backed up by several Regulators, approached Roberts and demanded that he give up. "Not much, Mary Ann," snarled Roberts. Bowdre fired, striking Roberts in the middle and slamming him backward. But Roberts began working his Winchester, wounding John Middleton in the chest and mangling George Coe's shooting hand.

Roberts staggered into the building, found a Sharps .50 buffalo gun, and propped himself on a mattress by the only window in the room. While the posse crouched for cover and tended their wounded, Brewer crawled carefully and circuitously to a pile of logs in front of Roberts' position at a distance variously estimated at 50 to 150 yards. Brewer squeezed off several shots, then ducked behind the logs. But when he raised his head again, Roberts was ready. The buffalo gun roared, and the heavy slug took off the top of Brewer's head.

Roberts exultantly shouted: "I killed the son-of-a-bitch! I killed him!" But when it became obvious that Roberts himself was near death, the posse decided to leave to find medical help for Middleton and Coe. After Roberts died, Dr. J. H. Blazer, owner of the mill, put together a pair of coffins and buried Roberts and Brewer side by side.

Sources: Keleher, *Violence in Lincoln County,* 83–84, 88–90, 96–100, 113–18, 128, 133–34, 227, 251–53, 260–76, 312, 325; Coe, *Frontier Fighter,* 64–69; Hunt, *Tragic Days of Billy the Kid,* 42–46, 56–60; Fulton, *Lincoln County War,* 64, 82–84, 87, 89–90, 112–13, 115–16, 125, 137–42, 147, 162, 172–79, 185, 191–92; Rickards, *Blazer's Mill.*

Bridges, Jack L.

(b. 1838 or 1839, Maine. Law officer.) Born either in Maine or, to quote the U.S. census of 1870, "at sea," Bridges was a peace officer for fifteen years in Kansas. A deputy U.S. marshal by 1869, Bridges lived for a time in Hays City, then moved to Wichita. There he was badly wounded in a shootout, and he returned to Maine to recuperate. Soon he resumed his career in Kansas, and about that time acquired a wife.

Bridges spent some time in Colorado, but in 1882 he was appointed city marshal of Dodge, and the next year he was aligned against Luke Short in the "Dodge City War." During his years as a peace officer he was involved in several minor incidents featuring gunplay, generally while making arrests. In 1884 he was replaced as marshal of Dodge by Bill Tilghman, and thereafter he faded into obscurity.

Gunfight: *February 28, 1871, Wichita, Kansas.* J. E. Ledford had recently married and purchased the Harris House Hotel in Wichita. Ledford was a suspected horse thief, and on a previous occasion he had whipped Bridges in a fist fight. Bridges secured a warrant for his arrest and at 4:00 A.M. approached the Harris House with a backup force of twenty-five soldiers.

While inquiring at the front door,

Bridges saw a man enter a nearby outhouse. Suspiciously, Bridges, scout Lee Stewart, and an officer closed in on the small building, with Bridges in the lead. Suddenly the outhouse door flew open, and Ledford bolted outside, blasting Bridges with a six-gun. Bridges and the other two men pulled their pistols and opened fire. All three men emptied their weapons as they pursued Ledford, and he was struck twice in the right arm and twice in the body.

Badly wounded, Bridges finally fainted and slumped to the ground. Ledford made it to a store across the street, but collapsed and died after being carried back to the hotel. Bridges was taken to the post hospital at Fort Harker and three months later went to Maine to complete his recovery.

Sources: Miller and Snell, *Great Gunfighters of the Kansas Cowtowns*, 33–41, 122–23, 325, 330, 377, 379, 394; Drago, *Wild, Woolly & Wicked*, 150.

Brooks, William L.

("Buffalo Bill," "Bully")

(d. July 29, 1874, Wellington, Kansas. Stage driver, buffalo hunter, law officer, mule thief.) Brooks's origin was hazy, but he was reputed to have engaged in fatal shootouts during his obscure past. He affected shoulder-length hair and almost always carried a Winchester. He became a stagecoach driver on the Newton–Wichita route, and when Newton was organized as a third-class city in 1872, he was elected the first city marshal.

Later in the year, after being shot up in a Newton gunfight, Brooks moved to Ellsworth and served briefly as a policeman. Soon he was in Dodge City, where he hunted buffalo and engaged in three gunfights before leaving the vicinity. By 1874 Brooks evidently turned to

Buffalo Bill Brooks, elected first marshal of Newton, Kansas. He was later lynched in his wife's presence for stealing cattle. *(Courtesy Boot Hill Museum, Dodge City, Kansas)*

stealing mules and horses, for a gang of thieves, including W. L. Brooks, was captured and lynched in July in southern Kansas. Brooks had moved to the Caldwell area with his wife, who was present when he was lynched.

Gunfights: *June 9, 1872, Newton, Kansas.* Several Texas cowboys on a spree had cornered a dance hall owner and were roughing him up in addition to harassing passersby with random pistol shots. Marshal Brooks rushed to the scene and ordered the revelers out of town. They went to their horses and started to leave, but cowhands James Hunt and Joe Miller suddenly turned and began firing at Brooks. One bullet nicked his collarbone, and two others struck his limbs, but he ignored his wounds and charged his assailants. A chase on horseback ensued, and Brooks chased the cowboys for ten miles before turning back to Newton to have his wounds tended. The two cowboys were soon arrested and tried.

December 23, 1872, Dodge City, Kansas. On a Monday night Brooks engaged in a quarrel with the Santa Fe Railroad yardmaster in Dodge, a man named Brown. Both men produced guns and squeezed off three shots each. Brown's first slug wounded his adversary, but Brooks's third shot nicked a bystander and slammed into Brown, killing him on the spot.

December 28, 1872, Dodge City, Kansas. After a festering disagreement with Matthew Sullivan, a Dodge saloon keeper, Brooks determined to kill his antagonist. On a Saturday night just five days after the previous killing, Brooks found Sullivan standing in his place of business. Brooks poked his gun through an open window and shot Sullivan. The saloon keeper was knocked off his feet and died immediately. Although Brooks was widely blamed as the assassin, no action was taken against him in those raw, fledgling days of Dodge.

March 4, 1873, Dodge City, Kansas. The fractious Brooks soon became entangled with another Dodge citizen, a

buffalo hunter named Kirk Jordan. The quarrel became violent, and upon encountering Brooks in the street, Jordan leveled his buffalo gun. Brooks dove behind a couple of water barrels just as Jordan fired. The heavy slug tore through both barrels but was stopped by an iron hoop. The next day Brooks prudently patched up the conflict.

July 28, 1874, near Caldwell, Kansas. Brooks was suspected of being a member of a gang of horse and mule thieves who probably had been organized by a stage line to drive a rival company out of business. A posse of 150 men descended upon the Caldwell area to engage in a mass roundup of the robbers. Brooks and two companions were cornered at a hideout near Caldwell and offered determined resistance, but after several hours the fugitives surrendered.

Brooks's two companions were released, but Brooks was imprisoned with two other suspects, Charley Smith and L. B. Hasbrouck, in the county jail at Wellington. The next day Brooks's wife came up from Caldwell, but at midnight a mob rushed the jail and took the three prisoners to a hanging tree. Smith and Hasbrouck died cleanly, but Brooks slowly and painfully strangled to death.

Sources: Miller and Snell, *Great Gunfighters of the Kansas Cowtowns,* 41–47; Streeter, *Prairie Trails & Cow Towns,* 138–39.

Brown, Henry Newton

(b. 1857, Cold Spring Township, Missouri; d. April 30, 1884, Medicine Lodge, Kansas. Farmer, cowboy, buffalo hunter, cattle rustler, gunman, law officer, bank robber.) Orphaned at a young age, Brown and his sister were reared on their uncle's farm, located near Rolla, Missouri. In 1875, at the age of seven-

Henry Brown, the dangerous marshal of Caldwell. *(Courtesy Kansas State Historical Society, Topeka)*

teen, Brown left Missouri and headed west. For a time he worked on a ranch in eastern Colorado, then he spent a season hunting buffalo. In 1876 he killed a man in the Texas Panhandle, and subsequently he gravitated to turbulent Lincoln County, New Mexico. Brown signed on as a cowpuncher and rustler with Major L. G. Murphy and worked for eighteen months while a bitter feud developed between Murphy and three local competitors—ranching magnate John Chisum, lawyer Alexander McSween, and rancher John Tunstall.

Early in 1878, disgruntled over a salary squabble, Brown switched sides and hired on with Chisum. About that time Tunstall was murdered, and Brown became an active participant in the all-out war that followed. He was one of

three men indicted for murdering Sheriff William Brady and Deputy George Hindman; he was present when Frank Baker, William Morton, and William McCloskey were killed; and he also participated in the Blazer's Mill shootout. There were numerous minor scrapes, and Brown finally found himself in the middle of the climactic battle in Lincoln. Afterward, Brown leagued with Billy the Kid and various other fugitives who formed a band of stock thieves.

In the fall of 1878 the Kid, Brown, Tom O'Folliard, Fred Wait, and John Middleton moved a herd of stolen horses to the Tascosa area of the Texas Panhandle, but by October the Kid and O'Folliard were ready to return to New Mexico, even though they were wanted by the law there. Middleton and Wait wisely decided to return to their homes in Kansas and Oklahoma, respectively, while Brown elected to stay in Tascosa.

For a while he was a cowhand for George Littlefield, but then he took a job tracking horse thieves. Next he wangled an appointment as a deputy sheriff of Oldham County, but he was soon fired because he "was always wanting to fight." In 1881 he again was hired by Littlefield, but he was discharged from that job, too, "because he was always on the war path." Brown then was hired by Barney O'Connor, foreman of a ranch in Woods County, Oklahoma, but shortly he drifted to Caldwell, a wild trail town just across the Kansas line.

In July, 1882, Brown was appointed deputy marshal of Caldwell, and within a few months he was promoted to city marshal. He imported a Texas hard case called Ben Wheeler (whose real name was Ben Robertson) to be his deputy, and the two gunmen immediately tamed Caldwell. On New Year's Day, 1883, Brown was presented a new Winchester with a silver plate saluting his "valuable services to the citizens of Caldwell, Kansas." Brown quieted the town still further by killing two troublemakers in ensuing months, and he otherwise enforced the law by helping track down area fugitives.

Brown was married in March, 1884, but his improving image as a solid citizen was ruined six weeks later when he was caught robbing a bank in nearby Medicine Lodge. Brown and Wheeler, accompanied by two Oklahoma desperadoes, slipped into Medicine Lodge, killed two men in the bank, and were chased down and lynched that night. Brown and his deputy had left Caldwell ostensibly to hunt outlaws, and later it was speculated that previous absences from town on "legal business" had also resulted in thievery.

Gunfights: *1876, Texas Panhandle.* In a Panhandle cattle camp the normally quiet Brown became involved in a quarrel with a cowboy. Angry words soon led to gunplay, and Brown pumped three slugs into his adversary, killing him on the spot.

April 1, 1878, Lincoln, New Mexico. Brown, Billy the Kid, John Middleton, Fred Wait, and Jim French concealed themselves behind an adobe wall in the rear of Tunstall's store with the intention of ambushing Sheriff William Brady. About 9:00 A.M. Brady and his deputy, George Hindman, strolled down the street, followed by Billy Matthews, Jack Long, and George Peppin. Suddenly and without warning the Kid's party jumped up and began shooting. The Kid, Brown, and Middleton fired the most telling shots, felling Brady, Hindman, and Matthews. Matthews scampered to cover, Brady died instant-

ly, and the mortally wounded Hindman writhed in the dusty street, begging for water.

The Kid opened the plank gate and ran to Brady's body, intending to steal his new Winchester, but Matthews began firing and grazed the Kid in the side. The Kid retreated quickly, and he and his men quickly mounted their horses and raced out of town.

April 4, 1878, Blazer's Mill, New Mexico. Three days later, Brown was with a group of Regulators who had ridden into Blazer's Mill to take a noon respite from their search for enemies. About half an hour after their arrival, a hostile gunman named Buckshot Roberts boldly rode into their midst. Brown, Charlie Bowdre, and George Coe pulled their guns and walked over to Roberts, and Bowdre ordered him to surrender.

"Not much, Mary Ann," snapped Roberts, whipping up his Winchester. Bowdre shot him through the middle, but Roberts began working his rifle, wounding Coe and John Middleton and scattering the others. He barricaded himself inside the building behind him, and later he succeeded in killing Regulator leader Dick Brewer. At that point Brown and the others meekly rode away with Coe and Middleton, leaving Roberts to die of his wound.

May 14, 1878, Lincoln County, New Mexico. Brown and several other Regulators raided a cow camp on the Pecos. They killed a man called "Indian," wounded two other herders, and rounded up a group of horses.

July 15 –19, 1878, Lincoln, New Mexico. During the big shootout in Lincoln, Brown spent most of his time in a little storehouse about thirty yards across an alley from Alexander McSween's store, where Billy the Kid and most of the other Regulators were stationed. Alongside Brown were George Coe and Joseph J. Smith, and from their vantage point the three sniped sporadically at the opposition.

The climax to the battle came after dark on the last day, when McSween, the Kid, and the others inside the blazing house tried to break out. In the flurry of shooting which followed, Bob Beckwith was the first to fall, and the Kid is popularly supposed to have killed him. But it is probable that Beckwith was gunned down from the storehouse where Brown was located. During the subsequent excitement and gunplay, Brown and his two companions slipped outside, clambered onto some barrels, and crawled over an eight-foot wall, thus making good their escape.

August 5, 1878, near the Mescalero Indian Agency, New Mexico. The Kid, Brown, George Coe, and six or eight Mexicans were riding to discover what had happened to Dick Brewer's corpse after the battle at Blazer's Mill. They pulled up to water their horses about a mile outside the Mescalero agency, and murdered a clerk, Morris Bernstein. The Mexicans were pursued, and they galloped back to their three astonished companions in a blaze of gunfire. Brown's horse was fatally wounded, and the Kid, who was dismounted, saw his frightened mount dash away. The party struggled to the cover of a stand of timber, discovered and roped a pair of Indian horses, then proceeded on to Coe's ranch.

April 11, 1883, near Hunnewell, Kansas. Late on a Tuesday morning Brown and Ben Wheeler were asked for assistance by Deputy U.S. Marshal Cash Hollister, who had located a band of horse thieves camped near Hunnewell. When the three officers passed through Hunnewell, they picked up two more lawmen, Deputy Sheriff Wes Thralls and the marshal of Hunnewell, a man named Jackson. By the following dawn the posse had surrounded the outlaws' camp, but the thieves opened fire when told to surrender. A rifle duel ensued, with the five lawmen facing a rustler named Ross, his wife, his daughter, his two sons, a daughter-in-law, and her child. After half an hour the older Ross boy had been killed, and his brother had suffered two or three serious wounds; the Ross gang then surrendered to custody.

May 14, 1883, Caldwell, Kansas. On a Monday morning in Caldwell a Pawnee named Spotted Horse was making a nuisance of himself, brandishing a pistol and demanding a meal for himself and his squaw. A complaint was registered with Brown, and the marshal promptly sought out Spotted Horse, locating him in Morris' grocery store.

Brown ordered the Indian to come with him, but Spotted Horse refused and began groping for his six-gun. Brown whipped out a revolver and told the Pawnee to stop, and when the Indian pulled on his weapon, the marshal opened fire. Brown fired three bullets point-blank, but the Indian finally managed to level his gun. The marshal then fired a fourth slug which tore through Spotted Horse's head, felling him and causing his death about two hours later.

December 15, 1883, Caldwell, Kansas. A Texas gambler named Newt Boyce had cut two men in a Caldwell saloon on a Friday evening, and Brown and Wheeler had thrown him in jail for the night. Boyce was released the next morning, and he spent Saturday drinking and proclaiming threats against the two lawmen. That night Wheeler told the marshal that Boyce had just threatened him with a pistol, whereupon Brown picked up his Winchester and went into the street to find the gambler. Boyce was standing in front of Phillips' saloon, and when Brown was about thirty feet away he ordered the gambler to stop. Boyce reached inside his coat, and Brown raised the rifle to his shoulder and squeezed off two rounds. One of the bullets struck Boyce, who staggered into the saloon, begging Brown not to kill him. Once inside, Boyce collapsed, and it was discovered that the slug had torn through his right arm, breaking a bone and then penetrating his side. He was carried to a nearby warehouse, and a doctor was summoned, but he died about 3:00 A.M.

April 30, 1884, Medicine Lodge, Kansas. Brown and Wheeler left Caldwell heavily armed on a Sunday afternoon, having obtained permission from the mayor to spend a few days in Oklahoma in search of a murderer. But the next day they were joined by two cowboys, William Smith and John Wesley, and the four men headed for Medicine Lodge, about seventy miles west of Caldwell. On Wednesday morning they staked fresh mounts in a canyon in the Gypsum Hills a few miles outside Medicine Lodge, and then they rode into town, arriving during a driving rain a little after nine.

Brown, Wheeler, and Wesley entered the Medicine Valley Bank and confronted the two men present—President E. W. Payne and Cashier George Geppert—with a demand for money. Payne went for a revolver, and Brown fatally wounded him, whereupon Wheeler and Wesley pumped two bullets into Geppert, who had raised his hands. Gep-

pert staggered to the vault and threw the lock, then slid to a sitting position and died. The robbers bolted out of town, followed by nine angry citizens led by Barney O'Connor, who once had employed Brown as a cowboy.

Hotly pursued, and with one of their mounts giving out, the outlaws headed for their spare horses, but they entered the wrong opening and found themselves trapped in a box canyon only thirty or forty feet deep. The four thieves held out for two hours, but it was clear that no escape from the flooding canyon was possible. Brown threw down his guns, asked for protection, and walked forward, followed by his three accomplices.

Infuriated townspeople met the prisoners with threats of lynching, and they were thrown into a log building under guard. The captives ate two meals during the day, had their pictures taken, and Brown wrote a letter to his bride, lamely stating that "it was all for you" and that "I did not think this would happen."

About 9:00 P.M. three shots were fired, and a mob overpowered the guards and opened the jail. Brown, anticipating a lynch party, had slipped out of his cuffs, and as soon as the door was opened, he dashed through the mob into an alley. Just as he broke into the clear, a farmer loosed both barrels of a shotgun and blew him in half. When he fell, a few rifle bullets thudded into his body, and he died on the spot. Wheeler also was wounded, and he was taken to a tree and hanged alongside Smith and Wesley.

Sources: Miller and Snell, *Great Gunfighters of the Kansas Cowtowns,* 47–64, 143; Keleher, *Violence in Lincoln County,* 99, 109, 112, 117, 122, 184, 231, 233, 253, 276, 315–16, 324–25; Coe, *Frontier Fighter,* 57–59, 64–69,

72–75, 77–79, 82, 86–88, 115–16, 119–23, 149; Hunt, *Tragic Days of Billy the Kid,* 51–53, 56–60, 80, 102, 113, 132–39; Rasch, "A Note on Henry Newton Brown," *Los Angeles Western-ers Brand Book,* V, 59–67; Fulton, *Lin-coln County War,* 137, 140, 158, 201, 215, 225, 264, 268, 333, 346.

Bryant, Charles

("Black Faced Charlie")

(d. August 23, 1891, near Waukomis, Okla. Gunman, train robber.*)* During a close-range shooting scrape in his youth, Bryant was blasted in the face by grains of black powder from a point-blank pistol shot which creased his cheek. The permanent disfigurement which resulted gave him his nickname. In 1891 he joined the Dalton gang of train robbers, and during a shootout with a posse he crowed, "Me, I want to get killed in one hell-firin' minute of action." He little realized how quickly his wish would be granted. Deputy U.S. Marshal Ed Short arrested him in a Hennessey, Oklahoma, hotel room, bed-ridden from illness. Short loaded him on a train for Wichita, Kansas, which was the nearest federal court district. But en route Bryant tried to escape, and in the process he and Short shot each other to death.

Gunfight: August 23, 1891, near Waukomis, Okla. Bryant had been ar-rested and was being transported to jail by Deputy U.S. Marshal Ed Short. Dur-ing the train ride Short decided to go to the smoker and left Bryant in the custody of the express messenger. Short checked Bryant's handcuffs, handed the outlaw's pistol to the messenger, then left the car. The messenger shoved the six-gun into a pigeonhole in his desk, then returned to his work.

Bryant sneaked toward the desk and suddenly seized the gun. At that mo-ment Short returned to the car, and Bryant shot him in the chest. Short began working his rifle, triggering a slug into the outlaw's chest which tore through his body and severed his spinal column. Bryant emptied his pistol, then died. Short helped pick up Bryant's body, then he laid down on a cot and expired within minutes. The train stopped at the next station, and the corpses were stretched out on the station platform.

Sources: Horan, *Pictorial History of the Wild West,* 157–58; Drago, *Road Agents and Train Robbers,* 180–83; Shirley, *Heck Thomas,* 135–36; Shir-ley, *Six-gun and Silver Star,* 32, 34–38, 73.

Burrows, Reuben Houston

(b. 1853, Lamar County, Alabama; d. 1889, Tennessee. Railroad employee, train robber.*)* Born in Alabama, Rube Burrows married and moved his small family to Texas in the 1870's. He be-came a member of the Masonic Lodge and was noted as a cracker-barrel phi-losopher. For fourteen years he lived quietly while working for the railroad, but in the late 1880's he became the leader of an outlaw band. His wife and two children returned to Alabama, while Rube, his brother Jim, and four other hard cases began holding up trains. Jim was captured in 1888, but Rube con-tinued to stage train robberies until he was killed a year later.

Gunfights: January 23, 1888, Montgomery, Alabama. Recognized while in Alabama, Rube and Jim were confronted in the streets of Montgom-ery by a posse seeking the large rewards posted for the Burrows brothers. Jim shot Neil Bray, a newspaperman who was trying to assist the officers, and the Burrows boys escaped.

1888, Nashville, Tennessee. An alert conductor spotted Rube and Jim on his train as it neared Nashville. The conductor notified the authorities, but when officers tried to close in, Rube shot his way to safety. Jim was captured, however, and died of consumption after a year in prison.

December 15, 1888, Illinois. Rube and two accomplices robbed an Illinois Central train later that year. During the holdup, shooting broke out, and passenger Chester Hughes was killed.

1889, Tennessee. Late in 1889 Rube was tracked down by a Southern Express Company detective. Again Rube tried to fight his way to safety, but the detective blasted him in the head with a shotgun.

Source: Horan and Sann, *Pictorial History of the Wild West,* 153–55.

Carson, Thomas

(Law officer, laborer.) A nephew of Kit Carson, Tom rated several notches lower as a frontiersman. His chief notoriety came as a peace officer, but he was frequently in trouble with city officials where he worked. Appointed to Abilene's police force in June, 1871, less than a week later he received a severe reprimand. Later that summer Carson was employed on the police force of booming Newton, arriving about the time of the bloody "Newton General Massacre."

Still later in the same year Carson was rehired in Abilene, but following an unprovoked shooting scrape he was quickly fired. Several weeks afterward he shot a fellow former policeman from Abilene,

but he broke out of jail before he could be tried.

Gunfights: November 22, 1871, Abilene, Kansas. Policeman Carson, allegedly acting "without provocation," fired at a local bartender named John Man. Man was wounded in the hip, and a few days later Carson was discharged from the police force, presumably because of this shooting incident.

January, 1872, Abilene, Kansas. Brocky Jack Norton had been fired from the Abilene constabulary at the same time as Carson. Two months later the two men had a falling out which led to gunplay. Carson wounded Norton and was arrested. Brocky Jack recovered, but Carson escaped from jail rather than face trial.

Sources: Miller and Snell, *Great Gunfighters of the Kansas Cowtowns,* 64–75; Streeter, *Prairie Trails & Cow Towns,* 84–85, 87, 137.

Chambers, Lon

(Law officer, train robber.) A Texan, Chambers wore a badge in the Panhandle, then drifted into New Mexico during the manhunt for Billy the Kid. Chambers was with Pat Garrett's posse when they ambushed the Kid in Fort Sumner, resulting in the death of Tom O'Folliard. A few days later the posse caught the Kid and his four surviving cohorts in an isolated rock house. They killed Charlie Bowdre and forced the rest to surrender. Within a year or two, however, Chambers decided that the rewards of carrying a gun for the law were not commensurate with the risks. Following a train robbery in Kansas, he won acquittal and disappeared from notoriety.

Gunfights: December 19, 1880,

Fort Sumner, New Mexico. Pat Garrett's posse had set an ambush in Fort Sumner for Billy the Kid and his gang. The posse gathered inside the old post hospital, and after dark fell, Chambers was posted outside as a guard. When the outlaws approached, Chambers passed the word.

Garrett stood beside Chambers and shouted, "Halt!" Tom O'Folliard and Tom Pickett rode in the lead, and O'Folliard went for his gun. Chambers and Garrett fired their rifles at the same time, and O'Folliard reeled in the saddle with a hole in his chest. With lead flying about them, the other outlaws raced to safety, and O'Folliard tried to follow them, but after 150 yards his wound forced him to turn back and surrender. He died within the hour, and the posse made ready to pursue those who had escaped.

September 29, 1883, Coolidge, Kansas. Shortly after 1:00 A.M. three masked men, one of whom was assumed to be Chambers, climbed aboard a westward-bound train which had made a brief stop in Coolidge. The leader, brandishing two pistols, ordered engineer John Hilton to "pull out." When Hilton did not obey, the bandit shot him in the heart, then turned upon fireman George Fadel and shot him with the other gun. Express messenger Peterson then opened fire, and after shooting wildly at the conductor, the thieves fled. A posse led by Dave Mather quickly rounded up Chambers and three other hard cases, but these suspects were tried and set free because of lack of evidence.

Sources: Miller and Snell, *Great Gunfighters of the Kansas Cowtowns,* 327–28; Garrett, *Billy, the Kid,* 111–28.

Champion, Nathan D.

(b. September 29, 1857, Williamson County, Texas; d. April 9, 1892, KC Ranch, Wyoming. Cowboy, cattle rustler.) Nate Champion was born near Round Rock, Texas, into a large and respected family. Champion became a cowboy, and after accompanying a herd up the Goodnight-Loving Trail in 1881, he and his twin brother, Dudley, decided to stay in Wyoming. The Champion brothers became top hands on several Wyoming ranches and began to side with Johnson County homesteaders and small ranchers in the growing feud with wealthy cattle barons of the area.

Like most cowboys, Nate occasionally appropriated stray cattle for his own use, and the big ranchers began to call him "King of the Rustlers." In the fall of 1891 Nate fought off a personal attack, but a few months later he was gunned down after a courageous fight against more than fifty "Regulators." Two weeks later his martyred remains were retrieved and buried at Buffalo. In May, 1893, Dudley was murdered by Mike Shonsey, a range detective who had feuded with Nate.

Gunfights: November 1, 1891, Powder River, Wyoming. Champion and Ross Gilbertson were living in a line shack owned by W. H. Hall on the Powder River. Just before dawn Joe Elliot, Tom Smith, Frank Canton, and Fred Coates crept up to the little log building, intent upon killing the outspoken Champion in the interests of their influential employers. The four gunmen kicked open the door, which was adjacent to the cabin's only bunk. One of the gunfighters shouted, "Give up. We have got you this time." Champion sat up beside Gilbertson, asked, "What's the matter, boys?" and then snatched his six-gun from the holster on the bedpost.

Champion and one of the intruders fired simultaneously; Nate was powder-burned in the face by one wild shot, and a second slug plowed into the bedding between the two partners. Champion nicked one of his assailants in the arm, and another was hit in the side, and the four gunmen scampered to safety. In their haste they left behind four overcoats, horses, a trail of blood, and a Winchester given to Canton by Smith. Champion ran out the door in pursuit, but he was chased back inside by Joe Elliott, with whom he traded shots.

Elliott later was arrested and charged with attempted murder, but Gilbertson, the only witness, disappeared, and the charges were dropped.

April 9, 1892, KC Ranch, Wyoming. Champion and Nick Ray, two men prominent on the death list of the Regulators, had recently leased the KC Ranch near the Hole-in-the-Wall country. On the evening of April 8 two trappers, Bill Walker, an out-of-work cowboy, and Ben Jones, spent the night with the partners, drinking, yarning, and singing to the accompaniment of Walker's fiddle.

At dawn Jones, an unemployed chuck wagon cook, went outside to get a pail of water, but he was quietly captured by the fifty or so Regulators who had just finished positioning themselves around the ranch. About half an hour later Walker emerged to hurry Jones, but he, too, was taken prisoner. A couple of minutes later Ray walked outside, and the Regulators opened fire.

Champion came to the door and traded shots with the posse members in the stable and a nearby creek bed before being driven back inside. As Ray crawled toward the house Champion suddenly reappeared, squeezed off several more rounds, then dragged his partner inside under heavy fire. Between tending Ray and firing at his attackers, Champion wrote a journal describing the siege.

Ray died about 9:00 A.M., and about 3:00 P.M. Champion saw two passersby unsuccessfully attacked by the Regulators. A wagon abandoned by the passersby was then loaded with hay and pitch pine wood, backed against the house, and fired with a torch. Revolvers blazing, Champion dashed for a ravine fifty yards away. But several Regulators were positioned in the ravine, and they shot him down. He fell on his back, and the Regulators continued to pump lead into him; twenty-eight wounds were discovered in his body.

The journal was found and given to Sam Clover, a correspondent from the *Chicago Herald* who had helped fire upon the cabin. A note proclaiming, "Cattle thieves, beware," was pinned to Champion's shirt, and the Regulators proceeded on to other dirty work.

Sources: Mercer, *Banditti of the Plains,* 22–23, 53–63, 86–88, 140–41, 157–58, 172, 181–87; Canton, *Frontier Trails,* 88–92; Brown, *Trail Driving Days,* 229–31, 245–50; Smith, *War on the Powder River,* vii, ix, xi, xii, 114, 145–46, 149, 152–55, 157–60, 182, 199–209, 214, 230–31, 246, 282.

Christian, Will

("Black Jack," "202")

(d. April 28, 1897, Black Jack Canyon, Arizona. Bandit, horsebreaker, cowboy.) Will and Bob Christian were Oklahoma outlaws who broke jail in 1895 following a killing and after two months of active thievery headed west. They passed through New Mexico and stopped in Arizona's Sulphur Springs Valley, where Will, using the alias Ed Williams, found work breaking horses and mules and later punching cows. His friends nicknamed him "202" because of his weight, then began calling the swarthy cowboy "Black Jack."

Soon Will returned to robbery, and

his gang, the "High Fives," plundered stagecoaches, trains, and banks, throughout 1896 and 1897. There was a series of battles and escapes from lawmen, and Will was chased down and killed by Deputy U.S. Marshal Fred Higgins.

Gunfights: April 27, 1895, Oklahoma. Deputy Sheriff Will Turner tried to arrest the Christian brothers and two confederates, but the lawman was slain. Soon arrested, Will and Bob shot their way out of an Oklahoma City jail on June 30.

August 6, 1896, Nogales, Arizona. At noon Christian led a band of thieves to the International Bank of Nogales. Christian, Three-Fingered Jack Dunlap, and George Muskgrave remained on horseback while Bob Hays and Jess Williams entered the bank.

While the robbery was in progress, a newspaperman named Frank King spotted the bandits and opened fire with a .41 Colt. Hays and Williams dropped the money and ran, pursued by bank clerk Frank Herrerra. King wounded two of the outlaw mounts, but the gang galloped out of town. King chased them on a buggy horse, but after another exchange of shots he returned to Nogales.

August, 1896, Skeleton Canyon, Arizona. A few days later the outlaws were intercepted by a posse from Tucson led by Sheriff Bob Leatherwood. Christian and his gang turned on their pursuers, and a sharp fight erupted. Deputy Frank Robson was killed, the other lawmen were routed, and the fugitives slipped across the border into Mexico.

1896, San Simon Valley, Arizona. Later in the year Christian and three of his followers had taken refuge in a horse camp in the San Simon Valley, where they were traced by eight lawmen. One

morning the bandits left camp, and when they returned the posse was waiting. At fifty yards Christian spotted the posse, and a battle broke out. Christian and Hays had their horses killed, but both jumped free and kept firing. Hays was shot to death, but Christian and the other two fugitives escaped into the rugged wilderness.

April 28, 1897, Black Jack Canyon, Arizona. Christian and two henchman were hiding in a cave located in a gorge which became known as Black Jack Canyon. A five-man posse discovered their whereabouts and set an ambush. When the shooting started, Christian was hit in the side and fell out of the saddle. The lawmen retired to nearby Clifton, and Christian's companions galloped away. Later in the day the dying outlaw leader was discovered, and after he expired, his body was hauled into town atop a load of lumber.

Sources: Haley, *Jeff Milton,* 267–74, 279.

Christianson, Willard Erastus

("Matt Warner," "Mormon Kid")

(b. 1864, Ephraim, Utah; d. December 21, 1938, Price, Utah. Farmer, cowboy, rancher, ferryman, rustler, bank robber, justice of the peace, bootlegger, law officer.) Matt Warner, as Willard Erastus Christianson was known, was the son of a Swedish father and a German mother who had come to Utah as Mormon converts. During a fight as a teen-ager in 1878 he thought he had killed an antagonist, and he ran away from his parents' farm near Levan to become a cowboy. He soon fell in with rustlers, however, and became known as the Mormon Kid.

For a time Warner operated out of Utah's Robbers Roost area, before leaguing with Butch Cassidy. While on the run, Warner married a girl named

Rose Morgan, and for a time he and Tom McCarty ran a cattle ranch in Washington's Big Bend country. After several robberies Warner returned to an old ranch of his on Diamond Mountain, Utah, and lived there with his wife and daughter, Hayda. But because of a shooting scrape in 1896 he was sentenced to five years in the Utah State Prison, and shortly thereafter his wife died, having given birth to a son just before her death.

Warner was released for good behavior in 1900, and he remarried and had three more children. He settled in Carbon County, Utah, where he was elected justice of the peace and served as deputy sheriff. Warner was also a night policeman and detective in Price, while moonlighting as a bootlegger. He died peacefully at the age of seventy-four.

Gunfights: *1892, Diamond Mountain, Utah.* Warner had established a little horse ranch on Diamond Mountain near the Green River, and he had a quarrel with a Mexican called "Pollito" over a brown mare. After an exchange of words the men went for their guns, and Pollito was hit high in the chest. The Mexican told Warner where the disputed animal was located and eventually recovered under a doctor's care.

ca. 1892, Roslyn, Washington. Warner and Bill and Tom McCarty—known in some circles as the "Invincible Three"—robbed a bank in Roslyn, and when citizens tried to stop them, shooting broke out. Tom McCarty wounded two men, and after a furious chase the outlaws escaped.

ca. 1892, Ellensburg, Washington. Warner soon was captured and jailed in Ellensburg to await trial for the Roslyn bank robbery. Warner and his cell mate,

George McCarty, obtained tools and pistols and, on a Sunday morning two days before the trial, squeezed through an opening in the brick wall of the jail. They wrapped themselves in blankets and blacked their faces in an attempt to effect a disguise as Indians, but cries of jailbreak quickly were raised.

As the two fugitives tried to find mounts, a livery stable door opened, and a shotgun blast superficially wounded McCarty. Warner winged one citizen, but he and McCarty soon were forced to surrender. Two days later, however, Warner and McCarty managed to beat the charges against them and left Ellensburg free men.

1896, Uinta Mountains, Utah. Warner was accompanying Bill Wall, Bob Swift, and prospector Henry C. Coleman to a mining camp in the Uinta Mountains. But Coleman wrangled with Dave Milton and Ike and Dick Staunton, and the three men vengefully ambushed the party. Warner's horse was felled in the first volley, but he leaped free, gripping his six-gun and Marlin .30-30 repeating rifle.

Warner pumped three pistol slugs into Milton, fatally wounding the bushwacker. Then Wall distracted the Staunton brothers with revolver fire, and Warner dove behind a tree as bullets ripped into his clothing. Holstering his six-gun, he charged the Stauntons, emptying his rifle by firing from the hip. Dick Staunton was killed, and Ike was wounded in the nose and knee.

When the shooting ended, Warner and Wall sent for the authorities, but they were both arrested and convicted of manslaughter.

Sources: Warner, *Last of the Bandit Raiders;* Horan, *Desperate Men,* 194–96, 210–13; Baker, *Wild Bunch,* 54–64, 152–53, 156, 159, 163, 185, 188.

Christie, Ned

(b. December 14, 1852, near Tahlequah, Oklahoma; d. November 3, 1892, Ned's Fort Mountain, Oklahoma. Blacksmith, gunsmith, whisky runner, horsethief.) Christie was a Cherokee blacksmith and gunsmith who served on the tribal council as a young man. In 1885, however, he killed a lawman who tried to arrest him for running whisky. For the next seven years he stubbornly drove invading lawmen away from his wilderness stronghold, about fifteen miles southeast of Tahlequah. After his home and shop were destroyed by a posse in 1889, he rebuilt about a mile away on a forbidding cliff that became known as Ned's Fort Mountain. A field of fire was cleared around the two-story fortification. The massive walls were two logs thick and lined with oak two-by-fours. Christie defiantly held out until 1892, when he finally was killed in a general assault.

Gunfights: *May 5, 1885, near Tahlequah, Oklahoma.* Deputy U.S. Marshall Dan Maples had come to the vicinity of Tahlequah to apprehend whisky runner John Parris. Parris and his confederate, Ned Christie, emerged from a secluded cabin and started across a foot log spanning Spring Branch. Maples rose from concealment and ordered the two men to halt and then triggered a pistol shot when they turned to run. Christie fired in return, and Maples tumbled dead into the stream.

May, 1885, near Tahlequah, Oklahoma. Deputy Joe Bowers approached Christie's cabin, intending to serve a murder warrant for the death of Maples. Christie ambushed him, wounding the lawman in the leg and sending him galloping away.

May, 1885, near Tahlequah, Oklahoma. Deputy John Fields had determined to talk Christie into surrendering, and he rode toward the Indian's home. When Christie burst out of his cabin brandishing a Winchester, Fields turned his horse. He was shot in the neck but managed to escape with his life.

ca. 1886, near Tahlequah, Oklahoma. When his cabin was approached by a posse, Christie responded with furious and accurate fire. Three deputies were wounded, and the lawmen fell back in defeat.

1889, near Tahlequah, Oklahoma. Deputy Marshals Heck Thomas, L. P. Isbel, and Dave Rusk and an officer known as Salmon crept toward Christie's home just before dawn. Alert watchdogs wakened Christie and his family, and Ned opened fire from a sleeping loft. Thomas set fire to Christie's little shop, but Ned spotted Isbel peering from behind a tree and drilled him in the shoulder. When the cabin caught fire, Christie's wife and son made a break for the woods, but the boy was wounded in the lung and hips by Rusk and Salmon. As the deputies gathered around Isbel, Christie bolted from the cabin. Thomas shot him in the face; the bullet shattered the bridge of his nose and put out his right eye. Christie scrambled to safety as his home burned to the ground.

1891, Ned's Fort Mountain, Oklahoma. Deputy Marshal Dave Rusk raised a posse of Indians and attacked Christie in his fort. Christie and a few companions screamed war cries and poured forth a deadly fire. Four posse members were wounded, and Rusk ordered a withdrawal.

On two later occasions Rusk approached the fort alone, only to be driven back by rifle fire. Eventually Christie slipped into Oaks, north of Tahlequah, and burned Rusk's general store.

October 11, 1892, Ned's Fort Mountain, Oklahoma. Charley Copeland, Milo Creekmore, D. C. Dye, and several other lawmen assaulted Christie's fortification, but two officers were quickly wounded. The posse fell back and then began to load brush into a lumber wagon Christie had used in constructing his fort. The brush was set afire, and the wagon was shoved toward the fort, but the burning vehicle careened into an outhouse and stopped short of its target. Several sticks of dynamite were hurled at the walls but bounced harmlessly onto the ground, and the posse retired in disgust.

November 2–3, 1892, Ned's Fort Mountain, Oklahoma. Three weeks later a sixteen-man posse, led by Deputy U.S. Marshal Paden Tolbert, closed in on Ned's Fort Mountain, equipped with a three-pounder cannon and six sticks of dynamite. At dawn on November 2 an Indian fugitive named Arch Wolf unsuspectingly emerged from the cabin's only door, and the lawmen shouted for him to surrender. Wolf dived back to safety, and an exchange of rifle fire erupted. When the little cannon was brought into play, the shells struck the thick walls without effect, and after thirty rounds the breech split.

When darkness fell, the posse members turned their efforts to constructing a portable barricade. They found the charred rear axle and wheels from the burned lumber wagon and built and mounted a thick wall from scrap-oak timbers. After midnight Tolbert, Charley Copeland, Bill Ellis, Bill Smith, and G. S. White rolled the barricade close to the cabin, while the two Indians blasted away at them from second-story gunports. Copeland lit the six dynamite sticks, dashed forward to place them against the south wall, and then raced with the others toward the tree line.

In a moment the dynamite exploded, shattering the wall and setting the structure on fire. Christie and Wolf tried to make it to the woods by running through the thick smoke, but Ned suddenly found himself face to face with Wess Bowman. Christie jerked up his Winchester and fired hastily but succeeded only in powder-burning Bowman's face. Bowman spun and got off a shot as Christie ran past. The rifle slug hit the tall Indian behind the ear and killed him on the spot. Young Sam Maples, whose father had been killed by Christie in 1885, came forward and emptied his revolver into Ned's body. Wolf somehow managed to escape, but later was apprehended and sentenced to a prison term.

Sources: Good, "Ned Christie," *Guns of the Gunfighters,* 39–44; Trachtman, *Gunfighters,* 153, 157, 159; Elman, *Badmen of the West,* 151, 161.

Claiborne, William F.

("Billy the Kid")

(b. October 21, 1860, Yazoo County, Mississippi; d. November 14, 1882, Tombstone, Arizona. Cowboy, mine employee.) Billy the Kid Claiborne should not be confused with Billy the Kid of Lincoln County fame. Claiborne drifted into Arizona as a teenager, arriving in Tombstone at the beginning of the mining boom. He hooked on as a ranch hand with John Slaughter's outfit, and because he was so tiny of stature, he was nicknamed "the Kid" by the crew. He later began working as a driver for a mining company and, it was

rumored, became linked with the Clanton-McLaury gang. He was involved in a couple of gunfights, and he was killed by Buckskin Frank Leslie in 1882.

Gunfights: *early October, 1881, Charleston, Arizona.* In this small mining town near Tombstone, Claiborne shot and killed a man named James Hickey who tried to force him to take a drink. He was arrested (possibly by one of the Earp brothers), but he soon managed to elude custody.

October 26, 1881, Tombstone, Arizona. Still under indictment for the Hickey killing, Claiborne turned up in Tombstone to back the Clantons and McLaurys. He was present when the Earp brothers and Doc Holliday approached the O.K. Corral. When they opened fire he hit the dirt, then watched as Billy Clanton and the McLaury brothers were shot. When Ike Clanton fled into C. S. Fly's photographic studio nearby, Claiborne scrambled after him, a bullet tugging at his pants leg.

November 14, 1882, Tombstone, Arizona. Claiborne was drinking heavily at the Oriental Saloon, and soon he exchanged harsh words with Buckskin Frank Leslie, whom he blamed for killing John Ringo. Claiborne left the premises and concealed himself behind a fruit stand which overlooked the front door of the saloon. But Leslie anticipated the ambush and crept out a side door. Startled, Claiborne snapped off a wild rifle shot, then doubled over as a slug tore into his left side. A bystander ran toward Claiborne to ease his fall, and as Leslie advanced, Billy moaned, "Don't shoot again, I am killed." A doctor dressed the entry and exit wounds, and Claiborne was carried to a private home, where he died while cursing Leslie.

Sources: Rickards, *"Buckskin Frank" Leslie,* 15–22; Erwin, *John H. Slaughter,* 136, 189–95, 250.

Ike Clanton, who fled from the gunfight at the O.K. Corral in 1881. Six years later he was shot to death in another altercation. *(Courtesy Arizona Historical Society)*

Clanton, Joseph Isaac

("Ike")

(d. 1887, Bonita, Arizona. Rancher, cattle rustler, freighter.) Ike's father, N. H. Clanton, took his family from California to a cattle ranch near Fort Thomas, Ari-

zona. He sold out in 1877 and moved one hundred miles south to another spread near Tombstone. For a time Ike and his brother Phineas ran a freight line, but mainly they were involved in "Old Man" Clanton's ranching, rustling, and stage robbing activities.

When the old man died, Ike took over the "ring" at the height of a growing feud with the Earp brothers. (Rumor and Ike's testimony after the O.K. Corral gunfight implicated the Earp brothers in various shady dealings.) On October 25 Ike and Tom McLaury drove into Tombstone to buy supplies. That night, while eating in a saloon, Ike was approached by Doc Holliday, who was backed by Virgil, Warren, and Wyatt Earp. Holliday cursed Clanton and challenged him to a fight, but Ike left the premises, pointing out that he was unarmed. Later, after a poker game with four other men, including City Marshal Virgil Earp, Ike was cursed again and pistol whipped by the lawman.

After the gunfight at the O.K. Corral, Ike was probably instrumental in the retribution ambushes of Virgil and Morgan Earp. Ike continued his illegal activities until he was killed by a deputy sheriff in 1887.

Gunfights: October 26, 1881, Tombstone, Arizona. Ike and Billy Clanton, Billy Claiborne, and the McLaury brothers were approached outside the O.K. Corral by three of the Earps and Doc Holliday. After a quick exchange of words, gunfire broke out, and Ike, who was not armed, rushed to Wyatt Earp, grabbed his left hand and implored him to stop the fight. "The fighting has now commenced," Wyatt retorted, "go to fighting or get away." With his brother and the McLaurys already shot, Ike dashed for a nearby doorway, bullets buzzing by his head and Billy Claiborne running at his heels.

1887, Bonita, Arizona. Ike and Phineas, charged with cattle rustling, were encountered near Bonita by Deputy Sheriff J. V. Brighton. "Finn" surrendered upon demand, but Ike resisted and was shot dead by the alert lawman.

Sources: Jahns, *Doc Holliday;* Miller, *Arizona;* Waters, *Earp Brothers of Tombstone,* 121–22.

Clanton, William

(b. 1862; d. October 26, 1881, Tombstone, Arizona. Rancher, cattle rustler.) N. H. ("Old Man") Clanton had been attracted to California by the gold rush, but eventually he led his family into Arizona. Assisted by his three sons, of whom Billy was the youngest, he operated a ranch one hundred miles north of Tombstone which he sold in 1877. He then located another ranch in the Tombstone area and was closely aided by Billy, whose older brothers, Ike and Phineas, operated a freight line.

Along with two other local ranchers, the McLaury brothers, the Clantons began raiding cattle herds in Mexico and selling them to Arizona ranchers. This lucrative racket attracted such outlaws as Curly Bill Brocius, Johnny Ringo, Buckskin Frank Leslie, Bill Leonard, Jim Crane, Harry the Kid, Billy Claiborne, and Frank Stilwell, who each dabbled in other forms of robbery and became involved in shooting scrapes from time to time.

The Clanton faction eventually came in conflict with the Earp brothers, who held various law enforcement offices in and around Tombstone and who were accused by their detractors of being just as guilty of rustling and stage robbery as the Clantons. The Earp-Clanton feud erupted violently at the O.K. Corral, and there Billy Clanton, through his death, attained his one claim to fame.

Gunfight: *October 26, 1881, Tombstone, Arizona.* Old Man Clanton had died a short time earlier (some said he was ambushed by angry *vaqueros* as the Clantons returned from one of their regular forays into Mexico), and Ike Clanton had assumed leadership of the Clanton-McLaury "ring." On October 25 Ike and Tom McLaury drove into Tombstone for a wagonload of supplies. That evening they were abused verbally and physically by Wyatt and Virgil Earp and Doc Holliday. The next day Billy Clanton and Frank McLaury rode to town, and there were dark threats from both sides.

That afternoon the Clanton and McLaury brothers and Billy Claiborne were near the O.K. Corral, about to leave town, when they were approached by Doc Holliday and Morgan, Virgil, and Wyatt Earp. The Earps produced weapons and ordered the Clanton party to throw down their guns. Billy Clanton threw up his hands and shouted, "Don't shoot me; I don't want to fight!" Tom McLaury opened his coat and declared that he had no weapons. In reply Morgan Earp shoved his gun toward young Clanton and fired point-blank. The bullet struck Billy just below his left nipple, and he was knocked backward off his feet, clutching at his breast.

The next thirty seconds were filled with gunfire. Ike Clanton and Billy Claiborne fled the scene, the McLaury brothers were shot down, and Billy Clanton and Frank McLaury managed to draw their guns and wound Virgil and Morgan Earp and Doc Holliday. Billy's right wrist had been broken by a bullet seconds earlier, but he had reached across and drawn his Smith & Wesson revolver with his left hand and was firing lying on his back with the gun propped on his knee. Then a final slug struck him in the stomach to the right of his navel.

The shooting stopped, and C. S. Fly, a photographer whose studio was next door, ran to Billy and snatched his gun from him as he weakly tried to fire again. Then Billy, writhing in agony, was carried into an adjacent building. As he was picked up, he asked where he had been shot. Told that he was dying, he said, "Get a doctor and put me to sleep." While being carried, he whimpered, "Pull off my boots. I always told my mother I'd never die with my boots on." After he was laid out, he began to cry, "They've murdered me! Clear the crowd away from the door and give me air; I've been murdered!" A doctor arrived and, while a bystander held Billy still, injected two syringe pills of morphine beside the belly wound. Ten or fifteen minutes after the injection Billy gasped, "Drive the crowd away," then died. His body was examined, then carried off in a wagon and interred the following day.

Sources: Waters, *Earp Brothers of Tombstone,* 121–22, 158; *Tombstone Epitaph,* October 27, 1881.

Clark, Jim Cummings

(b. 1841, Clay County, Missouri; d. August 7, 1895, Telluride, Colorado. Thief, soldier, laborer, law officer.) Born in Missouri, Clark was christened Jim Cummings, but his name soon was changed when his widowed mother married a man named Clark. At the age of seventeen Clark stole a mule from his stepfather and fled to San Antonio, where he and a friend sold the animal, stole fourteen hundred dollars from a

rancher, and then returned to Missouri.

Clark met William Quantrill, and when the Civil War broke out, he became one of the guerrilla leader's most trusted lieutenants. After the war he again turned to thievery for a time before moving to Leadville in the 1870's. There he fought a champion prize-fighter for a one-hundred-dollar fee, flirted with outlawry again, and left for Telluride in 1887.

Clark worked at digging a pipeline into town, then secured an appointment as city marshal. He enforced the law by clubbing ruffians with his fists, and he was widely rumored to have continued his criminal activities from time to time. He finally was fired and promptly began muttering threats to kill members of the city council for fifteen cents, or two for a quarter. Clark remained in Telluride and was shot to death there in 1895.

Gunfight: *August 6, 1895, Telluride, Colorado.* About midnight Clark was walking toward his cabin with a man called Mexican Sam. As the two men passed the Colombo Saloon, there was a gunshot, and Clark clutched his chest, crying, "I'm shot. Go for a doctor." He staggered up the street, collapsed, and was carried to a cabin. The slug had torn through a lung and had severed an artery, and Clark died in less than an hour.

Source: Rockwell, *Memoirs of a Lawman,* 186ff.

Clements, Emmanuel

("Mannen")

(d. March 29, 1887, Ballinger, Texas. Rancher.) Mannen and his brothers Gyp, Jim, and Joe were brought up on a cattle ranch south of Smiley, Texas. In 1871 Mannen's younger cousin,

Emmanuel ("Mannen") Clements, Sr., in 1879, eight years before his death in a saloon fight. *(Courtesy Western History Collections, University of Oklahoma Library)*

fugitive John Wesley Hardin, came to stay on the Clements ranch. Hardin went up the Chisholm trail with a Clements herd and later assisted the Clements boys in the notorious Sutton-Taylor feud. Mannen and his brothers were involved in several ambushes and sieges on the side of the Taylors, who were their relatives by marriage.

In October, 1872, Mannen helped Hardin to escape from jail by slipping him a file, then pulling him between the jagged bars by lariat. Throughout the 1870's Clements and his brothers were active in driving herds to the Kansas railheads, and Mannen ran spreads in San Saba and McCulloch counties. In 1877 Clements found himself in jail in Austin, along with Hardin, Bill Taylor, John Ringo, and members of the Sam Bass gang.

By 1880 Clements was suspected of rustling, and he had accumulated vast horse and cattle herds on his McCulloch County ranch. In 1887 he ran for sheriff of newly formed Runnels County, and the heated campaign climaxed with his death in a saloon fight.

Gunfights: July, 1871, southern Indian Territory. While leading a herd toward Abilene, Clements came into conflict with two of his cowboys just as the party crossed into Indian Territory. The two cowhands, Adolph and Joseph Shadden, resisted Clements' authority, and Mannen angrily went for his guns. There was an exchange of shots, both Shadden brothers were killed, and the trail drive proceeded toward Abilene in orderly fashion.

March 29, 1887, Ballinger, Texas. While drinking in Ballinger's Senate Saloon, Clements was approached by City Marshal Joe Townsend. Soon firing erupted, and Clements went down, fatally wounded.

Sources: Shirley, *Shotgun for Hire,* 11–13; Shoenberger, *Gunfighters,* 25–26, 81–82; Sutton, *Sutton-Taylor Feud.*

Clements, Emmanuel, Jr.

("Mannie")

(d. December 29, 1908, El Paso, Texas. Cowboy, law officer.) Mannie Clements was the son of violence-prone South Texas rancher Mannen Clements, and he followed his father's aggressive ex-

Emmanuel ("Mannie") Clements, Jr., like his father, killed in a saloon. *(Courtesy Western History Collections, University of Oklahoma Library)*

ample. Clements drifted to El Paso in 1894, and for the next fourteen years he wore a badge as a deputy constable, constable, and deputy sheriff. During the 1890's he was united in El Paso with his cousin John Wesley Hardin, just released from prison, and with his murderous brother-in-law Killin' Jim Miller. In 1908 Clements was indicted for armed robbery, and even though he was acquitted (after dire warnings against any juror who dared vote against him), his career as a law officer was ruined. He turned increasingly to drink, and soon he was killed—ironically enough, in an El Paso saloon.

Gunfights: *1894, Alpine, Texas.* In Alpine, which at that time was known as Murphysville, Clements was hired to kill a local hard case named Pink Taylor. Clements climbed into a tree overlooking a saloon frequented by Taylor, and when his prey appeared, he opened fire through a window. But he succeeded only in killing the wrong man, and he immediately fled town, soon turning up in El Paso.

December 29, 1908, El Paso, Texas. About 6:00 P.M. Clements entered El Paso's Coney Island Saloon and began talking with Elmer Webb. About ten minutes later there was a shot, and Clements dropped dead with a bullet in his head. The circumstances of his death were never made clear, but it is likely that Clements was shot by a hired killer, probably bartender Joe Brown, in connection with a local racket to smuggle Chinese into the United States.

Sources: Nordyke, *John Wesley Hardin,* 82–88, 113–19, 139–40; Sonnichsen, *Pass of the North,* 336–44.

Clifton, Dan

("Dynamite Dick")

(d. December 4, 1896, near Newkirk, Oklahoma. Cattle rustler, bank robber.) In the 1890's Clifton switched from rusling cattle to bank robbery by joining Bill Doolin's "Oklahombres." After he was finally captured, he was incarcerated with Doolin in the jail at Guthrie. The two confederates bribed a guard in July, 1896, and after releasing a dozen other prisoners made good their escape. Clifton, however, was tracked down and killed by a posse a few months later.

Gunfights: *1892, Oklahoma.* In the Osage country Clifton encountered lawman Lafe Shadley, who tried to arrest him. The men blazed away at each other with their pistols before Clifton managed to escape. But Shadley had wounded Clifton in the neck, and the bullet had to be cut out, leaving a prominent scar.

September 1, 1893, Ingalls, Oklahoma. Clifton was with the Doolin gang when they were jumped by a posse at Ingalls. He shot his way from the hotel to the stable, helped bridle the horses, then galloped away beside Doolin.

May 20, 1895, Southwest City, Missouri. While the Doolin gang was robbing a bank in Southwest City, Bill Dalton shot and killed J. C. Seaborn, a former Missouri state auditor. A fierce exchange of shots began, and the gang mounted up, guns blazing. Doolin was hit in the head, but he stayed in the saddle, and the outlaws fought their way out of town.

November, 1896, near Sapulpa, Oklahoma. Clifton and two other hard cases were camped in a ravine twenty miles west of Sapulpa,where they were found by a small posse led by Heck Thomas. There was a flurry of gunfire, but the outlaws made good their escape.

December 4, 1896, near Newkirk, Oklahoma. A hunted fugitive, Clifton had found refuge on the Sid Williams farm sixteen miles outside Newkirk. There he was located by Deputy Marshals George Lawson and W. H. Bussey, but when they intercepted him on horseback and called for his surrender, he opened fire with a Winchester. A slug from Lawson's rifle broke his arm and knocked him out of his saddle, but he escaped on foot into the brush. By dark the lawmen had trailed him to a cabin in the woods, and as they closed in, he burst through the door, firing as he ran. The officers gunned him down, and he died within minutes.

Sources: Croy, *Trigger Marshal,* 204–205; Canton, *Frontier Trails,* 132–35; Drago, *Road Agents and Train Robbers,* 201, 205–207, 209–10; Shirley, *Heck Thomas,* 205–206, 214–15; Shirley, *Six-gun and Silver Star,* 91–93, 145, 179, 181, 189–94, 198.

Coe, Frank

(d. September, 1931, Lincoln County, New Mexico. Cowboy, farmer, rancher.) As a young bachelor Coe drifted to Lincoln County, New Mexico, where he found employment with several relatives as a farmer and ranch hand. Frank and his cousin George, who regularly served together as the fiddlers at local dances, jointly invested in the county's first thresher. But just as their financial situation was improving, the Lincoln County War broke out, and both cousins found themselves fighting with the McSween faction.

When the shooting subsided, the Coes moved to San Juan County, then left New Mexico completely. In 1884 the Coes returned to Lincoln County, and Frank and his wife of three years settled on a ranch which in 1873 had been leased by the murderous Horrell brothers from Lampasas, Texas. Coe lived on this ranch until his death in 1931; he was survived by six children and his wife of fifty years.

Gunfights: April 4, 1878, Blazer's Mill, New Mexico. Coe was with a group of Regulators who had been scouring the countryside for members of the opposing faction. Their leader, Dick Brewer, had called a halt at Blazer's Mill for the noon meal, but within thirty minutes one of their prey, Buckshot Roberts, rode into their midst bristling with weapons. Roberts had just spent the night with Coe, who approached him and tried to persuade him to give up his guns without a struggle. But three other Regulators walked over with cocked weapons, and a vicious shootout ensued. George Coe and John Middleton were wounded, and Roberts and Brewer were killed.

April 30, 1878, near Lincoln, New Mexico. Coe and Ab Sanders had decided to accompany Frank McNab to his ranch near Lincoln, but about eight miles out of town they were ambushed by the "Seven Rivers Crowd." They had stopped at a spring to water their horses, and just as Sanders and McNab dismounted, the bushwackers began shooting.

Both men went down, severely wounded, and Coe spurred his horse in an attempt to escape. But the animal was shot in the head, and Coe scrambled to cover behind an embankment. He stood off his attackers until he had exhausted his ammunition, then they let him surrender. McNab had been killed while trying to crawl away, and with Coe in custody the ambushers rode off, leaving behind both the wounded Sanders and McNab's bullet-riddled body.

July 4, 1878, near Roswell, New Mexico. Frank and George Coe, Billy the Kid, and two other men had ridden from the Chisum ranch to buy tobacco and candy at Ash Upson's store. They began the return trip about 10:00 A.M. but soon they encountered a large party of riders. The riders opened fire at long range, and there was a running fight all the way back to the ranch.

1881, near Fort Lewis, Colorado. For some time local Indians had plagued area farmers and ranchers with livestock raids, and a neighbor of the Coes, Jack Buchanan, was robbed and wounded by three of the renegades. He went to the Coes for help, and they treated him and put him to bed, then rode in pursuit of the thieves. There was a running battle, and the Indians finally abandoned the stock and fled. After a final volley the Coes rounded up the animals and returned them to Buchanan. Before reaching home, however, Frank slashed his coat, then with a straight face he described a desperate hand-to-hand fight with the savages. But after arousing the admiration of his family, he removed his tongue from his cheek and confessed the exaggeration.

Sources: Coe, *Frontier Fighter,* 43, 45–46, 60, 65–66, 82–86, 90, 103–106, 143, 163–65, 177, 179, 181–82, 188, 192, 203, 212; Keleher, *Violence in Lincoln County,* 83, 114, 117, 128, 233; Fulton, *Lincoln County War,* 66, 125, 131, 173–75, 177, 213–15, 220.

Coe, George Washington

(b. December 13, 1856, Brighton, Iowa; d. November 12, 1941, Lincoln, New Mexico. Farmer, cowboy, gunman, rancher, storekeeper.) The son of a Civil War veteran who had migrated to a Missouri homestead, George Coe in 1874 went to Fort Stanton, New Mexico, to work on the ranch of a cousin. By 1878 Coe had leased his own spread in Lincoln County, but the area was on the verge of all-out war, and Coe soon found himself arrested unjustly by Sheriff William Brady. While he was in custody he was subjected to physical torture, and upon his release he bitterly determined to seek revenge. In the subsequent Lincoln County War he fought with the Regulators, figuring prominently in the gunfight with Buckshot Roberts and in assorted other shooting scrapes.

When the hostilities died down, Coe moved with his relatives to San Juan County, where he had further trouble with outlaws and where he acquired a wife. Eventually Coe obtained amnesty from Governor Lew Wallace, and, after brief sojourns in Nebraska and Colorado, in 1884 he returned to Lincoln County to make his permanent home. He homesteaded what became known as the Golden Glow Ranch and also operated a store there. Coe became a staunch family man, and, following a conversion to Christianity, he hung up his guns for the rest of his long life.

Gunfights: *April 4, 1878, Blazer's Mill, New Mexico.* Dick Brewer had just led several Regulators from George Coe's spread into Blazer's Mill for a meal when Buckshot Roberts rode up on a mule. A member of the opposing faction, Roberts was armed with a rifle and two six-guns, and Frank Coe tried to persuade him to submit to arrest peacefully. Other Regulators were more impatient, however, and Charlie Bowdre, George Coe, and Henry Brown walked up with cocked guns to demand his surrender. But when Bowdre ordered him to raise his hands, Roberts snapped up his Winchester and growled, "Not much, Mary Ann!"

Both men fired at the same time, and Roberts staggered back with a hole through his middle. The bullet from Roberts' rifle glanced off Bowdre's cartridge belt and struck George Coe's gunhand. His pistol went flying, the hand was shattered, and the slug took off his trigger finger. The stunned Coe then charged Roberts, who shot John Middleton in the chest, then turned his weapon on Coe.

Roberts fired three times, but managed only to drill a hole in Coe's shirt and vest. Roberts then ducked into the building behind him and barricaded himself inside. After he killed Brewer with a shot in the head, the Regulators left him to die and withdrew to seek medical aid for Middleton and Coe.

April 30, 1878, Lincoln, New Mexico. A number of McSween men had gathered at Isaac Ellis' store in Lincoln, and a group of their enemies began to menace them. Coe, stationed on the roof, saw Dutch Charlie Kruling sitting on a cow's skull in a distant field. "See that fellow yonder?" he asked Henry Brown, who was sitting beside him. "I am going to take a shot at him." The rifle bullet shattered Kruling's ankle; he leaped into the air, then collapsed, so badly wounded that he spent four months in the Fort Stanton hospital. Coe's shot ignited a general exchange of fire, and a major battle was averted only by the appearance of Lieutenant G. W. Smith and fourteen soldiers.

May 14, 1878, Lincoln County, New Mexico. A couple of weeks later Coe accompanied a band of Regulators in a raid on a cow camp. The herders were easily routed; one was killed, two were wounded, and a herd of horses was confiscated.

July 4, 1878, near Roswell, New Mexico. On the morning of the Fourth of July, George and Frank Coe, Billy the Kid, and two other men rode to Ash Upson's store to get tobacco and candy. In a holiday mood, they headed back to the Chisum Ranch about 10:00 A.M. but they soon spied a band of fifteen or twenty men approaching. A running fight was carried on all the way back to the ranch, but there were no casualties.

July 15–19, 1878, Lincoln, New Mexico. During the first day of the big shootout in Lincoln, Coe fought from Ike Stockton's saloon. After dark he shifted to the McSween headquarters, but on the last day he moved again to a nearby warehouse building, where he fought alongside Henry Brown and Joseph Smith. When McSween, Billy the Kid, and the others inside the burning house tried to break out on the last night of the siege, Coe and his two companions used the resulting violent moments as a distraction. They crept outside, clambered on top of some barrels, and vaulted over an eight-foot fence to safety.

1882, near Fort Lewis, Colorado. Frank and George Coe were living near a man named Jack Buchanan, who was attacked and wounded by Indians. The Coes chased the Indians, and after a flurry of shots routed the renegades and retrieved Buchanan's livestock.

Sources: Coe, *Frontier Fighter;* Keleher, *Violence in Lincoln County,* 114, 128, 184, 233, 312, 325, 329; Fulton, *Lincoln County War,* 69, 131, 173, 215, 225, 264, 268.

Coe, Philip Haddox

(b. Texas; d. October 8, 1871, Abilene, Kansas. Gambler, saloon owner.) A border-town gambler, Coe became friendly with members of the Second Texas Mounted Rifles when that regiment was stationed in the Rio Grande Valley in 1862. The six-foot-four-inch Coe was so popular that the company (in

which Ben Thompson served) elected him lieutenant. When regimental officials learned of this, Coe was directed to enlist in the army through proper channels or stop acting as an officer. When Coe ignored those orders, he was conscripted, although he chose to flee to Mexico rather than serve under such conditions.

After the Civil War, Coe and Tom Bowles opened a saloon in Austin and installed Ben Thompson as a house gambler. In 1871 Coe drifted to Abilene, Kansas, and, pooling resources with Ben Thompson, opened the Bull's Head Saloon. Decorated with an obscene sign, the Bull's Head was expensively equipped and located so that it was the first saloon cowboys encountered upon entering the booming cowtown. This prosperous partnership was broken up that summer, however, when Thompson and his family were severely injured in a buggy mishap and returned to Texas.

Coe sold his interest in the saloon, but continued to gamble there. At this point he came into conflict with City Marshal Wild Bill Hickok, with whom he had previously clashed. The town council had ordered Hickok to see that the sign above the Bull's Head was altered, but when Coe and Thompson resisted, Hickok sent painters up to daub over the offensive portion of the bull's anatomy. But when the paint dried, the distinctive part of the bull still was sharply outlined, and Hickok had earned the bitter enmity of Coe. Then Coe acquired a mistress—a girl who earlier had caught Hickok's fancy. The marshal's anger was so great, according to some versions, that a fist fight broke out between the two, and when Hickok was floored, he threatened Coe's life.

The feud came to a head on October 5, when Hickok fatally wounded Coe in

an infamous gunfight. A friend of Coe's, Bud Cotton, took the body to Texas, and at one point overtook Ben Thompson and his family. Thompson, previously unaware of the shooting, allegedly wept over the casket.

Gunfight: *October 5, 1871, Abilene, Kansas.* Coe accompanied about fifty friends from Texas, mostly cowboys, on a drunken spree through the streets of Abilene. They caught passersby, carried them on their shoulders into saloons, and made them buy drinks. In one saloon they found City Marshal Hickok, who treated them to a round of drinks but warned them against excessive rowdiness.

A short time later, about 9:00 P.M. Coe fired a shot, and Hickok ran outside to confront the merrymakers. Several of the Texans had six-shooters drawn, and Hickok asked who had fired his gun. Coe said that he had shot at a dog, and the marshal went for his guns. Coe drilled a hole in Hickok's coat, then a slug hit the gambler in the belly and tore out his back. As Coe fell, he fired another shot which went between Hickok's legs; Wild Bill, apparently aiming for Coe's head, muttered that he had shot too low.

At that point policeman Mike Williams alertly rushed around the corner. Hickok, surrounded by a hostile crowd and suffering from bad eyesight, whirled and put two bullets in Williams' head, killing him instantly. Wild Bill then closed up the town, and the wounded Coe was taken to his cabin. Shot on Thursday, he lingered in horrible agony until Sunday.

Sources: Streeter, *Ben Thompson,* 75, 87–90; Streeter, *Prairie Trails & Cow Towns,* 83, 84, 86, 89–91; Miller and Snell, *Great Gunfighters of the Kansas Cowtowns,* 131–33.

Colbert, Chunk

(d. January 7, 1874, Colfax County, New Mexico.) Colbert established a reputation as a gunman during the early 1870's, reputedly killing seven men in West Texas, New Mexico, and Colorado. Two of these fights are on record, as well as his last shooting scrape. In 1874 he ran afoul of Clay Allison, and during the subsequent gunfight Colbert was shot to death.

Gunfights: 1871 or 1872, Cimarron, New Mexico. Colbert suspected a man named Charles Morris of trifling with his wife, and he angrily confronted Morris in Cimarron. Gunfire quickly broke out, and Colbert succeeded in shooting Morris to death.

ca. 1873, Trinidad, Colorado. Colbert fell into a disagreement with one Walter Waller in Trinidad, and the two men soon resorted to their guns. In the shooting which followed, Colbert managed to wound his antagonist fatally.

January 7, 1874, Colfax County, New Mexico. Colbert challenged Clay Allison to a horse race at Tom Stockton's quarter-mile track, which was adjacent to Stockton's Clifton House, an inn and store on a Canadian River crossing in Colfax County. The race was declared a dead heat, and Colbert and Allison somewhat unhappily repaired to the Clifton House to eat.

Upon finishing their meals, the two gunmen began drinking coffee. Colbert decided to shoot Allison, and while reaching for the coffepot with one hand, he began sneaking his pistol into firing position with the other. But Allison alertly spotted Colbert's gun and snatched for his own revolver. Colbert hurried his shot, and the slug plowed into the tabletop. Allison fired more carefully, and his bullet slammed into Colbert's forehead just above the right eye. Colbert toppled over dead and was buried in a small cemetery behind the Clifton House.

Sources: Stanley, *Clay Allison,* 98–99; Schoenberger, *Gunfighters,* 5–6, 171–72; Clark, *Allison,* 19; Stanley, *Desperadoes of New Mexico,* 177; Stanley, *Grant That Maxwell Bought,* 68.

Cole, James

(Law officer.) Cole was a peace officer in the Indian Territory who proved himself a deadly gunman during the 1880's.

Gunfights: 1886. On a ferryboat a drunken bully attempted to abuse Cole, and a fight broke out. As the brawl worsened, Cole pulled his revolver and shot his antagonist to death.

November, 1887, Indian Territory. Cole and a small posse were fired upon from ambush by a Cherokee desperado named Big Chewee. Cole instantly began shooting back, and he succeeded in mortally wounding the Indian.

November 29, 1887, Cherokee Nation, Indian Territory. Cole and fellow Deputy Marshal Frank Dalton held warrants for a horse thief named Dave Smith. On a Sunday morning they located their prey in a tent near the Arkansas River. With Smith was his brother-in-law, Lee Dixon, Dixon's wife, and William Towerly, a youthful horse thief.

As the officers approached the tent, Smith shot Dalton in the chest, and Towerly ran over to the fallen lawman and emptied his Winchester into Dalton's head. By this time Smith, Dixon, and his wife had begun firing at Cole, and Smith sent a rifle slug into his side. But Cole began shooting from the hip, killing Smith and the woman and wounding Dixon in the left shoulder and back.

Cole transported Dixon to Fort Smith, where the outlaw died of his wounds. Towerly had managed to escape, but he was soon killed in a shootout with lawmen at his family home near Atoka.

Source: Shirley, *Heck Thomas,* 79.

Collins, Ben

(d. August 1, 1906, near Emet, Oklahoma. Law officer.) Ben Collins served as an Indian policeman in Indian Territory, and in 1898 he received an appointment as deputy U.S. marshal. Collins made a number of sensational arrests, including an incident in which he was forced to shoot Port Pruitt, an influential resident of Emet. Partially paralyzed, Pruitt and his brother Clint, a prominent citizen from Orr, swore revenge against Collins. In 1905 a gunman acquaintance of Collins told the officer he had been paid two hundred dollars to kill him, with an extra three hundred dollars to come after completion of the job. The hired gun skipped the country with a two-hundred-dollar profit, but the next year Collins was assassinated by Jim Miller.

Gunfights: 1905, Emet, Oklahoma. Collins was called upon to arrest Port Pruitt, who vigorously resisted the lawman. Shooting broke out, and Pruitt fell wounded. He was charged with assault with intent to kill, but the case was dismissed.

August 1, 1906, near Emet, Oklahoma. Returning to his home near Emet on a Wednesday evening, Collins was ambushed by Killin' Jim Miller and thrown out of the saddle by a shotgun blast in the stomach. Collins managed to fire four revolver slugs at Miller before taking another load of buckshot in the face, and his hysterical wife reached his side to find him already dead.

Source: Shirley, *Shotgun for Hire,* 64–71.

Cook, Thalis T.

(Law officer.) During the 1890's Thalis Cook served in Company D of the Texas Rangers. He was a crack shot, but his lethal inclinations were tempered by his activities as a church worker and Bible student. Although a knee wound resulted in a permanent limp, Cook saw repeated action while riding with Ranger Captain John Hughes.

Gunfights: ca. 1895, near Marathon, Texas. About fifteen miles northeast of Marathon, Cook and fellow Ranger Jim Putnam encountered Fin Gilliland, who was wanted for the death of rancher H. H. Poe. As the men passed each other on horseback, the wary fugitive produced a .45 and squeezed off a shot which struck Cook in the knee and knocked him off his horse. Putnam killed Gilliland's mount with a rifle slug, and the outlaw forted up behind the fallen animal while the two rangers scrambled for cover. There was an exchange of shots, but Gilliland suddenly stopped firing. Putnam drew a bead while Cook hobbled over to discover the fugitive dead, hit squarely between the eyes.

September 28, 1896, Nogalitos Pass, Texas. Cook was a member of a posse led by John Hughes which tracked a trio of rustlers to Nogalitos Pass. Horse thieves Art and Jubel Friar and Ease Bixler were trapped on a mountaintop, and they opened up with rifles as the lawmen approached. When Jubel Friar raised up to shoot Hughes, Cook killed him with a Winchester bullet in the head.

Art Friar had already taken two slugs, and he shouted, "I have got enough."

"Hands up then," ordered Cook, "and come out."

Cook and Hughes advanced on foot, but when they were just ten yards away, Friar began firing a pistol. The two rangers cut him down with one slug each, and he died on the spot. In the meantime, Bixler mounted one of the stolen animals and galloped bareback to safety.

Sources: Martin, *Border Boss,* 131–34, 136–41; Webb, *Texas Rangers,* 447–49.

Cooley, Scott

(d. ca. 1876, Blanco County, Texas. (Cowboy, farmer, law officer, gunman.) Cooley was a Texas frontiersman who pursued a variety of occupations before becoming a central figure of the Mason County War in 1875. At one time a member of Company D of the Texas Rangers, Cooley turned in his badge to pursue of more peaceful vocation. He trailed a couple of herds to Kansas for a Mason County rancher named Tim Williamson, and when Cooley contracted typhoid fever, he was nursed back to health by Mrs. Williamson.

Cooley later acquired a farm near Menard in a neighboring county, but when Williamson was murdered, Cooley bitterly returned to Mason County to seek vengeance. The Mason County War was essentially a clash between Anglos and Germans in the area, and the conflict was aggravated by local cattle thefts. There were assorted shootings, and Williamson was a victim of the German faction. When Cooley arrived on the scene, he promptly killed two men, then became the leader of several other gunmen and continued his path of violence.

Texas Rangers were called in and soon quelled the feud, but Cooley, who previously had served with several of the lawmen, managed to escape arrest. He returned to Blanco County, a former haunt, but he soon fell ill and died.

Gunfights: 1875, Mason, Texas. Having discovered the identity of Williamson's murders, Cooley rode to the home of Deputy Sheriff John Worley. Worley was working on a well, and Cooley dismounted and introduced himself. When Worley began to pull a helper up out of the well, Cooley asked his name. As soon as Worley's identity was confirmed, Cooley drew his pistol and shot him to death. The helper plunged into the bottom of the well, and Cooley scalped his victim and then fled the scene.

1875, Llano County, Texas. Cooley proceeded immediately to the western part of an adjacent county, where he confronted Pete Border, the second man on his list of suspects. Cooley gunned down Border, whose wounds proved fatal.

1875, Mason, Texas. Several local hard cases, eager for an opportunity to attack local Germans, quickly joined Cooley. Cooley and five of these men swaggered into Mason spoiling for trouble. They soon found it with a leader of the opposing faction, and there was a vigorous exchange of shots. Cooley and his gang killed a local citizen, then escaped the town on horseback.

1875, Mason County, Texas. An angry posse tracked Cooley's band and located them on the Llano River. A sharp fight ensued, and before Cooley and his men could escape, one of their number, Mose Beard, was killed.

Sources: Gillett, *Six Years with the Texas Rangers,* 46–52; Webb, *Texas Rangers,* 325–28; Polk, *Mason and Mason County,* 48–59.

Jim Courtright, who wielded his gun on both sides of the law before his death at the hands of Luke Short. *(Courtesy Western History Collections, University of Oklahoma Library)*

Courtright, Timothy Isaiah

("Longhaired Jim")

(b. 1848, Iowa; d. February 8, 1887, Fort Worth, Texas. Soldier, army scout, law officer, racketeer, mine guard, ranch foreman, private detective.) Courtright, a native of Iowa, fought during the Civil War under Union General John ("Black Jack") Logan. After the war Courtright drifted to Texas, where he was employed by Logan as an army scout. In 1876 he was appointed city marshal of Fort Worth, a job he held for three years. Three years later Courtright went to Lake Valley, a booming New Mexico silver camp, where he secured a job as an ore guard with the American Mining Company. He was then once more employed by General Logan, this time as foreman of the old officer's New Mexico ranch.

Prominent among his duties was the assignment of keeping Logan's range clear of rustlers and sodbusters, and after killing two squatters, Courtright fled New Mexico to avoid trial. He returned to Fort Worth and opened a private detective firm known as the T.I.C. Commercial Agency, but soon extradition papers were served on him. Friends fastened a pair of six-guns beneath a café table, however, and using these weapons and a saddled mount, Courtright escaped custody. He hid aboard a train headed for Galveston, and from there he took a ship to New York. He wandered through Canada and into Washington, and then he went to New Mexico and succeeded in clearing his name of all charges.

Courtright next returned to Fort Worth and reopened the T.I.C., although the agency's primary activity was a protection racket by which the town's gambling joints were "policed" in return for a piece of the action. Luke Short, part owner of the White Elephant Saloon, flatly refused to pay, and when Courtright confronted him, the little gambler shot Longhaired Jim to death.

Gunfights: 1882, near Lake Valley, New Mexico. Two Mexican *bandidos* tried to rob an ore shipment guarded by Courtright. A running gun battle ensued, and Courtright managed to kill both thieves with well-placed rifle shots.

1883, near Silver City, New Mexico. Ranch foreman Courtright rode up to the shack of two Frenchmen who had squatted on General Logan's land. Courtright ordered them off the property, and when gunplay broke out, he shot both squatters to death.

February 8, 1887, Fort Worth, Texas. Courtright's protection racket included Jake Johnson's White Elephant Saloon. Luke Short had purchased a one-third interest in the saloon and angrily protested Johnson's payment to Courtright. Longhaired Jim sent a warning to Short through Johnson on February 7.

Short and Bat Masterson met Courtright at a Fort Worth shooting gallery. Courtright and Short exchanged words, and Luke reached inside his coat. Courtright ordered him not to go for his gun, and Short replied that he never carried a pistol there. But Courtright already had jerked out one of his revolvers and squeezed the trigger. The hammer caught in Short's watch chain, however, giving Luke time to draw his weapon and fire a slug which shattered the cylinder of Courtright's six-gun.

Short then fired his other five bullets, two of which went wild. The other three slammed into Courtright's right shoulder, right thumb, and heart. Longhaired Jim died within minutes, and Short later was cleared on grounds of self-defense.

Sources: Schoenberger, *Gunfighters,* 143, 184; Looney, *Haunted Highways,* 173; Cheney, "Longhair Jim Courtright," *Real West,* Fall, 1973, pp. 14–17, 68.

Crane, Jim

(d. June, 1881, Mexico. Cattle rustler, stage robber.) Crane was connected with the notorious Clanton-McLaury "ring" in southern Arizona. He engaged in cattle rustling and in 1881 was involved in an abortive attempt to rob a stagecoach, during which he allegedly killed the driver. Crane and two accomplices, Harry Head and Bill Leonard, remained at large until Head and Leonard were killed while trying to hold up a store. In revenge Crane engineered the deaths of the owners of the store, but was himself hunted down and killed a short time later.

Gunfights: *March 15, 1881, Contention, Arizona.* Crane, along with Harry the Kid Head, Bill Leonard, and Luther King, planned to rob a Wells, Fargo bullion shipment. It also was rumored that one objective of the holdup was to kill Bob Paul, a special agent who had been sent out by Wells, Fargo to prevent robberies in the Tombstone area. (It was further rumored that the Clantons and the Earps were behind the attempt to kill Paul and that Doc Holliday was actually present and fouled up the robbery because he was drunk, thus causing the beginnings of the Earp-Clanton feud which led to the fight at the O.K. Corral. According to this theory, the Earps pursued the stage robbers not to bring them to justice, but to prevent any damaging revelations of Earp involvement. Indeed, Doc Holliday was indicted for robbery and murder but was acquitted for lack of evidence.)

The night coach originated in Tombstone and carried a shipment of $26,000 in bullion along with eight passengers. After reaching Contention, twelve miles from Tombstone, the team was changed, and Bob Paul traded seats on the box so that he could temporarily relieve driver Budd Philpot. About a mile down the road the stagecoach slowed at a steep grade, and out of the darkness stepped Crane, Head, and Leonard.

One of the outlaws shouted, "Hold," but Crane immediately fired at the guard's seat, striking the luckless Philpot in the heart. Philpot tumbled onto the horses, and they bolted in terror. Paul groped for his shotgun and managed to wound Leonard in the groin. The robbers blazed away at the lurching coach and killed a passenger who was sitting on top, a miner named Peter Roerig. The intrepid Paul leaped onto the wagon tongue and brought the team under control.

Paul later led one of three posses (the other two were headed by Sheriff John Behan and Wyatt Earp) which managed only to produce Luther King, who had held the stage robbers' horses. King revealed the identities of his accomplices, but they successfully eluded capture.

June, 1881, Eureka, New Mexico. Leonard and Head attempted to rob a store in Eureka but were killed by the owners, Bill and Ike Haslett. Before dying, Leonard named Crane as the man who shot Budd Philpot. But Crane, unaware of Leonard's deathbed testimony, organized several hard cases to wreak revenge on the Haslett brothers. The Hasletts were attacked twenty-six miles from Eureka but defended themselves just as gamely and skillfully as they had their store. They killed two and wounded three of Crane's party before finally being overwhelmed and killed.

June, 1881, Mexico. In desperation, Crane ducked across the border into Mexico, but soon he was tracked down by Mexican regulars and, after a brief fight, was shot to death.

Sources: Faulk, *Tombstone,* 145–47; Waters, *Earp Brothers of Tombstone,* 127–40.

Cravens, Ben

(b. 1868, Lineville, Iowa and Missouri; d. September 19, 1950. Horse thief, whiskey smuggler, train robber, convict, farmhand.) Often called the last of the notorious Oklahoma outlaws, Cravens was the troublesome son of farmer B. B. Cravens. Ben ran away to the lawless Indian Territory after being jailed for tearing up the local school. He became a horse thief, whiskey runner, and train robber. Frequently arrested, he just as frequently escaped from jail. He broke out of custody in Lineville and Corydon, Iowa, Guthrie and Tecumseh, Oklahoma, and Lansing, Kansas.

Cravens was married to a Missouri girl and worked as a farmhand for a time, but he was arrested under an alias for stealing hogs, and when his true identity was revealed, charges were brought against him. He was given a life sentence, although he won parole as an old man.

Gunfights: 1896, Blackwell, Kansas. Wanted for train robbery, Cravens was apprehended by the city marshal of Blackwell. Cravens pulled his gun, but was shot down. He was wounded so severely that it was thought he would die. He recovered, but was sentenced to fifteen years in the Kansas State Prison at Lansing.

1897, Lansing, Kansas. Assigned to work in the coal mines, convict Cravens whittled a wooden pistol and covered it with tinfoil from cigarette packages, then pulled his "gun" on a guard. The guard surrendered his weapon, then hoisted Cravens to the top of the shaft. Cravens shot the guard dead, then made good his escape.

1897, Emporia, Kansas. Having just broken out of prison, Cravens encountered two fellow convicts who had previously escaped. Cravens and the two other fugitives began quarreling, and Cravens shot them to death.

March 19, 1901, Red Rock, Oklahoma. Cravens and a former convict named Bert Welty entered a combination store and post office and, finding no one present, began looting the cash drawer and merchandise. The postmaster barged in and fired a shot, missing Cravens. Cravens whirled and shot the postmaster, killing him instantly.

The two outlaws left town in a buggy during a thunderstorm, but when the vehicle overturned, Cravens leveled his shotgun and blasted Welty. Cravens rode off with the team, but Welty recovered and later identified Cravens, who was already serving a jail sentence under an alias.

Source: Croy, *Trigger Marshal,* 222–28.

Crawford, Ed

(d. November, 1873, Ellsworth, Kansas. Law officer.) Crawford's major notoriety came while he was a member of the Ellsworth police force. Temporarily off the force the day Sheriff C. B. Whitney was shot by Billy Thompson, he was reappointed after Mayor Jim Miller angrily fired all of the officers. While wearing a badge, he killed Texan Cad Pierce (who had been a participant in the monte game which precipitated Whitney's death) and then again was fired a week later. Within three months he was shot and killed in an Ellsworth whorehouse, supposedly in revenge for killing Pierce.

Gunfights: *August 20, 1873, Ellsworth, Kansas.* After the killing of Sheriff Whitney there was hard feeling

against the Texans who remained in town. Vigilante groups were rumored to have issued "white affidavits" against a number of Texans, including Cad Pierce and Neil Cain, principals in the events which had led to Whitney's death.

About 4:00 P.M., Pierce, Cain, and another Texan, John Good, approached City Marshal Ed Hogue, Policeman Crawford, and several other men lounging in front of the store Happy Jack Morco had ducked into during the Whitney shooting. "Hello, Hogue!" shouted Pierce. "I understand you have a white affidavit for me. Is that so?"

Hogue replied that Pierce's remark was ridiculous and tried to calm the Texan, stating that there had been too much talk already. "Yes, a damn sight too much talk," interrupted Crawford, "bad talk on your side. What did you say yesterday when you had the shotgun in your hands? [This was a reference to a shotgun Pierce had given Ben Thompson—the weapon Billy Thompson had used to shoot Whitney just five days earlier.] You said this gun had killed one son-of-a-bitch, and that it cost one hundred dollars and you would not take two hundred dollars better for it."

Pierce mumbled a reply. "What is it that you say?" pressed Crawford angrily. "If you want a fight, here is the place for it—as good as any!" Crawford then stepped back, gripped his gunbutt, and drew when Pierce placed his hand behind his back. Crawford's first shot hit Pierce in the side, and the Texan ran inside the store. Crawford pursued, shooting Pierce in the arm and then clubbing him over the head. Pierce died within moments.

November, 1873, Ellsworth, Kansas. When Crawford was discharged from the police force after killing Pierce, bitter Texans grimly warned him to leave town. Crawford left, but came back early in November. Four nights after his return he was in Lizzie Palmer's house in the red light section of town. He drunkenly fired four shots through a door and kicked it open, revealing a prostitute and her customer, a man named Putnam who was a brother-in-law of Cad Pierce. Crawford wounded Putnam in the hand, but Putnam then emptied his six-gun, striking Crawford four times. At that point several other Texan patrons charged in and opened fire. Crawford died with thirteen slugs in his body.

Sources: Streeter, *Ben Thompson,* 103–106, 118; Bartholomew, *Wyatt Earp, the Untold Story,* 75–79; Drago, *Wild, Woolly & Wicked,* 114–18.

Cruz, Florentino

(b. Mexico; d. March 22, 1882, Tombstone, Arizona. Laborer, thief, gunman.) Cruz was a halfblood who was involved with cattle rustlers and stage robbers in the Tombstone area. He was associated with Ike Clanton, Curly Bill Brocius, Pete Spence, Frank Stilwell, and other archenemies of the Earp brothers. Cruz was one of five men who killed Morgan Earp, and he subsequently was chased down and shot to death by the Earp faction.

Gunfights: *March 18, 1882, Tombstone, Arizona.* During the afternoon Cruz was at the Tombstone house of Pete Spence, a stage robber who had been aligned against the Earps for some time. Morgan Earp passed by in the street, and Spence pointed him out to Cruz.

At 10:50 P.M. Earp was playing pool at Campbell and Hatch's Billiard Parlor, standing with his back to a glass door ten feet away which opened onto an alley. His brother Wyatt sat nearby watching the game. Spence, Frank Stilwell, a gambler named Freis, Cruz, and another halfblood called "Indian Charley" crept up to the glass door. A shot was fired into Morgan Earp's back, and a second slug struck the wall near Wyatt's head. The five assassins fled immediately, and Morgan died within half an hour.

March 22, 1882, Tombstone, Arizona. Two days earlier Wyatt and Warren Earp, Doc Holliday, Sherman McMasters, and Turkey Creek Jack Johnson gunned down Frank Stilwell in Tucson. This group, bent on further vengeance against Morgan Earp's murderers, promptly returned to Tombstone in search of the other suspects. The Earp party went to Pete Spence's wood camp outside town, arriving about 11:00A.M.

The county sheriff already had taken Spence, Freis, and Indian Charley into custody, but Theodore Judah, working at the Spence camp, told the Earp posse that Cruz was nearby chopping wood. The five avengers fell upon Cruz, Judah heard "ten or twelve" shots, and he later found Cruz's body riddled with bullets.

Source: *Tombstone Epitaph,* March 22, 23, 25, 27, 1882.

Cummings, Samuel M.

("Doc")

(d. February 14, 1882, El Paso, Texas. Sheep raiser, restaurant owner, hotel owner, justice of the peace, law officer.) Doc Cummings was a close friend and brother-in-law of Texas gunman Dallas Stoudenmire, having married his sister in 1870 in Columbus, Texas. Perhaps because of his association with hard cases, or perhaps because of his own

irascible nature, Cummings was involved in numerous altercations, some of which erupted into shooting scrapes. At various times Cummings was a hotel owner in San Marcial, New Mexico, a justice of the peace in Oldham County, Texas, a sheep raiser in West Texas, and the owner of various restaurants in El Paso. But his inclination to become embroiled in trouble caused his death in a gunfight in 1882, just one week after he had pinned on a deputy's badge.

Gunfights: April 17, 1881, El Paso, Texas. Cummings was accompanying Stoudenmire as the marshal made his evening rounds of El Paso. An attempt on the life of Stoudenmire had been planned, and from atop a pile of bricks a man named Bill Johnson leaped up with a shotgun. Johnson loosed a wild blast of buckshot at the marshal, and Stoudenmire and Cummings palmed their six-guns and returned his fire. Eight bullets hit Johnson, tearing open his chest and severing his testicles, and he slumped onto the bricks, dead on the spot. A few more shots came from across the street, but Stoudenmire charged and scattered those hidden assailants.

February 14, 1882, El Paso, Texas. Cummings shared Stoudenmire's hatred of El Paso's Manning brothers and suspected them of provoking Bill Johnson into his assassination attempt. Several months later Cummings encountered Jim Manning in the Coliseum Variety Theater. It was about 6:00 P.M., and Cummings had been drinking; he began to curse Manning to goad him into fighting. Manning repeatedly tried to back away from a shooting, but at last he removed his coat, buckled on a gunbelt, and grimly snapped, "Doc, we will have this out."

Cummings went for his gun, but Manning and bartender David Kling, who also had been abused by Doc, fired first. Both slugs tore into Doc's body, but he managed to squeeze of one wild shot. Then he staggered through the batwing doors, collapsed in the street, and died after gasping out one awful moan.

Sources: Metz, *Dallas Stoudenmire,* 31, 42, 51–53, 59, 74, 82–92; Sonnichsen, *Pass of the North,* 220, 222–24, 230, 239.

Curry, George

("Flat Nose," "Big Nose")

(b. March 20, 1871, Prince Edward Island, Canada; d. April 17, 1900, Castle Gate, Utah. Rustler, horsebreaker, train and bank robber.) Curry migrated with his family from Canada to Chadron, Nebraska, where he spent his childhood. At the age of fifteen he drifted west, eventually becoming a stock thief. At some time during his career a horse kicked him in the nose, producing the alteration which earned him his nicknames.

Curry joined the Wild Bunch in several bank and train holdups, and in 1897 he was wounded and taken prisoner by a posse. He and two cohorts escaped, however, and he spent the following summer breaking horses with Harvey Logan and the Sundance Kid on various ranches in Nevada.

In 1899 Curry was involved in a train robbery at Wilcox Siding, Wyoming, and after a lengthy pursuit he was chased down and killed in Utah. Following his death, souvenir hunters stripped skin from his chest and made it into wallets and moccasins, and he was dumped into a grave in Thompson, Utah. Several months later his father appeared, had his body disinterred, and shipped it back to Nebraska for final burial in Chadron.

Gunfights: *October, 1897, southern Montana.* Curry, the Sundance Kid, and Harvey Logan had drifted into Montana with vague plans to stage a train robbery. They camped just inside the Montana state line, where they were tracked down by Six-shooter Bill Smith and a bounty hunter. The two lawmen crept between the outlaws and their staked horses, then shouted out demands for their surrender. The fugitives scrambled for their guns, and there was a quick flurry of shots.

Curry took a slug in the arm, and when the wanted men realized they could not reach their horses, they stopped shooting and submitted to custody. They were taken to jail in Deadwood and were charged with robbing a bank in Belle Fourche, South Dakota, but they soon managed to escape.

June 5, 1899, near the Red Fork of the Powder River, Wyoming. Having just looted a train of eight thousand dollars at Wilcox Siding, the Wild Bunch split the money and scattered. Curry, Harvey Logan, and the Sundance Kid rode north together, establishing a camp near the Red Fork of the Powder River. As they were sitting down to a meal, a posse galloped up. Logan killed Sheriff Joe Hazen, and with guns blazing the three outlaws rode to safety.

April 17, 1900, Castle Gate, Utah. Curry, having resorted again to rustling, found himself being chased by a posse near Castle Gate, Utah. The lawmen were led by Sheriffs Jesse Tyler and William Preece, and Curry was unable to elude them. A six-mile running gunfight ensued, but no hits were scored until Tyler or ranch foreman Doc King

struck Curry in the head with a long-range rifle shot. Curry scampered into some rocks and forted up, and the posse surrounded his position. When Curry offered no further resistance, the officers cautiously moved in and discovered that their prey had died quietly, slumped against a rock with his rifle in his lap.

Sources: Horan and Sann, *Pictorial History of the Wild West,* 191, 198, 210–13; Baker, *Wild Bunch,* 86, 95–104, 109, 186, 216; Pointer, *Butch Cassidy,* 67–68, 70, 102-103, 127, 131, 153, 158–59, 161.

Dalton, Robert Reddick

(b. 1868, Cass County, Missouri; d. October 5, 1892, Coffeyville, Kansas. Farmer, law officer, train and bank robber.) Dalton's father, Lewis, was a Missouri saloon owner who turned to farming as a more fitting atmosphere for his fifteen children. In 1882 the family moved to Indian Territory, living for a time within a few miles of Coffeyville, Kansas, where the Dalton gang would be decimated in 1892. An older brother, Frank, was killed by a trio of whiskey runners while serving as a deputy U.S. marshal under the "hanging judge," Isaac Parker. Bob, although still a teenager, and two other brothers, Emmett and Grat, promptly pinned on deputy marshals' badges themselves. But Bob soon was fired for taking a bribe, and, amid rumors that they were engaging in cattle rustling on the side, Emmett and Grat also resigned.

Grat followed two other brothers, Bill and Littleton, to California, while Bob and Emmett drifted into New Mexico. There, after supposedly being cheated by house gamblers, they held up a faro game. Wanted by the law, Emmett returned to Oklahoma while

TIM EVANS   BOB DALTON   GROT DALTON   DICK BROADWELL

The bodies of the Dalton gang after the Coffeyville raid, propped up against the wall of a livery stable owned by John J. Kloehr, who fired shots into all three of the Dalton brothers during the shootout. *(Courtesy Kansas State Historical Society, Topeka)*

Bob fled to California. Bob and Grat then teamed with two other hard cases and attempted to rob a train, but after a good deal of shooting the attempt was aborted.

Bob decided to shift his illegal activities to Kansas and Oklahoma, where he knew the terrain. He returned home and with his aggressive personality became the leader of a band of outlaws which would terrorize the area for a year and a half. Members of the gang included Bob, Grat, and Emmett, Bill Doolin, Dick Broadwell, Black Faced Charley Bryant, William McElhanie, Bitter Creek Newcomb, Charley Pierce, and Bill Powers. Bob's girlfriend, Eu-

genia Moore, was the gang's advance agent until she died of cancer before the Coffeyville raid.

The Daltons pulled four Oklahoma train holdups in Wharton, Lelietta, Red Rock, and Adair and were blamed for a variety of other robberies in the vicinity. They then planned their most daring job: the robbery of two banks in Coffeyville, where their father and brother Frank had been buried. The citizenry resisted, however, and in the bloodbath which followed Bob was killed, and his gang was shot to pieces.

Gunfights: *winter, 1888, Coffeyville, Kansas.* Bob's sweetheart was a distant cousin named Minnie Johnson. When he left Coffeyville to serve as an Arkansas peace officer, Minnie was soon being courted by Charles Montgomery, who worked on a farm adjacent to the Dalton homestead. When Bob returned, he was enraged at the situation, and Minnie and Charles fled town on a train, with Dalton pursuing and firing his six-gun wildly.

Bob bitterly nursed his grudge, and when during the winter Montgomery came back to pick up his belongings, Bob met him on the road outside Coffeyville. Hot words ensued, and Bob shot Montgomery in the neck with his Winchester. Bob reported that the dead man was a horse thief, and the matter was quickly dropped.

February 6, 1891, Alila, California. Bob, Grat, and a couple of accomplices took over the depot in tiny Alila, and when the morning train chugged near, they flagged it down. The outlaws jerked up masks and, as the train slowed, two of them jumped into the cab. While some of the robbers kept the passengers pinned down with rifle fire, one masked man forced fireman George Radcliff to accompany him to the express car. The men inside refused to open up, but the thieves smashed through the door with picks. When the outlaws began to climb inside the car, Radcliff tried to slip away, but one of the robbers shot him fatally in the stomach. The bandits were unable to open the safe, and after futilely applying crowbars they fled the town.

July 15, 1892, Adair, Oklahoma. Bob and his gang had been camped near Adair for several days before this long-planned holdup. About 9:30 P.M. Bob and seven of his men rode into tiny Adair, followed by a spring wagon. They boldly walked into the depot, looted the

station at gunpoint, then calmly awaited the arrival of the 9:42 train.

When the train pulled in, the bandits commandeered the engine and approached the express car, backing the wagon up to the door. Threatening to use dynamite, and firing several shots through the door, the outlaws frightened the messenger into admitting them. Three of the bandits jumped into the car, forced the messenger to open the safe, then cleaned it out and threw the loot into the wagon.

While this was occurring, several guards opened fire on the gang, and a brisk exchange of shots began. Three guards were wounded: railroad detective L. L. Kinney, who suffered a flesh wound in the right shoulder; territorial Police Chief Charley LaFlore, who was nicked in the arm; and Deputy Marshal Sid Johnson, who had previously served as a peace officer with Bob and Grat and who was only scratched. Stray bullets wounded Doctor T. S. Youngblood and killed Doctor W. L. Goff, both of whom were sitting in a drugstore when the shooting started.

October 5, 1892, Coffeyville, Kansas. Six members of the gang—the three Daltons, Dick Broadwell, Bill Powers, and Bill Doolin—planned to loot a pair of Coffeyville banks, but on the way into town Doolin's horse supposedly went lame, and Bill did not participate. About 9:30 A.M. the rest of the gang rode into Coffeyville, leaving their horses in an alley instead of the town square because workmen had temporarily torn down the hitch rails.

The Daltons were recognized by a citizen named Aleck McKenna, who quietly began to spread the alarm. While Grat, Powers, and Broadwell walked across the street to the Condon Bank, Bob and Emmett ducked into the First

National Bank and held guns on teller W. H. Shepherd, cashier Thomas G. Ayres, and customers C. L. Hollingsworth, J. H. Brewster, and A. W. Knott, who was a deputy sheriff. But while Bob and Emmett scooped twenty-one thousand dollars into a tow sack, townspeople were shouting warnings and arming themselves in nearby hardware stores.

When Bob and Emmett emerged from the bank, they were pushing Shepherd, Ayres, and Knott before them. But gunfire forced them back inside the building, and they fled through the back door toward their horses. A young man named Lucius Baldwin waved a pistol and tried to block their path, but Bob fired a Winchester slug into his left breast, inflicting a fatal wound. As the two brothers raced past Rammel's drugstore, Bob spotted George Cubine and Charles Brown, bootmakers who had known the Daltons in their boyhood. Cubine held a Winchester, and Bob killed him with one shot. Brown angrily grabbed the rifle, and Bob shot the old man dead. Ayres had dashed from the bank into Isham's hardware store, and as he emerged from the building Bob dropped him with a bullet in the left cheek.

In the alley Bob and Emmett were joined by their three cohorts, who had managed to grab only fifteen hundred dollars before the shooting started. As they tried to mount their horses, heavy gunfire poured into the alley, and Bob and Powers had their animals shot out from under them. At that moment Marshal Charles Connelly, a former schoolteacher, rushed into "Death Alley" with his gun blazing, but Grat shot him to death.

John J. Kloehr, a livery stable owner, now stepped out five feet from the outlaws. Bob whirled toward him, but Kloehr dropped the bandit leader with a slug in the chest. Bob staggered back, sat down in the street, rolled over, and died. Grat turned his gun toward Kloehr, but the livery stable owner coolly pumped a bullet into the outlaw's neck.

Powers jumped onto Grat's horse, but a slug ripped into his heart, and he pitched to the ground. Broadwell, who had been shot in the arm inside the Condon Bank, climbed into the saddle and spurred his horse, but he was met by a deadly fusillade which tore the life from his body. By this time Emmett had been hit in the arm, but he mounted and, still clutching his grain sack, tried to pick up Bob. But Kloehr and barber Carey Seaman stepped forward and shot him out of the saddle.

The firing stopped. Citizens Charley Gump and T. A. Reynolds also had been wounded, and among the outlaws only bullet-riddled Emmett remained alive. Souvenir hunters snipped locks of hair from Bob's head, and Bob and Grat were held up to be photographed alongside the victorious townspeople.

Sources: Horan and Sann, *Pictorial History of the Wild West,* 156–65; Preece, *Dalton Gang;* Drago, *Road Agents and Train Robbers,* 177–93.

Dalton, Emmett

(b. 1871, Cass County, Missouri; d. July 13, 1937, Los Angeles, California. Farmer, law officer, train and bank robber, convict, building contractor, realtor, movie scenarist, actor.) Emmett and his fourteen brothers and sisters were born on a farm in Missouri but moved in 1882 to a homestead near Coffeyville, Kansas. His family later migrated to Kingfisher, Oklahoma, but by then Emmett had pinned on a badge in Arkansas. His brother Frank had been killed while making an arrest as

a deputy U.S. marshal, and Grat, Bob, and Emmett followed in his footsteps for a while. Bob soon was fired for taking a bribe, and Grat and Emmett quit before they were slapped with cattle rustling charges. Emmett then accompanied Bob to New Mexico, where they held up a faro game after presumably being "cheated" by house gamblers.

Bob went to California to join three other brothers, and Emmett decided to seek refuge in Oklahoma. While there, he built a large dugout which later became a hideout for the Dalton gang. Bob and Grat had attempted a train holdup in California, and when they rendezvoused in Oklahoma with Emmett, Bob organized a band of train robbers.

After one and one-half years of looting trains, the gang tried to rob a brace of banks in Coffeyville, but in the celebrated shootout which followed, only a badly wounded Emmett survived. Doctors wanted to amputate his arm, but he refused and slowly began to recover. When he regained his health, Emmett pleaded guilty to second-degree murder in the Coffeyville death of George Cubine, although Bob probably was the one who killed the man.

Although sentenced to a life term in the Kansas State Penitentiary, Emmett received a pardon in 1907. He married a woman who had been his sweetheart during his outlaw days and embarked on a successful career in honest enterprise. He was a building contractor and real estate agent, and after moving to Los Angeles in 1920 he wrote movie scenarios and even acted in a few bit parts. Until his death in 1937 he was a vigorous crusader against crime and for prison reform.

Gunfights: *July 15, 1892, Adair, Oklahoma.* At 9:00 P.M. the Dalton gang rode into Adair, took over the depot, and prepared to loot the 9:42 train. When the train chuffed into the station, the bandits took control of the engine, rolled a wagon up to the express car, and frightened the messenger into opening the door. Three bandits then climbed into the car, cleaned out the safe, and tossed their loot into the wagon.

By this time guards had opened fire from the smoking car, and the outlaws returned a heavy fusillade which slightly wounded three of the officers and allowed the gang to retreat from the village. Before the shooting ended, however, two bystanders were struck by stray bullets: Doctor W. L. Goff, who was fatally wounded, and Doctor T. S. Youngblood.

October 5, 1892, Coffeyville, Kansas. About 9:30 A.M. Emmett, Bob, Grat, Bill Powers, and Dick Broadwell rode into Coffeyville, tied their horses in an alley, and walked toward the two banks they intended to rob. Emmett and Bob entered the First National Bank, while the other three bandits crossed the square to the Condon Bank. Bob and Emmett quickly piled twenty-one thousand dollars into a grain sack, but when they emerged from the bank gunfire from the alerted townspeople drove them back inside.

They dashed out the back door and ran toward the alley. Along the way Bob pumped bullets into Lucius Baldwin, George Cubine, Charles Brown, and Thomas Ayres: all but the last man died, and Emmett later was charged with second-degree murder in the deaths of Cubine and Brown. Emmett took a slug in the right arm, but he still clutched the grain sack and managed to climb into the saddle.

Grat, Powers, and Broadwell ran toward their mounts with Marshal Charles Connelly right behind them. Grat shot

Connelly dead, then turned toward his horse. But livery stable owner John J. Kloehr suddenly appeared and methodically shot down Bob and Grat from a range of five feet. Powers and Broadwell climbed onto horseback, but just as quickly were shot out of the saddle by a deadly hail of lead.

Emmett tried to lean over and pick up Bob, but Kloehr shot him in the hip, and barber Carey Seaman blasted a load of eighteen buckshot into his back and shoulders. Emmett was slammed to the ground, then was carried to the Farmers' Hotel, where he eventually was nursed back to health by his sweetheart and his mother.

Sources: Horan and Sann, *Pictorial History of the Wild West*, 156–66; Preece, *Dalton Gang;* Dalton and Jungmeyer, *When the Daltons Rode;* Drago, *Road Agents and Train Robbers*, 177–93, 226.

Dalton, Grattan

("Grat")

(b. 1865, Cass County, Missouri; d. October 5, 1892, Coffeyville, Kansas. Farmer, law officer, train and bank robber.) One of fifteen children, Grat Dalton was reared on farms in Missouri and Kansas. Eventually the family moved to a homestead near Kingfisher, Oklahoma, but by that time Grat and three of his brothers had pinned on badges as deputy U.S. marshals. Frank Dalton was killed in 1887 in the line of duty, but Grat, Bob, and Emmett did not enjoy such honorable careers. Grat and Emmett resigned amid a flurry of rumors that they were rustling cattle on the side, and Bob was fired after taking a bribe.

Grat then went to California, where brothers Littleton and Bill had previously established themselves. Bob soon joined them, and Grat and Bob tried to rob a train in February, 1891. During their escape Grat's horse took a fall, and, suffering a gash in his side, Grat made his way to Bill's home in Tulare. A posse followed the trail of blood and arrested Grat and Bill, although the latter quickly obtained a release. Grat, however, was convicted and sentenced to twenty years, and on April 1, 1891, he was placed aboard a train to be transported to the penitentiary. Somehow Grat escaped custody in a spectacular incident.

After this fortunate escape Grat returned to Oklahoma to join Bob's gang of train robbers. A series of successful holdups ensued, but when the Daltons tried to loot two banks in Coffeyville there was a massacre in which Grat and seven other men were killed.

Gunfights: 1888, Oklahoma. Grat attempted to arrest an Indian desperado, who responded with gunfire. There was an exchange of shots, and Grat caught a slug in the left forearm.

February 6, 1891, Alila, California. Just before the passing of the morning train, Grat, Bob, and two henchmen commandeered the Alila village depot. When the train approached, the outlaws flagged it down, then donned masks and produced rifles. Two of the bandits began firing to hold the passengers inside the cars, while the other two hopped into the cab.

While Grat held a gun on the engineer, the other robbers forced fireman George Radcliff to lead the way to the express car. When the express messenger refused to open the door, the thieves ripped it apart with pickaxes. Radcliff then tried to break away, but he was shot down, mortally wounded in the abdomen. The bandits then entered the express car, but were unable to open the safe. They finally threw aside their crowbars in exasperation, mounted their horses, and spurred out of town.

July 15, 1892, Adair, Oklahoma. About 9:00 P.M. Grat and the other members of the Dalton gang rode into Adair from their campsite outside town. The outlaws took over the depot at gunpoint, and when the 9:42 train arrived they executed prearranged assignments. The engine was commandeered by two men, other bandits backed a spring wagon toward the express car, and the rest of the gang exchanged shots with guards in the smoking car.

Three of the guards were slightly wounded during the firing, and two citizens sitting in a drugstore, Doctors Youngblood and W. L. Goff, were struck by stray bullets, Goff fatally. While the shooting was going on, three of the outlaws jumped into the express car, threatened the messenger into opening the safe, scooped its contents into grain sacks, and tossed the sacks into the wagon. The gang then withdrew and escaped into the surrounding territory.

October 5, 1892, Coffeyville, Kansas. Grat, Bob, Emmett, Dick Broadwell, and Bill Powers rode into Coffeyville, located just a few miles from the old Dalton homestead, with the intention of robbing two banks on the town square. They had planned to hitch their horses in front of the banks, but a repair party had removed the hitch rails, and the gang tied their animals to a fence in a nearby alley. Bob and Emmett proceeded to the First National Bank, while Grat led Powers and Broadwell across the street to the Condon Bank.

Inside the Condon building Vice-President Charles Carpenter, bookkeeper T. C. Babb, and cashier Charley Ball were confronted with drawn guns and harsh orders to open the safe. Thinking quickly, Ball lied that the safe had

a time lock which would not open until 9:45, a three-minute wait. Already warnings were being shouted outside, but Grat calmly announced that he would wait for the "time lock" to open. The townspeople were arming themselves, however, and a harness maker named Miller fired a shot into the bank which hit Broadwell in the arm. When Bob and Emmett emerged across the street with a bulging grain sack, Grat scooped fifteen hundred dollars in loose bills into his bag and led his men around the corner toward the alley.

Bob already had shot four citizens, and when Grat dashed into "Death Alley" a heavy fire was pouring into it. City Marshal Charles T. Connelly, a former schoolteacher, ran toward the bandits firing rapidly, but Grat killed him with one shot. At that point livery stable owner John J. Kloehr stepped from behind a fence and fired his rifle into Bob's chest. As his brother fell, Grat turned toward Kloehr, but the man coolly shot Dalton in the neck.

When Grat collapsed, Powers jumped onto his horse, but was quickly shot out of the saddle. Broadwell also climbed aboard a mount, and he, too, was gunned down. When Emmett was blasted off his horse, the battle ended. Seven townspeople had been shot— three fatally—and among the outlaws only the buckshot-riddled Emmett remained alive. Curious citizens pumped Grat's arms up and down to watch the blood spurt, and his corpse was lifted to be photographed alongside the triumphant survivors.

Sources: Horan and Sann, *Pictorial History of the Wild West,* 156–65; Preece, *Dalton Gang;* Drago, *Road Agents and Train Robbers,* 177–92.

Dalton, William Marion

(b. 1866, Cass County, Missouri; d.

September 25, 1895, near Ardmore, Oklahoma. Farmer, politician, bank robber.) One of ten sons and five daughters born to a Missouri farmer and saloon keeper, Bill gained notoriety as a bandit but was never a member of the Dalton gang. When he reached adulthood, Bill married and obtained a minor political position in the California town of Tulare. In 1891 his brothers Grat and Bob, already in trouble with the law, came to California and tried to hold up a train. After the aborted robbery Grat sought refuge in Bill's house, and a trailing posse arrested both men. Bill was quickly freed, but Grat was convicted and avoided a stiff prison sentence only by means of a spectacular escape.

After the Coffeyville raid, in which the Dalton gang was decimated in a wild street fight, Bill turned up at his brother Emmett's bedside. Bill was bitter and resentful. Any hope of a political career was ruined by family notoriety; three of his brothers had died violently (Grat and Bob at Coffeyville, Frank while trying to arrest whiskey runners in 1887); and Emmett was facing a life prison term after being gunned down by the men of Coffeyville. Bill yearned to strike back at society, and when Bill Doolin offered him an opportunity, he promptly elected to hit the outlaw trail.

Doolin, a key member of the Dalton gang, had missed the Coffeyville massacre only because his horse had gone lame on the way into town. Doolin subsequently formed a band of robbers known as the "Oklahombres," and Bill Dalton became his second in command. The Oklahombres pulled a series of bank robberies in 1893 and 1894, and in September, 1893, there was a bloody shootout with lawmen in Ingalls, Oklahoma. The gang broke up in 1895, and Dalton tried to hide out with his wife and two children, but he was soon tracked down by a posse and killed at his wife's home.

Gunfights: *September 1, 1893, Ingalls, Oklahoma.* Doolin, Dalton, Bitter Creek Newcomb, Arkansas Tom Jones, Red Buck Weightman, Tulsa Jack Blake, and Dan Clifton were spending a brief period of recreation in Ingalls. Lawmen learned of their whereabouts and began to close in on the little town.

The shooting began at 10:00 A.M. when Newcomb, mounted on his horse, was fired upon by posse member Dick Speed. Newcomb was wounded but managed to escape, and the officers and remaining fugitives exchanged a furious barrage of fire. A local boy was killed, a bystander named N. A. Walker was wounded in the chest, and a stray horse was shot dead.

Arkansas Tom, trapped in an upstairs hotel room, killed lawmen Speed and Tom Houston with accurate rifle fire. But the posse concentrated their attack on the saloon which sheltered the main body of outlaws, and when the two saloon owners were wounded, the fugitives determined to make a run for it. Doolin led the way, dashing to the nearby livery stable and providing cover fire while Dalton and Red Buck came next. These three men then began shooting to cover Clifton and Blake, and when all five outlaws were inside, they readied themselves for the final flight.

Doolin and Clifton galloped to safety out the back door, while Dalton, Red Buck, and Blake burst into the street with guns blazing. John Hixon stopped Dalton's horse with a bullet in the jaw, but Dalton spurred furiously, and the animal bolted forward. But after just twelve more yards Lafe Shadley felled the poor beast with a rifle slug which broke its leg. Dalton hit the ground running, only to discover that his comrades had been stopped by a wire fence.

Dalton darted back to his horse, retrieved a pair of wire cutters, and began working on the fence. Just then Shadley approached, but as he crawled under the fence, Dalton spotted him and opened fire. The outlaw pumped three slugs into Shadley's body, forming a trio of holes so close together they could be covered with the palm of a hand. Dalton then turned from the fatally wounded officer, finished cutting the fence, and clambered up behind Doolin. As the outlaws galloped away, they turned at the top of a hill to fire one last volley, but they succeeded only in inflicting a shoulder wound in the fourteen-year-old son of Dr. Briggs.

April 1, 1894, Sacred Heart, Oklahoma. At 8:00 P.M. Dalton and Bitter Creek Newcomb entered a store at Sacred Heart owned by a former lawman named W. H. Carr. Carr was waiting on a seventeen-year-old boy named Lee Hardwick, but the old officer instantly recognized Dalton and reached for his gun. Newcomb whipped out a pistol and shot Carr in the wrist just as the crusty old lawman wounded the outlaw in the left shoulder. Carr dropped his weapon, and as he stooped to retrieve it, Dalton fired, sending a slug crashing into the floor. Hardwick reached for a shotgun, and Dalton triggered three more wild shots. Carr came up shooting, and although now wounded in the abdomen, he continued firing and chased the fugitives outside, whereupon they mounted and escaped.

Spring, 1895, near Dover, Oklahoma. Following an April 3 train robbery just outside Dover, the Doolin gang was jumped by a posse. Tulsa Jack Blake was fatally wounded, but the other bandits broke into the clear. Red Buck's horse was killed, but he climbed up behind Bitter Creek Newcomb, and the outlaws finally managed to escape the lawmen. When the gang reached a farm owned by an old preacher, Red Buck stole a horse and then gunned down the parson when he protested. Dalton and Doolin angrily decided to expel Red Buck; they counted out his share of the loot, tossed him the money, and ordered him to leave the gang.

September 25, 1895, near Ardmore, Oklahoma. Dalton was hiding at his wife's house on a ranch twenty-five miles from Ardmore. A posse surrounded the house while Dalton was on the porch playing with his youngest child, Grace, who was a cripple. The lawmen called out for him to surrender, but he turned to reach for his Winchester a few feet away. Deputy Marshal Loss Hart immediately fired, and the slug entered Dalton's back and ripped out just above his heart. He collapsed and died within moments.

Sources: Horan and Sann, *Pictorial History of the Wild West,* 157–58, 165–69; Preece, *Dalton Gang;* Drago, *Road Agents and Train Robbers,* 177–78, 188, 192, 194, 198–200, 205–209; Shirley, *Six-gun and Silver Star,* 26–30, 60–64, 91–94, 108–17.

Daugherty, Roy

("Arkansas Tom Jones")

(b. 1870, Missouri; d. August 16, 1924, Joplin, Missouri. Cowboy, bank robber, convict, restaurant owner, movie actor.) Daugherty was raised in Missouri in a highly religious atmosphere; his father was deeply devout, and his two brothers became preachers. But Roy rebelled against his family and ran away from home at fourteen. Calling himself "Tom

Roy Daugherty (alias "Arkansas Tom Jones"), who began robbing banks with Bill Doolin and did not stop until he was shot to death in 1924. *(Courtesy Western History Collections, University of Oklahoma Library)*

Jones," he claimed that he was from Arkansas (thus his nickname) and hired on at an Oklahoma ranch. He eventually decided to get his money the easy way, and in the 1890's he joined Bill Doolin's gang of bank robbers. He was captured after the shootout at Ingalls, convicted of manslaughter, and sentenced to a fifty-year prison term.

Largely through the efforts of his brothers Roy obtained a parole in 1910. After running a restaurant in Drumright, Oklahoma, for two years, he went to Hollywood to act in Westerns. Later he returned to Missouri, and in 1917 he helped rob a bank in Neosho. He was again imprisoned, but in 1921 he

was released. He immediately became involved in a bank holdup in Asbury, Missouri, and for three years he was a wanted man. In 1924, however, he was apprehended in Joplin and was shot to death while resisting arrest.

Gunfights: September 1, 1893, *Ingalls, Oklahoma.* Doolin led six members of his gang into tiny Ingalls to rest and recuperate from their most recent · activities. While his cohorts began drinking and playing poker in a saloon, Daugherty, who was ill, went to the City Hotel and retired to an upstairs bedroom.

But lawmen had quietly filtered into the town, and Daugherty was jolted out of his rest when officer Dick Speed and Bitter Creek Newcomb began trading shots in the street. Daugherty grabbed his Winchester and stepped to the window in time to see Speed wound Newcomb, who was mounted. As the lawman stepped forward to finish off Newcomb, Daugherty fired a bullet which caught Speed in the shoulder. Speed turned, and Daugherty fired another shot which killed him instantly, and Newcomb galloped out of town. Posse members and outlaws then began an exchange of shots so furiously that four citizens were wounded and one was killed.

Daugherty decided to improve his vantage point (the hotel was the only two-story building in town) by climbing a ladder to the attic. He poked a hole in the roof just as his companions were trying to escape on horseback. Daugherty spotted lawman Tom Houston moving in and squeezed off shots which fatally wounded his target in the left side and in the lower abdomen.

After Doolin led the other fugitives out of town, the posse ordered everyone to vacate the hotel while the building was surrounded. Daugherty knocked a hole in the other side of the roof and held out for an hour, but Jim Masterson produced two sticks of dynamite, and at 2:00 P.M. the besieged outlaw prudently surrendered.

August 16, 1924, Joplin, Missouri. Widely sought for bank robbery, Daugherty sought refuge in the Joplin home of a friend, Red Snow. Detectives found him there, babysitting in the absence of the Snow family. Daugherty caught sight of the officers, snatched up a pistol, and opened fire. After two shots his gun jammed, however, and he was killed by the lawmen.

Sources: Croy, *Trigger Marshal,* 207–209; Drago, *Road Agents and Train Robbers,* 201, 205–207, 210, 217, 227; Shirley, *Heck Thomas,* 171–74; Shirley, *Six-gun and Silver Star,* 62, 91–95, 97, 118, 190, 215–16.

Delony, Lewis S.

(b. October 21, 1857, Clinton, Texas. Laborer, clerk, law officer, carpenter, building contractor, cattleman, insurance executive.) Delony's father was an adventurer who was an early member of the Texas Rangers and who fought in the Mexican War and the Civil War. He later settled down to become a schoolteacher, a sheepman, and the surveyor and tax assessor for DeWitt County, which was the center of the violent Sutton and Taylor feud. By the age of twelve young Delony had acquired the habit of carrying a derringer to school, and within two years the self-reliant youth was in Louisiana and Mississippi, working at a variety of jobs. He soon returned to Clinton, his birthplace, where he became a store clerk, assistant postmaster, and deputy sheriff.

In 1877 and on several occasions thereafter Delony received a temporary appointment as a Texas Ranger, and for a time he served as a border guard in Laredo, engaging in several skirmishes with smugglers. Delony married in 1887 and entered a variety of business ventures in different Texas towns, but he continued to accept employment as a lawman from time to time, and he occasionally found himself involved in shooting scrapes.

Gunfights: 1879, Cuero, Texas. Riding into town for lunch, Delony was startled to see a suspected train robber bolt out of a café with Deputy Sheriff Add Killgore in hot pursuit. The fugitive threw a shot at Killgore, then vaulted onto his horse and spurred down the street. Delony promptly hauled out his Winchester and killed the outlaw's horse, but the desperado nimbly scrambled to his feet, found another mount, and galloped to safety.

Spring, 1882, Eagle Pass, Texas. Delony was traveling with Texas Ranger Spencer Adams, and the two lawmen camped in a wagon yard in Eagle Pass. About 4:00 A.M. they were awakened by a Mexican boy, who told them that a deputy sheriff and a Mexican woman had just been killed in a dance hall. The lawmen ran to the dance hall, where they found the killer coolly dancing near the bodies.

The two officers arrested the man, but suddenly a bartender shouted, "Look out, Ranger!" Delony whirled to see a Mexican charging him with a knife. Delony shot the man in the chest, then scampered outside with Adams to escape the enraged crowd. They later retrieved their prisoner, and the wounded Mexican recovered, but both men were eventually freed.

Fall, 1888, Dallas, Texas. While on night guard duty in the art department at the Texas State Fair, Delony heard a suspicious noise and crept into a darkened display room. He found two robbers looting jewelry showcases. Delony fired and wounded one of the thieves, but both robbers managed to scramble to safety. They were soon apprehended, however, and sentenced to prison terms.

Sources: Delony, *40 Years a Peace Officer;* Sonnichsen, *I'll Die Before I'll Run,* 53–54, 65, 97.

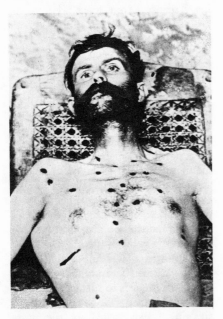

Bill Doolin, leader of the "Oklahombres." He was shotgunned to death by an Oklahoma posse in 1896. *(Courtesy Western History Collections, University of Oklahoma Library)*

Doolin, William M.

(b. 1858, Johnson County, Arkansas; d. August 25, 1896, Lawson, Oklahoma. Cowboy, bank and train robber.) The son of an Arkansas farmer, Bill Doolin drifted into Indian Territory in 1881 and worked as a cowboy for the H-X-Bar Ranch. Following a shooting, he became a member of the Dalton gang and was busy robbing banks and trains until the band was destroyed at Coffeyville. Doolin missed the massacre, perhaps because of a quarrel with Bob Dalton over how the money was to be divided or perhaps because his horse went lame on the way into Coffeyville.

In 1893 Doolin married a preacher's daughter, but, little reformed, he soon organized his own gang. Doolin's "Oklahombres" included Bill Dalton, Charley Pierce, Red Buck George Weightman, Little Bill Raidler, Bob Grounds, Tulsa Jack Blake, Little Dick West, Dynamite Dick (Dan Clifton), Arkansas Tom Jones (Roy Daugherty), Bitter Creek George Newcomb, Alf Sohn, and Ol Yantis. From 1893 through 1895 the Oklahombres specialized in robbing banks. In 1893 the gang shot their way out of Ingalls, Oklahoma, by killing three lawmen.

Finally, Oklahoma's "Three Guardsmen"—peace officers Chris Madsen, Heck Thomas, and Bill Tilghman—led a concentrated search for Doolin and his band, but the outlaws remained at large for well over a year. In January, 1896, Doolin was captured by Tilghman at the health resort in Eureka Springs, Arkansas, where the outlaw leader had traveled to find relief for his chronic rheumatism. Doolin escaped jail, however, and hid out in New Mexico. But when he returned to rejoin his wife and son, he was found and killed by a posse.

Gunfights: 1891, Coffeyville, Kansas. Doolin and a large number of other cowboys were having a beer bust just outside Coffeyville. Two constables appeared and asked who owned the beer. "Nobody owns it," replied Doolin, who was in charge of the party, "It's free.

Help yourselves." One of the constables then announced, "It is against the law to drink beer in this state, and we are going to pour the beer out." Doolin angrily retorted, "If you pour our beer out, you're going to get hurt."

The officers stubbornly began to roll one of the barrels over, and several cowboys drew their guns. A general shootout followed, and the two lawmen were killed. No one knew who fired the fatal shots, but Doolin was afraid he would be blamed, and he fled, soon to join the Dalton gang.

July 15, 1892, Adair, Oklahoma. Doolin and the rest of the Dalton gang rode into Adair planning to loot the 9:42 evening train. About fifteen minutes before the train was scheduled to arrive, the outlaws barged into the depot and scooped up all the currency on hand. When the train pulled in, they jumped aboard the cab, backed a wagon up to the express car, and threatened the messenger until he opened the door. Three bandits leaped inside, forced the messenger to unlock the safe, and began cleaning it out.

In the meantime, guards opened fire from the smoker, but several of the gang riddled the car with rifle slugs and wounded three of the lawmen. Two bystanders also were hit, one fatally. Finally the loot was dumped into the wagon, and the gang thundered triumphantly out of town.

May 30, 1893, Cimarron River near Ashland, Kansas. On May 26 Doolin had engineered a train robbery near Cimarron, Kansas. When he and three members of his band crossed the Cimarron River to return to Oklahoma, they were intercepted by a posse led by Chris Madsen. The outlaws and the posse began exchanging fire, and Madsen shat-

tered Doolin's right foot with a steeljacketed rifle bullet. Doolin then led his men as they galloped safely away from the ambush.

September 1, 1893, Ingalls, Oklahoma. Doolin and his gang rode into tiny Ingalls, a frequent stopoff. Doolin, Bill Dalton, Bitter Creek Newcomb, Tulsa Jack Blake, Red Buck Weightman, and Dan Clifton bellied up to the bar of the Ransom and Murray Saloon while ailing Arkansas Tom Jones went to an upstairs room of the City Hotel to collapse into bed. The authorities had been tipped off, however, and numerous lawmen closed in on the town.

The outlaws started a poker game in the saloon, but Newcomb soon stepped outside to check the street. Lawman Dick Speed took a shot at him, and a general fight erupted. Newcomb, despite a wound, managed to spur his mount out of town while Arkansas Tom and the fugitives in the saloon furiously exchanged shots with the officers. Speed was shot dead in the street, a boy named Dell Simmons was killed, and another bystander was hit in the chest.

There was a brief lull in the firing, and the lawmen began to move in, calling on the outlaws to surrender. Doolin defiantly shouted, "Go to hell!" and the shooting began again. As the posse poured volley after volley into the building, saloon owners Ransom and Murray were hit in the leg and in the side and arm, respectively. Doolin dashed out to the nearby livery stable, then provided covering fire while his cohorts ran to join him.

Doolin and Dan Clifton quickly bridled their horses and rode out the rear door toward a draw, while Dalton, Blake, and Weightman galloped through the front entrance. After bitter shooting in the street, the last three outlaws whirled their mounts and tried to follow Doolin and Clifton. Their path was blocked by a wire fence, but Dalton went to work with a pair of wire cutters. Lawman Lafe Shadley approached, but Dalton killed him and returned to his job. When the fence was cut, Doolin rode back, pulled Dalton up behind him, and the bandits thundered off to safety.

May 20, 1895, Southwest City, Missouri. Doolin led his gang into Southwest City with the intention of holding up the local bank. Doolin and several henchmen slipped inside and announced their intentions. But while the robbery was taking place, former State Auditor J. C. Seaborn tried to pull a weapon. The outlaws shot him to death, and before the gang could get out of town there was a brisk exchange of gunfire. Doolin was wounded in the head, but he stayed in the saddle, and the gang escaped to safety.

Spring, 1895, near Dover, Oklahoma. Tulsa Jack Blake was guarding the sleeping gang's camp on the Cimarron River near Dover. Suddenly a posse closed in, and a wild fight commenced. Blake was killed, but Doolin and the rest of his gang scrambled to safety after a running battle.

August 25, 1896, Lawson, Oklahoma. After escaping custody, Doolin had hidden at the New Mexico ranch of writer Eugene Manlove Rhodes. In August he determined to bring his wife and son to New Mexico, and he returned to the farm of his father-in-law, a minister, located just outside Lawson. Carrying a Winchester and leading his horse, Doolin was walking down a lane near the house in the bright moonlight.

Heck Thomas, however, had been tipped off, and there were lawmen stationed on both sides of the road. Thomas ordered Doolin to surrender, but the outlaw whipped up his rifle and began firing. A bullet from the posse knocked the Winchester from his hands, but Doolin jerked his pistol and squeezed off a round or two before Thomas, firing a rifle, and posse member Bill Dunn, armed with a shotgun, killed him by blasting twenty-one holes in his body.

Sources: Hanes, *Bill Doolin;* Croy, *Trigger Marshal,* 158–203; Drago, *Road Agents and Train Robbers,* 127, 180–82, 184, 194, 199, 198–202, 205–15, 217; Shirley, *Six-Gun and Silver Star,* 34, 44–45, 57–68, 82, 87–94, 104–11, 120, 142–48, 152, 159, 182–98.

Dow, Les

(b. Texas; d. May, 1896, Carlsbad. New Mexico. Hotel and saloon keeper, law officer, range detective, cattle inspector.) Dow was a Texan who drifted into New Mexico and after running a saloon and hotel became a deputy sheriff of Chaves County. Later he was a range detective and a cattle inspector for the Texas and New Mexico Sanitary Association, and for a time he served as sheriff of Eddy County and held a commission as a deputy U.S. marshal. Eventually he ran afoul of a Texas hard case named Dave Kemp, who shot him to death in 1896.

Gunfights: 1896, San Simon Valley, Arizona. Dow and seven other officers had trailed the outlaw band of Black Jack Christian to a horse camp in the San Simon Valley. The lawmen secluded themselves in the camp one morning as the fugitives were rounding up horses, and when the band returned, the officers ordered them to surrender. The outlaws went for their guns, and a sharp fight broke out. Dow squeezed off five rounds at Black Jack, and the desperado's horse went down, but Christian scrambled free and ran to safety. The posse killed Bob Hays's horse, but he jumped up shooting, managing to send splinters into lawman Fred Higgins' face. Hays was then shot to death, but the other two outlaws fought their way to freedom.

April, 1896, Carlsbad, New Mexico. Dow had gone to the post office, and he strolled outside reading a letter. Suddenly an enemy named Dave Kemp stepped forward and discharged a sixgun into Dow's face, shattering his jaw. As he staggered back, Dow pulled his gun, but he collapsed before he could fire. Kemp and a henchman sprinted away from the scene, and Dow died that night.

Sources: Sonnichsen, *Tularosa,* 95–96, 113–14, 117, 141–42, 312; Harkey, *Mean as Hell,* 45–46, 64, 82–85; Gibson, *Colonel Albert Jennings Fountain,* 221, 225–27, 229, 254, 262.

Dunlap, Jack

("Three-Fingered Jack")

(Bank and train robber.) Dunlap was a notorious Arizona outlaw about the turn of the century. Captured in 1895, he soon was loose again, and he joined the bandit gang of Black Jack Christian. Later Dunlap became involved with the Burt Alvord–Billy Stiles band of train robbers.

Gunfights: *August 6, 1896, Nogales, Arizona.* Christian, Dunlap, and George Muskgrave were guarding the street while two henchmen were looting the International Bank of Nogales. Suddenly a reporter named Frank King

opened fire on them with a handgun, and in the shooting which followed, two of the outlaws' horses were hit. The thieves shot their way out of town, but were forced to abandon their booty.

August, 1896, Skeleton, Canyon, Arizona. A week or so later the gang was jumped by a Tucson posse led by Sheriff Bob Leatherwood. The outlaws fought back viciously, succeeding in killing Frank Robson and driving off the other lawmen.

February 15, 1900, Fairbank, Arizona. As darkness fell, Dunlap, George and Louis Owens, Bravo Juan Yoas, and Bob Brown met just outside Fairbank to rob the incoming train. As the train rolled into the station, the bandits opened fire on the express messenger, Jeff Milton, shattering his left arm. But Milton scrambled for his shotgun and loosed a blast which drove eleven buckshot into Dunlap's side and one slug into the seat of Yoas' pants. Yoas fled, Dunlap collapsed, and the remaining three outlaws continued to fire futilely at the express car. Finally they dragged Dunlap away, lifted him into the saddle, and galloped out of town.

Source: Haley, *Jeff Milton,* 268–70.

Dunn, William B.

(d. November 6, 1896, Pawnee, Oklahoma. Rancher, bounty killer, cattle rustler, law officer.) Dunn and his brothers—Bee, Calvin, Dal, and George—ran a road ranch near Ingalls, Oklahoma, where travelers ate and slept. Prosperous, solitary voyagers often were robbed and murdered there, according to hearsay, and in 1895 two members of the Doolin gang were killed at the ranch. The Dunn brothers helped law officers track down outlaws from time

to time, and Bill Dunn fired the shotgun blast which finished off Bill Doolin.

Dunn also owned a meat market in Pawnee through which he and co-owner Chris Bolton disposed of stolen cattle. Charged with theft, Dunn directed his animosity toward lawman Frank Canton, who considered the fugitive "a dead shot, and . . . the quickest man with a revolver that I ever met." But Dunn apparently was not quick enough, because when he and Canton met in Pawnee, the peace officer whipped out his pistol and shot Dunn to death.

Gunfights: *May 2, 1895, Dunn Ranch on the Cimarron River, Oklahoma.* Charley Pierce and Bitter Creek Newcomb approached the Dunn Ranch after dark and went into the barn to stable their horses. The two men were wanted by the law, and there was a five-thousand-dollar dead-or-alive reward out for Newcomb. Bill and a brother picked up shotguns, and when the outlaws emerged from the barn, they were shot down in front of the house. Pierce groaned and was shot again. The next day the outlaws were taken into Guthrie for the rewards.

August 28, 1896, Lawson, Oklahoma. An ill and hunted Bill Doolin had sought refuge with his wife at the home of her father. Dunn was in the posse which surrounded the farm after dark. Doolin, heavily armed, was caught in the open and was ordered to surrender, but he fought desperately to escape. Dunn and posse leader Heck Thomas blasted him with a shotgun and a rifle, respectively, and Doolin died on the spot.

November 6, 1896, Pawnee, Oklahoma. There had arisen an indignant public furor over the way Bitter Creek Newcomb and Charlie Pierce had been killed, and Bill Dunn blamed Deputy Sheriff Frank Canton for starting the talk. Dunn repeatedly swore he would kill Canton, and his bitterness increased after he was charged with cattle theft. When he encountered Canton on the streets of Pawnee, he cursed the lawman and placed his hand on his pistol grip. But Canton instantly went for the revolver stuck in his waistband and snapped off a shot which sent a .45 slug into Dunn's forehead. Dunn sprawled on his back, trigger finger twitching, and died within moments.

Sources: Croy, *Trigger Marshal,* 185–87; Canton, *Frontier Trails,* 110–16, 119–21, 134–37; Shirley, *Six-gun and Silver Star,* 143–47, 157, 161–62.

Earhart, Bill

(d. fall, 1896, Pecos, Texas. Cowboy.) Reared in Jack County, Texas, Earhart came to New Mexico in 1883 with his friends Jim and Clay Cooper. Five years later, while directing a roundup on the Cooper ranch in the Tularosa country, he fell into a dispute with a rugged cattleman named John Good and thereby became involved in a range war directed against the bullying rancher. Later, Earhart returned to Texas, where he was killed in 1896.

Gunfights: *August, 1888, near Las Cruces, New Mexico.* John Good had recently found his murdered son's corpse in the White Sands, and while the bereaved rancher and five cohorts were returning home, they spotted a party of five rivals, including Earhart, who were suspected of the killing. The two groups opened fire at a distance of 150 yards, and more than one hundred shots were exchanged. Two horses were killed, and one was wounded, but none of the men were struck.

Fall, 1896, Pecos, Texas. Earhart had become involved in another feud in the Pecos country, and while in a Pecos saloon he encountered an antagonist. Shooting broke out, and Earhart was fatally wounded.

Source: Sonnichsen, *Tularosa,* 33–35, 44, 48, 52.

Morgan Earp, a victim of the violence in Tombstone, Arizona, that made him and three of his brothers famous as gunmen. *(Courtesy Kansas State Historical Society, Topeka)*

Earp, Morgan

(b. April 24, 1851, Pella, Iowa; d. March 18, 1882, Tombstone, Arizona. Gambler, laborer, shotgun guard, law offi-

cer.) Acknowledged to be the most pleasant and outgoing member of a highly clannish family, Morgan Earp was reared in Iowa and traveled with his parents to California in 1864. When he was nineteen he returned east to be with his older brothers, Jim, Virgil, and Wyatt. In 1870 Wyatt had become constable of Lamar, Missouri, and had married a girl who soon died. Wyatt had trouble with his dead wife's family, and the four Earp brothers engaged in a twenty-minute street brawl with five other men.

Morgan then drifted into Kansas, where he was arrested and fined for an unnamed offense in Wichita in September, 1875. Seven months later Morgan and Wyatt (who had just been fired from the police force) were run out of Wichita under a charge of vagrancy. During this period Morgan picked up a wife, probably of the common-law variety, known to history solely as "Lou."

Wyatt claimed that about that time he and Morgan visited Deadwood and that Morgan supposedly became marshal of Butte, Montana. Morgan then purportedly killed Billy Brooks, formerly marshal of Newton, Kansas, in a head-on gunfight; Brooks, however, probably died at the hands of a Caldwell, Kansas, lynch mob. For a short time Morgan served as a deputy sheriff of Ford County, Kansas, before joining his brothers in Tombstone early in 1880.

In Tombstone, Morgan's first steady employment came as a shotgun guard for Wells, Fargo—a position that had been recently vacated when Wyatt received an appointment as deputy sheriff. Soon Morgan resigned, however, so that he could begin dealing faro in the Occidental Saloon. As a posse member following a highly publicized stage holdup attempt and double murder, Morgan captured a ruffian named Luther King, who identified Jim Crane, Harry Head, and Bill Leonard as the culprits. A feud began to grow between the Earps and the Clantons and McLaurys, and on October 25, 1881, Morgan helped back up Doc Holliday as he bullied the Clantons. Morgan fought at the O.K. Corral the next day, but was himself killed in retribution a few months later.

Gunfights: October   26,   1881, Tombstone, Arizona. Along with Virgil, Wyatt, and Doc Holliday, Morgan approached Billy and Ike Clanton, Frank and Tom McLaury, and Billy Claiborne outside the O.K. Corral. There was a quick flurry of words, then Morgan fired the first shot of the celebrated gunfight. Standing only a few feet from Billy Clanton, Morgan went for his six-gun as the nineteen-year-old shouted, "Don't shoot me; I don't want to fight." But Morgan fired point-blank at Clanton, the slug striking just below his left nipple and knocking the youth off his feet.

Frank McLaury, now wounded in the stomach by Wyatt, and Billy Clanton began returning the Earps' fire, and Morgan was hit in the left shoulder. But he steadied himself and took aim at Frank McLaury, who was staggering forward with one hand at his middle and the other working his gun. Morgan's shot took Frank just under his right ear and threw him lifeless into the street. "I got him!" shouted Morgan exultantly. At that point the fight ended, with only Wyatt of the Earp party unwounded and with each member of the Clanton group having fled or suffered mortal wounds.

March 18, 1882, Tombstone, Arizona. Morgan was playing a Saturday night game of billiards with Bob Hatch in Campbell and Hatch's Billiard Parlor. A large number of men, including Wyatt, were watching. At 10:50 P.M., while Morgan was chalking his cue, several armed men crept up to the rear door of the pool hall, and two shots were fired into the room. The first slug entered the right side of Morgan's stomach, shattered his spinal column, and emerged to inflict a flesh wound in one of the onlookers, George Berry. Morgan collapsed, and Wyatt, who had been narrowly missed by the second bullet, went to his brother's side and, helped by Dan Tipton and Sherman McMasters, stretched the dying man out.

Three doctors rushed to the scene and stated that they could do nothing to help. Morgan was then carried into the adjacent card room and placed on a sofa, where he was surrounded by Wyatt, Virgil, James, Warren, and the Earp women. One attempt was made to place him on his feet, but he gasped, "Don't, I can't stand it. This is the last game of pool I'll ever play." He whispered a word into Wyatt's ear, then died less than an hour after being shot. It was generally thought that this revenge killing had been performed by Clanton sympathizers Frank Stilwell, Pete Spence, a gambler named Freis, and two half-bloods, Florentino Cruz and "Indian Charley."

Sources: Waters, *Earp Brothers of Tombstone;* Jahns, *Doc Holliday;* Lake, *Wyatt Earp;* Bartholomew, *Wyatt Earp, the Untold Story.*

Earp, Virgil

(b. July 18, 1843, Hartford, Kentucky; d. 1905, Goldfield, Nevada. Soldier, farmer, stage driver, ranch hand, laborer, prospector, law officer, detective.) Virgil moved from Kentucky with his restless family to Illinois and later to

Virgil Earp, who was shotgunned from ambush after the O.K. Corral shootout but survived to die of natural causes in 1905. *(Courtesy Arizona Historical Society)*

Iowa. At seventeen he ran away with a sixteen-year-old girl named Ellen, and although her parents annulled their marriage, she bore him a daughter, Jane. Eighteen at the opening of the Civil War, Virgil enlisted with his older brothers, Newton and James, and served the duration of the conflict in the Union army.

After the war Virgil drove a stagecoach out of Council Bluffs, Iowa, where he met his second wife, Allie. In 1870 he was involved with Wyatt, James, and Morgan in a marathon street brawl against five other men in Lamar, Missouri. He then followed his brothers

into Kansas, where he was appointed to the Dodge City police force. From there Virgil moved to Prescott, Arizona, where he farmed, drove a mail route, worked a timber stand, and prospected for gold.

Late in 1879 Virgil and other members of the Earp family moved to Tombstone, where Virgil worked at odd jobs until he became deputy marshal a year later. He was appointed marshal in June, 1881, just as a feud began to grow between the Earp and the Clanton factions. Virgil fought at the O.K. Corral, was discharged from his marshal's position as a consequence, and as a further consequence was shot from ambush. After Morgan was killed a short time later, Virgil and his wife were sent to California out of danger. (Minutes after he boarded the train, one of the chief suspects in his and Morgan's ambushes was killed a short distance away.)

Virgil convalesced for some time in Colton, California, home of his parents. In 1886 he opened a detective agency in Colton, returned to Arizona to search for gold, and then went back to Colton, where he was elected city marshal. Soon, however, he and his wife began prospecting again, living in a dozen mining camps until 1905, when Virgil died of pneumonia in Goldfield, Nevada.

Gunfights: 1876, Prescott, Arizona. Two hard cases began firing their guns in the streets and held the local sheriff, a man named Dodson, at gunpoint when he tried to arrest them. When the pair left town, Dodson deputized a few men and rattled after them in a buckboard. When the chase passed Virgil's house, he, too, was deputized and helped follow the two rowdies into a nearby canyon. When cornered, the two men tried to break away, and a shootout ensued. While one of the gunmen was reloading his pistol, Virgil killed him with two shots in the head. The other man surrendered after being shot in the leg.

October 28, 1880, Tombstone, Arizona. Virgil was deputized by Marshal Fred White to assist in arresting a drunk and disorderly Curly Bill Brocius, whom they cornered in an alley. A struggle ensued, and Curly Bill's gun went off, mortally wounding White. Curly Bill then was taken into custody, but White gasped out that the shooting was accidental, and Bill was later acquitted.

October 26, 1881, Tombstone, Arizona. The previous evening Virgil played poker with Ike Clanton, Tom McLaury, and two other men. After the game, Virgil had words with Clanton. Virgil drew his gun and clubbed Ike with the barrel, then dragged him off to night court. Early the following afternoon Virgil, accompanied by "deputies" Wyatt and Morgan Earp and Doc Holliday, approached five members of the Clanton faction near the O.K. Corral under the pretense of disarming them. Virgil shouted, "Throw up your hands," and the shooting began. Virgil was wounded in the leg, but he kept firing. Morgan and Holliday were also wounded, and Billy Clanton and Frank and Tom McLaury were killed. When the shooting stopped, a doctor ran up and began probing in Virgil's leg before discovering that the slug had passed all the way through his calf.

December 28, 1881, Tombstone, Arizona. About 11:30 P.M. Virgil left the Oriental Saloon, and as he crossed the street, several shotgun blasts roared out. Carried to a nearby hotel, he was placed on a table, and a doctor cut off his shirt, revealing buckshot wounds in his left side and back and left arm. When his wife appeared, he tried to comfort her: "Never mind, I've still got one arm left to hug you with."

"Wyatt," he said to his brother, "when they get me under, don't let them take my arm off. If I have to be buried, I want both arms on me." The doctor complied as well as possible, removing the buckshot and four inches of bone.

Sources: Waters, *Earp Brothers of Tombstone;* Jahns, *Doc Holliday;* Bartholomew, *Wyatt Earp, the Untold Story.*

Earp, Warren

(b. March 9, 1855, Pella, Iowa; d. 1900, Willcox, Arizona. Stage driver, law officer.) In 1864 nine-year-old Warren journeyed with his family to California, where he lived until 1880, when he went to Tombstone to be with his brothers. There he gambled at the Oriental Saloon and was deputized on occasion by Virgil, marshal of Tombstone. Warren, along with his brothers, was rumored to be in on rustling and stage robbing activities in the vicinity, but he was absent when the Clanton and McLaury boys (widely acknowledged to be rustlers) and the Earps shot it out at the O.K. Corral. After Morgan was assassinated, however, Warren was present at the revenge killings of Frank Stilwell and Florentino Cruz. Warren then went with Wyatt to Colorado for a time, but eventually he returned to Arizona, where he drove a stage between Globe and Willcox before being killed in a saloon fight.

Gunfights: March 20, 1882, Tucson, Arizona. Two days after Morgan's death, Virgil, wounded in an earlier ambush, was taken to Tucson to catch a train for California. Accompanying him were Warren and Wyatt, Doc Holliday, Sherman McMasters, and Turkey Creek Jack Johnson. It was rumored that Frank Stilwell, suspected of killing Morgan, was in Tucson, and just after placing Virgil on the train, the Earp party spotted Stilwell. Wyatt pursued, followed closely by Warren and the others. A few moments later Stilwell was cornered and murdered by a volley of shotgun and rifle fire.

March 22, 1882, Tombstone, Arizona. After killing Stilwell, Warren and the others returned to Tombstone in search of other victims. They traveled out of town to a wood camp owned by Pete Spence, another suspect in Morgan's death. An employee, Theodore Judah, told them that Spence was not there, but that Florentino Cruz, also a suspect, was nearby. The five avengers plunged after Cruz; Judah soon heard "ten or twelve" shots and found Cruz's bullet-riddled corpse.

1900, Willcox, Arizona. Warren was drunk in a saloon in Wilcox when he encountered Johnny Boyet, a cowhand who had clashed with Earp before. Warren challenged him to fight, drunkenly forgetting that he had left his gun in his hotel room. Boyet drew and fired, killing Earp, and was duly acquitted.

Sources: Waters, *Earp Brothers of Tombstone;* Jahns, *Doc Holliday;* Bartholomew, *Wyatt Earp, the Untold Story.*

Earp, Wyatt Berry Stapp

(b. March 19, 1848, Monmouth, Illinois; d. January 13, 1929, Los Angeles, California. Farmer, section hand, buffalo hunter, horse thief, saloonkeeper,

Wyatt Earp, who exaggerated his frontier exploits, portraying himself as the West's premier gunfighter. *(Courtesy Arizona Historical Society)*

gambler, bunco artist, sportsman, law officer, prospector.) Because of highly conflicting versions of his career, no individual has caused greater controversy in Western history than Wyatt Earp. The son of a restless frontiersman (Wyatt's father named him after his Mexican War company commander, Captain Wyatt Berry Stapp), he moved with his clannish family from Missouri to Iowa to California. When Wyatt reached his early twenties, he worked his way back to Missouri as a section hand.

In 1870 Wyatt was married in Lamar, Missouri, where that same year he defeated his half brother, Newton Earp, for the post of town constable. His wife, however, died just three and one-half months after their marriage. Then, according to Jahns *(Doc Holliday)*, Wyatt and three of his brothers, James, Morgan, and Virgil, "had a 20 minute street fight with her 2 brothers, Fred and Bert Sutherland and 3 Brummet boys, Granville, Loyd and Garden. . . ." The outcome, and whether or not this fight involved guns, is not known, but the Earps soon drifted into Kansas.

Wyatt spent a couple of years hunting buffalo, got himself arrested in Indian Territory for stealing horses, then increasingly turned to gambling, most frequently in Hays City. By 1875 he was a city policeman in Wichita, where he made routine arrests, nearly shot himself with his own gun, neglected to turn in fines he had collected from prostitutes, and was himself arrested for fighting. He was kicked off the force and out of town. Shortly thereafter, in May, 1876, Earp became a policeman in Dodge City, and after wandering around a bit in Texas, in 1878 he assumed the position of assistant marshal of Dodge, where he also acted as deacon of the Union Church. While in Dodge in 1876 he was beaten to a pulp by a huge cowboy named Red Sweeney in a fist fight over the affections of a dance hall girl.

In September, 1879, Earp left Dodge and went to Las Vegas, New Mexico, there joining other members of his family and Doc Holliday. En route to Las Vegas Wyatt stopped off in Mobeetie, Texas, long enough to be run out of town by Deputy Sheriff James McIntire for trying to work a "gold brick" swindle with Mysterious Dave Mather.

Within a few months Wyatt, James, and Virgil Earp moved to Tombstone, accompanied by their families. (Wyatt recently had acquired a second wife, Mattie, whom he deserted in 1882. She became a prostitute and committed suicide in the Arizona mining town of Pinal on July 3, 1888, at the age of thirty.) Wyatt became a shotgun guard for Wells, Fargo, and soon Morgan and Warren Earp and Doc Holliday appeared in Tombstone.

Wyatt twice tried unsuccessfully to obtain appointment as Cochise County sheriff, but in July, 1880, he became deputy sheriff of Tombstone. He also managed to acquire an interest in the flourishing Oriental Saloon. Within a year a feud developed between the Earps and the Clanton and McLaury brothers, possibly, according to rumor, because the Earps were infringing on the rustling and stage robbing activities of the Clanton "ring," but more probably because the Earps, who held various law enforcement offices in and around Tombstone, tried to thwart the ring. The feud was climaxed but not ended at the O.K. Corral. Following that famous gunfight, Virgil and Morgan were ambushed, and in revenge Wyatt, then a deputy U.S. marshal, and his cohorts killed two members of the Clanton faction.

Wyatt then began to wander throughout the West. In 1882 he was in San Francisco, where he married his third wife, Josie. In 1883 he was in Colorado and twice visited Dodge City, where he backed up Luke Short as a member of the celebrated but short-lived "Dodge City Peace Commission." He spent most of 1884 in Idaho at the Coeur d'Alene gold rush, although he did journey to Colorado later that year. In Idaho, Wyatt owned a couple of saloons, speculated with his brother Jim in several mining claims, and became involved in a combine which specialized in claim jumping.

After jaunts to Wyoming and Texas, Wyatt returned to California, running a saloon in San Francisco from 1886 to 1890. He then moved to San Diego and began to raise thoroughbreds, with time out in 1896 to referee the Bob Fitzsimmons–Tom Sharkey prizefight (which Wyatt was widely accused of throwing to Sharkey). He spent most of the time from 1897 until 1901 in the gold rush area of Alaska, where he operated a saloon in Nome. One night he brandished a revolver and was slapped and disarmed by U.S. Marshal Albert Lowe. He fared little better back in California, where, on a visit to San Francisco in May, 1900, he was knocked senseless in a fist fight with a local prizefighter named Mike Mulqueen, who was more than two decades younger than Wyatt.

Late in 1901 Wyatt returned to the Southwest, attracted by new mining discoveries. For five years he and his wife prospected widely in Nevada, and Wyatt also opened still another saloon in Tonopah. In 1905 he visited Virgil in the Nevada mining camp of Goldfield before settling permanently in Los Angeles. Aside from occasional prospecting trips to a mining claim near Parker, Arizona, Wyatt's primary activities seem to have been various confidence games. He also tried to find someone to publicize his adventures, unsuccessfully seeking out movie star William S. Hart and writer Walter Noble Burns before meeting his biographer, Stuart N. Lake, just months before his death at the age of eighty in 1929.

Gunfights: *July 26, 1878, Dodge City, Kansas.* At 3:00 A.M. three or four Texas cowboys began firing their guns into the air. Earp and fellow law officer Jim Masterson charged onto the scene, and the two parties began to exchange shots. As the drunken cowhands tried to ride off, one young Texan, George Hoy, fell from his saddle with a wound in the arm. Infection soon set

in, and Hoy, who was under a fifteen-hundred-dollar bond in Texas for cattle rustling, died four weeks later.

October 26, 1881, Tombstone, Arizona. The previous day, Ike Clanton and Tom McLaury had arrived in Tombstone to buy supplies. Wyatt, Morgan, and Virgil had backed Doc Holliday as he cursed Clanton, and later that evening Virgil also abused the rustler. The next morning Wyatt approached McLaury, and after an exchange of words Wyatt drew his Buntline Special and issued a challenge to fight. When McLaury refused, Wyatt slapped him with his left hand, then clubbed him to the ground with the twelve-inch barrel of his gun.

A short time later Wyatt saw Frank McLaury enter a store, and he went over to remove the man's horse from the boardwalk. McLaury emerged and growled, "Take your hands off my horse!"

"Keep him off the sidewalk," said Wyatt. "It's against the city ordinance."

McLaury left muttering curses, and about an hour later the two factions met outside the O.K. Corral. Sheriff John Behan tried to intervene, but both sides ignored him, and the three Earps and Holliday approached to within a few feet of the McLaury brothers, Ike and Billy Clanton, and Billy Claiborne. Wyatt said, "You sons of bitches, you've been looking for a fight and now you can have it!" Virgil ordered, "Throw up your hands!" Then Morgan shot Billy Clanton, and Wyatt pulled his pistol from his right pants pocket and began pumping lead at Frank McLaury, who was immediately hit in the stomach.

As the firing became general Ike Clanton, still unarmed, ran up to Wyatt, grabbed his left hand, and implored him to stop shooting. "The fighting has now commenced," replied Wyatt, "go to fighting or get away." Clanton fled into the adjacent photography studio, followed closely by Claiborne, and the firing continued. At last Billy Clanton and the McLaury brothers were sprawled on the ground, dead or dying, and Virgil, Morgan, and Holliday were wounded. Of those on the scene, only Wyatt was unscathed.

March 20, 1882, Tucson, Arizona. Two nights earlier Wyatt had seen his brother Morgan murdered from ambush; indeed, one shot had landed near Wyatt's head. Wyatt, his youngest brother Warren, Doc Holliday, Sherman McMasters, and Turkey Creek Jack Johnson had accompanied Virgil, wounded in an earlier ambush, to catch a train for California. This group, however, had another motive for being in Tucson—there they expected to find Frank Stilwell, chief suspect in Morgan's murder.

Stilwell was spotted near the train, and a chase ensued. He vanished into the evening darkness with Morgan's avengers hot on his heels, and after five minutes a ragged volley of shots was heard. Headed off by Wyatt, Stilwell apparently tried to shove Earp's shotgun aside by grabbing the barrels. But the weapon discharged, wounding Stilwell, and the entire party opened fire and finished him off.

March 22, 1882, Tombstone, Arizona. After killing Stilwell, the Earp party returned to Tombstone in search of other suspects. Seeking a Clanton sympathizer named Pete Spence, they arrived at Spence's wood camp at about 11:00 A.M. In fear of such vengeance, Spence had already surrendered himself to Tombstone authorities, but the Earps found another prime suspect, a half-blood named Florentino Cruz, in seclu-

sion at the wood camp. Wyatt, Warren, Holliday, McMasters, and Johnson jumped Cruz alone and killed him with a volley of gunfire.

September, 1884, Lake City, Colorado. Wyatt, frequently accused of cheating at cards, apparently resorted to the practice during a poker game in Lake City. A fight broke out, and Wyatt was shot in the arm; there were no other casualties.

Sources: Bartholomew, *Wyatt Earp: the Untold Story;* Bartholomew, *Wyatt Earp, the Man and the Myth;* Masterson, *Famous Gunfighters,* 53–65; Miller and Snell, *Great Gunfighters of the Kansas Cowtowns,* 12, 78–95, 141, 186–89, 222, 229, 234, 236, 263, 293–94, 313, 354–56, 387–88, 405–407, 410–12, 434, 444; Waters, *Earp Brothers of Tombstone;* Jahns, *Doc Holliday;* Lake, *Wyatt Earp;* Boyer, *Suppressed Murder of Wyatt Earp;* Schoenberger, *Gunfighters,* 15–17, 21–59, 96, 99–102, 104, 108, 113, 120–22, 136, 138, 141, 186, 187, 188.

Elliott, Joe

(Range detective, stock inspector.) Elliott's chief notoriety as a gunman came during the Johnson County War of the 1890's. Elliott was a range detective and stock inspector for the Wyoming Cattle Growers' Association, and he fought vigorously for the interests of the cattle barons. Elliott was banished from Wyoming in the aftermath of the conflict, and despite his threats to come back and kill his enemies, he did not return.

Gunfights: November 1, 1891, Powder River, Wyoming. Elliott and three other association employees— Frank Canton, Tom Smith, and Fred

Coates—were attempting to seize Nate Champion, ardent leader of the "rustlers" and small ranchers of Johnson County. Champion was discovered in a tiny cabin he was sharing with Ross Gilbertson, and the four gunmen closed in at dawn. Elliott covered the back while the others broke through the door. Champion got to a gun and wounded two of his attackers, and the three men fled. Champion came out to retrieve two rifles they had abandoned, but at that moment Elliott rounded the corner. The two men traded shots, and Champion ducked back inside while Elliott dashed after his cohorts.

April 9, 1892, KC Ranch, Wyoming. In a concentrated attempt to take over Johnson County, the cattlemen raised a force of fifty men, including Elliott. This impressive force stopped to surround and attack Champion's new ranch, which he and Nick Ray had leased. Elliott was carrying ten pounds of gunpowder with him, but it was decided not to try to blow up the cabin.

At sunrise Ben Jones, an unemployed ranch worker who had turned to trapping and who had spent the night with Champion and Ray, came outside to fetch water. Elliott and several others quietly took him prisoner, and they did the same thirty minutes later to Bill Walker, Jones's partner. When Ray emerged, he was shot down in a hail of rifle fire, but he made it back to the cabin with the help of Champion. Ray soon died, but Champion kept up a vigorous exchange of fire with the association "Regulators." At mid-afternoon the attackers finally ran a fire wagon against the cabin and forced Champion outside. There was a short, one-sided fight, and Champion collapsed, riddled with bullets.

Sources: Smith, *War on the Powder*

River, 158, 188; Mercer, *Banditti of the Plains,* 22–23, 157, 172, 175, 181–87, 194.

Estabo, Tranquellano

Of Mexican extraction, Estabo was active in New Mexico during the 1890's, and within a short span of time in 1895 he became involved in three gun duels.

Gunfights: 1895, Phoenix, New Mexico. On a spring evening Walter Paddleford led about fifteen other Carlsbad roisterers to nearby Phoenix, where a fight soon broke out with about an equal number of Mexicans. The Mexicans, led by Estabo, quickly resorted to guns, and general firing erupted. The Mexicans dove to their stomachs behind the railroad tracks, and Paddleford's intruders took cover fifty yards away, behind several barrels filled with empty beer bottles. Four Mexicans were wounded, three of them fatally, and on the other side saloon keeper A. Rhodes was shot dead.

At last lawman Dee Harkey rode between the factions and ordered them to stop shooting. Both sides complied, but Paddleford marched forward, opened his shirt, pointed to his bare chest, and proclaimed: "My dad was a war horse and I was his papoose, and you are afraid to shoot me." Harkey simply grabbed Paddleford's rifle, then marched the warriors off to jail.

1895, Phoenix, New Mexico. Later that summer Estabo was gambling in a Phoenix saloon and fell into a quarrel with one of the other players. Gunplay soon followed, and Estabo mortally wounded his opponent. He then blustered into the street, mounted his horse, and began shooting up the town. After a time Carlsbad lawman Dee Harkey and Cicero

Stewart wheeled into Phoenix on bicycles and ordered Estabo to surrender.

Estabo again resorted to his gun and
snapped a shot at Harkey, who pulled
a revolver and fired back. Estabo then
rode down the other lawman, but Stewart rolled free and emptied his pistol as
the Mexican roared out of town. Harkey pursued on horseback and caught
Estabo after a three-mile chase. "Don't
kill me, don't kill me," begged a subdued Estabo. "I will go with you." When
they returned to town, a bruised and
bleeding Stewart angrily wanted to kill
Estabo, but the Mexican instead was
thrown into jail.

Source: Harkey, *Mean as Hell,* 49–
50, 57–58, 72–74.

Evans, Chris

(Farmer, stagecoach robber.) Evans was
a Californian who owned a farm near
the mine of George and John Sontag,
a pair of train robbers. In 1892 Evans
helped the Sontag brothers escape from
a posse, and after George was captured,
Evans teamed up with John in stopping
stagecoaches. They claimed that they
were searching for lawmen to kill, but
they seemed to have no compunctions
against seizing whatever loot was available.

The manhunt continued for nine
months, and the two fugitives shot their
way out of trap after trap, wounding
seven deputies in the process. When
they were finally apprehended, John
was killed, and Evans, once he recovered from his wounds, was sentenced
to life in prison. On December 3, 1893,
he managed to escape, but he was recaptured the following February and
was returned to his cell.

*Gunfights: January, 1892, San
Joaquin Valley, California.* Evans and

the Sontag brothers were discovered by
a posse while hiding in a barn. The lawmen closed in, and shooting erupted.
George was taken into custody, but
Evans and John Sontag shot and killed
a deputy and escaped.

*September 13, 1893, Sampson's Flat,
California.* After a long, violent search,
a posse located Evans and Sontag, and
the fugitives inevitably offered resistance. Two deputies were killed, but
reinforcements soon arrived, and Evans
and Sontag were unable to escape. The
"Battle of Sampson's Flat" raged on for
eight hours until both outlaws were too
shot up to keep up the fight. Sontag
soon died, but Evans lived and was imprisoned for life.

Sources: Horan and Sann, *Pictorial
History of the Wild West,* 151–52; Conger, *Texas Rangers,* 134.

Evans, Jesse

(b. 1853, Missouri. Cowboy, rustler,
robber.) Evans left his Missouri home
at an early age, was employed as a cowboy in Lampasas County, Texas, and
then in 1872 migrated to New Mexico
and soon found work on John Chisum's
spread. Within a few years he turned
to outlawry, robbing stores and isolated
camps and organizing a band of rustlers
which included, at various times, Billy
the Kid, Tom Hill, Frank Baker, and
numerous other ruffians. Evans was
briefly jailed, and he was constantly under indictment. He became an early
member of the Murphy-Dolan faction
in the Lincoln County War. The country soon became too hot for him, however, and he shifted his rustling activities to Southwest Texas. In 1880 he
killed a Texas Ranger during a general
shootout, and he was sentenced to ten
years in the penitentiary. He escaped

from a work gang in May, 1882, and thereafter disappeared from verifiable history.

Gunfights: October 17, 1877, Lincoln County, New Mexico. Evans and three henchmen—Tom Hill, Frank Baker, and George Davis—had stolen valuable stock from the ranches of John Tunstall, who was visiting St. Louis, and Dick Brewer. Brewer and a fifteen-man posse finally cornered the rustlers in a dugout on the Beckwith ranch near Seven Rivers, and the two groups opened fire at sunrise. The outnumbered and trapped rustlers finally surrendered, but within a few weeks they succeeded in escaping from the flimsy jail in Lincoln.

January, 1878, Grant County, New Mexico. Evans and his gang stole a herd of horses from a Grant County ranch, but the rustlers were soon overtaken by angry pursuers. There was a sharp exchange of shots, and when Evans and Tom Hill both were hit, the outlaws abandoned the stolen animals and galloped away.

February 18, 1878, near Lincoln, New Mexico. Evans, Hill, and a large group of Murphy-Dolan followers located and surrounded opposing rancher John Tunstall as he rode toward Lincoln. After a brief flurry of words Evans, Hill, Frank Baker, and William Morton hauled out their pistols and murdered Tunstall, thus triggering the Lincoln County War.

March 13, 1878, Alamo Springs, New Mexico. Evans and Hill were in the process of plundering an unguarded sheep camp when a halfblood Cherokee returned from finding water. The two thieves held the halfblood at gunpoint,

finished looting the camp wagon, and threw saddles on a horse and a mule which belonged to the owner of the herd. Suddenly the Cherokee grabbed a Winchester, but when Evans and Hill opened fire, he turned and ran. He was hit in the leg, and after he fell the bandits prepared to leave. But the halfblood crawled to within point-blank range and began firing his rifle. Hill was killed with the first bullet, and Evans caught a slug in the wrist. Evans dropped his rifle and six-gun and spurred away on the stolen horse.

July 3, 1880, near Presidio, Texas. On Cibola Creek about eighteen miles north of Presidio, Evans and three other outlaws were discovered and attacked by a detachment of Texas Rangers led by Sergeant E. A. Sieker. When they saw the rangers approach them, the bandits opened fire. After a one-and-one-half-mile running fight the outlaws wheeled their horses up a steep mountain and took cover behind large rocks. As the rangers advanced, Evans killed Private George Bingham with a bullet in the heart. But a ranger named Tom Carson plugged outlaw John Gross between the eyes, and the remainder of the band soon surrendered.

Sources: Bartholomew, *Jesse Evans;* Rasch, "The Story of Jesse Evans," *PPHR;* Keleher, *Violence in Lincoln County,* 82–83, 88–89, 96–97, 100–102, 107–108, 114, 141, 204, 207–17, 233, 247, 251–76, 312; Webb, *Texas Rangers,* 406–409; Klasner, *My Girlhood Among Outlaws,* 60, 155–57, 171, 174–75, 249; Garrett, *Billy, the Kid,* 10, 22, 25–31, 36, 45, 50–51, 63–69, 82–83; Fulton, *Lincoln County War,* 51, 67, 70, 82–91, 103–104, 107–108, 112–13, 118–20, 125, 147–49, 201, 240, 251, 324–28, 331, 333, 347, 373–78.

John King Fisher, killed with Ben Thompson in a San Antonio theater at the age of thirty. *(Courtesy Western History Collections, University of Oklahoma Library)*

Fisher, John King

(b. 1854, Collin County, Texas; d. March 11, 1884, San Antonio, Texas. Bronco buster, cowboy, rancher, rustler, saloon owner, livery stable partner, law officer, gunman.) King Fisher led a somewhat unsettled life during his youth. His mother died when he was a small boy, and his father, after fighting for the Confederacy, established ranches in various parts of Texas. King lived in Collin County, Lampasas, Goliad, and Florence. When he was just fifteen he got into trouble in Florence over a stolen horse and escaped from the local constable. At sixteen he was sentenced to two years in the state penitentiary for housebreaking in Goliad, although he was forced to serve only four months.

After his release Fisher was employed as a cowboy in the "Nueces Strip" country of South Texas, where he broke horses, chased Mexican bandits, and learned to shoot. Soon he started his own spread, the Pendencia, became a dominant and colorful figure in the nearby border town of Eagle Pass, and nailed up the celebrated crossroads sign: "This is King Fisher's Road—Take the other one."

A gaudy dresser, sporting fringed shirts, crimson sashes, and bells on his spurs, King became widely feared as a rustler. During the 1870's he was arrested several times in San Antonio and Uvalde for gambling, and he reputedly killed several men in skirmishes with rivals. (When queried in 1878, he stated that he was responsible for seven deaths, "not counting Mexicans." The most persistent of these unauthenticated incidents concerned an argument which arose between King and four *vaqueros* at a cattle pen on the Pendencia. King whacked the nearest opponent on the skull with a branding iron, shot and killed a second man who drew a gun, then whirled and drilled the last two, who were still sitting on the fence.) In 1875 King was indicted for murder, and later warrants for his arrest on rustling charges were issued in numerous Texas counties.

Married in 1876 and eventually the father of four daughters, King's following years were marred by frequent arrests for murder and theft, even though he usually was found not guilty or was released after the charges were dismissed. By the late 1870's, however, he had begun to smooth over his troubles and expand his business interests. In 1879 his biggest problem was shooting himself in the leg by accident. Within two years he was cleared of his final murder charges, and in 1881 he was sworn in as deputy sheriff of Uvalde County. After serving as acting sheriff for a time, King announced his candidacy for county sheriff in the election of 1884. Before the election could be held, however, the thirty-year-old King was killed with Ben Thompson in San Antonio.

Gunfights: *December 25, 1876, Zavala County, Texas.* A cowboy named William Dunovan aroused King's temper. Fisher pulled a gun and pumped three bullets into Dunovan, killing him on the spot.

1877, Pendencia Ranch, Texas. King and several of his cowboys surprised several Mexicans stealing a horse from a Pendencia corral. One of the thieves snapped off a shot at Fisher, who then jumped off his horse onto the man. King wrestled the gun away from the assailant and began spraying lead, fatally wounding three of the Mexicans. In May, 1877, he was arrested on charges of murder by Texas Ranger Lee Hall in an Eagle Pass saloon, but Major T. T. Teel successfully defended Fisher in court.

1883, Leona River near Leakey, Texas. While acting as sheriff of Uvalde County, King trailed Jim and Tom Hannehan, suspected of robbing a stage, to their ranch on the Leona River. At the ranch King approached them and placed them under arrest. The brothers moved to resist, but King shot Tom dead. Jim then surrendered and gave up the loot. (It should be noted that after King's death the next year, Mrs. Hannehan would come to the cemetery in Uvalde on each anniversary of her son's death and, setting a brush fire atop King's grave, would "dance with devilish glee" around the mound.)

March 11, 1884, San Antonio, Texas. In Austin on official business, Fisher encountered old acquaintance Ben Thompson, and after the pair visited several bars together, Thompson gave King a personal photograph and decided to accompany him as far as San Antonio on his return to Uvalde. On the afternoon train the two gunfighters continued to drink and act boisterously, even though King once warned Ben to stop abusing a colored porter.

After arriving in San Antonio, the inebriated pair visited a saloon, saw a play at the Turner Hall Opera House, then at 10:30 P.M. went to the Vaudeville Variety Theater, a gambling hall where Ben had killed proprietor Jack Harris two years earlier. They had a drink at the bar, then went upstairs to watch the variety show, where they were joined in their box by bouncer Jacob Coy and by Billy Simms and Joe Foster, former partners of Jack Harris. Ben vindictively referred to Harris' death, then playfully stuck his six-gun into Foster's mouth and cocked the hammer. Coy jumped at Thompson and grabbed the cylinder. Fisher backed off and said something about leaving before trouble started, but he and Thompson were shot down in a sudden burst of gunfire.

It has been strongly suggested that Coy, Simms, and Foster were aided by three other assassins: a gambler called Canada Bill, Jewish performer Harry Tremaine, and a bartender known only as McLaughlin. These three men presumably armed themselves with rifles and shotguns and lurked in an adjacent box in case of trouble. Thompson was struck nine times, Coy suffered a flesh wound, and Foster was shot in the leg — probably when Coy grabbed Ben's gun — and died following amputation. King never drew his weapon, but was hit thirteen times in the head, chest, and leg, and died on the spot, his arm across Thompson's body.

Sources: Fisher with Dykes, *King Fisher;* Raymond, *Captain Lee Hall,* 54–56, 88–89, 172, 176–80, 183–84, 215–17; Streeter, *Ben Thompson,* 190–99.

Flatt, George W.

(b. 1852 or 1853, Tennessee; d. June 19, 1880, Caldwell, Kansas. Saloon keeper, law officer, range detective.) A native of Tennessee, Flatt achieved notoriety as a two-gun lawman in Caldwell, Kansas. Although he was alleged to have killed on previous occasions, Flatt's reputation as a gunman was established in Caldwell in 1879. Shortly afterward Flatt and William Horseman opened an "elegant saloon" adjacent to Caldwell's City Hotel. That same summer Flatt became Caldwell's first city marshal, but the next year he was replaced by Horseman.

Flatt next became a range detective, and during this same period he married an eighteen-year-old girl named Fanny. In June, 1880, Flatt was gunned down in the streets of Caldwell, and four days later Fanny Flatt gave birth to a son. William Horseman was suspected and tried for Flatt's murder, but he was acquitted, and the murderer was never brought to justice.

Gunfights: *July 7, 1879, Caldwell, Kansas.* On Monday afternoon two cowboys from the Cherokee Strip, George Wood and Jake Adams, galloped into Caldwell and, after an hour of heavy drinking in the Occidental Saloon, weaved into the street and began firing their six-guns. Constable W. C. Kelly and Deputy John Wilson, accompanied by a posse which included Flatt and W. H. Kiser, cautiously entered the Occidental.

Wood and Adams immediately leveled their guns at the lawmen, ordered them to keep their hands at their sides, and began to move toward the door. Flatt boldly stepped in front of the door, whereupon the two cowboys pointed their weapons at him and demanded his revolvers. "I'll die first," growled Flatt. One of the cowboys decided to accommodate him, but his shot whizzed by Flatt's head and grazed the temple of Kiser, who stood behind Flatt.

Flatt instantly went for his pistols. As Wood darted for the door, Flatt fired two shots; one slug went wild, but the other clipped off the end of Wood's forefinger, tore away the trigger of his gun, ripped through both his lungs, and came out under his right shoulder blade. The impact of the bullet rolled Wood into the street, and he died immediately.

Almost simultaneously Flatt squeezed off a shot from his other gun. Adams was struck in the right side, and the slug tore all the way through his body. He fired back at Flatt, but the bullet grazed John Wilson's wrist. Wilson pumped two slugs into Adams, who was hit in the right hand and stomach. As he went down, Adams shot Wilson in the leg, then breathed his last on the saloon floor.

October 29, 1879, Caldwell, Kansas. A man named John Dean rode into Caldwell one afternoon and quickly became drunk and disorderly. He was armed, a violation of city ordinances, and Marshal Flatt and his deputy, Red Bill Jones, marched to arrest him. Dean suspiciously mounted his horse and began riding out of town, firing into the air. Flatt ran toward Dean, declaring him to be under arrest. Dean pumped a shot at Flatt, then spurred away. The two lawmen pursued on foot, emptying their pistols as they ran, but Dean galloped to safety.

June 19, 1880, Caldwell, Kansas. Flatt, at times a heavy drinker, had spent Saturday evening becoming increasingly inebriated and raucous, and he had trouble with Frank Hunt and others. Finally, an hour past midnight, C. L. Spear and Samuel H. Rogers persuaded Flatt to leave for home, although he insisted on first stopping by Louis Segerman's restaurant to eat. As they walked toward Segerman's, a rifle or shotgun exploded from above and behind Flatt, wounding him in the base of the skull and severing his spinal cord.

Flatt dropped dead in his tracks, but a fusillade of shots from across the street spattered around him and sent three more slugs into his body. Flatt's killer or killers were never legally determined, but Frank Hunt and William Horseman, the dead man's former business partners, were widely suspected.

Sources: Miller and Snell, *Great Gunfighters of the Kansas Cowtowns,* 95–103, 142, 359–60; Drago, *Wild, Woolly & Wicked,* 208–12.

Bob Ford, who shot Jesse James in the back of the head while Jesse was straightening a picture. *(Courtesy Western History Collections, University of Oklahoma Library)*

Ford, Robert

(b. 1861; d. June 8, 1892, Creede, Colorado. Farmer, stage performer, saloon keeper.) Bob Ford moved with his family to a farm in Ray County, Missouri, in 1879. His older brother, Charlie, soon became involved with the James gang in train holdups, and although Bob apparently was not a professional robber, he regularly consorted with outlaws. In 1882 he and Dick Liddell killed Wood Hite in a gunfight in the home of Ford's sister, and a few months later Bob murdered Jesse James for the reward money. He was then tried and convicted of murder in the death of Hite, but Governor T. T. Crittendon gave him a full pardon because he had rid the state of James.

For a time Bob returned to his parents' home at Richmond, Missouri, but he was regarded with widespread contempt and scorn. Charlie also was met with distaste, and he committed suicide in 1884. Bob soon went on tour with a stage company, repeating the story of how he had killed Jesse James, but boos were the usual reaction. However, a chorus girl named Nellie Waterson fell in love with him, and they were married.

Ford spent the next two years in P. T. Barnum's freak show, and he began to drink and gamble heavily. Then he bought into a saloon in Las Vegas, New Mexico, but business was bad. Finally he was attracted to the Colorado boom town of Creede, where he opened a prosperous saloon in a tent. But in Creede he tangled with a hard case named Ed O. Kelly, and Kelly killed him with a shotgun. Ford was buried in Richmond.

Gunfights: January, 1882, Ray County, Missouri. Wood Hite, a member of the James gang, had sought refuge for a few days at the Ray County farmhouse of Martha Bolton, Ford's young widowed sister. Dick Liddell, another fugitive, was also present, and at breakfast an argument broke out between Hite and Liddell. Bob Ford was at the breakfast table, too, and when Hite and Liddell went for their pistols, Ford threw down on Hite.

Hite got off four shots, putting a slug into Liddell's right thigh, and Liddell emptied his weapon, hitting his adversary in the right arm. While these two were blazing away at each other, Ford quietly leveled his revolver and pumped one slug into Hite's head. The bullet entered two inches above Hite's right eye and came out near his left ear. Hite died within fifteen or twenty minutes. Ford wrapped the body in a horse blanket and, with the help of his brother, Cap, buried the corpse in the woods a mile from the house.

April 3, 1882, St. Joseph, Missouri. In January, Ford had met with the governor of Missouri and was encouraged to try to kill Jesse James. Governor Crittendon promised him a large reward and a full pardon, and Ford promptly persuaded his brother to enlist him in the James gang. A new robbery was being planned and the Fords were housed at Jesse's home in St. Joseph.

After breakfast on a Monday morning Bob and Charlie went to the barn to tend the horses, and when they returned to the house about 8:30 A.M. Jesse complained of the heat. He removed his coat, then unstrapped and laid aside his guns. He then climbed onto a chair to straighten a picture, and Charlie nodded at Bob. The brothers drew and cocked their pistols, and Jesse started to turn. But Bob quickly fired a bullet into the back of Jesse's head, and the notorious outlaw dropped dead to the floor.

Jesse's wife ran into the room, and Bob muttered, "The gun went off accidentally."

"Yes," Mrs. James sobbed, "I guess it did."

The Fords then darted out to a telegraph office to claim their reward.

June 8, 1892, Creede, Colorado. Ford suspected and loudly accused Ed O. Kelly of stealing his diamond ring. When Kelly angrily stomped into Ford's saloon to stop the rumors, Bob had him thrown out of the building. Kelly then procured a shotgun, barged back into the saloon, and confronted Ford. In a moment the shotgun roared, and Ford died on the spot, a collar button driven through his throat by a slug.

Sources: Settle, *Jesse James Was His Name,* 116–19, 123–24, 128, 170, 193; Horan, *Desperate Men,* 141–51; Horan and Sann, *Pictorial History of the Wild West,* 27, 34, 40–43, 45, 46; Robertson and Harris, *Soapy Smith,* 93, 99, 104, 110–18, 133–34.

Fountain, Albert Jennings

(b. October 23, 1838, Staten Island, New York; d. February 1, 1896, White Sands, New Mexico. Newspaperman, soldier, lawyer, county surveyor, cus-

toms collector, politician.) Albert Jennings (he later added Fountain to his name) traveled abroad extensively as a youth before settling in California in the 1850's. In 1859 he became a journalist for the *Sacramento Union* and covered William Walker's filibustering activities in Latin America. During the Civil War, Fountain joined the First California Infantry Volunteers, and in 1862 he came to New Mexico as a member of Carleton's California Column. In Mesilla he married fourteen-year-old Mariana Pérez, who eventually bore him a dozen children.

When the war ended, Fountain organized a militia company to fight Indians, and he was severely wounded in a skirmish in 1865. Soon he moved to nearby El Paso, where he became a deputy collector of customs, county surveyor, and attorney, with time out to fight in Mexico with Benito Juárez as a colonel of artillery. In 1868 he won election to the Texas Senate. Soon he was selected president of that body, and Governor E. J. Davis appointed him brigadier general of the Texas State Police. Fountain was involved in a fatal gunfight in 1870, his political career was turbulent, and in 1875 he moved back to Mesilla.

Fountain was a colorful and controversial lawyer, and at different times he served as an assistant U.S. district attorney and as a member of the New Mexico House of Representatives. On occasion he led Mexican supporters (who were derisively termed "Fountain's Greasers" by Anglos) against outlaw gangs and marauding Apaches.

In the late 1880's Fountain began a bitter power struggle with Albert B. Fall, who in time became secretary of the interior and a key villain in the notorious Teapot Dome scandal. Fountain and Fall first duelled through opposing newspapers, but soon the feud grew violent. In 1896 Fountain and his youngest child, nine-year-old Henry, were killed in the White Sands while returning to Mesilla, creating one of the great mysteries of the Southwest. Their bodies disappeared, an extensive manhunt and subsequent court proceedings failed to reveal the killers, and the subject remained obscure and dangerous to discuss.

Gunfights: *December 7, 1870, El Paso, Texas.* In Ben Dowell's El Paso saloon a lawyer named B. F. Williams began berating Fountain and District Judge Gaylord Judd Clarke. When Williams angrily brandished a pistol, Fountain, although armed only with a cane, charged his adversary. Williams warded off the stick and fired three shots, then darted out the back door while Fountain staggered to his home nearby. One slug had struck his left arm, one had gouged out a bloody but superficial scalp wound, and another had slammed into his breast, tearing through five letters in his pocket and finally being deflected by his watch.

Ignoring his pleading wife, Fountain wiped blood from his face with a towel, seized a rifle, and went back outside. In the street Williams was pursuing Judge Clarke with a shotgun; one load of buckshot missed, but a moment later Clarke was mortally wounded with a blast in the chest. At that point Fountain felled Williams with a shot from fifty yards. Williams rolled over and groped for his pistol, but Captain A. H. French of the state police dashed in and finished him with a bullet in the head.

March, 1883, Canutillo, Texas. Fountain and his son Albert had picked up three fugitives from Texas Rangers in El Paso, and on the train ride back to New Mexico an escape was attempted by Doroteo Sáenz. The young prisoner jumped Albert and threw him off the train as the cars slowed approaching Canutillo.

The senior Fountain was visiting friends elsewhere on the train, and upon spotting the commotion he jumped to the ground. His revolver slipped out of his holster, but in El Paso Ranger Captain John R. Baylor had loaned him a cord to attach to his weapon, and Fountain retrieved the gun and dropped to one knee. Sáenz was running for mesquite thickets which lined the Rio Grande, but as he topped a small hill Fountain sky-lined him and fired four shots. Sáenz fell fatally wounded, and the engineer backed up the train to take on the body.

Sources: Gibson, *Life and Death of Colonel Fountain;* Metz, *Pat Garrett,* 72–73, 104, 132–53, 159–63, 172–73, 178, 181–82, 186–89, 191–92, 194, 197, 216–17, 239, 246; Sonnichsen, *Tularosa,* 48, 54–68, 72–75, 78, 90–95, 106–49, 153–58, 171–94, 214, 216, 224–26, 235–36.

Frazer, G. A.

("Bud")

(b. April 18, 1864, Fort Stockton, Texas; d. September 14, 1896, Toyah, Texas. Law officer, livery stable owner.) The son of a county judge in West Texas, Bud Frazer began a law enforcement career by enlisting in the Texas Rangers at the age of sixteen. Later he was a deputy sheriff of Pecos County before being elected sheriff of Reeves County in 1890. One of his deputies was Killin' Jim Miller, who shot a Mexican prisoner to death. Miller said the Mexican had tried to resist arrest, but the prisoner had actually known that Jim had stolen a pair of mules.

Frazer fired Miller and charged him with theft, but Jim was soon released. He ran against Frazer for sheriff in 1892, and even though he was defeated, Miller was appointed city marshal of Pecos, the county seat. The feud grew, and two years later Miller and Frazer had a gunfight in the streets of Pecos.

In November, 1894, Frazer was beaten for a third term, and he left for New Mexico, where he operated a livery stable in Eddy (later Carlsbad). A visit to Pecos the next month resulted in another inconclusive duel with Miller, and Frazer was jailed for intent to murder. He won acquittal in May, 1896, and returned to New Mexico. Four months later, however, he visited his mother and sister in Toyah and was assassinated by Miller.

Gunfights: April 12, 1894, Pecos, Texas.* Frazer opened fire on Miller while the latter stood talking in front of a Pecos hotel. Struck in the right arm near the shoulder, Miller fired back but succeeded only in wounding a spectator. Frazer emptied his pistol into Miller's chest, and Jim collapsed. Frazer walked away, but later learned that Miller somehow had recovered.

December 26, 1894, Pecos, Texas. A month after his election defeat Frazer returned to Pecos from New Mexico to settle his affairs. He encountered Jim Miller in front of Zimmer's blacksmith shop and went for his gun. Frazer's first two shots tore into Miller's right arm and left leg, but Killin' Jim began firing left-handed. Frazer pumped two more slugs into Miller's chest, but when his antagonist did not go down, Bud fled the scene. Frazer later was arrested and then discovered that in their two clashes Miller had been protected by a hidden steel breastplate.

September 14, 1896, Toyah, Texas. While visiting his family, Frazer frequently dropped into a Toyah saloon. At 9:00 A.M. Jim Miller peered through the door to find Frazer playing seven-up with three friends. Miller discharged a shotgun into Frazer's face, taking away most of his head. Bud's distraught sister soon approached Miller with a gun, but Jim threatened to "give you what your brother got—I'll shoot you right in the face!"

Sources: Shirley, *Shotgun for Hire,* 6–7, 20–22, 25–32, 34–45, 48–49; Harkey, *Mean as Hell,* 47, 113–14.

French, Jim

(Cowboy, gunman, rustler.) French was noted primarily for his participation in the Lincoln County War, during which he aligned with the Tunstall faction alongside Billy the Kid, Henry Brown, and other vicious killers. French was a member of the posses which killed Frank Baker and Billy Morton in March, 1878, and Buckshot Roberts the next month. He was also one of the men who ambushed Sheriff William Brady, and he shot his way out of Alexander McSween's burning store. For a short time thereafter he joined Billy the Kid's gang of stock thieves, but he soon decided to leave turbulent New Mexico, and Jim French faded into obscurity.

Gunfights: March 9, 1878, Steel Springs, New Mexico. French was one of the "Regulators" who chased down suspected murderers Billy Morton and Frank Baker. On the return trip to Lincoln posse member William McCloskey was killed—possibly by Morton—and the two prisoners spurred away. But the posse quickly caught up with them and riddled both men with bullets.

April 1, 1878, Lincoln, New Mexico. French accompanied Billy the Kid, Henry Brown, John Middleton, and Fred Wait in setting up an ambush for Sheriff William Brady. They hid behind a low wall beside the Tunstall store in Lincoln, and about 9:00 on April Fool's morning Brady and Deputy George Hindman walked nearby, followed by Billy Matthews, Jack Long, and George Peppin. The bushwhackers suddenly opened fire, cutting down Brady and Hindman and wounding Matthews, who ducked for cover along with Peppin and Long.

The Kid darted out to relieve the dead Brady of his new rifle, but Matthews opened fire and drove him off. The five ambushers then rode away, although John Long fired four rifle shots after them, managing to hit French.

July 16–19, 1878, Lincoln, New Mexico. French was one of the dozen men defending Alexander McSween and his store during the climactic shootout of the Lincoln County War. There was only sporadic and ineffective firing until the nineteenth, when the adobe store was set afire. At nightfall, with nine of the building's twelve rooms reduced to smoldering ruin, McSween's men prepared to break out, while their adversaries crept to a low wall just a few yards from the door. When the door burst open there was a furious exchange of shots. Firing as he ran, French dashed past the wall and down a slope to the safety of the nearby river, leaving five of his comrades sprawled in the back yard of the store.

Sources: Keleher, *Violence in Lincoln County,* 69, 99, 109–12, 131, 150, 237; Hunt, *Tragic Days of Billy the Kid,* 42–54, 80; Fulton, *Lincoln County War,* 137, 140, 158–59, 234, 249, 267, 271, 282, 286–87, 333.

Pat Garrett in his mid-forties, when he was running a horse ranch in Uvalde, Texas. *(Courtesy Arizona Historical Society)*

Garrett, Patrick Floyd

(b. June 5, 1850, Chambers County, Alabama; d. February 29, 1908, near Las Cruces, New Mexico. Clerk, cowboy, buffalo hunter, café owner, gambler, bartender, law officer, rancher, livery stable owner, customs collector.) One of six children of a southern plantation owner, Pat moved his family in 1856 to three thousand acres of Louisiana cotton lands. But both of his parents died after the Civil War, and Pat soon was working full time in the plantation store.

In 1869, at the age of eighteen, the lanky southerner went West, where he spent the next several years punching cattle in the Texas Panhandle. He also hunted buffalo before drifting to Fort Sumner, New Mexico, where he herded cattle, tended bar, and opened a small restaurant. He was married in 1879, and after his first teen-aged bride died in premature childbirth, he quickly remarried and began raising a family.

An acquaintance of Garrett's during this period was Billy the Kid, and the two young men were called Big Casino and Little Casino, a reference to their respective sizes. By this time the Kid was a principal figure in the bloody Lincoln County War, and in 1880 Garrett was elected county sheriff to restore order to the area and, in particular, to recapture his former friend. By then the Kid had turned to a life of complete outlawry as the head of a band of ruthless fugitives and rustlers. After a lengthy manhunt, which included a shootout in Fort Sumner and a siege at an isolated hideout, Garrett captured the Kid and incarcerated him in Lincoln, pending trial. But Billy gunned down two guards and shot his way out of jail, and Garrett was forced to pursue him again. He caught the Kid on a summer night in 1881 in Fort Sumner and shot him to death.

Alternately praised and condemned by various factions for the shooting, Garrett presented his side in a biography of the Kid ghosted by Ash Upson, an itinerant journalist who spent the last fourteen years of his life in the Garrett home. Garrett had to hire a lawyer to get the reward money posted for the Kid and was not even renominated for sheriff by the Republican party.

Garrett started a cattle ranch near Fort Stanton, and in 1884–85 he headed a special group of the Texas Rangers against rustlers on the Texas–New Mexico border. Garrett then briefly managed a ranch for an English owner, operated his own spread near Roswell, and unsuccessfully tried to promote irrigation projects in the Pecos Valley.

Pat ran for sheriff of Chaves County in 1890, was defeated, and bitterly moved to a horse ranch in Uvalde, Texas. There he became friendly with young John Nance Garner, was elected a county commissioner in 1894, and left Texas in 1896 only because another New Mexico manhunting assignment was proffered. Judge Albert J. Fountain and his young son had disappeared and presumably had been murdered in the White Sands area, and Garrett became sheriff of Dona Ana County principally to capture the culprits. Despite his vigorous efforts, however, the case was never solved, and once again Garrett was not renominated for office.

Garrett briefly operated a livery stable in Las Cruces, then received an appointment from Teddy Roosevelt as a customs collector in El Paso. Refused appointment in 1905, he returned to ranching near Las Cruces. Hard pressed financially, within two years he was involved in a feud with a neighbor, and as a result he was shot to death in 1908.

Gunfights: *November, 1876, near Fort Griffin, Texas.* For three years Garrett had shot buffalo in the Texas Panhandle for Skeleton Glenn's hide-hunting outfit. One fall morning an Irish skinner named Joe Briscoe was washing his clothes in a muddy creek near camp; Garrett walked over and sourly grunted, "Anyone but a damn Irishman would have more sense than to try to wash anything in that water." The enraged Briscoe charged Garrett, and a furious fist fight ensued. The six-foot-four-inch Garrett soon bested his smaller opponent, but Briscoe broke

away and seized an ax. He brandished the weapon and ran toward Garrett, but Pat grabbed his Winchester and fired a slug into Briscoe's chest. Briscoe lasted less than half an hour, but just before dying he reduced Garrett to tears by asking, "Won't you come over here and forgive me?"

Early December, 1880, Lincoln County, New Mexico. Tom O'Folliard was riding to join Billy the Kid's band of rustlers when he was spotted by Garrett and a posse. Both sides opened fire, and a running fight commenced. There were no casualties, and O'Folliard, turning in his saddle to fire his Winchester, finally pulled away from the lawmen.

December, 1880, Puerto de Luna, New Mexico. Garrett and Barney Mason (who had served as each other's best man in a double wedding the previous July) had delivered prisoners to Puerto de Luna, about forty-five miles northwest of Fort Sumner. While Garrett and Mason were lounging in a store, a local hard case, Mariano Leiva, entered and belligerently announced that no *gringo* dared arrest him. He then marched outside and proclaimed, "By God, even that damned Pat Garrett can't take me!"

Garrett followed Leiva, whirled him around, and slapped him off the porch into the dusty street. Leiva, enraged, palmed his six-gun and snapped off a wild shot. Garrett drew his .45 and fired twice: the first bullet kicked up dust at Leiva's feet; the second slammed high into his body, shattering his left shoulder blade. Garrett allowed Leiva to be placed on a horse and led away, but the man later was fined eighty dollars for attempted murder.

December 19, 1880, Fort Sumner, New

Mexico. Garrett had led a posse to Fort Sumner in an effort to find Billy the Kid and his gang of outlaws. The lawmen stationed themselves in the old post hospital, where Charlie Bowdre's wife had a room and where Garrett felt the criminals would first come. A card game was begun, but about 8:00 P.M. a guard announced, "Pat, someone is coming." Garrett ordered his men to get their guns, then he walked onto the porch. Beside him Lon Chambers whispered, "That's them."

Tom O'Folliard and Tom Pickett were in the lead, and when they had nearly reached the porch, Garrett barked "Halt!" O'Folliard went for his pistol, and Garrett and Chambers fired simultaneously. All six outlaws turned their mounts and galloped away, and further volleys by the lawmen succeeded only in wounding Pickett and killing Dave Rudabaugh's horse. Pickett and Rudabaugh managed to escape, however, along with the Kid, Bowdre, and Billy Wilson. But O'Folliard, who had been shot in the chest by Garrett or Chambers, soon wheeled his mount and rode slowly back toward the lawmen, calling out, "Don't shoot, Garrett. I'm killed."

Posse member Barney Mason told O'Folliard to take his medicine, and Garrett ordered him to throw up his hands. But O'Folliard protested that he was dying and could not lift his arms, and the lawmen lifted him from his horse and carried him into the hospital. The card game resumed, and about forty-five minutes after the shooting Garrett warned, "Tom, your time is short." O'Folliard replied, "The sooner the better. I will be out of pain." He died a few minutes later after naming his five companions.

December 23, 1880, Stinking Springs, New Mexico. Garrett and his posse easily tracked the fugitives across the snow-covered terrain to an abandoned rock house. In the darkness the lawmen quietly surrounded the dilapidated structure, and Garrett passed the word to shoot the Kid when he walked outside in the morning.

At dawn Bowdre, who was the same size and general appearance as the Kid, came through the door, and Garrett raised his rifle to his shoulder. This gesture was a prearranged signal to begin firing, and two slugs slammed into Bowdre's chest, sending him reeling back into the cabin. Moments later Wilson shouted that Bowdre was dying and wanted to come out, and Garrett ordered that he have his hands up. The Kid shoved the dying man outside with an exhortation to "Kill some of the sons-of-bitches before you die," but Bowdre merely staggered toward Garrett and fell into his arms. Choking on his own blood, Bowdre gasped, "I wish —I wish—I wish—I'm dying." Garrett stretched him out on his personal bedroll, where he died within minutes.

Soon Garrett observed the surviving outlaws trying to pull the three horses tied outside into the house, but when the first animal reached the doorway Garrett killed it. The outlaws were then trapped inside, and Garrett asked the Kid how he was doing. "Pretty well," came the reply, "but we have no wood to get breakfast." "Come out and get some," invited Garrett. "Be a little sociable."

Later in the day Garrett was lamenting his execution of Bowdre, but he felt less remorse upon being told that Bowdre had wanted to ambush "that damned long-legged son-of-a-bitch" when Garrett had tried to arrange a meeting to persuade Bowdre to surrender.

That afternoon the outlaws, who had not eaten all day, were tantalized by the odors of food and cooking fires, and Rudabaugh came outside under a white flag. Garrett guaranteed safety to the outlaws, and after a brief conference they surrendered.

July 14, 1881, Fort Sumner, New Mexico. On April 28 the Kid had shot his way out of the Lincoln jail, and several weeks later Garrett came to believe that he could find the Kid at Fort Sumner. Accompanied by Frank Poe and Tip McKinney, Garrett slipped into the old military post on a Wednesday night, seeing but not recognizing the Kid on the way in.

Garrett decided to ask Pete Maxwell if the Kid was nearby and, leaving his two companions on the porch of the old officers' quarters building, he entered Maxwell's bedroom. Garrett quietly awakened Maxwell, sat on the bed, and began to talk with him. At that point the Kid walked into the unlighted room. He had been with his sweetheart and, deciding to eat a steak, had come to Maxwell to ask for a key to the meat house.

Hatless and in his sock feet, the Kid was carrying a butcher knife and had his six-gun stuck in his waistband. Passing McKinney and Poe, he pulled the revolver and entered Maxwell's bedroom, asking, "¿Quién es? ¿Quién es?" Maxwell whispered, "That's him," and Garrett whipped out his pistol and triggered a shot into the Kid's chest. Garrett instantly threw himself to the side and fired a bullet which went wild, then scampered out of the room on Maxwell's heels. The Kid died on the spot, and the following morning he was buried in the Fort Sumner cemetery between Charlie Bowdre and Tom O'Folliard.

July 13, 1898, Dona Ana County, New

Mexico. Garrett and a posse had tracked accused murderers Oliver Lee and James Gilliland to a small spread of Lee's at Wildy Well, about thirty-two miles south of Alamogordo. Before dawn the five lawmen moved in on the little adobe ranch house, advancing from the east so that the sun would be in the eyes of the fugitives.

Two posse members captured a sleepy guard named Madeson, who gurgled out a cry of alarm before being subdued. Then lawmen Ben Williams and Clint Llewellyn stationed themselves under a water tank to give supporting fire while Garrett, Kent Kearney, and José Espalin rushed into the house. But the cautious fugitives had slept on the flat roof of the adobe building, and the posse now heard them moving around.

Garrett and Kearney ran outside and climbed a ladder to the top of a nearby shed. Kearney shouted, "Surrender," and he and Garrett began firing their Winchesters. Lee and Gilliland shot back, hitting Kearney twice and grazing Garrett in the ribs. The hunted men then began shooting holes in the wooden water tank, drenching Williams and Llewellyn underneath. Espalin, who had taken off his boots to sneak up on the house, had run into sand burrs and was jumping around in pain.

Garrett parlayed briefly with Lee, who allowed the posse to withdraw in humiliation. Kearney soon died, Garrett's reputation was tarnished, and Lee and Gilliland eventually were acquitted after a sensational trial.

February 29, 1908, near Las Cruces, New Mexico. Garrett had leased a tract of land to Wayne Brazel, and when Brazel began to graze a herd of goats on the property, a personal feud and legal battle for the removal of the animals began. Jim ("Killer") Miller and

Carl Adamson appeared on the scene and offered to lease the land, but Miller apparently was on hand primarily to ply his deadly trade.

Garrett, Brazel, and Adamson were riding together about four miles outside Las Cruces, when Garrett stopped his buggy to urinate. Suddenly a slug slammed into the back of his head, tearing out above his right eye and spinning him around. A second bullet caught him in the belly and threw him to the ground, where he died within moments. Although Brazel claimed he killed Garrett in self-defense, it was generally assumed that Miller had gunned down the former lawman from ambush.

Sources: Metz, *Pat Garrett;* O'Connor, *Pat Garrett;* Keleher, *Violence in Lincoln County,* 74, 225, 285, 289–93, 296, 298, 303–304, 324, 332, 334, 337, 348, 351–52, 364; Garrett, *Authentic Life of Billy, the Kid;* Sonnichsen, *Tularosa,* 134, 142–47, 152–56, 158, 160–64, 166, 168–72, 178, 180, 183–84, 192–94, 211, 224, 228–44, 254, 257, 292; Fulton, *Lincoln County War,* 381–85, 391, 393–94, 398–402.

Gillett, James Buchanan

(b. November 4, 1856, Austin, Texas; d. June 11, 1937, Temple, Texas. Cowboy, law officer, railroad guard, rancher.) The son of a lawyer and modest landholder, Gillett was reared in Austin, where he learned to ride and shoot skillfully. At seventeen he left home and became a cowboy for two years until his enlistment into the Texas Rangers. For the next six and one-half years he was embroiled in Indian skirmishes and fugitive manhunts, and eventually he earned the rank of first sergeant. On December 26, 1881, he left the rangers to head a group of railroad guards, and soon he became the city marshal of El Paso.

On the side Gillett began building a cattle partnership with another former ranger near Marfa, Texas, and in 1885 he turned in his badge for good. Devoting his full-time activities to business, he eventually built up a thirty-thousand-acre spread at Barrel Springs in the vicinity of Marfa. After his death in Temple, Texas, in 1937, Gillett was buried in Marfa.

Gunfights: January, 1877, Menard County, Texas. Corporal Gillett led five other rangers on a scout to find fugitive Dick Dublin, who had been a cowboy with Gillett years earlier. On the fourth day out the rangers quietly closed in on a ranch where Dublin was hiding. When the law officers emerged into the open, the owner of the ranch, who was outside doing chores, shouted, "Run, Dick, run! Here come the Rangers!" The rangers spurred their mounts, and Dublin, cut off from the corral, sprinted into the brush. Gillett, twenty-five yards behind, ordered him to halt, then snapped off a shot from his carbine.

Dublin disappeared into a ravine, and Gillett followed. When Gillett spotted Dublin, he again ordered the man to stop, whereupon the fugitive whirled to run. Gillett fired a slug which hit Dublin above the right hip and coursed upward through his body, killing him instantly. At that point the other rangers galloped up, and before he could be restrained, Private Ben Carter pumped two more bullets into Dublin's body.

February, 1878, Menard County, Texas. A few weeks later Gillett and five other rangers, led by Lieutenant N. O. Reynolds, set out to escort five prisoners to Austin for trial. As the party rode on the Junction City and Mason road, they encountered an elusive fugitive named Starke Reynolds, who owned a nearby ranch. The wanted man, spotting the rangers at a distance of four hundred yards, wheeled his horse and headed for the Llano River bottoms. The lawmen gave chase, and after a mile and one-half Gillett outdistanced his comrades and began to close in on the fleeing figure. Finally both men pulled up, dismounted, and threw down on each other, but the other rangers soon galloped up, and the fugitive surrendered.

Sources: Gillett, *Six Years with the Texas Rangers;* Webb, *Texas Rangers,* 396, 398–99, 410, 447, 566.

Goldsby, Crawford

("Cherokee Bill")

(b. February 8, 1876, Fort Concho, Texas; d. March 17, 1896, Fort Smith, Arkansas. Bandit.) Cherokee Bill was part Cherokee, part white, part Mexican, and part Negro. His parents were separated, and he got into his first trouble over a shooting when he was just eighteen. He then fell in with two young hoodlums, Bill and Jim Cook, and he killed a lawman when a posse tried to arrest one of the Cook brothers. Goldsby then teamed up with the Cook gang, and over the next several years there was a series of notorious killings and robberies. He gunned down his brother-in-law, George Brown, for beating his sister; while looting a depot he murdered station agent Richard Richards; he killed conductor Samuel Collins when Collins tried to throw him off a train.

There were other incidents, but early in 1895 Cherokee Bill was captured while visiting his sweetheart. Judge Isaac Parker sentenced him to be hanged,

but his attorney, J. Warren Reed, Parker's oldest nemesis, cleverly delayed the execution. After Bill cold-bloodedly murdered a guard, however, the hanging was moved up and carried out in front of one hundred onlookers. Bill quietly exchanged words with his mother, and then when asked if he had any remarks, the twenty-year-old replied, "No. I came here to die, not to make a speech."

Gunfights: 1894, Fort Gibson, Oklahoma.* At a dance in Fort Gibson, Bill quarreled with a Negro named Jake Lewis. A fist fight followed, and when Bill began to be pounded, he produced a gun, wounded Lewis, then fled town.

June, 1894, near Tahlequah, Oklahoma. At Fourteen Mile Creek near Tahlequah, Bill and the Cook brothers encountered a posse. The officers wanted to arrest Jim Cook on a charge of larceny, but the three youths went for their guns. In the melee which followed Bill killed lawman Sequoyah Houston, then galloped to safety.

1894, Oklahoma. Maude Brown, Cherokee Bill's sister, was beaten by her husband, George. Bill angrily sought out Brown and shot him to death.

1894, Lenapah, Oklahoma. Bill and several accomplices were robbing the Shufeldt & Son General Store in Lenapah when Ernest Melton peered in the doorway. Bill whipped up his gun and fatally wounded Melton in the head. It was the death of Melton which earned Bill his original sentence of execution.

July 26, 1896, Fort Smith, Arkansas. Bill procured a gun and, hoping to break out of jail, threw down on guard Lawrence Keating. Keating, a father of four, defiantly resisted Bill's demand, and the prisoner shot him to death. Henry Starr, a fellow inmate, persuaded Bill to give up his gun, and Judge Parker immediately had Bill charged with a second count of murder.

Sources: Horan and Sann, *Pictorial History of the Wild West*, 145–47; Breihan, *Great Gunfighters of the West*, 110–12.

Good, John

(b. near Lockhart, Texas. Rancher, rustler, hotel owner.) John Good first became known as a big, bullying ruffian who ran a ranch, stocked with stolen beef, in the hill country west of Austin, Texas. After a cattle drive to Newton he was present when Cad Pierce was killed by Ed Crawford. Involved in a shooting in 1877, Good moved to Coleman and opened a hotel, but he soon became unpopular, and by 1880 he had moved again, this time to a ranch fifty miles northwest of Colorado City. A short time later he migrated to New Mexico, establishing a ranch near La Luz and a relationship with a notorious local woman known as Bronco Sue Yonker. (In 1884 Bronco Sue had killed a man in Socorro and was suspected of further violent deeds.)

The tryst soon ended when Mrs. Good and John's children arrived, but Bronco Sue merely took up residence nearby with a man named Charley Dawson, thus worsening the situation. In December, 1885, Good killed Dawson, then turned to more practical matters. He built a ten-room adobe house, imported his brother Isham and his large family, and ruthlessly began to accumulate wealth. In 1888 a young man named George McDonald clashed with Good, and when McDonald was assassinated, his friends blamed Walter Good, one of John's sons. A feud broke out, and

Walter Good was killed. The senior Good soon gave up the fight, disposed of his property, and drifted into Arizona. He was last noted working for wages in Oklahoma.

Gunfights: June 10, 1877, Blanco City, Texas. Good had just ridden into Blanco City from his ranch twelve miles away. A few minutes after entering town he was approached by a man named Robinson, who accused Good of stealing his horse. Robinson angrily went for his gun, but it caught in his clothing, and Good pumped four slugs into his adversary. Robinson managed to fire one shot, then he collapsed and died.

December 8, 1885, La Luz, New Mexico. Good and Charley Dawson had quarreled over a mutual mistress, Bronco Sue Yonkers. The dispute eventually erupted into gunplay in the streets of La Luz, but details are hazy.

August, 1888, near Las Cruces, New Mexico. Earlier in the day Good had discovered the decomposed body of his son, Walter, in the White Sands desert. While two of their number remained with the corpse, the rest of the large search party scattered toward home. With Good rode five other men, and when this group neared Las Cruces they encountered five adversaries suspected of Walter's death: Oliver Lee, Tom Tucker, Cherokee Bill Kellam, Perry Altman, and Bill Earhart. Shooting broke out at a distance of 150 yards, and more than one hundred rounds were fired. Good and his men retreated into a field of tall corn, and although three horses were hit, no one was wounded. When Good's band straggled into Las Cruces, a deputy sheriff was sent to recover Walter's cadaver.

Source: Sonnichsen, *Tularosa,* 17–19, 24–27, 32–36, 39–41, 44, 45, 49, 50, 52; Bartholomew, *Wyatt Earp, the Untold Story,* 75–76.

Graham, Dayton

(Law officer.) Dayton Graham was a peace officer in Bisbee, Arizona, when in 1901 he was tapped by Burt Mossman for the newly created Arizona Rangers. Mossman was the captain of the rangers, and there were to be twelve privates and a sergeant. Graham accepted the position of sergeant at seventy-five dollars per month, and his service with the rangers was the high point of his career in law enforcement.

Gunfights: 1901, Douglas, Arizona. A few months after his appointment to the rangers, Graham was stationed in Douglas to try to locate outlaw Bill Smith. One night Graham was with Tom Vaughn, a Douglas peace officer, when a local merchant approached Vaughn and asked him to remove a suspicious-looking stranger from his store. Graham accompanied Vaughn, and as they neared the man in question, who turned out to be Smith, he leaped up firing a six-shooter. Vaughn was hit in the neck, Graham went down with slugs in the chest and arm, and Smith hastily made his escape. Mossman was notified that the ranger was dying, and he gathered up Graham's family and drove them to Douglas. But Graham recovered, although he was bedridden for two months, and he vowed to find Smith.

1902, southern Arizona. As soon as he returned to duty, Graham began an exhaustive search of southern Arizona for the man who had shot him. At last

he entered a saloon one evening and spotted Smith sitting at a monte table. Both men scrambled for their guns, and when the smoke cleared, Smith was dead with two bullets in the belly and one in the head.

Source: Breihan, *Great Lawmen of the West,* 82–85.

Graham, William

("Curly Bill Brocius")

(b. Missouri. Cowboy, cattle rustler.) Graham was a cowhand in Texas who drifted into New Mexico, where he derived a colorful nickname from a *cantina* singer. He helped drive a herd of New Mexico cattle into Arizona, and there he assumed an inflated reputation as a gunslinger. He was one of the leaders of the Clanton cattle rustling gang, and in Tombstone he frequently went with his men on sprees during which he would "buffalo" the town—take over a saloon as headquarters and ride up and down the streets firing revolvers. On one such occasion he accidentally killed the first marshal of Tombstone.

A few months later a similar attempt to take over Galeyville, Arizona, resulted in the serious wounding of Curly Bill. As soon as he recovered, he left Arizona for good, although Wyatt Earp continued to scour the countryside for him. Curly Bill had supposedly vowed revenge upon the Earps for killing his cattle rustling cohorts at the O.K. Corral (even though Bill left Arizona well *before* the famous Earp-Clanton gunfight). Wyatt Earp later claimed to have killed Curly Bill in a gun duel, but Bill actually lived a quiet existence for years after leaving the Tombstone vicinity. He learned about his "death" at Earp's hand a decade later when he was passing through Arizona on the way to Texas.

Gunfights: *October 28, 1880, Tombstone, Arizona.* A number of cowhands, led by Curly Bill, had ridden into Tombstone and were drinking and discharging their guns in the streets. Fred White, appointed in January as Tombstone's first marshal, determined to restore peace and deputized Virgil Earp to assist him. The two men located Curly Bill in an alley, and in the ensuing struggle Bill's gun went off, wounding White in the stomach.

Wyatt Earp, trailing along to be in on the action, rushed up and clubbed Curly Bill on the head with the footlong barrel of his Buntline Special. Marshal White gasped out a dying statement to the effect that the shooting was unintentional, and a subsequent trial in Tucson resulted in Curly Bill's acquittal.

May 25, 1881, Galeyville, Arizona. Curly Bill had ventured into Galeyville and was drinking heavily along with seven or eight of his men (whose number included Jim Wallace, previously a hired gun in the Lincoln County War). Deputy Sheriff Billy Breakenridge of Tombstone passed through town and entered the saloon where the rowdies were drinking.

Wallace drew his gun and insulted Breakenridge, but the lawman laughed it off and set up drinks for everyone. Curly Bill, half drunk, forced Wallace to apologize, and Breakenridge tried to leave the saloon. But Curly Bill then began to exchange words with the lawman and followed him outside.

Breakenridge had investigated the shooting of Fred White, and he was taking no chances: as he mounted his horse he drew his gun and fired at Bill. Bill turned, but the bullet struck him in the left side of his neck and passed out his right cheek, knocking out a tooth but miraculously causing no other damage. After Bill healed, he decided to leave Arizona forever. On his way out in July he told a rancher that Virgil Earp had caused him to shoot Fred White, and then asked the man never to remember the sobriquet "Curly Bill."

Sources: Waters, *Earp Brothers of Tombstone,* 106–107, 120–22, 147, 181, 186, 189–91, 200–202; Sherman, *Ghost Towns of Arizona,* 27, 58.

Griego, Francisco

("Pancho")

(d. November 1, 1875, Cimarron, New Mexico. Cowboy, businessman.) Although his family resided in Santa Fe, by the 1870's Griego was living in Colfax County, New Mexico, where he acquired a local reputation as a dangerous *pistolero.* His most spectacular exploit came in May, 1875, when he felled three soldiers during a violent gunfight in Cimarron. A few months later Griego's friend and business associate, Cruz Vega, was lynched by a mob led by Clay Allison. Griego sought out Allison and was killed by the vicious Tennessean.

Gunfights: *May 30, 1875, Cimarron, New Mexico.* In Lambert's Saloon in Cimarron's St. James Hotel the touchy Griego became embroiled in a quarrel with enlisted men of the Sixth U.S. Cavalry. Griego had been dealing monte to the soldiers, but when he angrily knocked the money to the floor, they broke for the door. Griego whipped out a pistol and sprayed the fleeing soldiers with lead, killing two of them. He then leaped up and finished off the third man with a Bowie knife.

November 1, 1875, Cimarron, New Mexico. Griego, bitter over the recent death of Cruz Vega at the hands of Clay Allison and a lynch mob, encountered Allison at the doorway of the St. James Hotel. The two men talked for a moment, then went inside for a drink, accompanied by Cruz Vega's eighteen-year-old son and Florencio Donahue, Griego's business partner. After the drink, Allison and Griego withdrew to a corner for more conversation. Suddenly Allison whipped out his pistol, shot Griego three times, then bolted to safety. The lights went out, and Griego slumped to the floor, dead.

Sources: Schoenberger, *Gunfighters,* 83–84.

Gristy, Bill

("Bill White")

(Bandit, arsonist, convict.) Bill Gristy was a notorious criminal who became the chief lieutenant in the bandit gang of "Tom Bell!" (whose real name was Thomas Hodges). A known thief and arsonist, Gristy met Hodges while awaiting trial on a murder charge. Gristy, Hodges, and several other men escaped jail, and Hodges and Gristy organized a band of thieves. The gang was active throughout 1856, but in September, Gristy was captured, and, extracting promises of leniency, he informed on Hodges and then was imprisoned.

Gunfights: 1856, near Nevada City, California. Near Nevada City Gristy and the rest of the Tom Bell gang jumped a teamster who had just been paid three hundred dollars for a load of beer. The teamster pulled a pis-

tol, and a gunfight began, but Gristy darted in and made off with the money.

August 11, 1856, near Marysville, California. The Tom Bell gang attempted to hold up the gold-laden Camptonville stage, but driver John Gear, express messenger Dobson, a man named Rideout (who owned the gold and who was accompanying the vehicle), and several passengers opened fire. One outlaw was shot out of the saddle, and after a running fight the stagecoach rocketed clear of the trap. Gristy and Hodges picked up their dying cohort and, accompanied by variously wounded gang members, headed for their hideout. Three or four of the passengers also had been wounded, and a Mrs. Tilghman had been killed, and as a result there was an intensive manhunt for the bandits.

September, 1856, Mountaineer House, California. The Mountaineer House was a road ranch where travelers could obtain food, drink, and shelter, and the proprietor, Jack Phillips, was a former criminal who readily harbored fugitives. Gristy and four other outlaws were hiding in a tent near the Mountaineer House, and there a pair of Sacramento detectives named Anderson and Harrison found them. The detectives were accompanied by two other men and were led by bandit informer Tom Brown.

After dark the party burst into the tent, and shooting erupted. A fugitive named Walker was standing at the mirror, and he squeezed off one pistol shot before Harrison killed him with a shotgun blast. Robber Pete Ansara went down with a load of buckshot in his leg, and the other two outlaws surrendered. But Gristy burst through the side of the tent and, firing over his shoulder, bolted for his horse. Anderson grazed his scalp with a rifle bullet, but the bandit managed to reach his mount and gallop to temporary safety.

Source: Drago, *Road Agents and Train Robbers,* 14–20, 25.

Hall, Jesse Lee

("Red")

(b. October 9, 1849, Lexington, North Carolina; d. March 17, 1911, San Antonio, Texas. Schoolteacher, law officer, rancher, Indian agent, soldier, speculator.) Son of a surgeon who served the Confederacy during the Civil War, Lee Hall came to Texas in 1869 and taught school in Grayson County. The county seat was Sherman, and in 1871 Hall left teaching to become city marshal of that growing community. After two years Hall became a deputy sheriff and, operating out of nearby Denison, stalked and captured numerous horse thieves, murderers, and other unsavory characters. In 1876 he was appointed a lieutenant of the Texas Rangers in Captain L. H. McNelly's company.

During the bloody and widespread Taylor-Sutton feud, Hall once walked unarmed into the midst of a roomful of feudists and boldly arrested seven men wanted in the infamous Brazell murder. In 1877 Hall was promoted to captain, and by 1879 he and his men had captured more than four hundred individuals and, of course, were instrumental in quelling the feud.

During the 1870's Hall also was active in suppressing difficulties on the Texas-Mexico border. He was present at Round Rock when peace officers surprised and killed Sam Bass, and he tracked down other criminals with great efficiency. In 1880, however, Hall was married, and he resigned from the rangers to devote himself—quite successfully—to raising sheep and cattle.

For two years during the 1880's young Will Porter lived on Hall's large ranch to regain his health, and in the process he stored up material which he later used under the pen name O. Henry.

In 1885 Hall was appointed Indian agent at Anadarko, Indian Territory, where he had frequent dealings with Comanche chief Quanah Parker. Two years later he was removed from this position under charges of graft, but eventually he won complete exoneration. He moved his wife and four daughters to San Antonio and became a deputy marshal there, but in 1894 Mrs. Hall took their children and left him.

During the Spanish-American War, Hall organized two companies of "immunes"—men born or who had spent lengthy time in sections of the country subject to yellow fever. Unfortunately, he was unable to go overseas with his troops because of a hernia he had suffered twenty-five years earlier. In 1899, however, Hall obtained a commission as a first lieutenant and fought in the Philippines; he was breveted to the rank of captain, but was forced to leave the service because of malaria. Back from abroad, he was a guard for gold mines in Mexico and speculated in oil and mining leases, and he died in San Antonio at the age of sixty-one.

Gunfights: 1873, Indian Territory. Hall had been attempting to arrest a man wanted on a number of charges. The outlaw, realizing the probability of an eventual arrest, sent word to Hall that he would meet him in a fair fight. Hall accepted, and when the pair met, Hall shot the fugitive out of the saddle. Hall dismounted to take his adversary into custody, but the fallen outlaw opened fire from the ground. Hall shot him dead, but was himself wounded. However, two passing cowboys heard the gunfire and discovered and helped the unconscious lawman.

June, 1874, Indian Territory, twenty miles from the Red River. Hall and an associate crept up to a secluded cabin, hoping to capture outlaw Mike Gormly and his band. No sooner had they taken their positions than Gormly and three companions appeared behind them. The two lawmen opened fire, and Hall shot Gormly, but the wounded outlaw was carried off by a confederate.

November, 1879, Wolfe City, Atascosa County, Texas. A scout in Hall's ranger company learned of the plans of four outlaws to rob a prosperous store in Wolfe City. Hall and five of his men arrived at the store after dark. Two rangers were stationed inside, and after the four outlaws entered and began looting the store, the concealed pair ordered them to surrender. A general shootout followed. One thief, a Mexican, emptied his gun and was shot dead in the doorway. Another bolted out the door and was killed in his tracks fifty yards from the store. A third robber was severely wounded and was captured and sentenced to prison, but the fourth man shot his way out of the trap.

February 9, 1885, Las Islas crossing of the Rio Grande. Hall and Charlie McKinney, sheriff of LaSalle County, met with three Mexican representatives on an island in the Rio Grande to discuss festering problems between Texans and citizens of Mexico. Large numbers of armed men lined each bank of the border river.

After a lengthy consultation, Hall, McKinney, and several of their men were invited to a *fiesta,* but a mile deep into Mexico the appearance of *rurales* caused Hall to shout: "Boys, I move we

don't go! Quick, make a run for it!" The Americans galloped back to Texas, and the Mexicans pursued, firing ineffectively all the way.

Sources: Raymond, *Captain Lee Hall of Texas;* Webb, *Texas Rangers,* 228–94, 454.

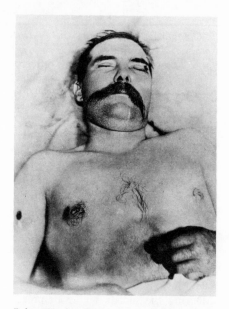

John Wesley Hardin, one of the most dangerous of the western gunmen, photographed after being gunned down by John Selman in El Paso. *(Courtesy Western History Collections, University of Oklahoma Library)*

Hardin, John Wesley

("Wes," "Little Arkansas")

(b. May 26, 1853, Bonham, Texas; d. August 19, 1895, El Paso, Texas. Schoolteacher, farmer, cowboy, businessman, convict, lawyer.) The son of a Methodist circuit preacher, Hardin's ancestors were prominent in Texas history (one Hardin fought at San Jacinto, another signed the Texas Declaration

of Independence, Wes's grandfather served in the Congress of the Texas Republic, and Hardin County had been named for Judge William B. Hardin). Wes's father selected the boy's name in hopes that he might become a minister, but was himself forced to teach school and practice law to make ends meet for his large family. When Wes was two, the Hardins moved to southeastern Texas, where the boy learned to handle guns as a hunter—and by shooting at effigies of Abraham Lincoln during the Civil War.

Wes had his first serious personal combat at the age of eleven, stabbing another boy in the chest and back during a knife fight. The boy lived, but Wes had revealed his killer instinct, and at fifteen he shot a former slave to death. Soon thereafter he ambushed and killed three soldiers who intended to arrest him. His father then took him to Navarro County, where Wes had many sympathetic relatives and where the sixteen-year-old killer taught school for a season at the secluded community of Pisgah Ridge.

The next year Wes worked in a cow camp near Corsicana, the county seat, where he became acquainted with another young fugitive, Bill Longley. Wes soon drifted to tiny Towash, where he killed another man. He then fled to an uncle's farm near Brenham, becoming involved in two more shootouts along the way.

After farming with his uncle for a few months, Wes decided to head for Louisiana. When he reached the East Texas town of Marshall, however, he was arrested by a deputy sheriff. Wes and several other prisoners were taken back to the interior of the state, but en route Hardin managed to escape after killing a guard. Wes then found safety at the ranch of relatives—including Mannen Clements and his brothers—near Smiley in South Texas.

Wes worked as a cowhand for a while, gambled, took part in a shooting scrape, and finally went up the Chisholm Trail with a herd bound for Abilene, killing an Indian in Indian Territory to keep in practice. After hunting down a Mexican killer in Kansas, Wes returned to Smiley, where he had another shootout with lawmen and escaped to marry Jane Bowen.

After his marriage Wes soon engaged in three more shootings, was wounded twice, and was taken into custody. Rescued from jail by Mannen Clements, he joined his Clements cousins in the violent Sutton-Taylor feud. Wes remained relatively inactive for about a year, but when he killed Deputy Sheriff Charles Webb in 1874, Texas placed a four-thousand-dollar dead-or-alive reward on his head, and the Texas Rangers began to track him.

Posing as "J. H. Swain, Jr.," Hardin took his wife and young daughter (a son arrived in 1875, and another daughter was born two years later) by steamboat to Florida. For three years in Florida and Alabama he bought and sold cattle and horses, operated saloon and logging businesses, and tried to remain anonymous. In 1877, however, Ranger John Armstrong and other officers captured him on a train near Pensacola, Florida.

Following trial, Hardin was sentenced to the penitentiary in Huntsville, Texas, where he put his time to good use and studied for the bar. In February, 1894, Hardin was released from prison and opened a law office in Gonzales; his wife had died a year and one-half earlier, but he lived in Gonzales with his children for a time. He soon moved his practice to Junction, however, where he married a young girl who left him on the day of their wedding. Hardin then opened an office in El Paso and began to run with a hard crowd in that notorious border town. He was killed in El Paso at the age of forty-two.

Gunfights: November, 1868, near Moscow, Texas. Wes, visiting an uncle's plantation near Moscow, got into a wrestling match with his teen-aged cousin and a former slave named Mage. Mage became angered and threatened to kill Wes, and the next day as Hardin was riding home, the Negro stepped into the road with a stick in his hand. Wes pulled his .44 and pumped three slugs into Mage, who died a few days later.

November, 1868, near Sumpter, Texas. While hiding at the farm of a friend, Wes learned that three soldiers were approaching to arrest him for the murder of Mage. Armed with a shotgun and a pistol, Wes set an ambush at a creek crossing. As the soldiers rode by, Wes fired both barrels, killing two of the men. The third soldier fired back, nicking Wes in the left arm. Hardin then drew his .44 and killed the man with pistol fire. Several former Confederates of the area concealed the bodies, and Hardin fled the scene.

December 25, 1869, Towash, Texas. While playing cards in Towash, Wes, who was a big winner, was threatened with a knife by a hard case named Bradly. Wes, who was unarmed, left the game and got his six-gun. Later that evening he encountered Bradly on the street. Bradly cursed Wes and fired a pistol shot at him. Wes shot twice, striking Bradly in the head and chest, then galloped out of town.

January, 1870, Horn Hill, Texas. On the run because of the Bradly killing, Wes and a companion decided to spend the night at Horn Hill, where local townspeople had clashed that afternoon with members of a circus troupe. Wes naturally was attracted to the circus, and just as naturally he got into a quarrel with a burly circus man. The man staggered Wes with a punch and reached for a pistol, but Wes already had his weapon out and shot his adversary in the head.

January, 1870, Kosse, Texas. Continuing on alone, Wes encountered a girl who, assisted by a male confederate, tried to roll the youth that evening. Wes threw his money onto the floor, and as the man stooped to pick it up, Hardin drew his six-gun and shot the thief between the eyes. Retrieving his money, Wes galloped out of town as usual.

January, 1871, near Marshall, Texas. In the custody of two state policemen, Wes and several other prisoners were being transferred from Marshall to Waco. The second night out, one of the guards went to a nearby farmhouse to procure feed for the animals. Wes produced a gun that he had obtained from a fellow prisoner in the Marshall jail, shot the remaining guard, and fled the camp on horseback.

February, 1871, Gonzales County, Texas. Wes, cousin Mannen Clements, and several other cowhands stopped at a Mexican camp to play monte. The dealer quarreled with Wes, who slugged him on the head with his gun barrel. When two other Mexicans went for their knives, Wes opened fire, wounding one in the chest and one in the arm.

May, 1871, Indian Territory. Wes strayed away from the cattle herd to hunt wild turkey and encountered an Indian, whom he shot in cold blood. His cousins and fellow cowboys helped him bury the body, hoping to avoid retribution by the dead man's tribesmen.

July 6, 1871, Abilene, Kansas. On the verge of leaving Abilene with a manhunt, Hardin fell into a quarrel with one Charles Cougar. With his usual murderous aggression, Hardin pulled a gun and shot Cougar to death.

July 7, 1871, Bluff City, Kansas. Two days earlier a Mexican named Juan Bideno had killed cowboy Bill Cohron, who was a friend of Wes Hardin, Jim Rodgers, and Hugh Anderson. This trio, armed with a warrant and accompanied by John Cohron, brother of the dead man, pursued Bideno until they found him at the tiny hamlet of Bluff City in southern Kansas. While the other three surrounded the café in which Bideno was eating, Hardin walked inside and ordered the Mexican to surrender. When Bideno tried to resist, Hardin shot him in the head at point-blank range.

September, 1871, Smiley, Texas. Green Parramore and John Lackey, a pair of Negro state policemen, had been searching Smiley for Hardin. Hearing of the search, Hardin boldly walked up to the lawmen while they were eating crackers and cheese in the general store. Wes asked the unsuspecting pair if they knew Hardin, and they replied that they had never seen him, but intended to seek and arrest him. "Well," said Wes, drawing his gun, "you see him now!" He emptied his gun at the officers, killing Parramore and wounding Lackey in the mouth. Lackey dashed out of the store and lived to see Hardin on another occasion.

June, 1872, Hemphill, Texas. Hardin, in town to sell a herd of horses, had a quarrel over a court case with a state policeman named Spites. Spites, who did not know Hardin's identity, warned him to back off or face arrest. Wes then palmed a derringer with his left hand and shot Spites in the shoulder. Spites ran away, and Wes spurred out of town with a posse on his heels.

July, 1872, Trinity City, Texas. Visiting relatives near his boyhood home, Wes and a cousin engaged in a bowling match, which Hardin intentionally lost. A bystander named Sublett challenged him to a series of matches at five dollars per set. After Wes won six games in a row, Sublett realized that he was being victimized, and he berated Hardin. Wes forced Sublett to finish the game at gunpoint, then generously bought him a drink.

Sublett stomped out of the building, returned a few moments later with a shotgun, and discharged a blast at Hardin. Struck in the side by buckshot, Wes drew his gun and staggered after Sublett, wounding the fleeing man in the back. Doctors dug out the buckshot, and friends carried Hardin into hiding.

August, 1872, Angelina County, Texas. Two state policemen rode up to a farmhouse where Wes, still recovering from his wounds, was hiding. Armed with rifles, the officers crept up to a window and fired into the room, wounding Wes in the thigh as he lay on a pallet. Wes crawled to the door and drove the men off with a shotgun.

April, 1873, Cuero, Texas. In Cuero to sell cattle, Wes visited a local saloon and began quarreling with a belligerent, half-drunk deputy of Jack Helm's named J. B. Morgan. When Wes left the saloon, Morgan followed him out and went for his gun, and he was shot dead by Hardin.

July, 1873, Albuquerque, Texas. While having a horseshoe replaced, Wes and Jim Taylor met Jack Helm, who was a leader of the Sutton faction in the Sutton-Taylor feud. Helm and six cohorts were passing by the blacksmith shop when he spotted Hardin and Taylor and impulsively approached them. Hardin abruptly blasted Helm in the chest with a shotgun, and Taylor emptied his pistol into the fallen man's head. Hardin and Taylor then frightened Helm's startled companions away from the scene.

May 26, 1874, Comanche, Texas. After celebrating his twenty-first birthday by winning heavily at horse racing, Hardin had words at a saloon with Comanche County Deputy Sheriff Charles Webb. The two men drew their weapons and fired. Hardin took a bullet in the side, and Webb was struck in the head. Webb jerked his trigger again when he was hit, and Hardin's two companions—Jim Taylor and Bill Dixon—pumped slugs into him as he went down. An enraged mob chased Wes and his party out of town, and even though Wes escaped, his brother Joe and Bud and Tom Dixon were soon caught and lynched in Comanche.

August 23, 1877, Pensacola, Florida. Hardin had been to Pensacola on business and intended to return with four cohorts to Alabama by train. Texas Ranger John Armstrong and several other officers gathered at a station just outside Pensacola to intercept the fugitive. Armstrong limped into Hardin's coach, supported by a cane because of a previous wound. The ranger pulled his .45, and Hardin shouted, "Texas, by God." But when Hardin went for his gun, the weapon, concealed in his waistband, hung in his suspenders.

Nineteen-year-old Jim Mann, sitting beside Hardin, drew his pistol cleanly and put a bullet through Armstrong's hat. Armstrong then shot Mann in the chest, and the youth jumped out the train window, ran several steps, and fell dead. In the meantime, Armstrong had grabbed Hardin's gun, and after a fierce struggle the ranger clubbed Wes senseless with his long-barreled .45. Hardin was then whisked by train back to Texas.

August 19, 1895, El Paso, Texas. Wes had had trouble with John Selman and John Selman, Jr., both peace officers in El Paso. Hardin had been seeing a married woman, a former prostitute named Mrs. Martin Morose, who recently had been arrested by John Selman, Jr. A short time later, Hardin encountered the elder Selman in the streets, tongue-lashed him, and threatened to kill him and his son.

Wes spent the evening of August 19 drinking and gambling in the Acme Saloon. Shortly after 11:00 P.M. he was shooting dice with H. S. Brown, a local grocer; Hardin's back was to the door. The senior Selman, a veteran gunfighter, walked inside and shot Wes to death. Hardin had just told Brown, "You have four sixes to beat," when a slug crashed into his head. As he fell, Selman fired again, but the bullet struck the floor. Selman then walked to the prostrate Hardin and fired two more shots. One hit Hardin in the arm, and the second struck him in the right side of the chest.

According to the coroner's report, the fatal bullet had entered the back of Hardin's skull, torn through his head, and emerged from his eye; Selman, however, claimed that he had spoken a word of warning and that the slug had entered Hardin's eye. At any rate, neither of the two pistols found on Hardin's body was fired.

Sources: Nordyke, *John Wesley Hardin;* Hardin, *Life of John Wesley Hardin;* Webb, *Texas Rangers,* 297–304; Metz, *John Selman;* Sonnichsen, *I'll Die Before I'll Run,* 67–72, 74, 76–81, 83, 86, 94, 154, 165, 317, 320; Haley, *Jeff Milton,* 226–29, 243–48; Horan, *Authentic Wild West,* 155–86.

Harkey, Dee

(b. March 27, 1866, Richland Springs, Texas; d. ca. 1948, New Mexico. Farmer, cowboy, law officer, miner, clerk, butcher, rancher.) One of eight children born to a Texas farm couple, Harkey was orphaned at the age of three and was reared by an older brother. As a youth, Harkey witnessed more than one Indian raid, and three of his brothers were killed in gunfights before they reached twenty-one. Harkey had little schooling, but earned his way as a farmhand and cowboy. When he was sixteen he began wearing a badge as deputy to his brother Joe, who had been elected sheriff of San Saba County. It was there that Dee first clashed with Jim ("Killer") Miller and various other hard cases.

After four years of serving warrants and arresting stock thieves, Harkey married and established a farm in Bee County. He soon came into conflict with a contentious neighbor named George Young, whom he killed in a knife fight in a corn patch. In 1890 he moved to Carlsbad, New Mexico, and found employment as a butcher. A quarrel with a customer named George High resulted in two shooting incidents in which Harkey acquitted himself well, and a delegation of citizens secured an appointment for him as deputy U.S. marshal to clean up the area.

Harkey served as a New Mexico peace officer until 1911 and eventually held a variety of official positions, ranging from town marshal to inspector for the cattle raisers' association. When he retired as a lawman, he engaged in ranching in Eddy County, and he died peacefully in his eighties.

Gunfights: 1884, Richland Springs, Texas. Harkey had arrested a mule thief named Quinn, and he and a deputy named Davis accompanied Quinn and his son to their hotel room for a change of clothing. Suddenly Quinn's wife and daughter Mary (whom Harkey had been courting) burst into the room. Mary held a pistol and said, "Dee, that's my father and I'm going to protect him." With that she shot Harkey in the stomach. Davis ran out of the room while Harkey slammed the girl to the floor and seized the pistol. But the elder Quinn picked up a machete and snapped, "Dee, I've got you."

"You sure have," replied Harkey.

This standoff was quickly broken when Davis led a mob of citizens to the rescue. Harkey wanted to shoot Quinn, but was restrained by the townspeople. A doctor arrived and discovered that the bullet had struck Harkey's watch and had merely burned a blister across his abdomen.

1895, Phoenix, New Mexico. Tranquellano Estabo, a local gunman, killed a man in Phoenix and then began shooting up the town. Harkey joined Carlsbad Sheriff Cicero Stewart, and the two lawmen rode the mile into Phoenix on bicycles. As they pedaled into town, they encountered Estabo, who was mounted on horseback and brandishing a Winchester. "Hold up, Tranquellano," ordered Harkey. Instead, the Mexican triggered a shot, and Harkey jerked his pistol and returned fire.

Estabo then rode down Stewart, who scrambled up and emptied his six-gun at the fleeing horseman. Harkey secured a mount, passed Estabo within three miles, and again ordered him to stop. This time Estabo threw up his hands and said, "Don't kill me, don't kill me! I will go with you."

1908, near Sacramento Sinks, New Mexico. For days Harkey and four other law officers had trailed an outlaw band led by Jim Nite, a former member of the Dalton gang who had recently escaped from the Texas penitentiary. One morning at daybreak the posse discovered Nite's secluded camp, but the outlaws spied the lawmen as they advanced. The fugitives seized their Winchesters and dashed for a depression in the ground, and Harkey led the posse in a downhill charge to the camp. Heavy fire drove all but Harkey away, and he dismounted to fight on foot.

Nite and a confederate named Dan Johnson ran toward Harkey, but he turned his fire toward them and sent them scurrying back to cover. From his elevated position Harkey poured a heavy rifle fire at the outlaws, and within minutes Johnson called out: "Dee, we will surrender if you won't kill us." The other posse members now rejoined Harkey, and the criminals were taken into custody.

Source: Harkey, *Mean as Hell.*

Hays, Bob

(d. 1896, San Simon Valley, Arizona. Bandit, cowboy.) Hays was involved with Black Jack Christian's band of robbers in Arizona. After a bank holdup in Nogales, the outlaws were pursued,

and Hays was killed in a shootout with a posse.

Gunfights: *August 6, 1896, Nogales, Arizona.* Black Jack's gang intended to rob the International Bank of Nogales, and while Christian and two others stayed with the horses, Hays and Jess Williams slipped inside. They held up bank clerk Fred Herrera and began stuffing money into sacks. A door slammed, and then newspaperman Frank King began to exchange shots with the outlaws outside.

Hays and Williams dropped the sacks and bolted for their mounts. Two of the thieves' horses were wounded, but the entire gang made it out of town. King pursued them singlehandedly, returning to Nogales only after another exchange of shots.

1896, San Simon Valley, Arizona. Christian, Hays, and two other fugitives were bushwacked by an eight-man posse at the gang's hideout in the San Simon Valley. As the firing broke out, Hays's horse was killed, but he leaped clear and squeezed off three slugs at Fred Higgins. He succeeded only in sending splinters into the lawman's face, but he took two bullets in return and fell fatally wounded. Christian's horse also was killed, but he and the other two outlaws managed to escape.

Head, Harry

("Harry the Kid")

(d. June, 1881, Eureka, New Mexico. Cattle rustler, stage robber.) Head was a cattle thief in southern Arizona and was associated with Ike Clanton's nefarious operations. In March, 1881, Head, Bill Leonard, and two other men were engaged in a bloody attempt to rob a stagecoach. Three months later

Head and Leonard were killed while trying to hold up a store in New Mexico.

Gunfights: March 15, 1881, Contention, Arizona. A stagecoach leaving Tombstone was loaded with $26,000 of Wells, Fargo money. There were eight passengers aboard, and the bullion was guarded by Bob Paul, a fearless lawman. The stage passed through Contention, about twelve miles from Tombstone, where driver Budd Philpot changed teams.

A mile outside Contention the coach slowed to negotiate a steep grade, whereupon Head, Leonard, and Jim Crane stepped from ambush and ordered the driver to stop. Paul and the bandits began to trade shots; Peter Roerig, a passenger sitting on top of the coach, was killed, as was Philpot, who was struck in the heart. Philpot pitched forward on top of the horses, and the animals bolted. Paul leaped onto the wagon tongue, managed to secure the reins, and brought the vehicle under control.

Luther King, who held the outlaws' horses, was captured a day later by Morgan Earp, and he divulged the names of his confederates. Wells, Fargo put up a reward of two thousand dollars each for Head, Leonard, and Crane, dead or alive, and Wyatt Earp, eager for the glory of apprehending the robbers, secretly offered the Clantons thirty-six hundred dollars if they would lure the escaped trio into a trap.

June, 1881, Eureka, New Mexico. Despite rewards and warrants issued for their arrest, Head, Leonard, and Crane remained at large for several weeks. Then in June, Head and Leonard attempted to rob a store in Eureka. The owners, Bill and Ike Haslett, produced guns, and after a sharp flurry of shots Head and Leonard were killed. Crane

later engineered the deaths of the Haslett brothers and was himself killed in New Mexico a short time later.

Sources: Waters, *Earp Brothers of Tombstone,* 127–40; Faulk, *Tombstone,* 145–47; Tombstone *Epitaph,* March 16, 1881.

Helm, Jack

(d. July, 1873, Albuquerque, Texas. Cowboy, law officer, inventor.) Helm first appeared in history just before the Civil War as a cowboy for Texas' fabulous Shanghai Pierce. During the late 1860's he joined the Sutton side in their bloody feud with the Taylors in South Texas, and he became one of the leaders of the two-hundred-strong Sutton "Regulators." In August, 1869, Helm arranged an attack which resulted in one of the bloodiest battles of the Sutton-Taylor feud.

On July 1, 1869, Reconstruction Governor E. J. Davis organized the Texas State Police, and Helm received an appointment as one of the four captains. But shortly thereafter he misused his authority to murder two members of the Taylor faction and to levy a tax of twenty-five cents per person to defray his hotel expenses. Therefore, in October, 1870, he was suspended from the state police, and he was permanently dismissed the following December.

Helm had managed to win election as sheriff of DeWitt County, however, and from that position he continued to be a leader in the area feuding. But in April, 1873, he moved to Albuquerque, Texas, where he worked to perfect an invention to combat cotton worms. A few months later he was killed in Albuquerque by Jim Taylor and John Wesley Hardin.

Gunfights: July, 1869, San Patri-

cio County, Texas. In San Patricio County, Helm and fellow regulator C. S. Bell encountered a pair of Taylor men, John Choate and his nephew, Crockett Choate. The two regulators attacked the Choates, and when the shooting stopped, both uncle and nephew were dead.

August 23, 1869, DeWitt County, Texas. Helm and Bell gathered several gunmen and organized an ambush near Creed Taylor's ranch. When Taylor's sons, Hays and Doboy, appeared, the Sutton posse opened fire. The Taylors fought back, but Doboy was wounded and Hays was killed.

August 26, 1870, DeWitt County, Texas. Henry Kelly, who was related by marriage to the Taylors, and his brother William had caused a disturbance at the hamlet of Sweet Home. That incident gave peace officer Helm an excuse to arrest the Kelly brothers, and he gathered Bill Sutton, Doc White, and John Meador to help him. The posse rounded up both men early in the morning at their adjacent farm homes.

A short distance down the road, the group stopped, and William Kelly dismounted and began to light a pipe. Sutton then fired at him and White promptly shot Henry out of the saddle. There was more shooting, and the Kelly brothers were killed.

July, 1873, Albuquerque, Texas. Helm and half a dozen friends were walking down the street when they spotted Wes Hardin and Jim Taylor in a blacksmith shop. Helm approached the shop, and Hardin suddenly leveled a shotgun and fired. The blast struck Helm in the chest, and he went down, and Taylor then emptied his revolver into the fallen man's head.

Sources: Webb, *Handbook of Texas,* I, 794, II, 693; Nunn, *Texas Under the*

Carpetbaggers, 45–48; Sonnichsen, *I'll Die Before I'll Run,* 43, 45–48, 56, 58, 61, 62, 64, 68–70; Sutton, *Sutton-Taylor Feud,* 8–9, 18–21, 23–24, 27–28, 40–45.

Hickok, James Butler

("Wild Bill")

(b. May 27, 1837, Troy Grove, Illinois; d. August 2, 1876, Deadwood, Dakota Territory. Hunter, teamster, laborer, stage driver, army scout and spy, Wild West show performer, gambler, law officer.) The fourth of six children, Hickok was the son of a Vermont couple who moved to the Illinois village of Troy Grove the year before James Butler was born. Hickok's father farmed and operated a general store, and he also established a way station of the Underground Railroad; young Jim was frequently required to help whisk fugitive slaves away from their pursuers.

By the time he was a teenager, Hickok had proved himself to be the best shot in northern Illinois, and he also seemed to be adept with his fists. In 1855 he brawled with a fellow teamster named Charlie Hudson, who was injured so badly that Hickok thought he had killed him. The eighteen-year-old Hickok fled to St. Louis, and soon drifted into Kansas, which then was being torn by strife over slavery. Hickok joined the Free-State Militia of General Jim Lane, but was involved in no real shooting frays.

In March, 1858, Hickok was elected constable of Monticello township in Johnson County, but his brief tenure was peaceful. He had hired out previously as a farmhand, and while in Monticello he worked his own homestead claim. Hickok next drove a stagecoach on the Santa Fe Trail, and in 1860 he was employed by Russell, Ma-

Wild Bill Hickok, a natty dresser. He killed seven men, and possibly another. *(Courtesy Kansas State Historical Society, Topeka)*

jors & Waddell as a wagon master of freight trains. A short time later, while leading a train through Raton Pass, Hickok was attacked by a bear. He killed the beast with his pistols and knife, but

was severely injured. His company sent him to Santa Fe and to Kansas City for treatment, then transferred him to light duties at their Rock Creek Station on the Oregon Trail in Nebraska. It was there that, a few months later, Hickok engaged in his notorious fight with Dave McCanles.

By that time the Civil War had begun, and Hickok associated himself with the Federal army. In October, 1861, Hickok hired on as a Union wagon master in Sedalia, Missouri, and later he operated as a spy and guide under General Samuel P. Curtis. During this period he had occasion to back down a lynch mob, and when a woman shouted, "Good for you, Wild Bill!" he was branded with his famous sobriquet. Hickok probably fought at the Battle of Pea Ridge, Arkansas, in 1862, and reputedly was in and out of one dangerous scrape after another during this period.

After the war Hickok became a gambler in Springfield, Missouri, and there he killed Dave Tutt in a street fight. After losing an election for chief of police of Springfield, Hickok moved to Fort Riley, Kansas, where his older brother was employed as wagon master, scout, and chief herder. On January 1, 1867, Hickok began scouting for Custer's Seventh Cavalry, and later in the year he was defeated as a candidate for sheriff of Ellsworth County, Kansas. Hickok nevertheless found employment in law enforcement as a deputy U.S. marshal, chasing army deserters and thieves of government livestock. On one occasion in April, 1868, Bill Cody assisted Hickok in bringing in eleven prisoners to Topeka.

September, 1868, found Hickok in Colorado in the company of several cattlemen who became surrounded by a hostile party of Cheyennes. Hickok was selected by the group to ride for help, and he dashed to safety past the Indians, receiving only a slight wound in the foot.

Back in Kansas, Hickok was elected sheriff of Ellis County in August, 1869. The county seat was Hays City, which, because of transient buffalo hunters and the raucous members of the Seventh Cavalry stationed nearby, was as wild and dangerous a frontier town as any in existence. In just three months Hickok killed two men, but he lost a November election to his own deputy, Peter Lanihan. Hickok moved to Topeka, but got into a street brawl and soon returned to Hays, where he shot two soldiers and again had to leave town.

Hickok next staged a Wild West show in Niagara Falls entitled "The Daring Buffalo Chase of the Plains." The show was a financial flop, and Wild Bill went back to the West. In April, 1871, he was hired to be city marshal of Abilene at $150 a month plus a percentage of fines. Hickok served throughout the remainder of the year and became involved in one tragic shootout.

Texas gamblers Phil Coe and Ben Thompson had opened the Bull's Head Saloon and had decorated it with a clearly depicted symbol of masculinity which offended the respectable citizens of Abilene. At the behest of the city council, Hickok ordered the alteration of the sign, and Coe resented this interference. Trouble between the two men grew, and eventually a gunfight occurred in which Hickok killed Coe and, by accident, his own deputy. Texans placed a price allegedly totaling eleven thousand dollars on Hickok's head, but Wild Bill avoided further trouble in Abilene and left his job at the end of 1871.

During the next couple of years there were several incorrect but widely circulated rumors that Hickok had been killed, and in 1872 he was a member of a royal Russian buffalo hunt in Kansas.

Throughout most of that time, however, Wild Bill was in the East traveling with Buffalo Bill Cody's troupe and somewhat ineptly performing in a production billed as "Scouts of the Prairie."

In 1874 Hickok drifted back to the West, but his eyesight was failing (probably as a result of gonorrhea), and so was his luck. Indeed, he was arrested in Cheyenne for vagrancy on several occasions in 1876. That same year he renewed an old acquaintance with a circus proprietor named Agnes Lake, and despite his longtime tendency toward profligacy, Hickok married her in Cheyenne on March 5. Two weeks later the lure of the booming gold fields around Deadwood, Dakota Territory, seduced Hickok away from his bride. After arriving in Deadwood, Hickok spent most of his time gambling at No. 10 Saloon, although he wrote his wife that he was hard at work as a prospector. A few months later he was murdered by Jack McCall and was buried owing a debt of fifty dollars to the saloon. A raffle of his possessions was conducted to pay the expenses of his funeral.

Gunfights: *July 12, 1861, Rock Creek Station, Nebraska.* For a short time Hickok had been working as a stock tender at the Rock Creek stage depot, which was operated by Horace Wellman, Wellman's common-law wife, and stable hand Doc Brink. The station attendants soon began to have trouble with Dave McCanles, who lived with his family at a ranch house across the creek and who kept a mistress, Sarah Shull, nearby. McCanles' financial difficulties with the freighting company of Russell, Majors & Waddell had originated the problems, but the greatest conflict grew between McCanles and Hickok, who secretly had been seeing Miss Shull. A further aggravation was McCanles' persistence in calling Hickok "Duck Bill," a slur upon his facial features, and "hermaphrodite," a slur upon certain other of his features.

On the afternoon of July 12 McCanles appeared at the stage station and was met first by Wellman's wife and then by Hickok, who refused to come outside. McCanles moved around to a side door, where he spotted Hickok lurking behind a curtain partition. "Come out and fight fair," demanded McCanles. He then threatened to drag Hickok outside. "There will be one less son-of-a-bitch when you try that," challenged Hickok. McCanles then stepped inside and was promptly shot to death by Hickok. Hickok had already pulled his revolver, and from behind the curtain he placed a ball into McCanles' heart.

At the sound of the shot McCanles' twelve-year-old son, Monroe; his cousin, James Woods; and an employee on his ranch, James Gordon, ran toward the stage station. At the side door Monroe McCanles cradled his father in his arms while Woods approached the kitchen door. Hickok shot Woods twice, then turned to wing Gordon, who suddenly appeared at the front door. Woods and Gordon then tried to flee, but Wellman and Brink, armed with a hoe and a shotgun, respectively, gave chase. Wellman easily caught Woods and hacked the life out of him, and Brink killed Gordon with a blast from his shotgun.

July 21, 1865, Springfield, Missouri. Dave Tutt, a former Union soldier and previously an acquaintance of Hickok's, began to clash with Wild Bill over the affections of a girl named Susanna Moore. The conflict was fatally aggravated on the night of July 20 because of a quarrel over a card game in the Lyon House. Hickok and Tutt exchanged threats, and at 6:00 P.M. the following day they confronted each other in the town square before a large crowd of onlookers.

At a distance of seventy-five yards Hickok shouted, "Don't come any closer, Dave!" In reply Tutt produced a pistol and squeezed off a shot. Hickok steadied his revolver with his left hand and fired a slug squarely into Tutt's chest. Tutt pitched onto his face, dead in an instant. Hickok surrendered himself to the authorities and was acquitted following trial.

July, 1869, Colorado Territory. A drunken Hickok became involved in a shooting fray. Wild Bill killed no one, but received three flesh wounds himself.

August 24, 1869, Hays City, Kansas. Shortly after being elected county sheriff, Hickok encountered John Mulrey, a drunken cavalryman. Mulrey belligerently refused to submit to arrest, and Hickok shot him down. Mulrey lingered through the night, but died the next morning.

September 27, 1869, Hays City, Kansas. A local troublemaker named Samuel Strawhim led a band of drunken teamsters through Hays on the evening of September 26. About one hour after midnight the raucous hard cases began to tear up a beer palace. Hickok and Deputy Peter Lanihan appeared on the scene and ordered a halt to the destruction. Strawhim turned on Hickok, and a riot ensued. Hickok deliberately shot Strawhim in the head, killing him instantly and stopping the trouble.

July 17, 1870, Hays City, Kansas. Under the influence of liquor, Hickok became involved in a brawl at Drum's Saloon with five inebriated troopers of the Seventh Cavalry. When Wild Bill was thrown to the floor and kicked by the soldiers, he pulled a gun and started shooting. Privates Jeremiah Lanigan and John Kile collapsed, severely wounded, and the other soldiers backed away. Hickok fled town, and Lanigan and Kile were taken to the post hospital. Kile died the next day, but Lanigan eventually recovered.

October 5, 1871, Abilene, Kansas. Phil Coe, with whom Hickok recently had clashed, led about fifty Texans on a drunken spree through Abilene. They forced several citizens to buy drinks for the group, and even Hickok was compelled to treat them. But Hickok warned the rowdies to control themselves, and he alerted Deputy Mike Williams.

That afternoon Williams had received a telegram from Kansas City asking him to come to the bedside of his ailing wife, and he planned to take the 9:45 evening train. But at 9:00 P.M. a shot rang out, and Hickok went to investigate it, ordering Williams to stay put. Hickok elbowed his way through the crowd of revelers and found Phil Coe, who, along with several other Texans, had his revolver in his fist.

Coe claimed that he had shot at a dog, but Hickok went for his six-guns. Coe fired hastily at Hickok, but only hit his coattails. Hickok's aim was better. Coe was standing just eight feet away, and Wild Bill's first slug tore through his belly and out his back. As Coe collapsed, his gun went off again, but the bullet breezed between Hickok's legs. Apparently having aimed for Coe's head, Hickok grumbled, "I've shot too low."

At this point Mike Williams broke through the crowd, hoping to help Hickok. Wild Bill saw the movement and, apprehensive at being surrounded by hostile cowboys, whirled and opened fire. Williams was struck twice in the head and died instantly. An enraged

Hickok dispersed the crowd and closed up the town. The mortally wounded Coe was carried away to die a lingering death three days later. One or two bystanders received treatment for flesh wounds, and Hickok paid Mike Williams' funeral expenses. (It should be noted that after the accidental death of Williams, Hickok is not known ever to have fired another shot at a man.)

August 2, 1876, Deadwood, Dakota Territory. In Deadwood's Saloon No. 10, Hickok entered a midafternoon poker game with three acquaintances: Carl Mann, one of the saloon's proprietors; gambler Charles Rich; and Missouri River pilot Frank Massie. Hickok twice asked Massie, sitting opposite him against the wall, to exchange seats, but Massie laughed and said that no one was going to shoot him in the back. After half an hour of play Hickok was cleaned out, and he borrowed fifty dollars from the house to stay in the game.

At 4:10 P.M. a drifter named Jack McCall downed a glass of whiskey, drew an old .45 Colt, and walked up behind Hickok. (McCall reportedly had lost $110 to Hickok the previous day, and there also was a strong possibility that local enemies of Wild Bill had offered McCall $200 to kill him.) Rich had just dealt Wild Bill a queen and two pairs, aces and eights, when a shot roared out. The slug tore into the back of Hickok's head, came out under his right cheekbone, and imbedded itself in Massie's left forearm. Hickok slumped to the floor, dead but still clutching his cards.

"Take that!" said McCall, as he turned to flee the building. Bartender Anson Tipple climbed over the bar to jump McCall, who tried to shoot him. But McCall's gun misfired (later it was discovered that the round which killed Hickok was the only one in the gun which was not defective). McCall was quickly apprehended and eventually executed.

Back in the saloon, Frank Massie, blood streaming from his arm, thought Hickok had begun shooting in anger over his card losses. Massie ran into the street, shouting, "Wild Bill shot me!" A crowd quickly gathered, to discover that the famous frontiersman was dead.

Sources: Schoenberger, *Gunfighters,* 61–91, 176–79; Miller and Snell, *Great Gunfighters of the Kansas Cowtowns,* 103–40; Rosa, *They Called Him Wild Bill;* Fiedler, *Wild Bill and Deadwood;* O'Connor, *Wild Bill Hickok;* Drago, *Wild, Woolly & Wicked,* 72–92; Streeter, *Prairie Trails & Cow Towns,* 84–86, 88–92; Rosa, *Alias Jack McCall;* Horan, *Authentic Wild West,* 81–122.

Higgins, Fred R.

(Law officer.) Higgins was an Arizona peace officer who fought outlaws during the 1890's. He held a commission as a deputy U.S. marshal, and after the turn of the century he was sheriff of Chaves County, New Mexico.

Gunfights: 1896, San Simon Valley, Arizona. Higgins was a member of an eight-man posse which had trailed Black Jack Christian and three other bandits to a hideout in the San Simon Valley. The lawmen set an ambush while the outlaws were out of camp, and when they returned, a vicious fight broke out. Christian's horse was killed, as well as that of a fugitive named Bob Hays. Hays jumped clear and fired three shots at Higgins, showering splinters into his face. Higgins then shot Hays twice, fatally wounding the outlaw, but the other criminals escaped.

*April 28, 1897, Black Jack Canyon, Ar-*izona. Higgins and four other officers had tracked Christian to a cave near Clifton, and there they ambushed Black Jack and his two companions. Christian was mortally wounded, but the posse was driven away, and the other two outlaws escaped.

Sources: Haley, *Jeff Milton,* 271–72, 279; Keleher, *Violence in Lincoln County,* 324; Harkey, *Mean as Hell,* 63, 93–94.

Higgins, John Calhoun Pinckney

("Pink")

(b. 1848, near Atlanta, Georgia; d. December 18, 1914, Kent County, Texas. Rancher, shop owner.) Pink Higgins was born in Georgia, but his family moved by wagon train to Texas a few months later, settling first near Austin before establishing a ranch in Lampasas County in 1857. As a young man Pink was an officer in the Ku Klux Klan, owned a combination meat shop and saloon until it burned, and was twice wounded while fighting Indians. Pink's best shooting was done with a Winchester, which he fired by pulling the trigger with his thumb when pulling back the lever.

Later he turned to ranching as a livelihood, and by the 1870's he was driving large herds to the Kansas railheads. At times he combined his cattle with those of the Horrell brothers, who ranched nearby. But in 1873 the Horrells killed three law officers, including Pink's son-in-law, and a vicious feud erupted. Pink was involved in several shooting scrapes, but finally he was prevailed upon by Texas Rangers to sign a truce. About the turn of the century he moved his ranching operation and large family to a spread thirteen miles south of Spur, Texas, where he died of a heart attack at the age of sixty-six.

Gunfights: ca. 1874, Lampasas County, Texas. Pink discovered Zeke Terrell, a Horrell cowboy, butchering a Higgins cow that he had just shot. From ninety yards Pink dropped Terrell with a Winchester slug. He then disemboweled the dead cow and stuffed Terrell's corpse inside. Pink next rode into town, found the local law officers, and told them where they could find a miracle taking place—a cow giving birth to a man.

ca. 1875, Lampasas County, Texas. At a waterhole used jointly by Horrell and Higgins stock, Pink encountered Ike Lantier. Lantier had ridden with Quantrill and had been a buffalo hunter, and he was employed by the Horrells. Upon meeting Higgins, Lantier went for his pistol, but Pink whipped up his Winchester, which he already had unsheathed, and pumped a slug into Lantier's belly, and the gunman dropped from his saddle and died within moments.

January 22, 1877, Lampasas, Texas. Claiming that Merritt Horrell had tampered with Higgins steers, Pink sought the accused man in Lampasas and found him in Jerry Scott's Matador Saloon, where the feud had so violently begun four years earlier. Higgins burst through the back door and shot the unarmed Horrell to death, methodically pumping four Winchester bullets into him.

March 26, 1877, near Lampasas, Texas. Higgins and several cohorts waylaid Sam and Mart Horrell as the brothers rode into Lampasas. The ambushers caught the Horrells about 10:00 A.M. some five miles outside town. Both brothers were wounded, but they put up such a spirited resistance that the Higgins group retreated.

June 14, 1877, Lampasas, Texas. A major shootout erupted in the streets of Lampasas at about 10:00 P.M. when Higgins and three of his men took on Mart, Sam, and Tom Horrell, Bill and Tom Bowen, John Dixon, and Bill Crabtree. Bill Wren, Higgins' top aide, was seriously wounded, and Higgins' brother-in-law, Frank Mitchell, was killed, but Pink managed to slip out of town. He soon returned with reinforcements, and the shooting did not stop until 1:00 P.M., when local citizens prevailed upon the two factions to cease fire.

July, 1877, Lampasas County, Texas. Determined to finish the Horrells, Higgins armed all fourteen of his hands with Winchesters and led them to the Horrell ranch. They pinned the brothers and their crew inside the ranch house and bunkhouse, but there was a vigorous return fire. Higgins sent back to his headquarters for food and settled down to a protracted siege. But after two days his ammunition ran low and, having succeeded in wounding just two Horrell men, he ordered a retreat.

ca. 1884, near Ciudad Acuña, Mexico. Higgins had traveled to Del Rio, Texas, to pick up 125 horses he had purchased from a Mexican, but when he crossed the Rio Grande the man tried to deny the sale. Higgins shot him to death, then was chased toward the river bank to make a stand. He held off his attackers until darkness fell, then swam to Texas and safety.

October 4, 1903, Kent County, Texas. Within sight of his ranch house near Spur, Higgins encountered a man named Bill Standifer, who had clashed with Pink previously. When they were sixty yards apart, the two antagonists dismounted and began exchanging rifle fire. Higgins' horse was struck, but Pink scored with a bullet that tore through Standifer's elbow and into his heart. Standifer shifted his rifle to the crook of his good arm, started to stagger away, then fell dead.

Sources: Sinise, *Pink Higgins,* 22–43; Webb, *Texas Rangers,* 334–39; Gillett, *Six Years with the Texas Rangers,* 73–80; Sonnichsen, *I'll Die Before I'll Run,* 134–39, 142–44, 149; Douglas, *Famous Texas Feuds,* 143–46; Douglas, *Cattle Kings of Texas,* 305ff.

Hill, Tom

("Tom Chelson")

(d. March 13, 1878, Alamo Springs, New Mexico. Stock rustler.) Known in Texas as Tom Chelson, by the late 1870's Hill was in New Mexico as rustler Jesse Evans' right-hand man. In October, 1877, Evans, Hill, and two other desperadoes raided the Tunstall and Brewer ranches in Lincoln County, and subsequently the bandits were chased down, captured, and incarcerated in Lincoln. But within weeks thirty-two of their cohorts boldly galloped into town and freed them from the unlocked jail. A few months later Hill was instrumental in the death of John Tunstall, which ignited the the murderous Lincoln County War. But Hill was not around for the rest of the fighting; within two weeks he was shot and killed while trying to rob a sheep camp.

Gunfights: September, 1877, Lincoln County, New Mexico. A few days earlier Hill, Jesse Evans, Frank Baker, and a young Texan named Davis rustled some valuable stock from the ranches of Dick Brewer and John Tunstall, who was on a trip to St. Louis. Brewer and two cowboys gave chase, and the outlaws offered to return Brewer's personal mounts if they could keep an excellent pair of Tunstall's mules. Brewer refused, returned to the ranch to organize a posse, and with fifteen men resumed the chase.

After a two-day search Brewer located the rustlers secluded in a dugout and began a siege at dawn. Following a furious exchange of shots, the posse members began to growl out a determination to take the thieves in dead or alive. At that point the four rustlers filed outside with their hands up—only to be rescued from jail a few weeks later.

January, 1878, Grant County, New Mexico. Evans, Hill, and several members of the gang stole a herd of horses from a Grant County ranch. Hotly pursued, the outlaws soon were overtaken, and a vigorous shootout ensued. Hill and Evans both were wounded, the herd was recovered, and the rustlers spurred away in defeat.

February 18, 1878, near Lincoln, New Mexico. Late in the afternoon John Tunstall was intercepted on the road from his ranch to Lincoln by a large group of enemies he had made in the growing Lincoln County feud. Tunstall was accompanied by four men, who were scattered out attempting to drive a herd of horses.

The posse, which included Hill and Jesse Evans, surrounded Tunstall, and after a brief exchange of words the rancher tried to submit to their custody. But Hill had sidled to the rear of Tunstall, and he suddenly cursed and shot the rancher in the back of the head. There were other shots, and the posse galloped away, leaving both Tunstall and his horse dead in the dust. After Tunstall had fallen, Hill had dispatched his half-thoroughbred mount with a rifle.

March 13, 1878, Alamo Springs, New Mexico. A sheep driver named Wagner had encamped near Alamo Springs and had gone to find water, leaving a half-blood Cherokee employee in charge. At this point Hill and Jesse Evans crept into camp, bent upon thievery. Pulling guns on the halfblood, they proceeded to rifle the wagon and to saddle a horse and mule belonging to Wagner.

The Cherokee suddenly seized a Winchester, but Hill and Evans quickly began pumping lead at him, and he tried to flee. He was hit in the leg and fell, and the two robbers returned to their work. The Cherokee then began to crawl back toward camp, and when he reached point-blank range, he opened fire. His first slug struck Hill, who dropped dead. Evans was wounded in the wrist, and he dropped his pistol and rifle and escaped on Wagner's horse.

Sources: Keleher, *Violence in Lincoln County,* 82, 88–90, 96–97, 100–101, 247, 251, 254–66, 269–70, 273–76; Fulton, *Lincoln County War,* 84, 88, 108, 112, 118–19, 125, 147–49, 240.

Hindman, George W.

(d. April 1, 1878, Lincoln, New Mexico. Cowboy, law officer.) Hindman was a Texas cowboy who drifted into New Mexico in 1875 with a cattle herd and decided to stay. After a nonfatal gunfight with his bosses, Hindman broke away and hired on at the Lincoln County ranch of Robert Casey. Shortly thereafter Hindman encountered a huge grizzly bear, and although he shot the creature, he entered a somewhat uneven wrestling match with it, which resulted in a severe mauling and the permanent crippling of his hand and arm. A couple of years later Sheriff William Brady appointed him a deputy, and in February, 1878, he was a member of the "posse" which assassinated John Tunstall, there-

by triggering the Lincoln County War. A few weeks afterward, Hindman and Brady were gunned down in the streets of Lincoln by Tunstall sympathizers.

Gunfights: 1875, Lincoln County, New Mexico. Hindman, participating in a cattle drive from Texas, decided to quit and take a job on a spread in New Mexico. Bill Humphreys, part owner of the herd, began to berate Hindman, who angrily snapped back and went for his six-gun. The two men fired at each other, and Hindman's slug grazed Humphrey's scalp and knocked him unconscious, but Humphrey's bullet smashed the cylinder of Hindman's pistol and drove metal splinters into his hand. Hindman then sprinted away, splashing across a river and darting across a meadow to a ranch house before calming down and returning to camp.

April 1, 1878, Lincoln, New Mexico. About 9:00 A.M. on April Fool's Monday, Hindman and Sheriff Brady were walking down the middle of Lincoln's main street trailed by Billy Matthews, John Long, and George Peppin. Brady was approaching a small adobe building used as a courthouse to change the notices. Suddenly the sheriff's party was fired upon from ambush by Billy the Kid, Henry Brown, John Middleton, Fred Wait, and Jim French. Brady collapsed and died instantly, and Hindman was also knocked to the ground, writhing in agony and begging for water.

Bystander Ike Stockton brought a hatful of water from the nearby Rio Bonito, but Hindman died within moments. Matthews, less seriously wounded, had scampered for cover, and when the Kid dashed into the street to seize Brady's rifle, Matthews opened fire and drove the ambushers away, and the shooting stopped.

Sources: Keleher, *Violence in Lin-*

Hite, Robert Woodson

("Wood")

(b. Kentucky; d. January, 1882, Ray County, Missouri. Soldier, train robber.) Wood Hite was a Kentuckian who fought with the Confederacy during the Civil War, eventually becoming one of Bloody Bill Anderson's raiders. When Jesse James rebuilt his gang after the Northfield disaster in 1876, Wood and his brother Clarence, who were first cousins of the James brothers, joined up willingly. But Wood, a gangling, stoop-shouldered man with prominent, decaying front teeth, was easily recognizable, and after a few train holdups he sought refuge at his father's home in Logan County, Kentucky. Soon he shot a Negro to death and was arrested, but he promptly escaped jail and headed west. He returned to Missouri late in 1881, but shortly thereafter he was killed in a gunfight by Bob Ford.

Gunfights: 1881, Logan County, Kentucky. A local Negro, John Tabor, incurred the wrath of Hite, and Wood gunned him down as he sat on a fence. Hite's stepmother witnessed the killing and swore out a warrant, and Wood soon found himself in jail in Adairville. Wood resourcefully produced a one-hundred-dollar bill, however, and after bribing a guard he escaped and left the state.

January, 1882, Ray County, Missouri. Hite was hiding at the home of Martha Bolton, the widowed sister of Bob Ford. Dick Liddell, a convicted horse thief and one of Jesse James's train robbers, was also there. Hite and Liddell clashed over the attentions of young Mrs. Bolton, and one morning after breakfast a quarrel broke out and guns were drawn.

Liddell emptied his revolver, wounding Hite in the right arm, and Wood fired four rounds, hitting Dick in the leg. But while Wood was concentrating on Liddell, Bob Ford coolly drew his pistol and fired a bullet into Hite's head. The slug entered above his right eye and tore through near his left ear, and he pitched to the floor. He was carried upstairs unconscious, where he died within fifteen or twenty minutes. After dark Ford and his brother Cap wrapped Hite in an old horse blanket and buried him in a scooped-out hole about a mile from the house.

Sources: Horan, *Desperate Men*, 130–42; Settle, *Jesse James Was His Name*, 114–16, 140–42, 148.

Hodges, Thomas

("Tom Bell")

(b. Tennessee; d. October 4, 1856, Merced River, California. Doctor, prospector, bandit.) Reared in Rome, Tennessee, Hodges enlisted at the outbreak of the Mexican War as a medical orderly. Following the war he moved to nearby Nashville and began practicing medicine, but within a few years he was attracted to California by the gold rush. Prospecting proved unsuccessful, and he assumed the alias "Tom Bell" and became a thief. He was arrested in 1855 and sentenced to the state penitentiary on Angel Island at San Francisco, but he soon managed to escape.

Assisted by a notorious criminal named Bill Gristy, Hodges formed the Tom Bell gang and began to prey regularly upon gold rush area stagecoaches and teamsters. After killing a woman in an unsuccessful robbery attempt, however, the gang was tenaciously pursued. There were violent escapes from the clutches of justice, but Hodges was finally captured by a posse near the Merced River. He wrote letters to his mother and to Elizabeth Hood, his mistress and partner in crime, and then at 5:00 P.M. on October 4, 1856, the vigilantes strung him up to strangle to death.

Gunfights: *1856, near Nevada City, California.* A teamster had delivered a load of beer in Nevada City and had just left town with three hundred dollars. He was confronted by Hodges gang and went for his gun to defend himself. There was a sharp exchange of shots, but the outlaws gunned him down and stole the money.

August 11, 1856, near Marysville, California. Hodges and his gang had concealed themselves along Dry Creek near Marysville to rob the Comptonville stage. When the vehicle—heavily laden with gold and passengers—drew into sight, the outlaws emerged. The driver whipped his horses, the guard and passengers opened fire, and a roaring battle ensued. The stage managed to elude the gang, leaving one dead robber and several wounded ones. Three or four passengers were wounded, and the wife of a Marysville barber was killed, and an enraged demand arose for the capture of Hodges and his confederates.

September, 1856, near Auburn, California. A posse led by Placer County Sheriff Henson located Hodges, outlaw Ned Conner, and a man known as Tex at an establishment near Auburn called the Franklin House. When Bell and his friends emerged, the lawmen closed in, and a gunfight erupted. Conner was killed, but Hodges and Tex shot their way out of the trap.

Source: Drago, *Road Agents and Train Robbers,* 12–21, 219–20.

John Henry ("Doc") Holliday, the most famous dentist in the West. *(Courtesy Kansas State Historical Society, Topeka)*

Holliday, John Henry

("Doc")

(b. early 1852, Griffin, Georgia; d. November 8, 1887, Glenwood Springs, Colorado. Dentist, gambler, saloon keeper.) The son of a prosperous Southern family, Holliday studied dentistry early in the 1870's. Also during this time he contracted turberculosis, and in 1873 he went west, seeking a climate which might postpone his imminent demise. His life was prolonged by fifteen years, during which time he acquired an exaggerated reputation as a beady-eyed killer. He occasionally practiced dentistry, but more frequently engaged in gam-

bling, usually as a house gambler. He appeared in numerous Western boom towns during their heydays, including Dallas and Fort Griffin in Texas; Cheyenne in Wyoming; Dodge City in Kansas; Denver, Leadville, and Pueblo in Colorado; and Tucson and Tombstone in Arizona.

In Tombstone, Holliday took part in the legendary gunfight at the O.K. Corral with his friend Wyatt Earp. Another famous friendship was with his mistress, the prostitute Big Nosed Kate Elder. (Frequently referred to as Kate Fisher, she was actually Katherine Elder from Davenport, Iowa. There is some possibility that she and Doc were married in St. Louis; they separated in 1881 after Kate unkindly implicated him in the killing of Budd Philpot during a notorious stage holdup.) As tuberculosis and alcoholism continually eroded his health, Holliday traveled to the Colorado health resort at Glenwood Springs, where he died at the age of thirty-five.

Gunfights: *January 1, 1875, Dallas, Texas.* Holliday exchanged shots with a Dallas saloon keeper named Austin. Neither party was wounded.

July 19, 1879, Las Vegas, New Mexico. Holliday ran a Las Vegas saloon in partnership with John Joshua Webb, formerly a peace officer in Dodge City. One of their saloon girls was the mistress of a former army scout named Mike Gordon. Gordon tried to persuade the woman to quit her job, and when she refused, he determined to shoot up the place. Standing in the street, Gordon fired two shots at the building, whereupon Doc stepped outside and felled him with one shot. Gordon died the next day.

June, 1880, Las Vegas, New Mexico. Newly returned to town, Holliday burst into the saloon where Charley White tended bar. A few months earlier Holliday had bullied White into leaving Dodge City, and while passing through Las Vegas, Doc pursued his quarrel with the bartender. After a rapid exchange of shots White was struck and collapsed behind the bar. Holliday left, assuming White to be dead, but White's wound proved to be superficial, and he recovered swiftly and completely.

April, 1881, Tombstone, Arizona. Mike Joyce, a local saloon owner, openly accused Holliday of participating in a recent stagecoach robbery. Enraged, Holliday charged into the saloon and opened fire, wounding Joyce in the hand. One of Joyce's bartenders, an innocent bystander, was struck in the foot.

October 26, 1881, Tombstone, Arizona. The previous day Holliday, ally and friend of the Earps and backed by Morgan, Virgil, and Wyatt, cursed an unarmed Ike Clanton in a Tombstone saloon. The next afternoon Holliday, technically a deputy city marshal, stood with the Earps against the Clanton faction at the O.K. Corral. As the firing commenced, Doc pulled a shotgun from under his long overcoat and turned on Tom McLaury.

McLaury stood behind his horse, unarmed except for a rifle in the saddle scabbard. Frank McLaury, already wounded by Wyatt, snapped off a wild shot which grazed Doc in the side. Holliday fired at Tom McLaury, who was hit by twelve buckshot under his right arm. Tom died on the spot, and Holliday then drew his pistol and fired at Ike Clanton, who fled unharmed into a nearby doorway.

March 20, 1882, Tucson, Arizona. Two days earlier Morgan Earp had been murdered in Tombstone, allegedly by a party of five whose number included Frank Stilwell. Wyatt and Warren Earp, Holliday, Sherman McMasters, and Turkey Creek Jack Johnson set out in pursuit of the killers. In less than forty-eight hours they found Stilwell at the train station in Tucson. After a short chase Stilwell suffered more than thirty shotgun and bullet wounds inflicted by Doc and the other four members of the avenging posse.

March 22, 1882, Tombstone, Arizona. The same vengeful group returned to Tombstone and two days later located Florentino Cruz, another suspect in Morgan's murder, in a nearby wood camp. Holliday and the others chased him down and executed him with "ten or twelve shots."

August 19, 1884, Leadville, Colorado. Down on his luck, Doc had borrowed five dollars from a Leadville bartender named Billy Allen. Allen threatened to "lick" Holliday if the five dollars was not promptly repaid, and he followed Doc into a saloon with the purpose of fighting him. Holliday, fifty pounds lighter, whipped out a pistol and snapped off a shot. Allen turned to run, but stumbled and fell. Holliday pumped a bullet into Allen's right arm, and Allen scrambled outside. Doc was taken into custody, tried, and acquitted.

Sources: Jahns, *Frontier World of Doc Holliday;* Myers, *Doc Holliday;* Schoenberger, *Gunfighters,* 24, 32, 33, 42–49, 51–54, 56, 93–105, 136, 187, 188, 191, 192; Masterson, *Famous Gunfighters,* 35–42.

Hollister, Cassius M.

("Cash")

(b. December 7, 1845, Cleveland, Ohio; d. October 18, 1884, Hunnewell, Kan-

sas. Hotel clerk, city mayor, law officer.) Cash Hollister was born near Cleveland, Ohio, and lived there until he was thirty-one years old. In 1877 he moved to Caldwell, Kansas, and the next year he married and moved to Wichita. Late in 1878 he returned to Caldwell and began clerking in the St. James Hotel. The next year mayor N. J. Dixon died suddenly, and Hollister won the special election to replace him.

While serving as mayor, Hollister was arrested and fined for assaulting Frank Hunt, and in subsequent years he was intermittently in trouble for fighting. Hollister did not choose to run for re-election in 1880, but three years later he was appointed a deputy U.S. marshal. During the next several months he served as marshal and deputy marshal of Caldwell and as a deputy sheriff of Sumner County, and he was particularly active in chasing down horse thieves. During the course of his duties he was involved in various shooting scrapes, and he met his death in such an incident in 1884.

Gunfights: April 11, 1883, Hunnewell, Kansas. On a quiet Sunday, Deputy U.S. Marshal Hollister was approached by Texan J. H. Herron, who requested help in tracking down a band of horse thieves. Encountering the suspects in a camp near Hunnewell, Hollister discovered that the gang consisted of several members of a family named Ross, and he decided to seek help with the arrest.

At dawn on Wednesday Hollister surrounded the Ross encampment with a party of area law officers: Henry Brown and Ben Wheeler, marshal and deputy marshal, respectively, of Caldwell; the city marshal of Hunnewell, a man named Jackson; and Sumner County Deputy Sheriff Wes Thralls. The lawmen ordered the thieves to surrender, but the

Ross group defiantly opened fire with rifles. The carefully positioned lawmen began pouring a heavy fusillade into the Ross camp, but the rustlers held out for half an hour. Finally, with one brother dead and another fearfully shot up, the Rosses stopped firing and submitted to arrest.

November 21, 1883, Caldwell, Kansas. On Tuesday, November 20, young Chet Van Meter beat his wife and teen-aged brother-in-law, fired at neighbors, and threatened to kill them. Hollister was authorized to arrest Van Meter and, accompanied by Ben Wheeler, drove in a wagon to the farm of Van Meter's father, located a few miles out of town. As the two lawmen approached the farmhouse, they discovered Van Meter outside, a Winchester at the ready. The officers jumped out of the wagon, and Wheeler ordered Van Meter to throw up his hands. Instead, Van Meter snapped off a shot at Hollister, who instantly fired a barrel of his shotgun. Wheeler also pumped a bullet at Van Meter, but even though he was wounded, the fugitive again tried to work the Winchester.

Hollister and Wheeler each fired a second round, and Van Meter fell dead in his tracks. His bullet-riddled carcass showed five wounds in the chest, a gaping hole in his right side, a slug in the belly, and one wound in each hand—and even his rifle had been struck by buckshot from Hollister's scattergun. Van Meter was dumped in the wagon, and the lawmen drove back to Caldwell.

October 18, 1884, Hunnewell, Kansas. Bob Cross was the son of a Texas minister, but he had repeatedly run afoul of the law while in Kansas. Although he had married one year earlier and had already fathered a child, Cross ran off with the young daughter of a Sumner

County farmer, then deserted the girl and returned to his wife on a farm a couple of miles from Hunnewell. The girl went back to her father, Joshua Hannum, who angrily swore out a warrant for Cross's arrest.

Deputy Sheriff Hollister received the warrant on Friday night, November 20, and enlisted the aid of Hannum, George Davis, and the marshal of Hunnewell, an officer named Reilly. Hollister and his posse reached the farm near Hunnewell about 3:00 A.M. While Hannum held the team, the other three men piled out of their wagon and approached the house. The lawmen ordered Cross to come outside, but his wife protested that he was not there.

The door was kicked open, and Mrs. Cross and her sister came out, swearing that Cross was not present and offering to let the posse search inside. But when the lawmen demanded that a lamp be lit, the women quickly reentered the house and shut the door. Just as quickly the officers kicked the door in again, and suddenly two shots were fired from inside.

The lawmen scampered for cover and warned that they were about to burn the house. The women again filed out, but Cross did not show, and Davis began to gather hay for a fire. Just as he was about to light the hay, another shot came from the house, and Davis dove behind a woodpile.

When the posse began to move in again, Davis discovered that Hollister was dead. Davis told Reilly, who ordered him to guard the window. Instead, Davis carried Hollister to the wagon, but the team shied and ran away. Finally the team was caught, and Hollister's corpse was loaded into the wagon bed. Meanwhile, Mrs. Cross went into the house and quickly returned, shielding her husband. Reilly leveled his gun, but Mrs. Cross leaped at him and pressed the muzzle to her breast. Reilly wrenched the gun free, but Mrs. Cross grabbed it again and Cross escaped into the night. The lawmen returned to town with Hollister's body, and Cross was captured the next day.

Source: Miller and Snell, *Great Gunfighters of the Kansas Cowtowns*, 141–51.

Hoover, Tuck

(d. ca. 1894, Alleyton, Texas. Rancher.) Hoover was a South Texas rancher who was in and out of trouble during his career. He was shot to death about 1894, following a killing in which he had been involved.

Gunfights: 1878, near Alleyton, Texas. Hoover was with Dallas Stoudenmire and several other friends who encountered a party of rival cattlemen near Alleyton. The opposing party, led by the Sparks brothers of Eagle Lake, Texas, were pressing a claim to the disputed ownership of a herd of cattle, and the quarrel ended with a flurry of gunfire. Two members of the Sparks faction—Benton Duke and his son—were shot to death, and one of the Sparks brothers was wounded.

ca. 1894, Alleyton, Texas. Hoover fell into an argument with an Alleyton saloon owner named Burtshell. The two men resorted to gunplay, and when the shooting ended, Burtshell lay mortally wounded.

ca. 1894, Alleyton, Texas. Hoover was soon released on bond, but shortly after being freed he was accosted in the streets of Alleyton by young Jim Coleman. Coleman, who was something of a local hard case, promptly produced a gun and shot Hoover to death.

Sources: Metz, *Dallas Stoudenmire,* 30; Sonnichsen, *I'll Die Before I'll Run,* 308–15.

Tom Horn, looking more like a prosperous merchant than a hired killer. *(Courtesy Arizona Historical Society)*

Horn, Tom

(b. November 21, 1860, Memphis, Missouri; d. November 20, 1903, Cheyenne, Wyoming. Cowboy, railroad employee, stagecoach driver, teamster, army scout, law officer, miner, Pinkerton detective, range detective, soldier, hired killer.) Horn was born and reared on a Missouri farm. He was a habitual truant from school, and after a whipping by his father the rebellious fourteen-year-old ran away to the West. He worked for the railroad in Newton, Kansas, and then was hired to drive a wagon to Santa Fe. Soon he was employed as a stagecoach driver, but by 1876 he had signed on with the army as a scout, and in

1885 he succeeded the famed Al Sieber as civilian chief of scouts. Horn was an important figure in the campaign which resulted in the final capture of Geronimo—although he did not play as significant a role as he later claimed. He hired out his gun in Arizona's Pleasant Valley War in 1887, then secured an appointment as a deputy sheriff of Yavapai County. Occasionally he worked a gold claim near Tombstone.

In 1890 Horn joined the Pinkerton Detective Agency in Denver, and in 1892 he enlisted as a range detective with the Wyoming Cattle Growers' Association. He helped recruit gunmen for the association, but he apparently missed the resultant Johnson County War. In 1894 Horn was hired by the Swan Land and Cattle Company—technically as a horsebreaker, but reputedly as a killer of rustlers and bothersome homesteaders. Once a member of the company turned in the name of a troublemaker, Horn supposedly would track him and methodically learn his habits. Then he would set an ambush and kill the offending individual with a high-powered rifle. He would carefully collect shell casings and other possible evidence, set two stones under the head of his victim as a sort of trademark, then leave the scene to collect his six-hundred-dollar fee.

Normally a reserved man, the tall, muscular Horn would periodically travel to Denver or Cheyenne to blow off steam with a drunken spree. When the Spanish-American War broke out, he rejoined the army and went to Cuba as the master of a pack train. When the war ended, he returned to Wyoming and to his trade as a hired killer.

Horn was employed in 1901 by John Coble, who owned a large ranch north of Laramie near Iron Mountain. Horn became friendly with the local schoolmarm, Glendolene Kimmel, whose family was conducting a feud with a neighboring homesteader named Kels P. Nickell. Coble also found Nickell to be a troublemaker, and Horn determined to kill the man. He mistakenly shot Nickell's fourteen-year-old son, however, and the subsequent furor put lawman Joe LeFors on his trail.

Tracking Horn to Denver, LeFors got him drunk and extracted what amounted to a confession. Taken down by eavesdropping deputies, this statement resulted in Horn's arrest and conviction for murder. Awaiting execution in a Cheyenne jail, Horn broke out, but was promptly taken back into custody by a local patrolman. He spent the months of his confinement writing an understandably one-sided autobiography. Despite the tearful pleas of Miss Kimmel and the legal efforts of the big cattlemen and their lawyers, Horn was hanged in November, 1903.

Gunfights: *July 8, 1900, Cold Springs Mountain, Routt County, Colorado.* The death of Matt Rash was typical of the shootings that Horn was involved in for a decade. Calling himself James Hicks, Horn quietly drifted into Rash's neighborhood and began scouting the rustler's activities. Early one summer afternoon Rash finished a meal of steak and potatoes and then stepped outside his cabin. Horn began firing a rifle from concealment. Rash was hit three times, and a fourth bullet killed his sorrel mare.

While Horn raced off to establish an alibi in faraway Denver, Rash stumbled inside and collapsed on his cot. He dipped a finger in his own blood and tried to write on an envelope, but he died before he could make any legible markings.

October 3, 1900, Routt County, Colorado. "Nigger Isom" Dart, a black cowboy, was suspected of rustling by the cattlemen who employed Tom Horn. Still posing as James Hicks, Horn armed himself with a .30-.30 rifle and established a sniper's position two hundred yards from Dart's cabin. After eating breakfast, Dart and five friends emerged from the cabin and walked toward the corral. Horn fired twice, and Dart dropped dead with a head wound.

Dart's companions fled inside, where they cowered all day before sneaking away after dark. Two days later a heavily armed party rode up and buried Dart's body.

July 18, 1901, Powder River Road near Cheyenne, Wyoming. Horn had checked out his next intended victim, homesteader Kels P. Nickell, and had decided to ambush him as he drove a hay wagon from his farm into Cheyenne. At midmorning he stationed himself on a ridge overlooking the Powder River Road and Nickell's homestead.

About 3:30 P.M. Nickell's fourteen-year-old son, Willie, hitched a team of horses to the hay wagon, threw a rifle into the vehicle, and drove to the pasture gate. Wearing his father's hat and coat, the tall youth resembled the senior Nickell from three hundred yards' distance. When the boy jumped down to open the gate, Horn drew a bead and shot him in the head. Young Nickell managed to rise to his feet, but as he staggered toward the wagon, Horn pumped another bullet into him. Horn then mounted and rode away as the Nickells ran frantically toward their dying son.

August 9, 1903, Cheyenne, Wyoming. About 8:40 A.M., Horn and fellow inmate Jim McCloud jumped Deputy Sheriff Richard Proctor. Proctor fired four shots, slightly wounding McCloud, but was overpowered. The two escapees made their way outside, where McCloud galloped away on the only horse in the jail corral. He was caught and subdued after a brief chase. Horn, fleeing on foot, was charged by a citizen named O. M. Eldrich. Eldrich fired several pistol shots, one of which grazed Horn in the head. Horn was unfamiliar with his revolver and could not release the safety, and Eldrich wrestled him to the ground. A swarm of officers beat him into submission and dragged him back to jail.

Sources: Paine, *Tom Horn;* Brown, *Trail Driving Days,* 232–35, 250–51; Faulk, *Geronimo Campaign,* 75–82, 85, 109, 117, 134, 198–202, 204; Horn, *Life of Tom Horn;* Thrapp, *Al Sieber,* 35, 36, 80, 221, 227, 229–30, 240, 251–52, 255, 263, 268, 271, 313, 315, 328, 381; Coolidge, *Fighting Men of the West,* 87–110; Raine, *Famous Sheriffs and Western Outlaws,* 80–91; Horan, *Authentic Wild West,* 221–54; Burroughs, *Where the West Stayed Young,* 204–207, 210, 214, 228.

Horner, Joe

("Frank Canton")

(b. 1849, Virginia; d. 1927, Oklahoma. Cowboy, outlaw, rancher, law officer, packing plant superintendent, prospector, soldier, bank robber.) Born fifteen miles from Richmond, Joe Horner moved to North Texas with his family while still a child. By the late 1860's Horner was herding cattle up to the Kansas railheads for Burk Burnett. Horner dropped out of sight from 1871 until 1878, engaging in a variety of illegal activities and becoming a fugitive from justice; in 1877 he was jailed for robbing a bank in Comanche, Texas,

Joe Horner (Adjutant General "Frank Canton," middle row, fourth from left) of the Oklahoma National Guard on a junket to the Philippines in the early 1900's. *(Courtesy Western History Collections, University of Oklahoma Library)*

although he managed to escape long incarceration. In 1878 he led a herd of cattle to Ogallala, Nebraska, and immediately thereafter he accepted the position of field inspector for the Wyoming Stock Growers' Association.

From that point on, Horner (who had now renamed himself "Frank Canton") sold his gun—technically, at least— only to the side of the law and order. In 1880 he stocked a ranch near Buffalo, Wyoming, and two years later he was elected sheriff of Johnson County.

During this period Canton was highly active in curtailing the rustlers of the area. In 1885 he married, eventually becoming the father of two daughters, although only one lived to maturity. He retired as sheriff in 1886, soon accepting another job with the Wyoming Stock Growers' Association along with a commission as a deputy U.S. marshal. He was a major figure on the side of the cattle barons in the notorious Johnson County War, but in 1893 he left the country to become superintendent of the Nebraska City Packing Company.

By the next year Canton had restlessly moved to Oklahoma Territory, where he again became a deputy U.S. marshal under Judge Isaac Parker and under-sheriff of Pawnee County. He was instrumental in subduing the wild Oklahoma outlaw gangs, but after three years he was again ready to move. In 1897 he left his wife and daughter in Buffalo and accepted an appointment as a deputy U.S. marshal in Alaska, thus embarking upon the most adventurous period of his life. He was snowed in for a winter, went prospecting on one occasion with Rex Beach, curtailed the lawless element in roaring Dawson, and otherwise enjoyed an exciting two years. But in 1899 he went snow blind and was forced to return to the states. He soon recovered, and once again pinned on a badge in Oklahoma.

Canton was a deputy sheriff in Comanche County, and he also was employed with the Cattle Raisers' Association of Texas to track down rustlers who sought refuge in Oklahoma. In 1907 he was appointed adjutant general of the Oklahoma National Guard, and over the next decade General Canton was successful in building up that organization.

Gunfights: *October 10, 1874, Jacksboro, Texas.* In a Jacksboro saloon, Joe Horner fell into a quarrel with Negro troopers from nearby Fort Richardson. Shooting erupted, and Horner killed one soldier and wounded another.

November 1, 1891, Powder River, Wyoming. Frank Canton, Tom Smith, Joe Elliott, and Fred Coates were assigned by the Wyoming Stock Grower's Association to apprehend Nathan Champion, a leader of the Johnson County cattle "rustlers." Champion was known to be living with Ross Gilbertson on the Powder River, and one night the four association gunmen quietly approached the cabin where the two were holed up. Just before sunrise one of the range detectives dropped his pistol and it discharged. Canton and his three cohorts then rushed the cabin and burst inside. Shots were fired at Champion, but he gamely leaped out of his bunk with a blazing six-gun. One of the range detectives was nicked in the side, and another was hit in the arm. The four gunmen then scattered as fast as they could run, dropping or abandoning articles of clothing, horses, and a rifle that Smith had recently given to Canton.

April 9, 1892, KC Ranch, Wyoming. As the feud intensified between the cattle barons and the small operators of Johnson County, Canton helped recruit gunfighters for the association. Early in April fifty or more association gunmen, under the leadership of Major Frank Wolcott and with Canton and Tom Smith as chief lieutenants, moved toward the town of Buffalo, which was the center of opposition to the association. Along the way they were told that Champion and Nick Ray, both of whom were prominent "rustler" leaders, had leased the nearby KC Ranch. Wolcott's "Regulators" promptly detoured and surrounded the ranch buildings just before dawn.

At sunrise Ben Jones, an old trapper who, along with his partner, had spent the night at the KC Ranch, emerged from the cabin to get a bucket of water. Canton quietly arrested Jones, and when his partner came outside half an hour later, he, too, was captured. Then Ray emerged, and he was shot down by a volley of rifle fire. Champion came to the door and covered the dying Ray as he crawled back to the cabin. The next several hours were spent in an exchange of shots between Champion and his besiegers.

At about 3:00 P.M. Jack Flagg, another man wanted by the Regulators, passed by the KC Ranch and was fired upon by the gunmen. He escaped to spread the alarm, but abandoned a spring wagon. The Regulators used it as a fire wagon and set Champion's cabin ablaze. Champion ran outside shooting and was gunned down, but the delay he had caused ultimately resulted in the failure and arrest of the Regulators.

1893, Pawnee, Oklahoma. Canton and fellow Deputy Sheriff George Hanner had received a telegram from a sheriff in Kansas requesting that they apprehend a murderer who was in Pawnee. The two lawmen found the fugitive in a livery stable owned by a hard case named Lon McCool. The officers arrested and handcuffed the murderer, and Canton sat on a keg and began to read the telegram to the prisoner.

Suddenly McCool entered the room and began to quarrel violently with Canton. McCool then slapped Canton and reached toward a hip pocket. Canton leaped back, kicked the keg at McCool, and shot his aggressor with a .41 derringer. McCool was hit above the left eye, and Canton thought he was dead, but a doctor later discovered him to be alive. McCool apparently recovered, but a few weeks afterward he got into a fist fight and died. Canton then threw away his derringer.

Winter, 1895, Pawnee County, Oklahoma. A pair of thieves named Bill and John Shelley had broken jail in Pawnee and holed up with a woman in their cabin located in the eastern part of the county on the Arkansas River. Sheriff Frank Lake led a posse, which included Canton, through a blinding snowstorm, and two hours before a winter dawn the officers reached the cabin. The posse surrounded the building, and Canton

positioned himself a few feet from the south door, directly opposite deputy John McCann.

At daybreak Lake ordered the Shelley brothers to surrender, but they barricaded the doors with furniture and shouted their defiance. Canton persuaded them to let the woman out, and as she passed through the door one of the brothers shot McCann. McCann staggered, but the bullet had glanced off a pistol in a shoulder holster. McCann and Canton then emptied their rifles into the door, and John Shelley was shot through the thighs. The brothers fired back, however, wounding a Dr. Bland in the arm. The posse then drew back to about twenty-five yards and systematically peppered the cabin.

More than eight hundred rounds were fired during the day, but the Shelleys continued to resist. About 3:00 P.M. Canton left the posse, secured a hay wagon from a farm a mile away, and returned to convert it into the type of fire wagon that had spelled Nate Champion's doom. When the blazing vehicle was pushed against the building, the outlaws surrendered and were taken to Fort Smith, where they unsuccessfully tried to help Cherokee Bill escape from jail.

November 6, 1896, Pawnee, Oklahoma. Fugitive Bill Dunn had long held a grudge against Canton and angrily confronted the lawman on a boardwalk near the Pawnee courthouse. "Frank Canton, goddamn you," snarled Dunn, "I've got it in for you." Canton had both hands inside his trousers pockets, but he instantly went for the .45 stuck in his waistband. Before Dunn could draw, the alert Canton whipped out his gun and pumped a slug into the wanted man's forehead. Dunn fell on his back, and his unfired gun dropped from his hand, but the dying man's trigger finger twitched convulsively for several moments.

Sources: Canton, *Autobiography of Frank M. Canton;* Mercer, *Banditti of the Plains;* Brown, *Trail Driving Days,* 226–31, 242–50; Smith, *War on the Powder River,* 70, 98, 112, 119–20, 145–47, 159–60, 162, 165, 167–78, 188, 194, 197, 201–202, 261, 263.

Horrell, Benjamin

(b. Texas; d. December 1, 1873, Lincoln, New Mexico. Cowboy, gunman.) Ben Horrell worked for his older brothers on their cattle spreads in Lampasas County, Texas. He was present during the early stages of the notorious Horrell-Higgins feud, then left with his brothers to establish a ranch on the Ruidoso River in Lincoln County, New Mexico. Within a short time he was killed in a gunfight with a local peace officer, and his brothers responded with vicious acts of retribution which sparked another feud. It is worthy of note that another brother, John, had drifted to New Mexico in earlier years and had been killed in Las Cruces.

Gunfights: March, 1873, Georgetown, Texas. Mart Horrell and Jerry Scott had been jailed in Georgetown following a minor massacre in Scott's Lampasas saloon. Mart had been wounded but was nursed in jail by his wife, who sent word to the Horrells when he had recovered. After dark a large Horrell party rode into Georgetown and assaulted the jail. There was a fierce fight with local citizens, but the escape attempt proved successful.

December 1, 1873, Lincoln, New Mexico. Ben and a few friends were in the process of drunkenly shooting up tiny

Lincoln. The disturbance attracted Constable Juan Martinez, who tried to arrest Horrell. There was an exchange of shots, and Ben pitched into the street, fatally wounded. Martinez also was killed, as were Dave Warner and Jack Gylam, two of Ben's companions. It is possible that Horrell and Gylam were killed after having surrendered. A thief took Horrell's gold ring by chopping off his finger.

Sources: Gillett, *Six Years with the Texas Rangers,* 9, 73–80; Rasch, "The Horrell War," *NMHR,* XXX (July, 1956); Askins, *Texans, Guns & History,* 151–60; Webb, *Texas Rangers,* 334–39; Keleher, *Violence in Lincoln County,* 13–15; Coe, *Frontier Fighter,* 213–14; Sonnichsen, *I'll Die Before I'll Run,* 126, 130–31.

Horrell, Martin

(b. Texas; d. December 15, 1878, Meridian, Texas. Soldier, cowboy, gunman.) Mart Horrell served with his brothers Sam and Tom in Terry's Texas Ranger brigade during the Civil War. After the war he helped his brothers build a ranching enterprise in Lampasas County, Texas, where he soon became a willing participant in the Horrell-Higgins feud. He then moved with his family and violence-prone siblings to Lincoln County, New Mexico. While there, the Horrells briefly terrorized the countryside, then were run out of New Mexico by vigilantes.

After returning to Texas with his brothers, Mart fought until the feud with Pink Higgins subsided in 1877, only to meet death at the hands of a lynch mob the following year. Mart, Tom, Bill Crabtree, John Dixon, and Tom Bowen were suspected of robbing and murdering a Bosque County merchant, and the two Horrells were jailed in Meridian. A group of irate citizens broke into the jail and shot both men to death.

Gunfights: March 19, 1873, Lampasas, Texas. Clint Barkley, Merritt's brother-in-law and an accused murderer who was using the alias Bill Bowen, had hired on with the Horrells. The Texas State Police, a detested force organized by carpetbag Governor E. J. Davis, sent Captain Tom Williams and three officers to Lampasas to arrest Barkley. Tom, Sam, and Mart, along with five or six of their hands, belligerently went with Barkley into town, where they swaggered into Jerry Scott's Matador Saloon and readied their weapons.

About dusk Williams and his policemen burst through the swinging doors, and a vicious shootout ensued. Mart and his brother Tom were wounded, and Williams and two of his men were killed. Mart, badly hurt, was carried to his mother's home nearby, and the other brothers disappeared in the hills. Mart and Jerry Scott were soon arrested and jailed in Georgetown, where Mart's wife came to nurse him. As soon as he began to recover, the Horrells arrived and freed both prisoners by force.

December 20, 1873, Lincoln, New Mexico. Having recently moved to the Lincoln area, the aggressive Horrells were enraged when Ben was killed by a constable. Local authorities refused to press the matter, and the brothers promptly took things into their own hands by raiding a Mexican wedding dance at a private home in Lincoln. At midnight Mart, Sam, Tom, and two accomplices rode up to the house and began firing through the windows and doors. Four Mexicans, Isidro Patrón, Isidro Padilla, Dario Balazár, and José Candelaria, were killed, and two were wounded, and rewards up to five hun-

dred dollars were posted for the Horrells.

January, 1874, Lincoln County, New Mexico. About a month after the attack on the dance, Lincoln County Sheriff Alex Mills led a posse of sixty Mexicans in surrounding the Horrell party in an adobe house on the Ruidoso River. After an all-day fight which produced no casualties, Mills and his followers withdrew.

March 26, 1877, near Lampasas, Texas. Having returned to Texas to settle on a ranch on Sulphur Creek near Lampasas, Tom Horrell determined to clear himself of past charges. On the morning of March 26, Tom, accompanied by Mart, was riding into Lampasas for a court appearance. About five miles outside town the Horrells were fired upon and wounded. Tom was thrown to the ground, and Mart jumped out of the saddle and dispersed the ambushers with a one-man charge. Mart then carried his brother to the nearby home of a Mr. Timmins and galloped into Lampasas for help.

June, 1877, Lampasas County, Texas. Members of the Horrell faction determined to raid a line camp owned by Pink Higgins, who presumably had conducted the ambush on Mart and Tom. They were discovered by two Higgins cowpunchers who emerged from the line shack at dawn. The Higgins men were instantly cut down by gunfire, and the Horrell party fled.

June 14, 1877, Lampasas, Texas. The two warring groups encountered each other on the square in Lampasas, and gunplay immediately followed. Higgins' group suffered two casualties—brother-in-law Frank Mitchell, dead when he fell, and a seriously wounded Bill Wren—but after three hours townspeople stopped the fight before further damage could be done.

July, 1877, Lampasas County, Texas. The Horrell ranch, ten miles outside Lampasas, was hit by Pink Higgins and fourteen cowboy-gunmen in a reprisal raid. Mart, his brothers, and the Horrell cowhands were pinned inside the ranch house and bunkhouse by rifle fire. Although two Horrell men were wounded, there was a spirited return of shots, and after two days the Higgins party retired.

July 25, 1877, Lampasas County, Texas. It was the Horrells' turn to retaliate, and a short time later they caught Carson Graham, a Higgins cowhand, in the open north of Lampasas. Graham was riding into town to purchase supplies, and the Horrell group gunned him down.

Sources: Sinise, *Pink Higgins,* 30–40; Webb, *Texas Rangers,* 334–39; Keleher, *Violence in Lincoln County,* 13–15; Gillett, *Six Years with the Texas Rangers,* 73–80; Rasch, "The Horrell War," *NMHR;* Coe, *Frontier Fighter,* 213–14; Sonnichsen, *I'll Die Before I'll Run,* 126–37, 141, 145–49; Fulton, *Lincoln County War,* 21–24.

Horrell, Merritt

(b. Texas; d. January 22, 1877, Lampasas, Texas. Cowboy, gunman.) A member of the violent Horrell clan of Texans, Merritt was present in Lampasas when the Horrell-Higgins feud broke out in 1873. He moved with his brothers to Lincoln County, New Mexico, and there joined with them in further shooting scrapes. The surviving brothers (Ben and John had been killed at different times in New Mexico) returned to Lampasas, and the feud quickly resumed. In 1877 Merritt was shot to death by Pink Higgins, leader of the opposing faction, in a Lampasas saloon.

Gunfights: March, 1873, Georgetown, Texas. Merritt accompanied his brothers when they sallied into Georgetown to break Mart Horrell and Jerry Scott out of the local jail. Citizens put up a stiff fight, but Merritt's brother-in-law, Bill Bowen, shattered the door with a sledgehammer. The Horrells drove the townspeople back with rifle fire, wounding lawyer A. S. Fisher and spurring out of town with the two fugitives.

January 22, 1877, Lampasas, Texas. On a cold Monday, Merritt, recently accused by Pink Higgins of tampering with his herd, was warming himself in Jerry Scott's saloon, where the feud had broken out four years earlier. Higgins slipped through the back door and shot Merritt with a Winchester. Hit in the body, Merritt fell, got to his feet, and leaned on the shoulder of a man named Ervin. Higgins then shot him again, and once more he fell down. Higgins pumped two more bullets into him, and he died within moments.

Sources: Rasch, "The Horrell War," *NMHR;* Gillett, *Six Years with the Texas Rangers,* 73–80; Webb, *Texas Rangers,* 334–39; Keleher, *Violence in Lincoln County,* 13–15; Sinise, *Pink Higgins,* 30–40; Sonnichsen, *I'll Die Before I'll Run,* 126, 133–36.

Horrell, Samuel W.

(b. Texas. Soldier, farmer, rancher.) Named after his father, Sam Horrell was one of the quarrelsome group of

brothers who fought together through the Civil War and through a variety of later conflicts. Following the war, John Horrell became the first of his clan to meet death in a shooting scrape, being gunned down in Las Cruces, New Mexico. In 1873 the remaining five brothers became embroiled in the Horrell-Higgins feud in Lampasas, Texas. Sam helped kill three state policemen in the initial battle, then temporarily left the country with his brothers and their families.

The Horrells tried to establish another cattle spread in Lincoln County, New Mexico, but almost immediately they became immersed in further violence. Ben Horrell was killed, and after his brothers took revenge they were chased back to Texas. They returned to a ranch ten miles southeast of Lampasas, and the feud resumed, climaxing after several gunfights in 1877. Sam was the only brother to survive the violence, and in 1880 he left Lampasas to make his life in New Mexico, peaceably rearing his two daughters and living a quiet existence.

Gunfights: *March 19, 1873, Lampasas, Texas.* The Texas State Police, instrument of a hated carpetbag government, came to Lampasas hunting Clint Barkley, an accused murderer who had hired on with the Horrells under an alias. The Horrells insisted upon defending their employee (Barkley was also Merritt's brother-in-law), and they led the wanted man and several cowboys into town. Bristling with pistols and Winchesters, the eight or ten members of the Horrell party swaggered into Jerry Scott's saloon and began drinking.

Early in the evening Police Captain Tom Williams, son-in-law of area rancher Pink Higgins, and three officers entered the saloon. There was an immediate outburst of gunfire, and Williams and two of his men were riddled with bullets. Before they went down, however, they shot Mart Horrell in the neck and drilled a hole through Tom's wrist.

March, 1873, Georgetown, Texas. Mart and Jerry Scott had been jailed in Georgetown, and the Horrells audaciously rode into town to effect an escape. Under fire from local citizens, Clint Barkley smashed the door with a sledgehammer, and the Horrell group swarmed inside. They seriously wounded A. S. Fisher and drove the rest of their attackers away, then dashed out of town with Mart and Scott.

December 20, 1873, Lincoln County, New Mexico. In revenge for the death of Ben Horrell at the hands of a Lincoln peace officer, Sam, Tom, and Mart, accompanied by E. Scott and Zachariah Compton, raided a house in Lincoln. A Mexican wedding dance was under way, and at midnight the five Anglos rode up to the house and began pouring rifle and pistol fire through the windows and doors. Six Mexicans were wounded—four fatally—and the Horrell party sped away into the night.

June, 1877, Lampasas County, Texas. As the feud was renewed, the Horrell brothers led a raid on a Higgins line camp. Under cover of darkness they let themselves into the stock corrals, but were discovered there when two cowboys came out of the line cabin to prepare an early meal. The Horrells poured a hail of fire into the Higgins men, then fled hastily. Pink Higgins arrived later in the day to discover one employee dead and the other wounded.

June 14, 1877, Lampasas, Texas. Sam, Mart, Tom, and four of their men encountered Pink Higgins, Bill Wren, and several of their gunhands in the Lampasas town square. Within moments shots were being exchanged, and Wren went down, seriously wounded. Also hit was Frank Mitchell, Higgins' brother-in-law, who died from his wound.

July, 1877, Lampasas County, Texas. Higgins soon led all fourteen of his surviving cowboys against the Horrell ranch. For two days his party poured rifle fire into the ranch buildings, but they only succeeded in wounding two men, and there was a spirited resistance. At the end of forty-eight hours, Higgins, running low on cartridges, called a retreat.

July 25, 1877, Lampasas County, Texas. The Horrells immediately went on the prowl for a means of reprisal. In the northern part of the county they found Higgins cowboy Carson Graham traveling into Lampasas for ranch supplies. Without hesitation the Horrells shot Graham to death, then outlined their brand in the dust beside the corpse. Soon afterward Texas Rangers came to the area and arrested all members of the Horrell faction.

Sources: Sinise, *Pink Higgins,* 30–40; Webb, *Texas Rangers,* 334–39; Gillett, *Six Years with the Texas Rangers,* 73–80; Keleher, *Violence in Lincoln County,* 13–15; Rasch, "The Horrell War," *NMHR;* Sonnichsen, *I'll Die Before I'll Run,* 126, 149; Haley, *Jeff Milton,* 24–26.

Horrell, Thomas W.

(b. Texas; d. December 15, 1878, Meridian, Texas. Soldier, rancher.) After the Civil War, Tom Horrell, a veteran of the Confederate army, established a ranch near Lampasas, Texas. Within a few years Horrell, aided by his four brothers, had built the ranch to the point that it was eclipsed in the area only by the nearby spread of Pink Higgins. In a joint drive to Abilene in 1872, Higgins and Tom Horrell had a saloon quarrel which almost led to gunplay and which did initiate a violent range feud. The conflict between the Higgins and Horrell factions erupted in March, 1873, and over the next few years there followed a series of gunfights and bushwhackings.

Late in 1873 the Horrell brothers—Tom, Mart, Sam, Ben, and Merritt—moved their livestock operation to Lincoln County, New Mexico, where they soon became embroiled in further hostilities. Ben was killed in Lincoln, and his brothers immediately sought revenge. Conditions soon grew so bad that the entire county became an armed camp, and a vigilante group was organized to overwhelm the Horrells. Early in 1874, therefore, the Horrells returned to Texas, where their feud with Pink Higgins soon was renewed.

The worst fighting was in 1877, but by August of that year John B. Jones, major of the Texas Rangers, had persuaded the two parties to sign a peace agreement, and major hostilities ceased. Tom and Mart were killed by a lynch mob the next year, following a robbery and murder of which they were suspected.

Gunfights: *March 19, 1873, Lampasas, Texas.* Tom Williams, a captain of the detested Texas State Police and son-in-law of Pink Higgins, had come to Lampasas in search of accused murderer Clint Barkley. Barkley, who was using the alias Bill Bowen, was employed as a cowboy at the Horrell ranch, and the Horrells determined to back him.

Tom, Mart, Sam, Merritt (who was Barkley's brother-in-law), and several other armed Horrell cowpunchers accompanied Barkley to the Matador Saloon on the afternoon of March 19. As darkness gathered, Tom Horrell ordered the bartender not to light the lamps, apparently hoping to obscure his party from easy detection.

Soon Williams entered the saloon, accompanied by three other members of the state police. Gunfire immediately broke out, with both groups blazing away with rifles and revolvers. Two policemen were riddled with slugs and died in the saloon, as did Williams, who was hit eight times. Mart was wounded in the neck, and Tom suffered a bullet through the wrist.

March, 1873, Georgetown, Texas. Mart, too badly wounded to hide out, had been arrested along with Jerry Scott, owner of the Matador Saloon, and the two men had been incarcerated in the Georgetown jail. Several days later a large party led by the Horrells rode into town and broke into the building. There was a sharp exchange of shots, and the rescue was effected with one casualty on each side.

December 20, 1873, Lincoln, New Mexico. Ben Horrell had recently been killed in Lincoln, and his brothers were set on revenge. About midnight on December 20, Tom, Sam, Mart, Zachariah Crompton, and E. Scott attacked a house in Lincoln where a large wedding dance was entertaining a major portion of the town's Mexican populace. The Horrell group poured a withering volley through the windows and doors, and six men were hit. Dario Balazár, José Candelaria, Isidro Padilla, and Isidro Patrón were killed, and Pilár Candelaria and Apolonio García were wounded.

When the surviving celebrants began to fire back, Tom swung his horse and led the other four attackers into the safety of darkness.

March 26, 1877, near Lampasas, Texas. Tom and Mart were riding into Lampasas for a session of court. About 10:00 A.M., when they were five miles outside town at a stream later named Battle Branch, they were ambushed by members of the Higgins faction. Both brothers were wounded, but they managed to drive off their attackers. Mart then galloped into town for help after carrying Tom to a nearby house.

June, 1877, Lampasas County, Texas. As the feud worsened, Tom Horrell determined to seek revenge for his most recent wounding. In June he led a party of his brothers and cowhands to a line camp owned by Higgins. At dawn the Horrell men were inside the stock corral when two Higgins riders emerged from the line shack to cook their breakfast. The surprised cowboys were gunned down with a volley of rifle fire, and the Horrells hastily rode away. Pink Higgins arrived later in the day and found one of his hands still alive, although the man died three days later of his chest wound.

June 14, 1877, Lampasas, Texas. Tom, Sam, Mart, and four of their gunmen were in Lampasas when they discovered that Pink Higgins and three of his men were in town. The two groups met on the square, and a volley of gunfire was exchanged. Two Higgins men went down: Pink's chief lieutenant, Bill Wren, and a dying Frank Mitchell, Higgins' brother-in-law. After three hours of shooting, concerned citizens prevailed upon the warring factions to stop firing.

July, 1877, Lampasas County, Texas.
Higgins led all fourteen members of his
crew on a retaliatory raid against the
Horrell ranch ten miles from Lampasas.
Armed with new Winchester 73 rifles,
the Higgins party besieged the Horrell
ranch house and bunkhouse for two
days. Their fire was vigorously returned,
and the Horrells kept their attackers at
bay. When Higgins began to run low on
ammunition, he ordered a withdrawal,
leaving two Horrell men slightly
wounded.

*July 25, 1877, Lampasas County, Tex-
as.* Higgins sent Carson Graham into
Lampasas to buy tobacco, whiskey, and
ammunition. While still in the northern
part of the county, Graham was intercepted by the Horrells and ambushed.
Beside his body the Horrells traced their
brand in the dust.

Immediately following this killing,
John B. Jones and seven rangers came
to Lampasas and arrested Tom Horrell,
his brothers, and all their cowhands.
Jones soon released all but Tom, Sam,
and Mart, and a truce was quickly arranged with Higgins.

Sources: Sinise, *Pink Higgins,* 30–40;
Webb, *Texas Rangers,* 334–39; Kele-
her, *Violence in Lincoln County,* 13–15;
Gillett, *Six Years with the Texas Ran-
gers,* 73–80; Rasch, "The Horrell War,"
NMHR; Coe, *Frontier Fighter,* 213–14;
Sonnichsen, *I'll Die Before I'll Run,*
126–49.

Houston, Tom

*(d. September 2, 1893, Stillwater,
Oklahoma.* Law officer.) During the early 1890's Houston served as a peace officer in Oklahoma Territory. He was
fatally wounded by Arkansas Tom Jones
during the shootout at Ingalls in 1893.

Gunfights: *November 29, 1892,
Orlando, Oklahoma.* Houston accompanied Heck Thomas and Chris Madsen to the Orlando farm of the sister of
bank robber Ol Yantis. Yantis came out
of the house at dawn, a sack of feed in
one hand and a revolver in the other.
Madsen shouted for him to give up, but
he squeezed off a shot in reply. Madsen
promptly wounded him, but he continued to fire until Houston sent him
sprawling with a well-placed shot. The
officers took him into town, but he died
that evening.

September 1, 1893, Ingalls, Oklahoma.
Houston was a member of the large
posse which battled the Doolin gang in
Ingalls. After a vicious fight the outlaws
escaped town, but they abandoned Arkansas Tom Jones. Jones armed himself with a rifle, poked loopholes in the
roof of the only two-story building in
Ingalls, and tried to fight off the posse
single-handedly. He had already fatally
wounded Dick Speed when Houston
tried to move in from across the street.
As Houston ran, Jones caught him with
bullets which slammed into his lower
abdomen and left side. After Jones surrendered, Houston, along with officer
Lafe Shadley and Speed's body, were
taken to Stillwater, but both wounded
lawmen soon died.

Sources: Drago, *Road Agents and
Train Robbers,* 199, 204–206; Croy,
Trigger Marshal, 207–209.

Hughes, John Reynolds

("Border Boss")

*(b. February 11, 1857, Cambridge, Illi-
nois; d. 1946, Austin, Texas.* Cowboy,
rancher, law officer.) John Hughes left
his native Illinois at the age of fourteen
and drifted to the Southwest to become

a cowboy. A year later his right arm was shattered during a brawl, causing him to switch gunhands. He became so skilled as a southpaw marksman that few people could guess that he was right-handed.

Hughes helped drive several cattle herds from Texas to Kansas, and in 1878 he started a seventy-six acre horse ranch of his own near Liberty Hill, Texas. In 1886 six rustlers stole nearly one hundred horses, eighteen of which belonged to Hughes, in the Liberty Hill area. Hughes tracked them for a year and finally killed three of the thieves, captured two others, and returned with the herd. In the process he traveled twelve hundred miles, used up nine mounts, and spent all but seventy-six cents of the forty-three dollars with which he had started.

Soon after his return Hughes helped a Texas ranger chase down and kill an outlaw, and shortly thereafter there were two ambush attempts on his life. On August 10, 1887, he journeyed to Georgetown and enlisted in the Texas Rangers. By 1893 he had reached the rank of sergeant of Company D of the famous Frontier Battalion. In June of that year Captain Frank Jones was killed, and Hughes was promoted to company commander.

Hughes was highly active as a ranger until 1915, when he retired following twenty-eight years of service. He became president of an Austin bank, although he continued to reside in El Paso, where Company D headquarters had been located through the years. In 1946, at the age of eighty-nine, the lifelong bachelor committed suicide.

Gunfights: *1872, Indian Territory.* Hughes and his employer, Indian trader Art Rivers, clashed with Choctaw farmers over a hog sale. An Indian tried to shoot Rivers, and Hughes jumped the man. In the ensuing scuffle the fifteen-year-old Hughes took a rifle bullet through his clothing, was nearly knifed, and was wounded in the right arm. The wound severely hindered his use of the limb throughout the rest of his life.

May, 1886, northwestern Texas. Having trailed six horse rustlers for almost a week, Hughes finally located their camp. As he closed in, however, the night guard spotted him, and a shootout ensued. Two of the outlaws fought Hughes while the other four drove off the stolen herd. Finally Hughes's horse was killed, and the fight ended as the last two rustlers galloped away.

April 15, 1887, northwestern Texas. During the following months the rustlers twice set ambushes for their pursuer, but both times Hughes shot his way to safety. One outlaw quit the band, and the others were unable to sell the horses. At last Hughes, along with Sheriff Frank Swafford and a deputy, caught the remaining outlaws, who were led by the Renald brothers. A fight broke out, and the four rustlers were fatally wounded. The other outlaws surrendered, and Hughes was soon on the way back to Liberty Hill with a large herd of recovered horses.

1887, near Mason, Texas. Unidentified assailants set an ambush for Hughes. He was hit, but it was only a flesh wound, and he managed to drive off the bushwhackers with quick return fire.

1887, near Mason, Texas. Another ambush attempt cut down Hughes's horse. He jumped free, produced a gun, and opened fire, and his antagonist quickly vanished.

July, 1887, Texas Panhandle. For a month Hughes had helped Texas Ranger Ira Aten follow the trail of escaped murderer Judd Roberts. Roberts finally turned up on a ranch in the Texas Panhandle, wooing the rancher's daughter. Aten and Hughes concealed themselves and intercepted the fugitive near the ranch house. Roberts tried to shoot his way out of the trap, but the two manhunters gunned him down. Riddled with six bullets, Roberts died in the embrace of his sweetheart.

1889, Shafter, Texas. Hughes, by now a Ranger corporal, went to work in a Shafter silver mine to discover who was responsible for a series of ore thefts. His undercover work revealed that a foreman was sneaking ore onto burro trains which quickly crossed the Rio Grande into Mexico. Hughes and fellow Ranger Lon Oden set a trap and intercepted a burro train at the mine entrance; there were four in the robbers' group, but one was undercover man Ernest ("Diamond Dick") St. Leon.

The thieves resisted with rifle fire, and shooting lasted for over an hour, with St. Leon firing the most effective shots against the thieves. The lawmen finally succeeded in killing three of the outlaws, and the next day they arrested the crooked mine foreman.

December 25, 1889, near Vance, Texas. Hughes led Texas Rangers Ira Aten and Bass Outlaw and Deputy Sheriff Will Terry in setting an ambush for cattle rustlers Will and Alvin Odle. The officers secluded themselves near tiny Vance, where the outlaws were expected to cross into Texas from Mexico.

Shortly after midnight on Christmas the two rustlers appeared in the moonlight, and Hughes ordered them to surrender. The brothers tried to fight, and the lawmen shot them out of their saddles. Will died immediately, and Alvin expired a few minutes later.

1893, San Antonio Colony, Texas. Rangers Hughes, Lon Oden, and Jim Putnam arrested Desidario Durán at San Antonio Colony, a Mexican village on the Texas side of the Rio Grande. Suddenly the lawmen spotted a trio of fugitives leaving town, and Hughes and Oden spurred after them. There was a short chase, and Oden's horse was killed by Florencio Carrasco, but the two rangers shot the Mexican off his mount, and he died within moments. In the meantime, Putnam, left to guard Durán, was surrounded by angry citizens, but his two comrades arrived in time to head off further trouble.

March, 1896, Bajitas, Texas. Hughes and three members of his company were in pursuit of a bandit leader named Miguel de la Torre, whom they located in Bajitas, a village on the Rio Grande. The four rangers rode into Bajitas leading a spare horse and immediately spotted de la Torre in the street. Hughes promptly dismounted, seized the astonished Mexican, and manhandled him onto the extra mount.

The bandit was handcuffed to the saddle, but before the rangers could leave town they were fired upon by de la Torre's *compadres.* The rangers dismounted, stood behind their horses, and quickly wounded three of their adversaries. Resistance melted, and the rangers proceeded without further problems.

September 28, 1896, Nogalitos Pass, Texas. Hughes was in pursuit of horse thieves, accompanied by Rangers Thalis Cook and R. E. Bryant, former Ranger and Sheriff J. B. Gillett, Deputy Sheriff Jim Pool, and two ranchers—Jim Stroud and Jake Combs—who had lost horses to the rustlers.

The three rustlers, Ease Bixler and Art and Jubel Friar, saw the lawmen approaching and tried to hold them off with rifle fire. Combs had an earlobe shot away, but Hughes led a charge. Reinforced by a cowboy named Arthur McMaster, the posse dismounted and forced the fugitives off the mountaintop. Jubel Friar raised up to fire at Hughes, but Cook drilled him through the head with a Winchester slug. Friar's brother, already wounded twice, announced, "I have got enough."

"Hands up then," replied Cook, "and come out."

Cook and Hughes moved in, but when they were within ten yards Art Friar jerked out a pistol and began firing. Cook and Hughes instantly pumped one bullet apiece into Friar, and he fell dead. The third outlaw managed to escape, mounted bareback on one of the stolen horses.

Sources: Martin, *Border Boss;* Webb, *Texas Rangers,* 428, 444, 447–51, 458, 460–62.

Hunt, J. Frank

(d. October 11, 1880, Caldwell, Kansas. Law officer.) Hunt attained a slight measure of notoriety as a gunman during a few months of 1880 in Caldwell's roaring boom period. Appointed a deputy marshal in 1880 by Mayor Mike Meagher, he was widely blamed for the death of former Marshal George Flatt and was assassinated a short time later in an apparent revenge killing.

Gunfights: *June 19, 1880, Caldwell, Kansas.* During a typical Saturday night in Caldwell, Hunt had trouble with a drunken George Flatt, whose brace of pistols and fearless reputation were widely respected. About 1:00 A.M. friends of Flatt's induced him to go home after a stop for food at Louis Segerman's Restaurant. As Flatt, C. L. Spear, and Samuel H. Rogers headed for Segerman's, a shot rang out which penetrated the base of Flatt's skull, tearing through his spinal cord and killing him instantly. As Flatt pitched forward, a volley of shots sent three more slugs into his body. Rogers ran back about thirty feet and shouted, "Let up, you have killed that man." Then a figure identified by witnesses as Hunt ran away from the scene.

October 11, 1880, Caldwell, Kansas. At night Hunt was sitting at an open window of Caldwell's notorious Red Light saloon and dance hall. While he drank and watched the dancers, an unidentified assailant crept up to the window and fired a bullet into the unsuspecting Hunt. Mortally wounded, Hunt collapsed writhing to the floor. He was carried away and given medical attention, but he died in great pain within hours.

Sources: Miller and Snell, *Great Gunfighters of the Kansas Cowtowns,* 100–102, 142, 359–60; Drago, *Wild, Woolly & Wicked,* 210–12.

Jackson, Frank

("Blockey")

(b. 1856, Texas. Tinner, bank and train robber.) Orphaned in his youth, Jackson long worked in the Denton tinshop of Ben Key, his brother-in-law. Jackson killed a Negro in 1876, and in 1877 he joined a bandit gang being formed by Sam Bass. During the next several months he participated in frequent skirmishes while robbing trains and eluding

posses. After the gang was decimated in an abortive bank robbery in 1878, Jackson managed to escape and disappear. He was rumored to have ended his days as a rancher in New Mexico, Montana, or Big Spring, Texas; as a drummer in Houston; or as a law officer in California.

Gunfights: Fall, 1876, near Denton, Texas. Jackson had threatened to kill a notorious horse thief named Henry Goodall for taking a mount which Frank had claimed. Goodall offered Jackson an animal in exchange, and the two men rode into the country together. Jackson later swore that Goodall dismounted to give his horse a drink, opened fire without warning, and was mortally wounded when Frank shot back. Goodall's body was found that night with a hole in his forehead and his throat cut. His death was considered a public service, and Jackson was neither arrested nor indicted.

April 10, 1878, Mesquite, Texas. The Bass gang had met light resistance before, but when they tried to rob a train in Mesquite, they were overwhelmed by vicious fire from convict guards, employees, and passengers. The outlaws fought back briefly, then beat a desperate retreat when several of their number were wounded.

June 13, 1878, Salt Creek, Wise County, Texas. Following minor clashes with posses, the Bass gang was attacked by lawmen in their camp at Salt Creek. During the ensuing "Salt Creek Fight" outlaw Arkansas Johnson was killed, but the others shot their way to safety on foot and escaped to Denton County atop stolen horses.

July 19, 1878, Round Rock, Texas. The only men left in the Bass gang were the leader, Jackson, Seab Barnes, and Jim Murphy. Murphy had informed lawmen that a bank robbery was planned in Round Rock, and officers converged on the town. The quartet rode in to case the community; Murphy warily dropped behind, and Bass, Jackson, and Barnes entered a store next to the bank.

Inside they encountered Deputy Sheriffs Morris Moore and Ellis Grimes, and when the latter asked Barnes if he had a gun, the three thieves began shooting. Grimes was killed and Morris seriously wounded, Bass was hit in the hand, and the outlaws dashed for their horses. In the street they were met by a hail of gunfire; Barnes was shot dead, and Bass was hit in the body.

Coolly firing his six-gun, Jackson picked up Barnes's saddlebags, untied Bass's horse and helped his chief into the saddle, then untied his own animal and rode out of town, helping Bass stay mounted. The two reached their camp near town, picked up two rifles, then headed into a thicket. Bass could go no further, and he insisted that Jackson escape while he could. Frank tended Bass's wounds, tied his horse nearby, then rode into the darkness and permanent anonymity.

Sources: Gard, *Sam Bass*, 39, 101–223, 231–32, 234, 238; Webb, *Texas Rangers*, 382–83, 386–88, 390.

James, Franklin

("B. J. Woodson")

(b. January 10, 1843, Clay County, Missouri; d. February 18, 1915, Clay County, Missouri. Farmer, guerrilla soldier, bank and train robber, race track employee, stock tender, clerk, Wild West show performer.) Frank James, slightly less notorious than Jesse, his younger brother, was the eldest child of an industrious frontier preacher and his

strong-willed wife. The year before Frank was born, his parents migrated from Kentucky and settled on a farm in western Missouri, where Frank's father, Robert James, assumed the pastorate of a nearby Baptist church. In 1850 Robert James caught gold fever and journeyed to California, where he quickly fell ill and died. His widow, Zerelda, soon remarried, but the union lasted only a few months.

In 1855 Zerelda entered her third marriage, with docile, prosperous Dr. Reuben Samuel. The growing family remained on the old James farm, began to acquire slaves, and were naturally sympathetic with the Confederacy when the Civil War broke out. In 1862 or 1863 Frank joined William Quantrill's infamous band of Missouri guerrillas and soon found himself involved in the notorious massacre at Lawrence, Kansas, among other bloody incidents.

After the war Frank enlisted with Jesse and the Younger brothers in a decade-long series of bank robberies in Missouri and adjacent states.

There were a number of shootings connected with these robberies, and Frank doubtless was involved in several of them, but since the robbers masked themselves, it is difficult in many cases to assign blame or credit in specific shooting incidents.

By 1873 the James-Younger gang had begun robbing trains, and soon Pinkerton detectives were trying to pin indictments on the James and Younger brothers. On March 10, 1874, detective John W. Whicher was shot in the head and heart in the vicinity of the Samuels' farm, and Frank and Jesse were assumed to have murdered him. In 1876 Frank eloped with a Kansas girl, Annie Ralston, who bore him a son two years later. On September 7, 1876, the James-Younger gang was decimated following an abor-

tive attempt to rob a bank in Northfield, Minnesota, although Frank and Jesse escaped capture.

For a few years Frank and Jesse lived with their families in Tennesseee before moving back to Missouri in 1881. Frank continued to help his brother rob banks, trains, and stores until Jesse was murdered in 1882. A few months later, on October 4, 1882, Frank surrendered himself to Missouri Governor Thomas J. Crittendon, throwing himself upon the mercy of the authorities. Frank issued a pathetic plea for sympathy and leniency, and after a lengthy series of trials and legal moves he achieved acquittal.

Frank was released from custody in 1885 and lived a quiet, honest existence for thirty years. He resided in New Jersey, Texas, Oklahoma, and New Orleans and on his mother's old farm in Missouri. He worked as a race starter at county fairs, as a theater doorman, and as an attraction in traveling stock companies, including a partnership in the James–[Cole] Younger Wild West Show in 1903. He died at the Missouri farm in 1915, and his ashes were kept in a bank vault until his wife's death in 1944, when their ashes were interred together in a Kansas City cemetery.

Gunfights: *March 21, 1868, Russellville, Kentucky.* Typical of robberies attributed to the James-Younger gang, this incident involved eight men, including one who had posed as a cattle dealer at the Russellville bank of Nimrod Long. Long tried to resist the thieves, but they opened fire and inflicted a scalp wound. Undaunted, Long grappled with the robbers, then dashed outside—only to be driven to cover by the fire of men stationed with the horses. The gang then escaped with twelve thousand dollars stuffed into a wheat sack.

December 7, 1869, Gallatin, Missouri.
Frank and Jesse entered the Gallatin
bank and asked cashier-proprietor John
W. Sheets to negotiate a minor trans-
action. As Sheets began writing, one
of the bandits shot him in the head and
heart. Clerk William McDowell bolted
outside and, although wounded in the
arm, shouted that Sheets had been
killed. The robbers emerged with several hundred dollars, but one failed to
secure himself in the saddle and was
dragged thirty or forty feet before he
could twist free. The other bandit picked
up his comrade, and the two brothers
galloped out of town on one horse. Outside town they stole a horse from farmer
Dan Smoot, then made good their
escape.

*December 15, 1869, Clay County, Mis-
souri.* A week after the holdup and murder at Gallatin, a small posse approached
the Samuel farm, hoping to capture
Frank and Jesse for the rewards that
had been offered. Alerted by a Negro
employee, the two brothers spurred out
of a barn when the four posse members
began to close in. There was a wild exchange of gunfire and a running chase.
Then Deputy Sheriff John Thomason
dismounted to fire more accurately, but
his horse shied and was killed by the
brothers as they pulled away safely.

April 29, 1872, Columbia, Kentucky.
For several days Frank and Jesse, Cole
Younger, and two unidentified confederates allegedly had been in the Columbia area posing as stock buyers. On April
29 the five men rode into town, and two
entered the Deposit Bank. When they
produced guns, cashier R. A. C. Martin
shouted, "Bank robbers!" Martin was
shot dead, there was a brief scuffle with
bystanders, and the thieves hastily collected six hundred dollars from the

counter. The five robbers then dashed
out of town to safety.

*September 7, 1876, Northfield, Minne-
sota.* Eight armed men, including the
James and Younger brothers, rode into
Northfield, and three of them entered
the First National Bank. Acting cashier
Joseph L. Heywood was ordered to open
the safe, but he stubbornly refused. One
of the robbers thereupon slashed Heywood's throat, then shot the fallen man
to death. Teller A. E. Bunker dashed
from the building, sustaining a shoulder
wound as he fled.

Citizens were quickly attracted by the
gunfire and began to exchange shots
with the outlaws. Townsman Nicholas
Gustavson was killed, along with robbers Clell Miller and William Stiles. Bob
Younger was severely wounded, and his
horse was killed, but one of his brothers
picked him up under fire and, with the
rest of the gang, galloped into the clear.
The shattered band was hotly pursued,
and Jesse reportedly tried to persuade
Cole to abandon or finish off Bob. When
Cole adamantly refused, Jesse and Frank
split away from the group.

A few days later one of the remaining
fugitives, Charlie Pitts, was killed, and
Cole, Bob, and Jim Younger were taken
into custody. The James brothers, however, managed to avoid apprehension.

Sources: Settle, *Jesse James Was His
Name;* James, *Jesse James, My Father;*
Wellman, *Dynasty of Western Outlaws;*
Drago, *Road Agents and Train Robbers,*
128–76, 225–26.

James, Jesse Woodson

("Dingus," "Thomas Howard")

*(b. September 5, 1847, Clay County,
Missouri; d. April 3, 1882, St. Joseph,
Missouri.* Farmer, guerrilla soldier, bank

and train robber.) The son of a Baptist preacher, Jesse was born in 1847 on his parents' Missouri farm. When he was three his father died in the California gold fields, and his mother, Zerelda, quickly remarried. This marriage soon failed, however, reportedly because their new stepfather was "mean" to Jesse and his older brother Frank. Zerelda married Dr. Reuben Samuel, a gentle and subservient man, and Frank and Jesse spent the next few years as the senior siblings of a growing farm family.

When the Civil War broke out, Frank and Jesse and the rest of the family aligned with the Confederate cause, primarily because they were slaveholders. On more than one occasion Jesse and his relatives were maltreated by Unionists, and by 1864 the teen-aged boy had joined Frank in William Quantrill's guerrilla band, then under the leadership of Bloody Bill Anderson. Jesse twice suffered severe wounds, but recovered to loot and kill until the end of the war.

In the years following Appomattox, Jesse and Frank and other former guerrillas turned to outright thievery. Among their exploits was the first daylight bank robbery in America during peacetime—the plunder of sixty thousand dollars from the Clay County Savings Bank on February 13, 1866. The chief associates of Jesse and Frank during these robberies were the Younger brothers—Cole, who had been one of Quantrill's lieutenants, James, Bob, and John. The gang, usually led by Jesse, successfully looted banks in Missouri and surrounding states for years.

There is no certainty as to which robberies the masked James-Younger band perpetrated, but there were numerous shootings. On several occasions these fights resulted in the deaths of bank officials or bystanders, and it may be safely assumed that Jesse was an active participant in a number of gun battles. Following each robbery that he was blamed for, Jesse customarily published a letter proclaiming his innocence and establishing an alibi.

In 1873 the James-Younger gang branched out and began robbing trains. Lucrative rewards were offered for the apprehension of the thieves, and by 1874 Pinkerton detectives were carefully scrutinizing the activities of the James and Younger brothers. Indeed, Jesse and Frank were widely suspected of murdering Pinkerton agent John Whicher in March of that year near their mother's farm.

On April 23, 1874, Jesse married his lifelong sweetheart, Zee Mimms, and within the next few years they became the parents of a son and a daughter. In 1868 Jesse had been baptized into the Baptist church, and, aside from numerous robberies and a few murders, he remained a devout Christian throughout his life. In 1875 unidentified persons set fire to the Samuels' farm during the night; the nine-year-old half-brother of Frank and Jesse was killed, and their mother suffered the amputation of a hand. Despite sympathy in some quarters—including certain area newspapers—for the James brothers, which resulted in one or two fruitless attempts to secure amnesty, Jesse and Frank continued to rob banks, stores, stagecoaches, and trains.

Using various aliases, Jesse and his wife lived in Texas, Tennessee (where their children were born), and Kansas City. Under the name of Thomas Howard, Jesse moved to St. Joseph late in 1881 to plan new depredations. But new rewards had been posted against him, and on numerous occasions he had been reported killed. Then on April 3, 1882,

Jesse was murdered at his home by Bob Ford, a new member of the gang who had secretly planned to collect the rewards since joining Jesse.

Although there were apprehensions that the report of his death was just another false one, and although impostors claimed for decades to be the outlaw, Jesse was buried in the front yard of his mother's farm in his thirty-fifth year. Mrs. Samuel allowed visitors to tour Jesse's home place and grave at twenty-five cents apiece. Somewhat melodramatically, she wept bitterly at the persecution of her sons, cursed detectives, and wished damnation upon the Ford brothers. She also sold pebbles from Jesse's grave at a quarter each and regularly replenished her supply from a nearby creek.

Gunfights: *September 27, 1864, Centralia, Missouri.* Bloody Bill Anderson led thirty followers, including Jesse, into Centralia on a looting raid. The guerrillas encountered twenty-five unarmed Union soldiers and promptly executed them in cold blood. Major A. V. E. Johnson led a Federal pursuit force, but Anderson joined two hundred nearby guerrillas and set an ambush. Johnson and one hundred of his men were killed, and Jesse was widely credited with shooting the Union leader.

February 13, 1866, Liberty, Missouri. During the morning a dozen men, including, it is often alleged, Jesse (who may have been bedridden at this time with a lung wound) and Frank James, rode into Liberty. Two of the robbers walked into the Clay County Savings Bank and produced revolvers. The cashier and his young son were locked inside the vault, and nearly sixty thousand dollars in currency were carried away in a wheat sack. Outside, the nervous robbers opened fire on passersby, killing George Wymore, a student at a local college. The bandits then galloped out of town, pursued by a posse.

March 21, 1868, Russellville, Kentucky. Jesse and Frank, Cole and Jim Younger, and four other bandits rode into Russellville to loot the Southern Bank of Kentucky. Jesse led several of his henchmen into the building and was forced to fire a number of warning shots before cashier Morton Barkley would begin to hand over the money. The president of the bank, Nimrod Long, heard the gunfire while eating lunch at his nearby home.

Long sprinted back to the bank, shouting a warning as he ran. He dashed through the back door and was met in the hallway by Jesse. The two men scuffled for a moment, then Jesse wrenched his pistol free and fired two shots. Long was grazed in the head and pitched to the floor. Jesse ran back into the front shouting that he had killed the president, and the bandits scrambled for their horses. Suddenly Long staggered outside and again sounded the alarm. The outlaws snapped several shots at him, then galloped away.

December 7, 1869, Gallatin, Missouri. Jesse and Frank, posing as customers, entered the Gallatin bank and began to transact business with proprietor John W. Sheets, a Civil War officer against whom they allegedly held a deep grudge. One of the brothers suddenly shot Sheets twice, killing him instantly. Clerk William McDowell was then fired upon and wounded in the arm, but he managed to make his way into the street and shout for help. The robbers dashed out with a sack full of loot, but one was unable to mount his unruly horse. The two men left town on one horse, stole another from a farmer, then escaped into Clay County.

December 15, 1869, Clay County, Missouri. Four men surrounded the Samuel farm, attempting to seize the James brothers for the three-thousand-dollar reward offered after the Gallatin murder and robbery. As Deputy Sheriff John Thomason approached the farmhouse, Frank and Jesse dashed out of the barn astride swift mounts. Shots were exchanged, and the posse galloped after them, Thomason in the lead. Thomason suddenly dismounted, rested his gun across his saddle, and fired deliberately at the fleeing brothers. The deputy's mount bolted unexpectedly and, riderless, soon pulled up alongside the Jameses. One of the brothers shot the horse dead, then the two men made good their escape.

September 26, 1872, Kansas City, Missouri. Three mounted men approached Ben Wallace, who was the ticket seller at the crowded Kansas City Fair. One of the men, supposedly Jesse James, grabbed the tin cashbox, seized its contents, then threw the box aside. Wallace grappled with the robber, who drew a pistol and fired a shot. The slug went wild and struck a small girl in the leg, and the thieves spurred into some nearby woods.

September 7, 1876, Northfield, Minnesota. Eight members of the James-Younger gang rode into Northfield to loot the First National Bank. Three men stopped at the edge of town, two stayed outside the bank with horses, and the remaining three entered the building. When cashier Joseph L. Heywood resisted their demands, one of the robbers slashed his throat, then finished him off with a bullet. A. E. Bunker, a teller, dashed outside, but was shot in the shoulder by one of the gang.

A number of citizens alertly began to fire on the outlaws, killing Clell Miller and William Stiles and seriously wounding Bob Younger. The robbers shot down townsman Nicholas Gustavson, then managed to fight their way out of town.

According to Cole Younger, Jesse wanted to abandon or kill Bob so that the gang could move faster. Cole refused, of course, and Jesse and Frank promptly set out on their own and made good their escape. Within several days outlaw Charlie Pitts was killed by a pursuing posse, and Bob, Cole, and Jim Younger were captured.

July 15, 1881, Winston, Missouri. On Chicago, Rock Island & Pacific Railroad the evening train out of Kansas City was boarded discreetly by half a dozen robbers when it stopped at Cameron and at Winston. By the time the train had left Winston, darkness had fallen, and the desperadoes made their move. Conductor William Westfall, collecting fares in the smoking car, was suddenly confronted by a bearded man in a linen duster (probably Jesse), who stood blocking the aisle. The outlaw produced a gun and ordered Westfall to raise his hands. Westfall abruptly turned, however, and the bandit shot him in the back. The conductor staggered out the door, but a second slug sent him tumbling from the rear platform. Westfall's murderer continued firing, as did one or two other members of the gang, and passenger Frank McMillan was struck fatally.

While several of the outlaws forced the engineer to stop the train on a siding, two of the bandits approached the express car. They forced their way inside, pistol whipped the messenger, then seized his key and opened the safe. The robbers then disappeared into the darkness.

April 3, 1882, St. Joseph, Missouri. For the past several months Jesse, under the name of Thomas Howard, had been living with his family and several cohorts in St. Joseph, laying plans for new robberies. After a Monday morning breakfast Jesse went into the living room with Charles and Robert Ford, a pair of brothers who ostensibly were planning to assist in a bank holdup the next day. Jesse set aside his guns and stepped up on a chair to straighten a picture. Bob Ford, who for a number of weeks had hoped to collect the large rewards on Jesse's head, immediately recognized his chance. Bob drew his pistol and fired a shot into the back of Jesse's head. Jesse collapsed and died instantly. The Fords fled the house, Jesse's grief-stricken wife rushed to his side, and townspeople swarmed to the house to view the notorious outlaw's body.

Sources: Settle, *Jesse James Was His Name;* James, *Jesse James, My Father;* Wellman, *Dynasty of Western Outlaws;* Drago, *Road Agents and Train Robbers,* 128–71, 185.

Jennings, Napoleon Augustus

(b. January 11, 1856, Philadelphia, Pennsylvania; d. December 15, 1919, New York, New York. Farmhand, clerk, surveyor's helper, law officer, cowboy, stage driver, sign painter, writer, and journalist.) The son of a Philadelphia merchant, N. A. Jennings was educated at St. Paul's School in Concord, New Hampshire. At eighteen he journeyed to Texas to find adventure, and he worked variously as a farmhand, quartermaster's clerk for the U.S. Cavalry, and surveyor's helper. In 1876 and 1877 he served in the Texas Rangers under L.

H. McNelly and John B. Armstrong, and it was during this period that he depended upon his gun for a living.

Jennings fought in border skirmishes with Mexicans and in scrapes with rustlers, and he was with Lee Hall in 1876 when the rangers tried to put a final halt to the Sutton-Taylor feud. In 1878 he left Texas upon the death of his father, but he soon went west again to ride as a cowboy, drive stagecoaches, paint signs, and prospect for gold. Finally, in 1884, he returned to the East to work the remainder of his life as a writer for magazines and newspapers.

Gunfights: *October 1, 1876, near Carrizo, Texas.* Jennings was with John B. Armstrong when he led a ranger patrol against an outlaw camp on Espinoza Lake near Carrizo. When Armstrong hit the camp at midnight, six bandits had already slipped away, but the four still present tried to fight their way through the rangers. When the shooting started, Jennings dropped an outlaw named McAlister with a rifle shot. McAlister had a gaping hole in his jaw, and he had also been hit in the leg, but, unlike his three cohorts, he survived his wounds. At about the same time, other members of the ranger detachment clashed with the other outlaws and killed two of them.

October 5, 1876, Carrizo Springs, Texas. A few days later Jennings and two other rangers were dispatched cross-country to warn a ranger patrol that an ambush might be set for them at Carrizo Springs. When they reached the Carrizo Springs crossing where the trap presumably would be set, they apprehensively hauled out their guns and spurred forward. They splashed through the water safely, but as they clambered up the bank they spotted a number of horsemen.

The three rangers dismounted and dove into nearby brush, and a flurry of gunfire erupted. The waiting horsemen charged the three rangers, but before anyone was wounded, Jennings discovered that their "adversaries" were the rangers they had been sent to help.

Sources: Jennings, *Texas Ranger;* Webb, *Texas Rangers,* 265.

Johnson, Jack

("Turkey Creek")

(Gunman, miner, law officer.) A prospector and miner, Turkey Creek was attracted to the gold rushes in Deadwood and Tombstone during the 1870's. In Tombstone he became involved with the Earp faction, receiving a temporary appointment as a deputy marshal to help Wyatt chase stage robbers and later assisting in the revenge killings of Frank Stilwell and Florentino Cruz. After the Earp-Clanton feud subsided, Johnson drifted into Utah and the Texas Panhandle with Sherman McMasters.

Gunfights: late 1876; *Deadwood, Dakota Territory.* Johnson had a quarrel in a Deadwood saloon with his two mining partners. The three men went out to the cemetery, followed by a large crowd. At a considerable distance the two partners opened fire and grazed Johnson, who coolly shot them dead. Johnson paid for the burials; their graves had to be blasted out of the frozen ground with dynamite.

March 20, 1882, Tucson, Arizona. Johnson accompanied Wyatt and Warren Earp, Doc Holliday, and Sherman McMasters in searching for Frank Stilwell, assumed to have fired the shot which had killed Morgan Earp two days earlier. Stilwell was sighted near the Tucson depot, where the Earp party had

taken wounded Virgil Earp to entrain for California. The five men chased Stilwell into the darkness, cornered him within minutes, and executed him with rifle and shotgun blasts.

March 22, 1882; Tombstone, Arizona. Still in pursuit of murder suspects, Johnson and the others returned to Tombstone. They found a halfblood named Florentino Cruz in a wood camp near town. Cruz supposedly confessed before being cut down by a volley of a dozen or so shots.

Sources: Jahns, *Frontier World of Doc Holliday,* 223, 228, 230–32, 234–35; Lake, *Wyatt Earp,* 158–59, 356.

Johnson, William H.

(d. August 16, 1878, near Seven Rivers, New Mexico. Soldier, rancher, gunman, law officer.) Johnson, a Confederate captain during the Civil War, drifted to New Mexico after the war and married the daughter of fellow Southerner Henry Beckwith. By 1876 Johnson was part owner of a ranch with Wallace Olinger, but when the Lincoln County War erupted two years later, both partners entered the fighting on the side of the Seven Rivers Crowd. Johnson served for a time as one of Sheriff William Brady's deputies, and he survived the general hostilities only to be shot to death by his father-in-law as a result of a family feud.

Gunfights: April 22, 1877, near *Seven Rivers, New Mexico.* John Chisum rode at the head of a number of cowboys on a punitive raid against the Beckwith ranch. (Chisum was convinced that the Beckwiths were rustling his stock.) No Beckwith males were present, and Johnson led the defenders. A rifle duel at seven to eight hundred yards ensued, and the Chisum party soon withdrew.

April 30, 1878, near Lincoln, New Mexico. Johnson had joined a posse which waylaid Frank McNab, Ab Sanders, and Frank Coe nearly eight miles from Lincoln. McNab and Sanders had dismounted to water their horses, and when the posse opened fire, both men were shot down. Coe's horse was killed, and he fought until he was out of ammunition. McNab, who tried to crawl away, was killed, the wounded Sanders was left where he fell, and Coe was taken into custody.

August 16, 1878, near Seven Rivers, New Mexico. Johnson and his father-in-law fell into an argument at Beckwith's ranch near Seven Rivers. The cantankerous Beckwith angrily seized a double-barreled shotgun charged with slugs and pistol balls and fired at Johnson. Johnson went down, mortally wounded in the chest and neck. Wallace Olinger shot Beckwith in the face, but the old man survived.

    Sources: Keleher, *Violence in Lincoln County,* 159, 223–24; Fulton, *Lincoln County War,* 37–39, 213, 217, 220, 288; Klasner, *My Girlhood Among Outlaws,* 67, 143, 172.

Jones, Frank

(b. 1856, Austin, Texas; d. June 30, 1893, Tres Jacales, Mexico. Texas Ranger.) Jones was a native Texan who entered the Texas Rangers, eventually rising to the command of Company D. He was highly active on the Mexican border, running to earth rustlers, train and bank robbers, and an assortment of lethal hard cases. He felt no compunction to stop at the Rio Grande in pursuit of fleeing fugitives, although he stated that

he "would not cross into Mexico where there are settlements and [where there] would be any danger of stirring up international trouble." He was killed in a shootout with Mexican rustlers in 1893, and he was succeeded as captain by the noted John Hughes.

Gunfights: *October, 1891, Crockett County, Texas.* In pursuit of a band of cattle and train robbers, Jones and a posse of seven men trailed four suspects into Crockett County. The lawmen intercepted the thieves near Howard's Well, and a running gun battle ensued. One outlaw's horse was shot from under him, and he quickly surrendered. The other three robbers were wounded, and two of them gave up after less than a mile of pursuit. The fourth outlaw, John Flint, was hotly chased by Jones and a few other posse members and galloped for eight miles. At last his wound weakened him so greatly that he knew capture was imminent; he scrawled his will on the back of an envelope, pressed his revolver against his head, and blew his brains out.

June 30, 1893, Tres Jacales, Mexico. Accompanied by Deputy Sheriff R. E. Bryant, Ranger Corporal Karl Kirchner, and Privates E. D. Aten, J. W. Sanders, and F. F. Tucker, Captain Jones went in search of cattle thieves Jesús María Olguín and his son Severio. The posse followed the trail south of the Rio Grande into Mexico and sighted their prey near the settlement of Tres Jacales. The Mexicans spurred their horses, and the Texans galloped after them, firing as they rode. Severio's arm was broken, and his father was hit in the right hand, but after a chase of just three hundred yards they dismounted and ducked inside one of a cluster of four adobe buildings.

    When the Texans came abreast of

the building, the five or six Mexicans inside opened fire, one slug hitting Kirchner's Winchester. Aten fired back with his revolver, and Jones pulled up within thirty feet of the door and opened up with his Winchester. A bullet slammed into Jone's thigh and knocked him from the saddle.

"Captain, are you hurt?" asked Tucker.

"Yes, shot all to pieces," replied Jones. But the plucky captain straightened his broken leg in front of him and began banging away with his rifle again. Suddenly a slug tore into his chest. "Boys, I am killed," he gasped, and fell back dead.

In the excitement the Olguíns escaped, and the Texans milled indecisively around their fallen leader. After three-quarters of an hour they decided that they were in danger of being cut off from the border, and they fled for the Rio Grande. Jones's body was delivered to San Elizario, Texas, two days later by Mexican authorities.

Sources: Webb, *Texas Rangers,* 438–44; Martin, *Border Boss,* 42–43, 48, 51, 53, 64, 68, 76–77, 82, 84, 90, 92–93, 102–104, 107–108, 111, 113–23, 125, 127, 134.

Jones, John

(b. Iowa; d. September, 1879, Lincoln County, New Mexico. Cowboy, rustler.)
One of ten children of Heiskell Jones, John moved with his family from Iowa to Colorado in 1861, and five years later from Colorado to Lincoln County, New Mexico. The Joneses operated several different spreads and on one occasion sold out to the homicidal Horrell brothers from Texas. John became dissatisfied with the tranquil life of a cowhand, and by 1878 he had become involved with rustlers and with the Murphy-Dolan crowd during the Lin-

coln County War. He killed Bill Riley and John Beckwith in quarrels over land and cattle, respectively, but was himself gunned down by peace officer Bob Olinger in 1879.

Gunfights: 1878, *Lincoln County, New Mexico.* Jones wrangled with Bob Riley, and their anger quickly led to gunplay. Jones shot his adversary to death, but escaped prosecution in the lawless atmosphere of Lincoln County.

July 15–19, Lincoln, New Mexico. Jones was a member of the forty-man party which besieged Alexander McSween and his gunmen during the climactic battle of the Lincoln County War. When the McSween house was set on fire, Jones and several others crept near and readied themselves behind a four-foot adobe wall close to the door. They opened fire when the dozen men inside came out, and McSween, Vicente Romero, Tom O'Folliard, Francisco Zamora, Harvey Morris, and Yginio Salazar were riddled with bullets. Only O'Folliard and Salazar survived, and it may safely be assumed that Jones fired several telling shots.

August 26, 1879, Seven Rivers, New Mexico. Jones and rancher John Beckwith began quarreling about the ownership of a herd of cattle, and the hot-tempered Jones soon went for his gun. In the shootout which followed Beckwith was fatally wounded.

September, 1879, Lincoln County, New Mexico. Lawmen Bob Olinger and Milo Pierce encountered Jones at a Lincoln County cow camp. John cocked his rifle and marched toward Olinger, growling, "I came to settle with you about those lies I've heard you told about my killing John Beckwith."

Olinger asked, "What sort of settlement do you want, John?" John snapped off a shot, whereupon Olinger pumped three slugs into him, killing him within moments.

Sources: Klasner, *My Girlhood Among Outlaws,* 63–64, 187–89; Keleher, *Violence in Lincoln County,* 105–106; Hunt, *Tragic Days of Billy the Kid,* 101–102, 181–84; Fulton, *Lincoln County War,* 69, 252, 271–73, 333, 347, 370–71.

Ed O. Kelly, who killed Bob Ford in Creede, Colorado *(Courtesy Western History Collections, University of Oklahoma Library)*

Kelly, Ed O.

("Red")

(b. Harrisonville, Missouri; d. January 13, 1904, Oklahoma City, Oklahoma.) Kelly was from Missouri and married a relative of the notorious Younger brothers. Over the years he acquired a

vague but apparently deserved reputation as a hard case. By the 1890's he had drifted to Colorado, where he encountered Bob Ford, the killer of Jesse James, in a Pueblo Hotel. Ford's diamond ring was stolen during the night, and Ford accused Kelly of the theft. When Ford returned to his saloon in Creede, he publicly repeated his accusations. Kelly promptly traveled to Ford's saloon, killed him, and soon found himself in prison. His life sentence was commuted to eighteen years, and he was released in 1900, but he managed to attract trouble and was killed in Oklahoma City four years later.

Gunfights: *June 8, 1892, Creede, Colorado.* Enraged at having been accused of robbery and at being thrown out of Bob Ford's saloon, Kelly loaded a shotgun and stormed back to confront Ford. Kelly blasted Ford and fled the premises, but a short time later he was arrested in Pueblo on murder charges.

January 13, 1904, Oklahoma City, Oklahoma. Kelly was called to task in the streets of Oklahoma City by a local policeman. After a desperate brawl the officer resorted to his gun, and Kelly was shot to death.

Source: Robertson and Harris, *Soapy Smith,* 111–12, 116–17.

Kemp, David

(d. ca. 1935, Higgins, Texas. Farmer, rancher, butcher, cattle rustler, gambler, law officer.) As a youth in Hamilton, Texas, Kemp killed a man named Smith. Kemp was sentenced to be hanged, and in panic he tore away from his guards and jumped out of a second-story courtroom window. He broke both ankles in the fall, but somehow clambered onto a horse before being surrounded and re-

captured. However, because of his age the governor commuted his sentence to life, then gave him a full pardon.

Kemp drifted into New Mexico, opened a butcher shop in Eddy (present-day Carlsbad), acquired an interest in a gambling casino in nearby Phoenix, and became sheriff when Eddy County was organized in 1889. He conducted his office in the interests of his gambling cohorts, and the county became quite rowdy. Dee Harkey was appointed deputy U.S. marshal to subdue the area, and Kemp and his friends threatened and on more than one occasion tried to kill the troublesome lawman.

Kemp also bought a ranch in the vicinity and turned to rustling to increase his ranching and butchering profits. He was cuaght red-handed by Harkey one night and agreed to leave the country. He stayed in Arizona for a few years, but returned when an old enemy, Les Dow, was elected sheriff of Eddy County. Kemp killed Dow, took up rustling again, and eventually returned to Texas to a ranch near Higgins. There he was shot and killed by his sister during the 1930's.

Gunfights: ca. 1885, Hamilton, Texas. A fight broke out in Hamilton's main street between men named Smith and Bogan. Kemp jumped into the fray, became angry, and shot Smith to death. The sheriff came running up, and Kemp backed away, triggering his pistol at the lawman. But the gun misfired, and a citizen named Tom Moss seized Kemp from behind and subdued him. Kemp was sentenced to die, but he eventually won a pardon.

April, 1896, Carlsbad, New Mexico. Kemp and a confederate, Will Kennon, lurked near the local post office when Sheriff Les Dow, an old antagonist, went inside. When Dow emerged reading a letter, Kemp poked a pistol in his face and shot him. Dow drew his gun in reflex action, but collapsed as Kemp and Kennon fled. Dow died that night, and Kemp, after running an eyewitness out of town, was acquitted on grounds of self-defense.

Sources: Harkey, *Mean as Hell,* 39–45, 63–65, 71, 74–75, 78–86; Haley, *Jeff Milton,* 230; Sonnichsen, *Tularosa,* 312.

Black Jack Ketchum posed for this portrait shortly before he was decapitated on the hangman's scaffold in Clayton, New Mexico. *(Courtesy Arizona Historical Society)*

Ketchum, Thomas

("Black Jack")

(b. 1866, San Saba County, Texas; d. April 25, 1901, Clayton, New Mexico. Cowboy, bank, train, and stage robber.)

Ketchum was a hard-drinking cowboy who displayed bizarre behavior from time to time. On one occasion, for example, he was rejected by a girl and reacted by beating himself alternately with a pistol and a lariat. In the 1890's he drifted into outlawry, robbing stagecoaches, banks, and trains in New Mexico. He was frequently assisted by his brother Sam, who was wounded in the arm during a train robbery and died following complications.

Black Jack was a deadly gunman, killing a pair of miners in an Arizona saloon fight and two officers who attempted to capture him. When apprehended, he was tried and sentenced to be hanged. He faced his fate with bravado, and at the gallows he dashed up the steps and announced, "I'll be in hell before you start breakfast, boys." After the hood was draped over his face, Black Jack gamely ordered, "Let her rip!" The trap was sprung, and the subsequent drop jerked his head from his torso.

Gunfights: *July 2, 1899, Camp Verde, Arizona.* In a saloon just outside Camp Verde, Ketchum began arguing with two miners over a card game. Shooting erupted, and Ketchum mortally wounded both miners before fleeing the premises.

July 12, 1899, Turkey Canyon, New Mexico. Ketchum and two fellow train robbers, Elzy Lay and G. W. Franks, were jumped by a posse at dawn while camping near Turkey Creek. An all-day battle followed during which three lawmen—Edward Farr, W. H. Love, and Tom Smith—were killed, and Ketchum was generally blamed for the deaths of Farr and Love. Lay was hit twice, and Ketchum took a slug in the shoulder, but the three outlaws slipped away that night. A few days later, however, the wounded Black Jack was taken into custody.

August 16, 1899, near Folsom, Arizona. Shooting erupted when Black Jack attempted singlehandedly to rob a Colorado & Southern train near Folsom, and Ketchum shot the express messenger in the jaw. Ketchum and conductor Frank Harrington exchanged fire and wounded each other simultaneously; Harrington was struck in the neck, and Black Jack's right arm was shattered by a load of buckshot. Black Jack dropped his revolver, crawled under the train, and escaped into the brush and darkness. The next day a freight train crew found him propped against a tree near the tracks, and doctors were forced to amputate his mutilated arm.

Sources: Burton, *Dynamite and Six-Shooters;* Horan, *Desperate Men,* 182, 228, 230–31; Nash, *Bloodletters and Badmen,* 307–308; Baker, *Wild Bunch,* 171, 176–77.

Larn, John M.

(b. 1849, Mobile, Alabama; d. June 22, 1878, Albany, Texas. Rancher, rustler, law officer, cowboy.) Reared in Mobile, Alabama, Larn ran away from home while in his early teens and wandered into Colorado. A few years later he killed a rancher, fled to New Mexico and killed a sheriff, then hastily repaired to Fort Griffin, Texas. He signed on as trail boss for Bill Hays, a local rancher, and in the fall of 1871 led a violence-filled cattle drive to California.

Larn then established a ranch near Fort Griffin and began to raise a family. In 1876 he was elected sheriff of Shackleford County, and he frequently deputized his close friend, noted gunfighter John Selman. Larn and Selman became deeply involved in cattle rustling, and Larn, under increasing pressure, resigned his sheriff's position on March 7, 1877.

Local anger over Larn's rustling activities and ensuing violence resulted in his arrest at his ranch on June 22, 1878. He was carried to Albany, and that night a masked mob broke into jail and executed Larn with rifle fire.

Gunfights: 1871, Colorado. Larn engaged in a quarrel over a horse with the owner of the ranch where he worked. Larn angrily pulled his six-shooter and killed his boss, then fled the scene.

1871, New Mexico. On the run in New Mexico, Larn encountered a suspicious sheriff. Taking no chances, Larn went for his gun and shot down the lawman.

1871, Texas, near the Pecos River. Larn, bossing a cattle drive to Colorado, became embroiled in a dispute with a pair of Mexicans. He settled the quarrel by shooting the men to death and then having their bodies thrown into the Pecos "to feed the catfish." (Larn supposedly killed another Mexican in a separate incident on this drive.)

June, 1878, near Fort Griffin, Texas. Larn had set an ambush for an antagonist, a local rancher named Treadwell. Larn opened fire too quickly, however, and Treadwell spurred his mount. Larn brought down the horse, but Treadwell made good his escape on foot.

Source: Metz, *John Selman,* 52–89, 211; Sonnichsen, *I'll Die Before I'll Run,* 152–66.

Lay, William Ellsworth

("Elzy," "William McGinnis")

(b. November 25, 1862, McArthur, Ohio; d. November 10, 1934, Los Angeles, California. Farmer, cowboy, rustler, train and bank robber, saloon keeper, oil wildcatter, gambler, irrigation

system manager.) Born in Ohio, Lay and his family migrated to farms in Iowa and near Laird and Wray in Colorado. In his late teens Lay went farther west to work as a cowboy. Lay soon married, but after he helped Butch Cassidy loot the Castle Gate, Utah, mining camp of eight thousand dollars in April, 1897, his wife quickly left him. Lay then became an active member of the Wild Bunch and was reputed to have planned several robberies.

On July 11, 1899, Lay helped the Ketchum gang pull a train robbery, and in the subsequent pursuit he was badly wounded. He escaped and began to recover from his wounds, but another posse found him, and after a fight he was arrested.

Lay was sentenced to a life term in the New Mexico Territorial Prison, but after he helped to quell a riot, he was pardoned on January 10, 1906. He then ran a saloon in Baggs, Wyoming, where he had once worked as a cowboy on the Calvert ranch. His first wife had divorced him while he was in prison. But in 1909 he married Mary Calvert, and they raised two daughters. For a while Lay tried his hand at drilling oil wells, but after he went broke, the family moved to California. Lay then disappeared for a few years, working as a professional gambler in Mexico. He spent the remainder of his career as the head watermaster of the Imperial Valley Irrigation System, and after suffering a heart attack, he retired to Los Angeles, where he died in 1934.

Gunfights: July 12, 1899, Turkey Creek Canyon, New Mexico. Following a train holdup at Twin Mountains on July 11, Lay, Tom Ketchum, and G. W. Franks galloped thirty-five miles to remote Turkey Creek and made camp. That night a posse led by Sheriff Edward

Farr surrounded them, and at dawn when Lay headed toward the creek with his canteen, the lawmen opened fire. Hit twice in the body, Lay rolled into an arroyo and joined his accomplices in defending themselves. A day-long gun battle ensued in which Ketchum was wounded and three lawmen—Farr, W. H. Love, and Tom Smith—were killed. That night the outlaws slipped away from the battered posse, although Ketchum was captured a few days later.

August, 1899, Eddy County, New Mexico. Lay, who had worked at the WS ranch in New Mexico, knew the surrounding country and hid out at an isolated cabin in the area to let his wounds heal. Upon returning to the cabin one day, Lay found a posse waiting as he walked inside the door. They ordered him to surrender, but he whipped out his gun and wounded one posse member in the wrist. The other lawmen jumped him, and after a brutal fist fight he was knocked unconscious and taken prisoner.

Sources: Horan and Sann, *Pictorial History of the Wild West,* 96–97, 180, 191–93, 208, 212–13, 240; Baker, *Wild Bunch,* 50, 59, 64, 81, 107–109, 132, 169–80, 188, 201; Pointer, *Butch Cassidy,* 18, 98, 107–108, 120–21, 123, 127, 148, 160–61, 194, 253–54.

Lee, Oliver Milton

(b. 1866, Buffalo Gap, Texas; d. December 15, 1941, Alamogordo, New Mexico. Rancher, law officer, state legislator, businessman.) The son of a Forty-niner from New York, Lee was reared in tiny Buffalo Gap in Burnet County, Texas. At the age of eighteen Lee and his older half-brother, Perry Altman, led their widowed mother and the rest of the family to a ranch in New Mexico's Tularosa Valley.

Widely known as a crack shot, Lee first fired his guns in anger during a feud with a neighboring rancher named John Good. Good's son, Walter, or another Good henchman murdered George McDonald, Lee's closest friend, and a brief but bitter range war resulted. Lee procured the bullet which had killed McDonald and carried it on a watch chain, and he was one of four men charged with Walter Good's death. After Lee was released from custody, he began to make great strides in extending his ranching enterprise, eventually carving out a prosperous spread called the Dog Canyon Ranch.

During these years Lee secured appointments as a deputy sheriff and as a deputy U.S. marshal, but in the 1890's he increasingly came under suspicion in the dastardly and mysterious murders of A. J. Fountain and his eight-year-old son. After routing a posse led by Pat Garrett, Lee and fellow fugitive James Gilliland sought refuge at the Bar Cross Ranch of Eugene Manlove Rhodes. Eventually the two men surrendered and, following a sensational trial in Hillsboro, won acquittal.

Lee returned to ranching, selling out in 1914 to a group of businessmen but staying on as manager. Later he was twice elected to the state legislature, and he served as an officer and director of numerous business organizations until his death in 1941 of a stroke.

Gunfights: mid-August, 1888, White Sands Desert, New Mexico. Lee, Jim Cooper, Cherokee Bill Kellam, and Tom Tucker jumped and captured Walter Good, the alleged murderer of George McDonald. One of the party—quite possibly Lee, McDonald's closest friend since boyhood—shot Good twice in the head with his own pistol, and the body was left in the desert.

August, 1888, near Las Cruces, New Mexico. Two weeks later John Good, accompanied by fifteen relatives and employees, discovered his son's body. Leaving two men to guard the decomposed corpse, Good sadly told his party to disperse. As Good and five men rode toward Las Cruces, however, they saw Lee, Tucker, Kellam, Perry Altman, and Bill Earhart. They immediately rode toward Lee's group, which hopped into a ditch and opened fire when Good's band drew within 150 yards. Good and his men scurried into a corn field, and before the shooting stopped, more than one hundred rounds had been fired. No one was hit, but two horses were killed and a third was wounded.

February 12, 1893, near El Paso, Texas. Lee and Bill McNew had trailed a herd of rustled cattle to within a short distance of El Paso, and they finally overtook the stock, which was being pushed toward Mexico by Charley Rhodius and Matt Coffelt. When Lee galloped up, Rhodius snapped off a wild shot, whereupon Lee opened fire with a borrowed rifle. Rhodius toppled out of the saddle, mortally wounded, just as his partner opened up on Lee. Lee turned on Coffelt and quickly, accurately shot him to death. Lee then went into El Paso, turned himself in, and easily won his release.

July 13, 1898, Dona Ana County, New Mexico. Lee and fellow murder suspect James Gilliland had taken refuge at Lee's property at Wildy Well, about thirty-two miles south of Alamogordo. Pat Garrett, Clint Llewellyn, José Espalin, Ben Williams, and Kent Kearney located the two fugitives and at dawn crept up to the little adobe house and captured a drowsy guard, who managed to croak out an alarm. Lee and Gilliland,

who cautiously had been sleeping on the roof, were awakened when bullets came crashing through from below.

Lee and Gilliland grabbed their rifles just as Garrett and Kearney climbed a ladder to the roof of a nearby shed. A bullet grazed Garrett's ribs, and he quickly jumped to safety, but Kearney tried to shoot it out. Two slugs tore into his body, and he fell to the ground, mortally wounded.

Williams and Llewellyn had taken shelter beneath a wooden water tank, and Lee and Gilliland methodically riddled the structure, drenching the lawmen. In the meantime, Espalin, who had removed his boots in the interests of stealth, had encountered sand burrs and was hopping around in anguish. After a brief parley the posse was allowed to withdraw in humiliation, and the victorious fugitives rode away to safety.

March 20, 1907, Dog Canyon, New Mexico. Two years earlier, five men had filed on water rights, the loss of which would have virtually destroyed Lee's Dog Canyon Ranch. During the ensuing period there was increasing trouble, which finally erupted when a man named James R. Fennimore and three assistants tried to build a fence on the disputed area. A brief, long-range rifle duel occurred when Lee rode up to stop them. Lee was fired at five times, and he squeezed off two rounds, nicking Fennimore in the hip.

Sources: Sonnichsen, *Tularosa,* 28–32, 38, 40–45, 49–53, 76, 77, 81–87, 90–93, 95, 96, 106, 109, 112–14, 127–30, 135–38, 140–45, 149, 151–90, 195–201, 216, 217, 222, 224–25, 236, 243, 257, 263, 270, 276; Harkey, *Mean as Hell,* 119–21, 125; Gibson, *Colonel Albert Jennings Fountain,* 201, 204–205, 208, 211, 214ff., 229, 236, 239, 242, 245–46, 249–50, 253, 258,

260ff., 266ff., 275ff., 281ff., 285, 287; Metz, *Pat Garrett*, 136, 140–43, 147–48, 151–88, 190–94, 200, 245.

Leonard, Bill

(d. June, 1881, Eureka, New Mexico. Jeweler, cattle rustler, stage robber.) Bill Leonard was a jeweler who in the late 1870's practiced his trade in Las Vegas, New Mexico. Drifting into Arizona, he became associated with cattle thieves, including N. H. ("Old Man") Clanton. In March, 1881, Leonard was involved in a bloody attempt to hold up a stagecoach near Tombstone, Arizona. He was wounded, but remained at large for three months until he was killed while attempting to rob a store in Eureka, New Mexico.

Gunfights: March 15, 1881, Contention, Arizona. For a week Leonard, Harry Head, Jim Crane, and Luther King camped in an abandoned adobe hut near the stagecoach road, planning a robbery. On the night of March 15, while King held their horses, Leonard, Head, and Crane crept into position at a steep grade where the coach would be slowed to a walk. That night's stage from Tombstone was loaded with eight passengers and twenty-six thousand dollars in bullion and was guarded by Bob Paul, a crack Wells, Fargo agent.

In Contention, twelve miles from Tombstone, driver Budd Philpot changed teams and was temporarily relieved by Paul. At the grade, about a mile outside town, Leonard, Head, and Crane stepped into the road and ordered the coach to halt. Paul threw down the reins and groped for his shotgun. Gunfire broke out, and Paul winged Leonard with a few buckshot in the groin. Budd Philpot was shot in the heart and dropped lifeless onto the horses' backs. The

animals bolted forward, and as the coach lurched past, the outlaws killed a passenger, miner Peter Roerig. Risking his life, Paul jumped down to the wagon tongue and retrieved the reins, while the robbers escaped.

June, 1881, Eureka, New Mexico. King was soon captured and revealed the names of his accomplices, and warrants and "dead or alive" rewards were issued for Leonard, Head, and Crane. But the three desperadoes managed to keep their freedom until June, when Leonard and Head attempted a robbery in Eureka. They entered a store owned by Bill and Ike Haslett, who boldly resisted the thieves. A gunfight broke out, and Leonard and Head both were shot down. The latter died almost immediately, but Leonard lived for several hours. The festering wound in his groin was discovered, and he admitted his identity, naming Crane as the killer of Budd Philpot.

Sources: Tombstone *Epitaph,* March 16, 1881; Waters, *Earp Brothers of Tombstone,* 127–40; Faulk, *Tombstone,* 145–47.

Leslie, Nashville Franklin

("Buckskin Frank")

(d. ca. 1925, California? Indian scout, bartender, bouncer, jailer, law officer, ranch foreman, convict.) A colorful, versatile frontiersman as well as a deadly gunman, Buckskin Frank was given his sobriquet because of the fringed leather shirt he affected. Reported (in the usual exaggerated fashion) to have killed thirteen men, Leslie attained his greatest notoriety in Arizona. A one-time Indian scout in Texas, Oklahoma, and the Dakotas, he drifted into Arizona during the early mining strikes and eventually opened the Cosmopolitan Hotel in

Tombstone. On occasion he wore a swivel gun, and he was known as an expert shot.

While in Tombstone Leslie was involved in a killing over another man's wife, rode in Bob Paul's posse to apprehend the Contention stagecoach robbers, pistol-whipped a man named Floyd, and shot Billy Claiborne to death. After the Claiborne shooting Leslie ramrodded a ranch for Tombstone saloon owner Mike Joyce (who once had survived a skirmish with Doc Holliday).

During the mid-1880's Leslie twice worked for the army during Apache outbreaks, and he also spent a few months as a mounted customs inspector along the Rio Grande. In 1887 his wife of seven years (who had become known as the "Silhouette Girl" because Leslie would practice by shooting her profile in bullets) divorced him; later she divorced her next husband to remarry Buckskin Frank.

Involved in another homicide in 1889, Leslie was sentenced to a twenty-five-year stretch in the territorial prison at Yuma. In 1897, however, his former military service and exemplary conduct as the doctor's chief assistant in the prison infirmary earned him a pardon. After his release he worked as a field assistant in Mexico to a Professor Dumell, a geologist who was searching for coal deposits for the Southern Pacific Railroad.

After drifting to the Alaska gold fields, Leslie was last heard from in 1925 working in a poolroom in Oakland, California. But after six months on the job he stole the proprietor's pistol and disappeared, possibly having committed suicide.

Gunfights: *June 22, 1880, Tombstone, Arizona.* Leslie had been seeing May Killeen, a married woman who worked in his hotel, and despite her sus-

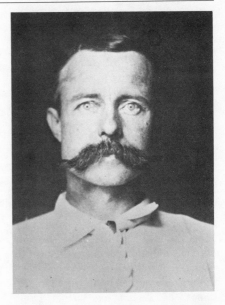

Buckskin Frank Leslie, who killed Billy Claiborne in Tombstone in 1882. *(Courtesy Arizona Historical Society)*

picious husband's threats Frank boldly squired her to a dance at Tombstone's Grand Hotel. At midnight he escorted her across the street to the porch of the Cosmopolitan, where he lived. The cautious Leslie first laid out his Colt six-gun (a borrowed revolver was in his hip pocket), then embraced Mrs. Killeen.

Moments later a friend of Leslie's, George Perine, arrived breathless to announce that a jealous Mike Killeen was hard on his heels. The irate husband stormed onto the scene, and all three men began firing. Leslie was grazed twice on the head and clubbed by Killeen before getting his guns into action. The shooting stopped when Killeen sprawled in the street, seriously wounded. He died five days later, and on August 6, one week after her husband's death, May Killeen became Mrs. Frank Leslie.

November 14, 1882, Tombstone, Arizona. While talking with friends at the Oriental Saloon, Leslie was belligerently approached by a drunken Billy the Kid Claiborne. Claiborne cursed and threatened Leslie, who collared Billy and shoved him through the batwing doors. Expecting an ambush, but remembering the benefits of self-defense, the always careful Leslie left the building by a side door and called out to Claiborne, who had hidden behind a fruit stand. Claiborne whirled and fired wild, then fell from a single fatal shot squeezed off by Leslie. The bullet ripped into Claiborne's left side and out his back, and Frank advanced brandishing his pistol. "Don't shoot again," gasped Billy, "I am killed." He died shortly afterward, and Leslie successfully pleaded self-defense.

July 10, 1889, Tombstone, Arizona. Leslie was operating a small ranch owned by Mike Joyce, and he lived there with a girl from the Bird Cage called Blonde Mollie Williams. Leslie returned drunk from Tombstone one day, quarreled bitterly with Mollie, and shot her to death. There was a witness, a young ranch hand named Jim Neal, and Leslie fired at him as he fled. Neal was wounded but managed to escape into the brush. Leslie searched for the youth, but Neal made it to a neighboring ranch.

Leslie decided that Neal had died in the brush, so he went back to town, making his usual claim of self-defense. But Neal's testimony netted Buckskin Frank a twenty-five-year prison sentence. Three and one-half decades later, Neal generously gave the elderly Leslie a job in a poolroom.

Sources: Rickards, *"Buckskin Frank" Leslie;* Jeffrey, *Adobe and Iron,* 79–80; Erwin, *John H. Slaughter,* 188–95, 205.

Lindsey, Seldon T.

(b. December 19, 1854, Minden, Louisiana. Cowboy, buffalo hunter, law officer.) Reared in Louisiana, Lindsey demonstrated his violent inclinations by participating in a knife fight while a schoolboy. When his father returned from the Confederate army after the Civil War, the family moved to McClennan County, Texas, where the elder Lindsey established a law practice. In 1870 sixteen-year-old Seldon found work as a cowboy, and over the next few years he trailed cattle to the Kansas railheads. He also spent a couple of seasons hunting buffalo, twice meeting Bill Cody.

Lindsey was wed in 1881, and during their thirty-two-year marriage his wife bore him eleven children. He was appointed a deputy U.S. marshal in 1890, operating for many years out of Paris, Texas, and engaging in several shooting frays with outlaws.

Gunfights: *1873, McLennan County, Texas.* Lindsey's father had clashed with a local gang and had decided to move out of McLennan County, and Seldon returned for a visit just before he was to leave. While the two men were riding in a wagon, they were followed by an adversary of the senior Lindsey. The gunman finally pulled a weapon, but Seldon alertly shot him out of the saddle. The gunman died, and Seldon was charged with his murder, but succeeded in winning acquittal.

1890, Winn Parish, Louisiana. Lindsey returned to his home state, Louisiana, in search of a man named Barber, who had killed his business partner in an Oklahoma village. Lindsey and a volunteer known as Jones located Barber in a log house in Winn Parish, and the two men entered the building through different doors. Barber produced a gun, but it misfired, and Jones grappled with him, at which point Lindsey rushed in and shot the fugitive to death.

1891, near Mill Creek, Oklahoma. Lindsey and fellow lawmen John Swain, J. D. Castleman, and George Stuart were scouring the country west of Ardmore for a band of ten thieves. During the evening they surrounded the fugitives' hideout on Mill Creek, and Lindsey sent Castleman back for help. A barking dog revealed the officers' presence, and a long-range rifle duel ensued. At daylight the posse was forced further back from the hideout cabin, and one outlaw bullet grazed the back of Lindsey's neck and blinded him for a few moments.

About 10:00 A.M. Castleman returned with three more officers, and after eating, the posse closed in. Lindsey and Castleman secluded themselves while the other five lawmen moved in from the other side. Finally the outlaws were flushed, and all ten robbers dashed toward Lindsey's position. Castleman winged the first fugitive, a man named Davis, in the arm, and Lindsey fired a shot which felled Bill Hutchins. The outlaws surrendered, and Hutchins eventually died from his wound.

1892, near Purcell, Oklahoma. Accompanied by John Swain and a new officer named Phillips, Lindsey was tracking Cornelius Walker, a Negro wanted for murder. Walker bolted out of a house toward Lindsey, who jumped up and fired a rifle bullet into him. Swain came around the house and also shot Walker, and the fugitive fell, mortally wounded.

1895, near Eufaula, Oklahoma. Lindsey and a posse were in pursuit of train robbers, and they located the outlaw camp in the country near Eufaula. The lawmen dismounted and crept through the woods, finding three outlaws lying on the ground and one cooking breakfast. The officers charged the camp, guns blazing; the man at the fire jumped into the woods and escaped, but his cohorts produced pistols and tried to fight. The shooting lasted only a few seconds, and all three of the remaining outlaws were fatally wounded.

September 25, 1895, near Ardmore, Oklahoma. Lindsey, Loss Hart, Ed Roberts, and W. H. Glover located Bill Dalton at a house near Ardmore. History records that Hart killed Dalton with a rifle bullet, but Lindsey later claimed to have fired the fatal shot. The lawmen tossed the corpse into a wagon, and on the way to Ardmore the day's heat caused the body to swell. Several buckets of well water were poured on the cadaver, but by the time the party reached Ardmore, it was distended to double the normal size.

Source: Lindsey, *The Story of My Life.*

Logan, Harvey

("Kid Curry")

(b. 1865, Tama, Iowa; d. June 8, 1904, Glenwood Springs, Colorado. Rustler, rancher, horsebreaker, gunman, bank and train robber.) Harvey and his three younger brothers were orphaned when they were children, and they were taken in to be raised by Mrs. Hiram Lee, their aunt who lived in Dodson, Missouri. At the age of nineteen Harvey and two of his brothers, Lonie and Johnny (eighteen and sixteen, respectively), left home to travel west. They were accompanied by a first cousin, Bob Lee, and they wandered to Wyoming. There the four youths became rustlers, and in 1888 they started a ranch near Landusky, Montana, with a stolen herd of cattle.

During the Johnson County War in the early 1890's the Logans sold their guns to the Red Sash Gang, but when leader Nate Champion was killed, they returned to the ranch. Harvey, always of a sour disposition and habitually a heavy drinker, killed the founder of Landusky in a murderous rage in 1894, and he and his brothers returned to Curry's gang of rustlers.

A year later the Logans engaged in a shootout with rancher Jim Winters, and when Johnny was killed, Harvey vowed revenge. Vengeance was postponed for a while, however, as Harvey spent the next few years as the "tiger of the Wild Bunch." He looted trains and banks with Butch Cassidy's gang, hid out in the Hole-in-the-Wall country, and acquired a reputation as a vicious killer. He killed sheriffs in Wyoming, Utah, and Arizona and was responsible for the death or injury of several other men, including the Norman brothers and Jim Winters.

By 1901 Harvey was one of the most wanted men in the country, and he sought refuge in Knoxville, Tennessee. But there he became involved in a wild saloon fight, and after shooting three policemen, he fled town on foot, bleeding badly from a shoulder wound. He was captured thirty miles away, and following the trial, he was to have been sent to the escape-proof prison in Columbus, Ohio. Before he could be transferred, however, he made a daring escape from the Knoxville jail.

With a small lasso he had fashioned from a wire on a broom, he snared a guard who walked too close to his cell. Holding him by the neck, Logan tied the guard with strips of cloth, found his keys, and procured two pistols. Using a second guard as a human shield, he found the local sheriff's mare, forced the guard to saddle his new mount, and rode out of town a free man.

At that point Logan tried to join Butch Cassidy and the Sundance Kid in South America, but he was unable to make the necessary arrangements and returned to the West. In Colorado he tried to organize another gang, but after an unsuccessful train robbery in 1904 he was chased down and killed. Rumors persisted that he escaped to join Butch Cassidy and the Sundance Kid in South America, where he supposedly was shot to death in 1910 or 1911.

Gunfights: *December 24, 1894, Landusky, Montana.* On Christmas Eve day Harvey, his brother Lonie, and rustler Jim Thornhill drank heavily, shot up the little town, and made general nuisances of themselves. Finally they roistered their way into a combination store and saloon where glowering old Pike Landusky stood, drinking and dwelling upon his hatred for Harvey.

Landusky was a fifty-five-year-old miner who had founded the town, and one of his four stepdaughters had borne Harvey Logan an illegitimate child. On this occasion the foul-tempered Harvey struck Landusky as he passed by, and the old prospector made an infuriated charge.

As the two men slugged it out, Lonie and Thornhill kept the crowd backed up with drawn pistols. Landusky at last began to cry for quarter, but the crazed Logan kept pounding his head against the floor. Landusky finally managed to pull his revolver from under his coat, but Harvey was quicker. He shot Landusky while the battered old miner was still on his knees, and Landusky died on the spot. Lonie and Thornhill continued to protect Harvey while he dashed outside and stole a buckboard, whereupon the three men escaped the scene of the shooting.

January, 1896, Montana. The Logan

brothers received word that Montana rancher Jim Winters had given incriminating information about them to the authorities. Loudly demanding revenge, Harvey, Lonie, and Johnny lost no time in riding to the Winters ranch. Winters, however, had been warned of their coming, and when they approached, he promptly opened fire. Johnny dropped from his horse, mortally wounded, and Harvey and Lonie groped for their weapons. They got off a few shots, but they were soon driven away by Winters' heavy fire.

September 24, 1897, near Lavina, Montana. Logan and two other men wanted for the robbery of the Butte County Bank of Belle Fourche had camped near Lavina on Montana's Musselshell River. Sheriff John Dunn of Carbon County, accompanied by W. D. Smith, Dick Hicks, and a constable named Calhoun, located the camp just as Logan was picketing his horse. When the posse called out a surrender demand, Logan's two companions dived for cover, and firing broke out. A bullet tore through the neck of Logan's horse and hit his right wrist. Logan dropped his gun, mounted, and galloped away. After a mile, however, the horse dropped dead, and Logan, along with his companions, was captured. But on October 31, Logan and the other robbers escaped from jail in Deadwood.

June 5, 1899, near the Red Fork of the Powder River, Wyoming. The Wild Bunch had just pulled a train robbery at Wilcox Siding, Wyoming. Logan had led the eight-thousand-dollar holdup, and afterward the outlaws scattered to the north. Logan, Flat Nose Curry, and the Sundance Kid made camp near the Red Fork of the Powder River and were eating supper when they were jumped by

a posse led by Sheriff Joe Hazen of Converse County. Logan cut down Hazen, fatally wounding the lawman with a rifle bullet through the stomach. Hazen died several hours later, while the three bandits fled on foot and escaped by swimming the turbulent, rain-swollen Powder River.

April 5, 1900, near San Simon, Arizona. Logan and a few other rustlers were being chased by veteran lawman George Scarborough and a man named Birchfield. The two officers ran the outlaws into a canyon, and Logan angrily unsheathed his rifle. He opened fire, and a slug ripped through Scarborough's leg and killed his mount. Birchfield raced to nearby San Simon and returned with a wagon, and by sundown Scarborough had been transported to the railhead. From there he was whisked to Deming, New Mexico, where his leg was amputated. Despite these efforts, however, he died the next day.

May 26, 1900, near Thompson, Utah. For three weeks a large posse had been combing the Book Mountains in search of Logan and several other rustlers. On this day the posse split into two groups, four men going with a Sheriff William Preece, and Moab County Sheriff Jesse Tyler leading Deputy Sheriff Day and posse member Sam F. Jenkins in another direction.

After about one-half hour Tyler's group discovered what they thought was an Indian camp, and Tyler and Jenkins dismounted to investigate. When they had walked to within a few yards of the camp, Tyler called out, "Hello, boys." Startled, Logan snarled a warning and went for his gun. Instead of fighting on the spot, Tyler and Jenkins turned and ran, hoping to reach their horses and holstered rifles. But Logan dropped both lawmen with a shot apiece in the back, each bullet tearing through its victim's chest.

Day, still mounted, wheeled his horse and galloped away, with bullets whizzing after him. When Preece heard the news, he courageously decided to seek more help, and it was not until a larger posse had been raised from nearby Thompson that the bodies of Tyler and Jenkins were retrieved.

June, 1900. A few weeks later Logan came into company with the Norman brothers. A quarrel developed, and the men quickly resorted to gunplay. When the smoke cleared, it was determined that Logan had inflicted mortal wounds on both his adversaries.

March 27, 1901, Paint Rock, Texas. Logan, by now perpetually on the run, was passing through the tiny Texas town of Paint Rock. He became involved in an argument with a local citizen named Oliver Thornton, and hot words soon led to gunfire. Thornton went down with fatal wounds, and Logan hurriedly left town.

July 26, 1901, Montana. Logan long had wanted revenge against Jim Winters, who had killed his brother Johnny five years earlier. Logan now had the opportunity to seek Winters out, and he shot the rancher to death.

December 13, 1901, Knoxville, Tennessee. Trying to duck the law by going east, Logan found himself in Tennessee. Entering a Knoxville saloon, he was soon involved in a high-stakes pool game, and a fight inevitably started. Logan's pool opponent tried to pull a gun, but Logan smashed the barrel of his .45 across the man's face, knocking him to the floor.

Several patrolmen burst into the saloon, and Logan and the lawmen promptly began to exchange shots. Three patrolmen went down, severely wounded, and Logan darted out the back door. But he fell thirty feet into a culvert, and as he scrambled to his feet a policeman pumped a slug into his shoulder. Logan then disappeared into the darkness, and ten miles out of town he stopped and bandaged his shoulder with his shirt. He managed to go another twenty miles before a posse and a pack of hounds cornered and captured him.

June 8, 1904, near Glenwood Springs, Colorado. The previous day Logan and two other outlaws had held up an afternoon train near Parachute, Colorado. To their dismay, when they blew open the safe, they found only a few dollars.

Within hours a posse was in hot pursuit, and by the next afternoon Logan's gang was cornered in a small canyon near Glenwood Springs. In the first exchange of gunfire a posse member wounded Logan as Harvey jumped from behind a rock. Logan collapsed, then crawled back behind cover.

During a lull in the firing one of his accomplices called out, "Are you hit?"

"Yes," Logan gasped weakly, "and I'm going to end it here."

There was a pistol shot from behind the rock, then the gun battle resumed. Logan's two confederates scrambled away to safety, and when the posse closed in they found Logan dead, a .45 in his hand and hole in his left temple. The posse did not know his identity, and he was dropped into a grave in Glenwood Springs. But detectives soon had his body exhumed, and at that time he was identified.

Sources: Horan and Sann, *Pictorial History of the Wild West,* 36, 191, 198–200, 210–18, 220–21, 224–26,

228–29; Baker, *Wild Bunch,* 87–88, 95, 102, 104, 107, 193; Pointer, *Butch Cassidy,* 100–101, 111–12, 118, 125–27, 130–31, 151–53, 156–57, 160, 165–68, 170–71, 180–82, 200–203, 257; Horan, *Authentic Wild West,* 187–220.

Logan, Lonie

(b. 1871, Tama, Iowa; d. February 28, 1900, Dodson, Missouri. Rustler, rancher, gunman, saloon owner.) Lonie and his brothers Harvey (the oldest), Johnny, and Henry were orphaned in the 1870's and were reared by their aunt, a Mrs. Lee, in Dodson, Missouri. In 1884 Harvey, Lonie, and Johnny left Missouri to go west and become cowboys. Joined by their cousin, Bob Lee, they reached Wyoming and began rustling livestock. About four years later the Logans and Lee drove a herd of stolen cattle into Montana and bought a small ranch near Landusky, a mining town.

During the Johnson County War the Logan brothers hired their guns to Nate Champion's Red Sash Gang, but they returned to their ranch after Champion was killed. Lonie and Harvey were members of Butch Cassidy's Wild Bunch, but in the late 1890's, when the Pinkertons began closing in, Lonie left the gang and bought a saloon in Harlem, Montana. But Charles Siringo and other detectives were hot on his trail, and he sold the saloon for fifteen hundred dollars and tried to find a safe refuge. At last he made his way back to Missouri, where he spent several quiet days with his aunt before being killed by a posse early in 1900.

Gunfights: December 24, 1894, Landusky, Montana. Lonie and Harvey and rustler Jim Thornhill spent Christmas Eve day drinking and "hurrahing" the town. At last they swaggered into a dry goods store–saloon where they encountered Pike Landusky, a rugged old miner after whom the town was named. Landusky, who held an old grudge against Harvey for making one of his stepdaughters pregnant, was suddenly knocked to the floor by Harvey. The enraged Landusky charged Harvey, and as Lonie and Thornhill held the crowd back with six-guns, a brutal brawl ensued.

Harvey soon whipped the middle-aged miner into submission, but he continued to slam Landusky's head against the floor. At last Landusky reached inside his coat and pulled out his revolver. But Harvey was quicker on the draw, and he shot Landusky to death. While Lonie and Thornhill still held the bystanders at bay, Harvey went outside and stole a buckboard, and the three men clattered out of town.

January, 1896, Montana. A Montana rancher named Jim Winters had given information on the whereabouts of the Logan brothers, and Harvey, Lonie, and Johnny rode to his spread to seek revenge. But Winters had been forewarned, and as the Logans rode up, he opened fire, killing Johnny with a shotgun blast. Lonie and Harvey returned Winters' fire, but they were exposed in the open, and the rancher quickly drove them away.

February 28, 1900, Dodson, Missouri. Pinkerton detective Bill Sayles had traced Lonie to his aunt's home, and Sayles gathered a local posse and approached the house at 8:00 A.M. Lonie saw them coming, and he dashed out the back door, firing a shot which nicked Sayles in the arm. Logan dived behind a mound of snow, and a furious exchange of shots continued for nearly half an hour. At last there was a lull in the firing while Lonie reloaded and steeled himself to a desperate try for freedom. He suddenly charged forward, firing as he ran, and a posse member shouted, "Here he comes!" A fusillade of lead met Logan, and he pitched forward into the snow, dying within moments.

Source: Horan and Sann, *Pictorial History of the Wild West,* 191, 198–99, 214, 227; Pointer, *Butch Cassidy,* 101, 127, 158.

Long, John

("Long John")

(Cowboy, law officer.) Jack Long was first involved in shooting troubles in Texas, where he killed two men at turbulent Fort Griffin. He then gravitated to Lincoln County, New Mexico, managing to secure an appointment as deputy sheriff. Long inevitably became involved in the Lincoln County War; he was a member of the posse which assassinated John Tunstall, thus triggering the conflict, and he was a prominent figure in the climactic four-day battle in Lincoln. Following these violent events, Long apparently retreated from the gunman's role, for his name was connected with no further shootouts.

Gunfights: ca. 1876, Fort Griffin, Texas. Long, visiting the dives of Fort Griffin's notorious "Flats," became embroiled in a wrangle which led to gunplay. In the shooting which followed, Long killed a man named Vergil Hewey and a black soldier assigned to the Tenth Cavalry at the fort.

April 1, 1878, Lincoln, New Mexico. Long was accompanying Sheriff William Brady, George Hindman, Billy Matthews, and George Peppin when the party was ambushed in Lincoln's main street. Rifle fire from Billy the Kid and four others felled Brady and Hindman with mortal wounds. The other three scampered for cover, and the Kid and his fellow bushwhackers soon were driven away. Long squeezed off four rifle rounds at the retreating quintet. Jim French was seriously wounded, and his cohorts returned Long's fire before galloping out of range.

April 28, 1878, near Lincoln, New Mexico. Four weeks later Long was a member of the three-dozen-strong "Seven Rivers crowd" who ambushed Frank McNab, Frank Coe, and Ab Sanders. Sanders and McNab were shot down in the initial volley, but Coe tried to fight his way free. After a hot exchange of shots he was forced to surrender, and McNab's corpse and the badly wounded Sanders were left behind.

July 13, 1878, near San Patricio, New Mexico. Long had been given a warrant to serve on Billy the Kid, but when he encountered his prey on the road near San Patricio, the Kid was in the company of Alexander McSween and nine other cohorts. Shots were fired, and Long's horse was killed, but he leaped free and sprinted to safety on foot.

July 15–19, 1878, Lincoln, New Mexico. During the siege of McSween's store, Long stationed himself atop the *torreón* (a round stone tower built years earlier for protection against Indians) and actively sniped at Billy the Kid and others of McSween's supporters.

Long's most important exploit, however, was setting the McSween house on fire. Accompanied by a man called "Dummy," Long crept up to the back of the rambling structure and saturated the kitchen floor with coal oil, but before he could get the fire to blazing, he was spotted. Under fire he darted for the nearest cover, a privy ditch in which he was pinned down until dark.

Following this unpleasant sojourn, his determination was greater than ever, and he soaked several sticks in oil, lit them, and threw them at the kitchen. The blaze finally erupted, and McSween's party was forced outside. Long joined in the explosion of firing which then occurred, but there is little certainty whose bullets caused which wounds.

Sources: Keleher, *Violence in Lincoln County,* 128, 141, 153, 224, 228, 232–34, 238, 273, 278; Metz, *John Selman,* 109–10, 112, 219; Fulton, *Lincoln County War,* 70, 103, 107, 110, 119, 126–28, 131, 158–59, 201, 213, 216, 232, 234, 251, 263–64, 318, 333, 347, 359.

Long, Steve

("Big Steve")

(d. October 19, 1868, Laramie, Wyoming. Law officer, thief.) Long's background is quite obscure, but the six-foot, six-inch northerner established himself as a vicious gunman in Laramie. In 1867 he obtained a postion as deputy marshal of Laramie and participated in a pair of bloody gunfights within two months. He became engaged, but when his fiancée discovered that he was moon lighting as a thief, she turned him in to local vigilantes. They promptly hanged him from a telegraph pole, and his fiancée erected a marker to his somewhat tarnished memory.

Gunfights: October 22, 1867, Laramie, Wyoming. Four cowboys from the Ox Yoke T were whooping it up in Laramie and decided to roust a quartet

of greenhorns who had just arrived from Shelby County, Illinois. Although unarmed, the immigrants were not at all intimidated by the cowhands, and they waded into their antagonists with fists flying. A large crowd of onlookers was attracted to the brawl, along with Deputy Marshal Long. Long futilely commanded a halt to the fight, then furiously whipped out his twin .44's and began pumping lead at the pugilists. Five men fell mortally wounded: three of the Illinois men and two cowboys.

December, 1867, Laramie, Wyoming. A pair of drunken prospectors began cursing each other over whose turn it was to set up the next round of drinks in the Baby Doll Saloon. Deputy Long arrived on the scene and gruffly ordered the men to settle down. The prospectors snarled a protest, whereupon the quick-triggered Long pulled his six-guns and began firing at them. Four men went down, three fatally wounded: the two prospectors, local bootmaker Upham Ransfield, and another bystander who survived the shooting.

October 18, 1868, Laramie, Wyoming. Long attempted to ambush and rob a prospector named Rollie ("Hard Luck") Harrison. Long's first shot grazed Harrison, who tumbled off his mule and played possum. As Long stepped from cover, Harrison squeezed off a slug which winged the bushwhacker in his left shoulder. Long scampered away and returned to town, where he had his wound treated in secret by his fiancée. When she discovered how he had been shot, she informed the head of the local vigilantes. Long was lynched the next day.

Source: Griswold, "The Outlaw Wore a Sheriff's Star," *Frontier West,* February, 1972, pp. 24–27.

The Wild Bunch on a vacation in Fort Worth, December, 1900. From the left: seated, Harry Longabaugh, Ben Kilpatrick, Butch Cassidy; standing, Will Carver, Harvey Logan. *(Courtesy Western History Collections, University of Oklahoma Library)*

Longabaugh, Harry

("Sundance Kid")

(b. ca. 1863, Mont Clare, Pennsylvania; d. 1908, San Vicente, Bolivia. Horse thief, cowboy, horsebreaker, cattle rustler, train and bank robber.) Reared in the East, Longabaugh migrated to Wyoming and while still a teenager served from August, 1887, to February, 1889, in the Sundance jail for horse stealing. Once released, he continued his criminal ways, becoming a regular user of the Robbers' Roost hideaway in the Hole-in-the-Wall country. In 1892, Longabaugh, Harry Bass, Bert Charter, and Bill Madden held up a train in Malta, Montana, and were soon captured. Longabaugh managed to escape custody, but his two associates were sentenced to long prison terms.

A few years later, while working on the Bar FS ranch in Wyoming, Longabaugh encountered Butch Cassidy, whom he had met years earlier at Hole-in-the-Wall. When Cassidy organized his notorious Wild Bunch of bank and train robbers, Longabaugh eagerly enlisted. Following an 1897 bank holdup in Belle Fourche, South Dakota, Longabaugh was arrested along with three other men, but Longabaugh and two others escaped from jail in Deadwood.

Longabaugh was active in all of the Wild Bunch robberies around the turn of the century, and he happily participated in vacation trips to such retreats as Denver, Fort Worth, and New Orleans.

In 1902 Longabaugh and his consort—a former schoolteacher and/or prostitute named Etta Place—met Butch in South America, where they used a government grant of land to set up a cattle ranch in Argentina. Etta developed appendicitis in 1907, and Longabaugh took her to Denver for medical care, but he soon returned to South America, where he and Butch alternated between robbing banks and working for a mining company in Bolivia. Following a payroll robbery which the two outlaws pulled in 1908, Longabaugh was killed in a fight with Bolivian soldiers, while Cassidy escaped and returned to the United States.

Gunfights: June 5, 1899, near the Red Fork of the Powder River, Wyoming. Following a train robbery at Wilcox Siding, Longabaugh, Flat Nose George Curry, and Harvey Logan headed north. They were jumped by a posse while they were encamped and eating supper. The outlaws managed to shoot themselves free, and in the melee Logan killed Sheriff Joe Hazen.

ca. 1905, Chubut Province, Bolivia. Longabaugh was visiting the wife of a local rancher when he was caught in her bedroom by her husband. The rancher was angrily brandishing a gun, but before he could fire Longabaugh produced his pistol and winged the man in the shoulder. Longabaugh then made a hasty exit.

1907, Denver, Colorado. After a gay holiday in New York, Longabaugh delivered Etta to a Denver hospital, then went out to spend a Saturday evening on the town. He quickly found some old friends, and within a few hours he was roaring drunk. He began shooting up a saloon, and when the bartender tried to stop him, Longabaugh turned his gun on the meddlesome barkeep and wounded him. Longabaugh's friends quickly hustled him away from the scene of the shooting.

1908, San Vicente, Bolivia. A day or two earlier Longabaugh and Cassidy had hijacked a money-laden mule train on a jungle trail. They then journeyed fifteen miles to San Vicente and found a place to eat after first tying their mules across the plaza. A local youth recognized the mules and told the police, who called in a troop of cavalry camped outside town.

When the soldiers had surrounded the plaza the *capitán* and several aides approached the two Americans and ordered them to surrender. Without hesitation Longabaugh pulled his six-gun and shot the commander out of his saddle. Cassidy drilled one of the other soldiers, and the outlaw pair ran inside the restaurant. They fortified their position with tables and chairs, but even though they seized the *capitán*'s cartridge belt, they were handicapped because their Winchesters and ammunition were loaded on the pack mules.

After dark, Longabaugh dashed across the plaza, grabbed the rifles and ammunition, and tried to run back. But the soldiers cut him down and also wounded Cassidy when he dragged his friend back inside. The siege quickly proved to be too one-sided, and Cassidy killed Longabaugh with a bullet in the head before managing to escape into the night.

Sources: Horan and Sann, *Pictorial History of the Wild West,* 96–97, 191, 194, 212–13, 215–21, 223, 227, 230–39; Baker, *Wild Bunch,* 59, 97–102, 104–106, 108, 185–86, 189–200; Pointer, *Butch Cassidy,* 6–8, 14–16, 18, 98–100, 125, 130, 160–62, 195–208, 211–13.

Longley, William Preston

("Wild Bill")

(b. October 16, 1851, Austin County, Texas; d. October 11, 1878, Giddings, Texas. Farmer, horsebreaker, cowboy, teamster, packmaster, woodcutter.) Born on Mill Creek in Austin County, Longley and his family moved to the little Texas town of Evergreen when he was two. Bill was reared in Evergreen, where he spent a large part of his boyhood learning to shoot. Two years after the Civil War, when Longley was fifteen, he killed a Negro soldier. Longley thus began a path of murder which was so often directed against blacks that he became known as "the nigger killer."

With another youth, Longley entered a horsebreaking partnership, but after shooting up a circus and killing three more Negroes in two incidents, he left home, finding work in Karnes County as a cowboy for John Reagon. He soon killed another soldier, and while on the run with a horse thief named Tom Johnson, he was lynched at the Johnson house. The job was bungled, however, and although Johnson died, Longley was cut down alive after the posse departed.

Longley then joined Cullen Baker's outlaw gang, but when Baker was killed in 1869, Bill again returned to Evergreen. He then started with a cattle

Wild Bill Longley facing the noose in Giddings, Texas, in 1878. *(Courtesy Western History Collections, University of Oklahoma Library)*

drive to Kansas, but after gunning down the trail boss, he went to Salt Lake City. When he finally made it to Kansas, he killed a soldier and was jailed, but he bribed a guard and escaped.

Wild Bill next ventured into Wyoming, where he was employed at Camp Brown (later Fort Washakie) as a teamster and packmaster. Since he was in charge of a number of pack mules and horses, he joined with a crooked quartermaster in a scheme to shortchange the government in stock sales and purchases. Longley soon fell out with his partner, however, and after killing him, Bill was thrown into the guardhouse for nine months. Eventually sentenced to thirty years in the Iowa State Prison, Longley escaped from Camp Brown before he could be transferred and headed for Indian Territory.

After spending a year with the Utes, Longley returned to his father's farm, working quietly at home before drifting to several other Texas locales. Arrested briefly in Mason County, he again bought his way to freedom, but he soon killed a man near home and was arrested in Delta County. On June 12, 1876, he escaped custody and fled to Indian Territory, Arkansas, and back to Texas. He soon killed again and fled to western Louisiana, where he rented some land near Keatchie.

Two lawmen from Nacogdoches slipped into Louisiana and, wielding shotguns, forced Longley to return to Texas. Jailed in Giddings and sentenced to death, Longley complained to the governor that his punishment was unjust because killer Wes Hardin had recently received merely a long prison term. Obtaining no response, Longley converted to Catholicism and, while awaiting appeal action, spent his time writing long, pious letters of regret to various newspapers.

When Longley was finally executed, five days short of his twenty-seventh birthday, he died with courage, although his knees dragged the ground and he had to be hoisted up and rehanged.

Gunfights: *1867, Evergreen, Texas.* The Camino Real—the old Spanish royal highway between San Antonio and Nacogdoches—ran within a mile of the Longley farm, and on the road Bill encountered a Negro member of the Reconstruction troops. An argument broke out, and the soldier, who was mounted, threw a rifle shot at his youthful antagonist. Longley jerked out his pistol and fired a ball into the soldier's head. Longley then hid the body in a shallow ditch.

1867, Lexington, Texas. Frustrated over a horse race, Longley and his partner, Johnson McKowen, decided to shoot up a Negro street dance. Guns blazing, they galloped through the victory celebration, leaving two dead and several wounded.

December, 1868, near Evergreen, Texas. Spoiling for a fight, Longley followed three abrasive Negroes to their camp about three miles from Evergreen. As he rode up, one the blacks squeezed off a shot at Longley, who then fatally wounded the Negro in the head. The other two men ran away, and Longley was forced to leave the country.

1869, Yorktown, Texas. In the employ of cattleman John Reagon, Longley rode into Yorktown and was mistaken for Charles Taylor. Reconstruction troops had been ordered to quell the violent Sutton-Taylor feud in that area, and several soldiers approached "Charles Taylor" to arrest him. Longley thought they wanted him for his most recent killing, and he immediately took flight. The squad sergeant was mounted and drew alongside Longley, ordering him to surrender. Longley promptly jammed his revolver into the sergeant's side and pulled the trigger. The soldier pitched to the ground, mortally wounded, and Longley escaped.

1869, Indian Territory. While helping to drive a cattle herd to Kansas, Longley fell into a quarrel with the trail boss, a domineering man named Rector. When words failed, Longley shot Rector to death, emptying his pistol into him. Longley then fled to the Salt Lake City home of relatives.

1870, Leavenworth, Kansas. In a Leavenworth saloon the touchy Longley wrangled with a soldier. Within moments the murderous Texan whipped out his pistol and killed the man. Longley sought refuge on a freight train, but at St. Joseph, Missouri, he was captured and returned to Fort Leavenworth.

1871, Camp Brown, Wyoming. Packmaster Longley and a quartermaster named Greggory were purposely miscounting army stock and selling the excess animals at a large personal profit. But when Longley sold some mules for five hundred dollars and told Greggory he had received only three hundred dollars, the quartermaster found out and threatened to kill his partner. Longley hid at the post corral, and when Greggory came in search of him, Wild Bill shot him down. Greggory died the next day, and Longley, who had tried to escape on a mule, was tracked down and arrested three days after the shooting.

1872, Parkersville, Kansas. Returning to Texas, Longley entered a card game and, predictably, began arguing with a young player named Charles Stuart. Within moments Longley snatched out a pistol and shot Stuart to death. Stuart's father posted a fifteen-hundred-dollar reward for the killer of his son, but "Tom Jones" (the alias Longley was then using) escaped safely to Texas.

1874, Comanche County, Texas. Longley learned that a black man had insul-

ted a Mrs. Forsythe, and he eagerly sought out the Negro. The man asked who the hell Longley was, and Longley answered by firing two slugs into the Negro's head. Longley was soon captured, but he was able to buy his way out of jail.

April 1, 1875, Bastrop County, Texas. While working at a Bastrop County farm, Longley learned that his cousin, Cale Longley, had been killed by Wilson Anderson, who had been one of Bill's boyhood friends. Longley rode directly to Anderson's farm, found his old friend working in the fields, and killed him with a shotgun. It was this murder which resulted in Longley's eventual arrest and execution.

November, 1875, Bell County, Texas. Longley and a man called Bill Scrier, whose real name was Lew Sawyer, had grown suspicious of each other. Longley, Scrier, and a youth named Hayes were riding toward Scrier's home when Longley abruptly drew his gun. Scrier alertly spurred his mount and fired over his shoulder at his attacker. Longley wounded Scrier in the right shoulder, but Scrier clung to his horse, still firing. As the chase continued, Scrier was hit four more times, and he finally wheeled his mount and triggered a shotgun blast at Longley. Longley's horse was killed, but by now Scrier had fallen out of the saddle, and the fight continued on foot. The men furiously exchanged shots at close range, and although Longley continued to wing Scrier, he did not die until a slug crashed into his head. Scrier's bloody corpse had taken thirteen bullets.

1876, Delta County, Texas. Longley had been working shares on a farm near Ben Franklin with a minister named Roland Lay. The two men had serious differences, and at last Longley armed himself with a shotgun and approached Lay in the corral. Lay's shotgun was resting against a corral post, and before he could reach his weapon, Longley cut him down with two barrels of turkey shot.

Sources: Bartholomew, *Wild Bill Longley;* Webb, *Texas Handbook,* II, 79–80; Breihan, *Great Gunfighters of the West,* 42–65.

Loving, Frank
("Cockeyed Frank")

(b. ca. 1854; d. April, 1882, Trinidad, Colorado. Gambler.) Loving was the victorious participant in one of the most celebrated gunfights of Western lore. A professional gambler, he was attracted to Dodge City during the 1870's and ultimately became involved in a fatal encounter with a local rowdy named Levi Richardson. Loving moved his operations to Las Vegas, New Mexico, and in 1882 he transferred to Trinidad, Colorado. A few days later Loving was killed by Jack Allen in a shootout in Trinidad, leaving a widow and two young children.

Gunfights: April 5, 1879, Dodge City, Kansas. A quarrel over a woman had grown between Loving and Levi Richardson, a twenty-eight-year-old freighter who had come to Kansas from his native Wisconsin. Between 8:00 and 9:00 P.M. on a Saturday night Richardson was in the Long Branch standing by the stove. He started to leave, but Loving entered and took a seat at a gambling table. Richardson followed him and sat down on the table, whereupon Cockeyed Frank stood up, and the two rivals began exchanging words.

"You damn son-of-a-bitch," said Loving, "if you have anything to say about me why don't you come and say it to my face like a gentleman."

"You wouldn't fight," sneered Richardson.

"You try me and see!" retorted Loving.

Richardson went for his pistol, and Loving clawed for his. Richardson fired first, and when Loving tried to shoot back, his gun misfired. Loving ran behind a stove, with Richardson in pursuit. Richardson fired twice more, and the crowd scampered for cover. Loving then began to empty his gun methodically at his opponent. Richardson was hit, but continued to trigger his .44 as he staggered back and fell against a table.

Suddenly bystander William Duffey rushed forward and seized Richardson's weapon as the wounded man slumped to the floor. Struck in the chest, side, and right arm, Richardson died within minutes; Loving suffered only a scratch on the hand.

April, 1882, Trinidad, Colorado. Loving had drifted into the mining territory of Colorado, where he continued to ply his trade. In Trinidad he encountered and began to quarrel with a former Dodge citizen, Jack Allen, who later became an evangelist. One night in Allen's saloon the two men exchanged sixteen shots, but none took effect. The next day Loving was emptying his revolver cylinder in George Hammond's hardware store when Allen suddenly appeared and shot the gambler to death.

Sources: Miller and Snell, *Great Gunfighters of the Kansas Cowtowns,* 28–30; Bartholomew, *Wyatt Earp, the Untold Story,* 298–300; Vestal, *Dodge City,* 162–68.

Lowe, Joseph
("Rowdy Joe")

(b. 1845 or 1846, Illinois; d. February,

Rowdy Joe Lowe, whose sobriquet accurately reflected his temperament. *(Courtesy Kansas State Historical Society, Topeka)*

1899, Denver, Colorado. Thief, dance hall proprietor, prospector.) Rowdy Joe Lowe and his wife Kate were natives of Illinois who wandered indiscriminately and notoriously throughout the West following the Civil War. Lowe, earlier an outright thief, was a rugged and prominent figure in Delano, a lawless and wide-open district just west of Wichita where he and Kate ran a combination saloon–dance hall–whore house. The Lowes also operated such establishments in Ellsworth and Newton during their railhead days, and in Newton in 1872 Rowdy Joe shot and killed a man named Sweet. The following year Joe killed Red Beard in Wichita, and although he surrendered himself to authorities, he soon escaped custody and fled to Osage Mission in Neosho County, Kansas.

In January, 1874, Lowe was arrested in St. Louis, but through bribery or some other device he was quickly on the loose again. This time he went to Texas, where he spent time in Denison and San Antonio. In the latter city he was fined one hundred dollars for assaulting Kate. He may have gone to the Black Hills during the gold rush, but eventually he drifted into Colorado, where he was killed in 1899.

Gunfights: *February 19, 1872, Newton, Kansas.* During a Sunday night dance at Lowe's Newton house, Joe slapped Kate for refusing the overtures of a customer. Another patron, A. M. Sweet, took advantage of the situation by plying the angry Kate with liquor, then shacking up with her at Fanny Grey's establishment. On Monday, Joe went to Fanny's house armed and ready. When Joe burst onto the scene, Sweet pulled a six-gun, but before he could fire, Lowe pumped two slugs into his body, and he died within three hours.

July 19, 1872, Wichita, Kansas. Rowdy Joe was celebrated for his ruthless ability to keep his place orderly. One of his "gunfights" aptly demonstrated his hardnosed technique. A reveler named Joseph Walters became drunk and disorderly in Lowe's Wichita house. When his antics began to disturb the other customers, Rowdy Joe drew his revolver and attacked Walters with the gun barrel. He clubbed and pistol-whipped Walters so badly about the head and face that doctors proclaimed the man's condition critical for a period of time.

October 27, 1873, Wichita, Kansas. Red Beard owned a dance hall adjacent to Lowe's establishment in Delano. On a Monday night Beard, drunk and always eager to use a gun, became incensed with and threatened to shoot a prostitute named Josephine DeMerritt. He aimed through a window and took a potshot at Lowe next door. Followed by Kate, Lowe charged toward Beard's place. Red drunkenly mistook a girl named Anne Franklin for Josephine and shot her in the belly.

Annie staggered toward the door as Lowe, quite drunk himself, jerked up a shotgun and discharged a wild blast at Beard. Beard fired back, then dashed outside with Lowe in pursuit.

At the bar Bill Anderson collapsed, blinded by a bullet in the head, while outside Lowe chased Beard down at the bridge across the Arkansas River. Bleeding from a neck wound, Rowdy Joe triggered a load of buckshot into Beard, shattering his right arm and hip. Beard lived for two weeks, but his wounds became infected and he finally succumbed.

February, 1899, Denver, Colorado. Lowe, in his usual inebriated state, grew increasingly belligerent and vociferous while drinking in a Denver saloon. When he insulted the local police department, a former member of the force took him to task. Angrily the two men went for their guns, and Lowe was shot to death.

Sources: Miller and Snell, *Great Gunfighters of the Kansas Cowtowns,* 151–68, 387–88; Streeter, *Prairie Trails & Cow Towns,* 145–47; Drago, *Wild, Woolly & Wicked,* 151, 161–62.

McCall, John

("Broken Nose Jack")

(b. 1850 or 1851, Jefferson County, Kentucky; d. March 1, 1877, Yankton, Dakota Territory. Buffalo hunter, laborer, freighter.) McCall was reared in Louisville, Kentucky, with his parents and three sisters. At the age of eighteen or nineteen he left home and drifted west. He joined a group of buffalo hunters, continued to wander, and in 1876 was attracted to Deadwood, where he referred to himself as "Bill Sutherland." A few weeks later he achieved his only notoriety by murdering Wild Bill Hickok. He was captured and quickly (and somewhat extralegally) brought to trial.

McCall testified that the day before the shooting he had gone $110 into debt to Hickok in a poker game. Then McCall "revealed" (falsely, of course) that he was the brother of Samuel Strawhim, who had been killed by Hickok in 1869 in Hays City. The jury thereupon acquitted McCall.

McCall journeyed as a freighter to Cheyenne, where he was arrested by a deputy U.S. marshal who overheard a drunken boast about lying to the Deadwood jury. McCall was sent to the federal court in Yankton, Dakota Territory, and was tried for first-degree murder. When asked, "Why didn't you go around in front of Wild Bill and shoot him like a man?" McCall replied frankly, "I didn't want to commit suicide."

McCall was convicted and sentenced to be executed. The hanging in Yankton was well attended, and newspapers reported that the twenty-five-year-old McCall "died game." The trap was sprung at 10:15 A.M., McCall gasped, "Oh, God," and he plunged to his death.

Gunfight: August 2, 1876, Deadwood, Dakota Territory. Possibly because of a poker debt, possibly because he had been paid two hundred dollars by enemies of Hickok, McCall determined to kill Wild Bill. Just after 4:00 P.M. McCall ordered a drink in Deadwood's Saloon No. 10, where Hickok was playing poker with Charles Rich, Carl Mann, and Frank Massie.

Hickok had just been dealt a pair of aces and a pair of eights when McCall crept up behind him, drew an old .45 Colt, and fired a bullet into the back of Wild Bill's skull. The slug tore through Hickok's head and out his right cheekbone, then bit into the forearm of Massie, who was sitting opposite Hickok. Wild Bill slid lifelessly to the floor, and McCall darted away.

Anson Tipple crawled over the bar to intercept McCall, who snapped his pistol ineffectually at the bartender. (A later examination revealed that McCall's gun was loaded with five defective bullets and only one good cartridge—the one which killed Hickok.) Outside, McCall was chased down the street by Harry Young. The murderer vaulted into the saddle of a nearby horse, but the saddle cinch broke, and McCall was dumped into the dust. He scampered away, but was captured a short time later when he tried to hide in a butcher shop.

Sources: Rosa, *Alias Jack McCall;* Schoenberger, *Gunfighters,* 86, 88–90, 179; Rosa, *They Called Him Wild Bill,* 148, 170, 193, 214–17, 219–20, 224, 226–45.

McCarty, Henry

("Billy the Kid," "William Bonney," "Henry Antrim," "Kid Antrim," "William Antrim")

(b. 1859, Indiana or New York; d. July 14, 1881, Fort Sumner, New Mexico. Teamster, cowboy, rustler, gunman.) Born Henry McCarty in New York or Indiana, this small, bucktoothed outlaw is often known as William Bonney and, of course, Billy the Kid. During the Civil War Billy moved with his parents and

Henry McCarty, better known as Billy the Kid. *(Courtesy Western History Collections, University of Oklahoma Library)*

older brother Joe to Kansas. After his father died, the family moved to New Mexico, where the widow McCarty married William H. Antrim in Santa Fe in 1873. The family settled in Silver City, and Mrs. Antrim died in September, 1874.

Billy soon became involved in petty theft, was jailed, and then managed to escape. He spent two years working as a teamster, cowboy, and general laborer in the Graham County area of eastern Arizona, and in 1877 he killed a man at Fort Grant. Indicted for murder, he again escaped and returned to New Mexico, where he spent the winter hunting with George Coe.

Soon thereafter the Kid was employed on the Lincoln County ranch of Englishman John Tunstall. When Tunstall was killed almost before his eyes a short time later, the Kid swore vengeance—and fully partook of it during the full-scale war which followed. He was a member of the posse which assassinated three gunmen of the opposing faction, he led the ambush which resulted in the deaths of Sheriff William Brady and Deputy George Hindman, and he participated in the battle at Blazer's Mill.

In July, 1878, the Kid led his faction in a four-day fight in Lincoln, and after a desperate escape from death he surrendered himself to the authorities in exchange for amnesty from Territorial Governor Lew Wallace. But the Kid became nervous over the formalities of his approaching trial, and he left "custody" in Lincoln, thus violating the terms of his amnesty agreement. He formed a band of stock thieves, which included Dave Rudabaugh, Charlie Bowdre, and Tom O'Folliard, and which ranged as far as the Texas Panhandle. The Kid killed gambler Joe Grant, fought off a posse at the Greathouse Ranch near White Oaks, and shot his way out of an ambush set by Pat Garrett.

Besieged by Garrett's posse in his hideout at Stinking Springs, the Kid finally surrendered and was incarcerated at Lincoln in December, 1880. Four months later, however, he killed two guards and escaped. But after three more months of freedom he was killed by Garrett at Fort Sumner. Subsequent accounts of the Kid's life have exaggerated and sensationalized his career, and while there is no doubt that he was a colorful and deadly individual, the facts remain that he was active as a gunfighter for less than four years and killed only about half a dozen men.

Gunfights: *August 17, 1877, Fort Grant, Arizona.* Seventeen-year-old

Billy had a quarrel with Irishman F. P. Cahill in George Adkins' saloon in Fort Grant. When the burly blacksmith threw Billy onto the floor and slapped his face, Billy pulled a revolver and shot him. Cahill died the next day, and Billy was indicted by the coroner's jury for "criminal and unjustifiable" murder.

March 9, 1878, Steel Springs, New Mexico. The Kid was a member of a posse which was led by Dick Brewer, John Tunstall's foreman, and which included Charlie Bowdre, William McCloskey, John Middleton, Frank McNab, Henry Brown, J. G. Scurlock, Wayt Smith, and Jim French. A few days previously this band of "Regulators" engaged in a five-mile chase which resulted in the capture of Frank Baker and William Morton, two of the chief suspects in Tunstall's murder a couple of weeks earlier.

There was bitter talk among the posse members about killing their prisoners, and as the party passed through Roswell, Morton posted a letter describing his situation and expressing fears for his life. The next day, about twenty-five miles up the road, Morton nudged his horse alongside McCloskey, seized his pistol, and shot him fatally. Morton and Baker then spurred away, followed closely by several members of the posse. There was a flurry of shots, and the fleeing prisoners fell to the ground, mortally wounded.

The Kid later claimed to have killed both men single-handedly, but at best he was merely one of several posse members who inflicted wounds upon Morton and Baker.

April 1, 1878, Lincoln, New Mexico. The Kid had determined to kill Sheriff William Brady and, accompanied by Henry Brown, John Middleton, Fred

Wait, and Jim French, he set an ambush behind a low adobe wall overlooking Lincoln's dusty main street. About mid-morning Brady walked by, with Deputy George Hindman beside him and Billy Matthews, Jack Long, and George Peppin trailing behind. The Kid and his party suddenly rose up and began firing, felling Brady and Hindman with mortal wounds. Matthews was also hit, but with Long and Peppin he darted for cover. Moments later the Kid and Wait opened the plank gate in the wall and approached the two dead lawmen, intending to steal their Winchesters, but Matthews opened fire, grazing Wait and nicking the Kid in the side. The two outlaws scampered back to the fence, and all five bushwhackers mounted up and galloped away.

April 4, 1878, Blazer's Mill, New Mexico. Three days later the Kid was with a large party of Regulators scouring the countryside for members of the opposing faction. The Regulators stopped for a meal at Blazer's Mill, and shortly after their arrival Buckshot Roberts, a heavily armed member of the opposition, wandered unsuspectingly into their midst.

Charlie Bowdre, Henry Brown, and George Coe walked up to Roberts, and Bowdre pulled a gun and ordered him to surrender. But Roberts whipped up his rifle and shooting erupted. Roberts wounded Coe and nearby Regulator John Middleton, but was himself shot in the middle by Bowdre. Roberts retreated inside the building while the Kid and the other Regulators scrambled around the corner.

The random shooting which followed was ineffective, and Regulator leader Dick Brewer tried to maneuver into position for sniping. Roberts blew off the top of his head, however, and the Kid and the rest of the Regulators soon rode away, leaving Roberts to die of his wound.

May 1, 1878, Lincoln, New Mexico. The Kid was one of several Regulators who encountered members of the opposing faction in the streets of Lincoln. Shots were exchanged for a few moments, but no one was seriously hurt.

May 14, 1878, Lincoln County, New Mexico. The Kid allegedly led a small party of McSween gunmen in a horse-stealing raid against a ranch east of Lincoln on the Pecos River. The wranglers half-heartedly tried to protect themselves, but they soon stopped firing. They were forced to walk back to headquarters, while the Regulators rode away with twenty-seven head of horses.

July 3, 1878, Lincoln County, New Mexico. The Kid and a posse of Regulators were skulking about the eastern part of the county when they were spotted by a group of cowhands. A long-range rifle duel ensued, but there were no casualties.

July 4, 1878, near Roswell, New Mexico. The Kid, Frank and George Coe, and two other riders were returning to the Chisum Ranch from Ash Upson's store when they saw fifteen or twenty of their enemies at a distance. Shooting broke out, and there was a running fight all the way back to the ranch.

July 13, 1878, near San Patricio, New Mexico. The Kid, Alexander McSween, and nine Regulators were riding near San Patricio when they encountered Deputy Sheriff Jack Long. At a distance of two hundred yards, Long, who was carrying warrants for the arrest of the

Kid and other Regulators, wheeled his mount and attempted to flee. But the Regulators opened fire and killed Long's horse, although the deputy hit the ground running and managed to escape on foot.

July 15-19, 1878, Lincoln, New Mexico. During the climactic battle of the Lincoln County War, the Kid fought from McSween's adobe house along with ten other gunslingers. Throughout the first days of the fight the men inside the building were required mainly to stay out of the way of incoming bullets and occasionally to support their comrades stationed outside in sniping at the opposition. On the final day, McSween's structure was set on fire, and the Kid and his cohorts steeled themselves to make a dash for freedom after dark.

When only three of the twelve rooms of the house remained intact, McSween walked outside, armed with just the Bible he clutched to his chest. Upon sighting McSween, the men who had crept near the burning building cut him down with a blast of rifle fire. Tom O'Folliard then burst outside, intending to shoot his way to the nearby riverbed. But when Harvey Morris was shot down behind him, he turned back to help and was wounded in the shoulder, although he stumbled to safety as his cohorts ran through the door. Three of them were riddled with bullets, but the Kid miraculously darted unscathed through the hail of lead.

One of the besiegers, nineteen-year-old Bob Beckwith, stepped from concealment to block an opening in the low adobe wall, but a pair of slugs slammed into his wrist and head and he fell dead. The Kid frequently has been credited with Beckwith's death, but the darkness and confusion of the moment rendered it quite impossible to determine Beckwith's killer with accuracy. At any rate, the Kid scrambled down the riverbed, splashed to the other side, and made good his escape.

January 10, 1880, Fort Sumner, New Mexico. During a boisterous evening in Bob Hargrove's saloon in Fort Sumner, the Kid was tipped off that a heavy-drinking hard case named Joe Grant intended to kill him. The Kid innocently approached Grant and asked if he could examine Grant's ivory-handled pistol. While admiring the weapon, the Kid discovered that only three cartridges were in the cylinder, and before handing it back, he set the cylinder so that it would next fire on an empty chamber. This precaution proved invaluable, because a short time later Grant belligerently challenged the Kid, then stuck the gun in Billy's face and pulled the trigger. The weapon merely clicked, and the Kid whipped out his revolver and pumped a slug in Grant's head. Grant dropped to the floor and died within moments.

November 29-31, 1880, near White Oaks, New Mexico. The Kid and fellow desperado Billy Wilson were intercepted by an eight-man posse in the mountainous countryside near White Oaks. The two outlaws aggressively opened fire, but the lawmen pressed forward, and a running gun battle began. The posse succeeded in killing the mounts of both fugitives, but the Kid and Wilson disappeared on foot.

The hunted pair united with notorious Dave Rudabaugh, and the next day the three hard cases boldly rode down the main street of White Oaks. Spotting Deputy Sheriff James Redman, they threw a wild shot at him, but quickly spurred out of town when a number of angry citizens ran outside to support Redman.

A posse led by Deputy Sheriff James Carlyle set out in pursuit, and at dawn it located the troublemakers at the ranch of Jim Greathouse. The Kid announced that Greathouse was a hostage, but Carlyle persuaded the outlaws to let him trade places with the ranch owner. After the switch was accomplished, Carlyle tried to talk the trio into surrendering. But at midnight Carlyle decided it prudent to escape, and he jumped through a window.

Firing erupted, and three slugs tore the life from Carlyle's body; it is not known whether the fatal bullets came from the outlaws or from the posse, who might have mistaken the lawman for an escaping fugitive. The Kid and his henchmen successfully fled the scene, and when the posse discovered the body to be Carlyle's they angrily burned the ranch house to the ground.

December 19, 1880, Fort Sumner, New Mexico. A few weeks later the Kid led Rudabaugh, Wilson, Charlie Bowdre, Tom O'Folliard, and Tom Pickett into Fort Sumner for food and recreation. Awaiting them in the old post hospital, however, was a posse headed by Sheriff Pat Garrett. The Kid—perhaps coincidentally, perhaps suspecting a trap—told O'Folliard beside him that he needed a chew of tobacco from Wilson, and he nudged his horse to the rear.

At that point the lawmen emerged from the hospital, and Garrett ordered the outlaws to halt. The fugitives immediately wheeled their mounts, and the lawmen opened fire. O'Folliard was hit in the chest, and Rudabaugh lost his horse, but all except the fatally wounded O'Folliard escaped into the darkness of the cold winter night.

December 23, 1880, Stinking Springs, New Mexico. The Kid and his four surviving followers hid in a dilapidated rock house, where they were trailed through the snow by Garrett's posse. Garrett ordered his men to kill the Kid on sight, and when an unsuspecting Charlie Bowdre emerged from the cabin at dawn, Garrett thought he was the Kid and gave the signal to fire. Bowdre reeled back inside, but the Kid stuck a gun into his hand said: "They've murdered you, Charlie, but you can get revenge. Kill some of the sons-of-bitches before you die." The Kid then shoved Bowdre out of the cabin, but the wounded man merely staggered forward to die in Garrett's arms.

Two horses were tethered inside, and the outlaws tried to pull their other three mounts into the building. But Garrett killed one of the animals, blocking the doorway, and later that day the fugitives surrendered.

April 28, 1881, Lincoln, New Mexico. The Kid had been sentenced to die on May 13, and he was incarcerated in the two-story courthouse in Lincoln to await hanging. Of his two guards, J. W. Bell was amiable and easy-going, but Bob Olinger had often abused the Kid verbally, and, with wretched timing, on the morning of the escape he threatened the Kid and shoved a shotgun into his face.

About 6:00 P.M. Olinger led the other prisoners across the street to eat at the Wortley Hotel while Bell remained in the courthouse with the Kid. The Kid asked Bell to let him use the outhouse, and on the way back upstairs the Kid slipped his small hands out of the cuffs and darted ahead of Bell, despite his leg irons. The Kid forced open the weapons closet and grabbed a six-gun (there is some speculation that the gun had been planted in the privy by prearrangement with young José M. Aguayo). Bell turned to flee, and the Kid fired. The slug ricocheted off the stairway wall and tore through Bell's upper body. Bell staggered outside and died in the arms of Godfrey Gauss, who then went to warn Olinger.

The Kid armed himself with Olinger's shotgun and hobbled to a window just as Olinger rushed across the street. "Hello, Bob," said the Kid, who punctuated the greeting by firing both barrels of the shotgun. The thirty-six buckshot took Olinger in the head and neck, and he died on the spot. The Kid shouted, "You won't follow me any more with that gun," and tossed the weapon into the dust beside Olinger's body. The Kid then took a Winchester and a gun belt, tried unsuccessfully to take off his leg irons, traded words with a few unoffending bystanders, and finally rode leisurely out of town.

July 14, 1881, Fort Sumner, New Mexico. The Kid had been hiding at a sheep camp near Fort Sumner, and on a Wednesday evening he ventured into the old post to rest and see Celsa Gutiérrez, a long-time sweetheart. As he passed a peach orchard adjacent to the post, he was noticed but not recognized by Pat Garrett, John Poe, and Tip McKinney, who were searching for the young fugitive.

Once at Celsa's two-room quarters, the Kid relaxed and partially undressed, but by midnight he decided he was hungry. He jammed his double-action .41 into his waistband, picked up a butcher knife, and padded in his stocking feet to Pete Maxwell's house to ask for the key to the meat house.

When he reached Maxwell's porch he saw McKinney and Poe, who were waiting outside while Garrett asked Max-

well about the Kid's whereabouts. The Kid asked *"¿Quién es? ¿Quién es?"* and when McKinney and Poe did not reply, Billy pulled his six-gun and entered Maxwell's unlighted bedroom. Seeing Garrett's dim form on the bed, the Kid repeated his question and began to back out the door. But Garrett promptly triggered two shots at the Kid, then followed Maxwell in scurrying out of the room.

Garrett's second shot had gone wild, but his first slug struck the Kid in the heart, knocking him onto his back and killing him instantly. Two men fashioned a coffin that night, and at noon the Kid was buried in the post cemetery between Tom O'Folliard and Charlie Bowdre.

Sources: Garrett, *Billy, the Kid;* Keleher, *Violence in Lincoln County;* Siringo, *Texas Cowboy,* 124–40, 168–77; Coe, *Frontier Fighter;* Hunt, *Tragic Days of Billy the Kid;* Fulton, *Lincoln County War;* Mullin, *Boyhood of Billy the Kid;* Adams, *Fitting Death for Billy the Kid;* Lyon, *Wild, Wild West,* 117–23; Klasner, *My Girlhood Among Outlaws,* 169–75, 177, 189–91, 217–18, 252, 328–29; Koop, "Billy the Kid," *Trail Guide;* Horan, *Authentic Wild West,* 9–80.

McCarty, Tom

(b. ca. 1855, Utah; d. ca. 1900, Montana. Cowboy, robber, sheepherder.) Tom, Bill, and George McCarty were associated with the Wild Bunch, although George never actively participated in outlawry. Reared on a Mormon ranch in Utah, Tom married Teenie Christiansen, sister of Matt Warner, when he was eighteen, but wedlock failed to settle him. He drifted into a life of banditry, frequently in alliance with Warner, his brother Bill, and other desperadoes. But Warner was finally

imprisoned, and Bill and his nephew Fred were killed while trying to rob a bank in Delta, Colorado. Tom secluded himself in Montana as a sheepherder, but he was shot to death around the turn of the century.

Gunfights: *ca. 1892, Roslyn, Washington.* While holding up a Roslyn bank, Tom, Bill, and Matt Warner were approached by an angry crowd. Tom opened fire, hitting a Negro in the stomach and wounding another man. The crowd hesitated, and the three thieves galloped away under a hail of lead.

September 7, 1893, Delta, Colorado. Tom, Bill, and Fred McCarty held up the Farmers and Merchants Bank of Delta. Fred held the horses while his uncles entered the bank, but cashier A. T. Blachey began shouting for help. Tom leaped over the railing and shoved his revolver into Blachey's ribs, while Bill began scooping money into a sack. Fred rushed in with news that a crowd was gathering, and the robbers began shooting. Blachey was killed, the assistant cashier was wounded, and the Mc-Cartys raced outside to mount up. When hardware merchant Ray Simpson heard the commotion, he grabbed a new repeating rifle and shells from his shelves and ran into the street as he loaded the weapon. As the robbers galloped past, Simpson knocked Bill out of the saddle with a slug in the head. Fred wheeled up to help his dying uncle, but Simpson dropped him with another mortal shot. Tom never slowed up, although Simpson fired a few rounds after his fleeing figure. After escaping a pursuing posse, Tom abandoned the owlhoot trail for the quieter existence of a Montana sheepherder.

ca. 1900, Montana. McCarty, always a fractious man, joined in a quarrel while in Montana's Bitterroot country. A gunfight broke out, and McCarty's antagonist fatally wounded the middle-aged outlaw.

Sources: Warner, *Last of the Bandit Raiders;* Burroughs, *Where the West Stayed Young,* 35, 121–23, 134–35; Baker, *Wild Bunch,* 56, 58, 64, 71, 149–57, 159, 185; Horan, *Desperate Men,* 194–96, 201; Pointer, *Butch Cassidy,* 46, 51, 120, 252.

McCluskie, Arthur

(d. June, 1873, Medicine Lodge, Kansas.) The brother of Mike McCluskie of Newton fame, Arthur's sole recognition as a Western gunman came from the bloody revenge he exacted from Mike's killer. Two years after his brother's death at the hands of Texan Hugh Anderson, McCluskie found Anderson in Medicine Lodge, at that time merely a handful of scruffy buildings. McCluskie called out Anderson, and the duel that followed resulted in the death of both men.

Gunfight: June, 1873, Medicine Lodge, Kansas. Arthur McCluskie—big, clad in buckskin, and armed with a pistol and a bowie knife—rode into Medicine Lodge with a guide named Richards. Inquiry revealed that Hugh Anderson was working as a bartender in the local trading post, and Richards was sent to tell him that McCluskie wanted a fight to the death with guns or knives. McCluskie, like his dead brother, was strong and husky, and the smaller Anderson accepted the challenge with pistols.

Late in the afternoon the two adversaries met outside, surrounded by a crowd of seventy onlookers. McCluskie and Anderson stood twenty paces apart with their backs to each other, and the owner of the trading post—a bearded man named Harding—fired a shot in the air. The antagonists whirled and fired without effect. Then McCluskie snapped off a quick second shot, and Anderson dropped to his knees, his left arm broken. But Anderson gamely fired again, and the slug tore into McCluskie's mouth. Roaring with rage and pain, blood smearing his face, McCluskie charged his fallen opponent. Anderson coolly pumped bullets into McCluskie's shoulder and stomach, and the big man finally collapsed to the ground.

The spectators thought the fight had ended, but the bullet-riddled McCluskie suddenly raised his head, leveled his gun and fired another shot. The slug caught Anderson in the belly and threw him onto his back. McCluskie then drew his knife and, with an agonized effort and leaving a trail of blood, began to crawl toward the still-breathing Anderson. Several men wanted to halt the gory brawl, but Harding insisted that the fight be finished.

As McCluskie inexorably approached, Anderson managed to rise to a sitting position, draw his knife, and slash his opponent in the neck. McCluskie then buried his own knife in Anderson' side, and the two men collapsed in death.

Source: Yost, *Medicine Lodge*, 75–77.

McCluskie, Mike

("Arthur Delaney")

(d. August 20, 1871, Newton, Kansas. Railroad employee, law officer.) McCluskie's background is hazy and is obscured partially by the fact that he sometimes referred to himself as Arthur Delaney. It is known that he was employed by the Atchison, Topeka & Santa Fe Railroad and that he eventually became foreman of a large crew. Known for his two-fisted ability to keep his men in line, he briefly moonlighted in Newton, Kansas, as a night policeman. His hot temper, however, embroiled him in two gunfights in Newton, and the second resulted in his death at the hands of Hugh Anderson. Two years later McCluskie's brother killed Anderson in a bloody fight in Medicine Lodge, Kansas.

Gunfights: August 11, 1871, Newton, Kansas. McCluskie's railroad crew had been in Newton a few weeks when a special election was held in town. An election deputy, a hard-drinking Texas gambler named Bill Wilson, was employed. Wilson reputedly had been involved in a couple of drunken shooting scrapes and, like Delaney-McCluskie, was employing an alias: William Bailey.

Drinking heavily throughout the day, Bailey began badgering the election officials and became generally obnoxious to everyone. The hot-tempered McCluskie seized Bailey, shoved him outside, and administered a profane tongue-lashing in his best railroad foreman style.

About 8:00 P.M. McCluskie encountered Bailey in the Red Front Saloon. Bailey abrasively ordered McCluskie to set up a round of drinks, and when the Irishman refused, Bailey swung at him. McCluskie countered with a stunning blow which sent Bailey reeling through the swinging doors of the saloon. When McCluskie followed him outside, he saw Bailey leaning on a hitch rail across the street—a six-gun in his fist. McCluskie went for his pistol and quickly fired two shots. The first went wild, but the second slug tore into Bailey's side.

Bailey was carried away and died early the next morning. When McCluskie heard the news, he left town on the morning train, hoping that Bailey's numerous Texas friends would cool off.

August 20, 1871, Newton, Kansas.

After a week in exile, McCluskie returned to Newton, defying the sinister threats of Texas cowboys like Hugh Anderson who were still bitter over Bailey's death. McCluskie hit town on Saturday, August 19, and spent the evening in Perry Tuttle's dance hall. An hour or so after midnight McCluskie was sitting at a faro table when Anderson approached with a drawn pistol. "You are cowardly son-of-a-bitch!" announced Anderson. "I will blow the top of your head off."

Without further ceremony Anderson fired a bullet somewhat inaccurately into McCluskie's neck. Blood spurting from his throat, McCluskie half rose, jerked his gun out, and squeezed the trigger. The first cartridge misfired, and Anderson shot McCluskie in the leg. As McCluskie went down, he furiously began firing slugs at Anderson. McCluskie then writhed onto his back, and Anderson fired into his body.

By this time several cowboys had produced guns and opened fire. A cowhand named Jim Martin was struck in the throat, and two railroad men—brakeman Patrick Lee and a shoveler named Hickey—were shot in the stomach and leg, respectively. As Martin staggered outside to die, Jim Riley, a young friend of McCluskie's, locked the door behind him and emptied his gun at the Texas cowboys.

When the gunsmoke cleared, the blood-spattered room revealed a squad of punctured cowhands: Anderson had been hit twice in the leg, Billy Garrett had been fatally wounded in the chest and shoulder, Henry Kearnes was dying from a chest wound, an unnamed cowboy had suffered a leg wound, and Jim Wilkerson's nose had been grazed. McCluskie was immediately carried away to his hotel room. He lived until eight the next morning, and before dying he claimed that his real name was Arthur Delaney and that his mother lived in St. Louis.

Sources: Miller and Snell, *Great Gunfighters of the Kansas Cowtowns,* 65–71; Streeter, *Prairie Trails & Cow Towns,* 131–36; Drago, *Wild, Woolly & Wicked,* 130–36.

McConnell, Andrew

(b. ca. 1835, Massachusetts. Homesteader, convict.) McConnell's background is vague; he is known chiefly as the killer of Abilene Marshal Tom Smith. A native of Massachusetts, McConnell came to occupy a Kansas homestead a few miles outside Abilene. In 1870 he killed a neighbor and subsequently clashed with local police officers, resulting in Smith's death and McConnell's imprisonment.

Gunfights: *October 23, 1870, Abilene, Kansas.* On a Sunday afternoon McConnell returned to his crude dugout, having spent the day hunting deer. He found a neighbor, John Shea, driving a herd of cattle across his land. The two men exchanged words, and Shea whipped out a pistol. Shea's gun snapped twice ineffectively, but he cocked the hammer for a third try. At that instant McConnell, who had been leaning on his rifle, shouldered the weapon and drilled a bullet into Shea's heart. McConnell went for a doctor and surrendered himself, but Shea was already dead. Subsequent testimony by one Moses Miles won McConnell an immediate release.

November 2, 1870, Abilene, Kansas. Soon, neighbors of Shea, who had left a widow and three children, shed doubt on Miles's statement. A warrant was sworn for McConnell's arrest, but a county officer was driven off his spread. Tom Smith, marshal of Abilene, offered to serve the warrant and, accompanied by Deputy J. H. McDonald, rode out to McConnell's dugout.

McConnell and Miles were together, and when Smith read the warrant, McConnell shot him in the right lung. Smith snapped off a return shot and winged McConnell; the two wounded adversaries then staggered together and began wrestling. Miles and McDonald had also exchanged fire, and although Miles was struck, McDonald fled the scene. Miles then turned upon Smith and beat him to the ground with his gun. Miles and McConnell hauled Smith about ten yards from the dugout, whereupon Miles seized an ax and chopped the lawman's head nearly from his body.

Within three days Miles and McConnell were taken into custody, and eventually they were sentenced, respectively, to terms of sixteen and twelve years in the penitentiary.

Sources: Miller and Snell, *Great Gunfighters of the Kansas Cowtowns,* 416–19; Streeter, *Prairie Trails & Cow Towns,* 78–81; Drago, *Wild, Woolly & Wicked,* 67–70.

McKinney, Thomas L.

("Tip")

(Cowboy, law officer.) Tip McKinney was a member of a noted Texas family. His grandfather, Collin McKinney, signed the Texas Declaration of Independence; Robert McKinney, Tip's uncle, died at the Alamo; and his cousin, Robert Moody McKinney, was owner and publisher of the *Santa Fe New Mexican.* Tip's father, John McKinney, owned a stock farm in East Texas.

During the late 1870's Tip helped his father drive a herd of horses to Palo Pinto County, where they traded their animals for a cattle herd. They drove the cattle to New Mexico's Seven Rivers country, where they soon became involved in fighting with the "Seven Rivers Warriors."

Tip later spent some time in Uvalde, Texas, and finally settled in Roswell. Pat Garrett appointed him deputy sheriff, and he was with Garrett when Billy the Kid was killed. McKinney's greatest notoriety as a gunman came during a close-range shooting scrape two months before the Kid's death.

Gunfight: *May 8, 1881, near Rattlesnake Springs, New Mexico.* Bob Edwards and three other rustlers had stolen twenty-one horses from John Slaughter's ranch in Arizona. McKinney located Edwards at a ranch on the Black River near Rattlesnake Springs, and he went directly to the ranch to encounter the horse thief. Edwards let the lawman ride abreast of him, but then he opened fire with his Winchester. McKinney jerked out his six-gun and began shooting back, and one of his slugs plowed into Edwards' head. Edwards fell out of the saddle and died within moments.

Sources: Keleher, *Violence in Lincoln County,* 342–44, 348–49; Hunt, *Tragic Days of Billy the Kid,* 309–15; Garrett, *Billy, the Kid,* 143–48.

McLaury, Frank

(b. late 1851 or 1852, Iowa; d. October 26, 1881, Tombstone, Arizona. Rancher, cattle rustler.) A native of Iowa, McLaury and his brother Tom came to Arizona in the late 1870's. They acquired two ranches in southern Arizona and became connected with the Clanton cattle rustling ring. Rumor suggested that the Earp brothers and Doc Holliday were associated with the Clanton-McLaury faction, but that trou-

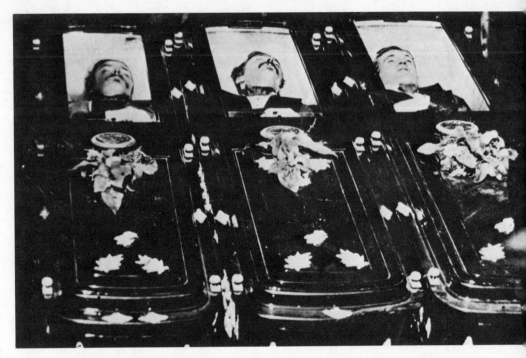

The McLaury brothers, Tom and Frank, and Billy Clanton, shown laid out after the fight at the O.K. Corral. *(Courtesy Western History Collections, University of Oklahoma Library)*

ble erupted between the groups over a gambling quarrel or over heated words between Doc Holliday and Frank Mc-Laury about the quality of food in Nellie Cashman's Russ House. Mrs. Virgil Earp even hinted that the origins of the feud could be traced to a midnight rendezvous between Hattie Earp, James Earp's sixteen-year-old stepdaughter, and one of the McLaury brothers.

Whatever the cause, the growing dispute came to a head on October 25, 1881, when Tom McLaury and Ike Clanton drove a wagon into Tombstone to pick up supplies. That night and the next morning the Earp brothers and Holliday cursed and bullied the pair, continually taunting them to fight. Before noon Billy Clanton and Frank McLaury rode into town, and a short time later Frank emerged from a store to see

Wyatt Earp pulling his horse by the bit.

"Take your hands off my horse!" snapped McLaury.

"Keep him off the sidewalk," demanded Earp piously, pulling the animal into the street. "It's against the city ordinance."

McLaury, cursing under his breath, rode to the O.K. Corral and tied his horse.

After making several trips to nearby stores, Frank was approached by Sheriff John Behan, who was attempting to head off trouble by trying to disarm everyone. McLaury refused to surrender his six-gun, saying that he intended to cause no trouble. Behan walked along with Frank to the O.K. Corral, still trying to persuade him to turn over his weapon. Behan then asked the entire Clanton party to give up their guns, but Ike Clanton and Tom McLaury protested that they were unarmed, and Frank vehemently declined again. Then the Earp brothers and Doc Holliday appeared, and Behan fruitlessly tried to intervene between the two groups. Both McLaury brothers, along with Billy Clanton, were killed in the gunfight that followed.

Gunfight: *October   26,   1881, Tombstone,   Arizona.* When firing broke out between the Earp and Clanton parties near the O.K. Corral, Frank McLaury   was   struck   immediately. (Wyatt Earp later said that he zeroed in on Frank because "he had the reputation of being a good shot and a dangerous man," and that it was his first shot which hit Frank in the stomach.) In shock, and clutching his belly with his left hand, Frank staggered into the street and managed to bring his gun into play. Billy Claiborne and Ike Clanton had fled the scene, and Tom McLaury had been shot down by Doc Holliday. But Frank and Billy Clanton, who had also been hit at the outbreak of gunfire, gamely inflicted wounds upon Holliday and Morgan and Virgil Earp.

Morgan, whose first shot had struck Billy Clanton and who had already been hit in the shoulder, squeezed off a bullet at Frank and yelled, "I got him." The slug caught Frank just beneath the right ear and pitched him face down into the street, dead on impact.

Sources: Waters, *Earp Brothers of Tombstone,* 122–23; *Tombstone Epitaph,* October 27, 1881.

McLaury, Thomas

(b. after 1852, Iowa; d. October 26, 1881, Tombstone, Arizona. Rancher, cattle rustler.) Tom McLaury and his

older brother Frank drifted into southern Arizona in the late 1870's and began to build up a ranching enterprise. While Tom improved their spread near Tombstone, Frank hired out to neighboring ranchers to raise money, and in so doing was introduced to the Clanton family.

The Clantons and the McLaurys soon were engaged in widespread rustling activities, and eventually they came into conflict with a faction led by the Earp brothers of Tombstone. The McLaury brothers testified against a key member of the Earp group, Doc Holliday, in connection with a stage robbery in March, 1881, in which two men were killed. Although the tubercular dentist was acquitted, the McLaurys had thus earned the vengeful resentment of the Earps in general and Holliday in particular.

On October 25, 1881, Tom McLaury and Ike Clanton went into Tombstone to buy supplies. That night Clanton was roughed up by Holliday and the Earps, and the next morning Wyatt Earp approached Tom on the street, and harsh words were exchanged. Wyatt drew his foot-long Buntline Special and challenged Tom to fight. Tom refused, and Wyatt slapped him with his left hand, then clubbed him on the head with his gun, knocking him down.

Frank McLaury and Billy Clanton rode into town to help their brothers, but Tom decided he wanted no further run-ins, and early that afternoon he turned over his revolver and gun belt to Andy Mehan, a local saloon keeper. About an hour later the Clantons and McLaurys were asked by Sheriff John Behan to surrender their guns, and Tom pointed out that he was unarmed. Then the Earps and Doc Holliday approached.

Gunfight: *October   26,   1881,*

Tombstone, Arizona. The Earp party was ordered by Sheriff Behan to turn over their weapons, but they ignored him and walked to within a few feet of the Clantons and the McLaurys. Tom McLaury was behind his horse, and although there was a Winchester in the saddle boot, he was still unarmed. Opposite him was Doc Holliday, a pistol in his belt and a shotgun beneath his long overcoat. The Earps ordered a show of hands. Billy Clanton shouted that he wanted no part of a fight, and Tom McLaury threw open his coat and said, "I'm not armed."

But the Earps began to fire, and Billy Clanton and Frank McLaury were shot immediately. Holliday leveled his shotgun and, when the horse shied at the gunfire, blasted Tom in the body. Twelve buckshot penetrated a four-inch area on his right side, and he staggered only a few steps before collapsing to the ground. Within a few seconds the firing stopped, and bystanders carried Tom and Billy Clanton into a nearby house.

Tom was stretched out on a carpet, and a pillow was placed under his head. A local carpenter who helped carry him inside asked him if he had anything to say before he died, but Tom could not talk. The carpenter unbuttoned Tom's shirt and took off his boots, then gave him some water, but he died within moments. At the burial services the next day the McLaury brothers were taken to their graves in the same hearse.

Sources: Waters, *Earp Brothers of Tombstone,* 122–23; *Tombstone Epitaph,* October 27, 1881.

McMasters, Sherman

(Gunman, law officer.) McMasters was in Tombstone during the Earp-Clanton feud. He sided with the Earps, was sworn in as a deputy marshal to help

Wyatt pursue stage robbers, and was present when Morgan Earp was shot from ambush while playing billiards. McMasters helped chase down and kill Frank Stilwell and Florentino Cruz, and when the vendetta ended, he drifted into the Texas Panhandle and Utah with Turkey Creek Jack Johnson.

Gunfights: March 20, 1882, Tucson, Arizona. After the death of Morgan Earp, it was decided to send Virgil Earp wounded in a previous ambush, to safety in California. Virgil was accompanied to the depot in Tucson by his brothers Wyatt and Warren, Doc Holliday, Turkey Creek Jack Johnson, and McMasters. It was rumored that Frank Stilwell, accused of Morgan's murder, was also in Tucson and the train was duly searched. Stilwell was spotted near the train, and a night chase ensued. Stilwell was run down within moments, and he was shot at close range by his five pursuers.

March 22, 1882, near Tombstone, Arizona. Still hunting participants in Morgan Earp's death, the five-man posse returned to Tombstone and went to the wood camp of suspect Pete Spence. Spence had already surrendered himself to Tombstone authorities, but another suspect, halfblood Florentino Cruz, was at the camp. Cruz was surrounded and executed just as Stilwell was.

Source: Jahns, *Doc Holliday,* 223, 227–28, 230–32, 234–35; Lake, *Wyatt Earp,* 266, 314–15, 321, 324, 329ff., 356.

McNab, Frank

(d. April 30, 1878, near Lincoln, New Mexico. Cowboy, ranch foreman, gunman.) A cowboy by trade, McNab was employed by cattle king John Chisum and eventually became one of the fore-

men on Chisum's South Spring Ranch in New Mexico. When the Lincoln County War broke out, McNab naturally aligned with the Chisum-McSween "Regulators." He was instrumental in the revenge murders of Frank Baker, Billy Morton, and William McCloskey, and after Dick Brewer was killed at Blazer's Mill, McNab became a leader of the Regulator's. A short time later, however, he was shot to death by a large posse of his adversaries.

Gunfights: March 9, 1878, Steel Springs, New Mexico. After a five-mile chase, a posse of Regulators captured Frank Baker and Billy Morton, who were known to have participated in the murder of John Tunstall. As the party headed back to Lincoln, there was a great deal of talk—vigorously encouraged by McNab—about shooting the two prisoners.

There are two versions concerning what finally happened. One suggestion is that Morton drew near Regulator William McCloskey, who had vehemently opposed any execution, and seized his pistol. Morton then shot McCloskey dead and spurred away with Baker, but the posse quickly caught their prisoners and killed them. The other version is that McNab rode up to McCloskey and shot him off his horse; then the posse turned on Morton and Baker and murdered them.

April 30, 1878, near Lincoln, New Mexico. McNab met fellow Regulators Frank Coe and Ab Sanders, Coe's brother-in-law, in Lincoln. About 3:00 P.M. they decided to go to Sanders' ranch. After riding about eight miles down the road, they stopped at a stream to get a drink.

When McNab and Sanders had dismounted, they were suddenly jumped by a posse of two dozen or more of the opposing faction. The first volley severely wounded the men on the ground, but Coe spurred his mount and almost made his escape. His horse was shot in the head, however, and he was forced to make a stand. When he emptied his pistol, the posse swarmed him and took him into custody.

In the meantime, McNab had crawled away in an attempt to escape. But the posse hunted him down, filled him with buckshot, and left his carcass to rot. Eventually friends buried his bones where he died. Sanders, wounded in the hip and legs, received medical treatment, and Coe later managed to secure his release.

Sources: Coe, *Frontier Fighter,* 82–84; Hunt, *Tragic Days of Billy the Kid,* 40, 45–46, 61, 66–67; Keleher, *Violence in Lincoln County,* 99, 128, 224; Fulton, *Lincoln County War,* 131, 137, 140, 158–59, 212–15, 220.

Madsen, Christian

(b. February 25, 1851, Schleswig-Holstein, Denmark; d. January 9, 1944, Guthrie, Oklahoma. Soldier, law officer.) The son of a professional soldier, at the age of fourteen Chris fought with the Danish army against the Germans. He then joined the French Foreign Legion and was stationed in Algeria until the outbreak of the Franco-Prussian War in 1870. His outfit returned to Europe and fought at the Battle of Sedan, where Chris was wounded and taken prisoner. He escaped confinement and fought with irregulars until hostilities ended, at which point he went to America.

Madsen landed in New York early in 1876 and joined the United States Cavalry. He was present when Buffalo Bill

Oklahoma lawman Chris Madsen, formerly of the Danish, French, and United States armies. *(Courtesy Western History Collections, University of Oklahoma Library)*

Cody scalped Cheyenne warrior Yellow Hand, and a short time later he was detailed to help bury dead troopers at the Little Big Horn. (In the first newspaper accounts of the Custer massacre Madsen was erroneously listed among the dead.) He campaigned continuously against hostile Indians through 1890. In 1887 he was married while stationed at Fort Reno, Indian Territory, and he soon produced two sons.

In 1891, having served fifteen years and having acquired sergeant's stripes and a Silver Star, Madsen resigned from the service and accepted an appointment as a deputy U.S. marshal operating from El Reno, Oklahoma. The next year he transferred to Guthrie and was highly active arresting fugitives until the outbreak of the Spanish-American War, when he joined the Rough Riders.

After returning from Cuba, Madsen reentered law enforcement and in 1911 was appointed United States marshal for Oklahoma. In 1916 he resigned and helped promote Bill Tilghman's motion picture on Oklahoma outlaws. From 1918 until 1922 he was a special investigator for Oklahoma Governor J. B. A. Robertson. His death came at the Masonic Home in Guthrie when he was nearly ninety-three years of age.

Gunfights: *November 29, 1892, Orlando, Oklahoma.* Madsen, Heck Thomas, and Deputy Tom Houston went to Orlando hoping to find bank robber Ol Yantis at his sister's farm three miles outside town. At sunrise Yantis emerged from the house carrying a sack of feed in one hand and a six-gun in the other. "Throw up your hands, Ol," ordered Madsen. "We're officers." Yantis snapped off a shot, then staggered from a wound from Madsen's rifle. The fugitive kept firing, but Houston hit him and he collapsed. The lawmen carried him into town, but he died that night.

1893, Beaver City, Oklahoma. Madsen had escorted a district judge to Beaver City, and the pair bedded down in the makeshift bedroom over a saloon. Drunken revelers began discharging their guns, and when a few slugs crashed through the ceiling, Madsen went downstairs. He jerked a six-shooter out of the grasp of one man, whereupon a second belligerently announced: "I'm a son-of-a-bitch from Cripple Creek."

"I knew who you were," replied Madsen, "but I didn't know where you were from."

The man swung at Madsen, who clubbed him to the floor with his gun. A third man pulled his pistol, but Madsen fired first, winging him in his shooting hand. Madsen then took the trio into custody.

May 12, 1894, El Reno, Oklahoma. An informer told Madsen that train robber Felix Young was in the street talking with a gambler. Madsen approached to within forty yards of the fugitive before Young recognized him and bolted toward a horse. Madsen ordered Young to stop, but the outlaw mounted his horse and snapped off two shots at the lawman. Madsen fired five times, and the horse fell dead. Young began running, but Madsen chased him down, and the outlaw eventually was sent to prison.

March 5, 1896, Cheyenne, Oklahoma. Red Buck George Weightman had been a vicious member of the Dalton and Doolin gangs and was at large in Oklahoma. Madsen and a posse finally located him at a dugout near Cheyenne. The posse surrounded the dugout and ordered Weightman to surrender. Instead, he tried to shoot his way out, and Madsen killed him with a rifle shot.

Sources: Croy, *Trigger Marshal;* Drago, *Road Agents and Train Robbers,* 182, 194, 199, 201, 207, 209; Shirley, *Six-gun and Silver Star,* 10, 40, 66–68, 78–80, 120, 122–24, 137, 150–53, 172, 190, 194, 214–15.

Manning, James

(b. ca. 1845, near Huntsville, Alabama; d. April, 1915, Los Angeles, California. Soldier, sailor, rancher, rustler, saloon owner, miner.) Born on a plantation near Huntsville, Alabama, Jim Manning was one of four brothers—

Doc, Jim, John, and Frank—who fought for the Confederacy, for Maximilian in Mexico, and against anyone who antagonized them. (Doc, for example, engaged in a bloody knife fight with the doctor who was his chief competitor in Giddings, Texas.)

After the Civil War the Mannings vowed never to shave until the South rose again, and then they moved to Texas' Gulf Coast. There they built a sloop, sailed to Mexico, and enlisted with Maximilian. Later they returned to Texas, settled in Belton, then restlessly scattered in various directions before reuniting in El Paso in 1881.

Jim, Frank, and John ran a ranch near Canutillo which became notorious as a haven for rustlers and other outlaws. The Mannings became involved in a bitter feud with lawman Dallas Stoudenmire, and Jim was largely responsible for killing both Stoudenmire and his brother-in-law, Doc Cummings, in separate gunfights.

Later, Manning was a saloon owner in El Paso and Seattle, and after an 1889 Seattle fire destroyed his business, he moved his family to Anacosta, Washington, and opened still another saloon. Soon he returned to the Southwest, investing in the silver and copper mines around Parker, Arizona. He died of cancer in Los Angeles in 1915, survived by his wife and many descendants.

Gunfights: ca. 1875, East Texas. While trailing a cattle herd to Kansas, the Manning brothers ran afoul of a man who later killed William, the youngest, from ambush. Frank, Jim, and John chased the bushwhacker, overtook him, and shot him to death.

February 14, 1882, El Paso, Texas. One evening Manning was approached in his Coliseum Variety Theater by a drunken

Doc Cummings, who, along with his brother-in-law, Dallas Stoudenmire, bitterly hated the Mannings. Cummings cursed Jim and his bartender, David Kling, and belligerently challenged Manning to fight. At first Manning tried to calm Cummings, but after a time Jim left the room, took off his coat, and returned with a gun belt strapped around his waist. "Doc, we will have this out," he growled, reaching for his pistol. Manning and Kling each fired a bullet into Doc's body, and Cummings snapped off a wild shot, then stumbled outside to die in the street.

September 18, 1882, El Paso, Texas. A fight had broken out between Dallas Stoudenmire and Doc Manning; Stoudenmire had been shot twice in the chest, and Doc was wounded in the right arm. When Jim came running onto the scene, his brother had dropped his gun, but was grappling on the sidewalk with Stoudenmire, who still gripped a pistol. Jim produced a .45 with a sawed-off barrel and no trigger, and he thumbed a shot at Stoudenmire. Despite a distance of just eight feet, Jim hit only a nearby barber pole. But he fired again, and his second slug caught Stoudenmire just behind the left ear, killing him instantly.

Sources: Metz, *Dallas Stoudenmire,* 37, 77, 86–93, 95–99, 113, 119–20, 123; Askins, *Texans, Guns & History,* 115, 120, 122–25; Sonnichsen, *Pass of the North,* 236–37, 239–40, 243–45.

Marlow, Boone

(b. 1865; d. January, 1889, near Fort Sill, Oklahoma. Farmer, laborer.) Boone Marlow was a member of a restless and clannish frontier family who lived at various times in California, Texas, Missouri, Oklahoma, New Mexico, Mexico, and Colorado. Boone had four brothers—Charley, Alf, Epp, and George—and their father was a stock raiser, farmer, and doctor.

In 1886, while the family was living in Wilbarger County, Texas, Boone killed a man, and the clan then left for Colorado. Two years later the five brothers were arrested on stealing charges, but the charges were dropped. They then moved back to Texas, settling near Vernon.

At Vernon local authorities tried to arrest Boone for murder, but he shot his way to freedom. His four brothers were arrested for complicity, and although they soon sawed their way out of jail, they were quickly rounded up again. Only their courageous defiance kept a mob from lynching them, and it was decided to transfer them to a safer jail. A short distance out of town, however, a mob opened fire from the darkness. One lawman was killed, and two others were wounded, and Alf and Epp Marlow fell dead. A prisoner named Clift was hit in the leg, George Marlow was shot in the hand, and Charley Marlow was wounded in the chest and jaw. But even though each was wounded and shackled to a dead brother, George and Charley picked up their guards' weapons and fought off the mob, killing three and wounding another.

George and Charley lived to be old men, but Boone was quickly found and killed by a trio of bounty hunters. The three men—Martin Beavers, J. E. Direkson, and G. E. Harboldt—located Boone on Hell Creek, twenty miles east of Fort Sill, Oklahoma. They apparently poisoned him for the seventeen hundred dollars' reward and packed his body into Fort Sill on January 28, 1889.

Gunfights: 1886, Wilbarger Coun-

ty, Texas. Boone was riding up to the house of his married sister when he was spotted by a man named James Holdson. Holdson was either drunk or nursing an old grudge, because he pulled a gun and opened fire on the unsuspecting Marlow. Boone quickly recovered and hauled out his Winchester. He coolly began pumping bullets at Holdson and shot him dead.

December 16, 1888, near Vernon, Texas. The Marlow family was eating dinner when Sheriff Marion Collier and Deputy Tom Wallace rode up to the house. Sheriff Collier burst through the door and barked, "Boone Marlow, I'm after you." Boone snatched up his Winchester, and the sheriff fired a wild shot. Boone then squeezed off two rounds: the first hit the sheriff's hat brim, and the second went through the door casing and struck Wallace as he ran toward the door. The slug tore through Wallace's body above the hips; both kidneys were damaged, and he died a week later.

Collier tried to flee, but Boone ordered him to return. As the sheriff walked back, Boone started to shoot him, but Charley Marlow, who was cradling Wallace's head, persuaded his brother not to fire.

Source: Sonnichsen, *I'll Die Before I'll Run,* 192–205.

Masterson, Edward J.

(b. September 22, 1852, Henryville, Canada; d. April 9, 1878, Dodge City, Kansas. Farmer, laborer, buffalo hunter, law officer.) Ed Masterson was the eldest of seven children of Thomas and Catherine Masterson. Born in Canada, Ed was reared in New York. A few years after the Civil War the family acquired an eighty-acre farm near Wichita and

Ed Masterson, brother of Bat, killed in a wild street fight while marshal of Dodge City, Kansas. *(Courtesy Kansas State Historical Society, Topeka)*

moved to Kansas. A few years later Ed and his brother Bat left home. They were active around Dodge City first as grading contractors, then as buffalo hunters during the heyday of that vicious but lucrative activity. In June, 1877, Ed was appointed deputy marshal of Dodge and quickly became popular and respected throughout the community. Just seven months after his appointment to the police force, he was promoted to city marshal. Five months later, however, he was killed in a street fight.

Gunfights: September 25, 1877, Dodge City, Kansas. Two or three shots split the air in Dodge, and Sheriff Bat

Masterson rushed to the scene. He ordered the careless celebrant, cowboy A. C. Jackson, to surrender. Jackson shouted defiance, fired twice more, and spurred his horse. Bat opened fire, along with Deputy Marshal Ed Masterson, who had just arrived on the scene. Jackson's mount was wounded, but managed to carry the cowboy to safety before collapsing.

November 5, 1877, Dodge City, Kansas. During the afternoon a quarrel broke out in the Lone Star Dance Hall owned by Texas Dick Moore and Bob Shaw. A bystander ran out in search of Deputy Marshal Ed Masterson, who burst into the Lone Star and ordered Shaw to surrender his gun.

In reply, Shaw took a shot at Moore, and Masterson clubbed Shaw on the skull with his gun butt. Unfazed, Shaw whirled and began firing at Masterson. The law officer was hit in the right breast, and the slug struck a rib and came out under his right shoulder blade. Masterson's right arm was paralyzed, and his six-gun thudded to the floor. Masterson dropped down and, clutching his revolver in his left hand, opened fire on Shaw. Shaw took bullets in the left arm and left leg and was knocked off his feet. During the fight a random slug hit Moore in the groin, but, like the other participants (including onlooker Frank Buskirk, who was hit in the arm by a stray bullet), he soon recovered fully.

April 9, 1878, Dodge City, Kansas. During the evening half a dozen cowboys were drinking and dancing at the Lady Gay, and Marshal Ed Masterson and Deputy Nat Haywood ambled over to keep a lid on the celebration. Especially raucous was Jack Wagner, who was carrying a pistol in disobedience of a city ordinance.

About 10:00 P.M. Masterson quietly disarmed Wagner, gave the pistol to Wagner's boss, A. M. Walker, then walked outside with Haywood. Walker returned the pistol to Wagner, and the intoxicated pair rushed after the lawmen. Masterson immediately grappled with Wagner for the gun, and a large crowd quickly gathered. Haywood stepped forward to assist, but Walker and another cowboy forced him back with drawn pistols; indeed, Walker tried to shoot Haywood in the face, but his gun misfired. Suddenly Wagner's gun went off, and a slug tore through Masterson's belly and out his back.

Despite his wound and the fact that the flash had set his clothes on fire, Masterson jerked out his gun and rapidly fired four shots. One bullet hit Wagner in the stomach, and the other three ripped into Walker. Two bystanders were grazed in the face by flying bullets.

Wagner staggered into nearby Peacock's saloon and collapsed on the floor. Friends carried him away, but he died the next day. Walker, a hole in his left lung and his right arm shattered by two slugs, ran through Peacock's saloon in shock and finally fell after he dashed out the back door. He eventually recovered.

Masterson, his clothes still aflame, calmly walked two hundred yards across the plaza and made his way over the railroad tracks and into George Hoover's saloon. He gasped to George Hinkle, "George, I'm shot," then sank to the floor. He was carried to Bat's room, where, surrounded by his brother and friends, he died about half an hour later. He was buried following a funeral attended by most of the saddened city.

Sources: Miller and Snell, *Great Gunfighters of the Kansas Cowtowns,*

169–85; O'Connor, *Bat Masterson,*
10–13, 64–71.

Masterson, James P.

*(b. 1855, Iroquois County, Illinois; d.
March 31, 1895, Guthrie, Oklahoma.*
Buffalo hunter, saloon owner, law officer.) Reared in New York state, Jim
Masterson moved with his family about
1871 to a small farm near Wichita, Kansas. Soon thereafter his older brothers,
Ed and Bat, went to Dodge City, and
teen-aged Jim quickly left the farm to
join them. He hunted buffalo for several
years and then, again following his
brothers' tracks, became a Dodge City
law officer.

Jim was appointed to the police force
in June, 1878, two months after Ed's
death in a gunfight. Jim was at the same
time a Ford County deputy sheriff (Bat
had been elected sheriff the previous
year), and he was a participant in several shooting scrapes. In November,
1879, Jim was promoted to the post of
city marshal, and he held the positon
for two years, until the defeat of Mayor
James H. ("Dog") Kelley and his administration.

Following a noted gunfight in Dodge
City's plaza, Jim spent a few years farther west. In 1889 he returned to Dodge,
hired his gun in the Gray County seat
war, then moved south to participate in
the Oklahoma land rush of 1889 and to
become one of the first settlers in
Guthrie. He served as a deputy sheriff
from Guthrie, and in 1893 he was appointed deputy U.S. marshal.

Masterson was active in pursuing the
numerous outlaws of Oklahoma Territory and was present at the bloody
raid on the Doolin gang in 1893. He
developed "galloping consumption" and
died two years later in Guthrie.

James Masterson, youngest of a trio of
gunfighting brothers, who was far more
active as a gunman than was the more
famous Bat. *(Courtesy Kansas State
Historical Society, Topeka)*

Gunfights: *July 26, 1878, Dodge
City, Kansas.* At 3:00 A.M. two or
three cowboys finished their evening's
celebration, retrieved their six-guns
from city officials, and headed back to
camp. As they passed the Comique
Dance Hall and Theater, they playfully
fired five or six shots which whizzed
across the stage and into the ceiling. Inside the Comique, 150 frightened revelers dived for the floor, dashed upstairs,
or darted for the doors.

Policemen Jim Masterson and Wyatt

Earp rushed to the scene and opened fire. Two or three shots whistled by in reply, then the cowboys spurred away. The officers emptied their guns without apparent effect, but a short distance from safety a drover named George Hoy fell from the saddle, his arm shattered by a bullet. Hoy was promptly treated, but he died from infection four weeks later.

June 9, 1879, Dodge City, Kansas. Several cowboys rode into Dodge for an evening on the town and declined to check their guns, as required by a local ordinance. Dodge policemen—probably including Jim Masterson—approached them and demanded their guns. The cowboys refused, whereupon both sides opened fire. One was struck in the leg, and the others then galloped out of town.

April 9 or 10, 1881, Dodge City, Kansas. Masterson and A. J. Peacock were co-owners of the Lady Gay Saloon and Dance Hall. A few weeks earlier Peacock had employed a bartender named Al Updegraff. Masterson disliked the new employee, and a quarrel erupted between him and the other two men. All three parties went for their guns, and Masterson blazed away at the other two men. No shot took effect, however, and the scrap was quickly broken up.

April 16, 1881, Dodge City, Kansas. Bat Masterson received a telegram in Tombstone, Arizona, describing his brother's predicament in Dodge. Bat promptly boarded a train and headed to Jim's rescue.

As Bat stepped off the noon train in Dodge, he spied Peacock and Updegraff walking across the street and shouted a challenge. The three men went for

their guns and darted for cover. Bullets began to whiz past startled bystanders as Bat plugged away from behind the rail embankment and his two antagonists fired from around the corner of the city jail.

Suddenly two men—probably Jim Masterson and Charlie Ronan—opened up on Peacock and Updegraff from a nearby saloon. Updegraff was hit in the chest, but it is not known who fired the lethal bullet. When the aggrieved parties paused to reload, Mayor A. B. Webster and Sheriff Fred Singer intervened with shotguns and demanded a halt to the hostilities. Bat paid a small fine, and Ronan and the Masterson brothers immediately left town.

January 14, 1889, Cimarron, Kansas. Cimarron and Ingalls, two villages situated six miles apart, desperately wanted to become the seat of newly formed Gray County. Cimarron held possession of the county records; therefore, Ingalls employed several Dodge City gunmen as "deputy sheriffs": Jim Masterson, Bill Tilghman, Fred Singer, Neal Brown, Billy Ainsworth, Ed Brooks, and Ben Daniels. These men, accompanied by a teamster and the Gray County sheriff and county clerk (both Ingalls men, drove a wagon into Cimarron about half an hour before noon on Saturday. While Masterson, Singer, Ainsworth, and County Clerk N. F. Watson boldly entered the Ingalls courthouse and began removing the records, the others remained on guard outside.

The Cimarron men quickly armed themselves, and when they menacingly approached the wagon, the Ingalls men lit out for safety. Both sides exchanged a torrent of lead, but the Ingalls group managed to break into the clear with only one serious casualty: Ed Brooks, who had been hit in the back and both legs, but who eventually recovered. The wagon driver was hit in the leg, and Tilghman sprained an ankle. The people of Cimarron suffered more grievously: J. W. English was killed by a bullet in the head, Jack Bliss was riddled with buckshot, Lee Fairhurst was shot in the chest, and a citizen named Harrington was struck in the hand.

In the meantime, the four men inside the courthouse found themselves trapped following the hasty flight of their comrades. Masterson, Singer, Ainsworth, and Watson, along with A. T. Riley, a Cimarron man who had been defeated but not yet replaced by Watson as county clerk, holed up in the second story of the courthouse. They remained pinned down until the next day, when the four Ingalls men let themselves be turned over to the county sheriff—an Ingalls sympathizer who of course released them immediately upon leaving Cimarron.

September 1, 1893, Ingalls, Oklahoma. Masterson was one of the lawmen who slipped into Ingalls to arrest the Doolin gang. Shooting erupted, and there were casualties on both sides, as well as five citizen bystanders who suffered wounds. Doolin and five other outlaws managed to escape town, but an ill Arkansas Tom Daugherty was abandoned in a second-story hotel room. Daugherty, who had already fatally wounded two posse members, held out for an hour, but Masterson produced two sticks of dynamite and threatened to destroy Daugherty's stronghold, and the fugitive prudently surrendered.

Sources: Miller and Snell, *Great Gunfighters of the Kansas Cowtowns,* 87–89, 186–92, 281–84, 433–37; Shirley, *Heck Thomas,* 171–74; Shirley, *Six-gun and Silver Star,* 81, 89, 91–94; Nix, *Oklahombres,* 103–16.

Bat Masterson took part in only three gunfights and killed just one man in a long career on the frontier. *(Courtesy Kansas State Historical Society, Topeka)*

Masterson, William B.

("Bat")

(b. November 26, 1853, County Rouville, Quebec, Canada; d. October 25, 1921, New York, New York. Farmer, laborer, buffalo hunter, army scout, gambler, saloon owner, law officer, gunman, sportsman, prizefight promoter, sports writer.) The second of seven children of Thomas and Catherine Masterson, Bat lived with his family on farms in Canada, New York, and Illinois, finally moving with them to a claim near Wichita, Kansas, about 1867.

In 1872 Bat and his older brother Ed left the farm and went to Dodge City, where Bat undertook a grading contract for the Atchison, Topeka & Santa Fe Railroad. Bat next turned to buffalo hunting, which reached the height of its slaughter and prosperity during this period. On July 27, 1874, he was a member of the party of several dozen hunters who fought off a large-scale Indian attack led by Quanah Parker. The assault fell upon the hunters' headquarters at Adobe Walls in the Texas Panhandle, but was repulsed by the professional sharpshooters.

Following the Battle of Adobe Walls, Bat joined the forces of General Nelson A. Miles as a scout for seventy-five dollars per month. He served for about three months, then was discharged on October 12, 1874. Bat then fell out of sight for a couple of years, but one notable incident presumably occurred during this hazy period: a gunfight between Bat and a soldier named King, during which King and a woman were killed.

By 1877 Bat had returned to Dodge, where he opened a saloon and got himself pistol-whipped by the marshal while helping a prisoner escape. But soon Bat wrangled an appointment as deputy sheriff of Ford County and was active in enforcing the law—along with his brother Ed, who was a policeman of Dodge City, the county seat. In November, 1877, Bat was elected sheriff of Ford County, and he distinguished himself by chasing down and arresting a variety of thieves and ruffians.

Bat's brother Ed was killed in a gunfight in April, 1878, but Bat stayed in Dodge and continued to capture horse thieves, train robbers, jail escapees, and confidence men. Adding to the summer's excitement was a local Indian scare involving Dull Knife and his band

of Cheyennes, along with the murder of dance hall girl Dora Hand by cowboy James Kenedy, who was captured and wounded by a posse led by Masterson. Bat found respite from all this activity on two occasions by traveling to the fair in Kansas City and to the spa in Hot Springs, Arkansas.

In January, 1879, Masterson was awarded additional authority by receiving an appointment as deputy U.S. marshal. Two months later, unconcerned by his responsibilites as sheriff, Bat left Dodge temporarily to hire his gun to the Atchison, Topeka & Santa Fe Railroad. He led a large posse of gunmen to back up the railroad in a dispute with the Denver & Rio Grande line over the right-of-way through Raton Pass, Colorado. Late in 1879 Bat was defeated for the post of sheriff after a hotly contested election campaign.

After leaving office, Bat drifted into Colorado and New Mexico, then traveled to Nebraska to rescue a seriously wounded Billy Thompson from the clutches of the angry populace of Ogallala. Bat lived in Kansas City for a while, then early in 1881 he joined several Dodge friends—including Wyatt Earp and Luke Short—at the Arizona boom town of Tombstone. But in April Bat was called back to Dodge to back his brother Jim in a fight which erupted into gunplay as soon as Bat stepped off the train. Bat immediately went back to Colorado, but he returned to Dodge in 1883 as a participant in the widely noted but decidedly nonviolent "Dodge City War."

By this time Bat had begun to dabble in newspaper writing, but soon he was in Fort Worth, Texas, again depending upon gambling as a livelihood. In addition to gambling and writing, Bat became increasingly active as a sportsman—especially as an official and promoter of horse races and prizefights. For the next several years he pursued these activities throughout the West, headquartering in Denver.

In 1891 Bat married Emma Walters, and eleven years later he moved to New York, where he spent the last two decades of his life as a sports writer for the *Morning Telegraph*. President Theodore Roosevelt appointed Bat a deputy federal marshal in 1905, but Bat resigned the post two years later when it increasingly interfered with his newspaper duties. Bat became a well-known figure around the night spots of New York, but he died at his work desk in 1921.

Gunfights: *January 24, 1876, Mobeetie, Texas.* While off duty from Fort Elliott near Mobeetie, a member of the Fourth Cavalry named King was struck by a pistol shot fired "by a citizen," and he died the next day. Also killed was a woman, Molly Brennan.

Apparently Bat Masterson killed King. According to legend, Molly and Bat were together in a saloon when a jealous Sergeant King roared into the building with a blazing six-gun. Molly and Bat both were hit before Bat managed to shoot King.

Molly and King died as a result of their wounds, and Bat supposedly was forced to adopt the cane which eventually yielded his famous nickname. (There has been the suggestion, however, that his sobriquet was short for "Battling," a common appellation given to scrappers of the day. "Bat" also may have derived from Bartholomew, the middle name which he later changed to Barclay.) It should be added that a contemporary newspaper indicated that Molly was shot by Masterson—possibly as she tried to intervene, possibly by a wild slug.

September 25, 1877, Dodge City, Kansas. A cowboy named A. C. Jackson rode into Dodge and gleefully fired his revolver several times into the air. After two or three shots Bat dashed into the street and ordered Jackson to halt. "I am going to skip out for camp," replied Jackson, squeezing off two more rounds. Bat began to fire at the fleeing figure and was joined in the fusillade by his brother Ed. The horse was struck, but it carried Jackson safely out of town before it died.

April 16, 1881, Dodge City, Kansas. Jim Masterson and A. J. Peacock had been partners in the Lady Gay Dance Hall and Saloon, and their personal relationship had steadily deteriorated. Their problems were aggravated by a bartender named Al Updegraff, who had been hired by Peacock and who Masterson immediately wanted to fire—especially after the three men exchanged wild shots.

Masterson felt that he needed help and telegraphed his brother Bat in Tombstone. Bat's train arrived in Dodge on the sixteenth at 11:50 A.M., and as he left his car he immediately spied Peacock and Updegraff walking together. The street was crowded, but Bat hurried over, and when he was about twenty feet away he shouted: "I have come over a thousand miles to settle this. I know you are heeled—now fight!"

All three men drew guns. Bat dove behind the rail bed, and Peacock and Updegraff darted around the corner of the city jail. The three antagonists opened fire, along with two men from a nearby saloon (probably Jim Masterson and Charlie Ronan), and bullets began to shatter windows and thud into the walls of surrounding buildings.

One slug kicked dirt into Bat's mouth, then ricocheted and struck James Anderson, a fleeing bystander, in the back. Updegraff was wounded in the right lung, possibly by Bat or possibly by one of the unkown assailants from the saloon.

After three or four minutes the antagonists paused to reload, and at that point Mayor A. B. Webster and Sheriff Fred Singer marched onto the scene brandishing shotguns. The firing stopped, and Bat paid a small fine and then boarded the evening train out of town. Updegraff recovered from his wound.

Sources: O'Connor, *Bat Masterson;* Miller and Snell, *Great Gunfighters of the Kansas Cowtowns,* 193–320; Jahns, *Doc Holliday,* 136–37, 168; Schoenberger, *Gunfighters,* 15–17, 24, 31, 33, 35–37, 41, 42, 97–99, 101–102, 107–31, 134, 136, 138, 141, 143, 161–62, 187, 192, 193, 194.

Mysterious Dave Mather, who used his gun on both sides of the law. His hatband identifies him here as an assistant marshal. *(Courtesy Kansas State Historical Society, Topeka)*

Mather, Dave H.

("Mysterious Dave")

(b. 1845, Connecticut. Horse thief, buffalo hunter, train and stagecoach robber, law officer, prospector, farmer, gambler, hotel employee.) Mysterious Dave was rumored to have been a descendant of Cotton Mather. His sobriquet accurately describes the true extent of knowledge about his background and final years. It is known that by 1873 this native of Connecticut was involved with rustlers in Sharp County, Arkansas. A year later he was hunting buffalo, but after suffering a stomach slash in a Dodge City knife fight he went to New Mexico, where he consorted with horse thieves and stage robbers. While in Mobeetie, near Fort Elliott in the Texas Panhandle, Mather reputedly killed a man following a quarrel.

In 1879 Mather and several other shady characters were arrested with the notorious outlaw Dutch Henry Born. Mather was soon released, but within months he was again arrested for complicity in a train robbery in the vicinity of Las Vegas. After trial he was acquitted, and almost immediately he secured an appointment as a constable in Las Vegas. For a few months he was quite active as a peace officer, but in the spring of 1880 he traveled with three other prospectors to the gold fields of Gunnison, Colorado.

By November Mather was back in Las Vegas. He helped some friends break from the city jail and then went to Texas. He was first in San Antonio, then went to Dallas and finally to Fort

Worth, where he was arrested for stealing a gold ring and chain from a Negro woman.

In 1883 Mather moved to Dodge City and was appointed deputy city marshal and deputy sheriff of Ford County. There were complaints that Mysterious Dave was a bully and was too cooperative with criminals, and when he ran for city constable in February, 1884, he was defeated.

A few months later an old feud with Deputy Marshal Tom Nixon erupted into bloodshed. In June, Nixon wounded Mather in the streets of Dodge, and three days afterward Mysterious Dave shot Nixon to death. Mather eventually won acquittal and briefly turned to farming, but in May, 1885, he became involved in another fatal gunfight in Ashland, Kansas. While awaiting trial, Mather jumped bail and turned up as city marshal of New Kiowa, Kansas. In 1887 he rode into Long Pine, Nebraska, where he had occasionally worked at the depot hotel. But after a year Dave mysteriously and permanently faded into anonymity.

Gunfights: *November 20, 1879, Las Vegas, New Mexico.* Several soldiers were indulging in a raucous night on the town. Constable Mather and other peace officers arrived on the scene, loaded the soldiers in a hack, and headed for jail. Suddenly one of the troopers jumped out of the vehicle and bolted away. Mather ordered him to halt, then ran in pursuit. The constable fired five or six pistol shots and struck the soldier in the thumb. The soldier then surrendered.

January 25, 1880, Las Vegas, New Mexico. Joseph Castello, a young railroad employee, had arrived in Las Vegas the previous day in charge of a repair crew. A little after 10:00 P.M. on the twenty-fifth, two of his workers drunkenly began to quarrel. Castello tried to intervene, but a crowd quickly gathered, and Castello and one of his men brandished pistols to keep the townspeople at bay.

At this point constable Mather arrived and ordered the railroad men to put up their weapons. In reply Castello leveled his six-gun at Mather and threatened to shoot him if he took another step. Mather whipped out his own revolver and without hesitation shot Castello. The slug penetrated Castello's left side, tore through his lung and stomach, and ranged down into his liver. He was carried to Hoodoo Brown's office, and a doctor was summoned, but he died at six o'clock the following morning.

July 18, 1884, Dodge City, Kansas. Mysterious Dave held a grudge against Tom Nixon, an old buffalo hunter who had recently replaced Mather as assistant city marshal of Dodge. At about 9:00 P.M. Nixon and Mather began quarreling outside the Opera House, where Mysterious Dave ran a saloon. Mather stood at the top of the stairs, while his antagonist was on the ground. Suddenly Nixon pulled a six-gun and fired a shot which plowed into the woodwork, spraying Mather with splinters. Sheriff Pat Sughrue appeared promptly and disarmed Nixon, who claimed that Mather had waved a weapon at him. Mysterious Dave swore that he was unarmed, and Nixon was forced to produce eight hundred dollars' bail.

July 21, 1884, Dodge City, Kansas. About 10:00 P.M. Nixon was standing on the Opera House corner amidst numerous passersby. Mather came to the foot of the stairs of the building and drew a Colt .42 revolver. "Tom," he whispered. "Oh. Tom." His gun still holstered, Nixon turned to face Mather. Without further warning Mysterious Dave fired. "Oh," gasped Nixon, "I'm killed," and he collapsed face down. Mather then began to walk toward his fallen adversary, methodically pumping three more slugs into his body. (After passing through Nixon, one of the bullets seriously wounded a cowboy bystander.) Nixon died on the spot, and Mysterious Dave surrendered his gun to Sheriff Sughrue.

May 10, 1885, Ashland, Kansas. On a Sunday evening about 8:30, Mather was visiting Ashland's crowded Junction Saloon, where his brother Josiah was tending bar. Dave began playing Seven-Up at fifty cents a game with a twenty-three-year-old grocer named David Barnes. Barnes won the first game, Mather the second, and Barnes the third, whereupon Mysterious Dave threw the cards at Barnes and picked up all the money on the table. Barnes protested, "I want my money," and was backed up by his brother John, who stepped forward and declared, "That man has some friends and he can't be robbed in such a manner."

Mysterious Dave shoved John and snarled, "What have you got to do with this?" As Barnes staggered back, he went for his pistol. Sheriff Pat Sughrue, an onlooker, shouted, "Here, that won't do," then pinned John's arms and finally managed to get his gun.

In the meantime, David Barnes had pulled a six-gun and fired a shot which creased Mysterious Dave's skull and tore a hole in his hat. From behind the bar Josiah Mather produced a weapon and began firing, and, according to certain witnesses, so did Mysterious Dave. David Barnes was hit and went down, and Josiah Mather squeezed off three more slugs at the fallen man.

When the shooting stopped, it was discovered that bystanders John Wall and C. C. Camp had suffered leg wounds from stray bullets. Sughrue arrested the Mather brothers, who posted a three-thousand-dollar bond, and then promptly jumped bail and left the area.

Sources: Rickards, *Mysterious Dave Mather;* Miller and Snell, *Great Gunfighters of the Kansas Cowtowns,* 31, 242–44, 297–98, 301, 320–43; Vestal, *Dodge City,* 212–20; Schoenberger, *Gunfighters,* 36, 38, 99.

Matthews, Jacob B.

(b. May 5, 1847, Woodbury, Tennessee; d. June 3, 1904, Roswell, New Mexico. Soldier, miner, court clerk, businessman, law officer, postmaster.) Billy Matthews was a native of Tennessee who fought through the Civil War with Company M of the Fifth Tennessee Cavalry. After the war he drifted west, and by 1867 he had become a miner in Elizabethtown, New Mexico. In 1873 Matthews moved to Lincoln, where he served as circuit court clerk and found employment with L. G. Murphy and James J. Dolan. He eventually worked up to a partnership with Dolan and John H. Riley—just in time to become embroiled in their feud with Alexander McSween and John Tunstall.

As a deputy of Sheriff William Brady, Matthews led the posse which assassinated Tunstall. He also was a principal in the gunfight which resulted in the deaths of Brady and George Hindman. In addition, he fought in the climactic four-day shootout in Lincoln, and he was later indicted for murder in the death of lawyer H. J. Chapman.

Years after Lincoln County had settled down, Matthews moved to Roswell, where in 1898 President McKinley appointed him postmaster. He was reappointed by Theodore Roosevelt in 1902, but he died two years later.

Gunfights: February   18,   1878, near Lincoln, New Mexico. Matthews was appointed deputy sheriff by William Brady to attach John Tunstall's livestock. Having accomplished this chore, Matthews' twelve-man posse encountered Tunstall and shot and killed the Englishman, thus setting off the Lincoln County War.

April 1, 1878, Lincoln, New Mexico. Sheriff Brady and Deputy George Hindman were walking down Lincoln's main street to post legal notices, and they were followed by Matthews, George Peppin, and John Long. Suddenly, from behind a low adobe wall next to Alexander McSween's store, Billy the Kid and four henchmen raised up and began to pour rifle fire at the law officers. Brady and Hindman fell, mortally wounded, and Matthews also was hit. But Matthews, along with Peppin and Long, scrambled to cover.

A few moments later the Kid and Fred Wait ventured into the street to steal the rifles of the two dead lawmen. Matthews, however, opened fire, grazing both bushwhackers and sending them diving back over the fence. The Kid and his party then mounted their horses and dashed out of town.

July 15–19, 1878, Lincoln, New Mexico. Matthews was recovered and ready for action by the time the two warring factions clashed in Lincoln. His primary position was in the round stone *torreón*, sniping at the McSween men from the old Indian-fighting stronghold.

February 18, 1879, Lincoln, New Mexico. Matthews was with James J. Dolan, Jesse Evans, and William Campbell when the four men encountered outspoken lawyer Huston Chapman near Lincoln's post office about 10:00 P.M. The drunken Campbell belligerently shot Chapman, and several bullets from the quartet knocked the lawyer to the boardwalk, dead as he fell.

Sources: Keleher, *Violence in Lincoln County,* 82, 86, 100, 109, 123, 141, 207–10, 223, 232–33, 251–58, 261–64, 275–76, 316, 321–22, 328–29; Hunt, *Tragic Days of Billy the Kid,* 31–35, 51–53, 153–57; Fulton, *Lincoln County War,* 49, 64, 76, 78, 112–14, 119, 158–59, 201, 213, 216–19, 225, 249, 251, 318, 331, 333, 347, 417.

Meagher, Michael

(b. 1843, County Cavar, Ireland; d. December 17, 1881, Caldwell, Kansas. Soldier, stage driver, law officer, Indian scout, mayor, carpenter, saloon keeper, gambler.) Natives of Ireland, Meagher and his younger brother John immigrated to the United States and settled in Illinois. They fought in the Civil War, and in the late 1860's they moved into Kansas as stage drivers. In 1871 Mike was appointed marshal of Wichita, and John became his deputy. Mike consistently distinguished himself by making arrests, often in the teeth of drawn guns, without violence and by frequently preventing bloodshed.

After three years Mike left the job, went to Indian Territory, dabbled in carpentry and drove a freight wagon, then returned to law enforcement in 1874 as a deputy U.S. marshal. That same year he was appointed first lieutenant of a militia company organized to scout Indians. In 1875 Meagher was reelected marshal of Wichita, and in 1877 he was forced to kill Sylvester Powell.

As the cattle boom waned in Wichita, Meagher moved to Caldwell, gambled, opened a saloon, and was elected mayor in 1880. The next year he served a brief term as city marshal, and a few months later he was killed by Jim Talbot in the streets of Caldwell.

Gunfights: *January 1, 1877, Wichita, Kansas.* Sylvester Powell, a city stage driver, spent New Year's Day drinking heavily with a friend. That afternoon the two men drunkenly took possession of a horse belonging to E. R. Dennison, who stepped to the hitch rail and made a joking comment. Powell grumpily slammed Dennison with a neck yoke and warned him not to report the incident. Dennison promptly told City Marshal Meagher, who hauled Powell away to jail.

That evening Powell's boss bailed him out, whereupon Powell swore he would shoot Meagher on sight. About 9:00 P.M. Powell found Meagher in an outhouse behind Hope's Saloon. In the moonlight Powell crept up to the little building and suddenly opened fire. One slug whipped through Meagher's coat, and a second bullet bit into his lower leg.

Without hesitation the startled marshal sprang at Powell and grappled with the assassin. Another slug grazed Meagher's hand, and Powell broke away and fled down an alley. Powell fired a fourth shot as he ran, and Meagher at last pulled his gun and squeezed off a round in return. The marshal then limped to the street and soon spied Powell standing in front of Charles Hill's Drug Store. Meagher deliberately took aim and fired a bullet straight into Powell's heart. Powell dropped in his tracks, dead when he hit the ground.

December 17, 1881, Caldwell, Kansas. Jim Talbot was a Texas cowboy who had been making a rowdy nuisance of himself in Caldwell for about a month. On a Friday night Talbot indulged in a rowdy drinking spree with Bob Bigtree, Dick Eddleman, Tom Love, Jim Martin, Bob Munson, and George Speers. During the evening Talbot had trouble with several citizens, including Mike Meagher.

Early the next morning Meagher went for help to City Marshal John Wilson, who arrested Love but was compelled to release him immediately by an angry Talbot and his cohorts. About 1:00 P.M. Wilson arrested Martin for carrying a gun. Martin was fined, and Deputy Will Fossett accompanied him to obtain the money. Suddenly Talbot, Love, Munson, and Eddleman converged on the pair and forcibly freed Martin. Talbot then fired two shots at Wilson, who was in the street. Talbot sprinted away, shouting at his friends to arm themselves, and Wilson and Meagher promptly went in pursuit.

On the sidewalk in front of the Opera House, Talbot whirled and began firing at Wilson and Meagher with his Winchester. One of the slugs slammed into Meagher, perforating his right arm and tearing through both his lungs and out the other side. Meagher dropped his rifle and six-gun and gasped, "I am hit, and hit hard." Wilson helped him to sit down, then resumed the chase. Ed Rathbun dashed to Meagher's side and blurted, "Good God, Mike, are you hit?"

"Yes," Mike managed to reply. "Tell my wife I have got it at last."

Meagher was assisted to a barber shop, and he died one-half hour later. As George Speers hastily saddled to leave town, a bullet from a citizen wounded him fatally. Talbot's other friends galloped out of Caldwell with a mob at their heels, and a furious chase continued into Indian Territory.

Sources: Miller and Snell, *Great Gun-*

fighters of the Kansas Cowtowns, 80–84, 99–103, 162–63, 343–69; Drago, *Wild, Woolly & Wicked,* 149–50, 155–59, 165, 183–84, 210–14; Streeter, *Prairie Trails & Cow Towns,* 149.

Meldrum, Bob

(b. 1865, New York. Harness maker, range detective, law officer, cowboy.) Before his arrival in Wyoming in 1899, Bob Meldrum had a vague reputation as a western killer. During the early 1890's he had supposedly aided Pinkerton detective Tom Horn in chasing and gunning down two horsemen, only to discover that their victims were the wrong men. Around the turn of the century Meldrum killed a man in Dixon, Wyoming, and then drifted to Colorado, where he was hired as a strike breaker against the United Mine Workers of America in Cripple Creek.

Meldrum returned to Wyoming in 1908 and was paid $250 a month by the Snake River Cattlemen's Association to rid the area of rustlers. He was made a deputy sheriff in Routt County and in Carbon County, but by 1911 he had been relieved of his duties. He soon found employment as town marshal of Baggs, and he quickly entered into a tempestuous marriage with a local girl. After killing a well-liked cowboy early in 1912, Meldrum was sentenced to the Wyoming Penitentiary for five to seven years for voluntary manslaughter. Following his release he worked as a harness maker in Walcott, Wyoming.

Gunfights: ca. 1899, Dixon, Wyoming. Meldrum was employed as a harness maker in a shop owned by Charley Perkins, of Dixon. Meldrum and a coworker named Wilkinson went to the local postoffice, where Meldrum received a dead-or-alive reward notice on his fellow employee. Meldrum shoved the notice into his pocket and walked outside with Wilkinson. As the two men strolled across a field, Meldrum pulled his side-breaking .44 Colt and killed Wilkinson with a bullet in the back of head. Meldrum later received the reward.

January 19, 1912, Baggs, Wyoming. A popular halfblood cowboy named Chick Bowen was enjoying an evening in Baggs with two cohorts. After the trio of celebrants had a few drinks in a saloon, they decided to go to the Elkhorn Hotel to eat. In the street Bowen gave a few high-spirited whoops and then entered the Elkhorn and ordered a meal. In a few minutes a waitress told Bowen that Marshal Meldrum was looking for him. The three men finished their meal and then strolled to Calvert's General Store. There Meldrum approached Bowen and asked if he had been shouting. When Bowen said no, Meldrum clutched at him to arrest him, knocking off his hat.

"I'll come as soon as I get my hat," said Bowen.

"I'll shoot you in the legs, and then you'll come, you son-of-a-bitch!" snarled the marshal.

"Don't you call me a son-of-a-bitch, Bob."

At that point Meldrum began firing his revolver, wounding Bowen in the knee and stomach and grazing him in the groin. Bowen hurled himself at Meldrum, wrestling Bob to the ground and pummeling him in the face. Bowen gasped to cohort George Salisbury, "For God's sake, Salsy, don't let them pull me off for I am shot in the belly, and if I let him up he will shoot me again."

But Deputy Sheriff Jim Davis arrived on the scene, pulled the wounded cowboy up and assisted him to the Red

Cross Pharmacy. Meldrum tagged along, muttering, "You damned son-of-a-bitch, I told you I would get you."

Dr. E. G. Condit tended Bowen and then had him removed to a hotel, where he soon died. Cattlemen who had sponsored Meldrum hired the best lawyers, but Bob was finally imprisoned in 1916.

Source: Burroughs, *Where the Old West Stayed Young,* 299–305.

Middleton, John

(d. 1885. Cowboy, gunman, rustler, grocer.) Middleton drifted into New Mexico from Kansas sometime in the 1870's. He was described by rancher John Tunstall as "about the most desperate looking man I ever set eyes on (& that is not saying a little.) I could fancy him doing anything ruffianly that I ever heard of, that is from his appearance, but he is as mild & composed as any man can be, but his arms are never out of his reach."

Perhaps because he was a hard case, Middleton was hired by Tunstall on the eve of the Lincoln County War. He was only a short distance away when Tunstall was killed, and he was member of the posse of "Regulators" who murdered Frank Baker, Billy Morton, and William McCloskey in retribution. Middleton was one of the men who ambushed Sheriff William Brady and Deputy George Hindman for further revenge, and a short time later he was severely wounded in the shootout at Blazer's Mill.

This brush with death apparently quenched his thirst for violence: he went to Fort Sumner to recuperate, then migrated to Sun City, Kansas, where he opened a grocery store. In later years he lived in several Kansas towns and continually, and unsuccessfully, tried to wheedle money out of Tunstall's father in England. In 1885 he was busy in Oklahoma with Belle Starr, whose husband Sam was temporarily absent. But that spring Middleton was ambushed and shot to death.

Gunfights: *March 9, 1878, Steel Springs, New Mexico.* Middleton was one of the Regulators who had captured Frank Baker and Billy Morton, key figures in the murder of John Tunstall. While riding near Steel Springs on the road back to Lincoln, Morton seized a pistol from posse member William McCloskey, a close friend of Middleton's. Morton shot McCloskey dead, then spurred away with Baker. The posse galloped after them and killed both men following a short chase. (It has been suggested that Regulator Frank McNab shot McCloskey because the latter had expressed sympathy for the two prisoners.)

April 1, 1878, Lincoln, New Mexico. Middleton, Billy the Kid, Henry Brown, Fred Wait, and Jim French had concealed themselves behind a wall adjacent to Tunstall's store in order to set an ambush for Sheriff William Brady. At mid-morning Brady and Deputy Sheriff George Hindman strolled down the street, heavily armed and trailed by Billy Matthews, George Peppin, and John Long.

Without warning the bushwhackers cut loose. The Kid, Middleton, and Brown fired the most effective volleys, hitting Brady, Hindman, and Matthews. Matthews was able to find cover, but Brady fell dead, and Hindman collapsed in the street and began moaning for water. The Kid ran toward Brady, hoping to steal his new Winchester, but Matthews began firing and nicked him in the side. The Kid retreated and led his men out of town on horseback.

April 4, 1878, Blazer's Mill, New Mexico. Three days after the Lincoln ambush a posse of Regulators had stopped in Blazer's Mill and were waiting for a meal when Buckshot Roberts, a member of the opposing faction, rode up on a mule. Cradling his Winchester in his lap, Roberts began talking with Regulator Frank Coe, an old acquaintance who tried to convince him to surrender peaceably. Suddenly Charlie Bowdre advanced, gun in hand, and ordered Roberts to give up. Roberts snarled a refusal, and the two adversaries began firing. Regulator George Coe was wounded in the hand, and Roberts stumbled back, a hole torn through his middle.

The other Regulators rushed forward, but Roberts, firing from the waist, drove them back. Middleton took a rifle slug in the chest, the bullet passing through the upper part of his left lung. He was propped up against the main building while Roberts barricaded himself inside. Roberts killed Dick Brewer and pinned down the rest of the posse, but he was near death, and the Regulators decided to withdraw, mainly to seek medical help for Middleton and Coe.

Helping the two wounded men onto their horses, the posse moved out at a walk, with two riders beside Middleton to support him. The surgeon from nearby Fort Stanton provided treatment, and Middleton survived and left the country.

Sources: Keleher, *Violence in Lincoln County,* 83–84, 97–101, 109, 112–17, 122–23, 128, 184, 231, 253, 261–66, 276, 315–16, 325; Hunt, *Tragic Days of Billy the Kid,* 36–60; Fulton, *Lincoln County War,* 83, 111–12, 115–16, 131, 137, 140, 158, 175, 177, 192, 201, 260–61, 333, 346.

Miller, Clelland

(b. Missouri; d. September 7, 1876, Northfield, Minnesota. Farmer, train and bank robber.) Clell Miller was born near the James homestead in Missouri. He worshiped Jesse and Frank James as heroes and eventually joined the gang. He was involved in the abortive Northfield raid and was shot dead in the streets.

Gunfights: *April 12, 1875, Clay County, Missouri.* Farmer Daniel H. Askew was suspected by the James brothers of housing a Pinkerton agent. At 8:00 P.M. on April 12 Askew went to his well and drew a bucket of water. Suddenly three shots rang out, and as Askew's wife ran to her dying husband, she saw three horsemen galloping away. There was never any positive proof, but it was widely suspected that the three assassins were Jesse and Frank James and Clell Miller.

September 7, 1876, Northfield, Minnesota. The James gang was embroiled in a large number of robberies and related shooting scrapes, and Miller was a frequent participant during the 1870's. But the bandits always tried to conceal their identity, and a great many holdups were unjustly blamed on the gang. Therefore, the only shootout with which Miller can be positively associated is the attempted Northfield bank robbery.

Eight members of the gang rode into town, and three dismounted and went into the First National Bank. Three other outlaws guarded the approach to town, while Miller and Cole Younger remained outside the bank. The bank door was open, and Miller moved to close it. But J. S. Allen, proprietor of a local hardware store, suspiciously approached the bank, and Miller ordered him away from the building. Allen ran around the corner and began shouting, "Get your guns, boys! They're robbing the bank!"

Killin' Jim Miller is said to have coolly asked for his hat to be placed on his head before he was lynched in Ada, Oklahoma, along with the three men who hired him to kill rancher A. A. Bobbitt (inset). *(Courtesy Western History Collections, University of Oklahoma Library)*

At that point shooting began inside the bank, then spread to the street as the townspeople were alerted. As Miller tried to remount, citizen Elias Stacy fired a shotgun at him. The weapon was loaded only with birdshot, however, and although Miller was hit in the face, he regained his saddle. But a young medical student named Henry Wheeler had helped spread the alarm and now stationed himself with a rifle in a second-story window. Wheeler missed his first shot at Jim Younger, then drew a bead on Miller. The slug tore through Miller's body, severing an artery in his chest and killing him instantly.

Sources: Croy, *Last of the Great Outlaws*, 107–24, 117; Settle, *Jesse James Was His Name*, 43–44, 57 89, 92–94, 104, 113; Drago, *Road Agents and Train Robbers;* Breihan, *Younger Brothers,* 149–51, 169–79.

Miller, James B.

("Killin' Jim," "Killer Miller," "Deacon")

(b. October 24, 1866, Van Buren, Arkansas; d. April 19, 1909, Ada, Oklahoma. Cowboy, rustler, law officer, saloon keeper, gambler, hotel owner, professional killer.) Born in Arkansas, Miller moved with his parents to Franklin, Texas, when he was one year old. A few years later Jim's parents died, and he was sent to live with his grandparents in Evant. When he was eight the old

couple was murdered in their home; Jim was arrested for the crime but never prosecuted. He was then sent to live with his sister and her husband, J. E. Coop, on their farm near Gatesville, and the hot-tempered boy frequently clashed with his brother-in-law. At seventeen Jim murdered Coop, but he was acquitted and soon became a cowhand on the McCulloch County ranch of Mannen Clements. Clements was killed in 1887, and his slayer was promptly ambushed in the Miller style.

For a couple of years Miller drifted around the Mexican border country, ran a saloon in San Saba, then began wearing a badge. He was a deputy sheriff of Reeves County and later became town marshal of the county seat, Pecos. During this period he reputedly killed several Mexicans while they were "attempting to escape." "I have lost my notch stick on Mexicans that I killed out on the border," he bragged.

In 1891 Miller married Sallie Clements, daughter of Mannen, and became such an outwardly devout Methodist that he was dubbed Deacon Jim. While in Pecos, Miller became involved in a feud with Sheriff G. A. ("Bud") Frazer, who accused Deacon Jim of stealing a pair of mules. The two lawmen exchanged shots in the streets of Pecos, and Miller later ended the feud by murdering Frazer. Although he eventually won acquittal on grounds that "he had done no worse than Frazer," Miller soon ambushed and killed Joe Earp, who had testified against him. Soon thereafter Judge Stanley, the district attorney who had vainly prosecuted Miller, died in Memphis, Texas, of supposed food poisoning, although there was widespread speculation that Killin' Jim had slipped arsenic to the lawyer.

Nevertheless, Jim somehow wangled his way into the Texas Rangers, becoming resident ranger at Memphis.

Later he served as a ranger in Hall County, and while there, he killed a man in adjoining Collingsworth County. In 1900 the Millers moved to Fort Worth; Sallie opened a rooming house, and Jim became known as a killer for hire. He killed two men near Midland, and the score mounted as word spread that his services were available for $150 per victim; between jobs, however, Deacon Jim spoke regularly at prayer meetings.

Perhaps Miller's most famous victim was Pat Garrett, whom Miller supposedly bushwhacked in 1908. The following year Killer Miller was paid his highest fee—two thousand dollars—to dispatch rancher A. A. Bobbitt in Ada, Oklahoma. The contract was successfully completed, and Miller returned safely to Texas, but he was extradited back to Ada, where he was promptly lynched along with the three men who had hired him.

Gunfights: *July 30, 1884, Plum Creek, Texas.* Miller, still a teen-ager, had a disagreement with his brother-in-law, John Coop. Coop lived at Plum Creek, a hamlet near Gatesville. One hot summer night while Coop was sleeping outside on a porch, Miller crept up to the house and shot his brother-in-law in the head. Miller tried to establish an alibi, but he was arrested, tried, and convicted of murder. He was sentenced to life imprisonment, but he soon won release on a legal technicality.

1887, near Ballinger, Texas. Miller had been working on the ranch of Mannen Clements, where he had become close to Mannen's son, Mannie Clements, and closer to his daughter, Sallie. The senior Clements was killed by Ballinger City Marshal Joe Townsend on March 29, 1887. Shortly thereafter, while riding home at night, Townsend was blasted out of his saddle by a shotgun fired from ambush by a vengeful Miller. Townsend recovered, but suffered the amputation of his left arm.

April 12, 1894, Pecos, Texas. Sheriff Bud Frazer had recently arrested Marshal Miller as a mule thief, and, perhaps fearing Miller's vengeance, he took a potshot at Killin' Jim without warning. Struck in the right arm, Miller pulled his gun with his left hand and began shooting. Miller managed to hit only bystander Joe Krans in the hip, then went down as Frazer emptied his six-gun into Jim's chest. But the bullets had struck a steel plate Miller often wore for protection, and Jim soon recovered from the fight.

December 26, 1894, Pecos, Texas. Standing in front of a Pecos blacksmith shop, Miller was suddenly fired upon by Bud Frazer. Miller was hit in the right arm and left leg, but he stood his ground and began operating his six-gun with his left hand. Two more bullets glanced off Miller's breastplate, and the demoralized former sheriff turned and ran.

September 14, 1896, Toyah, Texas. A frightened Bud Frazer had left Texas for Carlsbad, New Mexico, but returned to the Pecos area to visit his mother and sister. Miller learned of his nearby presence and immediately traveled to Toyah, where he found Frazer in a saloon. Miller pushed the swinging doors open with his shotgun, leveled the weapon, and calmly blasted away most of Frazer's head. When cursed shortly afterward by Frazer's irate sister, Miller threatened to shoot her, too.

1899, Coryell County, Texas. Joe Earp had testified against Miller in an unsuccessful attempt to charge him with murder in the death of Bud Frazer. Miller, of course, muttered grim threats of vengeance, and three weeks after the trial he shot Earp dead from ambush. Miller then spent the night in a grueling one-hundred-mile gallop to establish an alibi.

ca. 1900, Collingsworth County, Texas. Miller and a henchman, Lawrence Angel, tracked down a man Killin' Jim probably had been hired to eliminate. The luckless victim was assassinated with a shotgun, Miller's favorite weapon, and Jim was arrested. But Angel claimed he had committed the killing, Miller stated that Angel had fired in self-defense, and the pair went free.

Summer, 1902, Ward County, Texas. Miller clashed with three men near the Pecos River. He claimed that they were herding stolen cattle and opened fire when he approached. Miller wounded all three with his Winchester; two died with bullets in the head, but the third clung to his horse and escaped.

ca. 1903, West Texas. Miller was guarding a cattle herd near the New Mexico border in West Texas. When he caught two Mexicans butchering a rustled steer, he efficiently shot them to death.

ca. 1904, near Lubbock, Texas. Cattlemen had paid Miller five hundred dollars to dispose of Lubbock lawyer James Jarrott, who had won several cases on behalf of area nesters. As Jarrott watered his buggy team near his farm, Miller shot him in the chest from ambush, then quickly fired another rifle shot into him. Jarrott fell, then struggled to his hands and knees. Miller walked near and squeezed off a round which tore into Jarrott's neck and shoulder. The lawyer sank to the ground, but it took a fourth shot to finish him. "He was the hardest damn man to kill I ever tackled," admired Miller.

1904, Fort Worth, Texas. Miller had accepted a contract on a Fort Worth resident named Frank Fore. Miller stalked Fore into the lavatory of the Hotel Westbrook and shot him to death. Miller then went down to the lobby, where he found lawman Dee Harkey talking with Jinx Clark and Tom Coggins, who had accompanied Miller to the hotel. Miller tried to surrender to Harkey, but the peace officer declared that he wanted no part of the affair. Clark and Coggins later testified that they had been present in the washroom and that Miller had fired in self-defense.

August 1, 1906, near Emet, Oklahoma. U.S. Deputy Marshal Ben Collins had shot and partially paralyzed Port Pruitt in 1903, and the Pruitt family swore to "get" the officer. On a Wednesday evening Collins was approaching his home near Emet when suddenly a blast of No. 8 buckshot caught him in the stomach and hurled him out of the saddle. He triggered four six-gun rounds in the direction of his ambusher, then died when another load of buckshot struck him in the face. Jim Miller was indicted for murder, but eventually secured his release.

February 29, 1908, near Las Cruces, New Mexico. About four miles outside Las Cruces, Pat Garrett was in the company of fellow ranchers Wayne Brazel and Carl Adamson. Garrett stepped out of his buggy to urinate, and Miller, supposedly hired by an enemy of the famous former lawman, opened fire from concealment. Garrett was struck first in the back of the head by a .45 slug which tore out above his right eye. He spun around and was hit in the stomach by a second bullet. Garrett died almost immediately, and Miller galloped away from the scene to create an alibi. Brazel somewhat hysterically confessed to the killing but was acquitted, and widespread blame was placed on Miller.

February 26, 1909, Ada, Oklahoma. Miller was hired by three cattlemen who had been feuding with rancher Gus Bobbitt, whose spread was near Ada. Miller went to Ada, methodically reconnoitered the setup, then concealed himself near Bobbitt's ranch house. Bobbitt and a hand, Bob Ferguson, were driving supply wagons from town when Miller blasted away with both barrels of his shotgun. His left side riddled with buckshot, Bobbitt tumbled out of the lead wagon while Miller escaped past Ferguson. Mrs. Bobbitt dashed out to hold her dying husband, and word of the crime quickly spread. Miller fled to Fort Worth, but was extradited and, along with his three employers, was lynched in an Ada livery stable on April 19, 1909.

Sources: Shirley, *Shotgun for Hire;* Harkey, *Mean as Hell,* 20–22, 112–17, 119, 131; Sonnichsen, *Tularosa,* 230, 237–38, 240–41, 243; Metz, *John Selman,* 160–61, 226; Metz, *Pat Garrett,* 234, 239, 242–48.

Milton, Jeff Davis

(b. November 7, 1861, near Marianna, Florida; d. May 7, 1947, Tucson, Arizona. Farmer, clerk, cowboy, overseer, law officer, saloon keeper, customs inspector, rancher, train fireman and conductor, express messenger, prospector, oil driller, range detective.) Jeff Milton

was the youngest of ten children of the Civil War governor of Florida. His father died during the war, and Jeff was reared on the family plantation, Sylvania, near Marianna. In 1877 the sixteen-year-old boy moved to Navasota, Texas, to live with one of his sisters and work in her husband's general store. A year later Milton went west and found employment on a cattle ranch near old Fort Phantom Hill before overseeing a gang of convicts on a farm near the state penitentiary near Huntsville.

In 1880 Milton joined the Texas Rangers, serving for three years and finishing with the rank of corporal. In Fort Davis he resumed clerking in a general store, but he soon pinned on a deputy sheriff's badge with the assignment of policing nearby Murphyville (present-day Alpine). Later Milton opened a saloon in Murphyville, tying holstered pistols to posts throughout the building so that a gun would always be handy. In 1884 he drifted into New Mexico and took employment on a ranch near San Marcial, but he soon homesteaded a spread in the San Mateos and became a deputy sheriff of Socorro County. On one occasion Milton was attacked by a grizzly, but he managed to jam his six-gun into the beast's mouth and send a bullet into its brain.

Soon Milton added the capacity of range detective to his deputy's commission, and in 1885 he joined "Russell's Army," a group of volunteers who campaigned in Arizona against Apache marauders. In 1887 Milton took a job as a mounted inspector along the Arizona-Mexico boundary, operating out of Tucson and becoming one of twenty-five men who controlled nine hundred miles of border. Two years later he resigned and began operating a little horse ranch near Tucson, but by 1890 he was working as a fireman for the Southern

Pacific Railroad, soon earning a promotion to conductor.

In 1894 Milton was appointed chief of police of El Paso, although he left the job within a few months to become an express messenger for Wells, Fargo. A turn-of-the-century shooting scrape crippled his left arm, and at that point he began prospecting in the Sierra Madres. Soon he was attracted to the oil boom, exploring leases in Texas and in Lower California.

Finding no success in these ventures, in 1904 Milton joined the Immigration Service, assigned to stop the smuggling of Chinese aliens through Arizona and California. In 1919 he met a New York schoolteacher who had come to Arizona for her health, and they married a few months later. Shortly thereafter the Immigration Service assigned Milton to help safeguard a shipload of alien radicals being deported from the United States and sent to revolutionary Russia.

Milton did not retire until 1930, living out his old age in Tombstone, where he had a small ranch near town. He died at the age of eighty-five, and his wife scattered his ashes in the desert.

Gunfights: *May 16, 1881, Colorado City, Texas.* Rangers Milton, J. M. Sedberry, and L. B. Wells were on duty in Colorado City when they heard shooting near the Nip and Tuck Saloon. They ran toward the saloon, encountering cattlemen W. P. Patterson and Ab Adair. The lawmen asked who had done the shooting, and Patterson, a frequent troublemaker, blandly replied that he did not know. But when Sedberry asked to look at his gun, Patterson snarled, "Damn you, you will have to go examine somebody else's pistol." Sedberry and Wells attempted to seize Patterson, but he jerked loose, drew his gun, and fired at Sedberry, inflicting powder burns on the ranger's face. Milton then gunned Patterson down with his .45, and Wells pumped another slug into the fallen man, who died within moments.

October, 1881, Fort Davis, Texas. Milton and fellow Ranger Buck Guyse got drunk in Fort Davis and shot up the little frontier town. When a deputy named Fairchild approached the roisterers, Milton fired a warning shot. The rangers then started back to camp, but Milton finished the journey in the back of a wagon and staggered off to a spring hole to take a sobering dip. Fairchild soon appeared in camp, and Milton was assigned thirty days "on horse herd."

1884, Socorro County, New Mexico. While riding up the Gila River with a cowboy named Jim Hammil, Deputy Sheriff Milton was leading a pack horse when a volley erupted from ambush. One bullet killed Milton's horse and tore through his leg, but he seized his Winchester, and he and Hammil opened fire. When the shooting ended, three Mexican bandits lay dead, and Milton poured turpentine into his wound, bound it, and rode away on the pack animal.

May, 1889, near Bisbee, Arizona. At night Milton and Cap Kelton were scouring the border country near Bisbee for smugglers. The two inspectors had split temporarily when Milton encountered a smuggler. The man broke for the brush, and Milton squeezed off four shots, missing each time.

June 29, 1895, El Paso, Texas. Milton and his brother-in-law, Texas Ranger Frank McMahon, were waiting on the Texas side of the Mexican Central Railroad bridge to apprehend Martin Morose, who was supposed to meet with

George Scarborough there late at night. At 11:30 P.M. Morose and Scarborough appeared in the darkness, and Milton and McMahon emerged from hiding and ordered the wanted man to surrender. Morose instead produced a pistol and fired at Scarborough. Milton shot Morose in the chest with a .45, knocking him to the ground. But he came up shooting, only to be shot again in the chest by Scarborough, and this time Morose collapsed and died.

July, 1898, near Solomonville, Arizona. Milton and George Scarborough were searching eastern Arizona for an outlaw called Bronco Bill Walters. One morning they heard nearby shooting (which later turned out to be Walters and two henchmen, Red Pipkin and Bill Johnson, firing at a rattlesnake).

When the gang rode into sight, Milton called out, whereupon Walters began working his six-gun and turning his horse. Two slugs kicked up dust near Milton, who squeezed off a shot which tore through Walters' lungs and knocked him out of the saddle. Milton and Scarborough then began firing at Walters' companions. The officers killed Pipkin's horse, but the bandit leaped free and escaped into the brush. Johnson took cover behind a juniper and began throwing rifle fire, but Milton and Scarborough zeroed in, and the outlaw caught a bullet in the hip which ripped into his abdomen. Johnson died that night, but Walters survived to serve a prison term.

February 15, 1900, Fairbank, Arizona. Milton was guarding the express car of a train which pulled into Fairbank just as darkness fell. Five members of Burt Alvord's gang of bandits—Three-Fingered Jack Dunlap, George and Louis Owens, Bravo Juan Yoas, and Bob

Brown—converged on the train as it pulled in and loosed a volley which shattered Milton's left arm and threw him to the floor. He scrambled for his shotgun, however, and fired a blast which riddled Dunlap with eleven buckshot and which sent one stray slug into the seat of Yoas' pants.

Milton managed to shut the car door, and he began applying a tourniquet to his arm just as the outlaws sent another volley crashing into the door. Brown and the Owens brothers forced the engineer to open the express door, but Milton had hidden the keys and then fainted, and the bandits left the train empty-handed, carrying the seriously wounded Dunlap with them. Milton was rushed to Tucson, where he spent several months in the hospital. He never regained full use of his arm.

November 3, 1917, Tombstone, Arizona. Milton had begun traveling his territory in a stripped-down Ford, and as he drove into Tombstone at noon one day, a bank robbery took place. Banker T. R. Brandt had just been fatally wounded, and Milton and Guy Welch chugged off after robber Fred Koch. About two miles out of town the Ford drew near Koch, and Milton hopped out and stopped the murderer with a .38 slug in the arm.

Sources: Haley, *Jeff Milton;* Sonnichsen, *Pass of the North,* 246, 320, 325, 327, 329–30, 356–57; Erwin, *John H. Slaughter,* 220, 247–48.

Miner, William

("Old Bill")

(b. 1847, Jackson, Kentucky; d. 1913, Milledgeville, Georgia. Cowboy; bullwhacker; postman; stage, train, and bank robber; slave trader; convict.) Miner's mother was a teacher and his father a miner. When Bill was ten his father deserted the family, bequeathing only his restlessness to his son. At thirteen Bill ran away from home to become a cowboy. He worked his way west from ranch to ranch, and when he reached California he became a bullwhacker. In 1863 he made a courageous ride through Indian-infested country to deliver a message, and for a time thereafter he operated a mail service in southern California. But in 1869 he tried a stagecoach robbery, and when his horse stumbled, a posse captured him.

Sentenced to fifteen years in San Quentin, Miner won release in 1879 for good behavior. He promptly went to Colorado and teamed up with a notorious highwayman named Bill Leroy. But after several successful train and stage holdups, vigilantes were formed to catch them. Leroy was hanged, and Miner escaped only after a desperate shootout.

Miner then left the country and spent more than a year traveling in Europe, the Middle East, Africa, and South America. In Turkey he joined in a venture involving the abduction of desert women and their subsequent sale as harem girls.

Back in the United States by 1880, Miner returned to robbing stagecoaches, with occasional vacations to spend his ill-gotten loot under one of a string of aliases. Late in 1881 he was caught and again sentenced to a long stretch in San Quentin.

Released in 1901, Miner seems to have gone straight for a couple of years. But in September, 1903, he held up a train near Corbett, Oregon, and then one year later he robbed a train just outside Mission Junction, British Columbia. For three years he lived off his booty, but in 1905 he stuck up another train in British Columbia. Within two months the Canadian Mounted Police caught him, and he was sentenced to life in the New Westminster Penitentiary in Victoria, B.C. In August, 1907, however, he escaped through a thirty-five-foot tunnel and fled to the United States. In July, 1909, Miner robbed a bank in Portland, Oregon, and in February, 1911, he led four other thieves in holding up a train near White Sulphur, Georgia.

Captured after a fight with a posse, Old Bill was sentenced to life in the Georgia State Penitentiary in Milledgeville. Three times he broke out and was recaptured, and finally, after being chased down by dogs in a swamp, the sixty-six-year-old fugitive admitted, "I guess I'm getting too old for this sort of thing." He died quietly in his sleep in 1913.

Gunfights: *1879, Colorado.* Miner and fellow stage robber Bill Leroy were being chased by a posse in Colorado. When the vigilantes tracked them down, Miner began shooting. He wounded three of his adversaries and escaped, but Leroy was caught and hanged.

March, 1881, Colorado. Miner and a tough young Ohio hard case named Stanton Jones held up the Del Norte stagecoach, taking in a few hundred dollars. A posse soon was in hot pursuit, and for four days a running fight took place over ravines and mountains. At last, after Miner and Jones had wounded three lawmen, the posse turned back.

November, 1881, near Sonora, California. Miner led three other thieves in a holdup of the Sonora stage, but a posse quickly caught up with them. Miner tried to shoot his way out, but the four highwaymen were soon forced to surrender.

February, 1911, near White Sulphur, Georgia. Old Bill and four cohorts robbed a train of $3,500 near White Sulphur, Georgia, and the area soon was ringed by officers. A posse led by Pinkerton detective W. H. Minster located the outlaw camp in a swamp and moved in for the capture. Miner seized a rifle and began firing, but after two of his men were shot down, he surrendered.

Source: Horan and Sann, *Pictorial History of the Wild West,* 80–81.

Morco, John

("Happy Jack")

(d. September 4, 1873, Ellsworth, Kansas. Policeman, laborer.) In California, Morco, semiliterate and a drunken brawler, killed four unarmed men and fled the state. He wandered into Kansas, appearing in Ellsworth during its heyday as a railhead. Claiming to have killed a total of twelve men (the actual total of four was revealed when his estranged wife traveled to Ellsworth with a show troupe), Morco wangled an appointment to the police force. He participated in a quarrel with Ben Thompson which led to the death of Sheriff C. B. Whitney, and he was discharged, although not before he had run Texan Neil Cain (a participant in the card game which initiated the Whitney killing) out of town by threatening to shoot him. Soon thereafter Morco was killed in a gun duel with Ellsworth Policeman J. C. Brown.

Gunfights: *ca. 1868, California.* Morco had a drunken quarrel with his wife and proceeded to beat her. Four men heard her screams and came to her rescue, whereupon Morco produced a gun and murdered the unarmed men.

August 15, 1873, Ellsworth, Kansas.
About 3:00 P.M. Morco was drinking with gambler John Sterling when Ben Thompson strode into the saloon and demanded payment of a gambling debt from Sterling. The drunken Sterling, seeing that Thompson was unarmed, struck him in the face. Before Thompson could retaliate, Morco drew his gun and backed Ben off. Heated words were exchanged, and Morco and Sterling left the saloon together.

Sterling armed himself with a shotgun, and then, spoiling for trouble, the pair found Thompson with a number of friends in a different saloon. Morco and Sterling spat out a challenge: "Get your guns, you damn Texas sons-of-bitches, and fight!" None of the Texans was armed, in accordance with a town ordinance forbidding the carrying of firearms, so an enraged Thompson rushed to his hotel room to get his weapons.

Morco and Sterling next encountered Thompson, now armed with a six-gun and a Winchester, entering a saloon with his brother Billy and Sheriff C. B. Whitney, who was trying to calm down the brothers. Policeman Morco drew two revolvers and charged, followed by the unsteady Sterling. A bystander shouted, "Look out, Ben!" Ben stepped out and aimed his rifle, and Morco ducked into the doorway of a store just as Thompson's slug crashed into the door casing in front of Happy Jack's face. At that point the drunken Billy Thompson fired, accidentally striking Whitney, and all attention shifted to the mortally wounded lawman.

The next morning Morco failed to appear to press charges of attempted murder against Ben, and later that day he was dismissed in one motion and rehired in a succeeding one by the town council—although he was permanently fired less than two weeks later.

September 4, 1873, Ellsworth, Kansas.
Discharged from the Ellsworth police force on August 27, Happy Jack left town, carrying off a brace of expensive six-guns in the process. Authorities in nearby Salina took him into custody a week later, but refused to release him to Ellsworth policeman Charlie Brown, turning over only the stolen revolvers. That very night Morco hopped a freight into Ellsworth, and the next morning he boldly marched up and down the streets. Brown approached him and ordered Morco to surrender his gun. Instead, Morco tried to pull his pistol, but Brown beat him to the draw, drilling Happy Jack in the head and heart.

Sources: Drago, *Wild, Woolly & Wicked,* 103, 116–18; Miller and Snell, *Great Gunfighters of the Kansas Cowtowns,* 444–47; Schoenberger, *Gunfighters,* 155–58.

Morse, Harry N.

(b. February 22, 1835, New York, New York; d. January 11, 1912, Oakland, California. Prospector, butcher, expressman, cook, grocer, law officer, detective, businessman.) At the age of fourteen Harry Morse came from New York as an eager Forty-niner, but he soon turned to a variety of other jobs for a steadier livelihood. In 1863 Morse was elected sheriff of Alameda County, and he subsequently achieved renown as a relentless and resourceful manhunter. In 1871 he led an exhaustive search which ultimately resulted in the capture of the notorious Tiburcio Vásquez, and during the course of his career he located and killed two other vicious outlaws.

Morse retired as sheriff in 1878 and founded a detective agency in San Francisco. As a private detective his greatest coup came in 1883 when he was responsible for the arrest of the elusive stage robber Black Bart. Morse built a large home in Oakland in which to rear his family, and he engaged in a number of business interests other than his detective agency, including real estate, publishing, and mining. He died peacefully in Oakland at the age of seventy-six.

Gunfights: October, 1865, near Livermore, California. Morse and a deputy had traced Norrato Ponce, a wanted killer, to a hideout near Livermore. At midnight the two lawmen saw Ponce astride a horse, and Morse ordered him to give up. But Ponce drew and fired a pistol, and Morse and his deputy began shooting at his gun flashes. They wounded Ponce and felled his horse, but he scrambled to safety on foot. Morse set fire to nearby haystacks, but the illumination revealed only traces of blood, Ponce's hat, and his blood-soaked coat.

November, 1865, Contra Costa County, California. Six weeks after the Livermore fight Morse and two other officers discovered Ponce in the adobe house of José Rojos, and when the little posse approached the dwelling, a man ran desperately from the building. But he proved to be a decoy, and Ponce sprinted in the opposite direction. There was a flurry of gunfire, and Morse spurred toward his prey. Ponce turned and steadied his pistol, but Morse cut him down with rifle fire, and the fugitive died on the spot.

1871, Sausalito Valley, California. Morse and several other lawmen had trailed the "Human Wildcat," Juan Soto, to an isolated refuge in the Sausalito Valley. Morse and a deputy named Winchell entered a low adobe and found themselves face to face with Soto, who was seated at a table and surrounded by a dozen Mexicans. Morse covered Soto with a pistol, produced handcuffs with his left hand, and ordered Winchell to shackle the fugitive. But Winchell dashed outside instead, and Morse was jumped from behind by a man and a woman.

Morse struggled free and fired at Soto, but the outlaw burst out of the room with only a hole in his hat. Morse followed him through the door, but dove for the ground as Soto charged, firing four times. Morse fired and smashed Soto's pistol, then scrambled toward his horse to get his Henry rifle. Soto ran back inside, then emerged with a revolver in each hand and one in his belt. He tried to find a mount, but the horse shied, and Soto sprinted away from the lawman.

At a distance of 150 yards Morse drilled Soto through the shoulder, and the fugitive roared with rage and turned back toward the sheriff. But Morse stood his ground and calmly fired a bullet into Soto's head, killing him instantly.

Summer, 1872, near Arroyo Cantua, California. Morse was in Monterey visiting the sheriff of San Benito County when word arrived that a double holdup had occurred that day, engineered by Tiburcio Vásquez and accomplices Francisco Barcenas and García Rodríguez. The two sheriffs enlisted the aid of the constable of Santa Cruz and promptly dashed to cut off the bandits before they could reach their hideout in the Arroyo Cantua.

The three lawmen jumped the outlaws on the road, and a desperate shootout ensued. Rodríguez and Vásquez were badly wounded, and the constable killed Barcenas. The two wounded outlaws galloped away, and Vásquez, although shot in the chest, managed to elude his hunters in the mountains. Rodríguez, however, was captured two days later and was taken to San Quentin, where he soon died.

Sources: Shinn, *Pacific Coast Outlaws;* Drago, *Road Agents and Train Robbers,* 33, 35–36, 38, 45–47.

Burt Mossman, a businessman who earlier in his career served as the first captain of the Arizona Rangers. *(Courtesy Arizona Historical Society)*

Mossman, Burton

("Cap")

(b. April 30, 1867, Aurora, Illinois. Farmer, cowboy, rancher, law officer, stagecoach contractor, businessman.)

The son of a farmer, Burt Mossman moved with his family in 1873 to Lake City, Missouri, then three years later to a homestead in Marshall. The Mossmans moved again in 1882, this time to New Mexico, where Burt soon became a cowboy. By the age of twenty he was a ranch foreman, and soon he became manager of a big spread in Arizona. In December, 1897, he was employed as superintendent of the two-million-acre Hash Knife outfit, where his primary problem proved to be ridding the vast range of rustlers.

Appointed a deputy sheriff of Navajo County, Arizona, Mossman not only found time to subdue the rustlers and run the ranch, but he also was able to conduct a stagecoach line with a partner. In 1898 Mossman and three other associates built a brick opera house in Winslow, although he soon sold out for a nice profit and later built a store building in Douglas which he sold for thirteen thousand dollars. But as he began other ventures, his business career was interrupted by an appointment as the first captain of the newly created Arizona Rangers. After two of his rangers were killed, Mossman led a hardhanded effort against area outlaws, culminating in the capture and eventual execution of the vicious Augustín Chacón.

Mossman resigned in August, 1902, following a violent year in service which established him as a deadly gunman. Later he built a vast ranch in Dakota Territory, with time out in December, 1905, to become married in New York City. A son and daughter were born to the union, but after the birth of the girl in 1909, Mossman's wife died. There were numerous business and ranching ventures during the rest of his full life, which extended deeply into the twentieth century.

Gunfights: summer, 1896, Mazatlán, Mexico. Mossman had recently delivered a herd of cattle to Mexico, and he traveled slowly back to Arizona, enjoying something of a vacation. In a Mazatlán *cantina,* however, he quarreled with a young Mexican captain, who challenged him to a formal duel the next morning. The following dawn the antagonists and their principals met, loaded their weapons each with a single bullet, and stepped off fifteen paces. The men whirled and the Mexican fired his German Luger. The bullet missed, and Mossman pumped the .45 slug from his short-barreled Colt into the captain's shoulder. At that point a squad of local police arrived, and Mossman spent four weeks in the *calabozo* until he managed to escape with the help of a Mexican friend.

March 17, 1898, Water Canyon, Arizona. Mossman and Deputy Sheriff Joe Bargeman were searching for a rustler hideout in Water Canyon. Led to a cabin by a reluctant Mexican, they discovered a slaughtered beef, whereupon the Mexican bolted. Mossman sprang onto his horse, rode down the Mexican, and clubbed him with a Winchester. As he dismounted to help the man to his feet, three other Mexicans began firing at him from a range of one hundred yards.

Grazed on the nose, Mossman forced his prisoner back to the cabin. Bullets tore off Mossman's saddle horn and cut his reins, but with Bargeman providing cover fire, Burt reached the cabin with his prisoner. After a brief siege Mossman and Bargeman were able to transport their prisoner the sixty miles into Holbrook.

Fall, 1898, Springer, New Mexico. While trying to undress in a room above a rowdy bar in Springer, Mossman was startled when a bullet crashed upward through the floor near his chair. He began to roll up the mattress as a barricade when a second slug tore through the floor, and he angrily seized his Winchester and emptied it blindly into the bar below. The room was vacated in a stampede, with no worse injuries than a hole in one man's hat brim and a glass shot out of the hand of a stunned drinker.

1901, Paradise Valley, Arizona. The trail of an outlaw named Salivaras had led Cap to a water hole in desolate and ill-named Paradise Valley. Salivaras tried to ambush Mossman, firing a bullet which nicked the ranger captain's right leg. Mossman threw his rifle to his shoulder and snapped off a shot, then jumped off his horse. After a time, he worked toward the outlaw's position and discovered that his slug had taken off the top of Salivaras' head.

1901, Colorado River, Mexico. Mossman had learned that six suspected train robbers had holed up twenty miles below the border on the Colorado River, and Cap and three rangers rode to investigate. They discovered the six Americans in an abandoned house near the river, and just before dawn one of the rangers, who had handled explosives as a miner, exploded four sticks of dynamite against the adobe building. The fugitives staggered outside to be greeted by rifle fire from the four rangers. Five of the outlaws were killed, but one managed to escape on horseback.

Sources: Hunt, *Cap Mossman, Last of the Great Cowmen;* Coolidge, *Fighting Men of the West,* 247–79; Wagoner, *Arizona Territory,* 373–95; Raine, *Famous Sheriffs and Western Outlaws,* 236–52.

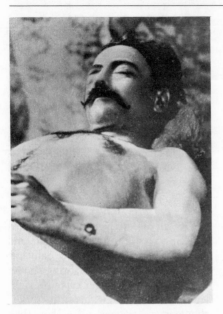

Bitter Creek Newcomb in 1895, dead at the hands of his brothers-in-law. *(Courtesy Western History Collections, University of Oklahoma Library)*

Newcomb, George

("Bitter Creek," "Slaughter's Kid")

(d. May 2, 1895, Dunn Ranch on the Cimarron River, Oklahoma. Cowboy, bank and train robber.) Newcomb was reared in Fort Scott, Kansas, but as a youth he left home for Texas, where he worked for cattleman John Slaughter, thus acquiring the sobriquet "Slaughter's Kid." In 1883 Newcomb drifted into Oklahoma, where he hired on as a cowboy in the Cherokee Strip ranching country. He so frequently sang, "I'm a wild wolf from Bitter Creek/And it's my night to howl," that his friends nicknamed him "Bitter Creek." He was a member of the Dalton and Doolin gangs and was involved in numerous train and bank holdups. At a county dance he met

fifteen-year-old Rosa Dunn, giving her renown as "the Rose of Cimarron." Eventually he sought refuge at the Dunn Ranch, but Rosa's brothers killed him for the five-thousand-dollar reward on his head.

Gunfights: *July 15, 1892, Adair, Oklahoma.* The Dalton gang rode into Adair about a quarter of an hour before the 9:42 P.M. train was due to arrive. They robbed the depot of everything of value, then attacked the train. While several of the bandits looted the express car, Newcomb was one of those who kept the passengers inside their car with rifle fire. Suddenly guards began shooting back from the smoker, and the outlaws concentrated their fire on that car. Within moments three of the lawmen— L. L. Kinney, Charley LaFlore, and Sid Johnson—had received flesh wounds, and the bandits were able to withdraw safely with their booty.

January 20, 1893, near Bartlesville, Oklahoma. Newcomb, Henry Starr, and Jesse Jackson were jumped by lawmen Rufe Cannon and Ike Rogers while traveling near Bartlesville. During a running fight Jackson was wounded and captured, but the other two outlaws shot their way to freedom.

September 1, 1893, Ingalls, Oklahoma. Bill Doolin had led Newcomb and five other gang members into tiny Ingalls for a brief rest. Arkansas Tom Jones, who was ill, bedded down in the hotel, but the others repaired to a saloon and began drinking and gambling.

At that point several lawmen slipped into town and began closing in on the saloon. Newcomb, sensing something amiss, left the poker game and went out to his horse. As he cautiously rode down the street, posse member Dick Speed asked a nearby youth, Del Simmons, who the rider was. "Why," chirped Simmons, pointing at the outlaw, "that's Bitter Creek Newcomb!"

The fugitive seized his Winchester, but Speed threw up his rifle and triggered a bullet which shattered the magazine of Newcomb's weapon, driving a piece of metal into his leg. Newcomb squeezed off one shot, and then his damaged gun jammed. Speed stepped forward to finish Newcomb, but Jones opened fire from his second-story window and killed the lawman. Newcomb then headed his horse out of town, and although other officers fired at him, he soon reached the safety of a stand of timber south of Ingalls.

April 1, 1894, Sacred Heart, Oklahoma. At 8:00 P.M. Newcomb and Bill Dalton entered a store run by an old law officer named W. H. Carr, who immediately recognized Dalton. Carr went for his six-gun, but Newcomb pulled his pistol from a coat pocket and warned, "I guess not." Carr resolutely shot Newcomb in the left shoulder, but Bitter Creek fired a slug which hit the old officer in the right wrist, causing him to drop his gun.

As Carr stooped to retrieve his weapon, a customer, teen-ager Lee Hardwick, grabbed at a shotgun. Dalton pumped four slugs at Carr and Hardwick, firing wildly each time. Newcomb then shot Carr in the stomach, but when the old man kept firing, the outlaws backed through the door and fled.

Spring, 1895, near Dover, Oklahoma. Having just robbed a train near Dover, the Doolin gang was jumped by a posse, and Tulsa Jack Blake was killed. A running gun battle began, and when Red Buck's horse was shot out from under him, Newcomb let his cohort ride double.

After the posse had been outdistanced, Red Buck stole a horse, murdered its venerable owner, and was expelled from the gang on the spot.

May 2, 1895, Dunn Ranch on the Cimarron River, Oklahoma. Newcomb and fellow fugitive Charley Pierce went to the Dunn Ranch. Bitter Creek hoped to see Rosa there, and the Dunn brothers owed him nine hundred dollars. But there was a five-thousand-dollar reward on his head, and when the two outlaws dismounted in front of the ranch house, two of the Dunn brothers opened fire. After Bitter Creek and Pierce fell, the Dunns emerged. When Pierce groaned, one of the brothers blasted him again.

The next morning the Dunns loaded the "bodies" in a wagon and drove off toward Guthrie to collect their reward. Bitter Creek was still alive, however, and gasped out a request for water. The Dunns' reply was another bullet, and this time Newcomb died.

Sources: Croy, *Trigger Marshal,* 173–76; Canton, *Frontier Trails,* 110, 119–21; Shirley, *Heck Thomas,* 123, 157, 171–74, 195–97; Shirley, *Six-gun and Silver Star,* 61, 86–92, 95, 105–106, 109, 145, 152–62, 179, 184.

Oden, Lon

(Law officer.) Oden served as a Texas Ranger during the late 1800's in Company D along the Mexican border. His most violent shooting scrapes occurred while following the noted ranger John Hughes.

Gunfights: *1889, Shafter, Texas.* Oden and John Hughes had secluded themselves near the entrance to an abandoned shaft where stolen silver ore had been hidden. Although painfully chilled by the night mountain air, the lawmen were finally rewarded when six burros appeared, driven by three ore thieves and undercover man Ernest St. Leon. Corporal Hughes ordered a surrender, and a fight erupted. St. Leon scrambled away and added his volleys to those of the rangers, and all three outlaws were fatally wounded.

1893, San Antonio Colony, Texas. Oden again accompanied Hughes and Jim Putnam on a border assignment. The three rangers arrested Desidario Durán at San Antonio Colony, a Mexican settlement, and as they prepared to leave, they spotted three other wanted men. Leaving Putnam with Durán, Oden and Hughes galloped to the chase. Fugitive Florencio Carrasco mortally wounded Oden's mount, but the lawman leaped clear and began firing. Carrasco was knocked out of the saddle, but he continued to resist, and the two officers finished him off. They then returned to town just in time to extricate Putnam from a menacing mob.

Source: Martin, *Border Boss*, 96–100, 109–11.

O'Folliard, Tom

(b. 1858, Uvalde, Texas; d. December 19, 1880, Fort Sumner, New Mexico. Horse thief, cattle rustler.) Born in Uvalde, Texas, as the son of an Irish immigrant, O'Folliard moved with his parents to Monclova, Mexico, before the Civil War. But Tom's parents soon died in a smallpox epidemic, and he was reared in Uvalde by relatives.

In 1878 the young man drifted into New Mexico, fell into bad company, stole some horses from Emil Fritz, a member of one faction in the Lincoln County War, and thus found himself entangled in the bloody feud. He quickly became friends with Billy the Kid, shot his way out of Alexander McSween's burning home with the Kid, and joined the Kid's band of rustlers.

O'Folliard and the Kid submitted to arrest together, and they also escaped custody together. For months they were active as stock thieves, ranging as far as the Texas Panhandle. During this period O'Folliard witnessed the murder in Lincoln of one-armed lawyer Huston Chapman at the hands of Jesse Evans, William Campbell, and Billy Matthews. On another occasion Pat Garrett's posse drew within three hundred yards, and after a furious chase, during which there was a heavy exchange of shots, O'Folliard outdistanced the lawmen.

Although O'Folliard's uncle, Texas Ranger Thalis Cook, tried to persuade him to surrender, O'Folliard remained a hunted fugitive until late in 1880, when he was shot and killed by Garrett's posse.

Gunfights: *July 15–19, 1878, Lincoln, New Mexico.* The great climactic battle of the Lincoln County War was a lengthy affair with about forty men on each side. O'Folliard was aligned with the "McSween crowd" centered inside McSween's rambling adobe building, while Sheriff George Peppin was in charge of the "Sheriff's party," which concentrated upon McSween's place, even though numerous McSween men were located in other structures. For two and one-half days the fighting consisted of sniping between the two factions, with the only casualty coming when Charlie Crawford was wounded by a slug coming from McSween man Fernando Herrera. Crawford was taken to nearby Fort Stanton for treatment.

On the third day of the fight a column of thirty-five soldiers trooped into Lincoln carrying two howitzers and a Gatling gun. Although the military declared its neutrality and warned both sides against killing soldiers, the commanding officer was known to sympathize with the anti-McSween group. Therefore, the McSween men felt compelled to desert the houses which protected McSween's place, and the adobe building was set afire. The women inside were allowed to leave, and as night fell on July 19 the dozen men trapped inside the slowly burning structure prepared to shoot their way free.

O'Folliard burst outside first, hoping to run from the back door past a low adobe wall to the river nearby. Behind him twenty-year-old Harvey Morris went down, and O'Folliard stopped to help him. But a slug tore into Tom's right shoulder, and he dropped his gun. Then he saw several of his compatriots, including Alexander McSween, who was armed solely with a Bible, riddled with bullets from gunmen crouched below the adobe wall.

Leaving his gun, Tom darted through a gate, stumbled down the river embankment, and collapsed in the underbrush. A short time later he rejoined the Kid and the others who had escaped.

Early December, 1880, Lincoln County, New Mexico. Pat Garrett and a posse intercepted O'Folliard in open country, but Tom began working his rifle and gradually outdistanced his pursuers.

December 19, 1880, Fort Sumner, New Mexico. The Kid, O'Folliard, Charlie Bowdre, Tom Pickett, Dave Rudabaugh, and Billy Wilson were riding into Fort Sumner for an evening of recreation, not realizing that a large posse led by Pat Garrett awaited them. With Lon Chambers standing lookout, the posse members were playing poker inside the old post hospital when the outlaw party rode in. O'Folliard and the Kid were in front, but the latter, perhaps suspecting danger, nudged his horse to the rear to get some chewing tobacco from Wilson.

Pickett moved up beside O'Folliard about the time Garrett shouted, "Halt!" O'Folliard reached for his gun, and several rifles went off. One slug tore through O'Folliard's chest on the left side just beneath the heart.

The rest of the outlaws galloped away unscathed, and O'Folliard, moaning with agony, wheeled and set off after them. But after he had gone perhaps 150 yards, he pulled up and walked his mount back, calling, "Don't shoot, Garrett. I'm killed." Deputy Barney Mason replied, "Take your medicine, old boy, take your medicine," and ran out to take custody of him.

Garrett barked a warning and ordered O'Folliard to throw up his hands. But O'Folliard repeated that he was dying and could not raise his hands, and he asked the lawmen to lift him from his horse and let him die as easily as possible. They complied, taking his cocked pistol from his hand and stretching him out inside the old hospital.

O'Folliard told Garrett that if he were a friend he would put him out of his misery, but the sheriff coldly declared that he was no friend to men of his kind. Mason continued to urge him to take his medicine, but the dying outlaw said, "It's the best medicine I ever took," then asked Mason to see that his grandmother in Texas was informed of his death. O'Folliard later moaned, "Oh, my God, is it possible I must die?"

Just before the end, Garrett said, "Tom, your time is short."

"The sooner the better," gasped O'Folliard. "I will be out of pain." He died less than an hour after being shot and was buried in the Fort Sumner cemetery where Bowdre and the Kid were later interred.

Sources: Hunt, *Tragic Days of Billy the Kid,* 54–60, 76–101, 105, 132–40, 151–62, 170–71, 179, 186–90, 195, 204, 213–17, 226, 229, 236–42; Keleher, *Violence in Lincoln County,* 124, 224, 291–93, 312; Garrett, *Billy, the Kid,* 103–104, 116–21; Siringo, *A Texas Cowboy,* 138–39, 170.

Olinger, John Wallace

(Rancher, law officer.) Olinger was a brother of Bob Olinger, who was killed by Billy the Kid in a jailbreak. Both brothers became involved in the Lincoln County War, being deputized by Sheriff George Peppin to fight against Alexander McSween's "Regulators." One month after the big four-day shootout in Lincoln, Wallace participated in a gunfight on behalf of his ranch partner, but from that point on he led a quiet existence.

Gunfights: *February 18, 1878, near Lincoln, New Mexico.* Olinger was a member of the posse which encountered rancher John Tunstall and shot him to death. Olinger helped lay out Tunstall's body, but later he claimed to have taken no part in the gunplay.

April 30, 1878, near Lincoln, New Mexico. Olinger and his brother Bob were also members of the posse which had a shootout with Frank McNab, Ab Sanders, and Frank Coe about eight miles from Lincoln. When the fighting ended, McNab was dead, Sanders was severely wounded, and Coe, having expended his ammunition, had surrendered to the posse.

August 16, 1878, near Seven Rivers, New Mexico. Olinger and William H. Johnson were partners in a cattle ranch on the Pecos River, and Johnson was involved in a family quarrel with his father-in-law, Henry Beckwith. The problem erupted into violence on Beckwith's ranch in the Seven Rivers coun-

try. Beckwith blasted Johnson with a double-barreled shotgun, inflicting fatal wounds in his neck and chest. Beckwith then argued bitterly with his son John and was restrained from killing him only by the intervention of bystanders. An enraged Olinger then pulled his pistol and opened fire, hitting the elder Beckwith in the cheek and nose. Olinger was arrested and taken to Fort Stanton, but he was later released when Beckwith recovered.

Sources: Keleher, *Violence in Lincoln County,* 141, 159, 224, 233, 255–59, 265, 276; Klasner, *My Girlhood Among Outlaws,* 67, 141, 172, 174; Fulton, *Lincoln County War,* 118–19, 213, 216, 251.

Olinger, Robert A.

("The Big Indian")

(b. ca. 1841, Ohio; d. April 28, 1881, Lincoln, New Mexico. Cowboy, law officer, farmer.) Bob Olinger moved with his family from Ohio to Oklahoma, then drifted into New Mexico about 1876 and obtained the position of town marshal of Seven Rivers in Lincoln County. Olinger was suspected of aiding local outlaws, and he soon turned to punching cattle for a living. Olinger also was involved in the Lincoln County War, playing a minor role as one of the besiegers of Alexander McSween's store in July, 1878. He later pinned on a badge again as one of Pat Garrett's Lincoln County deputies, and in January, 1881, he received an appointment as a deputy U.S. marshal, although months later he was arrested in Las Vegas for illegally carrying arms.

Olinger was killed by Billy the Kid during a bold jailbreak from the Lincoln courthouse. At the time of his death Olinger had completed arrangements to rent an irrigated farm for three thousand dollars per year, but he was gunned down before he could pursue those plans.

Gunfights: *April 30, 1878, near Lincoln, New Mexico.* Olinger was with the "Seven Rivers Crowd" which ambushed Frank McNab, Ab Sanders, and Frank Coe at a stream near Lincoln. McNab and Sanders were wounded, and when McNab tried to crawl away, the posse finished him off with shotguns. Coe's horse was shot when he tried to flee, and after a short fight he surrendered. The posse rode away with Coe in custody, leaving Sanders to fend for himself as best he could.

1878, Seven Rivers, New Mexico. On the main street of Seven Rivers, Olinger encountered Pas Chavez, with whom he had argued a few days earlier. Olinger extended his hand, and when Chavez took it, Bob suddenly jerked him off balance. Olinger then jammed his revolver into Chavez' middle and pulled the trigger, mortally wounding the Mexican.

1879, near Seven Rivers, New Mexico. John Hill was shot to death—apparently from ambush—near Seven Rivers, and it was commonly assumed that Olinger had fired the fatal shots.

September, 1879, Lincoln County, New Mexico. Olinger accompanied Deputy Sheriff Milo Pierce in tracking a killer named John Jones to a Lincoln County cow camp. Olinger had previously clashed with the accused man, and Jones snarled a challenge and squeezed off a rifle shot. Olinger then fired three slugs into Jones, killing him on the spot. One bullet passed through Jones and struck Pierce, causing a permanent limp.

April 28, 1881, Lincoln, New Mexico. Something of a blowhard, Olinger had steadily taunted Billy the Kid while the prisoner awaited execution. Olinger had ceremoniously crossed out the days preceding the Kid's hanging date of May 13, and he had often brandished a shotgun in the Kid's face.

About 6:00 P.M. Olinger left the Lincoln courthouse with four or five prisoners to take an evening meal at the Wortley Hotel down the street. J. W. Bell stayed behind to guard the Kid, but Billy obtained a gun and killed Bell. Olinger heard the shots and dashed toward the courthouse. Godfrey Gauss, who had just cradled the dying Bell in his arms, intercepted Olinger and began to blurt out his tale.

Suddenly the Kid leaned out a second-story window and said, "Hello, Bob." Gauss ducked for cover as the Kid fired both barrels of a shotgun. Olinger was riddled by a double load of buckshot in the head and neck, and he dropped dead in his tracks. The Kid threw the shotgun into the street, shouting, "You won't follow me any more with that gun!"

Sources: Keleher, *Violence in Lincoln County,* 141, 159, 223, 233, 257, 321, 333–35, 347; Hunt, *Tragic Days of Billy the Kid,* 265–67, 273–91; Klasner, *My Girlhood Among Outlaws,* 6, 151–52, 172, 178, 183–91, 199; Fulton, *Lincoln County War,* 213, 251, 370–71, 393, 395–96.

O'Rourke, John

("Johnny-Behind-the-Deuce")

(b. 1861; d. 1882, Sulphur Springs Valley, Arizona. Gambler.) O'Rourke was a young gambler who, according to legend, was saved from lynching by Wyatt Earp. That incident was blown

out of proportion, and the rest of his story is somewhat hazy. Earp, always a questionable source, repeated the rumor that O'Rourke was responsible for the death of Johnny Ringo in July, 1882, and that a friend of Ringo's called Pony Deal quickly chased the gambler and killed him in revenge.

Gunfights: January 14, 1881, Charleston, Arizona. After an all-night poker game, mining engineer Henry Schneider and heavy winner O'Rourke exchanged angry words. When Schneider pulled a knife, O'Rourke pulled a pistol and shot his adversary dead. Constable George Mc-Kelvey arrested the gambler and took him to Tombstone, where Wyatt Earp supposedly held off a vicious lynch mob. Actually, several lawmen, including Deputy Marshal Virgil Earp, loaded O'Rourke into a spring wagon and transported him with no complications to jail in Tucson.

1882, Sulphur Springs Valley, Arizona. Shortly after the death of Johnny Ringo, Pony Deal sought out O'Rouke in Sulphur Springs Valley, and a fight broke out in which Johnny-Behind-the-Deuce was shot to death.

Sources: Waters, *Earp Brothers of Tombstone,* 112–15; Jahns, *Doc Holliday,* 163–65; Erwin, *John H. Slaughter,* 205, 207.

Outlaw, Bass

(b. Georgia; d. April 5, 1894, El Paso, Texas. Law officer.) Reared in a good family in Georgia, five-foot-four Outlaw was well educated and possessed fine manners. However, he was feisty and a problem drinker. Reputedly he killed a man in Georgia, then ran away to Texas. In 1885 he enlisted in the Texas

Rangers and won rapid promotion to sergeant, but in Alpine he was discovered drunk on duty, and he was forced to resign. After a time he secured an appointment as a deputy U.S. marshal, although he was constantly warned to curb his drinking. He was killed during a wild gunfight in El Paso in 1894.

Gunfights: 1889, Sierra del Carmen, Coahuila, Mexico. Outlaw, John Hughes, and Walter Durbin had spent several weeks guarding bullion shipments from a silver mine in the Mexican state of Coahuila. One evening between trips Outlaw, drinking heavily, quarreled with a Mexican mine worker in the company store. The Mexican pulled a knife, and Outlaw shot him to death, then backed outside brandishing his guns. Hughes and Durbin subdued him, and the three Texans hastily headed for the Rio Grande.

December 25, 1889, near Vance, Texas. Outlaw, fellow Rangers Ira Aten and John Hughes, and Deputy Sheriff Will Terry sprang a midnight ambush on the outlawed Odle brothers as they tried to sneak into Texas from Mexico on Christmas. Will and Alvin Odle tried to resist, and both were fatally wounded within moments.

April 5, 1894, El Paso, Texas. In town as a court witness, Outlaw spent an afternoon drinking and visiting various El Paso dives. He fired a shot in Tillie Howard's sporting house; Constable John Selman was already on the scene, and Texas Ranger Joe McKidrict came running up, encountering Outlaw in the back yard. "Bass," challenged Mc-Kidrict, "why did you shoot?" Drunkenly, Outlaw replied, "You want some too?" He raised his pistol and fired a shot point-blank into McKidrict's head, then shot the ranger in the back as he fell.

Selman went for his gun, but Outlaw got off another shot, missing the constable but half blinding him with the powder blast. Selman's return shot hit Outlaw in the chest, tearing through his left lung and emerging out his back. Outlaw staggered back, fired two more shots, wounding Selman twice in the leg, and then stumbled away.

When he encountered Texas Ranger Frank McMahon, Outlaw surrendered his gun and was led into a nearby saloon, where he collapsed. A doctor arrived and placed Outlaw on a prostitute's bed in back. "Oh God, help!" cried Outlaw repeatedly. "Where are my friends?" At 9:15 P.M., about four hours after he was shot, Bass Outlaw died.

Sources: Metz, *John Selman,* 146–50; Sonnichsen, *Pass of the North,* 315, 317–19; Martin, *Border Boss,* 76–84, 102–107, 115, 117.

Owens, Commodore Perry

(b. July 29, 1852, Tennessee; d. 1918, Seligman, Arizona. Stage station employee, cowboy, horse rancher, railroad detective, express messenger, law officer, businessman.) Named after the War of 1812 hero of Lake Erie, Commodore Perry Owens was reared in Tennessee. As a youth he left home and spent a decade as a cowboy. He then drifted into Arizona as a stage station employee, also earning a reputation as a dead shot against Indians.

Owens began a horse ranch at Navajo Springs and later became sheriff of Apache County. After mowing down four opponents in an 1887 gunfight, Owens, who sported long hair, a brace of .45's, and two rifles, cut his mane and settled down to the peaceful occupation of rearing a family. After three

Commodore Perry Owens, a few years after he shot down four opponents in an 1887 gunfight. *(Courtesy Arizona Historical Society)*

years as sheriff, he became a detective for the Santa Fe Railroad and an express messenger for Wells, Fargo. He then became a businessman in Seligman, where he died in 1918.

Gunfights: *1886, Apache County, Arizona.* Owens had been hired by a railroad contractor to guard a horse herd. A band of Indian renegades tried to rush Owens and start a stampede, but he drove them off by fatally wounding two of the would-be rustlers. The fame he gained from this incident enabled him to become elected county sheriff.

September 4, 1887, Holbrook, Arizona. On a Sunday afternoon Owens rode up to the Holbrook house of widowed Eva Blevins, who recently had lost her husband and one of her four sons in the Pleasant Valley War. Owens was looking for her boy Andy "Cooper," who had adopted an alias becasue he had killed two sheepmen in the Pleasant Valley feud and because he was sought by Texas authorities for past misdeeds.

Owens approached the house with his Winchester cradled in his arms, and he spotted Andy, armed with a six-gun, peering through one of the two front doors. Owens and Andy fired simultaneously, and the lawman's bullet plowed through the door and sent Andy staggering back into the arms of his mother. Then John Blevins squeezed off a shot from the other front door, and Owens, still firing from the hip, shot him in the right shoulder.

Owens ran to the side of the house just as Mose Roberts, a Blevins brother-in-law from Texas, hopped out a rear window brandishing a revolver. Owens dropped Roberts with one shot, then wheeled to meet another threat. The youngest Blevins boy, sixteen-year-old Sam Houston, ran onto the front porch with a six-gun, but Owens drilled him in the heart.

Owens fired a few more shots through the thin walls of the house, but there was no one besides Eva Blevins and two other women left standing. Owens rode off, leaving only John Blevins to survive the shootout.

Sources: Coolidge, *Fighting Men of the West,* 113–33; Drago, *Great Range Wars,* 98, 113, 116, 118–30.

Parker, Robert LeRoy

("Butch Cassidy," "George Cassidy," "William T. Phillips")

(b. April 13, 1866, Beaver, Utah; d.

Robert LeRoy Parker, photographed in 1893 upon entering the Wyoming State Penitentiary. *(Courtesy Western History Collections, University of Oklahoma Library)*

July 20, 1937, Spangle, Washington. Cowboy, ore freighter, mine employee, sailor, butcher, rustler, train and bank robber, engineer.) Robert LeRoy Parker, whose father and paternal grandparents emigrated to Utah with the second Mormon handcart procession, was reared in Beaver, where his father ran a store. In 1879 the Parkers moved their growing brood, which eventually numbered thirteen, to a ranch near Circleville. This area had long been a hangout for outlaws, and in his mid-teens Robert LeRoy developed a hero worship for a ruffian named Mike Cassidy, who gave his young friend a saddle and a gun. At the age of sixteen Parker left home and began to run with Cassidy, ultimately becoming second-in-command of the rustling outfit.

Parker's activities brought him from time to time to Wyoming's isolated Hole-in-the-Wall country, where he met some of the men who later became members of his Wild Bunch. In 1887 he participated in an aborted train robbery in Colorado, and in 1889 he helped loot banks in Denver and in Telluride, Colorado. Following these jobs, Parker, using the alias "George Cassidy," returned to Wyoming and lay low, working in a Rock Springs butcher shop, which, of course, is where he gained the sobriquet "Butch." During those years he sometimes tried to go straight, working as a cowboy on various ranches, including a stint in the mid-1880's on the huge Swan Land and Cattle Company Ranch. But he soon returned to rustling, and in 1892 he was taken into custody. In 1894, following a delayed trial, Butch was sentenced to a two-year stretch in the Wyoming State Penitentiary. The man who swore out the warrants leading to Butch's arrest, rancher Otto Franc of the Big Horn Basin, was mysteriously shot to death in 1903.

After his release in 1896, Butch returned to crime, forming the notorious Wild Bunch to assist him. Surrounded by such men as Harvey Logan, Harry Longabaugh ("the Sundance Kid"), Ben Kilpatrick, Elzy Lay, Harry Tracy, and Big Nose George Curry, Cassidy engineered a number of train and bank robberies in the ensuing years. After a job the gang sometimes vacationed together in such cities as Fort Worth, San Antonio, and Denver. Between holdups Butch often rendezvoused with Mary Boyd and other sweethearts. He also sought refuge in various locales, once working as a sailor on the Great

Lakes and on another occasion serving on a steamer from Seattle to Los Angeles.

By the early 1900's the law was closing in, and in 1902, Cassidy, Longabaugh, and Longabaugh's mistress, Etta Place, fled to South America, following an extended vacation in New York. Cassidy sailed alone via Liverpool and the Canary Islands, and was joined by Longabaugh and Etta in Montevideo, Uruguay. The trio moved to Argentina, where they operated a cattle and sheep ranch, trailing their herds into Chile, finding a profitable market at the mines there. After a few years Etta began suffering attacks of appendicitis, and in 1907 Longabaugh took her to Denver for an operation. After he returned, the two *bandidos yanquis* shifted their activities to Bolivia, where they began robbing payroll shipments and banks, working in the tin mines between holdups. Early in 1908 they were caught by Bolivian soldiers, and Longabaugh was killed after a violent battle. Butch apparently escaped, however, returning to the United States and establishing his identity as William Thadeus Phillips. He claimed to be a mechanical engineer from Des Moines, Iowa, and on May 14, 1908, he married Gertrude Livesay in Adrian, Michigan.

Because Mrs. Phillips was an asthmatic, the couple soon moved to Globe, Arizona, and Phillips spent some time across the border as a mercenary in the Mexican Revolution. In 1910 they settled in Spokane, Washington, and within five years William had established the Phillips Manufacturing Company, producing adding machines and other business equipment. The company prospered, and Phillips became an Elk and a Mason and indulged his love of fine cars—just as Butch had always enjoyed fine horses. In 1919 the childless couple adopted an infant son. In 1910, 1925, and 1934, Phillips visited some of his old haunts, searching fruitlessly for buried loot from his Wild Bunch days. He also saw members of his family and former acquaintances—including his widowed sweetheart, Mary Boyd Rhodes.

Phillips was forced to sell his company during the Great Depression, and in 1934 he unsuccessfully tried to market a manuscript, "The Bandit Invincible," based on his career as Butch Cassidy. In desperation he concocted a scheme to kidnap for ransom a wealthy Spokane citizen, but the plan was never executed. By that time Phillips had contracted cancer, and he died in 1937 at Broadacres, the county poor farm at Spangle, near Spokane.

Gunfights: April 8, 1892, near Auburn, Wyoming. John Chapman and Bob Calverly, deputy sheriff of Uinta County, Wyoming, had traced Butch and his rustling partner, Al Hainer, to a hideout near Auburn. The daughter of a local rancher was consorting with them, and Chapman and Calverly picked her up when she tried to get the outlaws' mail. She revealed that Butch was in a nearby cabin and Hainer was working at a local sawmill. Chapman and Calverly went to the mill, and after a short fight they subdued Hainer and tied him to a tree. The two lawmen then went to the cabin and barged inside. Butch leaped for his six-gun hanging on a chair, seized it, and snapped off a wild shot. Calverly's pistol misfired three times, but on the fourth try a bullet grazed Butch's head, stunning him and allowing the lawmen to handcuff him.

Spring, 1908, San Vicente, Bolivia. On an isolated jungle trail Butch and Longabaugh hijacked a mule train loaded with bullion from the Alpoca Mine.

They traveled fifteen miles to San Vicente, tethered their pack animals in a corner of the plaza, and walked to a restaurant to get something to eat. In the meantime a young Bolivian recognized a mule stolen from a friend of his in the robbery and reported this information to the local authorities. They notified a troop of soldiers camped nearby, and soon armed men were quietly surrounding the plaza. When everyone was in position, a detail rode up to the two Americans and the *capitán* demanded their surrender. Longabaugh immediately shot him from his horse, and as the outlaws retreated inside, Cassidy shot another soldier. A barrage of gunfire came from the soldiers, and Cassidy and Longabaugh barricaded themselves behind tables and chairs. But their rifles and ammunition were with their pack animals, and Longabaugh decided to try to get them. When darkness fell he dashed across the plaza and reached the mules, but, burdened with cartridge belts and Winchesters, he was shot down as he tried to make it back. Cassidy dragged him inside the building, suffering a wound when he exposed himself. Butch held out for a while, but about nine or ten o'clock he fired a pistol shot into Longabaugh's head and then donned a uniform from the body of a nearby victim. In this disguise Butch slipped through the soldiers and eventually made his way to the coast.

Another version, described in "The Bandit Invincible" manuscript, states that Cassidy, Longabaugh, and two accomplices, Billings and Hains, were looting a pack train at midafternoon on a trail outside La Paz. Suddenly they were jumped by a Bolivian cavalry detachment. The bandits scrambled for cover behind boulders at the mouth of a gorge, and a sharp fight broke out. Billings was fatally wounded, but the other outlaws felled several troopers. Cassidy and the Sundance Kid killed a pair of soldiers, nearly blowing their heads off, and the wary cavalrymen withdrew to concealment. When the soldiers renewed their assault, they killed Hains and shot Longabaugh in the body and scalp. Cassidy crawled to him. Longabaugh gave him a letter from Etta, saying that he had legally married her and asked Butch to deliver his money belt to her. Cassidy shot two soldiers who crept near and then helplessly watched Longabaugh die as darkness fell. Butch fired at a noise and heard a body crash into the underbrush. Then he secured Longabaugh's money and crawled away. After an hour he made his way to the horses, which had remained undetected in their place of seclusion throughout the battle. Loading the food and water bottles onto his mount, he rode into the darkness, reflecting that the trio of dead Americans and three tied horses, along with identification he had left behind, should convince the authorities that Butch Cassidy was dead. Making his way to the coast, he sailed to Europe, submitted to facial surgery in Paris, and then embarked for the United States.

Sources: Pointer, *Butch Cassidy;* Horan, *Wild Bunch;* Horan and Sann, *Pictorial History of the Wild West,* 191, 196, 201, 204–10, 212–13, 215–21, 227–39; Baker, *Wild Bunch.*

Peacock, Lewis

(d. June 13, 1871, Pilot Grove, Texas. Farmer.) An influential landowner near Pilot Grove (also known as Lick Skillet), Texas, Peacock led a faction of local toughs in a post–Civil War feud in North Texas. Peacock wore the uniform of the Reconstruction Union League, an organization designed to help former slaves, and the conflict had racial overtones. The feud erupted in 1867 and lasted for four years, during which time the leaders of both sides (Peacock's opposition led by Bob Lee) were killed.

Gunfights: *April,   1868,   Pilot Grove, Texas.* After several bushwhackings and murders resulted in the deaths of three men, several members of the Lee and Peacock factions had a skirmish in Pilot Grove. Peacock was wounded, but there were no fatalities.

June 15, 1868, Hunt County, Texas. Peacock and his allies had congregated at the farm of an old man named Nance. While they were tending their mounts in his horse corral, Lee's men opened fire from ambush. A brisk battle ensued, and when the shooting stopped, three Peacock men had been fatally wounded, while Lee's party escaped unscathed.

December, 1868, near Farmersville, Texas. Peacock was leading a few of his men and a detachment of Union soldiers in a search for Lee when they were ambushed. There was an exchange of shots which resulted in the death of a soldier, the wounding of one of Peacock's men, and the narrow escape of Peacock himself.

June 13, 1871, Pilot Grove, Texas. Lee had been killed late in 1869, but there were further revenge killings, and Peacock began to spend most of his time in hiding. However, two friends of Bob Lee's—Dick Johnson and Joe Parker—spotted Peacock sneaking back home. Johnson and Parker set a vigil which lasted throughout the night. At dawn Peacock emerged to get firewood, and shooting broke out. Peacock was mortally wounded, and Johnson and Parker fled the scene.

Source: Sonnichsen, *I'll Die Before I'll Run,* 21–34.

Pickett, Tom

(b. 1858, Decatur, Texas; d. May 14, 1934, Pinetop, Arizona. Cowboy, law officer, rustler, gambler, prospector, bartender.) Reared in Decatur, Texas, Pickett got into trouble at the age of seventeen for stealing cattle. His father, a member of the state legislature and a former Confederate officer, mortgaged the family home and paid the heavy fine. Pickett then served briefly with the Texas Rangers, trailed a cattle herd to Kansas, and became a gambler in the wide-open cowtowns. He met rustler Dave Rudabaugh and followed him to New Mexico. There Tom served as a peace officer for a short time in Las Vegas and in White Oaks before hiring on as a cowhand for Charlie Bowdre in the Fort Sumner area. He soon fell into rustling with Bowdre, Rudabaugh, Billy the Kid, Billy Wilson, and Tom O'Folliard.

In December, 1880, O'Folliard was killed by Pat Garrett's posse in Fort Sumner, and Pickett and the others galloped away in a panic. A few days later they were captured after a siege in an isolated rock cabin. Released on three hundred dollars' bail, Pickett hung around Las Vegas for a while before drifting into northern Arizona. There he caught on with the Hash Knife outfit and participated in the Graham-Tewksbury feud.

After receiving a serious leg wound, Pickett returned to punching cattle. In 1888 he married Catherine Kelly, whose mother ran a boarding house in Holbrook, Arizona. A year later, however, his wife died in childbirth, along with the baby, and Pickett again began wandering.

Pickett gambled professionally, tended bar, prospected for gold, worked as a cowhand, and served as a deputy U.S. marshal during the Wilson administration. At last he was forced to have his leg amputated, and he returned to northern Arizona. He died at seventy-six in Pinetop and was laid to rest in Winslow.

Gunfight: December 23, 1880, Stinking Springs, New Mexico. Having just escaped from a Fort Sumner posse's ambush, Pickett, Billy the Kid, Dave Rudabaugh, Charlie Bowdre, and Billy Wilson found refuge in an abandoned one-room rock house. After a freezing, snowy night Bowdre went outside at dawn to feed his horse. He was met with a fusillade from Pat Garrett's posse, which had quietly crept up during the night. Mortally wounded, Bowdre staggered inside only to be sent back out by the Kid to "Kill some of the sons-of-bitches before you die." He died almost immediately, and a siege began.

The Kid's horse was already inside, and the outlaws tried to pull the other mounts in, hoping to make another galloping escape. But Garrett shot one horse dead in the open doorway, and the others were frightened away. The Kid and Garrett exchanged remarks for a while, then the posse went in shifts to a nearby ranch to eat.

About 4:00 P.M. a wagon arrived from the ranch with provisions, and the posse began cooking a meal upwind of the cabin. When the famished fugitives smelled the tantalizing odors, Rudabaugh waved a white handkerchief and asked to surrender. Dave went out to parley with Garrett and returned to tell his cohorts that they would not be harmed. After a quick discussion they all filed out and allowed themselves to be disarmed.

Sources: Hunt, *Tragic Days of Billy the Kid,* 217, 229, 239–52, 257–58; Keleher, *Violence in Lincoln County,* 291–93, 319–20; Stanley, *Desperadoes of New Mexico,* 143–52.

Pierce, Charley

(d. May 2, 1895. Dunn Ranch on the Cimarron River, Oklahoma. Race horse owner, train and bank robber.) After unsuccessfully racing horses in Pawnee, Oklahoma, Pierce became a member of the Dalton gang during the 1890's. After that band was decimated at Coffeyville, Kansas, he joined Bill Doolin's Oklahombres. He participated in several holdups, but in 1895 he was killed by bounty hunters in Oklahoma.

Gunfights: July 15, 1892, Adair, Oklahoma. The Dalton gang slipped into tiny Adair about fifteen minutes before the scheduled arrival of the 9:42 evening train. They took over the depot at gunpoint, robbed it of the cash on hand, then went to prearranged positions. When the train pulled in, they commandeered the cab, drove a wagon up to the express car door, and began firing to keep the passengers inside. Guards returned their fire from the smoker, and a brisk gun battle broke out. Three of the guards were quickly wounded, however, and the bandits left town with their loot.

May 2, 1895, Dunn Ranch on the Cimarron River, Oklahoma. After the Doolin gang split apart, Pierce and Bitter Creek Newcomb teamed up to avoid the law together. In May they rode to the Dunn Ranch to see Newcomb's sweetheart, the famed "Rose of the Cimarron," and to collect nine hundred dollars Rose's brothers owed Newcomb. But when the two fugitives approached the house, the Dunn brothers shot them out of the saddle, intending to collect the large bounty on their heads. When the Dunns walked near, Pierce groaned, but he was quickly finished off with another shot.

The next morning Pierce and Newcomb were thrown into a wagon to be taken into Guthrie so that the rewards could be collected. But Newcomb had lived through the night, and he began to beg for water. He was given another bullet instead, and the wagon continued toward town.

Sources: Croy, *Trigger Marshal,* 173–76; Horan and Sann, *Pictorial History of the Wild West,* 157–58, 167–69; Canton, *Frontier Trails,* 110, 119–21; Shirley, *Heck Thomas,* 195–97; Shirley, *Six-gun and Silver Star,* 104, 145, 153–61, 179, 184.

Plummer, Henry

(b. July 6, 1837, Connecticut; d. January 10, 1864, Bannack, Montana. Prospector, baker, law officer, gambler, convict.) Born in New England, Plummer ran away from home at fifteen and was drawn to gold-rich California. In 1853 Plummer and Henry Hyer opened the Empire Bakery in Nevada City, California. Plummer supplemented his income with gambling, and in 1866 the nineteen-year-old youth was elected marshal of the little mining town.

Just before the end of his year in office Plummer killed a man whose wife he was having an affair with, and he was sentenced to a ten-year prison term. He wangled a pardon within a year, however, and went into partnership with Henry Hyer in another Nevada City bakery. Plummer became involved with a prostitute, nearly killed a man with a blunt instrument in a brawl, and was suspected of robbing the Wells, Fargo office in Washoe. Then he was arrested for committing another murder, but he bribed a jailer and escaped. After that he was designated a suspect in the death of an Oregon sheriff named Blackburn, seduced a married woman in Walla Walla, Washington, and helped murder a man in Orofino, Idaho.

Plummer next turned up in Lewiston, Idaho, a booming mining town. He again took up gambling, but under cover he organized a band of thieves and highwaymen. When a band of vigilantes was formed to combat lawlessness, Plummer immediately joined, then quietly ordered the murder of one of the vigilante leaders.

By 1862 Plummer had moved his operations to the richer fields of Bannack, Montana, where he again outwardly dealt faro for a living. But his huge band of desperadoes continually preyed upon stagecoaches, payrolls, and unwary travelers. Plummer's riders called themselves the Innocents, identified themselves by secret handshakes and neckerchief knots, and marked stagecoaches with code symbols indicating that they were to be robbed.

After Plummer frightened the city marshal out of town, he assumed the office himself. But by this time a bonanza had been discovered in Virginia City, and Plummer once more transferred his operations to a more lucrative area. He again managed to become city marshal, but his attempt to obtain an appointment as deputy U.S. marshal was thwarted by a stalwart citizen named Nathaniel Langford.

As the Plummer gang's depredations mounted, Langford and others fostered a growing movement for law and order. A large vigilante group was organized,

and during the first five weeks of 1864, twenty of Plummer's henchmen were shot or hanged.

When the vigilantes began their activities, Plummer tried to escape, but he was tracked down and thrown into the Bannack jail. The vigilantes coldly ignored him when he begged for mercy because he did not want to leave his young wife in Connecticut alone. On a frigid January day Plummer was carried to a gallows he had earlier erected himself, and without ceremony he was executed. The gallows were crudely constructed, and a weeping, pleading Plummer and two confederates were lifted onto the shoulders of the vigilantes and then tossed into the air to strangle slowly to death.

Plummer's wife came to the area a short time later, claiming that her husband had been lynched because he was a Union sympathizer. Compassion briefly swelled for her, but Plummer's misdeeds were recalled too vividly, and she left Montana unvindicated.

Gunfights: *September, 1857, Nevada City, California.* John Vedder entered his home and discovered his wife in the embrace of City Marshal Henry Plummer. Vedder angrily confronted the pair and ordered Plummer to leave. Instead, the marshal shot Vedder to death.

1859, Nevada City, California. A brawl broke out in a bawdy house which Plummer was visiting, and he naturally became involved. He squared off against a man named Jim Ryder, and when the going became rough, Plummer went for his gun. Ryder collapsed, mortally wounded, and Plummer was thrown in jail.

1860, Lewiston, Idaho. A few days after Plummer had arrived in town, a local miner laughed at the Connecticut Yankee's accent. Plummer angrily snarled a retort, and the two men went for their guns. Plummer was quicker on the draw, and he sent the miner sprawling into the street, fatally wounded.

January 14, 1863, Bannack, Montana. Jack Cleveland was a criminal who was familiar with Plummer's secret operations and who came to Bannack to demand a cut of the action. Plummer and Cleveland argued about the matter in Goodrich's Saloon, and soon they hauled out their pistols and began firing. The drunken Cleveland missed, and Plummer's first shot tore into the ceiling. But then Cleveland was hit and slammed to the floor, and a butcher named Hank Crawford carried him to his own lodgings. Cleveland lingered for several hours, and before dying he told Crawford that Plummer was the secret leader of the local outlaws.

1863, Bannack, Montana. The courageous Crawford began to voice his knowledge of Plummer's activities, and he was soon elected marshal of Bannack. Plummer set an ambush for Crawford, but missed him. A short time later Plummer heard that Crawford was drinking coffee in a local restaurant without weapons. Plummer grabbed a shotgun and lay in wait for Crawford near his butcher shop.

When Crawford approached, Plummer stepped out, but before he could fire he was spotted by Frank Ray, a friend of the marshal's. Ray whipped out his pistol and snapped off a shot which broke Plummer's right arm — and which promptly ended the assassination attempt. Crawford decided his office was becoming too risky, however, and he unpinned his badge and returned

to his native Wisconsin. Plummer never regained total use of his shooting arm, and he had to teach himself to shoot with his left hand.

Sources: Breihan, *Badmen of the Frontier Days,* 28–49; Drago, *Road Agents and Train Robbers,* 84, 87, 95–99, 101, 103–104, 224; Langford, *Vigilante Days & Ways;* Boorstin, *The Americans,* II, 87–88.

Ponce, Norrato

(d. November, 1865; Contra Costa County, California. Horse thief.) A Chileno horse thief, Ponce gained his greatest notoriety in 1865, when he was involved in a saloon killing. For the next six weeks Ponce was the subject of a California manhunt that resulted in his death.

Gunfights: October 3, 1865, Hayward, California. At 2:00 A.M. a poker game in Governor's Saloon ended in bitter argument. Ponce soon went for his gun and fatally wounded a fellow participant named Joy. Ponce then had a drink at the bar, asked if anyone else wanted anything, coolly went outside, and rode off.

October, 1865, near Livermore, California. Ponce was in hiding in the Black Hills near Livermore, and there he nearly rode into a trap set by Sheriff Harry Morse and a deputy. Riding after dark, Ponce was startled to hear Morse order that he surrender. The fugitive opened up with his pistol, and the lawmen zeroed in on Ponce's gun flashes. Ponce was hit three times by pistol slugs, and he took thirteen buckshot wounds. Then his horse fell, shot in the leg, and Ponce escaped on foot in the midnight darkness.

November, 1865, Contra Costa County, California. Ponce recovered and sought refuge in the adobe house of José Rojos, located in Pinole Canyon at the west end of Contra Costa County. There he was trailed by Morse and two deputies, and when the lawmen approached, one of Ponce's friends ran away as a decoy. When the officers rode in pursuit, Ponce dashed out of the house. The fugitive soon was spotted by the lawmen, and there was an exchange of shots. Morse galloped toward Ponce, who stopped and leveled his pistol across his arm for a steady shot. But the sheriff's Henry rifle spoke first, and Ponce was shot dead.

Source: Shinn, *Pacific Coast Outlaws,* 60–61.

Powell, Sylvester

(d. January 1, 1877, Wichita, Kansas. Stage driver.) Powell was a man of normally quiet demeanor who was rash and deadly, "a perfect demon," when drinking. Wichita policemen and saloon keepers were well aware of this trait, and Powell was widely rumored to have killed two men—one by brutally employing brass knuckles—before coming to the cattle town. While in Wichita, Powell was hired as a city bus driver by the Southwestern Stage Company. He was killed after a vicious exchange of gunfire with Marshal Mike Meagher in 1877.

Gunfight: *January 1, 1877, Wichita, Kansas.* Powell and Albert Singleton celebrated New Year's Day by drinking and carousing. That afternoon they openly attempted to commandeer a horse owned by E. R. Dennison. Dennison stepped forward and made a good-natured comment, but was answered by a stunning blow from a neck yoke wielded by Powell. Powell then ordered Dennison not to turn him in, but within moments Marshal Mike Meagher was prodding Powell toward the city jail.

That evening W. A. Brown, a stage company official, obtained Powell's release. Powell threatened Meagher's life, then located a pistol and went in search of the marshal. At 9:00 P.M. Powell asked a policeman named McIvor if he had seen Meagher, and again announced dire threats. Moments later Powell discovered the marshal in an outhouse behind Jim Hope's saloon. Powell quietly approached the tiny building, then fired two bullets through the planks.

One bullet ripped into Meagher's calf, and the other perforated his coat, but the lawman instantly leaped toward Powell and tried to seize his gun. But the pistol went off again, grazing Meagher's hand, and Powell bolted down an alley, firing another shot as he ran.

Meagher fired once in Powell's direction, then limped in pursuit. Meagher finally saw Powell standing in front of Charles Hill's Drug Store and, taking deliberate aim, fired a bullet into Powell's chest. The slug went into Powell's heart, killing him instantly.

Source: Miller and Snell, *Great Gunfighters of the Kansas Cowtowns,* 356–58.

Raidler, William F.

("Little Bill")

(Cowboy, train and bank robber, convict.) Of Pennsylvania Dutch stock, Raidler was a man with a good education who drifted into Texas and became involved with Bill Doolin's band of outlaws, having met the bandit leader while both men were Oklahoma cowboys.

Bill Raidler received so many wounds at the hands of various lawmen that he spent his last days a cripple. *(Courtesy Western History Collections, University of Oklahoma Library)*

Tracked down in 1895 by a posse led by Bill Tilghman, Raidler was shot six times and captured. Tilghman later helped him gain a parole from an Ohio prison, and Raidler married after his release. But Little Bill never regained his health, and he died after several years as a cripple.

Gunfights: *Spring, 1895, near Dover, Oklahoma.* A posse jumped the Doolin gang's camp near Dover. During a forty-minute fight nearly two hundred shots were exchanged, and Tulsa Jack Blake was killed. But Raidler and his three surviving cohorts grabbed two horses and, mounted double, escaped down an unguarded ravine.

May 20, 1895, Southwest City, Missouri. While robbing a bank at South-west City, the Doolin gang was fired upon by irate citizens. As the outlaws tried to shoot their way out of town, brothers Oscar and Joe Seaborn stepped outside their store. Raidler galloped past firing pistol slugs, and one of his bullets passed through Oscar and hit Joe. Oscar was barely hurt, but Joe died on the spot.

September 6, 1895, near Elgin, Kansas. Raidler had sought refuge at the ranch of Sam Moore, located eighteen miles south of Elgin. At dusk Raidler was riding in to have supper, but when he dismounted, he was jumped by Bill Tilghman and two other officers. Raidler pulled his pistol and fired at Tilghman ten feet away, but Tilghman pumped a rifle slug into the outlaw's right wrist.

Raidler's wrist was broken, and his six-gun dropped to the ground, but he turned and began running. Deputy W. C. Smith stepped out from the shadows of the corral and blasted Raidler with a shotgun. The outlaw dropped, wounded in each side, the neck, and twice in the head. Moore and his wife ran out and carried Raidler inside. They bound his wounds, and he survived.

Spring, 1895, near Bartlesville, Oklahoma. Raidler was hiding in a cave near Bartlesville, but the hideout was discovered by Heck Thomas and two Osage scouts. Raidler saw them coming and opened fire with his rifle from ambush. Thomas fired back with a .45-90 Winchester, and a bullet tore into Raidler's right hand. He screamed, dropped his rifle, and dashed into the brush. The lawmen followed, and Raidler hacked off two mangled fingers, then successfully hid in a tree. A week later he was wounded and captured by Bill Tilghman and two other officers, tried, and imprisoned.

Sources: Shirley, *Heck Thomas,* 193–95, 199–201; Shirley, *Six-gun and Silver Star,* 62, 106, 145, 179–81, 184.

Reed, Charlie

(d. ca. 1883, Ogallala, Nebraska. Cattle rustler, cowboy.) Reed was a drifter on the cattle frontier who was known as something of a hard case. In the mid-1870's he became involved with the rustling ring operated by John Selman and John Larn in the vicinity of Fort Griffin, Texas. After a shootout in Fort Griffin, he wandered to Nebraska, where he was eventually killed.

Gunfights: January 17, 1877, Fort Griffin, Texas. Reed and fellow rustler Billy Bland galloped into town, quite drunk and firing their pistols. They entered the Beehive Saloon and Dance Hall and continued discharging their weapons. Deputy Sheriff W. R. Cruger and County Attorney William Jeffries rushed to the Beehive, intent upon arresting Reed and Bland. As they passed through the door, however, Bland whirled and fired a shot, grazing Cruger.

All parties began firing, and several men were wounded or killed. Bland was mortally wounded, and Jeffries was hit in the chest, although he survived. A cavalry officer, one Lieutenant Meyers, was killed, and Reed fired a wild shot which hit a young, recently married lawyer, Dan Barron, squarely in the chest. Reed fled the scene on foot, spent the night in the country, and, securing a horse the next day, left Texas.

ca. 1883, Ogallala, Nebraska. Reed, drinking in an Ogallala saloon, became embroiled in a quarrel with a man named Dumas. Reed angrily pulled his six-gun and shot Dumas to death. An enraged mob quickly gathered, however, and promptly hanged Reed.

Source: Metz, *John Selman,* 70–71, 214.

Reed, Jim

(b. 1844, Rich Hill, Missouri; d. August 6, 1874, near Paris, Texas. Farmer, guerrilla soldier, stagecoach robber, horse thief.) Reed was born eight miles from the Missouri hamlet of Rich Hill, where his father was a large landholder. When Jim was seventeen his family moved to Carthage, where he met a thirteen-year-old girl named Myra Belle Shirley, later to be known as Belle Starr. The two adolescents courted, and after a clash with her father, Reed had a bloodless shootout with John Shirley. By this time the Civil War had broken out, and Reed joined a group of guerrilla raiders. This taste of lawless plunder set the tone for the remainder of his life.

After the war Reed became embroiled in a Missouri feud and killed two men. He fled the state and went to Texas, where he again encountered Myra Belle. Her family had moved to Scyene, near Dallas, and she became his concubine. She already had a daughter named Pearl, whom she claimed was sired by Cole Younger.

Reed, Belle, and Pearl now migrated to Dallas, and the lovers soon produced a son they christened Eddie. After pulling a couple of holdups out of the state, Reed and his "family" returned to Texas, where he bought a farm near Scyene. On November 30, 1873, Reed, Belle, Dan Evans, and another thief ventured into Oklahoma and went to the cabin of Watt Grayson on the North Canadian River. Grayson was a Creek Indian chief who handled government subsidies for his tribe, and Reed's gang tortured him until he revealed where they could find thirty thousand dollars.

For this and a variety of other misdeeds Reed soon was hotly pressed by the law, and he was forced to leave Belle. On April 7, 1874, Reed and two other holdup men robbed a stagecoach near Blanco, Texas, and rewards totaling four thousand dollars were posted for him. Within a few months a close acquaintance killed him for the bounty on his head.

Gunfights: *1861, Carthage, Missouri.* Reed had wrangled with John Shirley over his amorous attentions to his young daughter, Myra Belle. Hot words finally led to gunplay, and Reed and Shirley traded shots. No one was hit, and the two men decided to settle their difficulties in less violent fashion.

1866, Vernon County, Missouri. Reed joined sides in a neighborhood feud and soon found himself confronted by two antagonists. The three men shot it out, and Reed fatally wounded both of his adversaries.

August 6, 1874, near Paris, Texas. Reed was riding with Deputy Sheriff John T. Morris, a friend who knew his true identity. About fifteen miles from Paris they stopped at a farmhouse to try to get a meal. They left their guns outside so as not to frighten the lady of the house.

During the meal the prospect of reward proved greater than friendship, and Morris slipped out to get his pistol. Upon reentering, he told Reed that he was under arrest. Reed instantly grappled with Morris, and the two men wrestled all over the room. Reed landed several heavy blows, but Morris finally freed his gun and shot the outlaw in

the stomach. Reed collapsed and died within minutes.

Source: Croy, *Last of the Great Outlaws,* 86–93, 167, 223.

Riggs, Barney

(d. ca. 1900, Fort Stockton, Texas. Cowboy, convict, rancher.) A West Texan, Riggs frequently became involved in altercations and seemed never reluctant to use a gun. Following one fatal fray in Arizona (cowboy Riggs killed his employer over a mutual sweetheart), he was sentenced to life in Yuma Territorial Prison. But he saved the warden's life during an attempted escape and won a pardon. Riggs then returned to Texas, where he began ranching near Toyah, married a sister of Bud Frazer, and became involved in the feud between Sheriff Frazer and Killin' Jim Miller. Riggs killed two of Miller's men in a saloon fight, but eluded further trouble until he was killed by his step-grandson in Fort Stockton.

Gunfights: *October, 1887, Yuma, Arizona.* As he strolled near the prison gate, Superintendent Thomas Gates was jumped by seven Mexican convicts who brandished knives and demanded their freedom. Assistant Superintendent Johnny Behan alertly closed the gate, and a general melee broke out as the desperate prisoners scrambled to obtain guns.

Guards ran up clubbing and firing at the convicts. Officer B. F. Hartlee shot convicts López, Bustamente, and Vásquez. Gates, who already had been shot and stabbed at, now had a knife buried in his neck by a wounded prisoner named Puebla. Vásquez then began to push Gates ahead of him as a shield, and the warden shouted at Barney Riggs to grab the fallen López' pistol and come to his aid.

Riggs, who was standing nearby watching the fight, darted forward, snatched up the gun, and put a slug into Puebla's chest. Hartlee started to shoot Riggs, but the guard suddenly realized the situation and shot Puebla in the back, just as Riggs fired another bullet into Puebla's leg. As the dying convict fell, a prisoner named Sprague rushed forward, clapped his hand over the warden's neck, and with Rigg's help carried Gates to his quarters.

1897, Pecos, Texas. John Denson and another hard case named Bill Earhart, who were friends with John Wesley Hardin and Jim ("Killer") Miller, were overheard in Fort Stockton muttering threats against Riggs. At that time Riggs was living in neighboring Pecos and was embroiled in difficulties with Miller. Denson, Earhart, and Hardin left for Pecos, supposedly to seek out Riggs, and lawman Dee Harkey wired a telegram of warning to the former convict. Throughout the next day the trio from Fort Stockton drank and bullied their way about town, and Riggs armed himself and warily avoided them.

Early the following morning, however, Riggs was alone in R. S. Johnson's saloon, substituting for a friend who was a bartender, when Denson and Earhart burst into the room. A shot from Earhart's six-gun grazed Barney, and Riggs instantly pulled a revolver from his waistband and killed Earhart with a bullet between the eyes. But Riggs had opened the guard on his pistol to prevent it from slipping into his pants, and as he jerked it up, some of the cartridges slid out far enough to keep the cylinder from revolving after the first shot.

As Riggs fumbled with his gun, Denson grappled with him for a moment.

Then Denson decided to flee the premises, and as he passed through the door Riggs managed to squeeze off a shot. Denson, unscathed, dashed down the street while Riggs ran to the door, aimed carefully, and fired a bullet into the back of his head, killing him on the spot. Riggs promptly surrendered himself, and Harkey soon arranged his release.

ca. 1900, Fort Stockton, Texas. A family dispute aroused the ire of Riggs's step-grandson. The youth eventually resorted to gunplay and shot Riggs to death.

Sources: Harkey, *Mean as Hell,* 72–73, 113; Jeffrey, *Adobe and Iron,* 89–92; Shirley, *Shotgun for Hire,* 22–26, 33–46, 41, 44–46.

Riley, Jim

(b. 1853.) Virtually nothing is known about Riley aside from his lethal activities during the bloody gunfight known as Newton's General Massacre. But his participation in one of the West's most remarkable shooting scrapes places him in any broad listing of frontier killers.

At the age of eighteen Riley appeared in Newton, which, in 1871, was a tough Kansas railhead and booming cowtown. Riley was a frail consumptive who attached himself to big Mike McCluskie, a brawling railroad crew foreman. McCluskie killed a Texas gambler and ten days later was threatened by several cowboys from the Lone Star state. Riley alertly was on the scene when the Texans attacked McCluskie, and within a few moments he earned himself a small share of notoriety in western history.

Gunfight: August 20, 1871, Newton, Kansas. On Saturday, August 19, Mike McCluskie returned to Newton just eight days after killing gambler William Bailey. Despite ominous threats from friends of Bailey, McCluskie spent the evening in Hide Park, a sleezy section of Newton containing numerous prostitute cribs and two dance halls about thirty yards apart—the Alamo and Perry Tuttle's establishment.

The Alamo closed at midnight, but Tuttle's place continued to entertain a large crowd, including McCluskie, seated at a faro table, and Riley, looking on quietly from the doorway. About 1:00 A.M. cowboy Hugh Anderson, who had sworn to avenge Bailey's death, drew a pistol and walked up to the faro table. "You are a cowardly son-of-a-bitch!" shouted Anderson, raising his gun. "I will blow the top of your head off." Anderson fired and hit McCluskie in the neck. McCluskie pulled his gun, half rose, and snapped a misfire at Anderson. Anderson sent a slug into McCluskie's leg, throwing him to the floor. McCluskie discharged his weapon as he fell, then took another bullet from Anderson in his back.

Other Texans began firing, and a cowboy named Jim Martin, who had stepped forward to try to stop the shooting, was hit in the neck. As Martin staggered past Riley to die in the dust in front of the Alamo, two friends of McCluskie's—railroad employees named Hickey and Patrick Lee—were shot in the leg and stomach, respectively (and fatally in the case of Lee). Then Riley coolly shut and locked the door of the dance hall, drew a gun, and descended upon the Texans who had killed his friend. Three cowboys were wounded, including Anderson, shot twice in the leg, and two others, Billy Garrett and Henry Kearnes, died of chest wounds.

Source: Miller and Snell, *Great Gunfighters of the Kansas Cowtowns,* 65–72, 74.

Riley, Thomas

(d. June, 1868, near Dayton, Nevada.) Riley was a hard case whose chief notoriety came in 1868. Within the span of a few days Riley gunned down a sheriff, fought off a posse, and killed himself.

Gunfights: June, 1868, near Carson City, Nevada. Riley encountered Sheriff Tim Smith near Carson City, and a dispute ensued. Smith tried to exert his legal authority, and Riley shot him to death.

June, 1868, near Dayton, Nevada. Shortly thereafter, one Asa Kenyon recognized Riley in the streets of Dayton and began enlisting help to arrest the killer. When the posse of citizens approached Riley, he retreated, found a horse, and galloped out of town. The citizens pursued him, and a running gunfight erupted. Riley succeeded in wounding posse member H. A. Comins, but his ammunition ran low, the posse began to close in, and he committed suicide.

Source: Ashbaugh, *Nevada's Turbulent Yesterday,* 104.

Ringo, John

(d. July 14, 1882, Turkey Creek Canyon, Arizona. Gunman, gambler, rustler, law officer.)* Johnny Ringo was a mysterious individual thought to be one of the deadliest gunmen of his time. Too little is known about the man, however, to accord him ranking among the elite of Western gunfighters. He was born probably in the early 1850's in Ringoes, N.J., or in Missouri, where he attended William and Jewell College in Liberty. His name likely was Ringo, not, as is suggested, Ringgold.

Rumored to have fought in Texas

range wars, in 1877 Ringo was jailed in Austin with Sutton-Taylor feud veterans Bill Taylor, John Wesley Hardin, and Mannen Clements. Ringo next drifted west to Shakespeare, New Mexico, and then on to Tombstone during its boom days.

Ringo was quite well cultured and was known to quote Shakespeare, but he had a serious drinking problem. He was an associate of the Clantons and the McLaurys, and he became involved in a handful of verifiable shooting scrapes. Although he rustled cattle in the Tombstone area, for a time he held a deputy's commission from Sheriff John Behan.

Following a two-week drinking trip with Buckskin Frank Leslie in the summer of 1882, Ringo was found dead in Turkey Creek Canyon. He had been killed by a bullet in the head, and suicide was proclaimed as the cause of death. But Ringo had been scalped, and on his person were found a rifle and two six-guns—all fully loaded. Billy Claiborne said that Leslie had killed Ringo, but Pony Deal, Ringo's friend and a fellow gambler, was convinced that another gambler named Johnny O'Rourke was responsible. Pony Deal sought out O'Rourke and in the ensuing gunfight shot him to death.

Gunfights: *December, 1879, Safford, Arizona.* Ringo was drinking heavily in a Safford saloon. He tried to press a drink on one Louis Hancock, who declined. The sullen Ringo took offense, hauled out his six-gun, clobbered Hancock over the head, and severely wounded him in the throat.

December 28, 1881, Tombstone, Arizona. At nearly midnight Virgil Earp left the Oriental Saloon and moments later was seriously wounded in the side and arm by concealed shotgun wielders. Earlier that night Ringo and three other Earp enemies had been seen carrying shotguns around town, and it was widely presumed that these men had gunned down Virgil Earp.

Sources: Waters, *Earp Brothers of Tombstone,* 152, 205, 222, 226, 234, 252; Lake, *Wyatt Earp,* 72, 234–35, 247, 271–72, 275, 278, 306–308, 310, 314–15, 319, 333–36, 346, 357; Hogan, *Life and Death of Johnny Ringo,* 125–26; Erwin, *John H. Slaughter,* 24, 195–96, 201–207, 213, 250.

Roberts, Andrew L.

("Buckshot")

(d. April 4, 1878, Blazer's Mill, New Mexico. Soldier, criminal, bounty hunter, buffalo hunter.) A native of the South, Roberts had a widespread but rather vague reputation as a desperado and gunman. He was rumored to have been an army deserter, a convict, a Texas Ranger, and an enemy of Texas Rangers. Supposedly he had come to New Mexico after having a shootout with the rangers, and his body movements were permanently impaired because he had been severely wounded in some obscure gun battle. He was lame and fired his rifle from the hip because he was unable to raise it above waist level.

Roberts acquired his sobriquet because he like to use a shotgun, because he carried a load of buckshot in his body, or because he had left Texas with shotguns blazing at his fleeing figure. He was a member of the Lincoln County posse which assassinated rancher John Tunstall, and a short time later he was himself shot to death by another posse in a bloody shootout at Blazer's Mill.

Gunfight: *April 4, 1878, Blazer's Mill, New Mexico.* Attracted by the two-hundred-dollar reward posted for the killers of Sheriff William Brady and his deputy, and aware that those same killers sought him for involvement in John Tunstall's death, Roberts had determined to dispatch as many of them as possible. The main group of these "Regulators," led by Dick Brewer and including Billy the Kid, Charlie Bowdre, Frank and George Coe, Henry Brown, John Middleton, and others, was at Blazer's Mill waiting for a meal when Roberts rode up on a mule.

Armed with a pair of six-guns and a Winchester, Roberts conversed with Frank Coe while the others were talking together. Coe tried to persuade his former friend to surrender, but the old gunman mentioned Billy Morton and Frank Baker, who had recently been killed after surrendering to the Regulators, and angrily declined.

Brewer then determined to arrest Roberts, and Charlie Bowdre, Henry Brown, and George Coe volunteered to take him into custody. As the three men rounded a corner of the house, they confronted Frank Coe still talking to Roberts, who had his cocked rifle in his lap. Bowdre held a gun on Roberts and ordered him to surrender.

"Not much, Mary Ann," snarled Roberts, snatching up his Winchester. The two men fired simultaneously, and a bullet ripped through Roberts' middle and out his back. His slug glanced off Bowdre's cartridge belt and shattered George Coe's right hand, severing his trigger finger. Roberts squeezed off three more rounds, managing only to shoot off Billy the Kid's hat, then he drilled John Middleton in the chest as the rest of the posse came running up.

Roberts staggered inside Blazer's bedroom, pulled a feather mattress in front of the lone window, and found a Sharps .50 buffalo gun to add to his armament.

While he propped himself up, the posse crouched behind the corner of the house, and Brewer called upon him to surrender. Answered only with curses, Brewer circled around to a pile of logs fifty yards or so in front of Roberts' position. Brewer fired at Roberts, then ducked behind the logs after hitting the window frame. As he cautiously peered above the logs again, the buffalo gun roared, taking off the top of Brewer's head.

Roberts shouted exultantly, then allowed Dr. J. H. Blazer, a retired dentist and owner of the mill, to enter the still open door and parley. "I'm killed," Roberts admitted. "No one can help me. It's all over."

Blazer reported to the posse that Roberts could not live an hour, and the Regulators promptly departed to find medical aid for Middleton and Coe. Roberts soon died and was buried alongside Brewer behind the mill.

Sources: Keleher, *Violence in Lincoln County,* 113–14, 120, 133, 206, 228, 252, 258, 262–63, 276, 292, 308, 312–14, 325; Coe, *Frontier Fighter,* 60, 64–71; Fulton, *Lincoln County War,* 112–13, 119, 172–77; Rickards, *Blazer's Mill.*

Roberts, Jim

(b. 1859; d. January 8, 1934, Clarkdale, Arizona. Gunman, law officer.) Roberts first appeared in western history as a gunfighter for the Tewksbury clan in Arizona's Pleasant Valley War. He was one of the suspects in killing the senior member of the Graham family, and he

was a known participant in subsequent shooting scrapes. Following the feud, he was cleared of legal charges, whereupon he pinned on a badge which he wore until his death.

Roberts was a law officer in several mining towns, including Jerome, Arizona, where he was marshal for a number of years. At the age of seventy he shot it out with bank robbers in Clarkdale, where he spent the last years of his life as a special officer for the United Verde Copper Company. He died of a heart attack in the streets of Clarkdale in 1934.

Gunfights: *August 10, 1887, Pleasant Valley, Arizona.* Roberts was one of half a dozen Tewksbury men who inflicted bitter damage on the opposing faction from inside a ranch cabin. Tom Tucker had led seven other cowboys to the cabin, and a shootout had ensued. From the cover of the building the Tewksbury party drove off the cowhands, wounding three and killing two. In the quick flurry of shooting it was difficult to credit specific shots, but when John Paine was pinned under his horse, Roberts clipped off his right ear with a rifle bullet, and Jim Tewksbury killed the man when he tried to run away.

September 2, 1887, Pleasant Valley, Arizona. Roberts was one of several Tewksbury men who held out inside a cabin after John Tewksbury and Bill Jacobs had been dry-gulched at dawn. After an all-day siege the Tewksbury party managed to sneak away, although they were forced to abandon the bodies.

September 16, 1887, Pleasant Valley, Arizona. The Tewksbury faction was surprised at daybreak in their camp near Cherry Creek. Roberts and Jim Tewksbury began shooting from their blankets, driving away the ambushers after drilling Joe Underwood in both legs and mortally wounding Harry Middleton.

1928, Clarkdale, Arizona. A pair of thieves had just looted Clarkdale's Bank of Arizona and were speeding away in an automobile when they were spotted by Jim Roberts. The septuagenarian hauled out his old single-action Colt and opened fire. One of the robbers was killed, and the car swerved and crashed. Roberts threw down on the other bandit, who meekly surrendered.

Source: Drago, *The Great Range Wars,* 108, 110–12, 115, 125, 130, 146, 291.

Roberts, Judd

(b. Williamson County, Texas; d. July, 1887, Texas Panhandle. Thief, horse rustler.) Roberts first achieved notoriety in 1885 when he led a gang of four men in robbing and killing a rancher named Brautigen in Fredericksburg, Texas. Texas Rangers captured Roberts and one of his confederates, and since lynching fever was high in Fredericksburg, the two outlaws were transferred to the new, "escape-proof" jail in San Antonio. (Indeed, a short time later a Fredericksburg posse captured a third member of Roberts' gang, and the local jail "immediately and mysteriously" burned down, roasting the desperado alive.)

After four months Roberts and his cohort escaped from the San Antonio jail, and Roberts soon was stealing horses in the Texas Panhandle. He periodically visited Williamson County to see relatives and friends, and Texas Ranger Ira Aten was dispatched to intercept him.

After several clashes and near misses, Aten and future Ranger John Hughes killed Roberts in the Panhandle.

Gunfights: April, 1887, Williamson County, Texas. Roberts, hunted in his home county by Ranger Ira Aten, discovered that the lawman had become friendly with local rancher George Wells. Seeking revenge, Roberts rode to Wells's ranch, where a waiting Aten surprised him and ordered, "Hands up!" Roberts went for his gun, and the two men fired simultaneously. Struck in the hand, Roberts wheeled his horse and galloped away. After being treated by a friendly doctor, Roberts escaped to the Panhandle.

June, 1887, Liberty Hill, Texas. Roberts returned to his home county and soon had a run-in with a young rancher named John Hughes. The vengeful Roberts determined to sneak up on Hughes at his spread near Liberty Hill, in adjacent Burnet County. At dawn the fugitive crept onto Hughes's front porch, only to be startled by the voice of the ever-present Ira Aten, who alertly had spent the night with Hughes. There was a quick trade of shots, and Roberts once again was wounded in his shooting hand—and once again made good his escape to the Panhandle.

July, 1887, Texas Panhandle. Within a month Roberts had established himself on a Panhandle ranch, where he ardently wooed the owner's daughter. One summer day Roberts was jumped two hundred yards from the ranch house by Aten and Hughes, who had trailed the outlaw for weeks. Although facing drawn guns, Roberts tilted his revolver handle and began firing through the open end of his holster. One round ripped Aten's brush jacket, but Roberts was stitched from chest to groin by six slugs. The dying man confessed to the murder of Brautigen, then was carried in a spring wagon to the ranch house, where he died in the arms of his sweetheart.

Source: Preece, *Lone Star Man—Ira Aten,* 144–60.

Robertson, Ben F.

("Ben Wheeler")

(b. 1854, Rockdale, Texas; d. April 30, 1884, Medicine Lodge, Kansas. Cowboy, law officer, bank robber.) Robertson was the son of a respected Texas family, and his brother became the general land agent for the state. Ben made nothing of himself, however, and following a shooting scrape, he deserted his wife and four children and went to Cheyenne. He worked as a cowboy for a few years, then drifted to Indianola, Nebraska.

There Robertson married Alice Wheeler in November, 1881, using the name Ben F. Burton. They lived with her parents until the next spring, when he deserted her and went to Caldwell, Kansas, where Marshal Henry Brown appointed him deputy in December, 1882. His second wife found him there, but he sent her back to Indianola, telling her that if she would stay at home he would send money to her and their child. After one and one-half years as an efficient peace officer, "Wheeler" (the alias he used in Kansas) was lynched because of his participation in one of the West's most notorious bank robberies.

Gunfights: 1878, Texas. Ben fell into dispute with a man, and he soon

Henry Brown (center, wearing a neckerchief) and Ben Robertson ("Ben Wheeler," the tall man at the right), who was Brown's chief deputy and accomplice in the Medicine Lodge bank robbery. Also captured were John Wesley, at Brown's right, and Billy Smith, between Brown and Wheeler. *(Courtesy Kansas State Historical Society, Topeka)*

resorted to his gun. Robertson's adversary was severely wounded, and Ben fled the state.

April 11, 1883, near Hunnewell, Kansas. Ben was one of five lawmen who had surrounded the camp of a stock thief named Ross and his family. At dawn the posse ordered Ross to submit to arrest, but Ross defiantly refused, and he and his two sons opened fire on the officers. After a thirty-minute fight the posse succeeded in killing one of Ross's sons and wounding the other, and Ross surrendered.

November 21, 1883, Caldwell, Kansas. Wheeler accompanied Cash Hollister to arrest Chet Van Meter. Van Meter met the lawmen outside his farmhouse, Winchester at the ready. Wheeler ordered him to put up his hands, but Van Meter opened fire. Wheeler and Hollister shot Van Meter to pieces, and the hauled his body to Caldwell.

April 30, 1884, Medicine Lodge, Kansas. Supposedly in search of a murderer, Henry Brown and Wheeler had left Caldwell and traveled to Medicine Lodge, intending to rob the Medicine Valley

Bank. Accompanied by William Smith and John Wesley, the Caldwell lawmen rode into Medicine Lodge during a hard rain, and Wheeler, Brown, and Wesley entered the bank at mid-morning. Inside they found bank President E. W. Payne and cashier George Geppert.

Payne went for a gun in an effort to fight the robbers. Brown fatally wounded Payne, and Wheeler in panic turned on Geppert. Geppert had raised his hands above his head, but Wheeler shot him twice. Geppert stumbled to the vault, locked the door, then collapsed and died.

The outlaws galloped out of town with a posse in pursuit, and they were soon chased into a box canyon. After a two-hour siege the robbers surrendered and were taken back to town.

The prisoners were locked up in a log building, but about 9:00 P.M. a mob brushed aside the guards and threw open the door. Brown darted through the crowd and was shot to death, and during this diversion Wheeler ran down the street in the opposite direction. But as he burst out of the mob his vest was set on fire by a gun flash. The burning garment was an easy target in the darkness, and Wheeler was gunned down before he had run one hundred yards. He had been hit three times in the body, a bullet had shattered his right arm, and two fingers of his left hand had been shot off.

Wheeler was carried with Smith and Wesley to a tree, and ropes were draped over a large limb. Wheeler, who earlier had tried to write his second wife but had tearfully found himself unable to compose the letter, now fell apart completely. He loudly begged for mercy and promised to reveal "many things that would interest the community at large," but the community impatiently strung him up alongside Smith and Wesley.

Sources: Miller and Snell, *Great Gunfighters of the Kansas Cowtowns,* 49, 52–63, 143, 145–46; Miller and Snell, *Why the West Was Wild,* 625–29; Rasch, "A Note on Henry Newton Brown," *Los Angeles Westerners Brand Book,* V (1953), 64–67.

Rudabaugh, David

(b. ca. 1840; d. February 18, 1886, Parral, Mexico. Stock rustler, stage and train robber, cowboy.) Dave Rudabaugh was a thorough scoundrel whose first notoriety came in the late 1870's as leader of a gang of thieves and rustlers in Texas. By 1878 he had shifted his activities to Kansas, where he led four men in a train holdup at Kinsley on Sunday, January 27. But a few days later Rudabaugh and Edgar West were caught in camp by Bat Masterson and a posse; Dave went for his gun, but was forced to surrender when John Joshua Webb threw down on him. Later, two of Dave's other accomplices were arrested, but Rudabaugh won release by giving evidence against his fellow thieves.

Rudabaugh piously pledged "to earn his living on the square," but he soon drifted to New Mexico and resumed his customary activities. In 1879 he was involved in stagecoach and train robberies in the vicinity of Las Vegas. In Las Vegas he was reunited with several Kansas associates who plagued the town for six months with thievery and confidence games. This "Dodge City gang" was supported by City Marshal John Joshua Webb, but when the marshal was arrested for murder in March, 1880, the gang dispersed.

Rudabaugh, who obviously had forgiven Webb for arresting him two years earlier, attempted to break the wayward lawman out of jail. Rudabaugh succeeded only in killing a peace officer, however, and he then fled and joined Billy the Kid's band of outlaws. With the Kid he was involved in rustling and shooting scrapes. Following a dogged pursuit by Pat Garrett, Rudabaugh surrendered with the Kid in December, 1880. Convicted of murder and sentenced to be hanged, he was incarcerated in Las Vegas, where John Joshua Webb was serving time.

Rudabaugh, Webb, and two others tried to shoot their way out of jail in September, 1881, and two months later Rudabaugh, Webb, and five other prisoners successfully escaped by digging through the walls. Rudabaugh and Webb went to Texas and on to Mexico, where Webb disappeared. Rudabaugh became foreman of a ranch owned by the governor of Chihuahua, but following rustling difficulties he fled to Parral, where, after robbing and shooting incidents, he was beheaded in 1886.

Gunfights: *April 30, 1880, Las Vegas, New Mexico.* Three weeks after John Joshua Webb had been sentenced to hang, Rudabaugh tried to engineer a jailbreak in his behalf. Deputy Sheriff Lino Váldez thwarted Rudabaugh's attempt, and the two men exchanged shots. Rudabaugh was driven away, but he mortally wounded Váldez. Rudabaugh fled to Fort Sumner, where he joined Billy the Kid.

November 30–31, 1880, near White Oaks, New Mexico. Rudabaugh, Billy the Kid, and Billy Wilson rode into White Oaks, which was a bold move, since Rudabaugh's companions had barely eluded a posse near town the previous day. When the three desperadoes encountered Deputy Sheriff James Redman, one of their number threw a shot at the lawman. Redman ducked

for cover behind Will Hudgen's saloon, but a large number of citizens surged into the street and chased the troublemakers out of town.

That night the outlaws took refuge at the ranch of Jim Greathouse, some forty miles from White Oaks. At dawn a posse closed in on the ranch house, but the fugitives bought time by trading Greathouse for Deputy Sheriff James Carlyle.

That evening at midnight Carlyle tried to escape by hopping out of a window, but he was fatally wounded by gunfire. The deadly shots may have come from lawmen mistaking their cohort for an escaping fugitive, or they may have been fired by the three outlaws, who promptly took flight. When the posse members discovered the dead man to be Carlyle, they angrily burned the ranch house, but Rudabaugh and his friends had already made good their escape.

December 19, 1880, Fort Sumner, New Mexico. The Kid, Rudabaugh, Wilson, Tom O'Folliard, Charlie Bowdre, and Tom Pickett wearily rode into Fort Sumner on a cold Sunday evening to seek refuge and recreation. A posse led by Pat Garrett had secluded itself in the old post hospital, and as the outlaws approached the building, Garrett ordered them to halt.

The fugitives, of course, tried to flee, and the posse opened fire. O'Folliard and Pickett were wounded, and Rudabaugh's horse was killed. Rudabaugh scrambled up behind Wilson, and the entire gang galloped safely out of town— except O'Folliard. Fatally wounded, he reined in and surrendered, and he died in the old military hospital within an hour.

Rudabaugh later secured another horse and along with the Kid, Wilson,

Pickett, and Bowdre, holed up in an abandoned stone cabin near Stinking Springs.

December 23, 1880, Stinking Springs, New Mexico. Garrett easily tracked the fugitives across the snow-covered terrain, and during the night his posse quietly surrounded the little rock building. At dawn Bowdre unsuspectingly stepped outside and was shot to death by the lawmen. The four remaining outlaws tried to pull their horses inside the house, but Garrett shot away the reins of two and killed a third, blocking the only doorway with its carcass. The outlaws held out all day, but they had no food, and escape was impossible. At last Rudabaugh waved a white flag and went out to parley with Garrett. When he returned, the outlaws surrendered, and Garrett loaded the fugitives into a wagon for delivery to jail.

September 19, 1881, Las Vegas, New Mexico. Rudabaugh, with a death sentence hanging over him, was locked up in Las Vegas with John Joshua Webb. Rudabaugh somehow obtained a six-gun and, accompanied by Webb, Thomas Duffy, and H. S. Wilson, attempted to break out of jail. Rudabaugh squeezed off two rounds at jailer Florencio Mares, but he quickly surrendered when assistant jailer Herculano Chavez mortally wounded Duffy. Within two months, however, Rudabaugh, Webb, and five other convicts secured a pick, an iron poker, and a knife and with these tools dug their way to freedom during the night.

February 18, 1886, Parral, Mexico. In a Parral cantina Rudabaugh entered a card game which soon broke up over cries of cheating. Rudabaugh and a Mexican stood up, and Dave killed him with a pistol shot in the head. Another player drew and fired wildly, then took a bullet in the heart from the gringo. Rudabaugh went to find his mount, but the animal was gone, and Dave returned to the building. The lights had now been extinguished, however, and Rudabaugh was jumped and his head was severed.

Sources: Keleher, *Violence in Lincoln County,* 281–99, 303, 319–20; Miller and Snell, *Great Gunfighters of the Kansas Cowtowns,* 93, 208–13, 215, 220–222, 320, 323; Garrett, *Billy, the Kid,* 93–97, 100–102, 114.

Rynning, Thomas H.

(b. 1866, Beloit, Wisconsin; d. June 18, 1941. Teamster, cowboy, soldier, wild West show performer, railroad employee, law officer, prison warden.) Orphaned by the time he was twelve, Tom Rynning drifted west as a teenager, working as a teamster and cowboy in Texas. In 1885 he enlisted in the Eighth U.S. Cavalry, and was soon transferred from Texas to Arizona, where he saw action in the final campaign against Geronimo. In 1891 he left the army, performed in Buffalo Bill Cody's Wild West Show, worked for the Southern Pacific Railroad, and then rode with Teddy Roosevelt's Rough Riders during the Spanish-American War. After his discharge Rynning married and settled in Arizona Territory. In 1902 he was appointed captain of the Arizona Rangers, serving for five years until his appointment as superintendent of the Territorial Prison at Yuma. He died in 1941 at the age of seventy-five.

Gunfights: ca. 1902, Douglas, Arizona. An Arizona ranger named Webb heard a gunshot in Douglas' Cowboy Saloon and hurried to investigate. Threatened at gunpoint by the saloon owner, Webb killed his antagonist with two shots. Rynning led two other rangers into the saloon, where one of his men was wounded in the chest by a half-blood gambler. Rynning ended the fight with a single shot; the bullet broke the gambler's arm and plowed into his side.

ca. 1904, Southern Arizona. A one-armed man had killed a schoolteacher and fled to a rock cabin in the Chiricahua Mountains. Rynning and fellow ranger Dave Allison trailed the killer to his hideout; the lawmen approached the only door unnoticed and burst inside. The fugitive jerked up a pistol, but Rynning shot him in the hip, and Allison wounded him in the leg, and he promptly surrendered.

Summer, 1906, northern Mexico. In 1906 a group of Mexican miners rebelled against their American engineers in the Cananea Mountains. The Mexican Army accepted three hundred American volunteers, and Rynning was appointed to a colonelcy and placed in command of the North Americans. The force traveled to the mining district by train and found the engineers under siege by the miners. During the ensuing battle Rynning made his way to the women who were tending the injured at the mining-complex hospital. Suddenly a trio of Mexican snipers opened up from a distance of two hundred yards. Rynning returned their fire with his rifle, wounding all three and quickly driving them away.

Source: Spangenberger, "Thomas H. Rynning," *Guns of the Gunfighters,* 31–37.

St. Leon, Ernest

("Diamond Dick")

(d. 1891, Texas. Soldier, law officer.) Reared in San Antonio, Ernest St. Leon was the son of a refugee Frenchman. As a youth he abandoned the study of law to join the U.S. Cavalry, and after several Indian campaigns he attained the rank of sergeant. On one occasion he was reputed to have gunned down three Indians who had killed one of his men.

In the 1880's St. Leon left the army and soon joined Company D of the Texas Rangers. Nicknamed "Diamond Dick" because he adorned himself with large diamonds, St. Leon developed a drinking problem and was dismissed from the rangers. Corporal John Hughes entrusted him with an undercover mission, however, and St. Leon performed so well that he was reinstated and handed further undercover assignments. A year and one-half later, unfortunately, he was killed in a saloon fight.

Gunfights: *1889, Shafter, Texas.* St. Leon, posing as an ore thief, accompanied three criminals in leading a mule train to a cache in an abandoned mine shaft. In the darkness waited Rangers John Hughes and Lon Oden, and they barked out an order to surrender. The three outlaws pulled six-guns, and a fight erupted. St. Leon opened up at close range, and two of the thieves collapsed. The third darted for cover, and the lawmen tried to talk him out. He tried to slip away, but was dropped by St. Leon with one shot. All three robbers were fatally wounded and were buried on the mountainside.

1891, Texas. St. Leon and a deputized citizen had arrested three cowboys, but the ranger decided to turn them loose, and all five men went to a saloon to smooth over any hard feelings. Drinking led to further disagreement, however, and shooting broke out. Both St. Leon and his deputy were cut down; the latter died on the spot, and Diamond Dick expired the next day.

Source: Martin, *Border Boss,* 94–100, 125, 129–30.

Salazar, Yginio

(b. February 14, 1863, New Mexico; d. January 7, 1936, Lincoln, New Mexico. Rancher.) Salazar's primary notoriety as a gunfighter stems from his participation in the Lincoln County War. Although just fifteen years of age, he signed on with the Alexander McSween faction, which was enlisting anyone willing to brandish a gun. He was in only one fight—the climactic battle in Lincoln in which he enjoyed a miraculous escape from death. After recovering from his wounds, he joined Governor Lew Wallace's "Lincoln County Riflemen," which existed briefly to assist the authorities in restoring order.

At about that time Salazar furnished Billy the Kid with a file and other tools which the outlaw used to free himself from his shackles just before he shot his way out of custody in Lincoln. When the hostilities finally ceased, Salazar remained in Lincoln for the rest of a long and peaceful existence.

Gunfight: July 15–19, 1878, Lincoln, New Mexico. For days Salazar had been one of the men holding the McSween house while the opposing faction gradually strengthened their position. When the adobe house was set afire and the ladies were evacuated on the nineteenth, Salazar and his comrades steeled themselves for a breakout attempt. When darkness fell, Salazar was one of the first to bolt out the back door of the smoldering building. A hail of lead poured from a low wall which protected members of the opposition. Three slugs hammered into Salazar's back, chest, and side, and he dropped, unconscious.

When he awoke, the shooting had stopped, and his adversaries were moving warily among the fallen. Salazar lay still, realizing that he might be shot again if it were suspected that he remained alive. Andy Boyle and a gunman named Pierce discussed putting one last slug into Salazar's sprawled body, but decided that he was already dead.

As dawn began to break, Salazar crawled down the nearby fifty-yard slope and drank greedily from the Rio Bonito. He then struggled to his brother's house, which was empty because the inhabitants were hiding in fear. He collapsed on a bed, and when he awakened, his brother and sister-in-law were standing over him. They located a doctor, military surgeon Daniel M. Appel, who dug out two of the bullets and stubbornly refused to let Salazar's enemies confront him.

Sources: Fulton, *Lincoln County War,* 249, 271, 275–76, 333; Keleher, *Violence in Lincoln County,* 150, 219, 339; Hunt, *Tragic Days of Billy the Kid,* 77–104; Coe, *Frontier Fighter,* 107–28.

Scarborough, George W.

(d. April 6, 1900, Deming, New Mexico. Cowboy, lawman, range detective.) Scarborough was a Baptist preacher's son who became a Texas cowboy. After a sojourn in rugged Fort Griffin, he served as sheriff of Jones County and as a deputy U.S. marshal in the El Paso

area during the 1890's. While in El Paso he had dealings with such gunmen as John Selman, Wes Hardin, and Jeff Milton. His acquaintance with Selman went back a number of years, but in El Paso the two men clashed, and in 1896 Scarborough shot Selman to death.

Scarborough resigned his deputy's commission, but after he was acquitted he found work as a detective in Deming, New Mexico, for the Grant County Cattlemen's Association. It was in that capacity that he was killed while chasing cattle rustlers in 1900.

Gunfights: June 21, 1895, El Paso, Texas. Late at night Scarborough met Martin Morose, wanted in Texas for cattle rustling, on a bridge spanning the Rio Grande. El Paso lawmen evidently had planned to lure Morose across the border either to obtain money from his wife, a former prostitute, or to gain revenge on John Wesley Hardin, who was having an affair with Mrs. Morose. As Morose and Scarborough crossed over the bridge, Deputy U.S. Marshal Jeff Milton and Texas Ranger Frank McMahon, Scarborough's brother-in-law, emerged from the darkness. The lawmen opened fire, and Morose, riddled with slugs, collapsed and died.

April 5, 1896, El Paso, Texas. John Selman, generally considered to be Scarborough's friend as well as a fellow lawman, had accused George of stealing money from the body of Martin Morose. At 4:00 A.M. on Easter Sunday Scarborough met Selman, who was drinking himself into a stupor in El Paso's Wigwam Saloon. The two men went into an alley to discuss their differences, but after a brief exchange of words Scarborough drew his gun and began firing. His first slug felled Selman, but Scarborough shot the old gunman three more times. "Boys," gasped Selman to a gathering crowd, "you know I am not afraid of any man; but I never drew my gun." Selman died, but Scarborough was declared innocent of murder.

July, 1898, near Solomonville, Arizona. Scarborough was helping Jeff Milton search eastern Arizona for an outlaw called Bronco Bill Walters, and they finally encountered him near Solomonville. A sharp fight broke out between the officers and Walters and his companions, Bill Johnson and Red Pipkin. Walters was shot out of the saddle, and Pipkin's horse was killed, although Pipkin scrambled to safety on foot. Johnson dismounted and opened fire with his rifle, but he soon received a mortal wound. Walters was taken into custody and recovered to serve a term in prison.

April 5, 1900, near San Simon, Arizona. Scarborough, working as a detective for a cattlemen's association, was assisted by a rancher named Walter Birchfield in tracing a group of rustlers who had been associated with Butch Cassidy's Wild Bunch. Scarborough and Birchfield, hot on the heels of the outlaws, chased them into a canyon. A bullet from the rifle of Harvey Logan ripped through Scarborough's leg and killed his horse.

Birchfield abandoned the chase and rode to nearby San Simon for a wagon. By nightfall Scarborough had been taken to the railroad, and from there he was transported to Deming, New Mexico. At Deming his leg was amputated, but he died on April 6, four years to the day after the death of John Selman.

Sources: Metz, *John Selman,* 163–67, 173–74, 177–81, 198–203, 229; Sonnichsen, *Pass of the North,* 315, 320, 329–31, 335–36; Haley, *Jeff Mil-*

Scurlock, Josiah G.

("Doc")

(b. Tennessee; d. ca. 1882, South Spring Ranch, New Mexico. Cowboy, rancher, rustler, gunman.) After a killing in his native Tennessee, Scurlock fled to South America, then worked his way back toward the States through Mexico. Scurlock appeared in New Mexico during the 1870's as a cowhand on John Chisum's huge ranch. (The two men had known each other in Tennessee, and Chisum tried to have Scurlock cleared of murder charges.) In 1876 Scurlock was involved in the shooting of his friend Mike Harkins, but it was determined that the latter's death was accidental.

Scurlock married a native New Mexican and acquired a tiny spread of his own, but when the Lincoln County War erupted, he hired his gun to the McSween "Regulators." He was a member of the possee which killed Frank Baker and Billy Morton, and he was present at the battle at Blazer's Mill which resulted in the deaths of Dick Brewer and Buckshot Roberts. He was a participant in the big shootout in Lincoln, then joined Billy the Kid's band of fugitives and cattle rustlers. He seemed to realize the futility of this way of life, however, and he soon rejoined his family and found employment on Pete Maxwell's Fort Sumner ranch. But his reform proved to be temporary, and he was killed in a gunfight in 1882.

Gunfights: ca. 1868, Tennessee.
Scurlock and his brother-in-law argued bitterly over a calf, and when the brother-in-law tried to drive the animal away,

Scurlock snarled, "Don't you dare drive that cow beyond my gate. I'll kill you if you do." When the man began to prod the calf, Scurlock picked up a shotgun and emptied both barrels into him, killing him on the spot.

March 9, 1878, Steel Springs, New Mexico. Dick Brewer led Scurlock and several other Regulators in chasing down suspected murderers Frank Baker and Billy Morton. There was a great deal of bitter talk concerning the prisoners, and on the way back to Lincoln the posse killed Baker and Morton, and Regulator William McCloskey also fell in the hail of lead.

May 1, 1878, Lincoln, New Mexico. Several McSween men were led by Scurlock in a brief flurry of shooting with the opposing faction in the streets of Lincoln. The skirmish was bloodless, however, for there were no casualties on either side.

May 14, 1878, Lincoln County, New Mexico. Scurlock led a Regulator raid on a cow camp in the Pecos country near Black River. Included in his party were Charlie Bowdre, George Coe, Henry Brown, three other Anglos (one of whom probably was Billy the Kid), and eleven Mexicans. Scurlock carried a warrant for a man called "Indian," and the Regulators also were trying to round up horses which had belonged to fallen comrades. When they descended upon the camp, the herders fled, but the Regulators wounded two and killed Indian. The party then rounded up all nearby horses and rode away.

ca. 1882, South Spring Ranch, New Mexico. At John Chisum's ranch Scurlock began cursing and waving a gun at Fred Roth, who was carrying a baby and could not defend himself. Roth angrily stomped inside the ranch house, put down the baby, and snatched up a Winchester.

When Roth emerged from the house, he shouted, "Come on now; say what you have to say; I'm ready for you." Both men then opened fire, Roth concealing himself at one corner of the house and Scurlock ducking behind a wagon. Roth splintered the wagon bed, and two or three of his slugs punctured Scurlock's body.

Finally Scurlock collapsed, gasping, "That's enough. You've got me, Fred. Don't shoot any more." But Roth dashed to the fallen man and was about to finish him off when bystander Elias Bly stopped him. This rescue proved only temporary, however, for Scurlock died within moments.

Sources: Keleher, *Violence in Lincoln County,* 69, 99, 120, 128, 131, 150, 184, 233, 308–309, 312; Hunt, *Tragic Days of Billy the Kid,* 42–46, 56–60, 79, 90, 107–108, 113–15, 124, 132; Klasner, *My Girlhood Among Outlaws,* 300, 305–306.

John Selman, shown here as he looked in 1878. He later killed Bass Outlaw and John Wesley Hardin. *(Courtesy Western History Collections, University of Oklahoma Library)*

Selman, John

(b. November 16, 1839, Madison County, Arkansas; d. April 6, 1896, El Paso, Texas. Farmer, rancher, butcher, saloon owner, soldier, law officer, rustler, gunman.) Selman's father was an Englishman who in America had become a schoolteacher, farmer, and small-scale slaveowner. John spent his early years on a farm in Arkansas, then moved with his family to Grayson County, Texas, in 1858. His father died, and John became responsible for his mother and four younger brothers and sisters.

After the Civil War began, John joined the Confederate cavalry and was stationed in Oklahoma. He saw no action, however, and in 1863 he deserted and led his family to Fort Davis, Texas, about twenty miles northeast of present-day Albany. (This Fort Davis was a fortification erected and named by settlers threatened by Indians, and should not be confused with the Fort Davis established by the U.S. Army in West Texas.)

In 1864 Selman enlisted in the state militia, which was responsible for frontier defense, and was elected lieutenant by his neighbors. In August, 1865, he married Edna deGraffenreid, and in 1869 the Selmans and the deGraffenreids moved to Colfax County, New Mexico. Indians stole all their livestock, however, and the following year Selman returned to ranching in Texas, about eight miles from wild and woolly Fort Griffin. During the 1870's Selman twice became involved in Indian troubles and reputedly killed several hostiles in skirmishes. He also was widely thought to have murdered a local bully known as Haulph.

Selman established close relationships with two Fort Griffin citizens: Hurricane Minnie Martin, a local prostitute who became his mistress, and John Larn, a vicious gunfighter and rustler who served for a time as sheriff of Shackleford County and who became Selman's close friend and business partner. In Fort Griffin Selman also came in contact with such frontier notables as Wyatt Earp, Bat Masterson, Doc Holliday, Killin' Jim Miller, Jesse Evans, and Pat Garrett.

Selman owned property in Fort Griffin, including a saloon, but increasingly he and John Larn resorted to rustling. Texas Rangers and local authorities were pressured to stop Larn and Selman, and bushwhacking attempts were perpetrated by both factions. Larn was arrested and killed by a mob in 1878, and Selman, who had witnessed Larn's arrest from concealment, fled the country. Warrants were issued for Selman's arrest, and while he remained at large, his wife died carrying their fifth child.

With his brother Tom, Selman drifted into Lincoln County in the summer of 1878, and John became the leader of a gang of hard cases. "Selman's Scouts" were involved in robbing stores and rustling cattle, but pressure from the army caused the gang to break up. The Selman brothers returned to Texas, and by March, 1879, John had organized another band of rustlers which operated throughout West Texas. The gang disintegrated when Selman was bedridden

with smallpox, and he then opened a butcher shop in the settlement adjacent to Fort Davis.

Selman soon began leading still another group of robbers and rustlers in the Fort Davis–Fort Stockton area, but in June, 1880, he was arrested in Fort Davis—two days after his second marriage. His brother and fellow outlaw, Tom Cat Selman, had been lynched when he was taken into custody, but when John was transferred back to Shackleford County for trial, he bribed his jailers and escaped.

Selman went to Chihuahua, Mexico, where he opened a saloon and gathered his family about him. After working a silver claim for a time, he returned to New Mexico, opened a saloon in Fort Bayard, and prospected in the mountains.

After a shooting scrape, Selman fled back to Mexico and sold John Deere farm equipment. Selman's second wife died, and when he received news in 1888 that he had been cleared of rustling charges in Texas, he and his two sons moved to wide-open El Paso. John peacefully went to work for a smelting company, but on one occasion an attempt was made on his life, and he was severely stabbed in the face. After recovering, he led a couple of cattle drives, then in 1892 was elected city constable.

The next year, at the age of fifty-three, Selman married a sixteen-year-old girl, who weathered their stormy marriage and wed three times after Selman's death. In 1894 Selman killed Bass Outlaw in the line of duty, and the next year he killed the famous John Wesley Hardin. A hung jury in the Hardin death caused a retrial to be scheduled, but Selman was slain before the case came to court. Selman was drinking heavily at this stage of his life, and he abrasively entered a quarrel with

George Scarborough and was killed in 1896.

Gunfights: *1876, Fort Griffin, Texas.* Selman frequently assisted his friend John Larn, Shackleford County sheriff, in making arrests. A man named Hampton, who was wanted by the law, was spotted on the streets of Fort Griffin by Larn and Selman. Hampton was unarmed and half deaf, but it is uncertain that Larn and Selman were aware of either condition. Larn ordered Hampton to surrender, and when he kept walking, Selman whipped out his pistol and emptied the weapon into him.

May, 1878, near Fort Griffin, Texas. While driving some steers down an arroyo on his ranch, Selman was ambushed by a local farmer angry over Selman's rustling activities. A shotgun blast tore off Selman's saddle horn, and John snapped off a return shot from his buffalo gun. Spurring into the brush, Selman discovered the farmer's corpse, which he ordered his men to carry off in a spring wagon.

September, 1878, Lincoln County, New Mexico. Selman had joined a Lincoln County band of desperadoes led by a gunman named Hart. Selman had contested Hart for leadership of the gang, and he seized a chance for control while the two men were waiting together in a cabin for a meal. Selman quietly drew his gun and shot Hart without warning. The slug ripped through the flimsy table and drilled into Hart's head, tearing off the top of his skull and killing him instantly.

October, 1878, Lincoln County, New Mexico. "Selman's Scouts" had encamped on the Pecos River, and John was playing poker with a few of the gang members. An argument broke out and quickly developed into gunplay. Without hesitating, Selman jerked out his revolver and killed the chief troublemaker on the spot.

1884, Fort Bayard, New Mexico. On the streets of Fort Bayard, where he operated a saloon, Selman encountered an old enemy of his from Fort Griffin, a man named Gotch. Both men hurled words at each other, then went for their guns. After an exchange of gunfire Gotch went down, wounded in the arm.

April 5, 1894, El Paso, Texas. About 5:00 P.M. Selman and Frank Collinson encountered a deputy U.S. marshal, Bass Outlaw, drunk and in El Paso as a court witness. The three men went to Tillie Howard's well-known sporting house, where Outlaw merrily discharged his pistol.

Texas Ranger Joe McKidrict (who previously had been a San Antonio policeman under the name Joe Cooly) charged onto the scene and found Outlaw in back of the establishment, gun in hand. Selman stepped onto the porch and said, "It was an accident, Joe. He's all right."

"Bass, why did you shoot?" persisted McKidrict. Outlaw jammed his six-gun against McKidrict's head and snarled, "You want some too?" He fired twice, hitting McKidrict above the ear and, as he fell, in the back. Selman jumped off the porch, clawing for his gun, but was almost blinded when Outlaw fired again. Outlaw missed Selman, but powder burns blurred John's vision. Selman got off a shot which ripped through Outlaw's chest, then was wounded himself. Outlaw pumped two slugs into Selman's right leg, then staggered off to die. Selman was forced to use a cane the rest of his life.

August 19, 1895, El Paso, Texas. A few weeks earlier, John Selman, Jr., appointed to the El Paso police force by Chief Jeff Milton, had arrested as drunk and disorderly Mrs. Beulah Morose, a former prostitute and wife of cattle rustler Martin Morose, recently killed by lawmen. Beulah had been seeing John Wesley Hardin, and the old gunfighter angrily quarreled with young Selman and then his father. (It was rumored that the actual source of trouble was that Hardin had taken a large sum of money from the body of Martin Morose and had refused to split it with the elder Selman, contrary to previous and secret agreement.)

Old John had never been one to take chances, and he decided to meet the trouble head-on. On the evening of August 19 Selman burst into the Acme Saloon and began firing, probably at Hardin's back. (A few bystanders testified that Hardin went for his gun, although neither of his guns was drawn or fired. The possibility has also been suggested that Selman saw Hardin's face in the saloon mirror, then fired and hit him as he turned. More probably Selman blazed away without warning, depending on his badge for legal exoneration.)

Hardin was struck in the head and dropped to the floor, and a second shot crashed into a board beside him. Selman then walked to the fallen Hardin and deliberately fired twice more. One slug drilled into Hardin's arm, and the other hit his chest. John Selman, Jr., rushed into the saloon and, grabbing his father by the arm, cried out, "Don't shoot him any more, he's dead." Old John then surrendered to his son and was later acquitted in court.

April 5, 1896, El Paso, Texas. On Easter Sunday at 4:00 A.M. Selman, thoroughly intoxicated, encountered fellow peace officer George Scarborough in a saloon. Apparently Selman had groused about town that Wes Hardin had split the money found on Martin Morose's body with Scarborough. At any rate, the two lawmen stepped into an alley, and Scarborough fired four shots into Selman, evidently without warning.

Hit in the neck, Selman fell without drawing his pistol. Scarborough pumped three more slugs into the fallen man, drilling him in the hip, knee, and side, the last wound paralyzing Selman from the waist down.

A crowd quickly gathered, and Selman gasped, "Boys, you know I am not afraid of any man; but I never drew my gun." The next day doctors operated and removed the bullet pressing on Selman's spine, but the old gunfighter died.

Sources: Metz, *John Selman;* Haley, *Jeff Milton,* 61–62, 209, 214, 217, 222, 247–49.

Shadley, Lafayette

(d. September 2, 1893, Stillwater, Oklahoma. Law officer.) Lafe Shadley was an Oklahoma peace officer who gained a measure of renown by clashing with outlaws during the 1890's. He was shot to death in a vicious gunfight with the Doolin gang at Ingalls in 1893.

Gunfights: 1892, Oklahoma. In the Osage country Shadley crossed the trail of rustler and bank robber Dan ("Dynamite Dick") Clifton. Shadley tried to take Clifton into custody, and a pistol duel erupted. Clifton took a nasty wound in the neck, but he managed to make good his escape.

September 1, 1893, Ingalls, Oklahoma. Area lawmen were informed that Bill

Doolin and six of his Oklahombres were busy whooping it up in Ingalls. A number of officers headed toward the little town, and by 10:00 A.M. two wagons filled with lawmen approached Ingalls from the south and west. Shadley came in from the south, along with Jim Masterson, W. C. Roberts, Henry Keller, Hi Thompson, George Cox, and H. A. Janson; this wagon circled town and stopped in a grove of trees at Dr. Pickering's residence. Dick Speed drove the second wagon; riding with him were John W. Hixon, Tom Houston, J. S. Burke, Red Lucas, and Ike Steel.

The posse members filtered into town, and the shooting began when Speed opened fire on Bitter Creek Newcomb. Speed was killed by Arkansas Tom Jones, who was firing from a hotel window, and the wounded Newcomb galloped out of town. Doolin and the other four outlaws began shooting from a saloon, and the battle that followed was so violent that a boy named Dell Simmons and a stray horse were killed and four other bystanders were wounded.

Doolin and his four men dashed to a livery stable next door, and Shadley took cover behind the dead horse and opened fire at the front door of the building. Suddenly Bill Dalton, Red Buck Weightman, and Tulsa Jack Blake burst through the door on horseback, while Doolin and Dan Clifton rode out the rear door. Houston was wounded by the sniping of Jones, and Hixon shot Dalton's horse in the jaw. Dalton spurred forward, but Shadley ran to the corner of a hardware store and dropped the animal with a bullet which broke his leg.

Dalton then snatched a pair of wire cutters from his horse and began working on a wire fence which blocked the way out of town. Shadley darted forward, crouching briefly behind a storm

cellar, then crawling under the fence. Dalton saw him, fired three slugs into his body, then finished cutting the fence. Dalton scrambled up behind Doolin, and the outlaws spurred away to safety. After an hour-long siege Jones surrendered, and the battle was ended.

Shadley, Houston, and the dead Speed were taken to Stillwater, where relatives and friends were summoned. The two wounded peace officers suffered through the night, then died.

Sources: Canton, *Frontier Trails,* 133–34; Croy, *Trigger Marshal,* 207–209; Shirley, *Heck Thomas,* 171–74; Shirley, *Six-gun and Silver Star,* 81, 89, 93–96, 190.

Shepherd, Oliver

(d. April, 1868, Jackson County, Missouri. Guerrilla soldier, bank robber.) Ol Shepherd fought and plundered with Missouri guerrillas during the Civil War, then lost no time in joining the James-Younger bandit gang. He was active in several holdups before he was tracked down and killed near Independence, Missouri.

Gunfights: February 13, 1866, Liberty, Missouri. Shepherd was one of twelve members of the James-Younger gang who pulled the first daylight bank robbery in the United States. The holdup went smoothly until the bandits began riding out of Liberty with the fifty-seven thousand dollars they had stolen. Shooting broke out, and a bystander, college student George Wymore, was killed.

March 21, 1868, Russellville, Kentucky. Shepherd and seven other members of the James-Younger gang galloped up to the Southern Bank of Kentucky, and Jesse led several henchmen inside.

Gunfire erupted, and bank president Nimrod Long suffered a head wound. The gang secured fourteen thousand dollars in loot, but had to battle their way out of town with their guns blazing.

April, 1868, Jackson County, Missouri. A vigorous manhunt immediately followed the Russellville holdup, and George Shepherd, Ol's cousin, was quickly captured. The gang then scattered, and Ol made his way back into Missouri, a posse from Kentucky hot on his trail. When he reached Jackson County, he encountered another posse, which demanded that he submit to investigation. Instead, he defiantly pulled a gun and tried to shoot his way through the lawmen. The posse threw a furious volley after him, however, and he collapsed, riddled fatally by twenty slugs.

Source: Breihan, *Younger Brothers,* 65–69, 83–85.

Sherman, James D.

("Jim Talbot")

(d. August, 1896, Ukiah, California. Cowboy, rancher.) James D. Sherman, who went by the name "Talbot," helped trail a herd of cattle from Texas to Caldwell, Kansas, in the fall of 1881. Upon arrival he rented a house and installed his wife and two children. Noted as something of a desperado in Texas, Talbot and several friends spent the next few weeks drinking and carousing about the town. In December Talbot killed former lawman Mike Meagher, but he managed to escape apprehension for fourteen years. By that time he had moved to a ranch in California, and in 1894 he was arrested—possibly for the murder of a man he had killed in Mendocino County.

The next year a trial for the murder of Meagher ended in a hung jury, and

a subsequent trial won him acquittal. He returned home to discover that his wife had taken a lover, and in 1896 Talbot was assassinated—probably by his amorous competitor.

Gunfights: December 17, 1881, Caldwell, Kansas. Talbot spent Friday night drinking heavily with Bob Bigtree, Dick Eddleman, Tom Love, Jim Martin, Bob Munson, and George Speers. The group was rowdy and abrasive, and Talbot drunkenly threatened the lives of a newspaper editor and former Marshal Mike Meagher.

The next morning Meagher complained to Marshal John Wilson, who arrested Love for firing his gun. Talbot, however, led his friends in rushing Wilson and forcibly freeing Love. Wilson asked Meagher for help, but the cowboys ganged up on Meagher and again threatened to kill him.

An hour after noon Wilson arrested Martin and had him fined for carrying a gun. Martin lacked the money to pay, and Deputy Marshal Will Fossett walked down the street with him to obtain funds. But again Talbot, Eddleman, Love, and Munson seized the prisoner, and Talbot impulsively squeezed off two shots in Wilson's direction. Talbot then began running with Wilson and Meagher in pursuit, but upon reaching the Opera House, he turned and began firing his Winchester. One slug ripped through Meagher's chest, and he died thirty minutes later.

An irate mob of citizens roared toward the cowboys. Speers was shot dead saddling a mount, and most of Talbot's friends' horses were wounded as they galloped out of town. The mob pursued the fleeing cowboys several miles into Indian Territory, and finally holed them up in a dugout. The fugitives wounded W. E. Campbell and damped the aggressiveness of the mob, then slipped away after darkness fell.

August, 1896, Ukiah, California. On a Tuesday evening Talbot was returning to his California ranch, not suspecting that an assassin lay waiting for him from concealment. When Talbot was within fifty feet of his gate, the assassin made his move. Before Talbot could react, a shotgun exploded behind him, severing his spinal cord and killing him on the spot. It was rumored that John Meagher had secretly avenged his brother's death, but a far more likely culprit was the lover of Talbot's wife.

Sources: Miller and Snell, *Great Gunfighters of the Kansas Cowtowns*, 361–68; Drago, *Wild, Woolly & Wicked*, 213–16.

Shonsey, Mike

(Cowboy, ranch foreman, gunman.) Of Irish and Canadian extraction, Mike Shonsey migrated to the cattle country of Wyoming from Ohio. Beginning as a cowboy, he soon worked his way up to foreman and served several outfits in that capacity. When the Johnson County War broke out, Shonsey sided with the big cattlemen and hired his gun to the Wyoming Cattle Growers' Association. On one occasion he had a fist fight with small rancher Jack Flagg, and twice he was forced to back down in clashes with Nate Champion; therefore, he willingly spied for the association and also killed Dudley Champion, Nate's twin brother. He left Wyoming for a few years, but eventually he returned and lived to an old age, one of the last survivors of the Johnson County War.

Gunfights: **April 9, 1892, KC Ranch, Wyoming.** Shonsey had gal-

loped excitedly into the camp of the association "Regulators," claiming that he had located fourteen rustlers at the KC Ranch. When the large party of gunmen closed in, however, they discovered only Nate Champion and Nick Ray, along with a pair of unemployed ranch workers named Bill Walker and Ben Jones.

The Regulators deployed before dawn, Shonsey stationing himself with five other men in a gulch to the rear of the cabin. At daylight Jones and Walker emerged and were captured, and when Ray came outside, the shooting started. Ray was shot down, but Champion covered him and helped his dying partner inside.

The firing continued until the middle of the afternoon, when Jack Flagg happened by. He was fired upon, but managed to escape. Flagg was forced to abandon a wagon, however, and the Regulators turned it into a fire wagon and shoved it against the cabin. Champion burst outside, firing a Winchester and six-gun and sprinting for the gulch in his bare feet. When he had almost reached the gulch, Shonsey and his five concealed cohorts opened fire and dropped Champion. Champion was riddled with twenty-eight bullets, and a note reading, "Cattle thieves, beware," was pinned to his shirt.

The Regulators proceeded on, but they soon encountered a large group of irate citizens and soldiers and, after a brief show of resistance, submitted to arrest.

May, 1893, near Lusk, Wyoming. In a cattle camp about twenty miles northeast of Lusk, Shonsey discovered Dudley Champion, twin brother of Nate. After a brief conversation Shonsey suddenly pulled his revolver, shot Champion, and fled camp. Champion gasped, "I can't cock it, I can't cock it," then died. His gun was jammed with dirt in the cylinder, and he had not fired a shot. Shonsey went straight to Lusk, was released on grounds of self-defense, and went to Cheyenne to board a southbound train.

Sources: Smith, *War on the Powder River,* xiii, 118, 145, 152–53, 162, 186, 189, 191, 201–204, 282–83; Mercer, *Banditti of the Plains,* xlviii, 51–106, 140–41, 179–87.

Shores, Cyrus Wells

("Doc")

(b. November 11, 1844, Hickville, Michigan; d. October 18, 1934, Gunnison, Colorado. Bullwhacker, hunter, trapper, freighter, cattleman.) Born in a Michigan village near Detroit, Shores received both his Christian name and his appellation from the man who brought him into the world, Doctor Cyrus Wells. In 1866 the young man left home for Montana Territory, finding work at Fort Benton as a bullwhacker.

Shores briefly turned to hunting and trapping, but soon he bought a wagon and spent the next few years hauling ties for the Union Pacific Railroad, running freight to various mining camps, and carrying government supplies from Fort Hays to Camp Supply, Oklahoma. In 1871 he sold his wagon and bought a small herd of Texas cattle, which he drove up the Chisholm Trail, and for the next seven years he bought and sold cattle in Kansas.

In 1877 Doc married, and three years later the Shoreses moved to Gunnison, Colorado, establishing a freighting outfit which supplied the area's booming gold camps. In 1884 Shores won election as sheriff of Gunnison County, and he served for eight years. He continued

his career as a deputy U.S. marshal and as a railroad detective for the Denver and Rio Grande, and in 1915 he was appointed chief of police in Salt Lake City.

Shores associated with men such as Wild Bill Hickok, Tom Horn, and Jim Clark, and among the numerous fugitives he apprehended was the notorious cannibal, Alfred Packer. The veteran lawman's first wife, an artist and poet, died in 1908, and he later remarried. Shores retired to Gunnison, where he survived to his ninetieth year.

Gunfights: October, 1880, near Gunnison, Colorado. While Shores was in his cabin rocking his infant son, a pair of ruffians named Jack Smith and Tom Lewis began shooting up the streets of Gunnison, seriously wounding a bystander. Shores sprang to his feet, grabbed a Winchester, and went outside to pursue the fleeing thugs. He exchanged shots with the two desperadoes, then was fired upon by a fifteen-man posse which tardily galloped onto the scene. Shores grumpily returned to Gunnison, and the posse soon captured Smith and Lewis.

December, 1891, Crested Butte, Colorado. About 250 Austrian and Italian coal miners had struck in Crested Butte, and Sheriff Shores rounded up two dozen deputies and boarded a special train to the troubled community to try to subdue the strikers. Upon arrival at midnight the posse was met by a charge from 150 angry miners, and Shores led his men in a retreat under fire.

The posse flattened behind the railroad track bed and began shooting. There was a heavy exchange of shots, and one of Shores's men became so flustered that he levered all fourteen cartridges out of his Winchester without once pulling the trigger. Shores ordered his men to fire low, and although thirty-six miners were wounded, only one was seriously hurt. None of the posse members were hit, and the strikers soon retreated and disbanded.

Source: Rockwell, *Memoirs of a Lawman.*

Dapper Luke Short, a gambler and the killer of Longhaired Jim Courtright. *(Courtesy Kansas State Historical Society, Topeka)*

Short, Luke L.

(b. 1854, Mississippi; d. September 8, 1893, Geuda Springs, Kansas. Farmer, cowboy, whiskey peddler, army scout, dispatch rider, gambler, saloon keeper.) Two years after his birth in Mississippi, Luke moved with his family to a farm in Texas. As a teen-ager Luke left home and hired on to trail cattle herds north to the Kansas railheads. After a few years of this rugged life he decided to seek a more pleasant and lucrative existence. In 1876 he drifted into Sidney, Nebraska, and soon joined up with some whiskey peddlers. The liquor merchants established a trading post 125 miles north of Sidney and began selling whiskey to Sioux Indians—a federal offense. Short later claimed that he killed six drunken braves on various occasions during this period.

Soon Short was arrested by soldiers, but he managed to escape and dropped out of sight for a couple of years. For a brief time in 1878 he carried dispatches and scouted for the army in Nebraska; then he was attracted to Leadville, Colorado, where he gambled professionally and engaged in a shooting scrape. In 1879 he moved to Dodge City and spent two quiet years as a house dealer in the Long Branch Saloon.

In 1881 Short gave booming Tombstone a look, becoming a house dealer in the Oriental Saloon along with Wyatt Earp and Doc Holliday. The three gamblers became known as the "Dodge City gang." While in Tombstone, Short killed a fellow gambler, Charles Storms, and after his release Luke returned to Dodge City and the Long Branch.

In 1883 Short bought an interest in the Long Branch, and shortly thereafter he became embroiled in the "Dodge City War." After a clash with reform-minded city officials, Short had a gunfight with policeman and City Clerk L. C. Hatman and was promptly run out of town. Lawyers were consulted, there was a series of charges and countercharges, and Short recruited a gang of gunfighter friends—the celebrated "Peace Commission," which included Wyatt Earp and Bat Masterson.

Eventually Short and his cohorts paraded into Dodge, but there was no violence, and Luke left town, ultimately settling his differences with the city out of court. Short then established his gambling residence in Fort Worth, buying a partnership in the White Elephant Saloon and acquiring a mistress named Hettie. Although gambling became illegal in the growing cattle town, Short went underground and made a fortune, frequently hobnobbing with the upper classes of Fort Worth society.

Always a fastidious dresser, Short regularly draped his small (five-foot, six-inch, 125-pound) frame in tailored clothes, and his right pants pocket was cut extra long and lined with leather to hold his six-gun. While in Fort Worth he had gunfights with Charles Wright and Longhaired Jim Courtright, with fatal consequences to both.

Short eventually developed dropsy, and as his condition worsened, he went to the mineral spa at Geuda Springs, Kansas, where he died in September, 1893.

Gunfights: *1879, Leadville, Colorado.* A man named Brown bitterly protested a gambling debt to Short. After a hot exchange of words the two men reached for their pistols. Short fired the first shot, wounding Brown in the face and promptly ending the fight.

February 25, 1881, Tombstone, Arizona. Short and gambler Charles Storms had an argument over a card game in Tombstone's Oriental Saloon, where Luke was a house dealer. Bat Masterson, another house dealer, intervened and restrained the two men, but Storms belligerently returned later in the day. After a bitter flurry of words the two gamblers went for their pistols. Aggressively, Short charged Storms, firing three times. One slug broke Storms's neck, and a second tore into his heart.

He slumped to the floor, dead, and Short later was cleared of all charges.

April 30, 1883, Dodge City, Kansas. A Dodge reform administration had arrested three female "singers" in the Long Branch Saloon, owned by Short and Will Harris. Short fumed and growled threats about the incident, and on Saturday night he encountered Special Policeman and City Clerk L. C. Hartman in front of a darkened general store on Front Street. "There is one of the sons of bitches," muttered Short to his companion, "Let's throw it into him."

Short jerked out his revolver and fired twice at Hartman, who dove for the ground. Thinking he had killed Hartman, Short walked away. But Hartman, unhurt, pulled his gun and pumped a slug at Short, who then disappeared into the darkness.

February 8, 1887, Fort Worth, Texas. Short had purchased a one-third interest in Jake Johnson's White Elephant Saloon, and the co-owners were approached by Longhaired Jim Courtright. Courtright was a notorious gunfighter who had formerly served as city marshal of Fort Worth and who currently was running a detective agency—along with a local protection racket.

Johnson had been willing to pay Courtright in exchange for a measure of security, but Short balked at the shakedown attempt. The quarrel grew, and although Short sold his interest in the saloon on February 7, the next day Courtright sent an ominous threat to Luke through Johnson.

Accompanied by Bat Masterson, Short encountered Courtright at a shooting gallery. The two men spoke together briefly, and Short reached inside his coat. Alarmed, Courtright warned him not to go for his gun. Short retorted that he never carried his pistol there, but Courtright was already pulling one of his six-guns.

As Longhaired Jim leveled his weapon, the hammer caught on Short's watch chain, and Luke snapped out his own revolver. Short emptied his gun rapid-fire: the first slug smashed the cylinder of Courtright's drawn pistol; two shots went wild; and three bullets tore into Courtright's right thumb, right shoulder, and heart. Courtright collapsed and died within minutes. Short was arrested, but was later released on grounds of self-defense.

December 23, 1890, Fort Worth, Texas. Another gambling dispute drew Short into his final gunfight. Charles Wright, a local saloon owner, vindictively ambushed Short with a shotgun blast from behind. Short was hit in the left leg, but produced his revolver and opened fire on his assailant. Wright managed to escape, but one of Short's bullets broke his wrist before he reached safety.

Sources: Cox, *Luke Short and His Era;* Schoenberger, *Gunfighters,* 133–45; Miller and Snell, *Great Gunfighters of the Kansas Cowtowns,* 369–415; Masterson, *Famous Gunfighters,* 7–24.

Slade, Joseph Alfred

("Jack")

(b. 1824, Carlyle, Illinois; d. March 10, 1864, Virginia City, Montana. Soldier, express company superintendent, rancher.) Reared in Illinois, Jack Slade left home in the 1840's and soon volunteered to serve in the Mexican War. He saw action in combat, and after his release he married and found employment with the Central Overland California and Pike's Peak Express Company.

By 1858 Slade was a line superintendent, and in his duties he ran afoul of a horse thief named Jules Reni, who nearly killed him. Slade recovered, resumed his duties, and a year later found and brutally murdered Reni.

Increasingly troubled with alcoholism, Slade became involved in a shooting in Wyoming and moved to Virginia City, Montana, where he tried to start a ranch. He soon fell into trouble in the booming mining town, however, and after a saloon quarrel citizens dragged him outside and threw a rope over a beam holding a sign. "My God! My God!" cried Slade. "Must I die like this? Oh my poor wife!"

Intending to bury her husband in his native Illinois, Virginia Slade sealed the corpse inside a tin coffin filled with raw alcohol. Upon reaching Salt Lake City, however, the body was so odorous that it was buried in the Mormon Cemetery on July 20, 1864—more than four months after the lynching.

Gunfights: 1858, Julesburg, Colorado. Jules Reni, a native of Canada, had been stealing horses from Slade's company. Slade came to Julesburg, Reni's center of operations, to investigate. Reni approached Slade in the street and fired twice at point-blank range. Slade collapsed, and Reni triggered three more shots into the fallen man. Reni ordered bystanders to bury Slade, but an angry mob chased the outlaw out of town. Slade then staggered to his feet, and after a lengthy convalescence he recovered his health.

1859, near Cold Springs, Colorado. The next year Reni was captured at Slade's ranch near Cold Springs. Slade assumed that Reni had been planning to bushwhack him, and he ordered his old adversary to be bound to a fencepost. Swigging deeply from a whiskey bottle, Slade began methodically to shoot Reni in the arms and legs. Finally he jammed his revolver into the wounded man's mouth and pulled the trigger, and it was reported that he then sliced the ears off the corpse.

1862, Fort Halleck, Wyoming. A drunken Slade became embroiled in a shooting scrape at Fort Halleck, and he nearly killed a civilian. A warrant was issued for his arrest, causing him to flee to Montana.

Sources: Langford, *Vigilante Days and Ways,* 360–76; Nash, *Bloodletters and Badmen,* 506–508.

Slaughter, John Horton

("Texas John," "Don Juan")

(b. October 2, 1841, Sabine Parish, Louisiana; d. February 15, 1922, Douglas, Arizona. Rancher, Indian fighter, law officer, state legislator, businessman.) John Slaughter was three months old when his pioneer family moved to a land grant in the Republic of Texas. Reared on a cattle ranch near Lockhart, he began fighting Indians during the Civil War as a "Minute Man of the Texas Rangers," and he continued to serve in this capacity during Indian alerts throughout the 1870's. Indeed, he eventually settled in the midst of Apache country, and as late as the 1890's he led punitive raids against renegades.

After the Civil War, Slaughter established his own ranch in Atascosa and Frio counties, and in 1871 he married and began to raise a family. Slaughter bossed a number of trail drives, and his ranch grew and prospered, but he de-

Texas John Slaughter in 1886, the year he was elected sheriff of turbulent Cochise County, Arizona. *(Courtesy Arizona Historical Society)*

cided to relocate in Arizona. In 1878, unfortunately, his wife contracted smallpox en route to her new home, and she died in Tucson.

During the Lincoln County War, Slaughter ventured into New Mexico and was arrested for killing Barney Gallagher, but he soon won release and returned to Arizona. In 1879 he remarried, and five years later he purchased the sixty-five-thousand-acre San Bernardino Grant, with range in both Arizona and Mexico.

Slaughter built dams and irrigation canals, and eventually he employed twenty or more cowboys, as well as thirty families who lived on the ranch to harvest grain, vegetables, fruit, and hay. When troubled by rustlers and other desperadoes, he used his guns to solve his problems, and in 1886 his Cochise County neighbors elected him sheriff to clean up the outlawry concentrated in Tombstone and Galeyville. In that same year he formed a partnership with trail driver George Lang, who owned the Bato Rico Ranch adjacent to Slaughter's San Bernardino spread. The two men regularly sent beef to California, and they also operated a slaughter house in Los Angeles. In 1890, however, Slaughter bought the Bato Rico from Lang.

During these years Slaughter had been highly active in taming Cochise County, chasing down criminals, breaking up lynch mobs, and winning reelection in 1888. By 1890 the area was orderly, and he retired to his business interests, although he was appointed a deputy sheriff in 1895, holding the commission until his death.

After Slaughter turned in his sheriff's badge, he was able to concentrate on his business interests, and he continued to improve his ranch and the meat market he operated in Charleston. In 1906 he won a seat in the territorial assembly, but he eagerly returned to business after one uncomfortable term. In 1910 he purchased two butcher shops in Bisbee. He was one of the founders of the Bank of Douglas, and he dealt in mortgages with many of his neighbors. As his wealth grew, Slaughter indulged his fondness for cards, frequently playing in high-stakes poker games for twenty-four hours at a stretch. Finally, at the age of eighty, the little cattle baron died peacefully in his sleep.

Gunfights: *1876, South Spring Ranch, New Mexico.* While herding cattle on John Chisum's South Spring Ranch, Slaughter encountered a drunken rustler named Barney Gallagher. Gallagher brandished a sawed-off shot-

gun and challenged Slaughter. The little cattleman rode toward Gallagher, suddenly whipped out a pistol, and triggered a bullet into the rustler's thigh before he could fire. Gallagher pitched out of the saddle, and his partner, a man named Boyd, galloped away. Gallagher was taken to a nearby store, but the bleeding could not be stopped, and he died about midnight.

ca. 1880, Mexico. Slaughter, two black hands named John Swain and Old Bat, and several cowboys had gone into Mexico to retrieve stolen stock. As they drove the animals back toward the ranch, *bandidos* appeared, and Slaughter's Mexican *vaqueros* fled into the brush. But Slaughter and the two Negroes drove the stock into a box canyon and readied their shotguns. The rustlers charged into the canyon, but were blasted and quickly driven away by Slaughter and his men.

1887, Fairbank, Arizona. Slaughter and Deputies Burt Alvord and Doc Hall tracked Gerónimo Baltiérrez, a murderer and bandit, to Fairbank. Baltiérrez and his *señorita* were inside a tent one-half mile from town, and three lawmen surrounded the tent and ordered the outlaw to come out. Baltiérrez slit an opening in the side of the tent and ran away, but he stopped at a nearby fence, and Slaughter killed him with two blasts from his shotgun.

May, 1888, Cochise County, Arizona. Three Mexicans who recently had helped rob a train had sought refuge in the Whetstone Mountains, and there they were discovered by Slaughter, Burt Alvord, and Cesario Lucero. The law officers jumped the fugitives while they were still in their bedrolls. There was a brief flurry of shooting, but when one of their number was wounded, the outlaws surrendered.

June 7, 1888, Cochise County, Arizona. Slaughter, Deputy Burt Alvord, and two Mexicans had trailed a group of bandits to their camp in the Whetstone Mountains. At dawn Slaughter, brandishing a shotgun, ordered the sleeping outlaws to surrender. Slaughter then opened fire, winging one of the fugitives. The bandit leader, Guadalupe Robles, jumped to his feet with a sixgun, and Slaughter shot him dead. An outlaw named Manuel sprinted out of camp, and Slaughter shouted, "Burt, there is another son-of-a-bitch. Shoot him!" Slaughter himself fired, felling Manuel, and he ordered his three posse members to chase and kill him. The deputies went in pursuit, but Manuel managed to escape.

September 19, 1898, San Bernardino Ranch, Arizona. About 7:00 A.M. Slaughter saw a man skulking about his property, and he soon discovered that the suspicious individual was Peg-Leg Finney, a wanted thief. Accompanied by four other men, Slaughter pursued Finney and located him asleep under a tree about one mile from the ranch house. Slaughter and his cohorts quietly approached Finney, and Slaughter picked up the sleeping man's Winchester and tossed it away. At that point Finney sat up and pointed a cocked pistol at Slaughter. Instantly Slaughter whipped up his rifle and triggered a bullet which tore through Finney's right hand and smashed into his chest. Two of Slaughter's men also fired, striking Finney in the head and hip, and he died where he lay.

ca. 1900, San Bernardino Ranch, Arizona. Gambler Little Bob Stevens held up a roulette game in Tombstone, stole a horse, and fled in the direction of the San Bernardino Ranch. Slaughter intercepted Stevens and shot and killed the man.

1901, Cochise County, Arizona. A young man had killed a mother, son, and daughter for three hundred dollars, and Slaughter joined the posse which pursued him. When they caught the murderer, he tried to resist arrest, and they readily shot him to pieces.

Sources: Erwin, *Southwest of John H. Slaughter, 1841–1922;* Klasner, *My Girlhood Among Outlaws,* 258–59; Harkey, *Mean as Hell,* 95–101; Faulk, *Tombstone,* 176–79.

Smith, Bill

(d. 1902, southern Arizona. Stock rustler, train robber.) Smith was a turn-of-the-century outlaw who led a gang of rustlers and train robbers in Utah and Arizona. After the Arizona Rangers were created in 1901, Smith clashed with the small band of lawmen, gunning down Rangers Bill Maxwell and Dayton Graham in separate gunfights. But Graham survived and killed Smith in 1902.

Gunfights: October, 1901, Black River, Arizona. The Smith gang had robbed a Union Pacific train in Utah, then had stolen a herd of horses and headed to Arizona to their hideout at the forks of the Black River. There they were located by three rangers and half a dozen cowboys, who decided that one of the rangers should go for help while the others watched the cabin.

At dusk Bill Smith and his brother were outside the cabin, and Rangers Carlos Tefio and Bill Maxwell threw down on them. The gang leader dashed into the cabin, but his brother walked toward the lawmen, dragging his rifle and feigning submission. Suddenly he brought up his rifle and pumped a slug into Tefio's stomach. The fatally wounded ranger emptied his Winchester, hitting one member of Smith's gang in the leg and another in the foot.

As Tefio staggered away, Bill Smith opened up on Maxwell with a rifle, clipping a hole in his hat and then killing him with a bullet in the eye. At that point the outlaws escaped into the darkness to parts unknown.

1901, Douglas, Arizona. Smith had been hiding in Mexico, but he occasionally ventured into Douglas to enjoy the nightlife. One evening he was approached in front of a store by Douglas Policeman Tom Vaughn and Ranger Dayton Graham. The lawmen asked the stranger what he was doing, but without reply Smith pulled a six-gun and began firing. Both officers were seriously wounded—Vaughn was hit in the neck and Graham in the arm and right lung —and Smith made an easy escape.

1902, southern Arizona. After his recovery, Graham doggedly tracked Smith, searching gambling dens throughout southern Arizona. At last Graham found the outlaw one night at a monte table. Smith jumped up, clawing for his gun, but Graham shot him in the head, then fired two more bullets into his belly. Steel hacksaw blades were found sewn into Smith's coat.

Sources: Breihan, *Great Lawmen of the West*, 83–85; Hunt, *Cap Mossman*, 149, 152–56, 170–74.

Smith, Jack

(d. ca. 1890, Cripple Creek, Colorado. Convict, hired gunman.) Smith was something of a desperado who was sentenced to a stretch in the Colorado penitentiary in 1880. Soon after his release he pistol-whipped a former lawman named Barrett in White Pine, then fled to Cripple Creek. There he led men in defiance of the authorities in the Bull Hill War, which resulted in riots, killings, and destroyed mines. During this violence, however, he was shot to death by the marshal of Cripple Creek.

Gunfights: *October, 1880, Gunnison, Colorado.* On a day late in October, Smith and Tom Lewis rode out of White Pine mining camp and began drinking heavily. On the road they encountered two officers escorting a counterfeiter, and for no apparent reason they held the lawmen at gunpoint and freed the prisoner. Then they rode into Gunnison and began shooting up the streets. After wounding a pedestrian, Smith and Lewis galloped out of town, pursued by nearly twenty men. There was a running fight during which the ruffians outdistanced the posse, although they were captured in Lake City the next day.

ca. 1890, Cripple Creek, Colorado. One of Smith's men had been arrested, and Smith marched into the Cripple Creek jail and began shooting at the cell locks. The city marshal rushed onto the scene and opened fire, and Smith was fatally wounded.

Source: Rockwell, *Memoirs of a Lawman*, 15–21.

Smith, Thomas J.

("Bear River Tom")

(b. 1830, New York, New York; d. November 2, 1870, near Abilene, Kansas. Railroad employee, law officer.) Of

Bear River Tom Smith, brutally slain while serving as marshal of Abilene, Kansas. *(Courtesy Kansas State Historical Society, Topeka)*

Irish descent, Smith was reared in the Catholic faith. He was rumored to have been a member of the New York police force. By 1867 Smith was in Nebraska working with the Union Pacific Railroad. The following year found him engaging in the same type of work in Wyoming, where he became involved in the violent Bear River Riot. Next he served as marshal of several "end-of-the-track" railroad towns before being appointed chief of police of Abilene, Kansas, in June, 1870.

Smith gained considerable renown for his adamant refusal to carry a gun, even during dangerous situations. On one occasion, for example, Smith marched toward a burly fellow named Wyoming Frank, who held a pistol on him. Unflinching, Smith slugged Wyoming Frank, seized his gun, then pis-

tol-whipped him with it. But in November Smith was brutally killed when he tried to serve a warrant. He was buried with a solemn and sincerely grieving community in attendance.

Gunfights: *1868, Bear River City, Wyoming.* A young friend of Smith's had been unjustly thrown in jail. Smith recruited several fellow railroad workers and descended upon the local hoosegow. A group of townspeople offered violent resistance, but the railroad men fought their way inside and freed their cohort. Smith was severely wounded, and he subsequently quit the railroad for work as a peace officer.

November 2, 1870, Abilene, Kansas. On October 23 Andrew McConnell had shot and killed a neighbor named John Shea. A warrant was sworn for McConnell's arrest, and Smith and Deputy J. H. McDonald rode out to McConnell's place, a small dugout about ten miles outside Abilene. McConnell and a friend, Moses Miles, were waiting, and the four men confronted each other.

Smith read the warrant, whereupon McConnell shot him in the chest. Smith just as quickly returned the shot, wounding McConnell. The two bleeding men then grappled, while Miles and McDonald began trading shots. Miles was hit, but continued firing and succeeded in driving McDonald off the premises. Miles then turned and clubbed Smith to the ground. McConnell and Miles dragged the fallen lawman several yards away from the dugout, and Miles picked up an ax and nearly severed Smith's head.

Sources: Miller and Snell, *Great Gunfighters of the Kansas Cowtowns,* 415–19; Streeter, *Prairie Trails & Cow Towns,* 75–80; Drago, *Wild, Woolly & Wicked,* 56–71.

Smith, Tom

(b. Texas; d. summer, 1893, near Gainesville, Texas. Law officer, range detective.) Smith was a Texan who entered law enforcement. He wore a badge in both Texas and Oklahoma, and at one time he held an appointment as a deputy U.S. marshal. In the late 1880's he was employed as a range detective by the Wyoming Stock Growers' Association, and he vigorously pressured area homesteaders and small ranchers on behalf of his cattle baron employers. On one occasion he killed a "rustler" and was indicted for murder, but the political connections of the association (which ultimately included the acting governor and both senators of the state) were sufficient to secure Smith's release.

During the spring of 1892 Smith was dispatched to Texas to recruit gunfighters for an all-out range war in Wyoming's Johnson County. He was authorized to offer five dollars per day and expenses, a three-thousand-dollar accident policy, and a bonus of fifty dollars to each gunman for any enemy shot or hanged. Smith enlisted twenty-six men in and around Paris and headed north. Frank Canton had recruited a similar number of hard cases, and Major Frank Wolcott was appointed to head the expedition, with Smith in charge of the Texans.

A one-hundred-thousand-dollar "extermination fund" had been raised to pay for the invasion, and the "Regulators" were given a list of seventy troublemakers to kill. The plan fell apart, however, and the Regulators were arrested in Buffalo. Strings were pulled, and the Regulators were finally released, but most of them immediately left Wyoming. Smith returned to Texas, where he was killed within a short time.

Gunfights: *November 1, 1891, Powder River, Wyoming.* Nate Champion, considered an outspoken, troublesome "rustler" by the association, was living with Ross Gilbertson in a tiny log cabin on the Powder River. Four association detectives—Smith, Frank Canton, Joe Elliott, and Fred Coates—were assigned to eliminate Champion, and they congregated near his little cabin in the predawn darkness. While they were deciding how to approach the building, one of their number dropped his revolver, and it discharged, being loaded in all six chambers.

The four men panicked, rushed the cabin, and burst through the door. One of the gunmen ordered the prone Champion to surrender, then snapped off a shot. Champion raised up firing, wounding one of his attackers in the arm and another in the ribs, and all four of the detectives promptly fled. They left behind clothing, horses, bloodstains, and a rifle given to Canton by Smith. Elliott was soon arrested, but when Gilbertson, the only eyewitness, disappeared, the charges were dropped.

April 9, 1892, KC Ranch, Wyoming. The Regulators, some fifty strong, were advancing toward Buffalo, where they hoped to surprise the enemy stronghold and hang Sheriff Red Angus and other homesteader leaders. But as they passed the Hole-in-the-Wall area, one of their detectives informed them that Champion and Nick Ray, prominent on their death list, had leased the nearby KC Ranch. The group decided to detour and exterminate Champion and Ray.

The Regulators deployed around the ranch before daybreak—with strict orders to carry only five loads in their revolver cylinders. At dawn Ben Jones, one of two trappers who had spent the night with Champion and Ray, walked out to fetch water, and he was captured. Half an hour later the other trapper, Bill Walker, was also quietly arrested, and within moments the unsuspecting Ray emerged from the cabin. A volley cut him down, but Champion stood in the door to provide cover fire, then dashed out to pull his dying partner inside. Champion's accurate fire nicked a few of the Regulators, and the hours passed by with no frontal assault.

About 3:00 P.M. Jack Flagg, who was on the death list, rode by the KC Ranch accompanied by his stepson at the reins of a supply wagon. When he was fired upon, Flagg cut one of the wagon animals loose for his stepson, and they galloped away with several Regulators in fruitless pursuit.

The Regulators realized that Flagg would spread the alarm, and they determined to finish Champion. Flagg's vehicle was turned into a fire wagon, and when Champion's cabin was engulfed in flames, he made a break. Twenty-eight bullets took the life from his body, and the Regulators pinned a note to his shirt-front reading: "Cattle thieves, beware." But the delay had been fatal, and Champion's courageous fight had caused the collapse of their plans.

Summer, 1893, near Gainesville, Texas. Immediately upon his release from custody Smith returned to Texas, but he lost no time in once more becoming embroiled in trouble. He boarded a train in Gainesville, Texas, which was bound for Guthrie, Oklahoma. But shortly after pulling out of the station, Smith began quarreling with a Negro hard case. Soon the men pulled their guns, and Smith was shot to death.

Sources: Mercer, *Banditti of the Plains,* xxix, 21–73, 122–32; Canton,

Frontier Trails, 88–106; Smith, *War on the Powder River,* 189, 192, 201, 213.

Sontag, John

(d. September 13, 1892, Sampson's Flats, California. Miner, train robber.) During the 1890's John Sontag and his brother George owned a quartz mine near Visalia, California. In 1891 they ventured east and were responsible for train holdups in Minnesota and Wisconsin. Within months they had returned to California, where they robbed a train at tiny Collis Station.

Wells, Fargo and Pinkerton detectives were hot on the trail of the Sontags, and their efforts resulted in the capture of George. For nine months there was a widespread manhunt during which John and accomplice Chris Evans wounded a total of seven posse members. But in September there was a final confrontation which resulted in a marathon gun battle. Two deputies were killed, and both outlaws were finally shot and captured. John died of his wounds, and when his brother heard the news in Folsom Prison, he went berserk and was killed by guards.

Gunfights: January, 1892, near Visalia, California. Suspecting that the Sontag brothers had recently robbed a train at Collis Station, a posse went out to their mine to bring them in. The Sontags defied arrest and began shooting. Two deputies were wounded, and John and George broke through to safety.

January, 1892, San Joaquin Valley, California. The Sontag brothers had been joined by Chris Evans, a crack shot. They were found by a posse while hiding in a barn a few days after the Sontags had shot their way to freedom. George was captured, but John and Evans killed a deputy and burst out of the trap.

September 13, 1892, Sampson's Flats, California. A posse finally located the hideout of John Sontag and Chris Evans, but the two fugitives opened fire and killed two of their pursuers, including former Texas Ranger V. C. Wilson. The posse was quickly reinforced, however, and the eight-hour "Battle of Sampson's Flat" began in earnest. All day Sontag and Evans darted from tree to tree in a desperate effort to escape, but at last both men were gunned down. John Sontag died that night; Evans survived and was sentenced to life imprisonment.

Sources: Conger, *Texas Rangers;* Horan and Sann, *Pictorial History of the Wild West,* 151–52.

Soto, Juan

("The Human Wildcat")

(d. 1871; Sausalito Valley, California. Thief.) Juan Soto, of mixed Indian and Mexican blood, was a large, ugly man who was a notorious California thief and murderer. In 1871 he was involved in a killing in Alameda County, and Sheriff Harry Morse made Soto the subject of one of his relentless manhunts. Morse found Soto several months later, and following a spectacular pistol duel, the fugitive was shot to death.

Gunfights: *January 10, 1871, Sunol, California.* Soto and two Mexican companions entered a Sunol store owned by former assemblyman Thomas Scott. Within moments shooting broke out, and Soto and his men killed clerk

Otto Ludovici. They then looted the store and fired a volley of shots at the apartment in the rear of the store where the Scott family lived. While the Scotts fled through a back door, Soto and his henchmen rode away.

1871, Sausalito Valley, California. Sheriff Harry Morse and a posse traced Soto to the Sausalito Valley in the Panoche Mountains about fifty miles from Gilroy, in a wild area known as the Picachos. While most of his men operated a short distance away, Morse and a deputy named Winchell marched into an adobe building and discovered Soto, along with a dozen other glowering men and women.

Morse instantly drew his pistol and ordered Soto to raise his hands while instructing Winchell to handcuff the fugitive. But when the Mexicans began to produce weapons, Winchell fled the room, and a man and woman seized Morse's arms.

Soto jumped up and drew a revolver, and Morse broke free and put a bullet through his hat. Soto bolted outside, and Morse followed, only to drop to the ground as the outlaw pumped four slugs at him. As Soto charged Morse, the sheriff ran toward his horse and the Henry rifle in a saddle scabbard. Then Morse squeezed off a pistol shot which struck and jammed Soto's revolver, and both men went for other weapons.

Soto ran back inside, shoved a pistol into his belt, clutched two others, and then dashed out to find a mount. The horse he approached bolted, and Soto headed on foot toward the nearest hill. At 150 yards Morse shot him through the shoulder, and Soto, enraged, began to shout and run back toward the law officer. Morse fired the Henry again, and Soto fell dead with a bullet in his head.

Source: Shinn, *Pacific Coast Outlaws*, 12, 38, 55–56, 67–75.

Spradley, A. John

(b. March 8, 1853, Simpson County, Mississippi; d. 1940, Nacogdoches, Texas. Farmer, laborer, law officer, saloon owner.) The oldest of nine children of a Mississippi farmer, A. J. Spradley lived with his family until 1871, when a local shooting scrape sent him scurrying to Texas. For a year he worked at the Nacogdoches farm of an uncle before accepting a job at a mill. In 1880 he was appointed deputy sheriff of Nacogdoches County, and a year later he stepped into the vacated sheriff's office.

In the following decades Spradley served thirty years as sheriff and four years as a deputy U.S. marshal. He was vigorous and shrewd in pursuing criminals, and on occasion he took the precaution of wearing a steel shirt beneath his clothing. He killed three men in gunfights, and twice he was nearly shot to death. As an extra source of income he owned an interest in a Nacogdoches saloon, but after a near-fatal wound he sold out and became an ardent prohibitionist. Following his retirement from law enforcement, Spradley farmed and took an active hand in politics until his death in 1940.

Gunfights: 1871, Simpson County, Mississippi. The eighteen-year-old Spradley had recently thrashed a local youth named Jack Hayes, and trouble occurred again when Hayes and his brother Bill approached Spradley and his brother Bill at the home of a friend. After an exchange of words the Spradleys walked away from the house, but the Hayes brothers produced derringers and opened fire. Bill Spradley went down with wounds in the hip and scalp, but A. J. hauled out an old cap and ball pistol and felled both of his antagonists. The Hayes boys died, and that night A. J. left for Texas.

Summer, 1884, Nacogdoches, Texas. Spradley had arrested a rowdy Saturday celebrant named Bill Rogers and was marching him toward jail when he was intercepted by Whig Rogers, Bill's drunken brother. Spradley told Whig that he, too, would be arrested if he caused any trouble, but Whig replied, "No, John, you are not going to put Bill in jail, not today, no how." Whig then went for his gun.

Spradley released his prisoner, jerked out his revolver, and snapped, "Don't do it, Whig, or I will kill you." But suddenly Bill produced a pistol, and as Spradley turned toward him, he fired twice. One of the slugs plowed into the lawman and tore out his back. Spradley took a few steps, collapsed, and was carried to a hotel. It was thought that he would die, but a silk kerchief was pulled through the wound to heal it, and in time he recovered and resumed his duties.

ca. 1887, Nacogdoches, Texas. On a Sunday morning Spradley had entered a meat market, where he was accosted by a young man who held a political grudge against him. The man pulled a pistol and fired at Spradley. The slug grazed Spradley's head, but he leaped upon his assailant. After a brief struggle the young man escaped, but he was arrested in the street and later imprisoned.

July 16, 1893, Logansport, Louisiana. Two years earlier Spradley had arrested a Logansport saloon keeper named Joel

Goodwin for killing a former employee. Although acquitted on grounds of self-defense, Goodwin bitterly nursed a grudge against Spradley, and when he learned that the lawman would be passing through town on a train, Goodwin determined to kill him. Forewarned, Spradley carried a shotgun to supplement his revolver.

Goodwin had stationed himself behind a tree near the depot, and when the train pulled in, he began flourishing his Winchester and daring Spradley to fight. Spradley was in the baggage car, and Goodwin spotted him and pumped a bullet through a window near the lawman's head. Spradley fired the shotgun, and fourteen buckshot slammed into Goodwin's chest. He died on the spot, and his crazed wife began firing at Spradley. The train left the station before anyone else was hit, but it was forced to return briefly when the engineer remembered that he had not yet picked up the mail.

Sources: Fuller, *Texas Sheriff;* Johnson and Greer, "The Legend of Joel F. Goodwin," *Interstate Progress.*

Standard, Jess

(b. December 13, 1854, Texas; d. March 19, 1935, Tuscola, Texas. Cowboy, gunman, carpenter, farmer.) A cowboy who worked for Pink Higgins during the 1870's, Standard became involved in the bloody Horrell-Higgins feud in Lampasas County, Texas. He later moved his growing family from the Lampasas area and spent the rest of his life as a farmer and carpenter near Tuscola, Texas.

Gunfights: *March 26, 1877, near Lampasas, Texas.* The Higgins faction ambushed Mart and Sam Horrell as they rode to court in Lampasas. Both

Jess Standard, who found himself using a Winchester instead of a lariat while riding for rancher Pink Higgins. *(Author's collection)*

brothers were hit in the first volley, and Sam was thrown to the ground. Mart jumped off his horse and angrily charged his attackers, firing as he ran, and the Higgins men hastily withdrew.

June 14, 1877, Lampasas, Texas. The Higgins and Horrell factions clashed in the streets of Lampasas in a brief but furious gun battle. Bill Wren was wounded, and Frank Mitchell was killed, but none of the Horrell men were hit.

July, 1877, Lampasas County, Texas. Standard and thirteen other men followed Higgins to the Horrell headquarters. They pinned the Horrells inside the ranch house and bunkhouse and wounded two men, but a lively return fire kept them from charging. After a two-day siege their ammunition ran low, and they returned to the Higgins ranch.

Sources: Webb, *Texas Rangers,* 334–39; Gillett, *Six Years with the Texas Rangers,* 73–80; interview with Mrs. Jessie Standard O'Neal, April 26, 1973.

Starr, Henry

("The Bearcat")

(b. December 2, 1873, Fort Gibson, Indian Territory; d. February 22, 1921, Harrison, Arkansas. Cowboy, horse thief, bank and train robber, convict, movie producer and actor.) Henry Starr, part Indian and a relative by marriage of Belle Starr, worked briefly as a cowboy in Oklahoma, then turned to stealing horses and to robbing banks and trains. In 1894, Starr was sentenced to hang for the death of Floyd Wilson, but in 1896, while the case was being appealed, he disarmed fellow-prisoner Cherokee Bill during an attempted jailbreak. Starr won a pardon for his efforts, and he was later pardoned again for good behavior after a stretch in Colorado (1909–13) and a term in Oklahoma (1915–19).

In the 1890's, Starr married a schoolteacher, and in 1920 he wed again, but he was never a model husband. During one period of freedom Starr produced and acted in a western movie filmed in Oklahoma. But he continued to stage bank robberies, and he was fatally wounded during a holdup attempt in 1921.

Gunfights: December 14, 1892, Lenapah, Oklahoma. Law officer Floyd Wilson encountered robbery suspect Starr on the streets of Lenapah (Starr had aided in robbing a Missouri Pacific agent the previous July at Nowata). Wilson swung out of the saddle, hauled

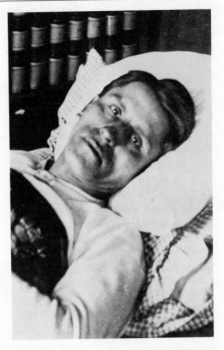

Henry Starr in 1915, after his left leg was shattered while he was trying to rob a pair of banks in Stroud, Oklahoma. *(Courtesy Western History Collections, University of Oklahoma Library)*

out his Winchester, and shouted, "Hold up! I have a warrant for you." Starr cradled his own Winchester and snapped back, "You hold up." Wilson fired one shot, missed, and then discovered that his rifle was jammed. Starr advanced, firing rapidly, and Wilson went down. The wounded lawman pulled his revolver, but Starr shot him twice more, and then fired a final round into his heart. Wilson's clothes smoldered from the point-blank muzzle blast, and Starr, whose own horse had run away during the shooting, mounted the officer's animal and rode away.

January 20, 1893, near Bartlesville, Oklahoma. Starr, Bitter Creek Newcomb, and Jesse Jackson were traveling near Bartlesville when they were spotted by lawmen Ike Rogers and Rufe Cannon. A running fight ensued, and nearly one hundred rounds were fired. Cannon shot Jackson in the side and right arm, and the wounded outlaw surrendered, but Starr and Newcomb managed to escape.

June 5, 1893, Bentonville, Arkansas. At 2:30 P.M., Starr and four accomplices robbed the Bentonville Bank of eleven thousand dollars, but before they could get away, officers and townspeople began shooting at them. Link Cumplin was hit several times and had to be helped onto his horse. The bandits then shot their way out of town, wounding several citizens.

March 27, 1915, Stroud, Oklahoma. Starr led six henchmen in a daring simultaneous robbery of Stroud's two banks. The double holdup began at 9:00 A.M., and within a few minutes the thieves were heading down the street with their loot, protected by human shields. Starr shot at a citizen carrying a shotgun, but the gang then came under the fire of a rifle-wielding seventeen-year-old named Paul Curry. Louis Estes was hit in the neck, Starr's left leg was shattered by a well-placed bullet, and both robbers were arrested.

February 18, 1921, Harrison, Arkansas. Starr and three confederates drove up to the People's National Bank of Harrison and proceeded with a holdup. But with great foresight former bank President W. J. Meyers had installed a back door in the vault and had placed a loaded shotgun inside the door. While Starr was gathering money, Meyers seized the shotgun and opened fire from inside the vault. Starr was slammed to the floor, and his accomplices fled in the car, abandoning their chief. Paralyzed by his wound, Starr died four days later and was buried at Dewey, Oklahoma.

Sources: Adelsbach, "Henry Starr," *Guns of the Gunfighters,* 169–72, 221–22; Drago, *Road Agents and Train Robbers,* 197–98, 208, 215; Shirley, *Heck Thomas,* 157–58; Graves, *Oklahoma Outlaws,* 127–28.

Stiles, William Larkin

(d. January, 1908, Nevada. Law officer, train robber.) Billy Stiles was a young gunman (rumored to have killed his father at the age of twelve) who gained notoriety in the Southwest at the turn of the century. After assisting lawman Jeff Milton, he was hired by Burt Alvord, marshal of Willcox, Arizona. The two law officers soon organized a gang of train robbers, however, including Three-Fingered Jack Dunlap, George and Louis Owens, Bravo Juan Yoas, and Bob Brown.

Stiles and Alvord eventually were exposed, and the next few years brought a series of chases, arrests, and escapes. In 1904 Alvord was captured, but Stiles fled the country and worked his way finally to China. He soon returned to the United States, where he was killed while working as a Nevada deputy sheriff under the alias "William Larkin."

Gunfights: April 8, 1900, Tombstone, Arizona. Stiles, recently released because of confession, entered the Cochise County courthouse at noon and asked jailer George Bravin if he could see Burt Alvord and other members of his gang. After talking with Alvord, Stiles was escorted back outside the cell by Bravin. Stiles then pulled a revolver and demanded the keys. Bravin resisted, and in the subsequent scuffle Stiles shot him in the leg, then released all of the prisoners.

February 17, 1904, Nigger Head Gap, Mexico. While hiding in Mexico, Stiles and Alvord were challenged by two Arizona Rangers who had crossed the border and located the outlaws at Nigger Head Gap. The fugitives tried to shoot their way to freedom, but both were wounded. Alvord, hit twice, surrendered, but Stiles, despite a bullet in the arm, managed to escape.

January, 1908, Nevada. Stiles, serving as a deputy sheriff, attempted to arrest a man, and the trigger-happy former outlaw shot his prey to death. Shortly thereafter Stiles rode back to his victim's house, where the killing had taken place. The victim's grief-stricken twelve-year-old son seized a shotgun and, before Stiles could dismount, killed him with a double blast from the weapon.

Sources: Erwin, *John H. Slaughter,* 232–36, 242, 246–47; Haley, *Jeff Milton,* 271, 302–12, 316–17, 343.

Stilwell, Frank C.

(b. ca. 1857, Kansas-Missouri border area; d. March 20, 1882, Tucson Arizona. Cattle rustler, stage robber, law officer, businessman, gunman, miner, teamster.) The younger brother of noted lawyer and former army scout S. E. ("Comanche Jack") Stilwell, Frank Stilwell came to Arizona in 1878 and worked as a miner and teamster at Signal Camp in Mohave County. Soon he was attracted to booming Tombstone, where he became an associate of N. H. Clanton and his ring of southern Arizona cattle rustlers.

Stilwell managed to secure an appointment as deputy sheriff of Cochise County, of which Tombstone was the county seat. He operated out of the copper mining town of Bisbee, south of Tombstone, but seemed more interested in his business activities with a Tombstone resident named Pete Spence: a Bisbee livery stable and a stage robbing partnership.

After the Tombstone-Bisbee stagecoach was looted of three thousand dollars by two bandits, Spence and Stilwell were arrested. They were acquitted, but soon were arrested again by Wyatt Earp, who was hoping to impress the electorate sufficiently to be elected county sheriff. The pair once more were released, but they nursed a grudge which they paid off after the O.K. Corral fight. An embittered Ike Clanton apparently engaged them to wreak vengeance upon the Earps, and after Virgil and Morgan Earp were ambushed, the surviving brothers knew where to look. While still a deputy sheriff, the twenty-seven-year-old Stilwell was gunned down by Wyatt Earp and four other men.

Gunfights: December 28, 1881, Tombstone, Arizona. While crossing the street half an hour before midnight, Virgil Earp was fired at from the darkness by several shotgun blasts. Although Earp lived, he was seriously wounded in the side and arm. Among the five suspects was Frank Stilwell.

March 18, 1882, Tombstone, Arizona. At 10:50 P.M. Morgan Earp was shot in the back while playing pool. The bullet passed through his body and struck a bystander in the leg. A second slug crashed into the wall near Wyatt, who was watching the game. Morgan died within half an hour, and heading the list of suspected assassins was Frank Stilwell.

March 20, 1882, Tucson, Arizona. Stilwell, either fleeing from Tombstone or in Tucson on court business pertaining to the Bisbee stage robbery, was apprehended by five members of the Earp faction. Morgan Earp's avengers had just placed Virgil and his wife on a train to California and were searching the train for Stilwell.

Stilwell and Ike Clanton were at the depot; spotting the Earps, the pair split up, Clanton heading toward his hotel and Stilwell plunging into the darkness. Stilwell was pursued by Wyatt and Warren Earp, Doc Holliday, Sherman McMasters, and Turkey Creek Jack Johnson, and after five minutes several shots were heard.

Apprehended, perhaps already wounded, Stilwell may have tried to fight off his attackers by grabbing the barrels of a shotgun; the palm of his left hand was blackened by powder burns. A load of eleven buckshot ripped apart his left leg. One bullet passed through his left arm and chest and lodged in his right arm, and another slug, possibly fired while he was on his knees, penetrated his left thigh and entered his calf. A final blast of eight buckshot tore through his chest. Stilwell's shattered body was discovered with his face "contorted with pain or fear."

Sources: Jahns, *Frontier World of Doc Holliday;* Waters, *Earp Brothers of Tombstone;* Breakenridge, *Helldorado.*

Stinson, Joe

(b. 1838, Litchfield, Maine; d. September 6, 1902, Los Angeles, California. Miner, soldier, saloon keeper.) Stinson migrated to the California gold fields during the 1850's. During the Civil War he marched with the California Column into New Mexico, where he remained when peace resumed. He once again fruitlessly pursued the miner's life, building up just enough of a stake to open a saloon in booming Elizabethtown.

In 1871 Stinson killed gunman Wall Henderson, and soon thereafter he moved his saloon business to Santa Fe. There he fractiously became involved in four other shooting scrapes, although he caused no further deaths. By 1890 alcoholism had so seriously debilitated him that he applied for and received a ten-dollar-per-month veteran's pension. In 1895 he was admitted as an invalid to the Pacific Branch of the National Home for Disabled Soldiers near Los Angeles, where he died in 1902.

Gunfights: October, 1871, Elizabethtown, New Mexico. A local hard case named Wall Henderson drunkenly threatened to burn Stinson's saloon, and Stinson stubbornly went for his Navy Colt. Henderson tried for his gun, but Stinson's Colt roared out, and Henderson pitched to the floor, mortally wounded.

1876, Santa Fe, New Mexico. Stinson spent the afternoon in his Santa Fe saloon drinking with an old friend named Van C. Smith. As the two men fell more and more heavily under the influence of liquor, an argument broke out, and the two men stomped away to find weapons. When Stinson emerged from his lodgings, he saw Smith crossing the main plaza armed with a rifle. Stinson immediately began popping away with his pistol. The hail of lead chipped the large Soldier's Monument in the plaza and wounded Smith in the hand and forearm. When Smith collapsed against the monument, Stinson tossed his gun aside and returned to his saloon.

ca. 1879, Santa Fe, New Mexico. Stinson angrily tried to use his gun to settle an argument with a man named Jack Davis. Both men fired several shots, but no one was hit.

ca. 1882, Santa Fe, New Mexico. The belligerent Stinson found himself in yet another quarrel, this time with Charlie Henry, another old friend. Stinson pulled his revolver and angrily pumped a slug into Henry. The wound proved superficial, and Stinson managed to suppress his latest outburst of rage.

June 24, 1886, Santa Fe, New Mexico. About 4:30 A.M., after a long evening of drinking with a friend, Reddy Mc-Cann, Stinson's temper flared, and he drunkenly threw McCann out of his saloon. McCann soon returned to resume the argument, and a flurry of curses filled the air. At last Stinson produced a gun and fired point-blank into McCann's face. McCann collapsed in a pool of blood, and it was thought that he would die. The base of his nose had been shot off, but there was no further damage, and he eventually recovered.

Source: Holben, "Badman Saloon-keeper," *Pioneer West,* February, 1972, pp. 14–18.

Stockton, Port

(b. 1854, Erath County, Texas; d. September 26, 1881, Farmington, New Mexico. Cowboy, gambler, law officer, rustler.) Born the son of a Texas rancher, Port Stockton and his older brother Ike early demonstrated a tendency toward wildness. At seventeen Port assaulted a man and was charged with attempted murder, but Ike helped him to escape the law. Port drifted to Dodge City, then in 1874 he went to Lincoln County, New Mexico, where Ike had opened a saloon. Ike was raising a family, and Port soon married a Baptist preacher's daughter named Irma. But within two years the brothers had moved to Colorado and settled in Trinidad.

In October, 1876, Port got into a shooting scrape in Cimarron, New Mexico, and Ike had to spring him with a predawn jailbreak. Two months later there was another gunfight in Trinidad, and the Stocktons hastily moved to Animas City, Colorado. Port gambled for a while, then secured an appointment as city marshal. But he was run out of town after he angrily chased and fired at a Negro barber who had nicked him with a razor. He briefly held the marshal's job in Rico, Colorado, but he was forced to leave there, too, when his past caught up with him.

Port next moved his wife and two small daughters to a shack just outside Farmington, New Mexico. Port teamed up with a pair of hard cases named Harge Eskridge and James Garret, and the trio was widely suspected of rustling. Then the three undesirables shot up a New Year's Eve party after being thrown out, and hard feelings grew. Port was killed in the violence that followed, and Ike swore revenge.

There was an outbreak of rustling soon thereafter, and when certain area citizens were shot up, Ike was blamed and Governor Lew Wallace issued a reward for his arrest. In September, 1881, Ike was shot in the leg in the streets of Durango, and he died following amputation.

Gunfights: October, 1876, Cimarron, New Mexico. In Lambert's Saloon in Cimarron the abrasive Port entered an argument with a Mexican named Juan Gonzales. Finally Port hauled out his pistol and shot Gonzales to death. Gonzales was found to be unarmed, and Port was arrested, but Ike soon arrived and helped his brother to escape.

December, 1876, Trinidad, Colorado. Once again Port was in a saloon—the barroom of Trinidad's St. James Hotel —and once again an argument broke out. Port had spent the afternoon playing cards, and he soon began quarreling with another player. This man, too, was unarmed, but the enraged Port murdered him. Port was soon captured by a posse, but Ike once more came to the rescue and arranged his escape.

January 10, 1881, Farmington, New Mexico. Alf Graves, a Farmington rancher who had clashed with Port, was riding by the Stockton cabin in the company of Frank Coe and several other friends. Port seized a Winchester, stepped outside, and shouted for Graves to come back and talk. Graves walked his horse back, but after a brief exchange of words he pulled a gun and began firing. He pumped five slugs into Stockton, and Port sank to the ground.

Irma Stockton ran out, picked up Port's gun, and hysterically fired a couple of wild shots, but then Graves squeezed off another round. The bullet hit a wagon spoke and sprayed splinters into her face and eyes, and the shooting stopped.

Sources: Coe, *Frontier Fighter*, 108, 168–70, 186–89, 192–94; Holben, "The Vengeance Vendetta of the Stockton Terror," *Frontier West*, August, 1973, pp. 26–29, 50–51.

Stoudenmire, Dallas

(b. December 11, 1845, Aberfoil, Alabama; d. September 18, 1882, El Paso, Texas. Soldier, farmer, carpenter, wheelwright, businessman.) A member of a large Southern farm family, young Dallas Stoudenmire joined the Confederate army in 1862 and served through the duration of the Civil War, suffering numerous wounds in the course of his duties. For several years after the war he farmed near Columbus, Texas, before becoming a member of Company B of the Texas Rangers.

After a couple of years of Indian fighting, Stoudenmire returned to civilian life as a carpenter and wheelwright in Alleyton, Texas. Between shooting scrapes he engaged in sheep ranching in Oldham County and in the merchandising business in Llano County. He became the city marshal of booming, violent El Paso in 1881.

A tall, rangy, impressive figure, Stoudenmire ceaselessly patrolled the teeming streets of El Paso with a brace of six-guns tucked inconspicuously under his coat in a pair of leather-lined hip pockets. (He also carried a snub-nosed revolver as a hideout gun.) Within days of his appointment as marshal he was involved in two bloody shootouts, and although he thus made bitter enemies, the city fathers were delighted with their new lawman. But Stoudenmire was an alcoholic, and his habits of drunkenly firing his guns in the streets —often in the dead of night—and of running around on his wife Belle soon dimmed his popularity. After a series of absences because of excessive drinking, Stoudenmire was censured, and Deputy Jim Gillett was groomed to replace him. Stoudenmire resigned after just over a year in office, and he then operated the Globe Restaurant, which his brother-in-law had willed him.

In July, 1882, Stoudenmire was appointed a deputy U.S. marshal, but he continued to drink and get into trouble. That summer he took a "cure" at the hot-springs bathhouses near Las Vegas, New Mexico, and by then he had developed such a severe tremor that a friend had to sign the hotel register for him. A short time later he became involved in a drunken saloon brawl in El Paso, and he was shot to death during the brutal gunfight which followed.

Gunfights: 1876, Colorado County, Texas. While riding across the prairie, Stoudenmire encountered a hard case with whom he had been wrangling for the past several months. The two antagonists reined in at some distance, dismounted, and began to hurl insults at each other. They drew their pistols, fired a few ineffective shots, then moved closer. At that point Stoudenmire drilled his opponent, walked over, and coldly watched him die.

1877, Alleyton, Texas. At a large party Stoudenmire became involved in a brawl in which shooting soon erupted. He wounded several adversaries, but was himself shot, bound, and placed under guard. His guard went to sleep, however, and Stoudenmire freed himself and escaped.

1878, near Alleyton, Texas. Stoudenmire and several friends encountered a party led by the Sparks brothers, who were ranchers below Eagle Lake, Texas. Both groups claimed a certain herd of cattle, and a violent melee broke out. When the shooting ended, one of the Sparks brothers was seriously wounded, and two members of the Sparks faction —Benton Duke and his son "Little Duke"—lay dead.

April 14, 1881, El Paso, Texas. Four days after becoming city marshal of El Paso, Stoudenmire watched as sullen crowds of Mexicans and Anglos glared and shouted at each other over the recent murder of two Mexicans. While Stoudenmire was eating a late lunch in the Globe Restaurant, Constable Gus Krempkau was approached by John Hale and George Campbell, a pair of heavy-drinking troublemakers who considered Krempkau a friend of the Mexicans. After an exchange of words, Hale fired a bullet into Krempkau.

As the wounded man staggered back, Stoudenmire pulled his revolvers and ran into the street. Stoudenmire fired at Hale, but the bullet went wild and struck a Mexican bystander. The Mexican had been trying to flee the scene, but Stoudenmire's slug caught him in the back, and he died the next day.

Hale ducked behind an adobe pillar, but when he stuck his head out to peer at Stoudenmire, the marshal sent a bullet crashing into his brain.

Campbell, who had recently threatened Stoudenmire, saw Hale die, and his whiskey courage vanished. He backed into the street, waving his pistol and shouting, "Gentlemen, this is not my fight." But the dying Krempkau had now produced his revolver, and he promptly emptied the weapon at Campbell.

The first bullet broke Campbell's right wrist, and as he scooped up his fallen six-gun with his left hand, another of Krempkau's slugs tore into his foot. At this point Stoudenmire turned on Campbell and pumped a bullet into his stomach. Campbell clutched his middle and gasped, "You big son-of-a-bitch, you murdered me." Campbell was carried away, and he died the following day.

April 17, 1881, El Paso, Texas. A drunken former marshal of El Paso, Bill Johnson, was duped into setting an ambush for Stoudenmire by enemies of the lawman. On Sunday night following the shootout with Campbell and Hale, Stoudenmire was patrolling the streets of El Paso, accompanied by Doc Cummings, the marshal's brother-in-law and close friend. Suddenly Johnson stood atop a pile of bricks and wildly discharged a load of buckshot in Stoudenmire's direction. Stoudenmire and Cummings whipped out six-guns and pumped eight slugs into Johnson, the final bullet severing the dying man's testicles as he collapsed. At this point other antagonists spontaneously opened fire from across the street, but Stoudenmire, ignoring a wound in the heel, charged and routed these enemies.

December 16, 1881, El Paso, Texas. Joe King, an El Paso thug, decided to murder Stoudenmire from ambush. He secluded himself behind a garbage pile near Stoudenmire's boarding house, and when the lawman returned home at 3:00 A.M., King opened fire. The nearby flashes temporarily blinded Stoudenmire, but King's bullets went wild, and the marshal pulled his guns. He fired several rounds and succeeded in sending King fleeing into the darkness.

July 29, 1882, El Paso, Texas. In El Paso's Acme Saloon, William Page, who once had served as Stoudenmire's deputy, entered an altercation with Billy Bell. Stoudenmire dragged Page away from the quarrel, and the two men spent the evening drinking in Doyle's Concert Hall. About midnight they returned to the Acme Saloon and almost immediately began arguing. Stoudenmire angrily drew a gun, but Page knocked the weapon upward just as it went off. Stoudenmire then produced a second revolver, but before he could fire it he was stopped by Jim Gillett, who had recently replaced Dallas as city marshal. Brandishing a shotgun, Gillett broke up the quarrel and marched Page and Stoudenmire to jail.

September 18, 1882, El Paso, Texas. Stoudenmire had long engaged in a feud with El Paso's Manning brothers, and when trouble flared anew, friends tried to arrange a truce. About 5:30 P.M. Stoudenmire and Doc Manning were brought together in the Manning saloon, while Jim Manning went out to find his brother Frank. But Stoudenmire belligerently faced Doc and snarled, "Some liars or damn sons-of-bitches have been lying on both parties and have been trying to make trouble."

"Dallas," retorted Doc, "you haven't stuck to the terms of your agreement."

"Whoever says I have not tells a damn lie," snapped Stoudenmire.

At these words J. W. Jones, co-owner of the saloon, stepped between the two enemies and pushed them apart. But both men pulled guns, and Manning, firing over Jones's shoulder, triggered the first shot. The bullet tore through Stoudenmire's arm and chest, and Dallas dropped his gun and staggered backward into the door. Doc charged his reeling opponent and again fired into his chest, but the slug drilled through papers and a photograph in Stoudenmire's shirt pocket, did not penetrate his body, and succeeded only in knocking the breath from him.

Outside, the two men grappled and fought, and Stoudenmire produced his little belly gun. He shot Doc in the arm, and Manning dropped his pistol, but the little man charged his larger opponent and again wrestled with him, preventing Stoudenmire from firing another shot.

As they fought and cursed up and down the boardwalk, Jim Manning came running back to the scene with a .45 in his hand. He fired at Stoudenmire, but the bullet thudded harmlessly into a nearby barber pole. Jim's second shot, however, ripped into Stoudenmire's head behind the left ear, and with a groan Dallas collapsed in death.

Doc Manning picked up Stoudenmire's short gun, straddled his body, and wildly pistol-whipped the corpse until he was pulled off by lawman Jim Gillett.

Sources: Metz, *Dallas Stoudenmire;* Sonnichsen, *Pass of the North,* 219–20, 223–25, 229, 234, 238, 240, 242–43, 245–46.

Strawhim, Samuel

(b. 1841 or 1842, Illinois; d. September 27, 1869, Hays City, Kansas. Teamster.) A frontiersman of vague background, Strawhim appeared in Kansas in the late 1860's and proved himself to be a troublemaker. He was warned to leave Hays City by local vigilantes, but he adamantly remained and engaged in gunplay with a vigilante leader. Sheriff Wild Bill Hickok shot him to death a few weeks later.

Gunfights: July 23, 1869, Hays City, Kansas. A vigilante committee, of which A. B. Webster was a leader, had ordered Strawhim and Joe Weiss— both ruffians and teamsters from Illinois—out of Hays. About 3:00 P.M. Strawhim and Weiss entered the post office where Webster worked as a clerk. The two hard cases cursed and slapped

Webster, threatening his life repeatedly. Weiss, a former convict, then drew a gun, but Webster produced his own weapon and began firing. Weiss was struck fatally in the stomach, and Strawhim scampered to safety.

September 27, 1869, Hays City, Kansas. A few weeks later Strawhim and several rowdy companions spent the evening of September 26 drinking and causing trouble. About 1:00 A.M. they began to break up a saloon, whereupon the newly elected sheriff, Wild Bill Hickok, appeared with Deputy Pete Lanihan to quell the trouble. A violent melee ensued, with Strawhim leading the ruffians. Hickok whipped out a six-shooter and blazed away. Strawhim was hit in the head and died on the spot.

Source: Miller and Snell, *Great Gunfighters of the Kansas Cowtowns,* 121–22.

Sutton, William E.

(b. October 20, 1846, Fayette County, Texas; d. March 11, 1874, Indianola, Texas. Law officer, rancher, soldier.) A native of South Texas, Bill Sutton served in the Confederate army and after the war moved his family to Clinton in DeWitt County. There he came into conflict with the Taylor clan, and the result was Texas' Sutton-Taylor feud. Texas Ranger Lee Hall held that the feud had begun a few decades earlier in the Carolinas and Georgia, but it flared anew in Texas in the late 1860's.

Sutton's band of "Regulators" at times numbered as many as two hundred and included such stalwarts as cattleman Shanghai Pierce, Indian fighter Old Joe Tumlinson, and vicious lawman Jack Helm. Aligned with the Taylors were the Clements brothers and their cousin from East Texas, the murderous John Wesley Hardin.

For several years there was a violent series of shootouts and ambushes which not even the Texas Rangers were able to halt. At last Sutton moved with his immediate family to Victoria, but Jim Taylor relentlessly sought him out and killed him in Indianola in 1874. The feud continued in bloody fashion until Taylor himself was killed a year and one-half later.

Gunfights: *March 25, 1868, Bastrop, Texas.* Sutton, who had wangled an appointment as deputy sheriff, led a posse from Clinton after a gang of horse thieves. The posse caught the stock rustlers in Bastrop, and a street fight commenced. Charley Taylor was killed, and James Sharp was captured, but on the return to Clinton, Sharp was shot to death while "trying to escape."

December 24, 1868, Clinton, Texas. Sutton encountered Buck Taylor and his friend Dick Chisholm in Clinton, and an argument erupted. Sutton and Taylor went for their guns, and Sutton was backed up by a party of his relatives and friends. When the smoke cleared, Taylor and Chisholm lay dying, and a full-scale feud was triggered by Taylor's demise.

August 26, 1870, DeWitt County, Texas. Henry Kelly, related by marriage to the Taylors, and his brother William created a disturbance at the tiny community of Sweet Home. Shortly thereafter Henry arose at his farm to find three men—Doc White, John Meador, and Jack Helm, a captain of the Texas State Police—waiting outside to arrest him. Kelly surrendered, and the party, now joined by Bill Sut-

ton, proceeded on one-quarter of a mile to the home of William Kelly.

After a couple of shots were fired, William joined the group, but Amanda Kelly, Henry's wife, was worried by the gunfire and hurried to the scene. She arrived just in time to see a general scuffle break out in which her husband was shot out of his saddle. When the shooting stopped, both Kellys were dead, and although Helm swore that they had tried to escape, he was fired from the state police.

April 1, 1873, Cuero, Texas. When Jim Taylor's father was killed by the Sutton faction, Jim had bitterly promised his mother, "I will wash my hands in old Bill Sutton's blood." Young Taylor soon located Sutton in Bank's Saloon and Billiard Parlor in Cuero, and, aided by friends, he attacked the enemy leader. Sutton was seriously wounded, but he recovered and ordered a continuance of the violence.

June 16, 1873, near Clinton, Texas. Riding in a buggy toward Clinton, and accompanied by Doc White, Horace French, John Meador, and Ad Patterson, Sutton was ambushed by a party of Taylor men. The attackers soon were driven off, but not before hitting Meador in the leg and killing French's horse.

December, 1873, Cuero, Texas. As Sutton and several of his friends left Clinton, they encountered a large group of Taylor men. A running fight broke out which lasted all the way into Cuero. Sutton and his followers holed up in the Gulf Hotel and traded potshots with the Taylors for a day and one-half. Then the Taylor party was besieged by Sutton reinforcements until angry Cuero citizens arose and forced the hostilities to end.

March 11, 1874, Indianola, Texas. Sutton and his young wife and child had boarded a New Orleans–bound steamboat when they were approached by Jim and Bill Taylor. Jim immediately opened fire, and while Sutton's horrified wife watched, he was cut down on the ship's deck by bullets in the head and heart. With Sutton was Gabe Slaughter, who was killed when Bill Taylor fired a slug into his head.

Sources: Webb, *Texas Rangers,* 222, 233–38; Sutton, *Sutton-Taylor Feud,* 28–40, 45, 48–52; Webb, *Handbook of Texas,* II, 693–94; Sonnichsen, *I'll Die Before I'll Run,* 50–52, 54, 57, 60, 61, 63, 66, 67, 72–75, 77–78, 82.

Taylor, Bill

(Farmer, gunman, horse thief, rustler, law officer.) The son of Texas farmer Pitkin Taylor, Bill became involved in the bloody Sutton-Taylor feud when his father was gunned down in the summer of 1872. When Pitkin died of his wounds six months later, Bill supported his brother Jim in a vow of revenge. There were two unsuccessful attempts to kill Bill Sutton, leader of the opposition, and these clashes were followed by a bloody progression of ambushes, sieges, and street fights.

Jim rapidly became the more prominent of the Taylor brothers, fighting his way to leadership of his clan against the Suttons, but Bill took part in his share of the bushwhackings and murders. In March, 1874, Bill and Jim finally succeeded in killing Sutton in Indianola, although Bill was later arrested and thrown into the Indianola jail. Luck was with him, however; on September 15, 1875, a fierce storm struck the Gulf Coast of Texas, and during the resultant chaos and destruction

in Indianola, Bill escaped—although before leaving he heroically rescued several people from the surging waters. The following December Jim Taylor was killed, and thereafter the fighting rapidly decreased.

Taylor's next notoriety came in 1877, when he was incarcerated in an Austin jail whose residents at the time included Wes Hardin, Mannen Clements, Johnny Ringo, and members of the Sam Bass gang. A year later rangers arrested Taylor in Cuero on charges of horse theft, assault, and forgery, but somehow he managed to evade imprisonment. In 1881 he was reported to be involved in altercations in Kimble County, but soon he left Texas and moved to Indian Territory. Relatives asserted that he became a law officer there and was killed by a criminal in the line of duty.

Gunfights: *April 1, 1873, Cuero, Texas.* Bill accompanied his brother Jim and several other men to a Cuero saloon in search of Bill Sutton. Sutton was inside, and a flurry of shots broke out in the saloon and billiard parlor. Sutton was seriously wounded, but survived, and when the Taylors set an ambush that summer, he escaped without a scratch.

March 11, 1874, Indianola, Texas. On a tip from Wes Hardin, the Taylor brothers rode to Indianola and boarded a steamboat which was about to leave the dock. On the deck they found Bill Sutton, Gabe Slaughter, and Sutton's wife and child. Mrs. Sutton stared aghast as Jim killed her husband and Bill fatally wounded Slaughter in the head. The Taylors escaped the scene, although Bill later was jailed in Indianola.

Sources: Webb, *Texas Handbook,* II, 693–94; Sonnichsen, *I'll Die Before I'll*

Run, 65, 66, 76–78, 83, 86, 90–91, 94, 95; Sutton, *Sutton-Taylor Feud,* 45, 49, 52–54, 63–66, 69–70.

Taylor, Hays

(d. August 23, 1869, DeWitt County, Texas. Cowboy.) Hays Taylor was a young member of DeWitt County's Taylor family and an early participant in Texas' murderous Sutton-Taylor feud. In 1867 he and his brother Doboy killed two soldiers and thus incurred the wrath of the authorities. Numerous members of the Sutton faction were officers of the law and were therefore able to take legalized action against the Taylors because of this and subsequent incidents. Hays was killed in an ambush near his father's ranch.

Gunfights: *November, 1867, Mason, Texas.* In Mason, Hays and Doboy wrangled with troopers from nearby Fort Mason. One soldier roughed up Hays, who calmly picked himself up and shot the trooper dead. In the firing which followed, a sergeant also was fatally wounded, and the Taylor brothers promptly fled the town.

August 23, 1869, DeWitt County, Texas. Near their father's spread Hays and Doboy rode into the midst of a posse of Sutton "Regulators" led by Jack Helm. In the predawn haze the Regulators opened fire just as Doboy dismounted. Doboy fought his way to safety, but Hays, seeing that his father was cut off, single-handedly charged the bushwhackers. He managed to wound five of the Regulators before they shot him to pieces.

Sources: Webb, *Texas Handbook,* II, 693; Sonnichsen, *I'll Die Before I'll Run,* 39–41, 47, 53; Sutton, *Sutton-Taylor Feud,* 14–20, 22.

Taylor, Jim

(b. 1852, Texas; d. December 27, 1875, Clinton, Texas. Farmer, gunman.) Jim Taylor was a young member of the large DeWitt County family which was embroiled with the Sutton clan in Texas' most violent feud. The Sutton-Taylor trouble had been raging since the late 1860's when, in the summer of 1872, Jim's father, Pitkin Taylor, was lured outside his house by Sutton drygulchers ringing a cowbell. Pitkin was gunned down in his cornfield, and he died six months later.

At their father's funeral Jim and his brother Bill and several other relatives vowed revenge. Over the next two months Jim twice tried to kill Bill Sutton, and he did succeed in putting to death three Sutton men, including the vicious Jack Helm. The day after Helm's death a Taylor party attacked the ranch of Sutton stalwart Joe Tumlinson, but a posse soon arrived, and a truce was signed.

A few months later, in December, 1873, Taylor ally Wiley Pridgen was killed at Thomaston, and the feud again erupted. The Taylors immediately besieged the Suttons in Cuero for a day and a night, then were themselves pinned down when Joe Tumlinson galloped up with a larger band of gunmen.

Within months Jim and Bill Taylor succeeded in killing Bill Sutton and a friend, but the Suttons retaliated by lynching Scrap Taylor, Jim White, and Kute Tuggle in Clinton on June 20, 1874. But after a few other incidents—notably the escape of Bill Taylor from the Indianola jail and the assassination of Rube Brown, marshal of Cuero and new leader of the Suttons—the feud climaxed with the death of Jim Taylor late in 1875. For three years he had been the

Taylors' most vigorous and aggressive leader, and when he was killed, the lengthy struggle rapidly subsided.

Gunfights: *April 1, 1873, Cuero, Texas.* Having sworn to kill Bill Sutton, Taylor located him in Bank's Saloon and Billiard Parlor in Cuero and led several cohorts in firing into the building. Moments later Taylor's party fled, leaving Sutton critically wounded. He recovered, however, and also survived an ambush set by Jim Taylor the following June.

June, 1873, DeWitt County, Texas. Scouring the countryside for Sutton men, Taylor and several friends encountered Jim Cox and a companion. The Taylor band opened fire, and when the shooting stopped, both of their victims were dead.

July, 1873, Albuquerque, Texas. Taylor was with John Wesley Hardin in an Albuquerque blacksmith shop when they saw Jack Helm, a murderous Sutton leader, walking down the street with six friends. Helm boldly strolled straight toward the shop, but Hardin seized a shotgun and blasted him in the chest. Taylor jerked out a pistol and emptied it into the dying man's head, and Helm's six companions quickly retreated.

March 11, 1874, Indianola, Texas. Taylor was told by Wes Hardin that Bill Sutton and his family were scheduled to sail aboard a steamer from Indianola on March 11. On that day Jim and his brother Bill galloped up to the dock and charged onto the steamboat. Standing on the deck were Sutton, his wife and child, and their friend, Gabriel Slaughter. A fight immediately broke out, and Jim Taylor fatally wounded Sutton in the head and heart. Bill Taylor killed Slaughter with a bullet in the head, and the two brothers fled the scene.

December 27, 1875, Clinton, Texas. Jim Taylor and a few of his friends had ridden into Clinton and left their mounts with Martin King when suddenly a Sutton posse rode into town and opened fire. King seems treacherously to have released the Taylor party's horses, and Jim and two of his cohorts named Arnold and Hendricks were cut off from their friends and their animals.

The three men dashed through King's house and tried to shoot their way to a log cabin in a nearby orchard. Sutton man Kit Hunter blocked the way, and Jim knelt and shot his hat off. Hunter hit Jim in the arm, and Taylor tried to run, but heavy fire dropped him and his two companions, and all three men died on the spot.

Sources: Webb, *Texas Handbook,* II, 693–94; Sonnichsen, *I'll Die Before I'll Run,* 63–66, 70, 73, 76–79, 86, 93–94, 112; Sutton, *Sutton-Taylor Feud,* 37–61, 67–68.

Taylor, Phillip

("Doboy")

(d. November, 1871, Kerrville, Texas. Outlaw, cowboy.) Creed Taylor, a veteran of the Texas Revolution, and his brothers Pitkin, William, Josiah, and Rufus were the elders of the DeWitt County family which battled the Suttons in Texas' bloodiest feud. Their sons were among the chief combatants of the murders and shootouts which lasted from the late 1860's until the middle 1870's. Phillip—always known as Doboy—was the son of Creed Taylor, and after the Civil War he was "wanted" by Reconstruction officials. (When he was married, the ceremony was con-

ducted on horseback in the open prairie should flight be necessary, and he took his bride to the Taylor gang hideout for her honeymoon.) Doboy was involved in early shooting scrapes of the Sutton-Taylor feud, and he was shot to death in 1871.

Gunfights: *November, 1867, Mason, Texas.* Doboy and his brother Hays fell into an argument with soldiers from Fort Mason. The antagonists went for their guns, and the Taylor brothers killed two troopers before fleeing. This incident put the Taylor family on the wrong side of the law, thus giving the Sutton faction—many of whom wore a badge in one capacity or another—an excuse to misuse their legal authority against the Taylors.

August 23, 1869, DeWitt County, Texas. Jack Helm, an aggressive leader of the Sutton "Regulators"—set an ambush near Creed Taylor's ranch. Taylor's sons Doboy and Hays rode into the trap, and Helm's posse began firing. After a desperate fight Hays was killed, and Doboy was wounded in the arm.

September 7, 1869, near Pennington, Texas. At the house of William Connor on the Neches River, Doboy and two friends named Kelleson and Cook were jumped at dawn by a party of Regulators. Kelleson was killed immediately, but Doboy and Cook retreated and fought back vigorously. They surrendered after running out of ammunition, but at dusk they managed to escape.

November, 1871, Kerrville, Texas. A man named Sim Holstein had been employed in a job that Doboy wanted, and one afternoon Taylor called him out of his hotel and threatened him. Doboy then pulled a pistol and fired, whereup-

on Holstein aggressively leaped a low gate and grappled with his antagonist.

Holstein tore the gun out of Doboy's hand and shot him. Doboy fell, rose to his feet, and was promptly shot down again. Doboy stood up once more, but Holstein shot him a third time. Again Doboy arose and staggered away, calling for help, but Holstein once more felled him with a final shot. Doboy lasted six hours, bitterly cursing Holstein until he died at 11:00 P.M.

Sources: Webb, *Texas Handbook,* II, 693; Sonnichsen, *I'll Die Before I'll Run,* 39–41, 47–49, 53; Sutton, *Sutton-Taylor Feud,* 14–18, 22–23.

Tewksbury, Edwin

(d. April 4, 1904, Globe, Arizona. Rancher, law officer.) Ed Tewksbury's family moved into Arizona's Pleasant Valley in 1880. The head of the clan was John D. Tewksbury, a restless wanderer whose Indian wife produced three sons—Edwin, James, and John, Jr. After he became a widower John married a Globe widow and sired two more sons.

The Tewksburys experienced difficulties with their ranching neighbors, the Grahams, and when the Tewksburys turned to sheep raising in 1887, a violent feud erupted. Ed was a frequent participant in the hostilities which followed, and he was probably one of the men responsible for the death of the leader of the opposing faction. After a long trial and two and one-half years' confinement in jail, Ed was cleared of all charges in 1896. Until his death in 1904 he served as constable of Globe and deputy sheriff of Gila County.

Gunfights: *1887, Pleasant Valley, Arizona.* The Tewksburys were in a hideout camp which was discovered by the opposing Graham faction. Several cowboys tried to crawl near the camp one night, but Ed, who was posted as a lookout, saw one of them in the moonlight. He called a warning, and Jim Tewksbury fatally wounded the man, thus halting the attack before it could begin.

September 2, 1887, Pleasant Valley, Arizona. Ed was repairing his cartridge belt after breakfast one morning when John Tewksbury and Bill Jacobs were ambushed and killed near camp. The surviving Tewksburys holed up in a hut, and a day-long siege ensued. That night the Tewksbury party managed to slip away, but the cowboys let hogs eat the two abandoned corpses.

August 2, 1892, near Tempe, Arizona. Years after the feud had supposedly ended, John Graham, who had posted rewards for the death of sheepmen, was driving a load of grain from his ranch into Tempe. He was jumped and fatally wounded, but before he died the next morning he stated that Ed Tewksbury and John Rhodes had shot him. The two men were arrested, but eventually they were acquitted by the court.

Sources: Forrest, *Arizona's Dark and Bloody Ground;* Raine, *Famous Sheriffs and Western Outlaws,* 226–35; Coolidge, *Fighting Men of the West,* 123–32; Drago, *Great Range Wars,* 98–146, 291–93.

Tewksbury, Jim

(d. December 4, 1888, Globe, Arizona. Rancher.) Jim Tewksbury was a deadly member of the half-Irish, half-Indian family who clashed in a vicious range feud with cattlemen in the Pleasant Valley War. In 1887 the Tewksburys, who for seven years had raised cattle near Globe, took on a herd of sheep and immediately fell into trouble with cowboys from the Hash Knife outfit and with a family named Graham. (The rumor persisted that a Graham added fuel to the fire by becoming involved in some way with a Tewksbury wife.)

After a Tewksbury collie was killed, the outnumbered sheepmen began sniping at their adversaries. The Grahams offered five hundred dollars for the death of any sheepherder and one thousand dollars for John Tewksbury, Sr. John and his son, John, Jr., were eventually killed, but Jim and other members of the faction extracted bloody vengeance. Jim did not long survive the feud, dying of consumption in 1888 in his sister's home.

Gunfights: *August 10, 1887, Pleasant Valley, Arizona.* Eight cowboys, led by Hash Knife man Tom Tucker, rode up to Jim Tewksbury's cabin looking for trouble. Tewksbury came to the door, and after an exchange of words, shooting broke out. A volley from Jim and his friends killed Hampton Blevins and John Paine outright, and Tucker, Bob Gillespie, and Bob Carrington were wounded. Tucker managed to empty his gun at Tewksbury and his companions, and he survived the fight to become a law officer in Santa Fe.

1887, Pleasant Valley, Arizona. The outnumbered Tewksburys were constantly on the move, driving their herds from one mountain camp to another. One moonlit night several cowboys crept toward the sheep camp, but one of their number was spotted by lookout Ed Tewksbury. Jim whirled and fired, breaking the man's leg. The other would-be attackers could not move for fear of discovery, and their wounded comrade bled to death.

September 2, 1887, Pleasant Valley, Arizona. John Tewksbury and Bill Jacobs left breakfast to round up horses—thereby walking into an ambush. Cowboy Andy Blevins opened fire, killing both men, and he drove away Mrs. Tewksbury when she tried to run to her fallen husband. Throughout the rest of the day there was sporadic sniping, but that night the Tewksburys escaped. The frustrated cowboys then let hogs devour the bodies of Jacobs and John Tewksbury.

September 16, 1887, Pleasant Valley, Arizona. Two weeks later the Tewksburys were camped just below John's home on Cherry Creek when they were attacked at dawn by several cowboy-gunmen. Jim Tewksbury and Jim Roberts opened fire from their blankets, fatally wounding Harry Middleton, hitting Joe Underwood in both legs, and driving off their other assailants.

Sources: Forrest, *Arizona's Dark and Bloody Ground;* Raine, *Famous Sheriffs and Western Outlaws,* 226–35; Coolidge, *Fighting Men of the West,* 123–32; Drago, *Great Range Wars,* 98–146, 291–93.

Heck Thomas, one peace officer who did not moonlight outside the law. *(Courtesy Western History Collections, University of Oklahoma Library)*

Thomas, Henry Andrew

("Heck")

(b. January 6, 1850, Oxford, Georgia; d. August 11, 1912, Lawton, Oklahoma. Soldier, railroad guard, detective, law officer.*)* Heck's parents intended that he become a Methodist minister, but the impetuous boy ran away during the Civil War and served in Stonewall Jackson's brigade as a courier. In 1871 Thomas married an Atlanta preacher's daughter and began raising a family, and soon he migrated to Texas and worked as a railroad guard. By 1879 he had been promoted to chief agent for the Texas Express Company in Fort Worth, where he learned a great deal about law enforcement from the local chief of police, Longhaired Jim Courtright.

At the age of thirty-five Heck left his job to run for the vacant office of chief of police, but after a narrow defeat he was employed by the Fort Worth Detective Association. Soon he tracked down a pair of long-sought fugitives, and shortly thereafter he was appointed a deputy U.S. marshal.

Thomas moved his wife and children to Fort Smith, Arkansas, and began scouring Indian Territory for wanted men under the jurisdiction of Judge Isaac Parker.

Within less than two years Thomas' wife, disgusted with frontier life in general and, specifically, with her husband's long absences and dangerous occupation (during this period fifteen Indian Territory officers were killed), took their five children back to Georgia and divorced him. But in 1888, while Thomas was in Tulsa recuperating from wounds, he met a schoolmarm and preacher's daughter named Mattie Mowbray, and three years later the couple married and Heck began siring a second family.

By this time Thomas was headquartered in Oklahoma, and he was highly active in trailing and hounding the Dalton and Doolin gangs. One of Thomas' greater accomplishments came late in 1893, when he was assigned to help Bill Tilghman tame "Hell's Half Acre," the tempestuous boom town of Perry, which boasted 110 saloons and twenty-five thousand vigorous citizens. During a three-year period, 1893–1896, Thomas was responsible for the arrest of more than three hundred wanted men, and he became noted as one of the "Three Guardsmen"—himself, Tilghman, and Chris Madsen. Later Thomas spent seven years as chief of police in Lawton, but he lost the job in 1909 when his health began to fail. He died within three years at the age of sixty-two.

Gunfights: March   18,   1878, Hutchins, Texas. At 10:00 P.M. the Sam Bass gang held up a train which Thomas was guarding. Several innocent men were used as shields so that Thomas could not fire at the outlaws. The express car was riddled with bullets, and Thomas was hit in the neck and nicked beneath the eye, Thomas hid the money packages, totaling twenty-two thousand dollars in the stove. When the outlaws chopped down the door, they looted the safe of decoy packages and rode off happily, their booty sack containing several fake money packages and cash amounting to eighty-nine dollars.

September 6, 1885, near Dexter, Texas. Thomas and Deputy U.S. Marshal Jim Taylor had been combing Cooke County and nearby areas for murderers Pink and Jim Lee, who had large rewards on their heads. At last, after a two-month search, the lawmen discovered the fugitive brothers at sunup cutting a fence on the prairie near Dexter, on their way from Indian Territory to a nearby hideout. When the Lees had ridden to within seventy-five yards, the bounty hunters stood, leveled their rifles, and ordered the outlaws to surrender.

The Lees went for their guns, and the lawmen began firing. Pink fell immediately, blood streaming from his head and ears. Jim Lee squeezed off three shots, then collapsed with a slug in the throat. The officers secured a wagon, loaded the corpses, and transported them to Gainesville, the county seat.

1886, eastern Indian Territory. Thomas had taken his wife for a buggy ride, and at a scenic stream he unhitched the horses to let them water themselves while he escorted his wife to the top of a hill to enjoy the view. At that point a halfblood tried to steal their horses, but Thomas spotted him and wounded the would-be thief. Thomas then handcuffed the half-blood and carried him to Fort Smith in the buggy.

June 27, 1888, Snake Creek, Indian Territory. Thomas and three posse members, Burrell Cox, Hank Childers, and Jim Wallace, were in search of a gang that had recently robbed a train. The lawmen located the outlaws at an illegal still on Snake Creek, but when Thomas ordered them to surrender, their leader, a moonshiner named Aaron Purdy, opened fire. Thomas was struck twice: one slug broke his right wrist, and the other opened an eight-inch wound in his left side. As Thomas pitched out of the saddle, his three deputies gunned Purdy down, then accepted the prompt surrender of the other outlaws.

1889, near Tahlequah, Oklahoma. Thomas led fellow officers L. P. ("Bones") Isbel, Dave Rusk, and a deputy named Salmon in an attempt to capture Indian fugitive Ned Christie. Christie's home was located in a heavily wooded area fifteen miles southeast of Tahlequah, and the posse closed in on the cabin and blacksmith-gunsmith shop at daybreak. Dogs began barking, and Christie alertly opened fire from a loft in the cabin. Thomas, crouching behind the shop, set the log building on fire. At that point Christie shattered Isbel's shoulder with a rifle slug, and Thomas ran to pull his cohort to cover. The fire soon spread to the house, and Christie's wife and son ran towards the woods. Rusk and Salmon blazed away, hitting the boy in the hip and a lung.

As his family struggled to safety, Christie dashed outside. Thomas fired a rifle shot that struck the Indian in the face, mutilating his nose and blinding his right eye. Christie fled to the woods, however, and made good his escape while the officers tended to the severely wounded Isbel.

January 26, 1890, Oklahoma. Thomas encountered Jim July, who had jumped bail after being charged with robbery. July tried to resist arrest, and Thomas shot him to death.

November 29, 1892, Orlando, Oklahoma. Thomas, Chris Madsen, and Tom Houston had journeyed to Orlando in an attempt to catch fugitive Ol Yantis at his sister's farm near town. At dawn they spotted Yantis coming outside to feed stock, cautiously carrying a revolver. When ordered to surrender, Yantis blazed away at Thomas. As Heck ducked behind a rock wall, his two cohorts cut the outlaw down.

Spring, 1895, near Bartlesville, Oklahoma. Thomas and two Osage scouts, Spotted Dog Eater and Howling Wolf, had trailed Little Bill Raidler to a cave near Bartlesville. Raidler saw them and opened fire as they approached. Thomas pulled out his .45-90 Winchester and fired back, shattering Raidler's hand and sending him running into the brush.

The little posse searched for the fugitive, but all they found were two mangled fingers Raidler had amputated. A week later, however, Raidler was wounded and captured by Bill Tilghman and two other officers.

August 25, 1896, Lawson, Oklahoma. Thomas and a posse had discovered that Bill Doolin was hiding with his family at a farm near Lawson owned by his father-in-law. Doolin came walking slowly down a moonlit lane, leading his horse and gripping a Winchester. Posse members were hidden on both sides of the lane, but when Thomas shouted for him to surrender, Doolin began throwing lead. A shot from the posse knocked the Winchester out of his hands, but he pulled a pistol and kept firing. Thomas and Bill Dunn then blew him off his feet with shotguns: twenty-one holes were counted in his body.

November, 1896, near Sapulpa, Oklahoma. Thomas, his son Albert, and two of the Dunn brothers found Dynamite Dick Clifton and a pair of henchmen camped twenty miles west of Sapulpa. There was a brief pitched battle, but the outlaws managed to slip away, leaving their baggage and one horse.

Sources: Shirley, *Heck Thomas;* Croy, *Trigger Marshal;* Drago, *Road Agents and Train Robbers,* 182, 194, 199, 209–17.

Thompson, Ben

(b. November 11, 1842, Knottingley, England; d. March 11, 1884, San Antonio, Texas. Printer, gambler, saloon operator, convict, soldier, law officer.) The oldest child of a British naval officer, Ben immigrated with his family in 1851 to Austin, Texas, where close relatives lived. Ben attended school through his middle teens, then spent the next two years working as a printer for an Austin newspaper. After a couple of adolescent shooting scrapes, Ben went to New Orleans in 1860, worked as a bookbinder, became involved in another violent incident or two, and soon returned to Austin.

At the outbreak of the Civil War Ben joined the Confederate army and served the duration in Texas, New Mexico, and Louisiana. All his activities were not

The deadly Ben Thompson, gambler, Texas Ranger, and gunman, who participated in fourteen gunfights. *(Courtesy Western History Collections, University of Oklahoma Library)*

military, however. He participated in high-stakes gambling; he injured a leg when his horse fell on him while he was smuggling whiskey; and while he was on furlough recovering from the leg injury, he married Catherine Moore, the daughter of a well-to-do Austin family. He was also rumored—inaccurately—to have shot an officer and two enlisted men in a fight following a quarrel.

There was a shootout caused by a gambling dispute, however, and after the war Ben was jailed in Austin because of still another shooting. He bribed a pair of guards and, accompanied by the dishonest pair and five other recruits, went to Mexico to enlist in Emperor Maximilian's forces. Awarded a commission in Matamoros, Ben fought bravely, engaged in gambling as often as possible, and escaped back to Texas after Maximilian was executed.

Ben continued to gamble, bought an interest in a saloon, helped his brother Billy escape after a killing, and had shooting trouble with his brother-in-law. When Ben threatened the life of an Austin justice of the peace, he was tried and sentenced to four years in prison. He served two years, being released in 1870 when Reconstruction ended in Texas.

The next year Thompson journeyed to Kansas, opening the Bull's Head Saloon in the roaring cattle town of Abilene. His partner in the saloon was an old Texas acquaintance, Phil Coe. Under their direction the Bull's Head prospered, and by summer Thompson sent for his wife and young son. Unfortunately, the day Ben met them in Kansas City, the buggy overturned, breaking Ben's leg, crushing the boy's foot, and so severely injuring Mrs. Thompson's arm that amputation was necessary. The family was laid up for three months, after which Ben sold his interest in the Bull's Head and returned to Texas.

Having sampled the prosperity of the cattle towns, however, he was lured back to Kansas in 1873, settling in June in that season's most promising railhead, Ellsworth. Billy arrived in town a few days later, and on June 11 the brothers were fined for discharging their weapons in the street.

More serious trouble arose the following month, trouble which culminated in the death of Sheriff C. B. Whitney at the hand of a drunken Billy. There was widespread ill feeling in Ellsworth, and after seeing that Billy had escaped, Ben left town himself, returning to Austin by way of Kansas City, St. Louis, and New Orleans.

Ben gambled, became involved in another shootout, helped Billy win acquittal in Ellsworth, then traveled with his brother to Dodge City in 1878. While there, Ben bullied performer Eddie Foy and met with his friend Bat Masterson, whom he soon would ask to rescue Billy after a shooting scrape in Nebraska.

The next year Ben went to booming Leadville, and while in Colorado he was a participant in the "Grand Canyon War" between the Denver and Rio Grande and the Atchison, Topeka and Santa Fe railroad lines. Hired by Santa Fe officials to lead the defense of their property in Pueblo, Ben was ultimately arrested, but after his release he used his five-thousand-dollar fee to open a string of gambling rooms in Austin.

Back in Austin he was involved in a series of minor scrapes and joined a group of volunteers who inflicted one of the last punitive expeditions upon the Comanches of Texas. In 1879 he was defeated for the office of Austin city marshal, but he ran again in 1881 and won.

Although Thompson proved to be an excellent peace officer, he resigned in 1882 after killing Jack Harris in Harris' Variety Theatre in San Antonio. After his resignation he began to drink heavily, his gambling activities went downhill, and he was repeatedly involved in minor disturbances.

In 1884 Ben and his friend King Fisher were killed in San Antonio at the Variety Theatre. Ben was mourned not only by his wife and children, but by the numerous orphans he very generously supported.

Gunfights: *October, 1858, Austin, Texas.* Ben had a quarrel with another teen-ager, a local Negro named Joe Smith. Ben ran home and came charging back with a single-barreled shotgun, which he discharged when Smith turned and ran. The Negro was struck in the back by a load of birdshot, and Ben was fined one hundred dollars and costs and sentenced to six days in jail. Because of Ben's age, however, Governor Hardin R. Runnels intervened and directed him only to pay court costs.

1859, Austin, Texas. A group of boys hunting geese near Austin split into two parties, aligning themselves on both sides of the Colorado River. When a flock of geese appeared, the group opposite Ben's side fired too soon, scaring the prey off. Angry words broke out, then the two groups began blazing away at each other with their shotguns. The shooting stopped when Ben and the leader of the other side agreed to fight a duel. The two boys faced off forty paces from one another and fired their shotguns. Both teen-agers were wounded, and Ben's opponent was hit so severely that his friends had to carry him home.

1860, near Austin, Texas. A party of Indians had boldly ridden into the outskirts of Austin and carried off five children. Ben joined the pursuing posse, which set an ambush in the hills. When the raiding party rode into the trap, Ben anxiously fired first, knocking the leader off his horse. In the melee which followed, the children were rescued, and only one Indian escaped.

1860, New Orleans, Louisiana. A man entered Samuel W. Slater's bookbindery and tried to steal several items. Ben, working as an apprentice, surprised him, grabbed a gun, and wounded the thief. Ben was taken into custody, tried, and acquitted.

1864, Laredo, Texas. Assigned to Colonel Rip Ford's regiment, Thompson found border duty tedious, and when off-duty he opened a monte game. One night he and his brother Billy, also a member of Ford's troops, played against a group of Mexican soldiers, who proceeded to lose their pay and sidearms to the *gringos.* By 2:00 A.M. the Mexicans were growing restive, and Ben whispered to his brother to go and arm himself.

Lieutenant Martino Gonzales soon appeared, declared the game closed, and demanded that Ben return the guns. Ben refused, whereupon Gonzales went for his gun, and a player named Miguel Zertuche jammed his pistol against Ben's chest and pulled the trigger. The gun misfired, and Ben shot Zertuche in the head, then whirled and pumped a slug into Gonzales' chest. Ben darted out the door and dove into a pool outside. When he emerged, he encountered Billy; the two brothers split up and escaped the angry Mexicans in the darkness.

1865, Austin, Texas. Ben and a few cohorts got into a fight with occupation troops just south of Austin. In the shootout which followed, two or three soldiers were killed, and Thompson was arrested and thrown in jail.

1866, Matamoros, Mexico. Having spent the early part of the evening gambling unsuccessfully, Ben stopped in at a dance. He had a quarrel with a Matamoros police officer over a *señorita.* The Mexican drew a knife and lunged at Ben. Ben stepped aside, clubbed the officer with his gun, then shot him four times. Later that night, however, Ben's troops moved into the interior, and there was no further trouble over the killing.

1867, Austin, Texas. Shortly after returning from Mexico, Ben intervened in a political quarrel between Judge Julius Schuetze and five other men. Becoming angry, the five men drew knives and apparently were about to carve up the judge when Ben drew his pistol and charged, driving the knife wielders away.

September 2, 1868, Austin, Texas. Five years earlier Ben had had a run-in with his brother-in-law, James Moore. Moore had sold all of Ben's mother's iron kitchenware to a local cannon factory, and an angry Ben, home on furlough, chased Moore down and fired at his feet and over his head.

The two were never reconciled, and when Moore struck Ben's wife, the gunfighter went after him again. Ben later claimed that, as on the previous occasion, he did not intend to wound Moore, merely to shame and frighten him. But one slug inflicted a slight wound in Moore's side, and although Ben turned himself in, he quarreled with a justice of the peace, threatening to kill the magistrate. Ultimately Ben served two years in the state penitentiary because of this incident.

August 15, 1873, Ellsworth, Kansas. Ben was running a game of monte in Joe Brennan's saloon and lined up some side bets with a gambler named John Sterling, who said he would split his winnings with Ben. Drinking heavily, Sterling won a large sum and left the saloon.

About 3:00 P.M. Ben found Sterling in a nearby saloon, drinking with Happy Jack Morco, a local policeman. There were angry words between the two gamblers, and Sterling finally hit Thompson in the face. Morco then drew his gun, and the unarmed Thompson was forced to back off.

Ben returned to Brennan's, and soon Morco and Sterling burst in and shouted, "Get your guns, you damn Texas sons-of-bitches, and fight!" Because of a local ordinance, none of Ben's friends were armed, so he bounded off to his hotel and picked up his Winchester and six-gun. Outside he encountered his younger brother, who had grabbed a shotgun.

Billy was staggering drunk, and just as Ben warned him to be careful, Billy pulled one of the triggers, nearly hitting Major Seth Mabry and Captain Eugene Millett with a load of buckshot. Ben seized the weapon and handed it to a bystander, then stepped out and bellowed: "If you, you damn sons-of-bitches, want to fight us, here we are!"

At that moment Sheriff C. B. Whitney and a former policeman named John DeLong intervened and tried to cool off the Thompson brothers. "Come on," said the unarmed Whitney, "let's go over to Brennan's and have a drink." By now Billy had recovered his shotgun, and as the four men walked to the saloon, Ben and Whitney again tried to talk him into giving up the weapon.

Just then someone shouted, "Look out, Ben," and Ben turned to see Morco and Sterling charging, guns in hand, with Morco in the lead. Ben threw up his rifle and fired at Morco, but the bullet smashed into the casing of a doorway into which Morco ducked. Before Ben could squeeze off another shot, there was a deep-throated report behind him, and he whirled to see Whitney stagger and fall, shot by Billy. "My God, Billy," exclaimed Ben, "you've shot your best friend!"

Ben got the drunken Billy to leave town, then stationed himself in his hotel. An hour passed, and when the city police force could not screw up sufficient courage to arrest Ben, Mayor James Miller approached the gunfighter and ordered him to surrender his weapons. When Ben refused, Miller stormed out and fired the entire police force. However, Deputy Sheriff Ed Hogue persuaded Morco to give up his arms, whereupon Ben allowed himself to be taken into custody.

The next morning Ben appeared in court to answer the charge of firing at Morco, but Happy Jack failed to show up, and Ben was released.

December 25, 1876, Austin, Texas. Mark Wilson, proprietor of an Austin variety theater, had a man named James Burditt ejected for rowdiness late in December. Burditt had given Billy Thompson a horse when he had tried to escape from Texas Rangers the previous fall, and Burditt threatened Wilson with Ben's name.

When it was rumored that Ben planned to make trouble Christmas evening, Wilson placed a small arsenal behind his bar and asked for police protection. When firecrackers broke out in the audience, Wilson asked a policeman named Allen to arrest Burditt, who was present.

Ben tried to intervene, and Wilson grumbled: "Who is running this house, you or I, Mr. Thompson? You attend to your business and I will attend to mine." A heated exchange followed, and Ben took a swing at Wilson, succeeding only in cutting Allen's face with his ring. Allen shoved Ben, who stepped back.

By this time Wilson had darted behind the bar and picked up a shotgun; bartender Charles Mathews armed himself with a rifle. Wilson aimed at Ben and yelled, "Clear the way there!"

The onlookers scattered, and one shouted, "Look out, there is going to be a shooting." Someone jostled Wilson as he fired, and a load of buckshot whistled over Ben's head.

By then Ben had palmed his six-shooter; he fired three times, each slug striking Wilson, who died instantly. As Ben pumped lead into Wilson, Mathews squeezed off a shot which grazed Thompson in the hip. Ben then severely wounded the bartender; his slug entered the man's mouth, knocked out several teeth and lodged in his neck. Ben surrendered to the authorities and was acquitted the following May.

1880, Austin, Texas. Ben was something of a dandy, and his cane, gloves, and stovepipe hat caught the attention of several drunken visitors to Austin from San Saba County. They stopped him on the street, and, seeing that they thought him a dude, Ben acted the part of an ill Easterner who was in Texas for his health.

After some rough joking, the men twice knocked Ben's new hat off his head. Ben's temper flared, and, drawing his pistol, he snarled, "You infernal scoundrel and coward, what do you mean? Is this the way you would act toward a stranger and sick man? I am Ben Thompson and equal to a dozen white-livered fiends like you."

The man Ben was dressing down jerked his gun, jumped behind an awning post, and snapped a shot at Thompson. Ben returned his fire, nicking the man's ear and, as the frightened drunk fled the scene, grazing his side. Ben was arrested, but cleared of a charge of assault.

July 11, 1882, San Antonio, Texas. For two years Ben and Jack Harris had feuded over a gambling incident which occured in 1880. Harris had been a seaman and a filibuster with William Walker in Nicaragua; had served as a policeman in San Antonio; and now owned and operated, along with partners Joe Foster and Billy Simms, the Vaudeville Theatre and Gambling Saloon, the most notorious night spot in San Antonio.

Ben entered the theater on the afternoon of the eleventh and, finding Harris absent, issued a belligerent challenge and left. Thompson returned later, had a drink at the bar, and exited through one door as Harris, alerted by an employee, entered through another. Outside, Ben stopped to talk with Simms, who was an old acquaintance.

In the meantime, Harris picked up a shotgun and, cradling it in his lame left hand, slipped behind the Venetian blinds on the door nearest Thompson. Several patrons, sensing trouble, stampeded outside, and one shouted, "Jack has got his gun."

Thompson peered inside and asked, "What are you doing with that gun?"

"Come on," replied Harris, "I'm ready for you."

Harris raised his weapon, but Ben drew and fired through the blinds. The shot ricocheted and struck Harris in the right lung. Harris lurched back, and Ben stepped inside and triggered a second shot, which missed. Harris then staggered upstairs, collapsed in the hall, and was carried to his home, where he died that night.

Ben surrendered himself, resigned as marshal of Austin, and was at length acquitted, and upon his return to Austin he was met with a spontaneous parade by well-wishers.

March 11, 1884, San Antonio, Texas. That day Ben met King Fisher, deputy sheriff from Uvalde who was in Austin on official business. The two men had

several drinks, then Ben decided to travel by train with Fisher as far as San Antonio, where Ben hoped to see a play scheduled to open the next day in Austin. On the train the men continued to drink and were quite rowdy.

After attending the play, at 10:30 P.M. Thompson and Fisher entered the Variety Theatre, where Ben had killed Jack Harris. Billy Simms, Joe Foster, and bouncer Jacob Coy apprehensively joined Thompson and Fisher upstairs in a booth overlooking the vaudeville show. The group had a drink together, but when the conversation turned to the Harris killing, Fisher arose and uneasily tried to talk Ben into leaving. But harsh words broke out between Foster and Thompson, and Coy told Ben to stop causing trouble. Ben then slapped Foster and jammed his six-gun into the man's mouth. Coy grabbed the cylinder of the revolver, and Foster scuffled with Ben.

A moment later gunfire erupted: Coy suffered a flesh wound, Foster was shot in the leg (and died following amputation), and King and Ben lay dead, with thirteen and nine wounds, respectively. King never drew his pistol, and the only shot Ben fired was when Coy grabbed his gun (this shot, incidentally, was probably the one which hit Foster).

Vaudeville performer Harry Tremaine, gambler Canada Bill, and a bartender named McLaughlin probably joined in the shooting, having been earlier alerted by Foster and Simms and stationed in an adjoining box. Most of the wounds in Thompson and Fisher were caused by shotgun and rifle fire, and there were powder burns on their faces.

Sources: Streeter, *Ben Thompson;* Paine, *Texas Ben Thompson;* Miller and Snell, *Great Gunfighters of the Kansas Cowtowns,* 73, 131, 280,

444–48; Schoenberger, *Gunfighters,* xvi, 24, 81, 82, 84, 85, 99, 113, 125, 147–70, 197; Masterson, *Famous Gunfighters,* 24–35; Raymond, *Captain Lee Hall of Texas;* Horan, *Authentic Wild West,* 123–54.

Thompson, William

("Texas Billy")

(b. ca. 1845, Knottingley, England; d. ca. 1888, Laredo, Texas[?]. Soldier, gambler, outlaw.) Younger brother of Ben Thompson, Billy moved as a boy to Austin, Texas, where the main occupations of his father were drinking and catching fish, which the two brothers sold around town. During the Civil War Billy enlisted in the Second Regiment of Texas Mounted Rifles—the celebrated "Horse Marines"—fought in Louisiana, and was assigned with Ben to border duty, where the brothers ran various monte games. In 1868 Billy killed a soldier and, aided greatly by Ben, escaped to the lawless Indian Territory.

Four years later Billy turned up in Abilene as a house dealer in the Bull's Head Saloon, co-owned by Ben. The next year Billy went with Ben to Ellsworth and took up with a prostitute named Emma Williams, who soon switched her affections to Wild Bill Hickok. Billy then began romancing Molly Brennan, who later was killed in the noted gunfight between Bat Masterson and Sergeant King. In Ellsworth in June, 1873, Billy and Ben shot their guns off in the street and the next day were fined for the offense. Graver trouble arose two months later when Billy, staggering drunk, accidentally shot and killed Sheriff C. B. Whitney. Friends helped him leave town, after which he dismounted, stretched out on

Texas Billy Thompson in Ellsworth, Kansas, in 1872, the year before he killed C. B. Whitney. *(Courtesy Western History Collections, University of Oklahoma Library)*

the prairie sod, and slept off his drunk. That night he wandered back into Ellsworth and saw Ben secretly, then after hiding in the vicinity for four or five days, he made his way to Buena Vista, Colorado, where the local outlaw element elected him mayor of the community. The governor of Kansas offered five hundred dollars for Billy's arrest, but it was three years before he was apprehended, after having returned to Texas. Captured by Texas Rangers, he was extradited to Kansas and eventually acquitted of Sheriff Whitney's murder.

Billy returned to Austin, went to Dodge City with Ben, then drifted into Nebraska, where he was wounded in a shootout in Ogallala. He was delivered out of that hostile town by Bat Masterson, after which he wandered back to Texas.

Billy continued to be a heavy drinker, but he was sober the night that Ben and King Fisher were killed. Billy was in San Antonio and, by coincidence, just three doors away when his brother was shot. He rushed to the scene, but was unarmed, and he merely walked the night streets in aimless grief.

Little is known of Billy's later years: in 1882 he hid in El Paso for several months to escape a murder charge in Corpus Christi, and it is rumored that he was killed in Laredo about 1888.

Gunfights: *September 2, 1868, Austin, Texas.* Billy and a U.S. Army sergeant named William Burke went together to a house of ill repute. Spotting three drunken soldiers sleeping in the yard, Billy suggested to Burke that they strip the trio and hide their clothes. Burke, insulted, stiffly refused, and later that night he burst in on a sleeping Thompson and threatened to drive him outside naked. Billy grabbed his pistol and shot Burke, who died the next day. Billy fled to the hills west of Austin and eluded search parties until Ben located him and helped him to travel out of the state.

August 15, 1873, Ellsworth, Kansas. About 3:00 P.M. a quarrel over a card game had involved Ben in harsh words and blows with gambler John Sterling and policeman Happy Jack Morco. Sterling and Morco, both armed, cursed the unarmed Ben and challenged him to fight. Ben dashed to his hotel room, armed himself, and went into the street, where he met his younger brother.

Billy, quite drunk when he heard of the trouble, found a shotgun and joined Ben. Just as Ben was warning his intoxicated brother to be careful, one barrel of the gun discharged and plowed into the sidewalk, nearly hitting two bystanders.

Ben gave the shotgun to a friend, but just then a warning was shouted, and the two brothers sallied forth to meet the danger. Sheriff C. B. Whitney appeared, however, and even though he was unarmed, he persuaded the Thompsons to step into a saloon and simmer down over a drink. Billy had retrieved the shotgun, and when Ben and Whitney tried to talk him into putting it down, he grumbled and snatched the weapon away.

Just as they entered the saloon, Sterling and Morco approached; the policeman, in the lead, shouted, "What the hell are you doing?" Ben dashed out and squeezed off a shot at Morco, who retreated into a doorway. Whitney followed and begged, "Don't shoot," but was himself trailed by Billy, who fired his remaining load wildly.

Mortally wounded, Whitney groaned, "My God, Billy, you've shot me," then collapsed.

"My God, Billy," shouted Ben, "you've shot your best friend!"

Billy mumbled something incoherent, and Whitney, according to one witness, replied, "He did not intend to do it; it was an accident. Send for my family."

Cad Pierce and Neil Cain, Texans who had been in the monte game which had started the trouble, shoved money and a pistol at Billy and got him onto a horse, and Ben said, "For God's sake leave town. You've shot Whitney, our best friend."

"I don't give a damn," retorted Billy. "I would've shot if it had been Jesus Christ." Billy finally rode out of town, cursing belligerently, and returned to Texas.

October 26, 1876, near Austin, Texas.
Billy was hiding out at the ranch of
Neil Cain, thirteen miles northeast
of Austin. Cain and several cowhands
were handling a herd of stolen cattle
on Cain's ranch. While Thompson sat
idly on a corral fence, ten Texas Rangers
led by Captain J. C. Sparks charged onto
the scene. Cain and several others escaped, but a man named Eb Stewart and
an unresisting Thompson were taken
into custody.

Charges of cattle rustling were filed
against Billy, but after an escape and
swift recapture in Austin and another
rumored escape plot he was shipped to
Kansas for trial in the death of Sheriff
Whitney.

June 26, 1880, Ogallala, Nebraska.
Billy had a quarrel with fellow Texan
Jim Tucker in the Nebraska cattle
town. Both parties went for their guns,
and Billy was riddled with five slugs.
None of his wounds proved mortal,
but there were widespread hints of a
lynching as soon as he recovered. Ben
persuaded his friend Bat Masterson,
who was unknown in Ogallala, to leave
Dodge City and rescue Billy. Bat had a
fight started as a distraction, and then,
with the aid of the male nurse in attendance, spirited Billy out of his hotel
to the train station. Bat and a fully recovered Billy rattled into Dodge in a
wagon in the middle of July.

Sources: Streeter, *Ben Thompson;*
Miller and Snell, *Great Gunfighters of
the Kansas Cowtowns,* 280, 444–48;
Schoenberger, *Gunfighters,* 147–70,
197; Metz, *Dallas Stoudenmire,* 122.

Tilghman, William Matthew, Jr.

*(b. July 4, 1854, Fort Dodge, Iowa; d.
November 1, 1924, Cromwell, Oklahoma.* Farmer, buffalo hunter, army

Bill Tilghman in 1912, while he was
in charge of the Oklahoma City police
force. *(Courtesy Western History Collections, University of Oklahoma Library)*

scout, law officer, rancher, saloon
keeper, state senator, businessman.)
Bill Tilghman moved with his family to
a farm near Atchison, Kansas, in 1856.
At sixteen he began hunting buffalo and
became well known among frontiers-
men. Operating out of Fort Dodge, Kansas, Tilghman scouted for the army until 1877, when he was appointed deputy
sheriff of Ford County.

In 1878 Tilghman was twice arrested
for theft, but that same year his reputation quickly improved when he married
and began raising children and livestock
near Dodge City. Over the years he also
operated two saloons in Dodge, and in
1884 he was appointed city marshal.
Friends presented Tilghman a unique
badge made of a pair of twenty-dollar
gold pieces, and he served Dodge well

for two years. In the late 1880's he saw action in two of Kansas' county seat wars, and on both occasions he was involved in killings.

Tilghman was attracted to the spectacular Oklahoma District Land Rush in 1889, and he managed to locate a claim near Guthrie, Oklahoma. For a time he was city marshal of Perry, then in 1892 he was appointed deputy U.S. marshal and moved his family to a stud farm near Chandler. Tilghman also served stints as sheriff of Lincoln County and as chief of police of Oklahoma City.

Over the next two decades Tilghman was instrumental in exterminating the outlaw gangs of Oklahoma, and in 1910 he was elected to the state senate. By that time he was rearing a second family: his first wife had died, having borne four children, and in 1903 Bill remarried and sired three more offspring. In 1911 he resigned his legislative position to head Oklahoma City's police force. He supervised the production of a motion picture, *The Passing of the Oklahoma Outlaws,* which was released in 1915 and exhibited by Tilghman for several years.

In August, 1924, the citizens of Cromwell, a booming Oklahoma oil town, persuaded Tilghman to leave retirement and become city marshal, but a few months later he was shot down in the street by a drunken prohibition officer.

Gunfights: June 25, 1874, Petrie, Indian Territory. Tilghman and several other buffalo hunters had camped near Petrie. On June 25 hunter Pat Congers was killed in Petrie by a local desperado known as Blue Throat. That night Tilghman and a cohort named Hurricane Bill rode into town to retrieve the body from the saloon where the shooting had occurred. Blue Throat and sev-

eral companions were still inside, and a fight broke out. Shots were exchanged, but a slug hit the lamp, and in the darkness the two buffalo hunters found Conger's body behind the bar. They carried it outside, rode out of town, and staged a decent burial the following day.

October 16, 1884, Dodge City, Kansas. A group of rowdy cowboys were raising a disturbance in Dodge at 10:00 P.M. on a weeknight. Marshal Tilghman approached the celebrants as they congregated on horseback near the toll bridge across the Arkansas River. Immediately, firing broke out, and when Tilghman emptied his revolver, he began operating his Winchester. After standing their ground for a few moments, the cowboys squeezed off a couple of parting shots, then thundered out of town.

July 4, 1888, Farmer City, Kansas. Farmer City was a hamlet jammed between Leoti and Coronado, and as these two communities were keen rivals for the seat of Wichita County, there was a great deal of hard feeling among the citizens of all three towns.

Ed Prather was a Farmer City saloon keeper who was known as an abrasive individual, and on the Fourth of July he went to Leoti and began drinking and firing his gun. Tilghman (who was celebrating his thirty-fourth birthday and his father's sixty-ninth) was asked to corral Prather, and when he did, Prather angrily returned to Farmer City, muttering threats against Tilghman.

About 7:00 P.M. Tilghman somewhat provocatively entered Prather's saloon. Tilghman, who may have been drinking, and Prather, who most certainly had been imbibing, quickly began arguing, and Prather placed his hand on his gun. Tilghman immediately whipped out his pistol and ordered Prather to remove his hand from his gunbutt. An instant later Tilghman fired, and the slug entered the left side of Prather's chest and tore out his back. Stunned, the wounded man stood motionless while Tilghman again ordered him to move his hand. Tilghman then shot him in the head, and Prather collapsed and died on the spot.

January 14, 1889, Cimarron, Kansas. When the Gray County seat war broke out, Tilghman hired his gun to the town of Ingalls. On a Saturday morning about a dozen Ingalls gunmen piled into a wagon and at 11:30 A.M. arrived at Cimarron with the intention of hijacking the county records. Tilghman and the others jumped out of the wagon and began looting the courthouse, but the local citizens soon discovered what was happening and angrily opened fire.

The outnumbered Ingalls men fired back, then scrambled to escape. Shooting on the run, Tilghman tumbled into a large irrigation canal and sprained an ankle. But he was helped into the wagon, and the vehicle rattled away toward Ingalls. Three of the Ingalls gunmen were abandoned, and after holding out in the courthouse for a while, they surrendered. Later they were released. Two of the Ingalls men were wounded during the skirmish, and four Cimarron citizens were hit, one fatally.

1894, near Pawnee, Oklahoma. Jennie ("Little Britches") Stevens and Cattle Annie McDougal were teen-aged consorts of the Doolin gang who were being hunted by Tilghman. Tilghman and lawman Steve Burke found the girls at a farmhouse near Pawnee, and when they fled, Tilghman went after Little Britches while Burke subdued Cattle Annie. Little Britches turned in her saddle and began to fire a Winchester at Tilghman. When the bullets began to whiz near his head, Tilghman reined in and killed her horse with a rifle shot. Then she tried to pull a pistol, threw dirt in his face, and clawed and bit him until he manhandled her.

September 6, 1895, near Elgin, Kansas. At Sam Moore's ranch eighteen miles south of Elgin, Tilghman located Little Bill Raidler, a member of the Doolin gang. Armed with a rifle, Tilghman and two deputies, W. C. Smith and Cyrus Longbone, secluded themselves at the ranch about dusk. When Raidler rode in to eat supper, Tilghman ordered him to surrender, but the outlaw drew his pistol. He snapped off a wild shot, and Tilghman, standing just ten feet away, fired a bullet which broke Raidler's right wrist and sent his gun flying. Raidler turned to run, but Smith blasted him to the ground with a shotgun. The outlaw squeezed off a couple of other stray rounds, then fainted. Tilghman nursed Raidler and later helped him obtain a parole, and the outlaw reformed and married.

November 1, 1924, Cromwell, Oklahoma. The seventy-year-old marshal of Cromwell had clashed with Wiley Lynn, a shady prohibition officer. One night Tilghman was seated in Murphy's Restaurant when a shot was fired outside. He rushed out to find Lynn drunkenly waving a pistol. A bystander seized the gun, and Tilghman began to lead Lynn toward jail. But Lynn produced a small automatic and began firing, and the old lawman crumpled to the ground and died within fifteen minutes.

Sources: Tilghman, *Marshal of the Last Frontier;* Miller, *Bill Tilghman;*

Miller and Snell, *Great Gunfighters of the Kansas Cowtowns,* 213, 222–23, 234, 296, 307, 330, 412, 420–37; Schoenberger, *Gunfighters,* 17, 28, 118, 121; Horan and Sann, *Pictorial History of the Wild West,* 167–72; Ray, *Wily Women of the West,* 31–32; Masterson, *Famous Gunfighters,* 42–53; Drago, *Road Agents and Train Robbers,* 182, 194, 197, 209–17, 227; Shirley, *Six-gun and Silver Star,* 17–18, 77–79, 142–47, 157, 161, 169–70, 179–90, 196, 203, 208–209, 214–15.

Tovey, Mike

(d. June 15, 1893, Amador County, California. Express messenger.) Tovey achieved renown by serving Wells, Fargo as a   shotgun guard for twenty-eight years. A veteran of numerous scrapes, he was involved in at least two fatal shootings, the second of which unfortunately resulted in his death.

Gunfights: *September 5, 1880, East Walker River Bridge, Nevada.* Road agents Milton Sharp and Bill Jones had planned a double holdup at the wooden bridge across the East Fork of the Walker River. In the moonlight they robbed the southbound Carson City–Bodie stage of three thousand dollars, then waited for a coach headed in the opposite direction on the same run. Tovey was guarding the second coach, which had encountered the the first vehicle and then proceeded onward, not suspecting that another robbery was audaciously planned. When they arrived at the bridge, Tovey hopped down without his shotgun to inspect the looted chest which seductively had been left at the scene.

Suddenly the hidden outlaws fired at Tovey, missing him but killing one of the horses. The driver tossed Tovey his

sawed-off weapon just as Jones emerged from seclusion. Tovey killed Jones with one blast of his shotgun, then turned toward Sharp. But Sharp fired and shattered Tovey's right arm and disappeared into the darkness. Tovey's wound was bleeding so badly that there was no pursuit.

June 15, 1893, Amador County, California. Tovey was riding shotgun for the Ione-Jackson stage when a holdup was attempted. As usual, he steadfastly offered resistance, but in the resulting exchange of shots he was fatally wounded.

Source: Drago, *Road Agents and Train Robbers,* 68–70, 223.

Towerly, William

(b. ca. 1870; d. December, 1887, near Atoka, Indian Territory. Horse thief.) Towerly made his mark as a gunman by killing two peace officers in separate shootouts, although he was himself shot to death in his last fight.

Gunfights: *November 29, 1887, Cherokee Nation, Indian Territory.* Towerly and fellow horse thief Dave Smith were camped in a tent on the Arkansas River. With them were Smith's brother-in-law, Lee Dixon, and Dixon's wife. On a Sunday morning the camp was approached by lawmen Frank Dalton (whose brothers later became the notorious bank robbers) and James Cole, who were carrying warrants for Smith's arrest.

Without hesitation Smith felled Dalton with a bullet in the chest, then he and the Dixons opened fire on Cole. Towerly ran toward the moaning Dalton and fired the last bullet in his Winchester into the lawman's mouth. Towerly then reloaded and blew Dalton's brains out.

By this time Cole, despite being hit in the side by Smith, had fatally wounded all three of Towerly's companions, whereupon the young thief unceremoniously scampered to safety.

December, 1887, near Atoka, Indian Territory. Towerly had fled to his family home near Atoka, where his parents and sister lived in a cabin on the Boggy River. Lawmen Ed Stokley and Bill Moody trailed him there and set an ambush which they sprang as Towerly emerged from the house at dawn. Stokley shouted, "Hands up," but Towerly went for his six-gun. Both officers fired at the same time, wounding Towerly in the leg and right shoulder.

Towerly dropped his gun and fell, but as Stokley ran toward him, the young killer grabbed his pistol with his left hand and shot the officer in the groin and heart. Towerly emptied the revolver into the dead lawman, then tossed the weapon toward his father, screaming: "Reload it and throw it back, so I can kill that other damned marshal!" In the meantime, Moody had been jumped by Towerly's mother and sister, who wrestled him into the cabin and locked the door. But Moody threw off the screaming women, broke out a window, and shot Towerly to death.

Source: Shirley, *Heck Thomas.*

Tracy, Harry

(b. Poughkeepsie, New York; d. August 5, 1902, near Davenport, Washington. Thief.) Harry Tracy was a vicious killer who radiated danger; Boston policemen were so intimidated that they refused to arrest him singlehandedly. After causing violence in the East,

Tracy prudently headed west, but soon was imprisoned in Utah for burglary. In 1897, Tracy and Dave Lant escaped and sought refuge with the Wild Bunch at Brown's Hole, a forbidding valley extending through Colorado, Utah, and Wyoming. Tracy killed Valentine Hoy in 1898, and when he was arrested, he escaped jail, was recaptured, and then escaped custody again.

He fled to Oregon, where he married the sister of Dave Merrill in 1899. The brothers-in-law began a series of store and bank robberies. Tracy and Merrill were apprehended and sentenced to the Oregon State Penitentiary, but they shot their way out of prison in 1902. An intensive manhunt ensued, during which in an act of treachery Tracy killed Merrill. Tracy terrorized the Northwest through the summer of 1902, but in August he was finally hunted down and shot to death.

Gunfights: March 1, 1898, Brown's Hole, Colorado. Tracy and two confederates, Dave Lant and Swede Johnson, were cornered in Brown's Hole by a posse led by Valentine Hoy. When Hoy approached on foot, Tracy warned him to stop and then shot him in the heart. The posse retreated, caught and hanged an outlaw named Jack Bennett, and then continued their pursuit until Tracy and his fellow fugitives surrendered.

June 9, 1902, Salem, Oregon. Tracy, standing in a line with fellow inmates at the Oregon State Penitentiary, suddenly seized a rifle from a box and shot guard Frank B. Ferrell in the throat. Ferrell dropped dead, and Tracy drew on guard Frank Girard. A convict named Frank Ingram wrestled with Tracy, but was shot for his trouble.

Tracy and Dave Merrill ran outside. Merrill found a ladder and placed it against a wall. Tracy provided cover, wounding guards Duncan Ross and B. F. Tiffany. The two convicts climbed to the top, and Tracy killed guard S. R. T. Jones. Using Ross and Tiffany as shields, the escapees crossed a creek bridge forty yards away. Tracy then began firing again, killing Tiffany. Ross collapsed and played dead, while Tracy and Merrill fled into the woods.

ca. July 1, 1902, Lewis County, Washington. One day in the forest in Lewis County, Merrill and Tracy began quarreling and decided to have a duel. They agreed to step off ten steps and then turn and fire. But Tracy whirled around prematurely and killed his brother-in-law with a bullet in the back.

July 3, 1902, Bothell, Washington. During a midafternoon rain Tracy ambushed a five-man posse at Bothell, near Seattle. He jumped up from behind a stump and opened fire with a .30-.30 rifle at point-blank range. Deputy Sheriff L. J. Nelson tumbled into a ditch, grazed in the face. A deputy named Raymond was hit twice and fell dead on top of a man named Anderson. Newspaperman Louis B. Sefrit exchanged shots with Tracy and was slightly wounded. Tracy then turned on Deputy Sheriff Jack Williams, shot him three times in the stomach, and vanished into the woods. Later in the day Tracy forced the residents of a nearby house to give him refuge. But that night he was found by a posse led by Sheriff Edward Cudihee. But Tracy killed two deputies and again eluded capture.

August 5, 1902, near Davenport, Washington. Lawmen discovered that Tracy was hiding at the Eddy Ranch, near

Davenport. A posse flushed him from a barn, but under heavy fire he sprinted behind a boulder and began shooting at the officers. He had to fire into the sun, however, and he decided to shift positions to a boulder in a barley field. He dashed seventy-five yards to the edge of the field. Suddenly a slug shattered his right leg, breaking both bones below the knee.

Bleeding profusely, Tracy dragged himself seventy-five yards through the grain field, occasionally firing a shot at the lawmen. The posse raked the field with volley after volley, and Tracy took another slug in the right thigh. At 5:30 P.M., his situation hopeless, Tracy jammed a revolver to his head and committed suicide. The lawmen had become so wary of Tracy, however, that they waited until the next morning and then, advancing cautiously, discovered Tracy's corpse.

Source: Horan, *Authentic Wild West,* 255–86; Horan and Sann, *Pictorial History of the Wild West,* 97, 153, 202–203, 243–45.

Tucker, Tom

(d. Texas. Cowboy, law officer.) Tucker was a cowboy who readily became involved in feuds. As a rider for Arizona's Hash Knife outfit he fought in the Pleasant Valley War until he was nearly shot to death. When he recovered, he went to New Mexico, hired on with Oliver Lee, and thus took sides in Lee's feuds with area ranchers. During the course of his career Tucker also wore a badge as a Santa Fe undersheriff, and he eventually died in Texas.

Gunfights: August 10, 1887, Pleasant Valley, Arizona. When the Pleasant Valley War intensified, Tucker led seven other cowboys to the cabin of sheepman

Jim Tewksbury. Tewksbury, who was backed by half a dozen gunmen inside the dwelling, spoke briefly with his antagonists, then gunfire erupted. Four of Tucker's companions were hit: Bob Gillespie was wounded in the right hip, Bob Carrington was struck in the right arm and right leg, and Hampton Blevins and John Paine were killed. Tucker took a bullet under the left arm which tore out through his other armpit, and the impact threw him out of the saddle. Tucker's horse had fallen on his rifle, but he jerked the weapon free and opened fire on the cabin. His surviving men retreated, and when Tucker's mount jumped up, he clutched a stirrup and managed to hang on until he had been dragged out of range.

Tucker spent the afternoon crawling toward a friendly ranch while blowflies and maggots went to work on his wound. He passed out, but a chilling rain and hailstorm roused him that night, and he finally struggled to the cabin of Bob Sigsby. Sigsby soaked the wound with creosote dip, and Tucker gradually recovered.

Mid-August, 1888, White Sands Desert, New Mexico. In the White Sands area Oliver Lee, Tucker, and two other men apprehended Walter Good, who supposedly had killed Lee's best friend. Good was killed with two bullets in the head, and his body was left to decay in the desert.

August, 1888, near Las Cruces, New Mexico. Two weeks later Lee, Tucker, and three other cowboys encountered John Good and five companions near Las Cruces. Good had just discovered his son's corpse, and a long-range duel broke out in which more than one hundred bullets were fired. No one was shot, but three horses were hit before the gunfire ended.

1889, Silver City, New Mexico. Tucker became involved in a shooting in Silver City, and he killed one Anglo and fatally wounded several Chinese. When brought to trial, Tucker was exonerated on grounds of self-defense.

1908, near Sacramento Sinks, New Mexico. Tucker and three other officers had helped Dee Harkey corner an outlaw band led by Jim Nite. When the shooting started, however, Harkey handled most of the action, and Tucker's only real activity was to help take the fugitives into custody after they surrendered.

Sources: Sonnichsen, *Tularosa,* 40, 44–45, 49–51, 81, 141, 156, 172, 177; Harkey, *Mean as Hell,* 124–28; Raine, *Famous Sheriffs and Western Outlaws,* 226–30; Drago, *Great Range Wars,* 97, 108–11, 292; Gibson, *Colonel Albert Jennings Fountain,* 214, 216–17, 224, 246, 249, 285.

Turner, Ben

(d. December, 1873, Lincoln County, New Mexico. Cowboy, gunman.) Turner was a cowboy in the employ of the Horrell brothers when the infamous Horrell-Higgins feud broke out in Lampasas, Texas. He helped gun down three state policemen in Lampasas, and he assisted in a jailbreak in Georgetown. He then accompanied the Horrells to New Mexico, where further violence soon erupted. Ben Horrell, Turner's brother-in-law, was killed in Lincoln, and in the shooting that soon followed, Turner met his death.

Gunfights: *March 19, 1873, Lampasas, Texas.* The Horrell brothers and their cowhands had determined to defend Clint Barkley from arrest by the detested state police. Mart, Tom, and Sam Horrell, along with Barkley, Turner, and half a dozen other heavily armed hard cases moved into Jerry Scott's saloon in Lampasas to await the lawmen. Four policemen entered the swinging doors, and gunfire immediately broke out. Mart and Tom Horrell were wounded, and three of the law officers were killed.

March, 1873, Georgetown, Texas. Mart Horrell and Jerry Scott soon were arrested and thrown into the Georgetown jail, and the other members of the Horrell faction lost no time in coming to their rescue. They rode into Georgetown, broke into the jail, and shot their way out of town with the freed prisoners.

December, 1873, Lincoln County, New Mexico. After the death of Ben Horrell his brothers and friends sought bloody retribution against the local Mexican population. Shortly after the worst of these incidents, Turner encountered a group of angry natives. Gunplay promptly ensued, and Turner was shot to death.

Sources: Gillett, *Six Years with the Texas Rangers,* 74–76; Rasch, "The Horrell War," *NMHR;* Webb, *Texas Rangers,* 334–39; Askins, *Texans, Guns & History,* 151–60.

Tyler, Jesse

(d. May 16, 1900, near Thompson, Utah. Law officer.) Jesse Tyler was a turn-of-the-century Utah lawman who operated against the Wild Bunch. As the sheriff of Grand County, Tyler was active in the pursuit of stock rustlers, but on one occasion he was sued by the wife of a horse thief for taking stolen

animals from their corral. In 1900 Tyler was killed by outlaws while leading a posse.

Gunfights: February, 1899, San Rafael Valley, Utah. Tyler and a five-man posse had spent several days trying to round up stolen horses. The lawmen closed in on a suspicious-looking campfire, and at dawn they ordered the first man to appear—a halfblood—to surrender. Startled, the man crawled to cover while the posse fired futilely. One of the outlaws warned the officers to leave, and a general exchange of shots erupted. After two hours of steady firing the posse ran low on ammunition and reluctantly withdrew.

May 16, 1900, near Thompson, Utah. For three weeks Tyler had led a posse in search of cattle rustlers. In Utah's Book Mountains, about forty-two miles from Thompson, the posse spread out, and Tyler and Deputy Sam Jenkins rode toward what they thought was an Indian camp. They dismounted and, leaving their rifles in their saddle scabbards, approached what was actually a band of rustlers led by Harvey Logan. Tyler shouted, "Hello, boys," but the reply alerted the lawmen, and they turned to run. But Logan opened fire and shot both officers squarely through the back. The other lawmen, badly frightened, retreated hastily, and the two bodies were left in the open for two days before they were retrieved.

Source: Baker, *Wild Bunch,* 86–89, 104, 135–36, 145–47.

Vásquez, Tiburcio

(b. ca. 1838, California; d. March 19, 1875, San Jose, California. Horse thief, cattle rustler, convict, stage robber,

bandit.) A halfblood with an Indian mother, Vásquez was reared in California and readily assumed the life of an outlaw. Between horse thieving and cattle rustling raids he spent his time and ill-gained money in Monterey. Arrested in 1857, the young criminal was sentenced to five years in San Quentin for stealing cattle. (Two years earlier he had eluded charges of murder for a stabbing death in Monterey.) In 1859 he escaped, but two months later he was rearrested on charges of larceny, and this time he was not released until August 13, 1863. Soon, however, he was returned to San Quentin for armed robbery, and the three-time-loser was behind bars until June 4, 1870.

Vásquez then began robbing stagecoaches and isolated stores, and he was suspected of killing an Italian butcher during a holdup. In 1873 three persons were killed during one of his robberies, and as a result the legislature offered eight thousand dollars for his capture, and a persistent manhunt ensued. A year later he was finally captured, and in 1875 he was hanged in Santa Clara County for the sake of an efficient execution.

Gunfights: *ca. 1856, Livermore Valley, California.* Vásquez, who considered himself an irresistible ladies' man, kidnapped the daughter of a Mexican rancher in the Livermore Valley. The rancher quickly rode in pursuit, and when he caught the couple, a fight developed. Vásquez' right arm was shattered by a bullet and, leaving his *inamorata* behind, he ingloriously spurred to safety.

Summer, 1872, near Arroyo Cantua, California. Earlier in the day Vásquez and two confederates, Francisco Barcenas and García Rodríguez, had held up a stagecoach and, as they were fleeing, a prosperous traveler whom they chanced to encounter. On the way toward their hideout at Arroyo Cantua they were intercepted by a posse consisting of Alameda County Sheriff Harry Morse, the sheriff of San Benito County, and the constable of Santa Cruz. A vicious fight broke out, and all three bandits were shot. Vásquez was hit in the chest, Rodríguez was seriously wounded, and Barcenas was killed by the constable. Vásquez and Rodríguez managed to outdistance the lawmen, but Rodríguez was captured two days later and died shortly thereafter. Vásquez reached safety in the mountains and in time recovered his health.

August 26, 1873, Tres Piños, California. Vásquez and six accomplices converged upon Andrew Snyder's store and, while Tiburcio and two henchmen stood guard, the other four entered the building and began to loot the premises. But when sheepherder William Redford approached the store, Vásquez nervously gunned him down. The other two men finished him off just as a pair of teamsters came running toward the scene of the shooting. Vásquez knocked one out with his pistol, then shot the other man, James Riley, through the heart.

At that point a man stepped out on the porch of a hotel seventy-five yards away, and when Vásquez pulled out his rifle and aimed it at him, he ducked back inside. Vásquez fired, and the bullet missed, but killed an old man named Davidson who was sitting in the hotel with his wife. In the meantime, Vásquez' lieutenant, José Chavez, had clubbed a boy unconscious, and following that unnecessary violence, the gang left town.

December, 1874, Los Angeles County, California. A posse closed in on Vásquez, who was hiding at the adobe house of Greek George Allen in Alison Canyon. When the posse burst inside, Allen's woman tried to block the way while Vásquez jumped out a back window in the direction of his horse. A deputy named Johnson fired a wild shot at Vásquez, and then George Beers, a journalist by profession, brought him down with a load of buckshot in his legs.

Source: Drago, *Road Agents and Train Robbers,* 30–38, 220.

Wait, Frederick T.

("Dash Wait," "Dash Waite")

(b. 1853, Indian Territory; d. September 24, 1895, Indian Territory. Cowboy, gunman, tax collector.) A quarter-blood Cherokee, Wait married an Indian woman and settled in Lincoln County, New Mexico. He was employed by English rancher John Tunstall just before the outbreak of the Lincoln County War. Wait followed Billy the Kid during the ensuing skirmishes, and when the Kid left New Mexico, Wait went with him to the Texas Panhandle. On one occasion, while riding alone in the Panhandle, Wait was jumped by a posse and escaped lynching only by flashing the secret distress signal of a Freemason. When the Kid and Tom O'Folliard decided to return to New Mexico, Wait went back to his home in the Cherokee Nation in Indian Territory. There he served as a tax collector, dying in 1895 at the age of forty-two.

Gunfights: April 1, 1878, Lincoln, New Mexico. Wait accompanied Billy the Kid, Henry Brown, John Middleton, and Jim French in setting an ambush for Sheriff William Brady in the streets of Lincoln. When Brady and four other lawmen walked near, the five bushwhackers rose up from behind an adobe wall and began firing. Brady and Deputy George Hindman were fatally wounded, but the other three officers ran for cover.

In a moment Wait and the Kid darted toward the dead men to seize their rifles, but Deputy Billy Matthews, who had been wounded, saw them and opened fire. The Kid and Wait both were grazed and scampered back behind the fence. All five ambushers then mounted up and rode out of Lincoln.

April 4, 1878, Blazer's Mill, New Mexico. Wait was one of the "Regulators" who encountered Buckshot Roberts at Blazer's Mill. When shooting broke out between Roberts and three Regulators, Wait and his companions threw lead in Roberts' direction and scrambled out of the line of fire. After Dick Brewer, the leader of the Regulators, was killed, Wait and the others retreated, leaving the severely wounded Roberts to die.

Sources: Keleher, *Violence in Lincoln County,* 109, 112–13, 128, 184, 253, 260–61, 263–64, 266, 276–78; Rickards, *Blazer's Mill;* Hunt, *Tragic Days of Billy the Kid,* 38, 50–53, 113, 132–33, 138–39; Fulton, *Lincoln County War,* 83, 110, 113–15, 126, 130–31, 137, 140, 158, 192, 201, 234, 333.

Walker, Joe

(b. ca. 1850, Texas; d. May, 1898, near Thompson, Utah. Cowboy, laborer, rustler, robber.) Walker's father, a Texas rancher, died when Joe was still an infant. His mother had turned their property over to her brother, a Dr. Whitmore, to manage. About 1870 Whit-

more merged the Walker herd with his own and moved to a ranch in northern Arizona, where he was soon killed in an Indian raid. Whitmore's widow sold out and migrated with her sons, George and Tobe, to Carbon County, Utah, where they became a prominent banking and ranching family.

When Walker's mother died, he went to Utah to make a property settlement with the Whitmores. They denied any relationship or property claims by Walker, and he found employment at local ranches and at a Huntington sawmill and began to hound the Whitmores.

After a shooting incident in 1895 Walker threw in with outlaws at nearby Robbers Roost and began to rustle cattle and horses. He frequently stole stock from the Whitmores, but on one such raid an accomplice named C. L. ("Gunplay") Maxwell informed the authorities of Walker's whereabouts after the two outlaws quarreled. Walker managed to escape only after a lengthy chase and siege. A few months later, on April 21, 1897, Walker cut telegraph wires and otherwise aided Butch Cassidy's Wild Bunch in pulling off the eight-thousand-dollar Castle Gate payroll robbery.

About one year later, following another raid on Whitmore livestock, Walker was chased by a nine-man posse in Utah. Encamped near the town of Thompson with a passing cowboy named Johnny Herring, Walker bedded down for the night with his gun in his blankets. But the posse surrounded the camp during the night, and when Walker stirred at dawn, the lawmen opened fire. Walker and Herring, who was assumed by the posse to be Butch Cassidy, were riddled with bullets and died in their bedrolls.

Gunfights: *summer, 1895, Price, Utah.* Walker, on a drinking spree,

pulled a gun and began to shoot up the town. Considerable property damage resulted, and when he finally rode away, complaints were filed which made him a wanted man.

1896, Robbers Roost region, Utah. As Walker rode toward Robbers Roost on the road near Granite, he was intercepted by a five-man posse of bounty hunters. Walker waved them off, but they continued to approach, and he opened fire. A running gunfight ensued, but Walker stayed far enough in the lead to be relatively safe. After a fifteen-mile chase he finally outdistanced his pursuers and galloped to safety in Robbers Roost.

1897, Mexican Bend of the San Rafael River, Utah. Having just stolen some horses from the Whitmore ranch, Walker and C. L. Maxwell hid the stock at a secluded cabin and corral near the San Rafael River. The two rustlers argued, and Maxwell grumpily left camp and told the Whitmores where to find the horses.

Sheriffs C. W. Allred and Azariah Tuttle immediately went in pursuit, and they surprised Walker on the river bank, cutting him off from the house. Walker waded across the river, climbed halfway up the canyon wall, and pulled his pistol. The two lawmen galloped after him, firing as they rode, but Walker knocked Tuttle off his horse with a slug in the leg, and the lawmen scrambled behind some boulders. They shouted at Walker to surrender, and when he refused, Allred rode for help, herding the horses in the corral ahead of him. Walker snapped off a few shots, but was driven behind cover by Tuttle's rifle fire.

The bleeding lawman kept Walker pinned down with accurate fire for two hours, but as the sun drew overhead, Tuttle was forced to ask for quarter. Walker agreed to fetch him some water if he would throw out his guns. Walker climbed down to Tuttle's position at the foot of the canyon wall, picked up the lawman's guns, and brought him a bucket of water. Walker then climbed out of the canyon, found a stray horse after a couple of miles afoot, and made good his escape.

Source: Baker, *Wild Bunch,* 48, 50, 64–82, 110, 174, 204.

Watson, Jack

(d. 1890, Price, Utah. Soldier, cowboy, law officer.) Jack Watson served the Confederacy during the Civil War and received a wound in his instep which caused a pronounced limp throughout the rest of his life. After the war he rode as a cowboy, enlisted in the Texas Rangers, and occasionally tracked rustlers on behalf of Texas ranchers. In 1884 he shot up Montrose, Colorado, and a six-hundred-dollar reward was posted for his capture.

Later Watson knifed a man in Crystal, a Gunnison County mining camp, and Sheriff C. W. Shores, who had once worked with Watson as a cowboy, arrested the fugitive. Watson was acquitted, then accepted a job as Shores's deputy. He served faithfully through 1890, when he was shot to death in Utah.

Gunfights: ca. 1880, Texas. A group of Texas cattlemen had employed Watson to overtake a horse thief. After nearly a week Watson located the man while the rustler was cooking breakfast. Watson killed the thief, then ate the dead man's meal.

February 7, 1884, Montrose, Colorado. Watson was arrested for drunkenness in Montrose, and the next day the city judge fined him eighty-five dollars, which cleaned him out. Infuriated, Watson marched to his horse and rode in search of the local marshal and the judge. He found them on Main Street and opened fire, hitting the lawman in the arm and wounding the magistrate in the side. Watson then rode out of town, reloaded, and roared back down the street, exchanging shots with the citizenry before finally galloping to safety.

1890, Price, Utah. While working under cover in Price, Watson made numerous local enemies, who hired a gunman named Ward to kill Watson. Ward secluded himself behind a hay wagon opposite a saloon which was frequented by the hard-drinking lawman. When the inebriated Watson stumbled out into the street, he was shot down by Ward. Watson had checked his gun in the saloon, and he tried to crawl back to the building, but he was killed by another volley from Ward.

Source: Rockwell, *Memoirs of a Lawman,* 213–32.

Webb, John Joshua

("Samuel King")

(b. February 13, 1847, Iowa; d. April 22, 1882, Winslow, Arkansas. Buffalo hunter, surveyor, teamster, law officer, convict.) By 1871 Webb, a native of Iowa, had gone west, supporting himself as a buffalo hunter and as a surveyor in Colorado. Later he drifted from Deadwood to Cheyenne to Dodge City, working for the law in Dodge during the late 1870's as a policeman, Ford County deputy sheriff, and member of various posses. He also hired out his gun in the struggle between the Santa Fe and the Denver & Rio Grande rail-

roads for right-of-way through the Grand Canyon of the Arkansas River. In 1878 he arrested train robber Dave Rudabaugh, who ironically became his close friend later in New Mexico.

Two years later Webb secured an appointment as city marshal of Las Vegas, New Mexico, but he moonlighted as a member of the notorious "Dodge City gang." Leader of this band of thieves and con men was Justice of the Peace and Acting Coroner Hoodoo Brown (Hyman Neill), who held court in a saloon and banged for law and order with a Winchester. The gang disbanded and scattered after Webb, who provided legal protection, was arrested for murder in March, 1880. On April 9 Webb was convicted and sentenced to be hanged, and on April 30 Dave Rudabaugh tried unsuccessfully to spring him from the county jail.

On appeal, Webb's sentence was changed to life imprisonment, but when Rudabaugh was incarcerated with him, they attempted (September 19, 1881) to escape, then succeeded (December 3, 1881). They fled to Texas and on to Mexico, where Rudabaugh was later killed. Webb returned to Kansas, assuming the alias "Samuel King" (his mother's maiden name was King). Later he worked in Kansas and Nebraska as a teamster for J. D. Scott & Co. In 1882 he died of smallpox in Arkansas.

Gunfights: *March 2, 1880, Las Vegas, New Mexico.* In Goodlet and Robinson's Saloon, Webb tangled with Michael Kelliher. When the argument grew heated, Webb shot and killed Kelliher. His marshal's badge notwithstanding, Webb was indicted and convicted of murder.

September 19, 1881, Las Vegas, New Mexico. Webb tried to break jail with Dave Rudabaugh, who had secured a gun, Thomas Duffy, and H. S. Wilson. There was an exchange of shots with guards, and when Duffy was killed, the other three prisoners surrendered. Two months later, Webb, Rudabaugh, and five other convicts dug their way out of jail with a knife, a pickax, and an iron bar and escaped to safety.

Sources: Miller and Snell, *Great Gunfighters of the Kansas Cowtowns,* 26, 188, 206, 211–13, 215–18, 222, 279, 322–23; Keleher, *Violence in Lincoln County,* 282, 286, 297–99, 303; Stanley, *Desperadoes of New Mexico,* 153–65.

Weightman, George

("Red Buck")

(b. Texas; d. February 14, 1896, Arapaho, Oklahoma. Horse thief, bank and train robber, convict.) Weightman was a vicious killer and horse thief from Texas. During the 1880's he drifted into Oklahoma, and in 1889 he was arrested by Heck Thomas for horse stealing. Following a three-year prison term, he joined Bill Doolin's gang of bank robbers.

On one occasion Weightman, in custody with two other prisoners, made a spectacular escape from a moving train. Although his two cohorts were killed and bullets were whizzing around him, Weightman jumped through a window and scrambled to safety. After a series of disagreements with Doolin, he was forced out of the band. He organized his own gang, but soon he was chased down and killed by lawmen.

Gunfights: *September 1, 1893, Ingalls, Oklahoma.* Bill Doolin, Red Buck, and five other outlaws had decided to seek recreation in the little community of Ingalls, where Doolin had once worked on a nearby ranch. A

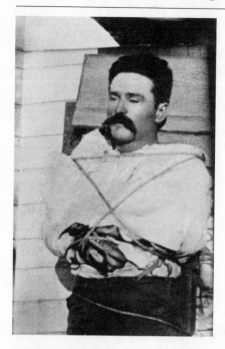

Red Buck George Weightman, in 1895, dead after a shootout with a posse. *(Courtesy Western History Collections, University of Oklahoma Library)*

large posse slipped into town while the fugitives drank and gambled in a saloon. When Bitter Creek Newcomb walked outside and mounted his horse, he was fired upon, but Arkansas Tom Jones (who had taken to a sickbed in the City Hotel) killed a lawman from his second-story vantage point, allowing Newcomb to escape.

A vicious fight erupted, and the outlaws in the saloon shot their way to a nearby livery stable. They mounted up, then dashed out through the building's two doors. Red Buck, Bill Dalton, and Tulsa Jack Blake burst out the front door into the street, firing desperately at the posse. Dalton's horse was gunned down, but he shot a lawman, cut a fence

which blocked the way, and climbed up behind Doolin. Except for Arkansas Tom, who was captured, the entire gang managed to escape.

April 3, 1895, near Dover, Oklahoma. The Doolin gang robbed a train just outside Dover, and a posse quickly formed and caught up with the outlaws. Tulsa Jack Blake was killed, but the rest of the gang broke away with guns blazing. During the running gun battle which ensued, Red Buck's horse was killed. Weightman vaulted up behind Bitter Creek Newcomb, and the gang finally outdistanced the posse.

When the outlaws passed a farm, Red Buck jumped into the corral and stole a horse. The owner, an old preacher, came out of the house to protest, but Red Buck murdered him in cold blood. In disgust Doolin conferred with his second-in-command, Bill Dalton, then tossed a share of the loot at Red Buck. The killer was told to go his own way, and Doolin led his men down the road.

December, 1895, north Texas. Red Buck and his gang were jumped in a shack by Texas Rangers. Red Buck was wounded, but the outlaws shot their way free.

February 14, 1896, Arapaho, Oklahoma. Peace officers located Red Buck in a hideout and, after a battle, shot him to death at the entrance to his dugout.

Sources: Drago, *Road Agents and Train Robbers,* 201, 207, 209; Shirley, *Six-gun and Silver Star,* 61, 91–93, 126, 145–46, 152, 181, 190.

Wells, Samuel

("Charlie Pitts")

(d. September 21, 1876, near Madelia,

Minnesota. Train and bank robber.) Sam Wells, who regularly used the alias "Charlie Pitts," was a member of the James-Younger gang. He was involved with them in a number of robberies and resultant shootouts, but it cannot be stated with any degree of certainty in which specific incidents he participated. It is known that he took part in a train robbery at Rocky Cut, Missouri, in July, 1876, because after the holdup he jilted his sweetheart, Lillian Beamer, to marry another girl, and Miss Beamer promptly informed on him to the authorities. It is also known that he was present in the abortive raid on Northfield, because he was killed during the subsequent manhunt.

Gunfights: September 7, 1876, Northfield, Minnesota. Wells accompanied the gang into Northfield to raid the local bank. Wells went inside with Jesse James and Bob Younger, while the other five robbers stood guard around town. When cashier Joseph L. Heywood refused to open the safe (which already was unlocked), Wells pistol-whipped him and inflicted a slash wound across his throat. Wells then grazed Heywood in the head with a revolver shot, at which point teller A. E. Bunker attempted to escape.

Bunker burst through a door and struggled to his feet, but Wells followed and put a bullet through his shoulder. Bunker scrambled to safety as the townspeople began to open fire, and the outlaws shot Heywood to death and fled out of the bank. Before the robbers could fight their way out of town, two of their party—Clell Miller and William Stiles—were killed, along with two citizens.

September 21, 1876, near Madelia, Minnesota. With the countryside thick with angry posses and the three Younger brothers wounded, the surviving gang members found it difficult to escape. When Jesse cold-bloodedly suggested killing the seriously wounded Bob Younger, the band split into two groups. The James brothers made their way back to Missouri, while Wells loyally struggled on with the Youngers.

There were occasional clashes with posses, and two weeks after the holdup the four men were spotted trying to buy food in the village of Madelia. A posse quickly organized and spread out to comb the area, and six officers located the fugitives somewhere in a thicket near the Watonwan River.

When the posse had advanced fifty yards, the outlaws opened up from thirty feet away. The lawmen stood their ground and vigorously fired back, although three of them—W. W. Murphy, G. A. Bradford, and S. J. Severson—suffered slight wounds. But all of the outlaws were hit, and Wells, with five holes in his chest, died on the spot. The bullet-riddled Youngers finally surrendered and were taken into custody. On Wells's body was found a derringer which bank employee A. E. Bunker had tried to reach and which Wells had seized.

Sources: Breihan, *Younger Brothers,* 169–81; Horan, *Desperate Men,* 107–22, 126; Settle, *Jesse James Was His Name,* 89, 93, 94; Drago, *Road Agents and Train Robbers,* 131, 149, 156–66.

Wheeler, Harry

(d. 1925. Indian scout, law officer, laborer.) Wheeler was the son of an army officer, and his career became one of public service in numerous capacities. He was a scout under Nelson A. Miles in the campaign against Geronimo, and during the Spanish-American War he

was a soldier in Cuba. In 1902 he joined the Arizona Rangers, and two years later he succeeded Thomas Rynning as captain, serving in that capacity until the organization was disbanded in 1909. Later he was elected sheriff of Cochise County, and during a 1917 labor dispute at the Bisbee copper mines he led the group responsible for the "Bisbee Deportation," in which nearly twelve hundred strikers and sympathizers were forcibly removed from the area.

During the First World War Wheeler reached the rank of captain in the U.S. Army. After the war he was defeated for the Cochise County sheriff's office, and he drifted from job to job until his death in 1925.

Gunfights: *February, 1902, Tucson, Arizona.* At 2:00 A.M. in Tucson's Palace Saloon, Wheeler, at the time a sergeant of the Arizona Rangers, apprehended a robber named Bostwick who had lined the patrons against a wall. When Wheeler burst through the swinging doors, he and Bostwick exchanged shots. Bostwick's shot missed, as did two shots from a "lookout" stationed across the street. The lookout escaped, but Wheeler grazed Bostwick's head, then mortally wounded him with a slug in the chest.

February, 1907, Benson, Arizona. At dawn a miner named J. A. Tracy accosted D. W. Silverton and his female companion as the couple approached the depot to board a train to El Paso. Tracy was infatuated with the woman and threatened Silverton with a pistol, but at that point Wheeler ran toward the group, ordering Tracy to drop his gun. Tracy, however, whirled and pumped two slugs into Wheeler, one into his thigh and one into his foot.

But Wheeler squeezed off five shots, sending four into Tracy's body. When the shooting stopped, both men shook hands and wished each other a speedy recovery, but Tracy died on the train to Tucson.

Sources: Coolidge, *Fighting Men of the West,* 283–99; Wagoner, *Arizona Territory,* 391–95; Hunt, *Cap Mossman,* 226.

Whitney, Chauncey Belden
("Cap")

(b. 1842; d. August 18, 1873, Ellsworth, Kansas. Indian fighter, law officer.) Whitney was one of the earliest settlers of Ellsworth, arriving in 1867, the year it was established by the railroad. He was the town's first constable, he built the first jail, and at various times he served as city marshal, deputy sheriff, and county sheriff. Twice he left Ellsworth on expeditions against Indians. In 1868, along with fifty other "scouts," Whitney fought at the celebrated Battle of Beecher Island; the following year he was elected first lieutenant of a militia company which manned a blockhouse near Ellsworth to guard against Indian depredations. Sheriff Whitney was killed in his thirty-first year by Billy Thompson in the streets of Ellsworth.

Gunfight: *August 15, 1873, Ellsworth, Kansas.* Whitney and former policeman John DeLong were standing outside an Ellsworth restaurant when they saw Ben and Billy Thompson squabbling over a shotgun. The Thompson brothers had armed themselves in response to a challenge by Happy Jack Morco and John Sterling over a gambling dispute. Billy was drunk, and no sooner had Ben warned him to be care-

C. B. Whitney, Indian fighter and lawman, gunned down in Ellsworth, Kansas, by Billy Thompson, brother of Ben Thompson. *(Courtesy Kansas State Historical Society, Topeka)*

ful than one barrel of the weapon went off, hitting the sidewalk.

Although they were unarmed, Whitney and DeLong alertly strolled over and, upon discovering the nature of the trouble, tried to calm the Thompsons. Whitney said, "Boys, don't have any row. I will do all I can to protect you. You know that John and I are your friends." He then invited the brothers to have a drink, and as the party headed toward a saloon, Ben and Whitney tried to persuade Billy to give up his shotgun. Billy refused, and at that point Morco and Sterling rushed toward the group, guns drawn. Ben snapped off a shot, and Whitney stepped toward him, shouting, "Don't shoot!" Billy, several feet behind, raised his shotgun and triggered

a blast which hit Whitney. The lawman staggered and gasped, "My God, Billy, you've shot me!"

Whitney collapsed and asked that his wife be summoned. Friends carried him to his house two blocks away, and doctors examined his wounds. The load of buckshot had struck his arm, shoulder, and breast, piercing his lungs and lodging against his spine. He lingered in great pain for three days, then died and was given a Masonic funeral.

Source: Miller and Snell, *Great Gunfighters of the Kansas Cowtowns,* 78, 437–48.

Wren, William R.

(Rancher, law officer.) Bill Wren owned a cattle spread in Lampasas County, Texas. Pink Higgins was a neighboring rancher who became embroiled in a bloody feud with the Horrell brothers, and when Wren lent his assistance, he became Higgins' chief lieutenant. Severely wounded in a street fight in 1877, Wren signed a truce at the urging of Texas Rangers Major John B. Jones and later used his gun only on the side of the law as a county sheriff.

Gunfights: *March 26, 1877, near Lampasas, Texas.* Wren and several other Higgins men ambushed Mart and Sam Horrell at what became known as "Battle Branch." Sam was shot from his horse, but Mart, despite a wound, jumped out of the saddle and, with a wild-eyed charge, dispersed the bushwhackers single-handedly.

June 14, 1877, Lampasas, Texas. At 10:00 P.M. Pink Higgins, Wren, and Frank and Bob Mitchell, Higgins' brothers-in-law, encountered seven of the Horrell faction in the Lampasas town square. Gunfire broke out, and Wren dashed to a wagon yard a block north of the square. Soon he tried to make it back to his horse, but at that point he was shot in the posterior. Wren dragged himself up a flight of stairs and forted up at a second-story window.

About noon Higgins slipped out of town and returned with reinforcements, but at 1:00 P.M. local citizens finally persuaded the combatants to stop fighting. Frank Mitchell lay dead on a side street, but aside from Wren there were no other casualties.

July, 1877, Lampasas County, Texas. Higgins led his men in an assault on the Horrell ranch. The fifteen gunmen positioned themselves and opened fire. Two Horrell men were hit, and they were pinned down inside the ranch buildings, but they returned volley for volley. When the Higgins party ran low on cartridges following a forty-eight-hour siege, Pink ordered a withdrawal.

Sources: Webb, *Texas Rangers,* 334–39; Gillett, *Six Years with the Texas Rangers,* 73–80; Sonnichsen, *I'll Die Before I'll Run,* 134–35, 137–44.

Wyatt, Nathaniel Ellsworth

("Zip," "Wild Charlie," "Dick Yaeger")

(b. 1863, Indiana; d. September 7, 1895, Enid, Oklahoma. Farmhand, robber.) The son of an Indiana farmer, Wyatt moved with his parents and brother to Oklahoma in 1889. After his brother, Nim ("Six-Shooter Jack"), was killed in Texline, Texas, Zip turned bad. He was involved in several fatal shootings and began robbing stores, post offices, and trains. He took refuge in Indiana, but was tracked down and arrested by Chris Madsen. He escaped

from jail in Guthrie, but in 1895 a posse surprised and shot him.

Gunfights: *June 3, 1891, Mulhall, Oklahoma.* Wyatt spurred his horse down the street, firing his pistol and otherwise enjoying himself. Several unamused citizens pumped a few shots at him, and Wyatt returned their fire, wounding two men before galloping out of town.

March 29, 1894, Todd, Oklahoma. Wyatt and a pair of accomplices robbed a Blaine County store owned by E. H. Townsend. Townsend attempted to bar the door, but was shot in the left wrist. He then knocked the lead outlaw to the floor with the bar, whereupon the other two thieves shot him to death before the eyes of his stunned wife and children.

April, 1894, Dewey County, Oklahoma. While pulling another robbery, Zip encountered County Treasurer Fred Hoffman. In his usual vicious manner, Wyatt killed Hoffman in cold blood.

May 9, 1894, Whorton (Perry), Oklahoma. Wyatt and other desperadoes held up a Santa Fe train. The station agent began telegraphing a message for help, but Wyatt saw him and shot him to death.

July 4, 1894, Pryor's Grove, Kansas. Wyatt had fled to Kansas, and after a theft he was trailed by Sheriff Andrew Balfour. Balfour found the outlaw in Pryor's Grove and announced, "Zip, I've got a warrant for you." Zip whirled and began pumping lead. Balfour was hit and died minutes later.

July, 1895, near Okeene and Watonga,

Oklahoma. On June 12 Wyatt (using the alias "Dick Yaeger") and Ike Black had robbed a general store and post office in Oxley and, accompanied by Black's wife and one Jennie Freeman, had encamped in a pasture in the hills between Okeene and Watonga. There they were jumped by Wood County Sheriff Clay McGrath and possemen Hadwinger, J. K. Runnels, and Marion Hildreth. The fight, interrupted by a furious storm, lasted throughout the day. Wyatt was hit in the left arm, and Black in the left side, and the two fugitives abandoned their women and slipped to safety up a canyon.

August 1, 1895, near Cantonment, Oklahoma. Wyatt and Black had picketed their mounts in a stand of timber on the North Canadian near Cantonment, about fifty miles southwest of Enid. An eight-man posse led by Deputy Sam Campbell found them and opened fire. Black was shot in the head and killed, and Wyatt was struck in the chest. He wounded one of Campbell's men, but a slug tore his Winchester from his grasp. He retrieved the weapon and, pumping shells continuously, managed to escape on foot.

August 3, 1895, Skeleton Creek, Oklahoma. Hunted by several posses, Wyatt had hidden and fallen asleep in a cornfield near Skeleton Creek. A large posse located him and crept quietly into position. He was spotted simultaneously by Ad Poak and Tom Smith, who fired their rifles, shattering his pelvis and tearing a hole in his belly. Within a moment Wyatt gasped, "Don't shoot any more. I'm bad hit." He was disarmed and taken to Enid, where he died from his wounds a few weeks later.

Sources: Croy, *Trigger Marshal,* 81–88; Shirley, *Six-gun and Silver Star,* 125–26, 148, 150, 173–79.

Younger, James

(b. January 15, 1848, Lee's Summit, Missouri; d. October 19, 1902, St. Paul, Minnesota. Farmer, soldier, bank and train robber, tombstone salesman, insurance salesman.) Born four years to the day after his brother Cole, Jim Younger followed Cole into the ranks of Quantrill's raiders in hopes of avenging the recent murder of his father. Jim stayed with Quantrill throughout the remainder of the war, raiding and looting and acquiring the outlook and attitude of the outlaw. He was with Quantrill at the end of the war when the dwindling band was tracked down near Smiley, Kentucky. Quantrill was mortally wounded, but Jim was confined to the military prison in Alton, Illinois, and released late in 1865.

Jim returned to Missouri, and for a time he quietly helped to work the home farm. But soon he began helping Cole and the James brothers rob banks, and over the next several years he was involved in a number of holdups. He was also a participant in the bloody 1874 shootout which resulted in the death of John Younger and two Pinkerton men. Two years later he was captured with his brothers, Cole and Bob, in the manhunt following the battle at Northfield.

Bob died in prison, but in 1901 Jim and Cole were paroled under a new Minnesota law which released lifers who had served a number of years. The paroles thus obtained under the Deming Act, however, restored no legal rights and required that the recipients stay in Minnesota.

Cole and Jim soon began selling monuments for the P. N. Peterson Granite Company, and Jim fell in love with newspaper writer Alice J. Miller. Legally, however, he was forbidden to marry, and his health was in steady decline, as evidenced by his emaciated frame. Furthermore, he turned to selling insurance only to discover that the policies he wrote as a former convict were invalid. Despondent over these problems, he repaired to the Reardon Hotel in St. Paul, procured a pistol, and committed suicide. He was laid to rest in the family plot in Lee's Summit, Missouri.

Gunfights: *March 21, 1868, Russellville, Kentucky.* Jim was one of eight members of the James-Younger gang who robbed the Southern Bank of Kentucky in Russellville. Shooting broke out, and before the gang galloped out of town, bank president Nimrod Long was slightly wounded.

June 3, 1871, Corydon, Iowa. Jim and six other armed men attempted to hold up the office of the county treasurer, but that official eluded robbery by referring the bandits to the nearby Obocock Brothers Bank. The gang went directly to the bank, looted it, and rode out of town. A posse soon caught them, and shots were exchanged, but the outlaws made good their escape without casualties on either side.

April 29, 1872, Columbia, Kentucky. Jim, Cole, Bob, and the two James brothers robbed Columbia's Deposit Bank of approximately fifteen hundred dollars. The bank officials offered resistance, and the outlaws began shooting. Cashier R. A. C. Martin was killed with a slug in the head, and another man was hit in the hand before the gang could fight their way out of town.

March 16, 1874, Monegaw Springs, Missouri. Following a train holdup, Jim and John Younger were hiding in Monegaw Springs at the home of a friend. There they were located by Pinkerton Agents Louis J. Lull and John Boyle, who, assisted by Deputy Sheriff Ed Daniels, began snooping around the area in an attempt to capture the fugitives. The Youngers quickly found out about their activities, armed themselves, and rode in pursuit.

The Youngers caught the lawmen on the Chalk Level Road about 2:30 P.M. Jim whipped out a brace of six-guns and John leveled a shotgun and forced the stunned officers to disarm themselves. Jim dismounted and began to collect the weapons when Lull suddenly produced a pistol from his hip pocket and pumped a slug into John's neck. John blasted Lull with the shotgun, mortally wounding the detective. Daniels managed to shoot Jim in the thigh, but the Youngers turned their fire on the deputy and gunned him down.

Boyle fled to safety, but his two cohorts lost their lives. John Younger collapsed and died on the spot, and Jim, who had only a slight wound, left the country after arranging for friends to take care of his dead brother. At this time Cole and Bob were in Mississippi, and they learned of the shooting several weeks later by reading a newspaper account. Stunned, they immediately embarked for Arkansas, where they soon found Jim.

September 21, 1874, Clay-Ray county line, Missouri. Flourney Yancey of the St. Louis Police Department was detailed to track down the James-Younger gang. For weeks he scoured the country unsuccessfully, but on the morning of September 21, near the Clay-Ray county line, he came upon two suspicious characters whom he identified as Jesse James and Jim Younger. Yancey reported with impressive precision that the three men exchanged three shots, and that he thought he had wounded Jesse. But the two fugitives fled and could not be found by posses.

September 7, 1876, Northfield, Minnesota. When the eight members of the James-Younger gang moved into Northfield to rob the First National Bank, Jim stationed himself at the bridge leading to the main part of town. When the shooting broke out, Jim spurred forward, reins in his teeth and working a pistol in each hand. By the time the gang fought their way out of town, the band had been horribly shot up, leaving two dead in the streets of Northfield.

The unfamiliar countryside soon was swarming with posses, and the James brothers split off to improve their chances of escape. Jim, Cole, Bob, and Samuel Wells stuck together, struggling on through a nightmare of misery. For two weeks there were clashes with posses, constant starvation, the agony of wounds, and desperate attempts to find safety in alien territory. At last, after one last fight on September 21 with a posse, the hunted men surrendered.

Wells was dead, Bob had been hit three times, Cole eleven times, and Jim five. Jim's worst wound came from a bullet that had shattered his jaw and lodged just below his brain. He was able to take only liquid nourishment, and the pain remained so great that three years later he prevailed upon a prison hospital intern to try to take out the bullet. After working at intervals of two days, the intern finally removed the slug. Jim's smashed jawbone was obtained after his death by the Minnesota Historical Society and placed on display.

Sources: Breihan, *Younger Brothers;* Croy, *Last of the Great Outlaws;* Horan, *Desperate Men,* 10, 100, 109–23, 171; Settle, *Jesse James Was His Name,* 23, 60–62, 68, 69, 73, 80–84, 92–97, 162–63, 181, 225; Drago, *Road Agents and Train Robbers,* 128, 131–66, 175, 226.

Younger, John

(b. 1851, Lee's Summit, Missouri; d. March 16, 1874, Monegaw Springs, Missouri. Farmer, clerk, train robber.) John Younger was one of fourteen children born to a Missouri landholder and politician. He helped his father with farm work, but the senior Younger was killed by Jayhawkers, and John became increasingly bitter and moody. He killed his first man at the age of fifteen, but he was exonerated. Two years later, however, he was alternately hanged and beaten in his own barn by a posse in an attempt to discover the whereabouts of Cole and Jim Younger.

John's mother died in 1870, and he grew even more temperamental and surly. He joined Cole, Jim, and a sister in Texas, and for a while he clerked at a store in Dallas. He soon got into trouble, and after gunning down the sheriff of Dallas County he left Texas. He returned to Missouri while a wound healed, then went to California in June, 1871. He soon headed back, and while aboard a train in Colorado he got into another gunfight. He jumped off the train, made his way to Denver, then joined a wagon train en route to Kansas. Finally, he arrived at the home of an uncle, Dr. L. W. Twyman, in Blue Mills, Missouri, and tried to drop out of sight.

It is possible that John rode from time to time with the James-Younger gang during this period, and in particular he was suspected of assisting with the robbery of a train at Gads Hill, Missouri, on January 31, 1874. A few weeks later John and Jim Younger shot it out with lawmen near Monegaw Springs, Missouri. John shot down two of the officers, but was mortally wounded. He was buried nearby, but later his remains were transferred to the family plot at Lee's Summit, Missouri.

Gunfights: *January, 1866, Independence, Missouri.* John became involved in an argument with a man named Gillcreas. Gillcreas angrily slapped the fifteen-year-old Younger with a dead fish, then stomped off to get his slingshot. When he returned with this weapon, John snatched up a revolver from his wagon and fatally wounded Gillcreas. The next day a coroner's jury acquitted Younger on grounds of self-defense.

January, 1871, Dallas, Texas. John was in the company of Thompson McDaniels when Dallas County Sheriff C. W. Nichols and Deputy John McMahan approached to arrest him. The warrant concerned a minor shooting incident involving a man named Russell, but Younger vehemently refused to go with the lawmen. At last the two officers tried to use force, and gunfire broke out.

At this point a brother of Russell ran up with a shotgun, and John was hit in the arm with buckshot. McDaniels wounded Sheriff Nichols, and Younger killed the other lawman. McDaniels and Younger then mounted and rode to the home of a friend, where John had his wound treated. The two men then fled to Missouri, finding refuge there in the home of a mutual friend near tiny Chalk Level.

1871, near Denver, Colorado. While returning to Missouri from California, the quarrelsome Younger tangled with fellow passengers. Shots were exchanged, and while no one was hurt, Younger knew that he could not stand up to the scrutiny of an investigation. Therefore, he jumped from the train and made his way to Denver on foot.

March 16, 1874, Monegaw Springs, Missouri. After the Gads Hill train robbery, John and his brother Jim took refuge at the home of a friend, Theodorick Snuffer, at Monegaw Springs. Pinkerton detectives discovered their whereabouts and determined to arrest them. Accompanied by Deputy Sheriff Ed Daniels, Agents Louis J. Lull and John Boyle spent a day in the vicinity posing as cattle buyers. When they stopped at the Snuffer home to "ask directions," the Younger brothers hid, then followed them when they rode off.

The Youngers quickly overtook the detectives on the Chalk Level Road. John leveled his shotgun, and Jim pulled two pistols, and the lawmen were directed to disarm themselves. After quizzing the "cattle buyers," Jim jumped to the ground and began to collect the guns.

Suddenly Lull reached behind his back, pulled out a concealed pistol, and shot John in the throat. John emptied both barrels of his shotgun into Lull, and the detective's horse bolted into the woods. Lull collapsed in the road and died the next day in a nearby house. Daniels shot Jim in the thigh, but John pulled his revolver and fired at the deputy. John then tumbled to the ground and died within moments.

Sources: Breihan, *Younger Brothers,* 4–5, 33, 59–64, 121–31; Drago, *Road*

Younger, Robert

(b. October, 1853, Lee's Summit, Missouri; d. September 16, 1889, Stillwater, Minnesota. Farmer, bank and train robber, convict.) Bob Younger was the baby of the Missouri brothers who followed the outlaw trail with Frank and Jesse James. Bob and his brother John were too young to fight in the Civil War, but after the older Cole and Jim began robbing banks, Bob and John joined them in the quest for easy money. There is little precise information about which robberies Bob participated in, but he proved to be a cool operator who pursued the outlaw's life quietly and with no regrets.

Bob was captured with his brothers in the manhunt following the Northfield disaster. The state of Minnesota provided a maximum sentence of life imprisonment if a guilty plea were entered in a murder trial, and rather than risk hanging, the Youngers proclaimed their rather obvious guilt. While awaiting trial in Northfield, the bedridden Bob unrepentantly declared to a newspaper reporter: "We are rough men and used to rough ways."

Behind bars Bob was a model prisoner and devoted several years to studying medicine. But he contracted tuberculosis, and after his death in 1889 he was interred in the family burial plot at Lee's Summit, Missouri.

Gunfights: April 29, 1872, Columbia, Kentucky. Bob accompanied four other members of the James-Younger gang in a holdup of Columbia's Deposit Bank. Two of the robbers stayed outside with the mounts, while the other three went in to loot the bank. They met resistance, and shooting erupted. Judge James Garnett was wounded in the hand, and cashier R. A. C. Martin was killed before the thieves dashed outside and vaulted onto their horses for the getaway.

September 7, 1876, Northfield, Minnesota. The James-Younger gang rode eight strong into Northfield to rob the First National Bank. Jesse, Bob, and Samuel Wells went inside and confronted bank employees Joseph Lee Heywood, F. J. Wilcox, and A. E. Bunker. When the bankers refused to cooperate, the outlaws began to work them over, but Bunker suddenly darted outside. Wells wounded him, then the three bandits tried to rejoin their cohorts outside. As they left the bank one of them turned and cold-bloodedly shot Heywood to death.

In the street the citizenry of Northfield angrily opened fire on the outlaws, and Clell Miller was peppered in the face with buckshot. As Jesse and Bob crouched behind their mounts, a merchant named A. E. Manning shot Younger's horse in the head, and Bob began to fire at Manning.

Suddenly Miller and Bill Chadwell were shot off their horses and pitched dead into the street, and Bob decided to seek better cover. He sprinted for an outside staircase nearby, still trading shots with Manning. But upstairs, stationed with a carbine in a second-story window, was a young medical student named Henry Wheeler, who had just killed Miller. Wheeler fired a slug which tore along Younger's right arm from his hand to the elbow, but Bob instantly executed a border shift and kept shooting. Cole galloped by and picked up

Bob, and the surviving outlaws raced out of town.

September 21, 1876, near Madelia, Minnesota. The following days were filled with danger and confusion as the gang tried to elude swarming posses in unfamiliar territory. Jesse and Frank James escaped on their own, but Samuel Wells and Cole and Jim Younger stayed with the weakened Bob. At last six possemen tracked the four bedraggled men to a thicket in a swamp near Madelia. There was a vicious shootout, and three of the officers were wounded. But Wells was killed, Bob was shot in the chest, Jim had five holes in him, and Cole had suffered eleven wounds.

At last Bob stood with his hands up and announced, "They're all down except me." Another shot rang out, and Bob was nicked in the cheek, but then the firing stopped, and the Youngers were taken prisoner.

Sources: Breihan, *Younger Brothers;* Croy, *Last of the Great Outlaws;* Horan, *Desperate Men,* 10, 100, 104–29; Settle, *Jesse James Was His Name,* 23, 69, 80–84, 89, 92–97, 162, 181; Drago, *Road Agents and Train Robbers,* 128, 134, 142–66, 174–75.

Younger, Thomas Coleman

(b. January 15, 1844, Lee's Summit, Missouri; d. February 21, 1916, Lee's Summit, Missouri. Farmer, soldier, bank and train robber, convict, tombstone salesman, insurance salesman, showman, lecturer.) The seventh of fourteen children, Cole Younger was reared on his father's land near Lee's Summit, Missouri. Although a slaveholder, the senior Younger was a Union sympathizer, and during the Kansas-Missouri border troubles Kansas Jayhawkers raided the Younger property.

Cole promptly joined William Clarke Quantrill's Missouri "Bushwhackers," and when his father was killed in 1862, he joined regular Confederate troops. At the age of eighteen he was appointed first lieutenant in a company in Upton B. Hays's Missouri regiment. He continued to participate in guerilla actions, however, and he was with Quantrill during the vicious massacre at Lawrence, Kansas. Late in 1863 Cole was stationed in Texas and Louisiana, and near Dallas he met sixteen-year-old Myra Belle Shirley. She would later become the notorious Belle Starr and would claim that her daughter Pearl had been sired by Cole. Various military assignments took Cole to Colorado, Mexico, and California, and he was on the Pacific Coast raising recruits when the war ended. He visited an uncle in Los Angeles, then headed for home, arriving the same week as his brother Jim. A short time later, in January, 1866, Cole ran into a neighbor who was an old Quantrill man, Frank James. Frank introduced Cole to his brother Jesse, also a Quantrill veteran. A few weeks later Frank and Cole teamed up to lead a bank holdup in Liberty, Missouri. With members of his family Cole then returned to Texas and Louisiana for several months to enjoy his illegally but easily gotten gains. When he went back to Missouri, he and his brothers united with the James brothers to form a bandit gang that would run rampant for years.

The aggressive, ruthless Jesse would become acknowledged as leader of "the Boys," but Cole never got along well with Jesse and led several robberies himself. In time, almost every bank, train, or stagecoach robbery was attributed to the James-Younger gang, and it is difficult to list the specific holdups in which Cole was involved. But until

Cole, Jim, and Bob were captured at Northfield in 1876, they were active, bold, and successful highwaymen. They committed robberies throughout Missouri and surrounding states and continued to make their home base in Missouri. Whenever pressure from the law became too great, the Youngers left the state, usually for Texas but on at least one occasion for California. Following the fiasco at Northfield, Cole, Bob, and Jim were wounded, and after desperately eluding posses for two weeks, they were taken into custody. They were thrown into a wagon and transported to the nearest town, where Cole, despite eleven wounds, stood up and made a sweeping bow to the astonished ladies who were present. Cole and his brothers pled guilty to escape hanging and were sentenced to life imprisonment.

Bob died in prison, but Cole and Jim were paroled in 1901. The next year Jim committed suicide, then in 1903 Cole received a pardon. He worked briefly and ineffectually as a tombstone salesman and as an insurance salesman, even though, as a convict, he was prohibited from drawing up legal contracts. He then teamed up with Frank James in a Wild West Show venture, and later he traveled widely, lecturing on his adventures and the evils of crime. He retired in Lee's Summit and died there in 1916 at the age of seventy-two.

Gunfights: *November 10, 1861, near Independence, Missouri.* Quantrill's men had a skirmish with Federal troops near Independence. During the shooting Cole killed his first man, downing him with a pistol shot measured at seventy-one yards.

December 25, 1862, Kansas City, Missouri. Younger had heard that the men responsible for the recent death of his father were spending Christmas in Kansas City. Cole and five of his men—Abe Cunningham, Fletcher Taylor, Zach Traber, George Todd, and George Clayton—spent Christmas Day searching barrooms. About midnight they entered a saloon on Main Street, and a fight quickly erupted with a man gambling at a table. Cole shot the man to death and then fled the premises with his men.

February 13, 1866, Liberty, Missouri. Cole and Frank James led ten other hard cases into Liberty with the intention of robbing the local bank. (No bank in the United States had ever been robbed before, aside from the bank in St. Albans, Vermont, which was looted by Confederate soldiers in October, 1864.) The desperadoes met in the town square, and two of them entered the bank at 8:55 A.M. Cashier Greenup Bird was alone, except for his young son, and at gunpoint he filled two grain sacks with more than fifty-seven thousand dollars. The two bandits leaped onto their horses, and the gang thundered out of town, whooping the Rebel yell and firing indiscriminately. A young student named George Wymore, on his way to William Jewell College with a friend, was shot down and killed.

March 21, 1868, Russellville, Kentucky. The James brothers, Cole and Jim Younger, Oliver and George Shepherd, John Jarrette, and Jim White rode up to Russellville's Southern Bank of Kentucky. Jesse led several of his men into the bank while the other bandits remained mounted to guard the street. There was shooting inside, and when the robbers emerged with their loot, bank president Nimrod Long, already grazed in the head by Jesse, dashed out and shouted an alarm. The robbers took several wild shots at him, then raced away.

December 7, 1869, Gallatin, Missouri. At noon Cole accompanied Jesse, Frank, and several other henchmen in a robbery of the Daviess County Savings Bank. Inside the bank Jesse shot and killed John Sheets, and townspeople armed themselves and ran toward the scene. Jesse's horse bolted, but he jumped up behind Frank, and the gang shot their way out of town.

April 29, 1872, Columbia, Kentucky. Cole and four other bandits rode into Columbia and stopped before the Deposit Bank. Three men went inside and proceeded to hold up the bank. Judge James Garnett began to shout a warning, and one of the robbers shot him in the hand. Cashier R. A. C. Martin reached into a drawer for a revolver, but the bandits killed him with a .45 slug in the head. The outlaws then hastily scooped fifteen hundred dollars into a grain sack, then rejoined their two mounted companions and galloped to safety.

September 7, 1876, Northfield, Minnesota. A few days earlier the James-Younger gang had planned to rob a bank in Mankato, Minnesota, but had been frightened away by an ominous-looking group of citizens who later proved to be idle onlookers at a construction project adjacent to the bank. At the suggestion of Bill Chadwell, they shifted their plans to the First National Bank of Northfield. The eight bandits donned linen dusters to hide their weapons and rode into town. Three of the thieves dismounted and walked inside the bank with a grain sack, but cashier Joseph L. Heywood refused to cooperate, and one of them angrily slashed his throat and shot him.

Cole, who was outside in charge of keeping people away from the bank, panicked when he heard the shooting and killed an innocent bystander, Nicholas Gustavson. Angry townspeople rushed to the scene and killed Clell Miller and William Stiles. Bob Younger was hit in the elbow, and his horse was shot down, but Cole picked him up, and, riding double, they fought their way out of town with the other four survivors.

The state was alerted, and the countryside soon was filled with posses. After a few days of pursuit Jesse wanted to abandon Bob Younger, who could not move rapidly. Cole stiffly refused, and Jesse and Frank went their own way, eventually returning to Missouri and safety. Cole, Jim, Bob, and Samuel Wells struggled on, skirmishing several times with manhunters. After two weeks of such pursuit, Cole had been wounded eleven times, Jim five, and Bob four. On September 21 a seven-man posse killed Wells, and the three Younger brothers surrendered.

Sources: Croy, *Last of the Great Outlaws;* Breihan, *Younger Brothers;* Younger, *Story of Cole Younger by Himself;* Drago, *Road Agents and Train Robbers,* 128, 131–68, 173–76.

Bibliography

Books

Adams, Ramon F. *A Fitting Death for Billy the Kid.* Norman: University of Oklahoma Press, 1960.

―――. *Burs Under the Saddle: A Second Look at Books and Histories of the West.* Norman: University of Oklahoma Press, 1964.

―――. *More Burs Under the Saddle: Books and Histories of the West.* Norman: University of Oklahoma Press, 1978.

―――. *Six Guns and Saddle Leather: A Bibliography of Books and Pamphlets on Western Outlaws and Gunmen.* Rev. enl. ed. Norman: University of Oklahoma Press, 1969.

Anderson, Frank W. *Bill Miner: Train Robber.* Calgary, Alta., Canada: Frontiers Unlimited, n.d.

Archambeau, Ernest R., ed. *Old Tascosa, 1885–1888.* Canyon, Texas: Panhandle Plains Historical Society, 1966.

Ashbaugh, Don. *Nevada's Turbulent Yesterday.* Los Angeles: Westernlore Press, 1963.

Askins, Charles. *Texans: Guns and History.* New York: Winchester Press, 1970.

Axford, Joseph Mack. *Around Western Campfires.* New York: Pageant Press, 1964.

Baker, Pearl. *The Wild Bunch at Robbers Roost.* New York: Abelard-Schuman, Ltd., 1965.

Ballert, Marion, with Breihan, Carl W. *Billy the Kid: A Date with Destiny.* Seattle: Superior Publishing Company, 1970.

Bard, Floyd C. *Horse Wrangler: Sixty Years in the Saddle in Wyoming and Montana.* Norman: University of Oklahoma Press, 1960.

Bartholomew, Ed. *Black Jack Ketchum: Last of the Hold-Up Kings.* Houston: Frontier Press of Texas, 1955.

―――. *Cullen Baker: Premier Texas Gunfighter.* Houston: Frontier Press of Texas, 1954.

———. *Henry Plummer: Montana Outlaw Boss.* Ruidoso, N.Mex.: Frontier Book Co., 1960.

———. *Jesse Evans: A Texas Hideburner.* Houston: Frontier Press of Texas, 1955.

———. *Wild Bill Longley: A Texas Hard-Case.* Houston: Frontier Press of Texas, 1953.

———. *Wyatt Earp: The Man and the Myth.* Toyahvale, Texas: Frontier Book Company, 1964.

———. *Wyatt Earp: The Untold Story.* Toyahvale, Texas: Frontier Book Company, 1963.

Bennett, Edwin Lewis. *Boom Town Boy in Old Creede Colorado.* Chicago: Sage Books, 1966.

Blankenship, Russell. *And There Were Men.* New York: Alfred A. Knopf, 1942.

Boorstin, Daniel J. *The Americans.* Vol. 2, *The National Experience.* New York: Random House, Inc., 1965.

Boyer, Glenn G. *Suppressed Murder of Wyatt Earp.* San Antonio: The Naylor Company, 1967.

Breakenridge, William M. *Helldorado.* Boston: Houghton Mifflin Company, 1928.

Breihan, Carl W. *Great Gunfighters of the West.* San Antonio: The Naylor Company, 1962.

———. *Great Lawmen of the West.* New York: Bonanza Books, 1963.

———. *Younger Brothers.* San Antonio: The Naylor Company, 1961.

Brophy, Frank Cullen. *Arizona Sketch Book: Fifty Historical Sketches.* Phoenix, Ariz.: Ampco Press, Arizona-Messenger Printing Co., 1952.

Brown, Dee. *Trail Driving Days.* New York: Bonanza Books, 1952.

Brown, Mark H. *The Plainsmen of the Yellowstone.* New York: G. P. Putnam's Sons, 1961.

Brown, Robert L. *An Empire of Silver: A History of the San Juan Silver Rush.* Caldwell, Idaho: Caxton Printers, Ltd., 1965.

Burroughs, John Rolfe. *Where the Old West Stayed Young.* New York: William Morrow and Co., 1962.

Burton, Jeff. *Black Jack Christian, Outlaw.* Santa Fe, N.Mex.: The Press of the Territorian, 1967.

———. *Dynamite and Six-Shooters.* Santa Fe, N.Mex.: Palomino Press, 1970.

Canton, Frank M. *The Autobiography of Frank M. Canton.* Norman: University of Oklahoma Press, 1954.

Castleman, Harvey N. *Sam Bass: The Train Robber.* Girard, Kans.: Haldeman-Julius Publications, 1944.

Chrisman, Harry E. *The Ladder of Rivers.* Denver: Sage Books, 1962.

Clark, O. S. *Clay Allison of the Washita.* Attica, Ind.: G. M. Williams, 1920.

Cleland, Robert Glass. *The Cattle on a Thousand Hills: Southern California, 1850-1870.* San Marino, Calif.: Huntington Library, 1941.

Coe, George W. *Frontier Fighter.* Albuquerque: University of New Mexico Press, 1934.

Coe, Wilbur. *Ranch on the Ruidoso: The Story of a Pioneer Family in New Mexico, 1871-1968.* New York: Alfred A. Knopf, 1968.

Collins, Dabney Otis. *The Hanging of Bad Jack Slade.* Denver, Colo.: Golden Ball Press, 1963.

Conger, Roger N. *Texas Rangers: Sesquicentennial Anniversary, 1823-1973.* Fort Worth: Heritage Publications, Inc., 1973.

Coolidge, Dane. *Fighting Men of the West.* New York: E. P. Dutton & Co., Inc., 1932.

Cox, William R. *Luke Short and His Era.* Garden City, N.Y.: Doubleday and Company, Inc., 1961.

Crichton, Kyle S. *Law and Order, Ltd.: The Rousing Life of Elfego Baca of New Mexico.* Glorieta, N.Mex.: Rio Grande Press, Inc., 1928.

Croy, Homer. *Jesse James Was My Neighbor.* New York: Duell, Sloan and Pearce, 1949.

————. *Last of the Great Outlaws.* New York: Duell, Sloan and Pearce, 1956.

————. *Trigger Marshal: The Story of Chris Madsen.* New York: Duell, Sloan and Pearce, 1958.

Cunningham, Eugene. *Triggernometry: A Gallery of Gunfighters.* New York: Press of the Pioneers, Inc., 1934.

Dalton, Emmett, and Jungmeyer, Jack. *When the Daltons Rode.* Garden City, N.Y.: Doubleday, Doran and Co., Inc., 1931.

Delony, Lewis S. *40 Years a Peace Officer.* [Privately printed by the author, probably in Abilene, Texas, ca. 1937].

Douglas, C. L. *Famous Texas Feuds.* Dallas, Texas: Turner Company, 1936.

Drago, Harry Sinclair. *The Great Range Wars.* New York: Dodd, Mead & Company, 1970.

————. *Outlaws on Horseback.* New York: Dodd, Mead & Company, 1964.

————. *Road Agents and Train Robbers.* New York: Dodd, Mead & Company, 1973.

————. *Wild, Woolly & Wicked.* New York: Clarkson N. Potter, Inc., 1960.

Dunlop, Richard. *Doctors of the American Frontier.* Garden City, N.Y.: Doubleday and Company, 1965.

Dykstra, Robert R. *The Cattle Towns.* New York: Atheneum, 1970.

Elman, Robert. *Badmen of the West.* Secaucus, N.J.: Ridge Press, Inc., 1974.

Erwin, Allen A. *The Southwest of John H. Slaughter, 1841-1922.* Glendale, Calif.: Arthur H. Clark Company, 1965.

Faulk, Odie B. *The Geronimo Campaign.* New York: Oxford University Press, 1969.

————. *Tombstone: Myth and Reality.* New York: Oxford University Press, 1972.

Fiedler, Mildred. *Wild Bill and Deadwood.* New York: Bonanza Books, 1965.

Fisher, O. C., with Dykes, J. C. *King Fisher: His Life and Times.* Norman: University of Oklahoma Press, 1966.

Forrest, Earle R. *Arizona's Dark and Bloody Ground.* Caldwell, Idaho: Caxton Printers, Ltd., 1953.

Frink, Maurice. *Cow Country Cavalcade.* Denver, Colo.: Old West Publishing Company, Fred A. Rosenstock, 1954.

Fuller, Henry C. *A Texas Sheriff.* Nacogdoches, Texas: Baker Printing Co., 1931.

Fulton, Maurice Garland. *History of the Lincoln County War.* Ed. Robert N. Mullin. Tucson: University of Arizona Press, 1968.

————. *Roswell in Its Early Years.* Roswell, N.Mex.: Hall-Poorbaugh Press, Inc., 1963.

Gard, Wayne. *Frontier Justice.* Norman: University of Oklahoma Press, 1949.

————. *Sam Bass.* Boston: Houghton Mifflin Co., 1936.

Garrett, Pat F. *The Authentic Life of Billy, the Kid.* Norman: University of Oklahoma Press, 1954.

Gaylord, Chic. *Handgunner's Guide: Including the Art of the Quick-Draw and Combat Shooting.* New York: Hastings House, Publishers, 1960.

Gillett, James Buchanan. *Six Years with the Texas Rangers.* New Haven: Yale University Press, 1925.

Gibson, A. M. *The Life and Death of Colonel Albert Jennings Fountain.* Norman: University of Oklahoma Press, 1965.

Graves, Richard S. *Oklahoma Outlaws.* Fort Davis, Texas: Frontier Book Co., 1968.

Greenwood, Robert. *The California Outlaw, Tiburcio Vásquez.* Los Gatos, Calif.: Talisman Press, 1960.

Gregg, Andrew K. *New Mexico in the Nineteenth Century: A Pictorial History.* Albuquerque: University of New Mexico Press, 1968.

Haley, J. Evetts. *Jeff Milton: A Good Man with a Gun.* Norman: University of Oklahoma Press, 1948.

Hamlin, Lloyd, and Hamlin, Rose. *Hamlin's Tombstone Picture Gallery.* Glendale, Calif.: Western Americana Press of Glendale, 1960.

Hamlin, William Lee. *The True Story of Billy the Kid.* Caldwell, Idaho: Caxton Printers, Ltd., 1959.

Hanes, Colonel Bailey C. *Bill Doolin, Outlaw O.T.* Norman: University of Oklahoma Press, 1968.

Hardin, John Wesley. *The Life of John Wesley Hardin.* Seguin, Texas: Smith and Moore, 1896.

Harkey, Dee. *Mean as Hell.* New York: Signet Book Edition, 1948.

Hayes, Jess G. *Boots and Bullets: The Life and Times of John W. Wentworth.* Tucson, Ariz.: University of Arizona Press, 1968.

Hendricks, George D. *The Bad Man of the West.* San Antonio: Naylor Company, 1942.

Hening, H. B. ed. *George Curry, 1861–1947: An Autobiography.* Albuquerque, N.Mex.: University of New Mexico Press, 1958.

Hertzog, Peter. *A Dictionary of New Mexico Desperadoes.* Santa Fe, N.Mex.: Press of the Territorian, 1965.

Hogan, Ray. *The Life and Death of Johnny Ringo.* New York: New American Library, Inc., 1963.

Hollon, W. Eugene. *Frontier Violence: Another Look.* New York: Oxford University Press, 1974.

Hoover, H. A. *Early Days in the Mogollons.* El Paso, Texas: Western Press, 1958.

Horan, James D. *Across the Cimarron.* New York: Crown Publishers, Inc., 1956.

————. *Desperate Men.* New York: Bonanza Books, 1949.

————. *The Wild Bunch.* New York: New American Library, 1958.

————, and Sann, Paul. *Pictorial History of the Wild West.* New York: Crown Publishers, Inc., 1954.

Horn, Tom. *Life of Tom Horn: A Vindication.* Denver: Louthan Company, 1904.

House, Boyce. *Cowtown Colonist.* San Antonio: Naylor Company, 1946.

Hubbs, Barney. *Robert Clay Allison, Gentleman Gunfighter, 1840–1887.* Pecos, Texas: n.p., 1966.

Hungerford, Edward. *Wells Fargo: Advancing the American Frontier.* New York: Random House, 1949.

Hunt, Frazier. *Cap Mossman: Last of the Great Cowmen.* New York: Hastings House, 1951.

————. *The Tragic Days of Billy the Kid.* Caldwell, Idaho: Caxton Printers, Ltd., 1959.

Hutchinson, W. H. *A Bar Cross Man: The Life & Personal Writings of Eugene Manlove Rhodes.* Norman: University of Oklahoma Press, 1956.

————, and Mullin, R. N. *Whiskey Jim and a Kid Named Billie.* Clarendon, Texas: Clarendon Press, 1967.

Jackson, Joseph Henry. *Anybody's Gold: The Story of California's Mining Towns.* New York: Appleton-Century Company, Inc., 1941.

————. *Bad Company.* New York: Harcourt, Brace and Company, 1949.

Jahns, Pat. *The Frontier World of Doc Holliday.* New York: Hastings House, Publishers, 1957.

James, Jesse, Jr. *Jesse James, My Father.* Independence, Mo.: Sentinel Publishing Company, 1899.

Jeffrey, John Mason. *Adobe and Iron.* La Jolla, Calif.: Prospect Avenue Press, 1969.

Jennings, N. A. *A Texas Ranger.* Dallas: Southwest Press, 1930.

Keithley, Ralph. *Bucky O'Neill: He Stayed with 'Em While He Lasted.* Caldwell, Idaho: The Caxton Printers, Ltd., 1949.

Keleher, William A. *The Fabulous Frontier: Twelve New Mexico Items.* Santa Fe, N.Mex.: The Rydal Press, 1945.

———. *Violence in Lincoln County, 1869–81.* Albuquerque: University of New Mexico Printing Plant, 1957.

Kemp, Ben W., with Dykes, J. C. *Cow Dust and Saddle Leather.* Norman: University of Oklahoma Press, 1968.

Klasner, Lily. *My Girlhood Among Outlaws.* Tucson: University of Arizona Press, 1972.

Knight, Oliver. *Fort Worth: Outpost on the Trinity.* Norman: University of Oklahoma Press, 1953.

Lake, Stuart N. *Wyatt Earp: Frontier Marshal.* Boston: Houghton Mifflin Company, 1931.

Langford, Nathaniel Pitt. *Vigilante Days and Ways.* Missoula, Mont.: University of Montana Press, 1957.

Lefors, Joe. *Wyoming Peace Officer.* Laramie, Wyo.: Laramie Printing Company, 1953.

Liggett, William, Sr. *My Seventy-Five Years Along the Mexican Border.* New York: Exposition Press, 1964.

Looney, Ralph. *Haunted Highways.* New York: Hastings House, Publishers, 1968.

Lyon, Peter. *The Wild, Wild West.* New York: Funk & Wagnalls, 1969.

McCarty, John L. *Maverick Town: The Story of Old Tascosa.* Norman: University of Oklahoma Press, 1946.

McKennon, C. H. *Iron Men: A Saga of the Deputy United States Marshals Who Rode the Indian Territory.* Garden City, N.Y.: Doubleday and Company, Inc., 1967.

McNeal, Thomas Allen. *When Kansas Was Young.* New York: Macmillan Company, 1922.

Martin, Douglas D. *Tombstone's Epitaph.* Albuquerque, N.Mex.: University of New Mexico Press, 1951.

Martin, Jack. *Border Boss.* San Antonio: Naylor Company, 1942.

Masterson, W. B. *Famous Gunfighters of the Western Frontier.* Fort Davis, Texas: Frontier Book Company, 1968.

Mercer, A. S. *The Banditti of the Plains.* Norman: University of Oklahoma Press, 1954.

Metz, Leon C. *Dallas Stoudenmire: El Paso Marshal.* Austin: Pemberton Press, 1969.

———. *John Selman: Texas Gunfighter.* New York: Hastings House, Publishers, 1966.

———. *Pat Garrett: The Story of a Western Lawman.* Norman: University of Oklahoma Press, 1974.

Middagh, John. *Frontier Newspaper: The El Paso Times.* El Paso: Texas Western College Press, 1958.

Miller, Floyd. *Bill Tilghman: Marshal of the Last Frontier.* New York: Doubleday and Company, Inc., 1968.

Miller, Joseph. *Arizona: The Last Frontier.* New York: Hastings House, 1956.

Miller, Nyle H., and Snell, Joseph W. *Great Gunfighters of the Kansas Cowtowns, 1867–1886.* Lincoln: University of Nebraska Press, 1963.

———. *Why the West Was Wild.* Topeka: Kansas State Historical Society, 1963.

Monaghan, Jay. *Last of the Bad Men.* New York: Bobbs-Merrill Company, 1946.

Mullin, Robert N. *The Boyhood of Billy the Kid.* El Paso: Texas Western Press, 1967.

Myers, John Myers. *Doc Holliday.* Boston: Little, Brown & Company, Inc., 1955.

———. *The Last Chance: Tombstone's Early Years.* New York: E. P. Dutton & Company, Inc., 1950.

Myers, S. D. ed. *Pioneer Surveyor, Frontier Lawyer: The Personal Narrative of O. W. Williams, 1877–1902.* El Paso: Texas Western College Press, 1966.

Nash, Jay Robert. *Bloodletters and Badmen.* New York: M. Evans and Company, Inc., 1973.

Nordyke, Lewis. *John Wesley Hardin: Texas Gunman.* New York: William Morrow & Company, 1957.

Nunn, W. C. *Texas Under the Carpetbaggers.* Austin: University of Texas Press, 1962.

O'Connor, Richard. *Bat Masterson.* New York: Doubleday and Company, Inc., 1957.

———. *Pat Garrett.* New York: Ace Books, Inc., 1960.

———. *Wild Bill Hickok.* New York: Ace Books, Inc., 1959.

Pace, Dick. *Golden Gulch: The Story of Montana's Fabulous Alder Gulch.* Butte, Mont.: n.p., 1962.

Paine, Lauran. *Texas Ben Thompson.* Los Angeles: Westernlore Press, 1966.

———. *Tom Horn, Man of the West.* Barre, Mass.: Barre Publishing Company, 1963.

Parsons, John E. *The Peacemaker and Its Rivals: An Account of the Single Action Colt.* New York: William Morrow and Company, 1950.

Peavy, Charles D. *Charles A. Siringo, a Texas Picaro.* Austin, Texas: Steck-Vaughn Company, 1967.

Pence, Mary Lou, and Homsher, Lola M. *The Ghost Towns of Wyoming.* New York: Hastings House, 1956.

Poe, John William. *The Death of Billy the Kid.* Boston and New York: Houghton Mifflin Company, 1933.

Pointer, Larry. *In Search of Butch Cassidy.* Norman: University of Oklahoma Press, 1977.

Polk, Stella Gipson. *Mason and Mason County: A History.* Austin: Pemberton Press. 1966.

Preece, Harold. *The Dalton Gang: End of an Outlaw Era.* New York: Hastings House, 1963.

————. *Lone Star Man: Ira Aten.* New York: Hastings House, Publishers, 1960.

Raine, William MacLeod. *Famous Sheriffs and Western Outlaws.* Garden City, N.Y.: Garden City Publishing Company, Inc., 1903.

Rascoe, Jesse Ed. *Some Western Treasures.* Cisco, Texas: Frontier Book Company, 1964.

Ray, G. B. *Murder at the Corners.* San Antonio, Texas: The Naylor Company, 1957.

Ray, Grace Ernestine. *Wily Women of the West.* San Antonio: The Naylor Company, 1972.

Raymond, Dora Neill. *Captain Lee Hall of Texas.* Norman: University of Oklahoma Press, 1940.

Rennert, Vincent Paul. *Western Outlaws.* New York: Crowell-Collier Press, 1968.

Rickards, Colin. *"Buckskin Frank" Leslie: Gunman of Tombstone.* El Paso, Texas: Western College Press, 1964.

————. *The Gunfight at Blazer's Mill.* El Paso: Texas Western Press, 1974.

————. *Mysterious Dave Mather.* Santa Fe, N.Mex.: Press of the Territorian, 1968.

Ridings, Sam P. *The Chisholm Trail.* Guthrie, Okla.: Co-Operative Publishing Company, 1936.

Robertson, Frank C., and Harris, Beth Kay. *Soapy Smith, King of the Frontier Con Men.* New York: Hastings House, Publishers, 1961.

Rosa, Joseph G. *Alias Jack McCall: A Pardon or Death?* Kansas City, Mo.: Kansas City Posse of the Westerners, 1967.

————. *The Gunfighter: Man or Myth?* Norman: University of Oklahoma Press, 1969.

————. *They Called Him Wild Bill: The Life and Adventures of James Butler Hickok.* 2d ed. Norman: University of Oklahoma Press, 1964.

Schaefer, Jack. *Heroes Without Glory: Some Good Men of the Old West.* Boston: Houghton Mifflin Company, 1965.

Schoenberger, Dale T. *The Gunfighters.* Caldwell, Idaho: Caxton Printers, Ltd., 1971.

Schultz, Vernon B. *Southwestern Town: The Story of Willcox, Arizona.* Tucson: University of Arizona Press, 1964.

Scobee, Barry. *Old Fort Davis.* San Antonio, Texas: Naylor Company, 1947.

Settle, William A., Jr. *Jesse James Was His Name.* Columbia, Mo.: University of Missouri Press, 1966.

Sheller, Roscoe. *Ben Snipes: Northwest Cattle King.* Portland, Oreg.: Binsford & Mort, 1957.

Sherman, James E., and Sherman, Barbara H. *Ghost Towns of Arizona.* Norman: University of Oklahoma Press, 1969.

Shinkle, James D. *Fifty Years of Roswell History, 1867–1917.* Roswell, N.Mex.: Hall-Poorbaugh Press, Inc., 1964.

Shinn, Charles Howard. *Graphic Description of Pacific Coast Outlaws.* Los Angeles: Westernlore Press, 1958.

Shirley, Glenn. *Buckskin and Spurs: A Gallery of Frontier Rogues and Heroes.* New York: Hastings House, 1958.

———. *Heck Thomas, Frontier Marshal.* Philadelphia: Chilton Company, 1962.

———. *Henry Starr, Last of the Real Badmen.* New York: David McKay Company, Inc., 1965.

———. *Shotgun for Hire: The Story of "Deacon" Jim Miller, Killer of Pat Garrett.* Norman: University of Oklahoma Press, 1970.

———. *Six-Gun and Silver Star.* Albuquerque: University of New Mexico Press, 1955.

Sims, Judge Orland L. *Gun-Toters I Have Known.* Austin: Encino Press, 1967.

Sinise, Jerry. *Pink Higgins: The Reluctant Gunfighter.* Quanah, Texas: Nortex Press, 1974.

Siringo, Charles. *A Texas Cowboy.* Lincoln: University of Nebraska Press, 1950.

Sloane, Howard N., and Sloane, Lucille L. *A Pictorial History of American Mining.* New York: Crown Publishers, Inc., 1970.

Smith, Helena Huntington. *The War on the Powder River.* Lincoln: University of Nebraska Press, 1966.

Smith, Wallace. *Prodigal Sons: The Adventures of Christopher Evans and John Sontag.* Boston: Christopher Publishing House, 1951.

Sonnichsen, C. L. *I'll Die Before I'll Run.* New York: The Devin-Adair Company, 1962.

———. *Pass of the North.* El Paso: Texas Western Press, 1968.

———. *Ten Texas Feuds.* Albuquerque: University of New Mexico Press, 1957.

————. *Tularosa.* New York: The Devin-Adair Company, 1960.

Sprague, Marshall. *Money Mountain: The Story of Cripple Creek Gold.* Boston: Little, Brown and Company, 1953.

Stanley, F. *Clay Allison.* Denver: World Press, Inc., 1956.

————. *Dave Rudabaugh: Border Ruffian.* Denver, Colo.: World Press, Inc., 1961.

————. *Desperadoes of New Mexico.* Denver: World Press, Inc., 1953.

————. *The Grant That Maxwell Bought.* Denver: World Press, Inc., 1952.

————. *Jim Courtright: Two Gun Marshal of Fort Worth.* Denver, Colo.: World Press, Inc., 1957.

————. *No More Tears for Black Jack Ketchum.* Denver, Colo.: World Press, Inc., 1958.

————. *The Private War of Ike Stockton.* Denver, Colo.: World Press, Inc., 1959.

Steen, Ralph W., ed. *The Texas News: A Miscellany of Texas History in Newspaper Style.* Austin, Texas: Steck Company, 1955.

Streeter, Floyd B. *Ben Thompson, Man with a Gun.* New York: Frederick Fell, Inc., 1957.

————. *Prairie Trails and Cow Towns.* Caldwell, Idaho: Caxton Printers, Ltd., 1971.

Sutton, Robert C., Jr. *The Sutton-Taylor Feud.* Quanah, Texas: Nortex Press, 1974.

Swallow, Alan, ed. *The Wild Bunch.* Denver: Sage Books, 1966.

Thompson, Mary, et al. *Clayton: the Friendly Town of Union County, New Mexico.* Denver, Colo.: Monitor Publishing Company, 1962.

Thrapp, Dan L. *Al Sieber: Chief of Scouts.* Norman: University of Oklahoma Press, 1964.

Tilghman, Zoe A. *Marshall of the Last Frontier.* Glendale, Calif.: Arthur H. Clark Co., 1949.

Tombstone Map and Guide. Tombstone: Devere Publications, 1969.

Trachtman, Paul, and the editors of Time-Life Books. *The Gunfighters.* New York: Time-Life Books, 1974.

Vestal, Stanley. *Dodge City: Queen of Cowtowns.* New York: Bantam Books, Inc., 1957.

Wagoner, Jay J. *Arizona Territory, 1863–1912.* Tucson: University of Arizona Press, 1970.

Waller, Brown. *Last of the Great Western Train Robbers.* South Brunswick, N.Y.: A. S. Barnes and Company, 1968.

Warner, Matt. *The Last of the Bandit Raiders.* New York: Bonanza Books, 1940.

Waters, Frank. *The Earp Brothers of Tombstone.* London: Neville Spearman, Ltd., 1962.

Webb, Walter P., ed. *The Handbook of Texas.* 2 vols. Austin: Texas State Historical Society, 1952.

———. *The Texas Rangers.* Austin: University of Texas Press, 1935.

Wellman, Paul I. *A Dynasty of Western Outlaws.* Garden City, N.Y.: Doubleday and Company, Inc., 1961.

Wharton, Clarence Ray. *L'Archevêque.* Houston: Anson Jones Press, 1941.

Yost, Nellie Snyder. *Medicine Lodge.* Chicago: Sage Books, 1970.

Younger, Coleman. *The Story of Cole Younger, by Himself.* Chicago: Henneberry Company, 1903.

Articles

Adelsbach, Lee. "Henry Starr," *Guns and Ammo Guide to the Gunfighters,* 1975.

Cheney, Louise. "Longhair Jim Courtright, Fast Gun of Fort Worth," *Real West,* Fall, 1973.

Forrest, Earle R. "The Killing of Ed Masterson, Deputy Marshal of Old Dodge City," *Brand Book of the Los Angeles Westerners,* 1949.

Good, Clyde. "Ned Christie," *Guns and Ammo Guide to the Gunfighters,* 1975.

Griswold, John. "The Outlaw Wore a Sheriff's Star," *Frontier West,* February, 1972.

Holben, Richard E. "Badman Saloonkeeper," *Pioneer West,* February, 1972.

———. "The Vengeance Vendetta of the Stockton Terror," *Frontier West,* August, 1973.

Johnson, Jay, and Greer, Maxine. "The Legend of Joel F. Goodwin," *Interstate Progress,* Logansport, La., January 23, 1974.

Kellner, Larry. "William Milton Breakenridge: Deadliest Two-Gun Deputy of Arizona," *Arizoniana* 2 (Winter, 1961): 20–22.

Kelsey, Harry E., Jr. "Clay Allison: Western Gunman," *Brand Book of the Denver Westerners,* 1957.

Koop, W. E. "Billy the Kid: The Trail of a Kansas Legend," *Trail Guide* 9 (September, 1964).

Kutz, Jack. "Elfego Baca, Lawman," *Great West,* April, 1973.

Penn, Chris. "A Note on Bartholomew Masterson," *Tally Book of the English Westerners Society,* April, 1967.

Rasch, Philip J. "The Horrell War," *New Mexico Historical Review* 30 (July, 1956).

———. "A Note On Henry Newton Brown," *The Los Angeles Westerners Brand Book* 5 (1953).

———. "The Story of Jesse Evans," *Panhandle Plains Historical Review* 33 (1960).

Roberts, Gary L. "The West's Gunmen: I, The Historiography of the Frontier Heroes," *American West* 8 (January, 1971): 10–15, 64.

———. "The West's Gunmen: II, Recent Historiography of Those Controversial Heroes," *American West* 8 (March, 1971): 18–23, 61–62.

Sonnichsen, C. L. "Tombstone in Fiction," *Journal of Arizona History* 9 (Summer, 1968): 58–76.

———. "The Wyatt Earp Syndrome," *American West* 7 (May, 1970): 26–28, 60–62.

Spangenberger, Phil. "Thomas H. Rynning," *Guns and Ammo Guide to Guns of the Gunfighters,* 1975.

Streeter, Floyd Benjamin. "Tragedies of a Cow Town," *The Aerend: A Kansas Quarterly* 5 (Spring and Summer, 1934).

Miscellaneous

Arizona Daily Citizen (Tucson), 1882.

Arizona Daily Star (Tucson), 1881.

Interview with Mrs. Jessie Standard O'Neal, April 26, 1973.

Lindsey, Seldon T. "The Story of My Life." Unpublished manuscript, Carthage, Texas.

O'Neal, Bill. Personal files, Carthage, Texas.

Tombstone Epitaph, 1880–82.

Tombstone Nugget, 1881.

Index

361